Social Work

Social Work

A Profession of Many Faces

Sixth Edition

Armando T. Morales
University of California at Los Angeles

Bradford W. Sheafor
Colorado State University

ALLYN AND BACON
Boston   London   Toronto   Sydney   Tokyo   Singapore

DEDICATED TO

Our Wives, Cynthia and Nadine
our Mothers, Lupe and Maria,
and Roland and Gary,
and Christopher, Perry, Brandon, and Laura

Managing Editor: Susan Badger
Series Editor: Karen Hanson
Series Editorial Assistant: Deborah Reinke
Production Administrator: Rowena Dores
Editorial-Production Service: Helyn Pultz
Text Designer: Glenna Collett
Composition and Manufacturing Buyer: Louise Richardson

Copyright © 1992, 1989, 1986, 1983, 1980, 1977 by Allyn and Bacon
A Division of Simon & Schuster, Inc.
160 Gould Street
Needham Heights, Massachusetts 02194

Library of Congress Cataloging-in-Publication Data
Morales, Armando.
    Social work : a profession of many faces / by Armando T. Morales
and Bradford W. Sheafor.—6th ed.
        p. cm.
    Includes bibliographical references and index.
    ISBN 0-205-13127-1
    1. Social services—United States.   2. Social work education–
–United States.   3. Social case work—United States.   4. Social
service—Vocational guidance—United States.   5. Social work with
minorities—United States.   I. Sheafor, Bradford W.   II. Title.
HV91.M67   1992
361.973—dc20   91-21612
                                                        CIP

 This book is printed on recycled, acid-free paper.

Photo Credits: Page ii, © Rhoda Sidney/Stock, Boston, Inc.; page 4, © Eric A. Roth/The Picture Cube, Inc.; page 34, © AP/Wide World Photos, Inc.; page 56, © Bryce Flynn/Stock, Boston, Inc.; page 92, © Steve Hansen/Stock, Boston, Inc.; page 120, © Michael Weisbrot and Family/Stock, Boston, Inc.; page 148, © Bob Daemmrich/The Image Works, Inc.; page 176, © Richard Wood/The Picture Cube, Inc.; page 210, © Michael Hayman/Stock, Boston, Inc.; page 244, © Bohdan Hrynewych/Stock, Boston, Inc.; page 282, © Peter Menzel/Stock, Boston, Inc.; page 316, © Judy S. Gelles/Stock, Boston, Inc.; page 346, © Emilio Mercado/The Picture Cube, Inc.; page 382, © Robert Kahaian/The Picture Cube, Inc.; page 418, © Peter Menzel/Stock, Boston, Inc.; page 450, © Leonard Freed/Magnum Photos, Inc.; page 490, © Janice Fullman/The Picture Cube, Inc.; page 516, © Lionel Delevingne/Stock, Boston, Inc.; page 534, © MacDonald Photography/The Picture Cube, Inc.; page 556, © Jean-Claude Lejeune/Stock, Boston, Inc.; page 580, © Elizabeth Crews/Stock, Boston, Inc.; page 606, © Hazel Hankin/Stock, Boston, Inc.

Printed in the United States of America
10 9 8 7 6 5 4 3 2 1   96 95 94 93 92 91

Contents

Preface

*I*n his best-selling book, *Cultural Literacy: What Every American Needs to Know,* E. C. Hirsch, Jr., convincingly makes the point that a problem experienced by many Americans, especially our youth, is that they have limited awareness of their cultural background. In Hirsch's terms, they lack adequate cultural literacy to comprehend a substantial amount of today's important communication. For example, the person who does not appreciate the meaning of Supreme Court decisions such as *Brown* v. *Board of Education,* the *Gault* decision, or *Roe* v. *Wade*; who fails to recognize the significance of the Three Mile Island or Chernobyl catastrophes; who is not aware of the significance of the contributions of Abraham Lincoln, Franklin D. Roosevelt, or Martin Luther King, Jr., to American society; or who is not knowledgeable about the implications of such major events as the Great Depression, the Vietnam War, or Watergate cannot fully comprehend much of what is reported by the media. Unless one is culturally literate, it is not possible to fully participate in and contribute to society.

Thus one goal of this book is to prepare the reader with sufficient background knowledge on the profession of social work to become what Hirsch might label "social work literate." *Social Work: A Profession of Many Faces* presents an overview of social work, introducing many of the terms, concepts, key people, and critical events that shaped this profession. To be "social work literate," one must appreciate the contri-

butions of Jane Addams and Mary Richmond to the social change and individual service missions of social work; understand the reasons social work has emerged as a central human service profession; be familiar with the several career paths available to social workers; recognize the purpose of the Code of Ethics in protecting vulnerable clients and preserving social work's professional integrity; know the roles of the National Association of Social Workers and the Council on Social Work Education in maintaining and strengthening social work; recognize the importance of the social welfare institution in American society and the function of human service agencies in either enhancing or diminishing the quality of services provided; and have some empathy for what it is like to be poor or to experience the impact of institutional racism, sexism, ageism, and homophobia. In short, this book intends to give the reader a sufficient working knowledge of social work to intelligently read, comprehend, and begin to understand the literature of the social work profession.

A second goal of this book is to help the reader recognize the relevance of social work to today's social issues. Far from being on the periphery of the critical events that shape the quality of life for people in this society, social workers are on the front lines of developing social programs that are responsive to such human needs as homelessness, poverty, family break-up, mental illness, physical and mental disabilities, alcohol and substance abuse, domestic violence, and many others. At the same time, social workers directly help people who are victims of these problems so that they may change their own lives or change the relevant aspects of their environments affecting their social functioning. Indeed, social workers operate from values that recognize each person as relevant to society and believe that, when needed, society should help each person to achieve his or her fullest potential. Social workers also work from the perspective that the society is often a cause, or at least a contributor, to most social problems. Our social institutions must be helped to become more just in their operation and more adaptable to changing human needs. Throughout this book the reader will find this focus on the interactions, or transactions, between people and their environments at the heart of our interpretation of social work. In working to enhance the quality of these transactions, social workers perform a critical role in the improvement of the well-being of all people in the society, and therefore for the maintenance of society itself. Social work's relevance to the successful functioning of American society should become evident in the following pages.

As we prepared the sixth edition of *Social Work: A Profession of Many Faces,* we were aware that we have spent nearly two decades seeking to understand and interpret the profession of social work. Our work has helped us become acutely aware that developments in the social work profession are intertwined, perhaps more than for any other profession, with changes in the society. We began the first edition just as Richard Nixon took office for his second term, and we concluded the manuscript for this edition as George Bush was completing his first two years as president. Regretably, during that period we saw an overall decline of social concern in the United States. Resources for human services were exchanged for a military build-up throughout the world, and the national debt increasingly drained the economy of funds that might have been used to improve the quality of

life for rich and poor alike. Hopes for a reversal of that trend associated with the "peace dividend" emerging from the dramatic changes in Eastern Europe during 1989 and 1990 were dashed as hundreds of savings and loan companies failed and military action in the Middle East drained the treasury. It is also noteworthy that many quality-of-life indicators have not improved during the time we have worked on this material. For example, the poverty rate increased from 12.1 percent of the population in 1969 to 13.5 percent in 1987, and for children—the Nation's future—the poverty rate was a shocking 22.4 percent. Political decisions made in the 1980s reduced the disposable income of the lowest one-fifth of the American families by 8 percent, while the upper one-fifth gained 9 percent. Social workers would argue that we are moving in the wrong direction.

The changes we have observed in the social attitudes of American society have been mirrored by the students who attend our colleges and universities, and ultimately those who elect to prepare for careers in social work. We have observed that student concern in the mid-1970s over the plight of the poor, the ill, and the aged; militant campaigns against racism and sexism; and outrage over U.S. military action in Vietnam have all too often been replaced by social apathy and a narrow vocational approach to careers. The question once heard by the university faculty member, "What can I do to help people?" has too often been replaced by, "What can you do to prepare me for a career that offers good pay and job security?" Admittedly decent pay and job security are desirable, but the shift in motivation and loss of idealism reflected in many of today's students concerns us.

Certainly the change of intensity in social concern has not been limited to students. We have also seen a rather dramatic shift in social work practice as many social workers have moved away from work with the most vulnerable members of society and into private practice or employment with for-profit agencies primarily serving the middle class. We have seen the zeal for social change as a prime activity of social work erode in favor of overemphasis on clinical skills for practice with individuals and families. While we believe that entrepreneurial and clinical social work practice is appropriate for social workers, we decry the fact that these approaches have expanded at the expense of social work's historical commitment to social action and services to society's most vulnerable people.

On a more positive note, we believe that during the years we have worked on this book social work has made great strides in clarifying its unique role among the helping professions and stabilizing a relatively clear career path that embraces baccalaureate-, master's-, and doctoral-level preparation. In addition, remarkable shifts have occurred in the settings where social workers have the opportunity to provide their services. Occupational social work, for example, has expanded rapidly, and increasingly health insurance companies are providing direct reimbursement to social workers who treat the social problems experienced by their clients. As it has done throughout its history, social work has adapted to prevalent public attitudes. Today that attitude is to restrict human services, forcing social workers to leave the streets and, we believe temporarily, expand services in the less controversial clinical aspects of practice. However, by maintaining its clear focus on the interaction between people and the world around them, social workers are poised to again become actively engaged in social change activities when the political climate supports more aggressive action.

It is perhaps useful to confess some of our biases, which will become evident as one reads this book. We frankly seek to appeal to the social conscience of those who read these pages. We strive to project the social worker as one who maintains a balanced perception of person *and* environment. Our view of the social worker is a generalist one in that we expect the social worker to serve multilevel clients (i.e., individuals, families and other households, groups, organizations, and communities) with a range of interventive approaches and in relation to various social problems. We also expect a disciplined approach to social work practice, characterized by an "informed passion" for improving the quality of life, for all people but especially for the most vulnerable members of our country. Finally, we are convinced that social work has an essential role to perform in helping people deal more effectively with the world around them and conclude that few occupations can offer the personal satisfaction of the social worker who successfully helps people to more effectively live out their lives.

This book, then, provides the basic information for becoming literate in social work and reveals the special relevance social work has for helping people live rewarding lives today. It is intended for the person who wants to learn about social workers—what they do and why they do it. As an introduction to this important profession, *Social Work: A Profession of Many Faces* helps the newcomer to this discipline or the person considering a career in social work to acquire a solid grounding.

The title, *Social Work: A Profession of Many Faces,* reflects the important point that this profession comprises people from widely diverse backgrounds, who serve people with a range of social problems, under the auspices of a wide variety of human service agencies, using quite varied knowledge and techniques. Nonetheless, social work practice has many common features that help to bind social workers together into one profession.

The authors themselves reflect some of the different faces of social work. One has devoted most of his practice experience to working with individuals, families, and groups, while the other has worked mostly with organizations and communities. Both are employed by universities. However, one is primarily engaged in direct clinical practice with the poor, and in teaching and training psychiatric residents and psychology and social work interns in a department of psychiatry. The other is engaged in teaching baccalaureate- and master's-level students in professional social work education. One is a member of a minority group, and the other is part of the majority. One has always lived in a large urban area on the West Coast, while the other is a product of smaller communities in the Midwest and Rocky Mountain regions. One has filled national leadership roles with the National Association of Social Workers and the other with the Council on Social Work Education. Despite the "different faces" of these two social workers, they are in substantial agreement in their enthusiasm for social work and their perception of the factors that make this profession essential to American society.

The preparation of each new edition requires many choices in regard to what to leave unchanged, what to revise, and what to replace. In our ongoing attempt to keep this book current with evolving trends in social work, we have made several revisions in this edition that are of note. We have, for example, updated the statistical material to include the most recent data available that portrays the current status of both social work and social welfare. We have also inserted material on the generalist and ecosystems practice perspectives in Chapters 1 and 7 to provide an orientation to how many social workers go about assessing client situations and helping them to bring about needed change. In addition, we have added a description of NASW's newly developed Academy of Certified Baccalaureate Social Workers (ACBSW) and more clearly described the differences between certification, accreditation, job classifications, and licensing. In the chapter on the fields of social work practice (Chapter 5), we have expanded our discussion of several fields and inserted new information on the employment patterns of social workers in each. Knowing that many students learn most effectively by examining case illustrations, we have placed case examples in most chapters to help the reader understand the connections between the conceptual material and the realities of day-to-day social work practice. Finally, in an effort to hold down the length, and thus the cost of this edition, we have devoted considerable effort to streamlining the presentation of our material. We found, to our surprise, that we could communicate our message just as effectively in fewer words.

In Part Four, "Social Work Practice with Special Populations," we have included four new chapters we believe will update and enhance our readers' understanding of social work practice with various population groups. Diane Kravetz prepared an insightful new chapter (Chapter 11) for this edition, which takes a fresh look at special issues related to women and affecting the practice of social workers. We also commissioned George A. Appleby and Jeane W. Anastas to prepare what we believe to be the most comprehensive chapter-length description of social work practice with gay and lesbian clients published to date (see Chapter 12). In Chapter 13, Manual R. Miranda and Armando T. Morales developed an interesting new chapter on practice with the growing aged population in the United States. Finally, Chapter 17, our chapter on social work with American Indians, had gotten quite dated and we substituted some very informative materials on American Indian families prepared by John Red Horse. We believe that these changes have made this the strongest of our six editions.

A special note to instructors who teach from this book is in order. We want to be sure that you are aware of the *Instructor's Manual/Test Bank* that we have prepared as a teaching aid. In the *Manual* we share teaching techniques developed over two decades of teaching this material. We have also brought another perspective to this work by engaging Dr. Mona Schatz (Colorado State University) in the preparation of these materials. For each chapter in *Social Work: A Profession of Many Faces,* the *Manual* gives a synopsis of the most important content covered, lists the key concepts and terms the student should master, offers suggestions and sample exercises for teaching the materials, and provides sample discussion, essay, and multiple-choice questions. A computerized version of the test bank is available for IBM personal computers.

The Baez Family Fire case is missing from this edition of *Many Faces*. We elected to disperse case material throughout the book rather than devoting a whole chapter to a single case. The Baez case, however, continues to be available for teaching purposes in the *Instructor's Manual*. We have prepared the material so that the case unfolds a few pages at a time, allowing an instructor to process the material with students before continuing to the next events in the case. We believe this format provides greater flexibility for use of this case material as the basis for class discussion, group projects, term papers, and even examinations. In addition, Allyn and Bacon, in cooperation with the Office of Instructional Services at Colorado State University, has made available a one-hour videotape containing four case examples of social work practice designed specifically for use with this book. In short, we believe the *Instructor's Manual/Test Bank* and videotape are important supplements to *Social Work: A Profession of Many Faces* and urge you to contact your Allyn and Bacon sales representative to secure your copy, or write to Allyn and Bacon, 160 Gould Street, Needham Heights , Massachusetts 02194. An audio version of this text is available for the visually impaired from Recording for the Blind, 20 Roszel Road, Princeton, New Jersey 08540.

Many people directly or indirectly influenced our ideas and gave support to make the preparation of this work possible. We wish to acknowledge our universities, the University of California at Los Angeles and Colorado State University, as well as our colleagues and students who have in countless ways helped by sharing ideas and offering critical reviews of these materials. Their critique has often led to revisions that improved the quality and readability of this material. Special thanks are particularly in order for Angie Esparza, who typed numerous revisions of this manuscript, with never a complaint, yet as timely as "yesterday"!

Finally, our families and loved ones must be thanked for sacrificing some of our precious time together so that the activity of preparing this manuscript could be included in our already crowded schedules. Their love, support, and encouragement provides meaning to our work and our lives.

The Profession of Social Work

*I*f the world were a perfect place, it would provide for everyone warm and safe housing, an adequate supply of nutritious food, challenging jobs, good health care, and love and caring from friends and family. It would be a world with minimal stress, crime, and suffering. All people would find their lives satisfying and fulfilling. Social work exists because the world is less than perfect. Social workers serve people and the institutions of society as they confront this imperfection.

Social work is a humanizing profession and social workers are action-oriented people. The social worker is not satisfied with this imperfect world that sends too many children to bed hungry at night, has effectively declared too many older people useless, restricts too many physically handicapped people from productive living, allows too many women and children to be physically and sexually abused, deprives too many members of minority groups of the full opportunity to share in the benefits of this affluent society, has too many single parents trying to raise children in substandard housing without enough money for proper nutrition and food, and deprives too many emotionally and intellectually impaired people of satisfying lives because they behave or learn differently from the majority in the society. In fact, when even one person is a victim of loneliness, hunger, discrimination, poor housing or clothing, domestic violence, or emotional upset, there is a need for social work.

Social work emerged during the twentieth century as an important profession in U.S. society. Its development has paralleled a seeming roller coaster of public interest in human welfare and social services. At times when the national political climate placed a high priority on human welfare, jobs were plentiful and the number of people entering social work increased dramatically. These social workers found it refreshing to be part of a profession that addressed the overall well-being of people. In a world where terrorist attacks have become commonplace and where nuclear stockpiles grow annually, it is little wonder that social work, a profession concerned with the enhancement of human potential, has attracted many bright and socially concerned young people.

However, the tides of the political climate periodically yield a conservative orientation more concerned with defense than human welfare, with big business than human rights, and with cutting social programs to balance the budget rather than increasing the taxes of the wealthy. In such times the appeal of social work to many young people declined and the supply of competent social workers prepared to help people lead more satisfying lives was reduced. Paradoxically, the decline in support for human services has occurred at times when social and economic conditions dictated the greatest need for the services of social workers. When the demand for human services by needy citizens has increased within the society, social work positions have been viewed as a luxury that can be reduced when it is time for budget cutting. In effect, when there is a poorly functioning economy society increases the burden on its most vulnerable members by reducing the supports available to them.

Since it does not appear that the world will become perfect any time soon, it is reasonable to assume that large numbers of social workers will continue to be needed. Employment opportunities may decline or shift from public to private auspices and there may be variations in the number of human service programs the public is willing to support, but the need for the services the social workers can provide will still exist. Although employment cannot be assured for the new social worker, professional education programs continue to graduate fewer social workers than the U.S. Bureau of Labor Statistics projects will be needed.

Why is social work important to American society? Social workers provide important services to help people solve problems that limit their social functioning and enhance the quality of their lives. Social workers provide these services in a variety of ways.

Sometimes the social worker offers a *direct service* or helps individuals, families, or other groups on a face-to-face basis. In some situations they help people solve specific problems, while at other times social workers counsel people to solve problems or engage in activities that will enhance the quality of their lives—whether or not they experience an identifiable problem.

The services of the social worker might also be provided on behalf of individuals or groups of people. These *indirect services* help to make social institutions such as organizations, neighborhoods, communities, or even the policies of a government or laws of a country more responsive to the needs of people.

Employment opportunities are an important factor for an individual to consider when making a career choice. Yet, as a review of the development of social work will indicate, the political climate has acted like a swinging pendulum that affects the availability of social-work jobs. As it has swung from a conservative to a liberal climate and back, social work has adapted its employment patterns to these changes and has continued to provide needed services. The combination of attrition and the creation of new arenas of social work practice has always enabled the competent and professionally prepared social worker to find satisfying employment.

Providing needed human services and contributing to an improvement of the quality of life for all people are personally rewarding experiences. A social worker can make a small but important contribution to the well-being of society. When one makes a career choice, these personal rewards must be considered.

This book presents an overview of social work for the person considering this profession as a possible career choice. It does not attempt to "sell" social work but to portray it honestly, and with its strengths and limitations in clear view. Because we are interested in recruiting qualified people to our profession—a profession in which we take great pride—we hope this book will enable people to discover whether social work is for them.

Social work is not easy work. It can be as emotionally draining as it is rewarding. It can be as frustrating as it can be satisfying. The prerequisite to developing the knowledge, values, and skills necessary for competent social work practice must be a basic commitment to social betterment and a willingness to invest oneself in facilitating the process of change.

Part One is devoted to the excitement, promise, and realities of social work's growth in the United States during this century. It provides a general review of the profession and stresses the commonality of purpose in this diverse field.

Wherever possible we present conceptions of social work that enjoy general acceptance in the field rather than those that reflect our exclusive biases. Although we may be accused of presenting a "consensus" view of social work, we do so because of our belief that familiarity with the field should begin in the "mainstream." Once this material is mastered, then the tributaries can be explored.

To understand the current status of social work, one must perceive the field within the context of its historical development. Particular chapters include brief historical perspectives relevant to the subject of the chapter. In addition, case materials are used to illustrate the more academic parts of the book. A concerted effort was also made to avoid jargon or technical language unfamiliar to the reader.

Chapter 1 provides a general framework for viewing the profession. It describes and defines this field so the reader may have a base on which to build a more thorough knowledge of social work. In subsequent chapters many of these points are examined more thoroughly.

Chapter 2 combines an understanding of the many helping professions with the specific place social work occupies among them. The chapter demonstrates how the motivation to establish social work as a profession has contributed both positively and negatively to the field.

Chapter 3 is especially geared to the person considering social work as a career. Using the National Association of Social Workers' classification system for identifying the several levels of social service personnel as an organizing theme, the chapter examines entry points, qualifications, expected competencies, and termination points for each level. The three chapters in Part One, then, provide an orientation to the social work profession—its purpose, its growth and development, its structure.

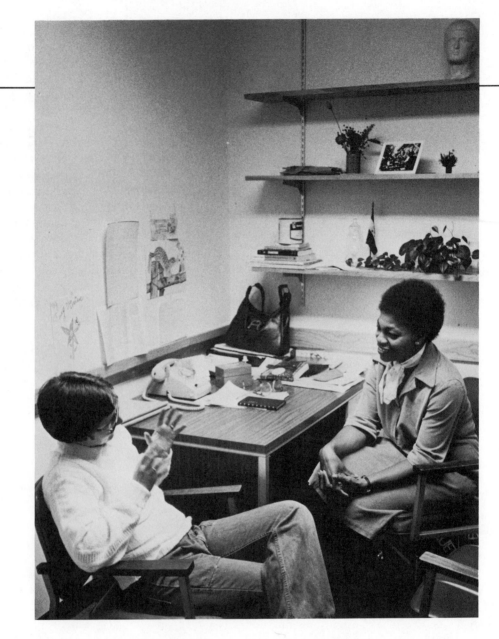

CHAPTER 1

Social Work: A Comprehensive Helping Profession

The profession of social work is made up of people dedicated to helping others change some aspect of their social functioning. In simplest terms social workers help people improve their interaction with various aspects of their world—their children, parents, spouse, family, friends, co-workers, or even organizations and whole communities. Social work is a profession committed to improving the quality of life for people through various activities directed toward social change.

UNDERSTANDING THE SOCIAL WORKER

Social work is a profession that is full of contradictions. Social workers may deal with very successful people, but more often they work with the more vulnerable members of our society. They relate to problems ranging from marital conflict to juvenile delinquency and from mental illness to unsafe housing. They provide services that vary from counseling to group therapy, to fund raising, and even social action. Social work itself strives for professional status that inherently restricts the number of people who can be recognized as professional, yet is philosophically anti-elitist.

How does one understand this complex profession? Five themes serve to characterize social work and provide a foundation on which to build more in-depth understanding of this profession.

Commitment to Social Betterment

The fundamental importance of improving the quality of life, i.e., *social betterment* must be a central value in the belief system of the social worker. As a

profession social work has maintained an idealism about the ability and responsibility of this society to provide opportunities and resources that allow each
person to lead a full and rewarding life. It has seen its mission as being particularly
concerned with the underdog—the most vulnerable people in the society. This
idealism must not be confused with naïveté. Social workers are often the most
knowledgeable people in the community about the plight of the poor, the abused,
the lonely, and others who for a variety of reasons are out of the mainstream of
society or experiencing social problems. When social workers express that perspective, it is often an uncomfortable one for people who wish to protect the
status quo. At times criticized as "bleeding heart do-gooders," social workers
would contend that if this label implies that they care for and advance the cause
of the less successful members of society, then they wear it proudly.

Desire to Enhance Social Functioning

A second theme that provides an understanding of social work is the focus of
this profession on helping to improve *social functioning*. Social functioning is
the manner in which people interact with their environments—with the people
and social institutions with which they come into contact. Social workers help
to facilitate change in the social functioning between people and social institutions in order to solve problems or to enhance the quality of already adequate
functioning.

The social work profession emerged to help people change in relation to a
rapidly changing world. Where once change was more gradual, today the world
in which we live has become a dynamic and rapidly changing environment. The
technology explosion, information explosion, population explosion, and even the
threat of nuclear explosion dramatically impact our lives. Those people who can
readily adapt to these changes—and are not limited by discrimination due to
race, cultural background, gender, age, or physical, emotional, or intellectual
abilities—seldom use the services of social workers. Other have become victims
of this too rapidly changing world and its unstable social institutions. They require
help from the social worker in dealing with this change.

Action Orientation

Moreover, it is a profession of doers. Social workers are not handwringers who
contemplate social issues in hopes that they will disappear. Rather, they take
action to prevent problems from developing and to help people deal effectively
with situations that cannot be changed, as well as to attack those situations that
can be changed.

Social work is an applied science. While social workers draw on considerable
knowledge about people and various social groups and institutions, their primary
activity is not the development of this knowledge. They tend to borrow their
basic knowledge from other disciplines, such as cultural anthropology, economics, political science, psychology, human physiology, and sociology. Selecting

carefully from the important work of these and other disciplines, social workers translate that knowledge into action, or services, that will benefit their clients and the institutions of society.

Appreciation of Human Diversity

To deal effectively with such a wide range of individual and institutional change, social work has become a profession characterized by diversity—diversity of clientele, diversity of knowledge and skills, and diversity of services provided. In addition, the social workers themselves come in all sizes, shapes, colors, ages, and descriptions.

Social workers view diversity as a strength. They consider human difference desirable and appreciate the richness that can be offered a society through the culture, language, and traditions of various racial, ethnic, and cultural groups. They value the unique perspectives of persons of different gender, sexual preference, or age groups, and they recognize and develop the strengths of persons who have been disadvantaged.

What's more, social workers view their own diversity as an enriching quality that has created a dynamic profession that can respond to human needs in an ever-changing world. Indeed, social work *is* a profession of many faces!

A Versatile Practice Perspective

The wide range of human problems with which social workers deal, the variety of settings in which social workers are employed, the extensive scope of the services they provide, and the diverse populations they serve make it unrealistic to expect that a single practice approach could adequately serve the social worker. Rather, the social worker must have a comprehensive repertoire of knowledge and techniques that can be used to meet the unique needs of individual clients or client groups. The social worker who is locked into a limited helping approach simply lacks the versatility to be of maximum effectiveness.

The versatile social worker, then, must have a solid foundation of knowledge about the behavior of people and their social institutions in order to understand adequately the situations that their clientele bring to them. They also need to understand that differing beliefs may affect the way people will understand and react to those situations. And, finally, they must have mastered a number of helping techniques they can imaginatively select and skillfully use to help individuals, families, groups, organizations, and communities improve their social functioning.

How can we characterize the social worker? As we have seen, the social worker must possess a fundamental commitment to social betterment, a basic desire to use his or her talents to enhance social functioning, the ability to translate concerns into action, an appreciation of human diversity, and the ability to be versatile in approaching practice situations.

A GLANCE AT SOME SOCIAL WORKERS IN ACTION

Examining the day-to-day work of members of a profession helps one to appreciate the manner in which the goals of that profession are operationalized. Perhaps observing some case examples of social workers as they apply their knowledge and skills will reveal a clearer picture of this profession. Consider the following social workers as they go about their work.

> In twenty minutes Nadine Harrison, a social worker with the local welfare department, has an appointment with Ms. Kim Lee. Ms. Lee is terribly worried about her future and that of her two small children. Her husband was killed two months ago in a construction accident. In addition to her grief and loneliness, Ms. Lee found that, after paying funeral expenses, little money was left for raising the children. She asked Ms. Harrison for help.
>
> Brandon Ford is a social worker employed in a psychiatric hospital. Although he works with some patients individually, this afternoon he will meet with a group of adolescent boys who expect to be released from the hospital in a few weeks. Mr. Ford will help the boys explore their feelings about leaving the hospital and their friends and will discuss problems they may face when they return to their homes.
>
> Laura Jackson is executive director of the Council on Aging in her community. This council identifies and seeks solutions to problems experienced by older people in that community. As executive director, Ms. Jackson provides leadership to the citizen board as it considers new programs. Tonight the board will consider initiating a new program for older people: a telephone hook-up between shut-ins.
>
> Perry Garcia is a social worker at a storefront neighborhood center in a large city. His job is to help residents rectify substandard housing conditions in the area. Tonight Mr. Garcia is helping a group from the neighborhood plan a strategy for pressuring some of the landlords to improve the quality of housing.
>
> This afternoon Christopher Warren will testify before a committee of the state legislature that is considering the need for new laws and programs related to the state parole system. After seven years as a probation officer for a large juvenile court and now as parole officer for the district court, Mr. Warren is well prepared to serve as an expert witness.

In each of these situations, the social worker is planning to provide some form of help that will enable a person or a group of people to make a change in their social functioning. Nadine Harrison's primary concern is for an *individual,* while Brandon Ford's responsibility is for a *group* of boys. Laura Jackson is helping an *organization* respond to the needs of older people, and Perry Garcia works to help a *neighborhood* and *community* improve the quality of housing. At the more comprehensive *state* or *national* levels, Christopher Warren is helping to improve the laws affecting people on parole. In these examples one can see that social workers are involved with a variety of *client systems,* or work with a number of different levels of clientele.

They also are employed by a variety of social agencies. They were found working in a public welfare department, a psychiatric hospital, a local council on aging, a neighborhood center, and a parole office. Clearly, social workers serve a very diverse group of people experiencing a wide range of problems.

Although social workers usually begin helping at one particular practice level, they often reflect their versatility of approach by moving to other levels in order to be of maximum help to their clients. For example:

> Brandon Ford learned from the group discussion that one of the boys, Artie Chambers, was afraid to leave the hospital because he believed his father was "mad at me for acting crazy." Mr. Ford met several times with Artie and his parents to help them examine Artie's fear and understand his improved behavior since hospitalization. Also, several boys in the group talked about what a drastic change it would be to leave the hospital, where life is highly structured, and go home to a life with a great deal of freedom. Taking his cue from this discussion, Mr. Ford gained permission to plan several excursions into the community and a few weekend visits home for the boys. He also learned that three of the boys could have been released several weeks earlier if there had been supportive mental health services in the small town where their parents lived. This information led him to convene a group of interested citizens in that town for considering ways in which the community could make such services available.

The work of Brandon Ford reflects that of a generalist social worker. He views the problems presented from a perspective that is not encumbered by any single practice approach or by working at any single client level. He began with a group of clients, but soon found it necessary to deal with both a child's family as well as a community in order to reduce or eliminate the problems in social functioning that he encountered.

THE MISSION OF SOCIAL WORK: SOCIAL BETTERMENT

While social work can be characterized by its variability, it has maintained a fundamental purpose for its nearly one century of existence in the United States: directly serving people in need and, at the same time, making social institutions more responsive to all people. However, the ability to specify this fundamental purpose clearly in precise terms has been difficult as the social work profession has evolved several patterns of operation through the years. Meyer notes:

> The development of social work as a profession has been a tortuous effort to develop boundaries within which an integral identity could be carved out while maintaining an open exchange with society. All enduring professions adapt to social change and pursue their interests, but they maintain the same purposes at the core. Architects design buildings, doctors deal with sickness and health, lawyers practice law, and educators teach. Social workers are concerned with _____. With what? Fill in the blank. With people? Psychosocial functioning? Delivery of social services? Management of human service agencies?

Policy analysis? Social change? Developmental services over the life span? Residual services to people with defined problems? All of these or some of these?[1]

To understand social work, it is useful to briefly examine its historical development so that the roots of its unique mission can be identified.

Influences from Practice Roots

Social work sprang from the need to institutionalize the response of U.S. society to an increasing number of people who were experiencing social problems in the late 1800s. Although some form of human service, people helping people in need, has no doubt always been present, the rapid social changes partially created by industrialization and urbanization required that these services be formalized. It was evident that many basic needs could not be met by the traditional resources of the market economy or the family.

Human services took shape within various organizations, or social agencies, that were created in response to these problems. While volunteers played an important role in the provision of services, it was soon learned that many social needs were most effectively met by paid personnel who were trained in the best methods of providing services. These emerging professionals, social workers, took their orientation from the agencies in which they were employed and only much later developed a professional identification that would transcend the scope of any one agency. Because social work began from this agency orientation, the roots of social work's mission can be found in the three dominant agencies in which social workers were first employed.

One development began in 1863 with the founding of the Massachusetts State Board of Charities. That organization, the forerunner of the present public human services agencies, was quickly imitated in other states and provided a base of operation for social work practice. The purpose of the state boards was to supervise the *care* given by the state-supported institutions responsible for the poor, the physically and mentally ill, and prisoners. The boards also collected information on all financial relief activities in the state in an effort to understand the problems and improve the quality of services.

Another development was the Charity Organization Society (COS) movement, which began in Buffalo, New York, in 1877 and spread to about 125 other cities in the United States in the late nineteenth century. The COS offered a range of services aimed at *curing* individuals who experienced problems in social functioning (or perhaps, more accurately, helping people cure themselves) and, at the same time, coordinating and evaluating existing services throughout the community.

Finally, the settlement house movement emerged in urban areas, beginning in New York with the Neighborhood Guild in 1886 and in Chicago with Hull House in 1889. Settlement houses originally focused on providing services to European immigrants who were flooding into the metropolitan centers and were ill-prepared for the demands of this urban environment. Many were subjected to inhumane treatment in factories and other workplaces. The settlement house workers were actively engaged in social reform aimed at *changing* laws and conditions that created these hardships.

From these and other social agencies that developed during this time, social work established its commitment to serving the more helpless and vulnerable members of society. The means of achieving this mission—caring, curing, and changing—have continued to characterize social work practice activities to the present time. Today, however, the range of agencies in which social workers are employed is much more varied. Richan and Mendelsohn comment that:

> At first glance it is surprising to discover that the arena is so wide and varied in size and depth. Social workers are all over the society; they turn up everywhere. Some are self-employed, engaged in private practice, but the bulk of them are employed in private or public agencies. You meet social workers in schools, hospitals, welfare departments, correctional institutions, residential treatment settings, adoption agencies, community service organizations, veterans' bureaus, the military, nursing homes, and children's services. They work in courts, in prisons, in literally all types of service agencies; they are even found tucked away in private industry. Social workers populate government bureaus and civil service at every level; many are involved in social work education as well.[2]

Although the degree of emphasis on the different aspects of the social work mission varies according to the type of agency in which social workers are employed, important commitments continue to be shared by most social workers.

Social Work's Three Purposes

Social work emerged with not just one, but three, purposes that reflect its particular mission among the helping professions: caring, curing, and changing.

Caring.   At the heart of the social work value system is a concern for the well-being of all people. From the efforts to enhance the quality of life in prisons and poorhouses more than a century ago to the effort to humanize services in nursing homes and juvenile detention facilities today, social workers have continually sought to improve care for limited or helpless groups in the population. At times this caring role has taken a back seat to social change and treatment efforts in social work. Keeping this vital function in the conscious view of the profession is essential if social work is to perform its role adequately in society. Morris has provided a clear summary of this situation:

> Social work in the United States began by filling a very basic, caring function. The need for this function has increased over time, and social work has flourished beyond the expectations of its founders. But . . . we have become attracted to new physical and psychological sciences that have led us to believe that we can prevent or cure, and this has become a central dynamic for our professional growth, displacing the earlier caring function. But the curative powers we have embraced have proved less than adequate. We now need to consider whether

our historic contribution lies in restoration of the caring function, while relegating the search for a cure for social problems to the exploratory and experimental frontier.[3]

The best knowledge we can muster is inadequate to prevent or cure the many social problems encountered by the disabled, elderly, and other persons with limited capacity for social functioning. Adequate care to make people comfortable and help them cope with limitations is, at times, the most important service a social worker can provide. In addition, there is an important leadership role for social work in helping communities create the necessary services to provide such care. This fundamental purpose continues to be a part of the mission of social work.

Curing.   In recent years, the dominant thrust of social work practice has been to treat people experiencing problems in social functioning. A variety of helping techniques have been developed for providing direct services to individuals, families, and groups. These range from general counseling techniques to more specialized approaches such as transactional analysis, family therapy, behavior modification, reality therapy, and gestalt therapy. In addition, a variety of lesser known approaches such as neurolinguistic programming, psychomotor therapy, existential therapy, and psychodrama are also used by some social workers.

These individually focused approaches do not necessarily cure problems in social functioning. Much depends on the ability of the social worker to use these techniques and the appropriateness of the technique for a given client and situation. In fact, most social workers would argue that at best they can only help clients help themselves. Yet, having the ability to make appropriate judgments, knowing how to engage clients in the helping process, and having a suitable environment for the provision of services are essential to good social work practice. In addition, the social worker brings to the helping process knowledge of human and societal behavior that aids both the client(s) and the social worker in understanding the practice situation, as well as the specific practice techniques that can be used to change that situation.[4]

Changing.   Social change has always been a part of social work. Many of the pioneer social workers were active reformers who worked to improve conditions in slums, hospitals, prisons, and poorhouses. Today social workers actively seek to impact social legislation related to social programs and conditions that maintain or increase racism, sexism, and poverty. They make efforts to reform; that is, to incrementally improve the existing system, to tinker with laws, procedures, and attitudes until these are more responsive to human needs.

Social workers also seek to affect negative public attitudes about the more vulnerable members of society through public education and facilitating the empowerment of the affected members of the population to advocate for their own interests. Social workers, then, seek change either by directly representing the interests of their clientele and/or indirectly making it possible for clients to convince decision-makers at the local, state, or national levels to respond to human needs.

DEFINING SOCIAL WORK

Social work has been a product of an increasingly complex world that makes it difficult for people to meet their needs effectively through conventional inter-action with family, friends, neighbors, and the various social institutions. As society changed, it became clear that professional services would be required to meet human needs, and social work began to be recognized as the profession that could best help people respond to social needs. However, finding a clear conceptualization or professional definition that encompassed the breadth of this emerging occupation was elusive.

Initially social workers, or those human service providers who wanted to identify themselves as social workers, tended to identify themselves by field of practice and intervention approach. Thus, a social worker might characterize him- or herself as a psychiatric caseworker, a medical group worker, or a community organizer. Not only did a certain amount of elitism develop around these identities, but they also distracted social workers from the effort to identify the common elements in these various forms of practice.

Three concerted efforts have been made to arrive at a clear definition of social work. First, the American Association of Social Workers convened a meeting of agency executives in Milford, Pennsylvania, in 1923, in order to define "social casework" (i.e., practice with individuals, couples, and families). Because these representatives of a range of settings were not immediately successful in their effort, four subsequent meetings of the Milford Conference were held, and each successive year the commonalities hidden among differing expressions of social work became clearer. Still, the committee was unable to conceptualize social work in a manner that would provide a satisfactory umbrella for the profession.[5]

The 1950s brought a second surge of interest in developing a clear conceptualization of social work. The merger of several specialized social work practice organizations (e.g., American Association of Hospital Social Workers, American Association of Visiting Teachers, American Association of Psychiatric Social Workers, and the more generic American Association of Social Workers) into the National Association of Social Workers (NASW) was completed in 1955. For a time a spirit of unity dominated the social work profession, and the effort to find a definition of social work that would reflect the commonality in the diverse practice activities began in earnest. A critical step was the publication of the "Working Definition of Social Work Practice" in 1958. Although not yet providing a comprehensive definition of social work, the efforts of the committee charged with developing this document established an important basis for subsequent definitions by identifying three common purposes that characterize all social work practice, namely, (1) to assist individuals and groups to identify and resolve or minimize problems arising out of disequilibrium between themselves and their environment, (2) to identify potential areas of disequilibrium between individuals or groups and the environment in order to prevent the occurrence of disequilibrium, and (3) to seek out, identify, and strengthen the maximum potential of individuals, groups, and communities.[6] Thus the "Working Definition" established that social workers are concerned with curative or treatment goals, as well as emphasizing the importance of social change or prevention. In addition, the definition recognized the focus of social work on the interactions between people and their environments and the responsibility of social workers to address people as individuals, parts of various groups, and as members of communities.

➤ Third, in the 1970s and 1980s NASW published three special editions of *Social Work* that generated substantial debate and discussion, but not conclusions, about the nature of social work.[7] While this activity enhanced understanding of the central features that characterize social work, it did not lead to a definition of this profession that has either general acceptance or official sanction. However, as part of a larger package of recommendations, the NASW Board of Directors adopted a definition of social work proposed by the task force that drafted the *NASW Standards for Social Service Manpower.*[8] That definition (Box 1–1) has become the generally accepted definition of social work. In three sentences it defines social work, describes what social workers do, and identifies the general areas of knowledge a social worker needs to possess.

> *A General Definition of Social Work:* Social work is the professional activity of helping individuals, groups, or communities enhance or restore their capacity for social functioning and creating societal conditions favorable to that goal.

This sentence provides a concise description of social work appropriate for use in giving a one-sentence "dictionary definition" of the profession. At this level of abstraction, general boundaries are drawn around social work. It is *professional activity* that requires a particular body of knowledge, values, and skills, as well as a discrete purpose, to guide the practice of the social worker. Community sanction to provide this professional activity is assumed to be present and social work is, in turn, expected to be accountable to the public for the quality of services provided.

The remainder of the sentence captures the uniqueness of social work. It makes it clear that social workers serve a range of client systems that include individuals, families or other household units, groups, organizations, neighborhoods, communities, and even larger units of society. However, the unique preparation and competence of the social worker are directed toward helping those systems interact more effectively with persons or social institutions that have an impact on them. The term *social functioning* captures the social worker's effort to help people, whether individuals or collectives, change their functioning to create more satisfactory forms of social interaction. Gordon describes this viewpoint more precisely:

> The central social work focus is placed at the interface between or the meeting place of person and environment—at the point where there is or is not matching

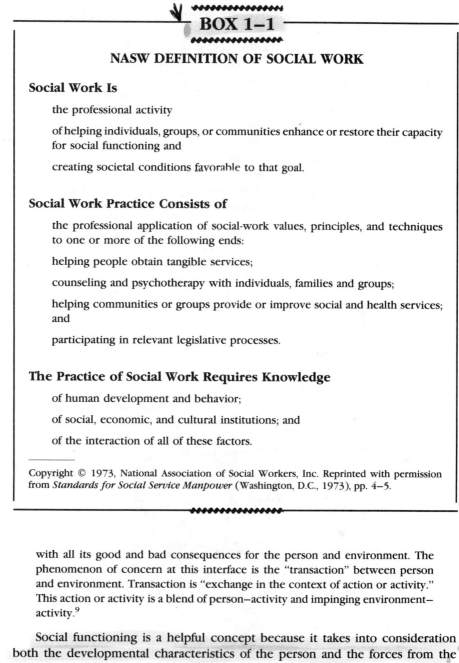

BOX 1–1

NASW DEFINITION OF SOCIAL WORK

Social Work Is

the professional activity

of helping individuals, groups, or communities enhance or restore their capacity for social functioning and

creating societal conditions favorable to that goal.

Social Work Practice Consists of

the professional application of social-work values, principles, and techniques to one or more of the following ends:

helping people obtain tangible services;

counseling and psychotherapy with individuals, families and groups;

helping communities or groups provide or improve social and health services; and

participating in relevant legislative processes.

The Practice of Social Work Requires Knowledge

of human development and behavior;

of social, economic, and cultural institutions; and

of the interaction of all of these factors.

Copyright © 1973, National Association of Social Workers, Inc. Reprinted with permission from *Standards for Social Service Manpower* (Washington, D.C., 1973), pp. 4–5.

with all its good and bad consequences for the person and environment. The phenomenon of concern at this interface is the "transaction" between person and environment. Transaction is "exchange in the context of action or activity." This action or activity is a blend of person–activity and impinging environment–activity.[9]

Social functioning is a helpful concept because it takes into consideration both the developmental characteristics of the person and the forces from the environment. It suggests that a person brings to the situation a set of behaviors, needs, and beliefs that are the result of his or her unique experiences from birth. Yet it also recognizes that whatever is brought to the situation must be related to the world as that person confronts it. It is in the transactions between the person and the parts of that person's world that the quality of life can be enhanced or damaged.

Herein lies the uniqueness of social work. The social worker is prepared to work with both the person and the relevant environment to improve the quality of their interaction. In contrast, the physician is primarily prepared to treat physical aspects of the individual, and the attorney is largely concerned with the operation of the legal system in the larger environment (although both the physician and the attorney must give secondary attention to other, related systems). The social worker, however, gives secondary attention to the individual and environment separately, and directs primary attention to the manner in which they relate to each other. In other words, the social worker is primarily engaged in facilitating transactions between the person and the environment. Figure 1–1 depicts this unique focus of social work and will be developed more fully in later

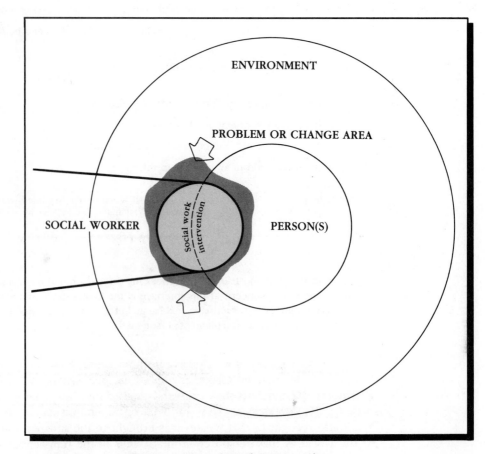

FIGURE 1–1   *Focal Point of Social Work Intervention*

chapters to illustrate the dimensions of social work in more detail. It should be noted that this figure overstates the sharpness of the focus of social work to highlight the point that social-work intervention involves both person and environment.

> *A Description of Social Work Practice:* Social work practice consists of the professional application of social work values, principles, and techniques to one or more of the following ends: helping people obtain tangible services; counseling and psychotherapy with individuals, families and groups; helping communities or groups provide or improve social and health services; and participating in legislative processes.

This part of the NASW definition directs attention to what social workers do. The payoff for the clients of social workers, whether they are individuals, groups, or various social institutions, is in the services provided. These services might take the form of providing access to *social provisions* or tangible items such as food, housing, clothing, or financial assistance. They might also include *social services* or more intangible forms of helping, such as using counseling or group process skills to help people solve problems or to improve their functioning relative to their interactions with other people or with various social institutions. Finally, social workers engage in the use of *social action* techniques to improve the functioning of community groups and organizations or to influence the legislative process to make the laws more responsive to human needs.

> *Knowledge Requirements for the Social Worker:* The practice of social work requires knowledge of human development and behavior; of social, economic, and cultural institutions; and of the interaction of all of these factors.

The NASW definition of social work concludes with a recognition that social work practice must also be guided by knowledge. The social worker is obligated to provide the best service possible. To improve the success rate with clients over one's natural helping abilities, it is necessary to draw on the best knowledge of human behavior and of the larger society. First, the social worker must gain both general knowledge about aspects of the human condition and specific technical knowledge required for social work. This can be gained through completing one of the baccalaureate and/or master's-level educational programs accredited by the Council on Social Work Education (CSWE). The knowledge one would expect to acquire in these programs includes a liberal arts perspective as well as a professional foundation that includes the basic knowledge, values, and skills required for competent social work practice. Second, the social worker must be dedicated to a lifetime of study as a skillful reader of the professional literature and as a student in staff development, continuing education, or advanced degree programs.

SOCIAL WORK PRACTICE APPROACHES: VERSATILE AND ACTION-ORIENTED

Social work also has had difficulty in arriving at a practice approach that was sufficiently flexible and encompassing to relate to this complex profession. In fact, social work can be characterized during much of its history as a profession in search of a practice approach. That search included the development of several distinct practice methods, i.e., casework, group work, community organization, administration, and research, as well as the more recent emergence of a generalist perspective and the development of a number of specialized practice approaches.

Traditional Practice Methods

As part of its drive to become identified as a unique profession, social work sought to identify a distinctive method of practice that would distinguish it from the other helping professions such as law, medicine, and psychology. The first practice method to develop, *social casework,* had its roots in the Charity Organization Society movement and was expressed in the first significant publication on social work practice, *Social Diagnosis.*[10] In this book Mary Richmond focused on the requirements for effective practice with individuals and families, regardless of the type of problem presented, and filled an important void in social work by introducing a practice literature. The principles of social casework identified by Richmond were enthusiastically adopted by social workers, and the profession moved to an almost exclusive focus on individuals and families. The popularity of Freudian psychology in the 1920s and 1930s, coupled with conservative opposition to more aggressive social change strategies, directed social work toward less controversial individual approaches. Edith Abbott noted that Richmond later had expressed concern over the exclusive nature of this trend and had stated that social workers should simultaneously be concerned with preventing problems.

> The good social worker, says Miss Richmond, doesn't go on helping people out
> of a ditch. Pretty soon she begins to find out what ought to be done to get rid
> of the ditch.[11]

Social workers concerned with providing services to groups took longer to develop a set of guiding principles, partially because those social workers involved in the Settlement House Movement disagreed as to whether they should identify professionally with the emerging fields of social work, recreation, or continuing education. This disagreement among the *social group workers* was resolved in the 1930s in favor of identifying with social work, and thus a second distinct method evolved.

The third practice method to develop was *community organization.* The Charity Organization Societies provided a coordinative and evaluative function among the emerging agencies in most communities, a function that was later moved to more autonomous councils of social agencies and is now frequently a United Way function. This form of practice was concerned with the distribution of financial resources and services within communities. Specific practice approaches that emerged within these organizations gradually were identified with social work.

In addition to using one of these three primary practice methods in their work, many social workers also found themselves responsible for administering social agencies and conducting research on the effectiveness of social work practice. Their experience and education usually left them with little preparation for these indirect service activities. By the late 1940s *administration* and *research* had evolved as practice methods in social work. Viewed as secondary methods, they were seen as a supplement to one's ability as a caseworker, group worker, or community organizer.

Multimethod Practice Approach

Concurrent with the development of these five distinct practice approaches was the growing commitment to the identification of social work as one profession with a unifying practice method. A major study of social work and social work education, the Hollis-Taylor Report, was concluded in 1951. It recommended that because the breadth of social work practice required social workers to intervene in more than one level of client system, social work education should prepare students with a beginning level of competence in each of the five practice methods.[12]

The multimethod practice approach proved a better fit with the varied demands for social work practice, but failed to yield the unifying practice theme the profession needed. Practitioners continued to identify with a dominant method and use the others sparingly. Elitism within the profession based on practice method and setting interfered with the search for commonality and unity within social work.

Generalist Practice Approach

Supported by concepts drawn from social systems theory, the generalist approach to practice began to emerge in the late 1960s. As Balinsky has stated, "The complexity of human problems necessitates a broadly oriented practitioner with a versatile repertoire of methods and skills capable of interacting in any one of a number of systems."[13] The generalist model provided that versatility and met the requirement for a flexible approach to social work practice demanded by the increasing complexity and interrelatedness of human problems.

→ Generalist practice contains two fundamental components. First, it provides a perspective from which the social worker views the practice situation. Social system theory helps the social worker to maintain a focus on the interaction between systems—i.e., the person–environment transactions. Second, rather than attempting to make the client's situation fit the methodological orientation of the social worker, the situation is viewed as determining the practice approach to be used by the social worker. Thus, the social worker is required to have a broad knowledge and skill base from which to serve clients or client systems and to have the ability to appropriately select from that base to meet the needs of the clients.

To summarize with a definition of *generalist social work,* we define it as

> ... an approach to practice characterized by a) a focus that is equally attentive to person and environment, b) a process that begins with the unique situation brought for help by the client or client system and then selects the most appropriate theory or theories to explain the situation and applies intervention strategies (ranging from individual to community change) that fit that situation, and c) a commitment to maximizing humanism, democracy, and client empowerment when carrying out practice activities.[14]

Although many social workers contend that the generalist approach has been part of social work practice since its inception, there have been limited careful analysis and explication of this practice approach. However, with an accreditation requirement that baccalaureate-level social workers be prepared as generalist practitioners[15] there has been a resurgence of activity aimed at clarifying the nature of generalist practice in recent years. In their article entitled "Milford Redefined: A Model of Initial and Advanced Generalist Social Work," Shatz, Jenkins, and Sheafor further describe the key elements of generalist social work at both the initial and advanced generalist levels as they are understood today.[16] Their model is based on research that identified areas of agreement among experts who have written about generalist social work practice or administered educational programs that prepared students for generalist practice. This model recognizes that there is a *generic foundation* for all social work, whether generalist or specialist, that includes such factors as knowledge about the social work profession, social work values, the purpose of social work, ethnic/diversity sensitivity, basic communication skills, understanding of human relationships, and others.

The *generalist perspective* is, according the Schatz-Jenkins-Sheafor model, (1) informed by sociobehavioral and ecosystems knowledge, (2) incorporates ideologies that include democracy, humanism, and empowerment, (3) requires a worker to be theoretically and methodologically open when approaching a practice situation, (4) is client-centered and problem-focused, (5) involves both direct and indirect intervention awareness, and (6) is research-based.

At the *initial generalist* level of practice the social worker builds on the generic foundation and, using the generalist perspective, must at least be capable of (1) engaging effectively in interpersonal helping, (2) managing change processes, (3) appropriately selecting and utilizing miltilevel intervention modes, (4) intervening in multiple-sized systems as determined by the practice situation, (5) performing varied practice roles, (6) assessing and examining one's own practice, and (7) functioning successfully within an agency.

The *advanced generalist* social worker, according to Schatz, Jenkins, and Sheafor, operates from an expanded knowledge base about individuals, groups, organizations, and communities. The advanced generalist also develops increased skills to intervene in direct service provision with individuals, families, and groups, at one end of the multiple-level practice spectrum, and, at the other end, to address more complex indirect practice situations such as supervision, administration, and policy or program evaluation. Finally, the advanced generalist is exected to approach social work practice from an eclectic but disciplined and systematic stance and to simultaneously engage in both theoretical research and practice evaluation.

Specialist Practice Approach

In contrast to the generalist approach, a number of specialized practice approaches have emerged. *Specialist social work* practice, as it is defined for use in this book, is an approach characterized by the application of selected knowledge and skills to a narrowed area of practice based on practice setting, population group served, social problems addressed, and/or practice intervention mode used. In other words, this practice approach begins with a specified expectation about the knowledge and skills required for practice in that specialized area and fits the client into those more narrow, but in-depth, worker competencies.

While education for generalist practice usually is offered in baccalaureate social work programs or the early part of master's-level programs, specialist education has increasingly been designated as the prerogative of the latter part of a master's degree. The Curriculum Policy Statement of the Council on Social Work Education that guides the accreditation of these programs identifies the following specializations that schools might offer:

Fields of Practice: Services to families, children, and youth; services to the elderly; health; mental health; developmental disabilities; education; business and industry; neighborhood and community development; the justice system; and income maintenance and employment.

Population Groups: Children, youth, adults, middle-aged adults, the aged, women, men, families, ethnic populations, groups defined by income levels, migrants.

Problem Areas: Crime and delinquency, substance abuse, developmental disabilities, illness, family violence, neighborhood deterioration, poverty, racism, sexism.

Practice Roles and Interventive Modes: Practice with individuals, families and groups, consultation, training, community organization, social planning, program planning and development, administration, policy formulation, implementation and analysis, and research.[17]

In addition, schools might offer an opportunity for students to concentrate in "advanced generalist" practice, where the student adds both more detailed information about the practice competencies learned in the generalist model and greater breadth of knowledge, values, and skills required for practice.

Today, like many disciplines, social work embraces both generalist and specialist approaches to practice. The generalist viewpoint supports the commonality that unites social work into one profession; the specialist approach helps to delineate unique areas for in-depth social work practice. In tracing the history of this generalist–specialist issue, Leighninger notes that "debates of optimum levels of breadth and depth in social work education and practice, and the relationship between these, recur in each decade."[18] At this point social work appears to have achieved a reasonably comfortable position regarding the balance of generalist versus specialized practice.

SOCIAL WORKERS: THEIR MANY FACES

It is possible to understand the diversity of social workers better by knowing their competencies, their career patterns, and their personal characteristics. The colleagues with whom one works and the trends in one's profession are important considerations when one is making a career choice.

Competencies of Social Workers

We have seen that to practice social work effectively, one must be able to provide a variety of helping services. The social worker not only must be able to work directly with a client or clients, but also must be prepared to understand and work to change the environment of these clients. One must understand the culture in which the practice occurs, the cultural background of the people served, and the functioning of the social agency where the services are provided as well as know what other services are available in the community, the reasons the clients have sought services, and alternate means by which to provide these services. In short, the social worker must be competent in knowledge, values, and skills to help clients resolve a broad range of existing or potential problems in social functioning.

What are the basic competencies that are fundamental to social work practice? Depending on the particular job a social worker occupies, the type of agency, client capabilities, problems being addressed, and resources available, the social worker will need to have differing competencies. With a generalist perspective and a repertoire of helping techniques, the social worker is prepared to begin most social work jobs. As one becomes experienced and jobs become more specialized, additional skills may be required.

As social work gradually has reached greater consensus regarding how it should be defined, it has become possible to be more precise about the competencies required to fulfill that role. Throughout social work's recent history several efforts have been made to identify the critical tasks performed by social workers. The primary limitation of these approaches was their reliance on experts to describe what social workers do in their daily practice. Too often these descriptions were more assertions about what social workers should be doing than factual statements of what tasks social workers actually perform. In the early 1980s NASW conducted a project designed to address its concern that many human service agencies were reducing the professional education requirements for many social work jobs and, therefore, reclassifying them to lower level positions (see Chapter 3). In an effort to establish a method to determine if there is a valid relationship between the content of professional education programs and social work practice activities, the NASW Classification Validation Project constructed a "job analysis" approach for studying social work practice that yields important empirical data about the activities of social work practitioners.[19]

The "job analysis" strategy invites frontline social workers to rate a series of approximately 135 different tasks typically performed by social workers according to their importance in their work, and a profile of their work activity is obtained through analysis of these answers. Through the statistical technique of cluster analysis it is possible to reduce the many tasks into a few groupings of activity performed by social workers, with the specific tasks that are correlated with each cluster serving as the basis for its definition. This self-reported analysis of the work of social workers yields perhaps the best description available of the type of activities in which social workers actually engage.

Several studies have been completed in which the job-analysis methodology has been used. One such study using this methodology, reported in 1987, yielded the following sixteen clusters of practice activity as performed by social workers in both governmental (public) and voluntary (private) social agencies:

1. *Formal Intervention with Individual Clients.* Use specific assessment or intervention techniques to provide support, improve client functioning, or bring about changes in the presenting needs of individual clients and their immediate support groups.

2. *Ongoing Case Management for Specific Clients.* Organize work and make arrangements for carrying out an ongoing plan of services for a specific client. . . . Activities include dictating and recording actions, reviewing files prior to client contact, carrying out procedures to protect client rights, and establishing a working relationship with clients.

3. *Teaching of Adaptive and Daily Living Skills.* Give informal instruction to help clients, volunteers, and agency personnel acquire adaptive skills for daily living. These areas include hygiene, basic communications, money management, orientation to new living arrangements and communities, and insight into human development processes.

4. *Linking Clients to Resources.* On behalf of clients, engage in interactions with agency personnel, natural helpers, and potential employers in order to connect clients with resources. These linkages involve using established connections. They include making contacts with professionals for purposes of team building and networking as well as putting clients with similar backgrounds and problems in contact with one another.

5. *Resource Assessment and Aggressive Client Brokering.* Identify service providers, services, and resources and assess their suitability for use by clients. Aggressively solve delivery problems and mediate on behalf of specific clients to insure eligibility and protect their rights.

6. *Initiation and Adjustment of Service Plan.* Carry out activities, for individual or multiple clients, to develop a service plan (at intake) or change it at

strategic points in the episode of service. Activities include arranging for resources inside or outside the agency, assessing the need for changes, and evaluating progress.

7. *Assessment of the Need for Protective Services.* Observe children and adults and assess the hazards associated with their living conditions or placement settings in order to determine whether various types of abuse or neglect (psychological, sexual, or physical) have occurred or are likely to occur.

8. *Arrangement of Specific Services for Clients.* Make referrals and engage clients and family members in making various types of linkages (e.g., transportation, medical care, appointments). Conduct case follow-ups and prepare individuals and families for changes in living arrangements.

9. *Formal Intervention with Groups.* Use formal interventive techniques with groups in order to teach skills in group participation to group members or to improve social functioning by taking part in the group process.

10. *Self Development/Information Transmission.* Engage in activities designed to develop self-awareness with regard to one's knowledge, skills, and values as such self-awareness relates to improvement in job functioning. Keep current by reading various materials, attending workshops, and exchanging various types of information.

11. *Quality Assurance Monitoring.* Communicate organizational performance expectations in order to insure compliance with organizational standards. Activities include reviewing agency records, conducting job performance evaluations of workers, carrying out orientation and training, and holding performance review conferences with workers.

12. *Staff Management.* Clarify job duties and agency rules, establish work schedules, and assign cases and other responsibilities to staff members.

13. *Internal Paper Flow.* Fill out and/or sign vouchers, requisitions, or standard data collection forms to purchase materials, pay vendors, or provide data for agency records.

14. *Ongoing Program/Unit Administration.* Perform tasks associated with day-to-day operation of a program or administrative unit. Activities include budgeting, monitoring, and documentation of expenditures, keeping track of supplies and inventory, monitoring the status of buildings and equipment, and summarizing information about staff.

15. *Management of Organizational Change/External Relations.* Propose and negotiate plans for implementing program and other organizational changes. Internal activities include recruiting and screening program personnel and conducting staff meetings. External activities involve serving as a buffer to protect staff from external pressures, negotiating with consumers, and interpreting programs to the community in order to maintain their viability.

16. *Program Planning/Design/Evaluation.* Assess the need for new services, establish program goals, design programs, plan service delivery mechanisms, secure support and resources, prepare staff, and evaluate program differences.[20]

Analysis of rankings of the importance of each of these sixteen clusters of practice tasks indicated that persons engaged in direct service jobs were most likely to engage in the activities described in clusters 1–9 while those in supervisory or administrative jobs were likely to find clusters 11–16 most important in their work. All workers were somewhat evenly involved in cluster 10, Self Development/Information Transmission. It is evident from these data that social workers have varied jobs that require competence to perform many tasks. It takes rigorous professional education to master the necessary competencies to enter social work practice prepared to provide the services required by persons in need.

The professional social worker, then, differs from the *natural helper*.[21] Before reaching a social worker or other professional helpers, clients often have asked for or have been given help by family, friends, neighbors, or volunteers. When that help is successful, people usually do not seek out professional help. Natural helping is an important resource for problem solving. It is based on a mutual relationship among equals, and the natural helper draws heavily on intuition and life experience to guide the process. Professional help is different. It is a disciplined approach focused entirely on the needs of the client that requires the helper consciously to apply specific knowledge, values, and skills in the helping process. Both natural and professional helping are valid means of helping people resolve problems in social functioning. In fact, at times the social worker will help activate natural helping systems in order to supplement professional help and maintain support for clients after the services of the social worker have been terminated, but they are not a substitute for competent professional help in addressing serious problems or gaining access to needed services.

Career Patterns of Social Workers

Varying social work career patterns have evolved as demands for social workers have changed over time. The early social workers were volunteers or paid staff who required no specific training or educational program to qualify for the work. When formal educational programs were instituted at the turn of the century, they were training programs located in the larger social agencies. In fact, it was not until 1939 that standards required that all recognized social work education must be offered in institutions of higher education. There was also controversy over whether appropriate social work education could be offered at the baccalaureate level as well as at the more professionally acceptable master's level. The reorganization, or perhaps more accurately organization, of social work into a single professional association (the National Association of Social Workers) and one professional education association (the Council on Social Work Education) in the 1950s yielded a single-level profession. At that time, only the master's degree from an accredited school of social work was considered "legitimate" social work preparation. In 1961 the NASW established another level of professional recognition by creating the Academy of Certified Social Workers (ACSW). It was the first step in creating a multilevel career pattern.

Although today the MSW is considered the terminal practice degree in social work, a small number of social workers are also completing doctoral degrees in social work (DSW or Ph.D.). The number of persons completing the doctorate at a school of social work in the United States averaged 238 per year during the 1980s.[22] Most doctoral-level social workers are employed in teaching or research positions, but an increasing number of doctoral programs aimed at preparing people for direct social work practice are emerging.

It was not until 1970 that the NASW recognized baccalaureate-level social workers as members of the Association when they had completed a social work major approved by the Council on Social Work Education. By 1989 there were a reported 26,154 social work majors in 362 accredited programs in the United States.[23] Another career level had evolved.

NASW publishes a classification system that helps to clarify the various entry points to social work and defines the educational and practice requirements at each level. This system sorts out the somewhat mixed practice levels that have evolved in social work over the past thirty years.

Basic Professional	Requires a baccalaureate degree from social work program accredited by the Council on Social Work Education (CSWE)
Specialized Professional	Requires a master's degree from a social work program accredited by CSWE
Independent Professional	Requires an accredited MSW and at least two years of post-master's experience under appropriate professional supervision
Advanced Professional	Requires special theoretical, practice, administrative, or policy proficiency or ability to conduct advanced research or studies in social welfare, usually demonstrated through a doctoral degree in social work or a closely related social science discipline.[24]

This classification scheme has several benefits. First, it identifies and clarifies the practice levels existing in social work, and it distinguishes the competencies that both clients and employers can expect (see Chapter 3 for a more complete specification of the competencies). Second, it describes a continuum of social work education with several entry points for the person wishing to make a career in social work. Finally, it suggests a basis for job classification that can increasingly distinguish among the various levels of social work competence in task and salary.

Characteristics of Today's Social Workers

In 1991, Teare and Sheafor merged data from three studies of social work practitioners to yield a profile of the work performed by professional social workers.[25]

The studies were conducted to provide a profile of social work practice that serves as the basis for the Academy of Certified Baccalaureate Social Workers (ACBSW) examination, NASW's Academy of Certified Social Workers (ACSW) examination, and an analysis of occupational social work practice. The data set includes 7000 respondents (1449 BSW and 5551 MSW) from these representative samples of social workers from throughout the United States. Although the task analysis of these workers' activities has not yet been released, the demographic and employment data that are available present an informative comparison of baccalaureate- and master's-level social workers. Table 1–1 identifies several characteristics of these respondents that provide insight into today's social workers.

These data indicate that the practicing social workers are predominantly female, particularly those working with a baccalaureate social work degree, who are more than 87 percent women (as opposed to 60 percent of the master's-level social workers). The number of minority group social workers practicing at the bachelor's and master's levels is about equal, with about 10.8 and 12.1 percent of minority background respectively.

Examination of Table 1–1 (see Current Employment Setting) reveals that social workers at both the baccalaureate and master's levels work in virtually every type of human service organization. There are, however, some marked differences in the preponderance of the two levels in different settings. Nearly one-half of the BSW workers, as compared to one-fourth of the MSWs, are employed by more general social service agencies such as small private agencies and public welfare agencies. BSWs are also much more likely than the MSWs to work in nursing homes and group homes or residential centers. Master's-level social workers are much more likely than their BSW counterparts to be employed by hospitals, outpatient mental health centers, schools, colleges and universities, and to be engaged in the private practice of social work.

The practice areas in which social workers work with their clients touch virtually every aspect of human life. The study reported in Table 1–1 identifies some rather substantial differences, however, in the primary practice areas addressed by baccalaureate- and master's-level social workers. BSWs are more likely to work with people at both ends of the age spectrum, i.e., children and youth as well as the aged population, and to serve the mentally retarded and developmentally disabled.

Concerning the earnings of social workers, the National Association of Social Workers recommends minimum salary levels for each of the four social work practice levels. These recommendations are intended to assist social agencies in establishing fair and competitive minimums in their salary structures. NASW recommends that the minimum annual income for a BSW social worker should be $20,000, as compared to $25,000 for the MSW, $30,000 for the MSW with two or more years of experience, and $45,000 for the highly skilled and experienced, advanced social worker.[26]

Recommended salaries often exceed the actual pay scales. Insight into the actual earnings of social workers can be gained through analysis of salary data NASW collected through a survey of 26,338 social workers who initiated or

TABLE 1–1 *Characteristics of Baccalaureate- and Master's-Level Social Workers*

Social Worker Characteristic	BSW	MSW
Gender: Female	87.5%	59.5%
Minority Group Member	12.1	10.8
Current Employment Setting		
Social service agency	46.7	26.0
Hospital (medical)	13.8	20.9
Nursing home/Hospice	11.6	1.0
Outpatient facility (mental health)	8.7	18.9
Group home/Residential center	6.4	1.6
Institution (psychiatric)	4.4	3.7
Court/Criminal justice system	2.8	1.4
Elementary/Secondary School	2.1	7.0
Non–social service agency	1.2	2.9
Private practice	.9	9.3
Membership organization	.6	1.2
College/University	.6	6.9
Primary Practice Area		
Children and youth	18.8	12.7
Services to the aged	16.6	3.6
Family services	13.7	13.5
Medical/Health	12.8	13.3
Mental health	9.9	28.3
Developmental disability/Mental retardation	9.6	3.4
Alcohol/Substance abuse	3.3	2.1
Public assistance/Public welfare	3.1	1.5
Corrections/Criminal justice	2.7	1.3
Schools	1.5	6.1
Other disabilities	.8	.5
Occupational social work	.6	1.1
Community/Organizational change	.5	1.5
Education	.3	4.9
Primary Employment Function		
Direct services	85.1	52.0
Management/Administration	8.3	27.4
Supervision	6.6	9.8
Education/Training	2.2	7.0
Consultation	.9	2.1
Policy planning and analysis	.6	1.3
Research	0.0	.2

Source: Robert J. Teare, Bradford W. Sheafor, and Barbara W. Shank, "Demographic and Employment Characteristics of BSW and MSW Social Workers." Paper presented to Baccalaureate Program Directors' Association, Minneapolis, Minn., September, 1990.

renewed their NASW memberships between July 1986 and June 1987[27] and from the 1989 study of BSW graduates reported above.[28] These data show the median salary of BSW social workers at $19,890 and the MSW workers at $27,800. The average salaries of DSW/Ph.D social workers is estimated at 28 percent above the MSW workers, or $35,600 per year. Analysis of regional differences in salaries suggest that social workers on the East and West coasts earn an average of roughly $1000–$1500 more than the amounts reported above and those in the South earn $1000–$1500 less.

Substantial salary differentials were related to job function, gender, and practice setting. The NASW salary study reveals that, at least for MSW social workers, the indirect service positions were paid the highest salaries and were primarily occupied by men. Specifically, managers and administrators averaged $35,200, policy developers and analysts $33,600, persons involved in education and training earned $32,300, while those in planning, research, and supervisory positions averaged $29,000. The direct service workers, on the other hand, averaged $25,300. The contention that women are less likely to hold the higher paying indirect service positions is confirmed by a salary differential of 30.5 percent. The data also indicated that social workers employed in colleges and universities or in private practice were at the high end of the pay scale and that workers employed in group or residential homes or nursing homes were at the low end.

Employment Projections for Social Workers

What are the employment prospects for social workers? It is especially difficult to project future social work employment patterns because social workers are usually lumped with other human service providers when the U.S. Bureau of Labor Statistics (BLS) makes its projections. Further, due to the fact that social work practice is intertwined with the larger society and subject to political and economic swings, projections require assumptions that over time a somewhat steady level of social programs will be maintained. In the past, however, the BLS middle-range projections have proven a reasonably accurate predictor of social work employment patterns and serve as a useful indicator of employment trends.

The U.S. Bureau of Labor Statistics projected that the number of social work jobs will increase from 385,000 to 495,000 (a 2.4 percent annual growth rate) between the years 1988 and 2000.[29] Further, the BLS estimates that each year 10.1 percent of the people holding social work jobs will leave the field, resulting in the need for a total of 13.5 percent, or approximately 52,000 new social workers each year. It is further estimated that only 49.3 percent of those persons classified by the BLS as social workers hold degrees from accredited social work education programs. For the preparation of professional social workers to keep pace with the estimated demand, then, the accredited schools need to graduate more than 25,500 new social workers annually. The Council on Social Work Education (based on data from 84.8 percent of the BSW programs and 98.9 percent of the MSW programs) reported 16,718 graduates in 1989.[30] Thus, it is reasonable to conclude that social work education is producing only about two-thirds of the anticipated supply of professional social workers that will be needed in the next decade. Although jobs for social workers may not be plentiful in any particular year, geographic location, or type of employment, long-range projections for those with professional social work education are favorable.

CONCLUDING COMMENT

Since its inception almost a century ago, social work has emerged as a comprehensive helping profession. From the beginning social workers have sought that elusive common denominator that would make a clear conception of this diverse discipline possible. It is quite possible that social work might have developed into several different disciplines, but the common task of helping people negotiate a more satisfying and productive existence with the world around them served to make the profession a cohesive entity.

The basic mission of social work has been to provide a combination of caring, curing, and changing activities in order to help people improve their social functioning—that is, to help people and their social environment change to enhance the quality of life for all. In addition to helping people deal with their environments, social workers are also charged to bring about social change in order to prevent problems or make social institutions more responsive to the needs of individuals.

To accomplish these goals, social workers are employed in settings that provide services ranging from child welfare to mental health to corrections work. An increasing number are employed in private practice where they contract directly with clients to provide services. Some are generalist in their practice perspective, while others are specialists and provide in-depth services related to particular helping activities.

The social workers themselves are prepared with the knowledge, values, and skills, or the competencies, to respond to a great variety of human problems. They are professionally educated at both the baccalaureate and master's levels of education and have evolved a career pattern that prepares them to provide this broad range of human services. Despite the conservative political/economic climate in the 1980s, employment projections for the next decade continue to be above the capacity of the professional social work programs to produce. The future for the person choosing a career in social work looks quite positive.

SUGGESTED READINGS

BARTLETT, HARRIET M. "Toward Clarification and Improvement of Social Work Practice." *Social Work* 3 (April 1958): 3–9.

GORDON, WILLIAM E. "A Critique of the Working Definition." *Social Work* 7 (October 1962): 3–13.

LEIBY, JAMES. "Moral Foundations for Social Welfare and Social Work: A Historical View." *Social Work* 30 (July-August 1985): 323–330.

MINAHAN, ANNE N. "Purpose and Objectives of Social Work Revisited." *Social Work* 26 (January 1981): 6.

MORALES, ARMANDO. "Beyond Traditional Conceptual Frameworks." *Social Work* 22 (September 1977): 387–393.

NATIONAL ASSOCIATION OF SOCIAL WORKERS. *Social Work* 19 (September 1974), 22 (September 1977), and 26 (January 1981). (Three issues devoted to conceptual frameworks for the profession.)

ENDNOTES

1. Carol H. Meyer, "Social Work Purpose: Status by Choice or Coercion? *Social Work* 26 (January 1981): 71–72.
2. Willard C. Richan and Allan R. Mendelsohn, *Social Work: The Unloved Profession* (New York: New Viewpoints, 1973), p. 20.
3. Robert Morris, "Social Work Function in a Caring Society: Abstract Value, Professional Preference, and the Real World," *Journal of Education for Social Work* 14 (Spring 1978): 83.
4. Bradford W. Sheafor, Charles R. Horejsi, and Gloria A. Horejsi, *Techniques and Guidelines for Social Work Practice* 2nd ed. (Boston: Allyn and Bacon, 1991).
5. American Association of Social Workers, *Social Casework: Generic and Specific* (Washington, D.C.: National Association of Social Workers, 1929), p. 11.
6. Copyright 1958, National Association of Social Workers, Inc. Reprinted with permission from Harriet M. Bartlett, "Towards Clarification and Improvement of Social Work Practice," *Social Work* 3 (April 1958): 5–7.
7. See *Social Work* 19 (September 1974); *Social Work* 22 (September 1977); and *Social Work* 26 (January 1981).
8. National Association of Social Workers, *Standards for Social Service Manpower* (Washington, D.C.: The Association, 1973), pp. 4–5.
9. William E. Gordon, "Basic Constructs for an Integrative and Generative Conception of Social Work," in Gordon Hearn, ed., *The General Systems Approach: Contributions toward a Holistic Conception of Social Work* (New York: Council on Social Work Education, 1969), p. 7.
10. Mary E. Richmond, *Social Diagnosis* (New York: Russell Sage Foundation, 1917).
11. Edith Abbott, "The Social Caseworker and the Enforcement of Industrial Legislation," in *Proceedings of the National Conference on Social Work, 1918* (Chicago: Rogers and Hall, 1919), p. 313.
12. Ernest V. Hollis and Alice L. Taylor, *Social Work Education in the United States* (New York: Columbia University Press, 1951).
13. Rosalie Balinsky, "Generic Practice in Graduate Social Work Curricula: A Study of Educators' Experiences and Attitudes," *Journal of Education for Social Work* 18 (Fall 1982): 47.
14. Bradford W. Sheafor and Pamela S. Landon, "Generalist Perspective" in Anne E. Minahan, ed., *Encyclopedia of Social Work,* 18th ed. (New York: National Association of Social Workers, 1987), pp. 660–669.
15. Council on Social Work Education, *Handbook of Accreditation Standards and Procedures,* rev. ed. (New York: Council on Social Work Education, 1984): Appendix 1, p. 126.

16. Mona S. Schatz, Lowell E. Jenkins, and Bradford W. Sheafor, "Milford Redefined: A Model of Initial and Advanced Generalist Social Work." Unpublished manuscript, Colorado State University, Fort Collins.

17. CSWE, *Handbook of Accreditation,* Appendix 1, pp. 128–129.

18. Leslie Leighninger, "The Generalist–Specialist Debate in Social Work," *Social Service Review* 54 (March 1980): 1.

19. Robert J. Teare et al., *Classification Validation Processes for Social Service Positions,* vols. I–VII, (Washington, D.C.: National Association of Social Workers, 1984).

20. Robert J. Teare, Bradford W. Sheafor, and Thomas P. Gauthier, "Establishing the Content Validity of Social Work Credentials." Photocopy materials accompaning a paper presented at the 33rd Annual Program Meeting of the Council on Social Work Education, St. Louis, Missouri, March, 1987.

21. Shirley L. Patterson, "Toward a Conceptualization of Natural Helping," *Arete* 4 (Spring 1977): 161–171; Alice H. Collins and Diane L. Pancoast, *Natural Helping Networks* (Washington, D.C.: National Association of Social Workers, 1976); and James K. Whittaker and James Garbarino, *Social Support Networks: Informal Helping in the Human Services* (New York: Adeline de Gruyter, 1983).

22. Allen Rubin, ed., *Statistics on Social Work Education in the United States: 1984* (Washington, D.C.: Council on Social Work Education, 1985), p. 49; and Elaine C. Spaulding, ed., *Statistics on Social Work Education in the United States* (Washington, D.C.: Council on Social Work Education, 1990), p. 36.

23. Spaulding, *Statistics, 1989,* p. 34.

24. Reprinted with permission from *NASW Standards for the Classification of Social Work Practice,* Policy Statement 4 (Silver Spring, Md.: 1981), p. 9.

25. Robert J. Teare, Bradford W. Sheafor, and Barbara W. Shank, "Demographic and Employment Characteristics of BSW- and MSW-Level Social Workers." Unpublished paper presented at meeting of Baccalaureate Program Directors' Association, Minneapolis, Minn., 1990.

26. "NASW Recommended Minimum Salaries," *NASW News* 35 (September 1990): 22.

27. "First-Time Look at Members' Salaries Finds Their Average Income Is $27,800," ©1988 National Association of Social Workers, Inc. *NASW News,* Vol. 33, January, 1988, pp. 1 and 18.

28. Robert J. Teare, Barbara W. Shank, and Bradford W. Sheafor, "Career Patterns of Baccalaureate Social Workers." Unpublished manuscript, Colorado State University, Fort Collins.

29. Bureau of Labor Statistics, *Occupational Projections and Training Data,* 1990 ed. (Washington, D.C.: U.S. Department of Labor, 1990), p. 21.

30. Spaulding, *Statistics, 1989,* pp. 1, 34, and 36.

CHAPTER 2

The Emergence of Social Work as a Profession

The growth and development of social work has not been a planned event. It just happened. It is a response to human suffering that began in several different parts of American society and eventually coalesced into a single, diverse profession.

Because its development has not been guided by a clear master plan, social work has been heavily influenced by a variety of factors. It has been pushed in one direction by external forces such as periods of political and economic conservatism, the stress of wars and other major international events, and by competition from other emerging helping disciplines. At the same time, social work has been pulled in other directions by its own goals and aspirations, such as the need for a coherent concept of the profession that could incorporate its different roots and its intense desire to be recognized as a legitimate profession.

In order to understand and appreciate social work more fully, it is useful to trace its emergence and identify key historical events and professional actions that have shaped the profession. While one could gain insight into the emergence of social work by examining the influence of external events, this chapter is guided by an examination of social work's internal professional development. It begins with a review of professions, particularly the helping professions, in U.S. society. It traces the emergence of social work during the past century, with emphasis on the choices made that affected its acceptance as a profession, and concludes with an analysis of its current professional status.

THE NATURE OF PROFESSIONS

A field of sociological inquiry has developed that is devoted to the definition and description of the nature of professions. One of the central figures in this field,

Wilbert Moore, concluded that "to have one's occupational status accepted as professional or to have one's occupational conduct judged as professional is highly regarded in all post industrial societies and in at least the modernizing sectors of others."[1]

Professions are highly regarded because they have been granted sanction to perform essential services that ensure survival and enhance the quality of life. For individuals, professionalism is usually personally satisfying, financially rewarding, and productive of high social status. For professions, this recognition is essential: it enhances the ability to recruit qualified people and ensures the respect of other professions and the general public. From the clients' point of view, the designation of professionalism signals those persons who are qualified to provide particular services and provides at least a minimum level of protection against incompetent and unethical behavior by practitioners. Recognition as professional, then, has been an important motivation driving many occupations.

How is it determined whether or not an occupation is a profession? One approach to the study of professions, known as the *absolute approach,* has been to examine the traditional professions of medicine, law, the ministry, and higher education to isolate their fundamental elements. These studies revealed that professions could be characterized by such factors as their requirements for specialized skill and training, a specific base of knowledge, the formation of professional associations, and the development of codes of ethical behavior governing professional practice.[2] Other occupations were then evaluated to determine whether they, too, contained these elements and could be considered professions. Using this approach, occupational groups were classified in one of two categories: professional or nonprofessional.

More recently the prevalent approach to the study of professions has been to identify the key attributes common to professions and assess the degree to which any other occupational group possesses these attributes. This *relative approach* to professionalism allows for the placement of any occupational group along a continuum from nonprofessional to professional. Using this approach, Moore, for example, identifies the primary characteristics of a profession as a full-time occupation, commitment to a calling, identification with peers, specified training or education, a service orientation, and autonomy restrained by responsibility.[3] Using such criteria, it is possible to place each occupational group on a scale of professionalism relative to other occupations. The point at which an occupation sufficiently meets the criteria to be considered a profession is not absolute, but determined by judgment.

As more has been learned about professions, three elements have been delineated to help explain the unique characteristics of the occupations that are considered to be professions.

First, professionals must be free from constraints that might limit their ability to act in the best interests of their clients. The protection of this *professional autonomy* has been most successful in professions that contract directly with clients to provide services on an entrepreneurial or private practice basis. In these situations few constraints are imposed on the manner in which practice is conducted. In agency-based professions, however, the organizations employ the professionals and contract with the clients to provide service. The agency's rules and regulations, intended to improve organizational efficiency and accountability, limit the professional's autonomy to exercise independent judgment regarding the manner in which services are provided.

Second, professions possess a monopoly in their field of expertise. Society has granted *professional authority* to a few people who have acquired the necessary knowledge and skills to provide the needed services in a given area of professional practice. Society grants this authority because it has in effect determined that it is inefficient, if not impossible, for every person to acquire all the knowledge and skill needed to meet complex human needs. Thus, these professionals are given the exclusive right to make judgments and give advice to their clients. In granting this professional authority, society in essence gives up the right to judge the competence of these professionals except in extreme cases of incompetent or unethical practice. Society depends on the members of that profession to determine the requisite entrance preparation and be sure those who are practicing as members of that profession do so competently.

To be able to operate within the authority of a given profession, each member must master the knowledge and skills the profession has determined to be essential. Through the accreditation of its educational programs and the content of examinations that govern certification by a profession, the technical information and competencies fundamental to that profession are assured. However, human problems typically extend beyond the purview of any one profession. To be of maximum effectiveness it is important that the professional not only has the technical training required for his or her profession, but must also possess a fund of general knowledge gained from the study of history, literature, philosophy, theater, and other fields that will help to provide a broad understanding of the human condition. In short, professionals must be both technically and generally educated.

Third, when the right to judge practice is relinquished by granting professional authority, the public becomes vulnerable and rightfully expects the professions to protect them from abuses that may accrue from the professional monopoly. Hughes indicates that the motto of the professions must be *credat emptor* ("buyer trust"), as opposed to the motto of the marketplace, *caveat emptor* ("buyer beware").[4] For example, where the layperson would rarely question the prescription of a physician, that same person might be very cautious when buying a used car and might have it thoroughly tested by an independent mechanic before making a purchase. To maintain this buyer trust, the professions must be accountable to the public that has granted them the sanction to perform these services. In order to establish and maintain this *professional responsibility,* professions develop codes that identify the expected ethical behavior of practitioners and establish mechanisms for policing their membership regarding unethical or incompetent practice.

In a sense, the professions and society struck a deal. In exchange for responsible service in sensitive areas of life, the professions were granted exclusive authority, i.e., a professional monopoly, to offer these services.

HELPING PROFESSIONS: A RESPONSE TO HUMAN NEED

All helping professions began as a response to unmet human need. As people experienced suffering or insufficient development in some aspect of life, when natural helping networks were not sufficient to meet the resulting needs, various forms of professional help emerged. Physicians, teachers, clergy, and other professional groups began to appear and to be given approval by the society to perform specific helping functions. The buyers', or clients', vulnerability was intensified in the area of helping services because they dealt in especially sensitive areas where unwitting persons could be harmed by the incompetent or improper actions of the professional. In addition to the codes of ethics and bodies established to investigate situations where abuses of this monopoly were alleged, the helping professions also characteristically have had external sources of client protection. For the entrepreneurial professions and private practitioners, this additional protection has taken the form of licensing professional practice, while clients of agency-based professions are usually considered to have adequate supplemental protection through the monitoring of practice by the agencies and organizations.

It was soon realized that the effectiveness of these helpers was increased when their skills were supported by specific knowledge and values that could guide their interventions into the lives of clients or groups of clients. As this professional knowledge expanded through the development of theories and concepts, as well as through experience, trial and error, or practice wisdom, the professions expanded their technical knowledge requirements and their membership became increasingly exclusive. There was a time when each profession could respond to a number of human needs. For example, the clergy traditionally provided help for both spiritual and social needs. However, the increasingly specialized knowledge necessary to provide effective helping services has led to a proliferation of helping professions, each with its own specializations.

What are these needs to which the helping professions have responded? In simplest form, people have two fundamental needs. The first is to possess security; that is, to love and be loved, to relate to others, and to have material comforts. The second is to experience growth by achieving maturity and developing one's maximum potential. Such broad definitions of need did not provide sufficient focus for emerging professions. Too much knowledge and skill was required of any individual to meet these broad needs adequately. A more precise description of needs, provided by Brill, helps to clarify the primary focus of the several helping professions as they exist today.[6]

- *Physical Needs:* functioning of the physical structures and organic processes of the body (Medicine and Nursing)

- *Emotional Needs:* feelings or affective aspects of the consciousness that are subjectively experienced (Psychology)
- *Intellectual Needs:* capacity for rational and intelligent thought (Education)
- *Spiritual Needs:* desire for a meaning in life that transcends one's life on earth (Religion)
- *Social Needs:* capacity for satisfying relationships with others (Social Work)

While the helping professions have tended to organize around a single need, there are exceptions, such as psychiatry, in which both emotional and physical needs—and their interaction—are the focus of professional service.

The increase of helping professions from few to many, and their overlap when providing services to people who experience more than one need, has inevitably led to problems in defining professional boundaries. As newer professions like social work, occupational therapy, and music therapy have emerged, they have devoted considerable energy to staking out their professional boundaries. That activity is important because it identifies for each profession, the other professions, and the public the unique contribution made by each to meeting human needs. It also helps to focus their education and training programs, research activities, and the development of appropriate professional knowledge.

How a profession stakes out its professional boundaries has significant influence on that profession. The more elitist professions limit the people they claim as their target of service to those with narrowly defined problems, typically charging high fees to the few people who require that service. These professions usually require extensive and highly technical training; few people acquire the credentials to be recognized as part of that profession. This limited supply of professionals yields high prestige and financial reward for those who hold the proper qualifications. Other professions have been far more open in their membership requirements and more general in the type of issues for which they provide service. This lack of exclusiveness has at times been viewed as less professional and has resulted in lower prestige and less financial remuneration for the persons identified with these professions.

Two models of professionalism have developed in the United States. One is the *private model,* where the individual client contracts directly with the professional for service. Law and medicine are clear examples of professions that have followed this model. A second model, typified by teachers and city planners, is the *public model of professionalism* in which the professionals primarily operate under the auspice of formal organizations and direct their services to the common good. Howe notes:

> For any given profession, the pattern of whether it serves primarily individual clients, the public, or both groups equally is determined in large part by the nature of the service it provides and by whether its beneficiaries are individuals or larger groups. When the beneficiary is one individual client, the service would be what an economist would call a private good; if the service benefits the collectivity, it would be a collective or public good.[7]

For social work, with its dual focus on person and environment, both the private and public models of professionalism apply. It must balance concern for the individual client and the public welfare.

Thus, it is evident that the nature of the services provided, the needs of the clientele served, and the professional model adopted will influence the orientation of any emerging profession. In addition the aspirations of that profession for a particular place among the professions will have a significant impact on the choices it makes at various points during the development.

How, then, has social work emerged? Where does it fit among the helping professions?

SOCIAL WORK AS A PROFESSION: A HISTORICAL PERSPECTIVE

From Volunteers to an Occupation (Prior to 1915)

The roots of social work may be found in the extensive volunteer movement during the formative years of the United States. In the colonial period, for example, it was assumed that individuals or families would care for themselves, but if further difficulties existed, friends, neighbors, or representatives of the community would volunteer to meet their needs. A description of such voluntary service is given by William Bradford, Governor of Massachusetts, concerning the smallpox epidemic of 1620:

> In ye time of most distress, there was but 6 or 7 sound persons, who to their great comendations be it spoken, spared no pains night nor day, but with abundance of toyle and hazard of their owne health, fetched them woode, made them fires, drest them meant, made their beads, washed their loathsome cloaths, cloathed and uncloathed them; in a word did all ye homly and necessarie offices for them ... all this willingly and cherfully, without any gruding in ye least, shewing herein true love unto their friends and brethern.[8]

These voluntary acts of service gradually became more formalized as numerous social agencies were formed. Some organizations carried such descriptive names as the Home for Little Wanderers, the Penitent Females' Refuge, and the Home for Intemperate Women. In the early 1800s, Alexis de Tocqueville commented on this development:

> Americans of all ages, all conditions, and all dispositions constantly form associations.... The Americans make associations to give entertainments, to found seminaries, to build inns, to construct churches, to diffuse books, to send missionaries to the antipodes; in this manner they found hospitals, prisons, and schools.[9]

The volunteer activities of some of these organizations involved interaction with the needy, the ill, and those with other social problems. These volunteer efforts were, however, frequently marked by a condescending attitude toward recipients of these services.

Developing out of this background came social work as an *occupation*. The first paid social work–type positions in the country were jobs in the Special Relief Department of the United States Sanitary Commission. Beginning as a voluntary agency and then receiving public support as the Civil War progressed, the Special Relief Department and its agents served Union soldiers and their families experiencing social and health problems due to the war. The wartime needs temporarily opened the door for women to provide social services, and their outstanding performance helped pave the way for other positions in social work. Several women involved in the war effort performed important leadership roles in the development of human services. For example, Dorothea Dix (Superintendent of Nurses in the U.S. Sanitary Commission) previously had provided leadership in an attempt to secure federal government support for mental hospitals; Clara Barton later founded the American Red Cross; Josephine Shaw Lowell helped start the Charity Organization Society in New York and also headed the Consumers' League, which worked to protect shopgirls from exploitation; Sojourner Truth gave leadership to the National Freedman's Relief Association; and Harriet Tubman, a central figure in the Underground Railroad, subsequently established a home for elderly blacks. Following the war the Special Relief Department was closed and social work temporarily disappeared as an occupation.

Social work reappeared a few years later when the Massachusetts Board of Charities was established in 1863. Founded under the leadership of Samuel Gridley Howe, an advocate for the physically and mentally handicapped, this agency coordinated services in almshouses, hospitals, and other institutions of the state. Although its powers were limited to inspection and advice, the Board gained wide acceptance under the leadership of Howe and its paid director, Frank B. Sanborn. The concept of boards overseeing state services spread to other states in the 1870s and became the forerunners to today's state departments of social services and institutions.

The Massachusetts Board of Charities also introduced social research into human service delivery. A 1893 report, for example, identified the causes of poverty as "first, physical degradation and inferiority; second, moral perversity; third, mental incapacity; fourth, accidents and infirmities; fifth, unjust and unwise laws, and the customs of society."[10] To deal with problems of such complex roots, paid staff members who could specialize in providing services were secured.

Another significant development leading to the emergence of social work was the establishment of the Charity Organization Society (COS) of Buffalo, New York, in 1877. Copied after an organization in London, charity organization societies sprang up in a number of communities with the dual purposes of finding means to help the poor and preventing the poor from taking advantage of the numerous uncoordinated social agencies that provided financial assistance. Leaders in social work from the COS movement included Mary Richmond, who helped identify a theory of practice in her books *Friendly Visiting among the Poor*

(1899) and *Social Diagnosis* (1917); Edward T. Devine, a founder of the New York School of Philanthropy in 1898 and its first director; and Porter Lee, who was instrumental in founding the American Association of Schools of Social Work in 1919.

Another important development that contributed to the emergence of social work was the Settlement House Movement initiated in 1886. Patterning settlement houses after London's Toynbee Hall, people such as Stanton Coit and Jane Addams established settlements in New York and Chicago. Within fifteen years, about one hundred settlement houses were operating in the United States. The settlements helped the poor learn skills required for urban living and simultaneously provided leadership in political action efforts to improve the social environment. Bremner sums up the impact of the settlement movement:

> Where others thought of the people of the slums as miserable wretches deserving either pity or correction, settlement residents knew them as much entitled to respect as any other members of the community. Numerous young men and women who lived and worked in the settlements during the 1890s carried this attitude with them into later careers in social work, business, government service, and the arts.[11]

The residents of Chicago's Hull House are a good example. Its founder, Jane Addams, won the Nobel Peace Prize in 1931; Julia Lathrop was the first director of the U.S. Children's Bureau and was succeeded by other Hull House alumnae Katherine Lenroot and Grace Abbott, thus contributing to the protection of children and youth for several decades. John Dewey was a philosopher and expert in educational theory, and Sophonisba Breckinridge helped form and was dean of the Chicago School of Civics and Philanthropy; while Edith Abbott contributed to the development of state public welfare programs.

The efforts to integrate the black population into the mainstream of U.S. society following the Civil War also contributed to the development of social work. George Haynes, the first black graduate of the New York School of Philanthropy, for example, helped found the National Urban League, while Mary McLeod Bethune gave leadership to the education of black women, was a founder of the National Council of Negro Women, and was influential in making New Deal policies more equitable for the black population.

Social work practice in hospitals began at the Massachusetts General Hospital in the early 1900s. Under the leadership of Richard C. Cabot, physician to outpatients, Ida Cannon established the first medical social work department in the United States and devoted nearly fifty years to the growth and development of this practice specialty. These social workers provided services for patients experiencing health-related social problems and also worked to strengthen the services of related health and welfare agencies throughout the community. Lubove identifies the significance of this development for the professionalization of social work:

> The enlistment of medical social workers marked an important stage in the development of professional social work. A casework limited to the charity orga-

nization and child welfare societies provided too narrow a base for professional development, associated as it was with problems of relief and economic dependency. Medical social work added an entirely new institutional setting in which to explore the implications of casework theory and practice.[12]

Medical social workers became interested in professional education as a means of moving beyond social work's "warm-heart" image and into an understanding of the psychic or social conditions as the base of patient distress. Further, with professional education it would be possible to move into more of a collegial relationship with the physician. In 1912, with Ida Cannon's participation, a one-year course in medical social work was established in the Boston School of Social Work.

Through these years social work jobs were springing up in other practice areas such as mental hygiene (mental health), prisons, employment and labor relations, and schools. Beginning in 1873 an organization designed to draw together members of this diverse occupation was formed, the National Conference on Charities. Later renamed the National Conference on Charities and Corrections, this organization brought volunteer and professional staff members of social agencies together to exchange ideas about the provision of services, discuss social problems, and "give more intensive study to 'practical' work."[13] Through the leadership of a remarkable group of social work pioneers, by the time World War I began social work was an established occupation distinguishable from the many volunteer groups and other occupations concerned with the well-being of the most vulnerable members of U.S. society.

Professional Emergence (1915–1950)

With social work firmly established as an occupation, attention then turned to its development as a profession. As opposed to relying on the day-to-day practice activities of its charismatic leaders, social work's professional development depended on the creation of a unifying professional organization. At the 1915 meeting of the National Conference on Charities and Corrections, Abraham Flexner addressed the subject, "Is Social Work a Profession?" Dr. Flexner, an authority on graduate education, had previously done a penetrating study that led to major changes in medical education. The organizers of this session of the National Conference apparently hoped Flexner would assure them that social work was, or was about to become, a full-fledged profession. However, that was not in the cards. Flexner, using an "absolute approach" to his study of professions, spelled out six criteria that an occupation must fully meet to be considered a profession:

1. Professions are essentially intellectual operations with large individual responsibility.
2. They derive their raw material from science and learning.
3. This material is worked up to a practical and clear-cut end.
4. Professions possess an educationally communicable technique.

5. They tend to self-organization.
6. They become increasingly altruistic in motivation.

After evaluating whether social work met these criteria—but not evaluating to what degree they were met—Flexner concluded that social work had not yet made it into the professional elite.[14] Following Flexner's admonition to "go forth and build thyself a profession," social workers busily attended to these functions over the next thirty-five years.

One effort was to develop a code of ethics. In 1921 Mary Richmond indicated that, "we need a code; something to abide by, or else we will have low social standing."[15] One code, the "Experimental Draft of a Code of Ethics for Social Case Workers," was discussed at the 1923 meeting of the National Conference on Social Welfare. Although this proposal was never acted upon, it represented a beginning effort at formulating a statement of professional ethics.

Probably the greatest effort was devoted to building a professional organization. The National Social Workers Exchange was opened in 1917 to provide vocational counseling and placement and later became actively involved in the identification and definition of professional standards. In 1921 its functions were taken over by the broader American Association of Social Workers, which made significant efforts to develop a comprehensive professional association. This effort was later weakened by attempts of some specialties to develop their own professional organizations. A chronology of the development of these specialized groups follows:

- 1918 American Association of Hospital Social Workers
- 1919 American Association of Visiting Teachers
- 1926 American Association of Psychiatric Social Workers
- 1936 American Association for the Study of Group Work
- 1946 American Association for the Study of Community Organization
- 1949 Social Work Research Group[16]

The need for a unified thrust for professional status was clearly evident.

Another development during this period concerned the methods of preparation to enter the social work profession. Social work education had begun in agency-based training, but a concerted effort was made during this period to transfer it to colleges and universities, where other professions had located their professional education. In 1919 the Association of Training Schools for Professional Social Workers was established with seventeen charter members—both agency and university affiliated schools.[17] The purpose of that organization was to develop professional standards in social work education. By 1927 considerable progress toward that purpose had been made and the Association of Training Schools reorganized into the American Association of Schools of Social Work (AASSW). Where the education programs had been offered in agencies as well as at both undergraduate and graduate levels in colleges and universities, the AASSW determined that by 1939 only university affiliated programs with two-year graduate programs would be recognized as professional social work education.[18]

That action led to a revolt by schools whose undergraduate programs prepared professionals to meet the staffing needs of the social agencies in their states. A second professional education organization was formed in 1942, the National Association of Schools of Social Service Administration, made up largely of public universities in the midwest that offered baccalaureate and one-year graduate level professional education programs. Harper described this development as "a protest movement against unrealistic and premature insistence upon graduate training and overemphasis upon professional casework as the major social work technique."[19]

With leadership from governmental and voluntary practice agencies, the two organizations were later merged (1951) into the Council on Social Work Education (CSWE) following the landmark Hollis-Taylor study of social work education.[20] The outcome of that decision favored the two-year master's program as the minimum educational requirement for full professional status. Undergraduate social work education temporarily faded from the scene.

Another important area of concern that was given only limited attention during this period was strengthening the knowledge and skill base of social work practice. Richmond's rich contribution, *Social Diagnosis,* was the first effort to formalize a communicable body of techniques applicable to the diverse settings in which social caseworkers were found.[21]

Momentum from this thrust, however, was lost as social work slipped into the grasp of the popular psychoanalytic approach. Cohen comments, "The search for a method occurred just at the time the impact of psychoanalysis was being felt. Did social work, in its haste for professional stature, reach out for a ready-made methodology for treating sick people, thus closing itself off from the influence of developments in the other sciences?"[22] This question must be answered in the affirmative. By adopting the helping methodology that was currently in vogue, social work became firmly, but perhaps inappropriately, wedded to the private model of professionalism. Writing in *Harper's Magazine* in 1957, Sanders accurately criticized social work for "floating with the ghost of Freud."[23] One might speculate about what would have happened if the model adopted had been the one for public education or public health.

Lowe, perhaps appropriately, critiques this period of social work's professional development by indicating that social workers incorrectly placed emphasis on the development of their skills and credentials (which split the profession) and failed to adequately develop the power to control their occupational arena. Lowe notes,

> The dimensions of control and power supporting monopoly are central to the professional notion. . . . Social work leadership between 1915 and 1952 misunderstood or ignored these crucial dynamics. This "mistake" led to practice methodology (casework) and educational policies (graduate-only) that sought status rather than occupational control. This flawed analysis split the occupation in its formative years.[24]

Consolidating the Gains (1950–1970)

The move to consolidate the accrediting bodies for the schools of social work into the CSWE set an important precedent for the field and was part of a broad movement to treat social work as a single and unified profession. In 1950 the several specialized associations and the American Association of Social Workers agreed to form the Temporary Inter-Association Council of Social Work Membership Organizations (TIAC). The purpose behind the formation of TIAC was the organization of one central professional association. After considerable efforts by the specialties to maintain their identities, TIAC proposed a merger of the several groups in 1952. By 1955 this was accomplished, and the National Association of Social Workers (NASW) was formed. The purposes of the NASW were:

1. To improve administration of social work services
2. To advance research in social work
3. To improve social work practice
4. To improve social work education
5. To recruit to the profession
6. To improve social conditions
7. To gain public understanding of social work
8. To improve salaries and working conditions
9. To develop, promulgate, and enforce a Code of Ethics
10. To certify the competence of social workers
11. To promote the development of the profession in other countries.[25]

The basic membership requirement for the NASW was graduation from a school of social work accredited by the CSWE and, of course, payment of dues. By 1964, 88.7 percent of NASW members held at least a master's degree, and 4.1 percent had completed the two-year educational program but had not completed all degree requirements.[26] The remainder were members under the "grandparent clause" for non-degree members of the predecessor organizations.

NASW membership rose from 28,000 to 45,000 between 1961 and 1965, largely because of the formation of the Academy of Certified Social Workers (ACSW), which required both NASW membership and a two-year period of supervised experience. Many job descriptions were revised to require membership in the Academy, forcing social workers to join the NASW and obtain certification.

The late 1950s were a time of great introspection, and the professional journal, *Social Work,* was filled with articles such as "The Nature of Social Work,"[27] "How Social Will Social Work Be?"[28] and "A Changing Profession in a Changing World."[29] Perhaps the most significant work was Ernest Greenwood's classic article, "Attributes of a Profession," in 1957.[30] Greenwood, using the "relative approach" to the study of professions, identified five critical attributes of professions that, depending on the degree to which they have been accomplished, determine the degree of professionalism for any occupational group:

1. A systematic body of theory
2. Professional authority

3. Sanction of the community
4. A regulative code of ethics
5. A professional culture

He related the development of social work to each of these five criteria and placed social work on a scale of professionalism. He concluded:

> When we hold up social work against the model of the professions presented above, it does not take long to decide whether to classify it within the professional or nonprofessional occupations. Social work is already a profession; it has too many points of congruence with the model to be classifiable otherwise.[31]

To the credit of social workers, they were as stimulated by Greenwood's declaration that they had become a profession as they were by Flexner's conclusion that they were not yet in the select circle. In 1958 the NASW published the "Working Definition of Social Work Practice," a valuable beginning to the difficult task of identifying professional boundaries.[32] This was followed by Gordon's excellent critique, which helped strengthen and clarify some parts of the working definition, particularly in relation to knowledge, values, and practice methodology.[33] In 1960 the NASW adopted a Code of Ethics to serve as a guide for ethical professional practice,[34] thus completing the steps to become a fully recognized profession.

At what price has professional status been attained? Sanders pointedly noted that social work had become a profession but had lost a mission. She indicated that social work had avoided controversial issues to keep its image clean, had become rigid in efforts to control service provision, and had developed jargon to maintain exclusiveness.[35]

Turning Away from the Elitist Professional Model (1970–Present)

From the turn of the twentieth century to the late 1960s, social work displayed a pattern typical of an emerging profession. It created a single association to guide professional growth and development; adopted a code of ethical professional behavior; provided for graduate-level university-based professional schools and acquired recognition to accredit those educational programs; successfully obtained licensing for social work practice in some states; conducted public education campaigns to interpret social work to the public; achieved recognition for social work among the helping professions; and moved in the direction of other professions by increasing specialization and limiting access to the profession. Indeed, social work was on its way to carving its niche among the elite group of helping professions.

However, social work did not vigorously pursue the path that would lead to even greater professional status. Perhaps influenced by a renewed spirit of concern emanating from the Civil Rights, Welfare Rights, and Women's Rights movements, the development of social work as a profession during the 1970s and

1980s was marked by an ambivalence over continued change in the more traditional format of the established professions.

First, there was a resurgence of social change activity on the part of social workers. A legacy from Lyndon Johnson's Great Society programs was federal support in the form of jobs and other resources toward efforts to eliminate social problems and alleviate human suffering. Social work was already committed to those goals, and social workers were prepared to move away from their clinical orientation and onto the front lines of social action. In 1966 Schorr reflected on this change:

> For one reason or another, the dazzle that once hovered over casework—especially psychiatric social work—now lights up social policy. Those interested in social policy ten years ago could have held their conventions in a telephone booth (if they had a dime); today they deliver the major addresses at our national conferences.[36]

For social workers bent on achieving higher professional status, the activist social workers were sometimes unpopular. Their somewhat controversial activities at times created an unwelcome public image of the profession characterized by activists on the front lines of social change. This change in the balance of activities performed by social workers helped to bring social work back to its roots and reestablish the "change" orientation in its mission of caring, curing, and changing (see Chapter 1).

The more liberal political climate that supported social work activism was short-lived. The federal support for programs encouraging social change dwindled and was nearly nonexistent under the Reagan and Bush administrations. Social workers again turned toward a more clinical orientation, and the social policy addresses at their national conferences were more nostalgic than immediately applicable.

Second, in 1970 NASW made a dramatic move by revising its membership requirements to give full membership privileges to anyone who had completed a baccalaureate degree in social work from an undergraduate program approved by CSWE. In opposition to the pattern of professions becoming more exclusive, social work opened its membership to more people, and a generalist approach to practice was embraced. Beginning in 1970, professional qualifications could be gained by obtaining professional education at the undergraduate level. However, social work has been uneasy about operating as a multilevel profession and, although the NASW classification system is clear about the "basic social worker" being viewed as professional, the social worker at this level has never been fully accepted by many MSW social workers. Some advocates for the baccalaureate social worker contend that NASW has not devoted sufficient attention to this practice level and that its program priorities in the 1980s "centered too much on licensing, vendor payments, private practice and other issues that were not sufficiently relevant to the baccalaureate worker."[37] NASW's creation of the Academy of Certified Baccalaureate Social Workers in the early 1990s represents movement from that overemphasis on the interests of master's-level social workers.

With NASW's formal recognition of baccalaureate social work as fully professional, in 1974 the Council on Social Work Education began implementing the full accreditation for baccalaureate social work education programs. Initially, 135 schools met the undergraduate accreditation requirements, and by 1990 more than 360 schools in the United States and Puerto Rico enjoyed accredited status. Of particular importance was the increased accessibility of these programs to persons wishing to become social workers. Where most of the ninety-seven accredited MSW programs were located in urban areas, undergraduate programs were found in both urban and rural communities. A study of 1449 baccalaureate practitioners in 1989 found that 40.7 percent worked in communities of 40,000 or less (as compared to approximately 22 percent of the U.S. population), and 11.1 percent were employed in communities of 10,000 or less.[38] These data suggest that the professionalization of baccalaureate social work opened educational opportunities to people who could not attend schools in urban areas and who enriched the provision of services in smaller communities by filling human service jobs in these areas.

Similarly, the emergence of professionally sanctioned baccalaureate-level social work education programs increased the opportunity for members of minority and lower socioeconomic backgrounds to enter social work as they could complete the requisite education preparation without needing both bachelor's and master's degrees. To illustrate, in 1989, 23.3 percent of the 26,154 full-time baccalaureate majors were of minority background, as opposed to 16.5 percent of the 15,777 full-time MSW students.[39]

The return of a conservative political climate in the United States during the 1980s created a perception that few jobs would be available in social work when the Reagan Administration completed its objective of dismantling the Great Society programs. After peaking at nearly 28,000 undergraduate social work majors in the late 1970s, that number declined by more than one-fourth by 1983. Enrollments then began to increase, gradually, and most of the loss had been regained by the beginning of the 1990s. Similarly, the number of full-time MSW students declined by one-fifth between 1978 and 1983 but almost returned to the pre-Reagan level by the end of the 1980s. The decline in enrollment was not matched by a comparable decline in social work jobs, yielding an undersupply of social work graduates. Often less qualified, or at least differently prepared, personnel were hired to fill social work jobs, and too often clients received services from personnel who were not qualified.

A third trend occurring in the past two decades has been the growing acceptance of a generalist orientation as a basis for social work practice. Where professions have tended to become increasingly specialized, social work has made a distinct move in the opposite direction. The search for a common practice approach that could embrace the breadth of social work practice has at least temporarily ended with general agreement that the generalist perspective is a viable approach for beginning-level social workers. At an elementary level the generalist approach can be described as directing the social worker to address practice situations unencumbered by a specific practice method and to select the most appropriate intervention techniques to fit the unique needs of the client or group.[40] The generalist approach is reinforced by the accreditation standards of the Council on Social Work Education, which require that the baccalaureate programs make preparation for the initial level of generalist practice their primary educational objective and permit the master's-level programs to offer an advanced generalist curriculum.

The adoption of the generalist model has not meant that social work has given up the development of specialized practice. Many specialized MSW programs prepare students with a generalist base and then add on content that emphasizes practice with unique population groups (e.g., age, race, gender), particular fields of practice (e.g., developmental disabilities, mental health, services to families), unique social problems (e.g., family violence, neighborhood deterioration), or specialized practice roles or intervention modes (e.g., practice with families, community planning, research).[41]

THE EMERGENCE OF INTERPROFESSIONAL
PRACTICE AND EDUCATION

With their own identity as a profession firmly established, social workers have begun to join other professions in efforts to strengthen interprofessional practice and education. One vehicle for this development is the National Consortium on Interprofessional Practice and Education, where the Council on Social Work Education and the National Association of Social Workers have joined parallel associations from medicine, law, theology, education, nursing, psychology, and the several "allied health disciplines" to explore ways of improving human services through cooperation among the professions. As opposed to previous attempts to create a new professional group blended from disenchanted members of existing professions (i.e., the "human services" movement), the major professions are beginning to explore means to better prepare practitioners to work collaboratively in the provision of services in a manner that builds on the unique contributions of each profession.

The growing complexity and rapid change in U.S. society have made it important to develop means to increase interprofessional collaboration.[42] For example, the expansion of specialization in all professions requires that a means be found to orchestrate the work of health and human service professionals so that there are neither problems of overlap (and therefore professional competition and/or waste of scarce resources) or problems of clients not getting services because they fall through the gaps between professional boundaries. Also, as noted by Dunn and Janata, "rapid technological advances and the resulting increase in the knowledge pool require new modes of problem solving and new collaboration among the professions in the delivery of services."[43]

Clients of human services are the primary losers when there is professional specialization without interprofessional collaboration. The committed professional must be prepared to engage in collaboration with other disciplines to maximize client services. The social worker, who is responsible for paying special attention to both person and environment, should give leadership to this interprofessional collaboration.

CONCLUDING COMMENT

In the past three-fourths of a century, social work has developed in a manner that it meets the generally accepted criteria for professions. Concensus about its unique purpose among the professions has been reached, and social work has achieved sanction as the appropriate profession to help people resolve problems in their interaction with their environments. Social workers have been granted the professional autonomy to provide the necessary helping services for people in need, although social workers are constrained by the fact that most are employed in social agencies that limit their ability to exercise professional judgment. Increasingly, they are entering private practice where the constraints are less severe.

Social work has taken its authority to provide these professional services seriously. Its national professional organization, the National Association of Social Workers, has worked through the decades to clarify social work's knowledge, value, and skill base. Social work has developed educational programs that prepare new people to enter this profession and established a process for accrediting the programs that meet qualitative educational standards at both the baccalaureate and master's levels. Accredited programs exist in more than 400 colleges and universities and enroll more than 42,000 students each year.

Social work has also adopted a comprehensive Code of Ethics (see Chapter 8) and established procedures for dealing with social workers who might violate that code. A process has been established through the National Association of Social Workers that allows the profession to carry out its professional responsibility to protect clients and the general public from abuses that might arise from the professional monopoly it has achieved.

One might expect social workers to feel satisfied with these accomplishments. Yet, within a profession of many faces, there are inevitably varied opinions. While most social workers believe the progress made in becoming a recognized profession is desirable, some believe that it has become too elitist and is targeting its services too much to the white middle class. Others believe that it has lowered professional standards by opening its membership to those with less than graduate-level credentials. Some believe it should meet the requirements of a private profession, and still others believe it should more fully embrace the model of the public professions and be satisfied with its professional status. Some also believe that social work's unique role in interprofessional practice should be that of the generalist who orchestrates or coordinates the client services provided by several disciplines, while others view social work's role as providing more specialized social treatment services on a parallel with the other helping professions as they respond to clients' physical, emotional, spiritual, and intellectual needs. As the twenty-first century approaches, these issues will be on social work's agenda.

SUGGESTED READINGS

Austin, David M. "The Flexner Myth and the History of Social Work," *Social Service Review* 57 (September 1983): 357–377.

Brieland, Donald. "History and Evolution of Social Work Practice," in Anne Minahan, ed., *Encyclopedia of Social Work* 18th ed. Silver Spring, Md.: National Association of Social Workers, 1987, pp. 739–754.

Day, Phillis J. *A New History of Social Welfare.* Englewood Cliffs, N.J.: Prentice-Hall, 1989.

Greenwood, Ernest. "Attributes of a Profession," *Social Work* 2 (July 1957): 45–55.

Howe, Elizabeth. "Public Professions and the Private Model of Professionalism," *Social Work* 25 (May 1980): 179–191.

Leighinger, Leslie. *Social Work: Search for Identity.* Westport, Conn.: Greenwood, 1987.

Lowe, Gary R. "Social Work's Professional Mistake: Confusing Status for Control and Losing Both," *Journal of Sociology and Social Welfare* 14 (June 1987): 187–206.

Lubove, Roy. *The Professional Altruist.* Cambridge, Mass.: Harvard University Press, 1965.

Trattner, Walter I. *From Poor Law to Welfare State* 4th ed. New York: Free Press, 1989.

Trolander, Judith Ann. *Professionalism and Social Change: From the Settlement House to Neighborhood Centers, 1886 to the Present.* New York: Columbia University Press, 1987.

ENDNOTES

1. Wilbert E. Moore, *The Professions: Roles and Rules* (New York: Russell Sage Foundation, 1970), p. 3.
2. A. M. Carr-Sanders and P. A. Wilson, *The Professions* (Oxford: Clarendon Press, 1933), pp. 3–31.
3. Moore, *Professions,* pp. 5–6.
4. Everett C. Hughes, "Professions," *Daedalus* (Fall 1963): 657.
5. Naomi I. Brill, *Working with People: The Helping Process* 3d ed. (New York: Longman, 1985): 23.
6. Ibid., pp. 24–28.
7. Elizabeth Howe, "Public Professions and the Private Model of Professionalism," *Social Work* 25 (May 1980): 181.
8. Ralph E. Pumphrey and Muriel W. Pumphrey, eds., *The Heritage of American Social Work* (New York: Columbia University Press, 1961), p. 12.
9. Alexis de Tocqueville, *Democracy in America* (New York: Alfred A. Knopf, 1945 reprint), p. 106.
10. Pumphrey and Pumphrey, *Heritage,* p. 146.

11. Robert H. Bremner, *From the Depths* (New York: New York University Press, 1956), p. 66.
12. Roy Lubove, *The Professional Altruist* (Cambridge, Mass.: Harvard University Press, 1965), p. 32.
13. Pumphrey and Pumphrey, *Heritage,* pp. 161–163.
14. Ibid., pp. 301–307.
15. Ibid., p. 310.
16. John C. Kidneigh, "History of American Social Work," in Harry L. Lurie, ed., *Encyclopedia of Social Work* 15th issue (New York: National Association of Social Workers, 1965), pp. 13–14.
17. Bradford W. Sheafor and Barbara W. Shank, *Undergraduate Social Work Education: A Survivor in a Changing Profession* (Austin: University of Texas School of Social Work, 1986), Social Work Education Monograph Series 3. 4.
18. David M. Austin, *A History of Social Work Education* (Austin: University of Texas School of Social Work, 1986), Social Work Education Monograph Series 1: 8.
19. Herbert Bisno, "The Place of Undergraduate Curriculum in Social Work Education," vol. II, in Werner W. Boehm, ed., *A Report of the Curriculum Study* (New York: Council on Social Work Education, 1959), p. 8.
20. Ernest V. Hollis and Alice L. Taylor, *Social Work Education in the United States* (New York: Columbia University Press, 1951).
21. Mary E. Richmond, *Social Diagnosis* (New York: Russell Sage Foundation, 1917).
22. Nathan E. Cohen, *Social Work in the American Tradition* (New York: Holt, Rinehart, & Winston, 1958), pp. 120–121.
23. Marion K. Sanders, "Social Work: A Profession Chasing Its Tail," *Harper's Monthly* 214 (March 1957): 56–62.
24. Gary R. Lowe, "Social Work's Professional Mistake: Confusing Status for Control and Losing Both," *Journal of Sociology and Social Welfare* 14 (June 1987): 187.
25. David G. French, "Professional Organization," in Harry L. Lurie, ed., *Encyclopedia of Social Work.* 15th issue (New York: National Association of Social Workers, 1965), p. 576.
26. Ibid.
27. Werner W. Boehm, "The Nature of Social Work," *Social Work* 3 (April 1958): 10–18.
28. Herbert Bisno, "How Social Will Social Work Be?" *Social Work* 1 (April 1956): 12–18.
29. Nathan E. Cohen, "A Changing Profession in a Changing World," *Social Work* 1 (October 1956): 12–19.
30. Ernest Greenwood, "Attributes of a Profession," *Social Work* 2 (July 1957): 45–55.
31. Ibid., p. 54.
32. Harriet M. Bartlett, "Towards Clarification and Improvement of Social Work Practice," *Social Work* 3 (April 1958): 5–7.
33. William E. Gordon, "Critique of the Working Definition," *Social Work* 7 (October 1962): 3–13; and "Knowledge and Values: Their Distinction and Relationship in Clarifying Social Work Practice," *Social Work* 10 (July 1965): 32–39.
34. National Association of Social Workers, *Code of Ethics* (Washington, D.C.: The Association, 1960).
35. Sanders, pp. 56–62.
36. Alvin L. Schorr, "Editorial Page," *Social Work* 11 (July 1966): 2.
37. Sheafor and Shank, p. 25.
38. Robert J. Teare, Barbara W. Shank, and Bradford W. Sheafor, "Career Patterns of the BSW Social Worker." Unpublished manuscript, Colorado State University, 1990.
39. Elaine C. Spaulding, ed., *Statistics on Social Work Education in the United States, 1989* (Alexandria, Va.: Council on Social Work Education, 1990), pp. 34 and 36. (Data

based on reports from 84.8 percent of the accredited baccalaureate programs and 98.9 percent of the accredited MSW programs).

40. Bradford W. Sheafor and Pamela S. Landon, "Generalist Perspective," in Anne Minahan, ed., *Encyclopedia of Social Work* 18th ed., vol. 1 (Silver Spring, Md.: National Association of Social Workers, 1987), pp. 660–669.

41. Council on Social Work Education, "Curriculum Policy Statement for the Master's Degree and Baccalaureate Degree Programs in Social Work Education," in *Handbook of Accreditation Standards and Procedures* rev. ed. (Washington, D.C.: The Council, 1988), pp. 128–129.

42. Richard C. Snyder, "A Societal Backdrop for Interprofessional Education and Practice," *Theory into Practice* 24 (Spring 1987): 94.

43. Van Bogard Dunn and Mary M. Janata, "Interprofessional Assumptions and the OSU Commission," *Theory into Practice* 24 (Spring 1987): 99.

CHAPTER 3

Entry to the Social Work Profession

Selecting a career is one of the most important decisions a person must make. Whether that decision is to become a homemaker, physician, salesperson, teacher, chemist, or social worker, it should be based on a thorough understanding of the physical, emotional, and intellectual demands of the field and a close look at one's own suitability for that type of work. Whatever the choice, it will dictate how a person spends a major part of each day. It will also spill over into other aspects of life, including life style, general satisfaction with self, and quality of life.

Making a career choice is difficult because of the wide range of careers to choose from but, more importantly, because of the problems an outsider experiences in gaining an adequate and accurate understanding of a career. Too often, only after a person has made substantial commitments in time, energy, and money or has cut off other opportunities by taking steps to enter a career does he or she find that it is not what was expected or wanted.

Another difficulty lies in having a clear perception of one's own needs, interests, and abilities. Personal introspection, occupational preference testing, guidance counseling, and experience in activities related to the career are all resources for making this choice.

The person contemplating a career in social work must consider a number of factors. It is evident that social work is extremely broad in scope—ranging from social action to individual therapy—and is constantly changing, with a *knowledge base* that is far from stable or well developed. Thus, explicit guidelines for social work practice do not exist, leaving the social worker with the responsibility for exercising a great deal of individual judgment.

The *value base* calls for a view of the human condition compatible with the social work approach of helping people improve their social functioning. Furthermore, the *skills* demanded of the social worker vary widely and require a flexible, creative, and introspective person to practice them. The pressures of a social work job are great since the outcome of the work is critically important to the clients. In addition social workers are regularly criticized by both clients and the general public, frequently in regard to programs social workers administer but over which they have little policy-making influence.

If a person can tolerate the ambiguity, responsibility, pressures, and criticism that are a part of social work; if the values, skills, and interests required of social workers are compatible; and if it is rewarding to work constructively to help people improve their level of social functioning, social work offers a rich and satisfying career. Before selecting social work as a career, one needs a general knowledge of this profession. In addition, volunteer experience, summer or part-time jobs in social agencies, and personal interaction with social workers may also help to determine one's suitability for a career in social work. The information contained in this chapter provides an orientation to a social work career.

ISSUES IN SOCIAL WORK PREPARATION AND EMPLOYMENT

Membership in any profession requires that the persons aspiring to enter it acquire the specified qualifications. The very act of defining professional membership is inherently elitist in that whenever qualifications are established, some persons who operate with similar knowledge and values but lack the identified qualifications will be excluded. In social work, for example, completion of the education and practice experience specified by the National Association of Social Workers (NASW) in its membership qualifications is necessary to gain professional recognition. However, social workers are cognizant that many other helping people with different education and experience make important contributions to the delivery of human services. For the person entering social work, or considering becoming a member of this profession, it is important to be aware of several issues that relate to professional qualifications.

Education and Accreditation

The social work profession contends that a person must have the requisite social work education; that is, either a bachelor's degree with a major in social work or a master's degree in social work (MSW) from an accredited social work education program, as a minimum for professional recognition. The *accreditation* process is administered by the Council on Social Work Education (CSWE) and has become a significant factor in social work because the graduate of the accredited program is assumed to be prepared to enter practice as a beginning-level professional social worker—ready to apply the appropriate knowledge, values, and skills in the service of clients. For all practical purposes education is the primary gatekeeper of the profession. This does not mean that all graduates are equally prepared to enter practice, that some people who do not have all the required social work courses are unable to perform many tasks of the social worker, or even that all schools offer the same opportunity for learning the essentials of social work. Rather, accreditation attests to the fact that the public can have confidence that graduates are at least minimally prepared for beginning-level social work practice because they have completed an instructional program that is soundly designed and taught by competent faculty.

Does social work education make a difference? Dhooper, Royse, and Wolfe conducted a study of employees of the Kentucky Department of Social Services in an attempt to answer that question.[1] Since that agency hired both baccalaureate- and master's-level social workers, including persons with and without social work education, the research team was able to determine if those employees with professional social work education were better prepared than their colleagues for the work demands. These researchers examined merit test scores, employees' quality assurance scores, ratings of supervisors, measures of the workers' commitment to social work values, and measures of the employees' own confidence in their educational preparation. Statistical analysis of these data indicated that the employees who had graduated from accredited social work education programs, both at the baccalaureate and master's levels, ranked higher than their colleagues on these measures of performance. Although additional research of this nature with additional samples of human service practitioners is needed to better substantiate this finding, it is noteworthy that the empirical evidence points clearly to the success of social work education in preparing graduates for social work practice.

Certification

The National Association of Social Workers provides a second level of confirmation to clientele and employing human service agencies that social workers are adequately prepared to engage in practice, i.e., *certification.* Where accreditation is testimony to the quality of an education program, certification is the profession's testimony regarding the individual's knowledge, values, and skills.

In 1990 NASW initiated a certification program for the basic social worker, i.e., the graduate of the accredited baccalaureate program. To accomplish this certification, the NASW Board created the Academy of Certified Baccalaureate Social Workers (ACBSW) and established an evaluation process to recognize those workers who are deemed qualified to become members of the Academy. The criteria established by the Competency Certification Board of NASW were "educational requirements (completion of an accredited baccalaureate degree in social work), a minimum practice-related requirement (two years of post-baccalaureate practice experience with favorable evaluations by supervisors), and successful completion of an examination that would address the knowledge and skills required for effective practice at the baccalaureate level."[2] With successful completion of these requirements, a BSW-level social worker is in a favorable position to compete for jobs and will have the professional recognition

that accompanies membership in the Academy of Certified Baccalaureate Social
Workers.

The ACBSW is modeled after the Academy of Certified Social Workers
(ACSW) that was created in 1960 to recognize the "independent" social worker.
Qualifications for the ACSW include membership in the National Association of
Social Workers, completion of an MSW from an accredited school of social work,
a satisfactory score on the ACSW examination, practice for at least two years
under the supervision of an ACSW social worker, and favorable evaluation of
practice competence by peers. Many advanced level social work jobs require the
worker to be a member of the Academy in order to qualify for employment.

NASW is also developing specialty certifications at the independent-practice
level of social work. After intensive litigation with two organizations concerned
with clinical social work practice, NASW was granted legal sanction to offer the
Qualified Clinical Social Worker (QCSW) certificate beginning in 1991. To attain
this certification the worker is required to have at least five years of post-master's
practice experience, to commit to upholding the NASW Code of Ethics, and to
pass a qualifying examination. A similar certificate is also being developed for
school social workers, and others are expected to follow.

Job Classification

Does completion of an accredited social work degree or meeting the requirements for membership in the Academy of Certified Baccalaureate Social Workers
or the Academy of Certified Social Workers in fact prepare people for social work
jobs? Some social agencies have been concerned it could be difficult to demonstrate that these credentials are valid minimum requirements for their positions
if an unsuccessful job applicant should challenge the requirement for a professional degree or professional certification. Court decisions in related fields have
held that, if challenged, an employer must be able to prove that any job requirement is valid. Rather than risk not being able to validate the relationship between
a curriculum or a qualifying examination and the requirements of a particular
job, a number of agencies have redefined social work positions so as to make
them open to people with other preparation. This activity, known as *declassification,* or perhaps more accurately as *reclassification,* has been of major concern to social work. Social workers are concerned that the reclassification trend
means that clients will receive services from less qualified persons and that other
disciplines will take over what has been social work's professional turf.

In 1979 the U.S. Children's Bureau began funding NASW to conduct a project
that would help employers determine if a social work degree would provide the
content necessary to perform social work jobs. The Job Validation Project examined court decisions and the research literature relative to job classification
and produced a set of procedures for determining the correlation between curriculum and job content in social work.[3] Two applications of this methodology
have identified a reasonably strong relationship between the content of social
work jobs and the content of the curricula of social work education programs.[4]

The job analysis section of the job validation methodology has also been used to supply the empirical data about social work practice on which the ACBSW and ACSW examinations were constructed. Although additional job validation is required in other jurisdictions to reverse the declassification trend and improve the chances of placing appropriately qualified personnel in social work positions, the success of the NASW Job Validation Project encourages optimism about the potential for such a development in the future.

Licensing or State Regulation of Social Work Practice

The social work profession, through the Council on Social Work Education, has shaped its educational programs through accreditation requirements and, through NASW, sought to identify its competent and experienced practitioners at the baccalaureate and master's levels by creating its certification programs. However, over the past two decades perhaps the most dominant issue on NASW's agenda has been to encourage the licensing of social workers throughout the United States.

As described by the American Association of State Social Work Boards, *licensing* is—

> . . . a process by which an agency of state government or other jurisdiction acting upon legislative mandate grants permission to individuals to engage in the practice of a particular profession or vocation and prohibits all others from legally doing so. By ensuring a level of safe practice, the licensure process protects the general public. Those who are licensed are permitted by the state to use a specific title and perform activities because they have demonstrated to the state's satisfaction that they have reached an acceptable level of practice.[5]

The intent of licensing is to have neutral sources, i.e., state governments, identify those social workers who are properly prepared through professional education and experience to provide client services. Both consumers of service (particularly in private practice settings) and health insurance companies that reimburse for the cost of social work services have looked to licensing as a desirable way to determine a social worker's practice competence. In order to attract clients and to be eligible for third-party vendor payments from insurance companies, social workers have embraced state licensing for social work.

The National Association of Social Workers has developed a model statute to instruct the states in the profession's recommendations regarding licensing. This Model Licensing Act for Social Workers incorporates the requirement of graduation from an accredited social work education program and suggests that three levels of practice be licensed—basic, specialized, and independent. The Model Act also describes social work in comprehensive terms that include service and action to affect human behavior and the social conditions of individuals, families, groups, organizations, and communities, which are influenced by the interaction of social, cultural, political, and economic systems.[6] Although the states vary considerably in their approaches to social work licensing, by the end of 1990, only the states of Indiana, New Jersey, and Wisconsin did not provide for some form of licensing of social workers.

Professional Standards

A profession is required by society to take responsibility for protecting the public from those members who abuse the professional monopoly (see Chapter 2). To conduct this self-policing, any profession must establish standards and develop procedures for evaluating complaints and imposing negative sanctions if a member has been found guilty of incompetent or unethical practice.

NASW has devoted considerable attention to matters of professional standards. The most important single document for specifying social work practice expectations is the *Code of Ethics.* The Code identifies expected behaviors of the professional social worker in the following areas: (1) conduct and comportment, (2) ethical responsibility to clients, (3) ethical responsibility to colleagues, (4) ethical responsibility to employers and employing organizations, (5) ethical responsibility to the social work profession, and (6) ethical responsibility to society.[8] When a social worker joins NASW, he or she must profess willingness to practice within the guidelines prescribed by the Code of Ethics. The Code, then, serves as the baseline for evaluating the professional behavior of social workers.

Because social work is primarily an agency-based profession, NASW has also established standards for appropriate personnel practices in agencies that employ social workers. These guidelines describe personnel standards and practices that uphold the fair treatment of social workers in the hiring process, assure necessary working conditions for social work practice, and identify proper procedures for the termination of a social worker's employment.[9] These standards serve as the basis for judging the validity of claims by social workers that they have been wrongfully treated by their employers.

The process established for complaints begins with the local chapter of NASW. An individual or organization may lodge a formal complaint about the practice of a social worker or the personnel practices of an agency. A committee of the chapter will then conduct an investigation of the complaint and make a determination that the complaint is or is not substantiated. Either party has the right to appeal to the NASW National Committee on Inquiry, which reviews the charges and makes a final judgment. If the Committee on Inquiry concludes that standards have been violated, an individual's membership in NASW may be suspended, and the action taken against either an individual or agency is published in the *NASW News.* The sanctions remain in effect until the terms established by the Committee on Inquiry are satisfied.

RELATED HUMAN SERVICE PRACTICE

Addressing complex human needs requires a range of service providers equipped with a variety of knowledge and skills. The human services, therefore, are made up of many people—from volunteers to members of related disciplines—who provide many different forms of helping. The person considering a career in a helping profession should carefully compare social work with other human service providers to determine if serving as a social worker would be the most satisfying way to spend one's work life.

Volunteers

One cannot fully examine the human services without recognizing the important role played by volunteers. For many people who have other vocations, one way to be involved with human services is to volunteer. The willingness to give of oneself, without monetary reward, in order to help others is characteristic of human societies and is expressed in the activity of millions of people who give their time, energy, and talents to make this a better world. It was from efforts to prepare volunteers to provide more effective human services that social work became a paid occupation and, later, a significant helping profession.

Today, social workers work closely with volunteers in many agencies. Their jobs often include the recruitment, selection, training, and supervision of volunteers. Although most commonly found in youth-serving agencies, such as scouting organizations or the YMCA, volunteers also serve on the boards of, or in a direct working capacity in, every human service agency imaginable—from nursing homes to crisis hotlines to mental hospitals.

The qualifications of volunteers vary from activity to activity. At times professionals volunteer their services beyond their jobs in their own agencies or to help in other agencies. These volunteer activities may use their professional abilities but may also require skills unrelated to professional training. Like any other good citizen, the social worker has an obligation to donate his or her talents in order to improve social conditions.

Most volunteers, however, are not professionals. They are housewives, bankers, auto mechanics, or retired persons, to name but a few. They receive personal gratification from helping others. It is important that volunteers are engaged in activities that fall within their competence and that the experience is personally satisfying.

Nonprofessional Service Providers

Not all human service practice requires the competencies of a social worker or someone with related professional skills. Many important services can be provided by persons who bring to the helping situation the perspective of the client population. These people have been referred to in the literature as *indigenous workers.* They may be clients, former clients, or others who have rapport with low-income or other client groups based on having similar experiences to the client population. At times indigenous workers can build relationships with clients when professionals have difficulty establishing working relationships with these people.

[handwritten margin note: Indigenous Those who get recruited and who workers work well w/ people. Also can interpret]

Indigenous workers can be found in human service organizations ranging from neighborhood centers to welfare agencies. A sample of tasks an indigenous worker may be expected to perform includes:

- Interviews applicants for services to obtain basic data and provide information on services available

- Interprets programs or services to special cultural groups and helps such groups, or individuals, express their needs

- Assists people in determining eligibility for services and assembling or obtaining required data or documentation

- Participates in neighborhood surveys, obtaining data from families or individuals

- Conducts casefinding activities within the community, encouraging people to make use of available services

- Provides specific instructions or directions concerning the location or procedures involved in obtaining help

- Serves as liaison between an agency and special groups or organizations in the community.[10]

The indigenous worker's own life experience and knowledge of the individuals or groups being served are his or her most important qualifications. At the same time the worker is employed in a rewarding job that has the potential through additional education and experience to advance to professional status.

Another important source of nonprofessional personnel for human service agencies are the *graduates of community colleges.* These Associate of Arts (AA) degree programs vary considerably from school to school but focus on preparing for very specific human service jobs with titles such as mental health technician, community service aide, child welfare worker, case aide, or eligibility worker.

The AA degree programs usually include the study of human growth and behavior, social problems, the social service delivery system, personal values and self-awareness, and basic communication skills. These programs may provide field experiences so students have an opportunity to apply knowledge acquired in the classroom. The tasks the AA graduate can be expected to perform are very concrete and require limited individual judgment. They include such activities as fact finding relative to specific cases, interviewing to obtain data, locating sources of assistance, organizing community groups around specific issues, making social provisions (e.g., money, food stamps, and housing) available to people, and screening applicants for service.

Other Baccalaureate-Level Disciplines

Several disciplines offer majors in colleges and universities that are closely related to social work. Completing these degrees can serve as helpful preparation for some human service jobs and can also be good preparation for a subsequent degree in social work. However, these programs of study should not be confused with social work degree programs that, if accredited, carry professional recognition.

Social Science Disciplines.   Social work has traditionally had a close relationship with the social science disciplines, for two reasons. First, social work has drawn on basic knowledge from the fields of psychology, sociology, anthropology, economics, and political science as it developed its theoretical base for understanding the individual, family, group, organization, community, and the impact of culture on all these. Second, in higher education, social work has had close administrative ties with these disciplines at the baccalaureate level. It is not uncommon to find a social work major housed in a sociology department or in a multidisciplinary social science department. Moreover, the social work student sometimes completes a double major or minor in one of the social sciences. Although master's-level social work education has traditionally isolated itself from other units of the universities in which it is located, in recent years there has been movement toward developing working relationships and joint master's degree programs with other disciplines.

The U.S. Bureau of Labor Statistics defines as social scientists the following occupational groups: anthropologists, economists, geographers, historians, political scientists, psychologists, sociologists, and urban/regional planners. The Bureau estimates the social sciences disciplines will grow "as fast as average" at 1.9 percent per year, even though many of the jobs in these disciplines are in higher education, where employment forecasts through the end of the century anticipate only a .25 percent per year growth. The number of graduates in these disciplines, however, is expected to exceed the number of new positions, creating strong competition for social science jobs.[11]

With the exception of the clinical branch of psychology and the (small) applied branch of sociology, the social sciences do not intend to engage in the provision of human services. Their purpose is to develop and test theories that will increase understanding of the aspects of life they study. Take sociology, for example, the social science discipline most commonly confused with social work. It is estimated that 80 percent of the 17,000 sociologists in the United States are teachers of sociology at two- or four-year colleges or universities, with most of the other 20 percent employed in research positions with business, industry, and governmental agencies.[12]

Related Helping Professions.   When making a career choice within the helping services, a person should examine a range of helping professions that might fit his or her individual talents and interests. The more established professions are medicine, law, nursing, teaching, dentistry, and psychology. Some newer helping professions such as physical therapy, music therapy, speech pathology and audiology, occupational therapy, recreation therapy, urban planning, and school counseling also offer challenging and rewarding careers.

Each of these is an established profession and has prescribed and accredited educational programs a person must complete to be recognized as a member of that profession. Like social work, these professions identify standards for competent and ethical practice and take responsibility for policing the membership for compliance with these standards. The clientele of these professions, then, have some protection from the possible misuse of professional authority. Employment opportunities in these professions vary considerably, but most jobs are defined as requiring the requisite professional education for entry. It is instructive to compare estimates of the demand for social workers with that of other helping professions. Table 3–1 provides a comparison of selected helping professions based on the projections of the U.S. Bureau of Labor Statistics.

Emerging Human Service Occupations.   During the 1970s a new occupational group began to emerge in the social services field, known generally as *human services* or *human development.* Human services differ from the helping professions we have reviewed because they intend to be nonprofessional. Most people giving leadership to this developing occupation are professionally trained in other disciplines and have been largely involved in corrections and mental health services—although they branch into every aspect of the social services.

The development of the human services field was stimulated by dissatisfaction with the service delivery system. Fundamental to the philosophy behind this field are two viewpoints:

1. The human services have been fragmented by division into problem areas (e.g., public welfare, mental health, corrections, developmental disabilities, public health, and vocational rehabilitation) that create barriers to client services because, to receive help, the client is often required to work with multiple agencies and multiple professionals. The human services philosophy calls for the integration of services through the development of "umbrella agencies" that will offer a wide range of services with a single staff member providing the help to a client.

2. The integration of services blurs the boundaries between professions and, therefore, requires that a professional orientation be abandoned in favor of a more generic service orientation. The approach is pragmatic. It is oriented to task completion as opposed to treatment; it is concerned with worker skill development as opposed to knowledge acquisition; it is interested in worker flexibility as opposed to worker professional identification; and (like social work) it is interested in the impact of social institutions, social systems, and social problems on clients.[13]

Social workers would agree that the fragmented methods of delivering social services often make it difficult for clients to locate help. However, the profession does not regard service integration as a solution (division lines can exist just as rigidly within one large agency as in several smaller ones) and believe that the professional model, with all its limitations, continues to be the most valid means of identifying the people who are prepared with the knowledge, values, and skills

TABLE 3–1   *Employment Projections among the Helping Professions*

Profession	Estimated Workers 1988[1]	Estimated Annual Growth Rate[1]	Estimated Annual Replacement Rate[2]	Annual New Workers Needed	Annual Supply Estimate[2]	Annual Supply as % of Demand
Much Faster Than Average						
Physical Therapists	68,000	4.2%	4.9%	6664	4021[3]	60.3%
Occupational Therapists	33,000	4.1	7.0*	3663	2273[3]	67.1
Registered Nurses	1,577,000	3.3	7.6	171,839	83,652[4]	48.7
Faster Than Average						
Lawyers	580,000	2.6%	5.7%	48,888	35,946[5]	73.5%
Social Workers	385,000	2.4	10.1	48,125	18,359[3]	38.2
Physicians	535,000	2.3	3.8	32,635	15,359[5]	47.1
Psychologists	104,000	2.3	5.0	7592	11,041[6]	145.1
School Counselors	124,000	2.3	11.1	16,616	9853[3]	59.3
Speech Pathologists/ Audiologists	53,000	2.3	8.5	5724	5416[3]	94.6
As Fast As Average						
School Teachers	2,798,000	1.3%	10.1%	318,972	178,820[3]	56.1%
Dentists	167,000	1.1	.4	2505	4413[5]	176.2

[1] George Silvestri and John Lukasiewicz, "Projections of Occupational Employment," *Monthly Labor Review* (November 1988): 51–52.

[2] Bureau of Labor Statistics, *Occupational Projections and Training Data, 1990 Edition* (Washington, D.C.: U.S. Department of Labor, 1990): 21 and 86–92.

[3] Includes baccalaureate/master's/PhD degrees

[4] Includes pre-baccalaureate/baccalaureate/master's/PhD degrees

[5] Includes professional degree only

[6] Includes master's/PhD degrees

* Projections not provided by Bureau of Labor Statistics. A 7.0% annual replacement rate is estimated by the authors.

to respond to specific human needs. Social work would argue that clients are better served through greater efforts at service integration through interdisciplinary practice, rather than the emergence of new human service disciplines that have no clear service focus or practice approach, no established standards for ethical conduct, no professional responsibility for quality control, and no standardized educational preparation.

LEVELS OF SOCIAL WORK PRACTICE

As has been seen, social work emerged as a single-level profession—the MSW level—and has evolved into a multiple-level profession. To help bring some order to this patchwork of entry points and differing practice expectations, NASW has developed a helpful classification plan. That scheme is used as a format for the remainder of this chapter. It defines four practice levels: Basic Professional, Specialized Professional, Independent Professional, and Advanced Professional; establishes the requirements of each; and differentiates them on the basis of the following factors:

1. Knowledge required by the position
2. Responsibility for one's own practice (autonomy)
3. Type and complexity of skills required
4. Complexity of the situations faced by clientele
5. Social consequences of service to society or community
6. Degree of client vulnerability
7. Social function (i.e., inherent value of the service to the individual and community).[14]

Table 3–2 provides a means of comparing these four practice levels on the basis of the expectations for the practitioner and the requisite education and experience preparation at each level.

Basic Professional

The practice at this first level has been formally recognized as professional only since 1970, when the NASW first admitted to full membership persons with a BA or BSW from a social work program approved by the Council on Social Work Education. This recognition not only reflected a movement away from professional elitism but also reinforced the increased quantity and quality of undergraduate social work programs that had emerged since the mid-1960s.

Some baccalaureate-level social work education has existed for many years.[15] A few schools offered social work courses at this level as early as the 1920s. However, the thrust of social work was toward graduate education. In 1932 the American Association of Schools of Social Work (AASSW) declared that, to be recognized as professional, a social worker must graduate from a four-year college

TABLE 3–2   *Levels of Social Work Practice*   HANDOUT

PRACTICE LEVEL	DESCRIPTION OF LEVEL	PREPARATION FOR PRACTICE
1. Basic Professional	Practice requiring professional practice skills, theoretical knowledge, and values that are not normally obtainable in day-to-day experience but that are obtainable through formal professional social work education. Formal social work education is distinguished from experiential learning by being based on conceptual and theoretical knowledge of personal and social interaction and by training in the disciplined use of self in relationship with clients.	Requires a baccalaureate degree (BSW) from a social work program accredited by the Council on Social Work Education (CSWE).
2. Specialized Professional	Practice requiring the specific and demonstrated mastery of therapeutic technique in at least one knowledge and skill method, as well as a general knowledge of human personality as influenced by social factors, and the disciplined use of self in treatment relationships with individuals or groups, or a broad conceptual knowledge of research, administration, or planning methods and social problems.	Requires a master's degree (MSW) from a social work program accredited by the CSWE.
3. Independent Professional	Achievement of practice based on the appropriate special training, developed and demonstrated under professional supervision, which is sufficient to ensure the dependable, regular use of professional skills in independent or autonomous practice. A minimum of two years is required for this experiential learning and demonstration period following the master of social work program. This level applies both to solo or autonomous practice as an independent practitioner or consultant and to practice within an organization where the social worker has primary responsibility for representing the profession or for the training or administration of professional staff.	Requires an accredited MSW and at least two years of post-master's experience under appropriate professional supervision.
4. Advanced Professional	Practice that carries major social and organizational responsibility for professional development, analysis, research, or policy implementation, or is achieved by personal professional growth demonstrated through advanced conceptual contributions to professional knowledge.	Requires proficiency in special theoretical, practice, administration, or policy or the ability to conduct advanced research studies in social welfare; usually demonstrated through a doctoral degree in social work or a closely related social science discipline.

Source: Copyright © 1981, National Association of Social Workers, Inc. Reprinted with permission from *NASW Standards for the Classification of Social Work Practice* (Washington, D.C.: The Association, September 1981), p. 9.

and complete at least one year of graduate education. In 1937 this position was revised to establish two years of graduate education as the minimum level for professional practice.

In response to the AASSW policy, in 1942 several schools created a competing organization, the National Association of Schools of Social Administration (NASSA), for the purpose of having undergraduate programs recognized as professional preparation. After several years of conflict over the legitimacy of undergraduate education, thirteen organizations interested in the resolution of this issue and in the overall enhancement of social work education formed the National Council on Social Work Education. As an initial activity of this organization, the Hollis-Taylor study of social work education was commissioned.[16]

The Hollis-Taylor report, released in 1951, urged that undergraduate education maintain a broad focus and avoid teaching social work skills or preparing students for social work practice on graduation. However, the process by which this study was conducted created harmony between the AASSW and the NASSA, which then merged with the National Council in 1952 to create what is now the single accrediting body for social work education: the Council on Social Work Education (CSWE).

The CSWE offered membership to both undergraduate and graduate schools and undertook a thirteen-volume curriculum study of social work education at both levels. One volume of this study recommended establishment of professional social work education at the undergraduate level with a continuum developed from undergraduate to graduate programs.[17] This recommendation was initially rejected by the CSWE and was not implemented until the NASW and CSWE took action in 1970 to recognize that quality undergraduate programs could prepare professional-level social workers.

During most of the 1960s, undergraduate programs operated under CSWE guidelines based on the following objectives:

1. To contribute to liberal education by developing a citizen who is knowledgeable about social work and other human service professions;
2. To improve the preparation of persons who wish to enter schools of social work; and
3. To train personnel who can perform social welfare functions for which a baccalaureate degree is sufficient.[18]

These programs might best be described as a traditional liberal arts education oriented toward social welfare. They were usually taught in departments of psychology or sociology, offered no more than three or four social work courses, and often had no social workers as faculty. With little independent identity on their campuses, and with the failure of both employers and graduate social work programs to give preference or credit for completion of these programs, they were not popular—even among students who planned to enter social work. It is still not uncommon for the social worker who is unaware of the significant developments in undergraduate education since the 1970s to recommend that college students interested in social work complete a major in psychology or sociology.

Disenchantment of students, employers, and professional social workers with undergraduate education contributed to the establishment of a Joint CSWE-NASW Ad Hoc Committee on Manpower Issues in 1968. The Committee's recommendations contributed to concurrent actions in 1970 by NASW members to grant full membership to graduates of approved undergraduate programs and by the CSWE to establish standards for approval of these programs. The standards adopted were essentially structural: they contributed to the visibility of social work programs, required that social workers be included in faculty, and demanded specification of educational objectives.[19]

CSWE "approval" was granted to 220 schools by 1973, but was at best a limited and informal type of accreditation. It was primarily concerned that the schools have an adequate structure for the growth and development of a baccalaureate program. Specification of curriculum content was slower to develop because a workable division between baccalaureate- and master's-level education had not evolved. One study indicated that most approved programs offered courses introducing the student to the social welfare institution and to social work as a profession, with at least one social work practice course, while about one-half offered a social welfare policy course, one-third offered courses in human behavior and the social environment, and all required a practicum or field experience, which varied from four hours per week for one term to as much as twelve hours per week for four terms.[20]

In 1973 CSWE took the second step to complete legitimate accreditation: it adopted much more substantial standards for baccalaureate degree programs, placing the primary focus on preparation for professional social work practice. Some previously "approved" programs could not meet the new standards, but most were able to secure the necessary resources to upgrade their programs and achieve accredited status. The number of BSW programs gradually increased, and by 1980 a total of 261 met the accreditation requirements.[21]

In 1984 another significant step to upgrade the quality of baccalaureate social work education was taken when the Council on Social Work Education operationalized a new set of accreditation standards and a much more substantive Curriculum Policy Statement. These standards spelled out the expectations for each program relative to its purpose, structure, and resources and also required that each school's curriculum be consistent with the Curriculum Policy Statement.[22] While the 1984 standards did not dictate how a school should organize its curriculum, they were considerably more explicit than the 1974 accreditation standards about the content of the student's learning experience. Rigorous application of the accreditation standards did not deter colleges and universities of all sizes in all states from building and maintaining undergraduate social work education programs. As of 1990, 362 colleges and universities had BSW programs accredited by the Council on Social Work Education.[23]

With NASW recognition came the gradual acceptance of baccalaureate-level social work, both by employers as preparation for practice and by the graduate programs as preparation for advanced standing. Increasingly, jobs were defined to recognize the competence and abilities of social workers who had completed this type of educational program, and salary and work assignments were differentiated from those without this preparation. Furthermore, in 1972 CSWE granted approval for graduate schools to accept up to one full year credit for special groups of students. By 1989, 70 percent of the graduate programs offered some form of *advanced standing* to graduates of accredited programs that typically amounted to waiving one to two terms of graduate work.[24]

The NASW classification system presents expectations for the basic social worker in relation to the seven factors that characterize social work practice. Clearly, the developments in the 1970s and 1980s enhance the conclusion that the social worker who has completed an accredited undergraduate social work program should be prepared with the competencies for the level of professional practice identified in Box 3–1.

Perhaps the most valid test of the acceptance of baccalaureate or basic social workers is whether they find employment as social workers. One study of 5228 graduates of BSW programs found that 71.4 percent found their first job in social work; 86.8 percent secured employment within six months after graduation. Over time 84.3 percent of the BSW graduates were employed as social workers. These data suggest that the human service agencies found baccalaureate-level social workers attractive, especially in direct service positions, in which 90.2 percent were employed in their first job.[25]

Specialized Professional

Prior to the re-emergence of baccalaureate-level social work education and the basic social worker, the generally accepted level of preparation for social work practice was that of the specialized social worker. At this level the social worker must have completed a master's degree from one of the accredited master's-level social work education programs. Although it is expected that the MSW social worker, too, will make use of professional supervision, he or she should have sufficient competence to appropriately exercise independent judgment and initiative.

Historically, social work education began much like the more sophisticated in-service training programs of today. The first formal education program was initiated under the auspices of the New York Charity Organization Society in 1898. This school, the New York School of Philanthropy, began with a six-week summer course for social workers. It evolved into a one-year program in 1904 and expanded into a two-year program in 1911. From the settlement house movement, another root of social work, cooperative extension courses were offered for college graduates, beginning in 1901, by the Chicago Commons Settlement in cooperation with the University of Chicago. In 1907 these courses became part of the Chicago School of Civics and Philanthropy and in 1920 became affiliated with the University of Chicago—the first school of social work entirely under university auspices. The first full-time school of social work was established

BOX 3–1

ILLUSTRATIVE PRACTICE COMPETENCIES FOR THE BASIC PROFESSIONAL SOCIAL WORKER

Knowledge

Basic and general knowledge of human behavior, social systems, and social institutions.

Awareness of social problem areas—their cause and impact on individuals, families, and communities, and the appropriate resources and methods involved in dealing with them.

Knowledge of basic theories and methods of casework or group work.

Working knowledge of at least one specific method of intervention or treatment.

Working knowledge of basic research techniques and sources of specialized, professional knowledge.

Specific knowledge of social planning and community organization methods.

Responsibility

Functions under direct and regularly provided professional supervision.

Is instructed in specific details of tasks, assuming a general knowledge of professional methods, functions, and objectives.

Casework or other professional judgments must be renewed to confirm decisions that affect clients in complex situations.

Acts professionally on one's judgment within an assigned scope of practice.

Determines client's or community's needs for service within one's practice area. Initiate or terminate one's own or another's services.

Supervises others in services they are qualified to provide.

Is advised of administrative requirements or consultative supervision.

Requires regular direct supervision. Requires regular direct supervision for learning specialized practice.

Skill

Ability to relate in positive or appropriate relationships under adverse conditions.

Ability to recognize primary behavior dysfunction of individuals and groups.

Ability to make a basic social assessment and service plan.

Awareness of community resources relevant to identified needs.

BOX 3-1 (Continued)

Ability to relate as a professional participant in an agency program.

Ability to carry out basic techniques of social research.

Ability to conduct or participate in methods of community organization and planning.

Ability to conduct a comprehensive social study or treatment plan within a given service.

Ability to initiate and develop community-group programs within given standards.

Situational Complexity

Routine service or tasks whose goal is easily achievable.

Single function of limited difficulty.

Clear expectation of clients.

Clients with noncompetitive interests when resources are available.

Temporary, uninvolved helping relationship.

Identified emotional and social needs with only limited or potential resources.

Some degree of unconscious motivation.

Service goals are achievable.

Social Consequences

Minor potential effect, the impact being limited to one or a small number of clients.

Potential errors or shortcomings limited in scope.

Benefits significant, but not essential to health or life.

Service or program involves a significant social problem.

Client Vulnerability

Minimal risk to persons or groups.

Potential risks temporary or correctable.

Client or groups with a clear and valid expectation of service.

Actions closely or regularly supervised or evaluated.

Actions or decisions governing a client's situation subject to prior approval.

Actions or activities have no significant impact on costs.

Significant health or emotional need or risk of injury involved.

Service or treatment errors not readily corrected or ameliorated.

BOX 3–1 (Continued)

Clear identifiable impact on the client or community.

Administration and planning of a program have a minor impact on costs.

Social Function

To provide information on rights, benefits, and services.

To obtain social and personal information or data within specified limits of ethics and confidentiality.

To advise the public or clients of social expectations and requirements in a constructive, helping relationship.

To develop data or other research information for the analysis or study of social problems.

To deal with negative or mildly hostile persons or groups on behalf of society.

To enable clients or persons seeking aid to understand, accept, or use help in relation to a social problem.

To interpret and build trust among resident individuals or groups in services designed to provide help.

To enable individuals or groups to involve themselves in socially-constructive activities or changes in conduct.

To work with hostile persons or groups to achieve or improve understanding or cooperation.

Source: Copyright © 1981, National Association of Social Workers, Inc. Reprinted with permission from *NASW Standards for the Classification of Social Work Practice* (Washington, D.C.: The Association, September 1981), pp. 20–21.

---

as a joint program between Simmons College and Harvard University in 1904. Harper summarized the situation in the early 1900s when he stated that "at the beginning of the present century education for social work was predominantly at the undergraduate level."[26]

As Chapter 2 indicates, the growing interest in social work becoming a profession was an important factor in the development of educational programs at the graduate level. In 1915 the first fully-graduate school was established at Bryn Mawr. Further, as many of the undergraduate and agency-based educational programs matured, they were elevated to the master's level.

The early curricula of these schools involved preparation for a range of services, from individual helping approaches to economic and reform theory. They included a heavy investment in internships or field experience as a tool for learning practice skills and tended to be organized around practice settings, such as hospital social work and school social work. Their greatest emphasis was on preparation for the services offered by private social agencies, and they tended to neglect the growing demand for social workers in the public social services.

By the 1940s the two-year MSW had become the minimum requirement for professional practice, although a few schools with strong undergraduate programs were resisting that requirement. The two-year programs were organized around what was known as the "Basic Eight," in reference to the eight primary divisions of social work practice: public welfare, social casework, social group work, community organization, medical information, social research, psychiatry, and social welfare administration. Although not every school offered all the Basic Eight, these practice divisions reflected the major areas of social work practice and education.

The period from 1950 through 1965 was one of rapid growth in the number of MSW programs and the relative standardization of these programs. By 1965 there were sixty-seven accredited graduate schools and nearly 9000 students.[27] The schools had largely abandoned programs structured on the basis of practice setting and instead organized curricula around the practice methods of casework, group work, community organization, administration, and research.

Three factors have significantly influenced social work education at the graduate level in the last quarter-century. First, the re-emergence of baccalaureate-level social work forced some reorientation of master's education; it was necessary to adapt to the student who entered the MSW program with a substantial social work education in a baccalaureate program. For this student, provision was made for advanced standing in the graduate-level program, which typically meant waiving or testing out of up to one semester of graduate work. A continuum of education between the baccalaureate and master's programs began to emerge.

Second, the Council on Social Work Education's Standards for Accreditation and Curriculum Policy Statement allowed individual schools increased flexibility in determining curriculum content. As the typical two-year MSW program evolved, it offered a general orientation to social work practice during the first year and then provided more specialized content based on population served, social problem addressed, practice intervention approach, or client group served during the second year. Prior to that development, students attending MSW programs could expect pretty much the same basic curriculum regardless of which school they attended. Today, this selection is appropriately based on the specialization the student desires to develop. In a real sense, graduate social work education has become what has traditionally been the expectation of graduate-level work; that is, it is more substantive and specialized than that which one would find at the baccalaureate level.

Finally, the conservative philosophy that dominated the United States during the 1980s initially eliminated some social work jobs and created a tighter job market in the human services. The fear of a dismantling of the human service delivery system, however, was greater than the ultimate impact of the Reagan and Bush administrations. Student interest shifted toward the clinical aspects of social work, and particularly to private practice, where one could avoid the risks of employment in an agency that might lose its funding as a result of a conservative administration. Also in the early 1980s, there was a dramatic decline in applications for MSW programs.[28] By increasing the rate of admissions, the graduate schools avoided a serious decline in the number of students, and by 1989 the number of applications had nearly returned to the 1980 level.[29] A surprising number of new graduate programs were initiated in the late 1980s, bringing the total to ninety-seven with ten more in the process of development.

The difference between the basic social worker and the specialized social worker has been a point of contention in social work. A comparison of Box 3–1 and Box 3–2 reveals that the specialized or master's-level prepared social worker has a more extensive knowledge base in one or more areas of specialization and operates with greater autonomy in more complex practice situations. Although the NASW classification system begins to clarify these differences, an important next step in understanding these two levels is to utilize carefully controlled research and analysis to determine the degree to which social workers at these levels do, in fact, differently perform the functions identified in this classification scheme.

Independent Professional

This classification identifies the experienced specialized social worker. It requires no additional academic preparation but assumes a person has achieved greater competence from increased experience and professional supervision.

The independent social worker is expected to have developed and integrated the knowledge, values, and skills of social work in at least one practice area. From this experience, he or she should be able to develop sufficient expertise in that field to function independently and skillfully in sensitive situations and should be prepared to practice outside the auspices of a social agency, that is, in private or entrepreneurial practice. Furthermore, the independent social worker should be able to provide leadership in at least one practice arena and to supervise and consult with other social workers.

One indicator of reaching the independent professional level is membership in the Academy of Certified Social Workers (ACSW). The ACSW was established in 1960 to protect clients from the abuses and incompetence of inadequately prepared practitioners. The Academy also was intended to establish a more favorable public image, to obtain societal sanction, and to increase confidence and understanding in social work.[30] Requirements for becoming a member of the Academy include maintaining membership in NASW, having a minimum of two years full-time practice experience, completing an application form that includes a curriculum vitae, providing reference letters from professional peers, and achieving a sufficient score on the ACSW exam (a multiple-choice, written test).

According to the *NASW Standards for the Classification of Social Work Practice,* the factors influencing practice reported in Box 3–3 reflect the expected level of competence for the independent professional.

BOX 3-2

ILLUSTRATIVE PRACTICE COMPETENCIES FOR THE SPECIALIZED PROFESSIONAL SOCIAL WORKER

Knowledge

Knowledge of personality theory, interpersonal communications, social group relations, or community organization theory.

A working knowledge of several methods of interpersonal helping or treatment. Knowledge of at least one psychotherapeutic technique.

A broad and beginning specialized knowledge of at least one such knowledge area.

Knowledge of the theory and techniques of professional and personnel supervision and organizational administration.

Basic knowledge of the administration of social programs.

Knowledge of the appropriate techniques and methods of research or planning.

Responsibility

Normally functions under periodic or consultative supervision. Requires learning for specialized practice.

Is advised of administrative requirements and expected to adhere to them adequately.

Requires instruction only in highly complex, specialized, or new methods or procedures.

Directs or administers a program staffed by professional social workers and other personnel.

Reviews work of subordinate professional workers. Assigns and evaluates social work activities.

Skill

Ability to establish constructive relationships with resistant clients by overcoming strong initial resistance or dealing with conflict-laden or complex situations.

Ability to design and conduct research.

Ability to provide psychotherapeutic treatment under supervision.

Ability to administer a social service program of limited scope within a larger setting.

Ability to determine differential treatment needs.

BOX 3–2 (Continued)

Ability to provide professional social work training or supervision.

Ability to represent the discipline of professional social work within an interdisciplinary program.

Ability to develop and conduct a treatment-therapy program or service without direct supervision.

Ability to provide a specialized treatment or method of service.

Situational Complexity

Involves two or more clients with divergent interests.

Multiple service functions with responsibility for coordination of services or personnel.

Goals present major difficulties.

Clients who are emotionally confused or have conflicting social needs.

Resources not readily available.

Social Consequences

Activity requires interdisciplinary coordination.

Actions have a serious but temporary impact and involve more than one client.

Service or program involves a significant social problem.

Client Vulnerability

Actions involve the potential for a long-lasting but not life-threatening condition or a risk to mental stability.

Ability of client or groups to identify needs is severely limited.

Social Function

To overcome strong resistance to participation or use of socially required assistance or conduct involving the protection of others.

To achieve socially desirable changes in conduct involving significant emotional and mental growth and change.

To achieve long-lasting or broad-scale change toward socially desired objectives.

Source: Copyright © 1981, National Association of Social Workers, Inc. Reprinted with permission from *NASW Standards for the Classification of Social Work Practice* (Washington, D.C.: The Association, September 1981), p. 24.

BOX 3–3

ILLUSTRATIVE PRACTICE COMPETENCIES FOR THE INDEPENDENT PROFESSIONAL SOCIAL WORKER

Knowledge

Sufficient expert knowledge to teach or communicate social work practice and theory to professionals in other disciplines or in an interdisciplinary service.

A thorough knowledge of at least one method of professional practice and specialized knowledge of others.

Responsibility

Acts professionally on his or her judgment.

Determines clients' or the community's need for service within one's own practice area. Initiates or terminates one's own or another's services.

Requires instruction only in highly complex, new, or specialized methods or procedures of treatment, research, planning, or other mode of work.

Obtain professional supervision on a consultative basis, as needed.

Skill

Ability to conduct psychotherapy of a highly complex or demanding nature.

Ability to conduct differential diagnoses of individuals or groups, involving complex and unconscious factors.

Ability to administer an autonomous social work, health, or mental health program of limited scope or one of major scope within a larger organization.

Ability to take full professional responsibility in a multidisciplinary setting or for general community development or services.

Situational Complexity

Severe conflicts between persons or groups served.

Multiple causative factors—major lack of resources.

Clear evidence of unconscious needs that restrict the ability of a client to change.

Highly complex emotional and social goals of service.

BOX 3–3 (Continued)

Social Consequences

Actions with the potential for a major or long-lasting impact.

Activities that provide the basis for reviewing, studying, or developing a policy.

Vulnerability

Administration, planning, or research involve moderate costs or risks.

Actions involve the potential for a risk to mental stability.

Inability of clients or groups to identify their own needs.

Social Function

To negotiate and mediate among deeply opposed persons or groups to achieve socially sanctioned objective.

To conduct broad-scale research studies that deal with specific social or community issues.

To provide treatment to overcome major problems involving social dysfunctions, behavior, or severe risk to others.

Source: Copyright © 1981, National Association of Social Workers, Inc. Reprinted with permission from *NASW Standards for the Classification of Social Work Practice* (Washington, D.C.: The Association, September 1981), p. 24.

Advanced Professional

This classification represents the most highly experienced and advanced education level of social work. It calls for extensive practice or research skills and implies the completion of either a doctoral degree in social work (DSW or Ph.D) or a doctoral degree in a closely related social science discipline. In contrast to many professions, few social workers achieve—or even aspire to achieve—the advanced professional level.

Doctoral education in social work was initiated more than three quarters of a century ago but experienced its major growth only relatively recently. Holland and Frost summarize the historical development of doctoral programs as follows:

The early years of doctoral education in social work were marked by slow growth of programs. Expansion has accelerated in recent years. In the three decades after Bryn Mawr College accepted its first doctoral student (1915), five more universities began offering the doctorate in social work—the University of Chicago (1924), Catholic University (1934), the Ohio State University (1934), the University of Pittsburgh (1945), and Saint Louis University (1947). In the 1950s, eight new programs were opened and in the 1960s seven more swelled the ranks.

A sharp expansion occurred over the next decade—sixteen new programs were launched. Another eleven have opened their doors since 1980, and four more new programs are scheduled to open before this decade ends.[31]

The purposes for establishing doctoral programs in social work have been mixed. The organization formed to provide an arena for discussing common issues experienced by doctoral programs, the Group for Advancement of Doctoral Education, has constantly wrestled with the problem of identifying an appropriate purpose for doctoral education. Should these programs be viewed as research, or clinical? Should the research focus be academic, or directed to social work practice? Should these programs devote their efforts to preparing the advanced practitioner, or the teacher/researcher? Should the main goal be to credential social workers so they might more effectively compete with other professionals, or should the main goal be to create a cadre of leadership that can further the development of this profession? Each program answers these questions in its own way. Since the doctorate is not viewed as an entry degree for the social work profession, these programs receive their sanction only from their universities and do not participate in a professional accreditation process. Therefore, the schools have considerable flexibility to determine the focus of their curricula and have taken on unique identities.

By the beginning of the 1990s, forty-seven doctoral programs in social work were available throughout the United States. In a typical year these programs would enroll a total of about 900 full-time students, 1000 part-time students, and would award doctoral degrees to 200 graduates.[32] These numbers do not, however, reflect the total number of social workers completing doctoral degrees, since some complete doctoral-level work in related fields such as sociology, psychology, higher education, and public administration.

At this time the advanced social worker represents a very small part of social work and is rarely recognized in job-classification or licensing criteria. The competencies and credentials of these social workers are listed in Box 3–4 and are sought by social workers with increasing frequency.

CONCLUDING COMMENT

The NASW classification plan represents an important step in the difficult task of differentiating practice at the several levels that have evolved in social work. Periodic revisions of these standards and research into the accuracy with which they portray social work practice will not only help to further define social work levels, but also will help to make a better distinction between social work and related disciplines.

There is no uniform acceptance within the social work field of these multiple practice levels nor of a range of professional levels extending from the basic to the advanced social worker. It may well be several more years before the public,

BOX 3–4

ILLUSTRATIVE PRACTICE COMPETENCIES FOR THE ADVANCED PROFESSIONAL SOCIAL WORKER

Knowledge

Advanced and expert knowledge in practice, research, administration, planning, or teaching.

Highly specialized and expert knowledge in a social work content area.

A thorough knowledge of several types of vulnerable populations, corresponding service delivery systems, methods for assessing needs and planning to relate the service delivery systems to human needs that are high priorities.

Responsibility

Directs major research study involving design, staffing, management, technical responsibility, writing, and budget.

Has chief administrative responsibility for major social service or multiservice department or organization.

Has responsibility for a major planning or policy-setting function.

Skill

Ability to design and conduct complex or extended research or planning studies involving multiple or discordant factors.

Highly specialized expertise in at least one social work method.

Ability to administer a major social work, social welfare, mental health, or health program or department with broad management and budgetary responsibilities.

Situational Complexity

Multiple, complex technical operations.

Broad-ranging organizational and administrative requirements and policies.

Long-range planning for the development of resources.

Social Consequences

Actions that have major public or social consequences.

BOX 3–4 (Continued)

Client Vulnerability

Administration, planning, and research involve long-lasting or major public costs or risks.

Social Function

To develop techniques or policies designed to further social objectives.

To conduct, write, and present social research studies of major scope.

Source: Copyright © 1981, National Association of Social Workers, Inc. Reprinted with permission from *NASW Standards for the Classification of Social Work Practice* (Washington, D.C.: The Association, September 1981), p. 24.

---

social agencies, clients, and even social workers themselves fully appreciate this range of levels as legitimate parts of social work. When that happens, clients will have more ready access to social workers who are equipped to supply the specific services they need and social workers, hopefully, will devote more energy to strengthening the quality of practice at each level.

For the person considering a career in social work, knowledge of these levels of practice helps to identify possible entry and terminal points. The selection of a particular practice level as a goal for any individual must depend on personal interest, the desire to provide a particular type of service for which that level offers the necessary preparation, and the ability to arrange one's life to acquire the necessary professional education to prepare for practice at that level. Recognizing that a person's goals and aspirations may change, social work offers an advantage over many other professions by presenting the opportunity to enter at a basic practice level and build on that background to achieve more advanced levels.

SUGGESTED READINGS

AUSTIN, DAVID M. *A History of Social Work Education.* Austin: University of Texas at Austin School of Social Work, 1986, Social Work Education Monograph Series, #1.

BERENGARTEN, SIDNEY. *The Nature and Objectives of Accreditation and Social Work Education.* Austin: University of Texas at Austin School of Social Work, 1986, Social Work Education Monograph Series, #2.

HOLLAND, THOMAS P., and FROST, ABBIE K. *Doctoral Education in Social Work: Trends and Issues.* Austin: University of Texas at Austin School of Social Work, 1987, Social Work Education Monograph Series, #5.

KARL, BARRY D. "LO, the Poor Volunteer: An Essay on the Relation between History and Myth," *Social Service Review* 58 (December 1984): 493–522.

NATIONAL ASSOCIATION OF SOCIAL WORKERS. *NASW Standards for the Classification of Social Work Practice.* Washington, D.C.: The Association, September 1981.

PECORA, PETER J., and AUSTIN, MICHAEL J. "Declassification of Social Service Jobs: Issues and Strategies." *Social Work* (November–December 1983): 421–426.

RUBIN, ALLEN. *Current Statistical Trends in Social Work Education: Issues and Implications.* Austin: University of Texas at Austin School of Social Work, 1986, Social Work Education Monograph Series, #4.

SHEAFOR, BRADFORD W., and SHANK, BARBARA W. *Undergraduate Social Work Education: A Survivor in a Changing Profession.* Austin: University of Texas at Austin School of Social Work, 1986, Social Work Education Monograph Series, #3.

ENDNOTES

1. Surgit Singh Dhooper, David D. Royse, and L. C. Wolfe, "Does Social Work Education Make a Difference?," *Social Work* 35 (January 1990): 57–61.
2. American College Testing Service, *The BSW Job Analysis and Test Specifications Project* (Iowa City: ACT, 1990), p. 1–1.
3. Robert J. Teare et al., *Classification Validation Processes for Social Service Positions* vols. I–VII (Silver Spring, Md.: National Association of Social Workers, 1984).
4. Bradford W. Sheafor, Robert J. Teare, Mervyn W. Hancock, and Thomas P. Gauthier, "Curriculum Development through Content Analysis: A New Zealand Experience," *Journal of Education for Social Work* 21 (Fall 1985): 113–124; and Robert J. Teare, *Validating Social Work Credentials for Human Service Jobs: Report of a Demonstration* (Silver Spring, Md.: National Association of Social Workers, 1987).
5. Robert R. Wohlgemuth and Thomas Samph, *Summary Report: Content Validity Study in Support of the Licensure Examination Program of the American Association of State Social Work Boards* (Oak Park, Ill.: The Association, 1983), p. 2.
6. National Association of Social Workers, "The Model Statute," *Handbook on the Private Practice of Social Work* (Washington, D.C.: The Association, 1974), pp. 58–59.
7. Leila Whiting, *State Comparison of Laws Regulating Social Work* (Silver Spring, Md.: NASW, 1990).
8. *NASW News* 26 (January 1980): 24. (See Chapter 8 for reprint of the entire Code of Ethics.)
9. National Association of Social Workers, *Standards for Social Work Personnel Practices: Policy Statement #2* (Washington, D.C.: The Association, 1971).
10. National Association of Social Workers, *Standards for Social Service Manpower* (Washington, D.C.: The Association, 1973), p. 14.
11. George Silvestri and John Lukasiewicz, "Projections of Occupational Employment, 1988–2000," *Monthly Labor Review* 112 (November 1989): 45 and 51.
12. Everett K. Wilson and Hanan Selvin, *Why Study Sociology?: A Note to Undergraduates* (Belmont, Calif.: Wadsworth, 1980), pp. 9–10.
13. Joseph Mehr, *Human Services: Concepts and Intervention Strategies* 4th ed. (Boston: Allyn and Bacon, 1989): 11–19.
14. National Association of Social Workers, *NASW Standards for the Classification of Social Work Practice* (Washington, D.C.: The Association, 1981), p. 8.
15. A comprehensive analysis of the growth and development of baccalaureate-level social work can be found in Bradford W. Sheafor and Barbara W. Shank, *Undergraduate Social Work Education: A Survivor in a Changing Profession* (Austin: University of Texas School of Social Work, 1986).

16. Ernest V. Hollis and Alice L. Taylor, *Social Work Education in the United States* (New York: Columbia University Press, 1951).

17. Herbert Bisno, *The Place of Undergraduate Curriculum in Social Work Education,* Social Work Curriculum Study vol. 2 (New York: Council on Social Work Education, 1959).

18. Council on Social Work Education, *Social Welfare Content in Undergraduate Education* (New York: The Council, 1962), pp. 3–4.

19. Council on Social Work Education, *Undergraduate Programs in Social Work* (New York: The Council, 1971).

20. Alfred Stamm, *An Analysis of Undergraduate Social Work Programs Approved by CSWE, 1971* (New York: The Council, 1971).

21. Allen Rubin, *Statistics on Social Work Education in the United States: 1980* (New York: Council on Social Work Education, 1981), p. 1.

22. Council on Social Work Education, *Handbook of Accreditation Standards and Procedures* (Washington, D.C.: The Council, 1984).

23. Council on Social Work Education, "Directory of Colleges and Universities with Accredited Social Work Degree Programs" (Alexandria, Va.: The Council, 1990).

24. Council on Social Work Education, *Summary Information on Master of Social Work Programs: 1989* (Alexandria, Va.: The Council, 1990), pp. 1–73.

25. Robert J. Teare, Barbara W. Shank, and Bradford W. Sheafor, "Career Patterns of the BSW Social Worker." Unpublished manuscript, Colorado State University, Fort Collins.

26. Ernest V. Harper, "The Study of Social Work Education: Its Significance for the Undergraduate Educational Institutions," *Social Work Journal* 22 (October 1951): 179.

27. Raymond DeVera, ed., *Statistics on Social Work Education, 1965–66* (New York: Council on Social Work Education, 1966), p. 6.

28. Allen Rubin, *Current Statistical Trends in Social Work Education: Issues and Implications* (Austin: University of Texas at Austin School of Social Work, 1986), pp. 5–10.

29. Elaine C. Spaulding, *Statistics on Social Work Education in the United States: 1989* (Alexandria, Va.: Council on Social Work Education, 1990), p. 36.

30. Phillip Klein, *From Philanthropy to Social Welfare* (San Francisco: Jossey-Bass, 1968), pp. 215–216.

31. Thomas P. Holland and Abbie K. Frost, *Doctoral Education in Social Work: Trends and Issues* (Austin: University of Texas at Austin School of Social Work, 1987), p. 1.

32. Spaulding, p. 36.

PART TWO

The Context of Social Work

*O*ne characteristic of Western societies is their tendency to create social institutions to meet human needs. Two social institutions have been dominant in U.S. society—the family and the market economy. During the past 150 years rapid change created by industrialization and urbanization has strained the ability of these two institutions to adequately respond to human needs. For example, specialization and the increased use of modern technology has made it more difficult for the physically and mentally handicapped person to find employment. Or, as individuals became more mobile in order to use their more highly specialized skills in business and industry, they also became isolated from the support of their extended families. Thus, the need for a social welfare institution that could help meet some of these social needs evolved.

Today a number of professionals deliver social programs that are intended to meet these human needs. These professionals include social workers, physicians, recreation specialists, public health nurses, occupational therapists, psychologists, and others. The so-cial programs take the form of direct provisions, social services, and social action efforts. Most of these programs are delivered through public and voluntary social agencies that employ these professionals, but some are offered through profit-oriented organizations or through private practice situations.

Particularly in the social provision programs, such as those giving food, clothing, or money, volunteers and nonprofessionals provide valuable services. Among the nonprofessionals are receptionists, eligibility technicians, food stamp clerks, and homemakers, to name but a few. For most services, however, professional knowledge and skills are required. The different professional disciplines each bring their special knowledge, values, and skills to the helping process. In the various practice fields one also finds different roles performed by the disciplines. For example, in a family service agency the social worker is the primary professional, while teaching is the primary discipline in a school and other disciplines are viewed as supportive to this effort. In still other settings, such as a mental health

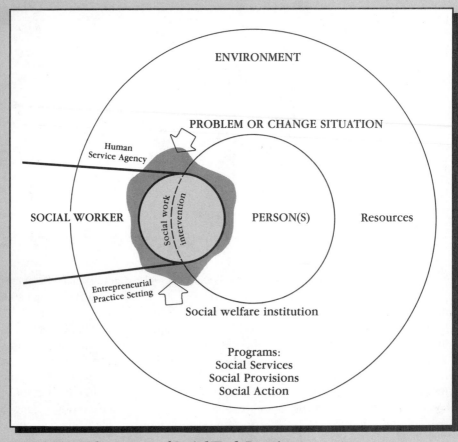

FIGURE II–1   *The Context of Social Work Practice*

center, several disciplines may be equal partners as a premium is placed on interdisciplinary teamwork.

   The social programs, the various disciplines, and the human service agencies or entrepreneurial practice settings provide the
context in which social work exists. Figure
II–1 depicts this context as an important dimension of the social worker's focus on people interacting with their environment. The
social worker helps the person and the rele-

vant parts of the environment as they seek to
improve their interaction. For the agency-
based social worker, that agency becomes a
part of the environment that can help or
hinder the services given to the client. In addition, the social worker must help client(s)
gain access to other agencies and the services
and programs they offer. If the resources available are not adequate or if there are factors in
the environment that contribute to potential
or existing problems of social functioning, the

social worker is charged to deal with these issues as well.

The social worker, then, not only must be prepared to deal with clients as individuals, families, or small groups on a face-to-face basis but also must acquire the necessary knowledge, values, and skills for enhancing the ability of social agencies to provide services. In fact, the social worker works within the context of the entire social welfare institution and must seek to make that institution more responsive to human needs.

Part Two helps the reader acquire a general understanding of the context in which social workers practice. Chapter 4 reviews the development of the social service delivery system in the United States. It discusses the various meanings of the term *welfare* and provides an understanding of the human needs that the social welfare institution is intended to meet. The chapter also examines social programs and services as they are now provided.

Chapter 5 surveys thirteen unique fields in which social workers apply their trade. The selection of fields varies from social work with children to social work in business and industry, from corrections to mental health settings, and from hospitals to group service agencies. Despite the differences in these fields of practice, a basic pattern of the social worker helping people interact more effectively with the world around them emerges.

Chapter 6 examines those public and private social agencies where most social workers are employed. Agency structure and functioning are discussed, with special attention given to the inherent conflicts that exist between the professional practice model and the bureaucratic model of organization usually found in social agencies. Some social workers have adopted an entrepreneurial approach, and many have opted for private practice, but that approach, too, is fraught with problems. It is possible, however, to minimize the problems of working within both the agency and the private practice in order to meet human needs more effectively.

CHAPTER 4

Understanding the Social Welfare Institution

The Constitution for the United States expresses a commitment to promote the "general welfare" of the people:

> We, the people of the United States, in order to form a more perfect Union, establish justice, insure domestic tranquility, provide for the common defense, promote the general welfare, and secure the blessings of liberty to ourselves and our posterity do ordain and establish this Constitution for the United States of America.

> —Preamble for the Constitution

How does a nation go about achieving such lofty goals as "insuring domestic tranquility" and "promoting the general welfare" of the people? Indeed, through the more than 200 years since the Constitution was adopted there has been continuing debate and changing public policy regarding the requirements to meet this constitutional imperative. Yet the resolve to achieve this objective has remained unchanged. A nation must assure that certain basic human needs are met if it is to survive.

Since the adoption of the Constitution, U.S. society has undergone dramatic changes making it necessary to adapt the social institutions to fit emerging needs of the population. For example, moving from an agriculture-based economy to one based on machines, and then on electronic technology, radically altered the structure of the work force. The related movement from a rural to an urban society influenced the ability of the primary social institution, the family, to perform its traditional role in meeting the needs of family members. One result of these changes has been the growth of the social welfare institution from a relatively minor role in U.S. society to a central place in fulfilling the constitutional commitment.

Social work emerged during this period as the profession sanctioned to bring the resources of the environment to bear on the needs of people. The person wishing to understand social work must understand this background as it is constantly evolving and will ultimately influence the social worker's ability to conduct effective practice.

HUMAN NEEDS

Each individual has his or her own special needs. The configuration of needs that each person experiences, the intensity with which they are felt, and the ability to discover ways to meet them are part of what makes human beings unique. Each person varies, for example, in the degree of need for expressions of affection, for approval from friends and colleagues, and for intellectual growth. Some people can manage pain and illness or limited financial resources quite satisfactorily, while others suffer greatly. Some ignore the many injustices that prevail, while others are motivated by injustice to seek corrections that create a more equitable society.

Society need not develop programs that are responsive to each and every human need. In fact, people are expected to develop their own means of satisfying most of their needs without help from others. If that fails, they look to family and friends, natural helpers in the community, and only then to the various human services to help meet these needs. The professionals who provide these services are often the "resource of last resort" for people seeking help.

Fundamental differences in viewpoint about the appropriate role of human services appear when the line is drawn between an individual's and society's responsibility for meeting need. A conservative philosophy leans toward placing the full responsibility on the individual; a liberal position favors a more substantial responsibility by society. Social work values, as we shall see in Chapter 8, are weighted in the latter direction.

Although each of us has a unique constellation of needs, there are some common needs that affect all people. Romanyshyn described these as needs of the flesh (survival and creature comforts), needs of the heart (love, intimacy, and exchange of tenderness), needs of the ego (sense of adequacy and self-assertiveness), and needs of the soul (transcending self to define the meaning of life beyond one's own biological existence).[1]

Human needs are not all of equal importance. Some must be fulfilled before people are able to address others. According to Maslow's research, people attempt to fulfill their needs in the following order:

- *Physiological survival needs:* nourishment, rest, and warmth, for example
- *Safety needs:* preservation of life and sense of security
- *Belongingness needs:* to be part of a group and to love and to be loved

- *Esteem needs:* approval, respect, acceptance, appreciation, etc.
- *Self-actualization needs:* to be able to fulfill our fullest potential.[2]

When sufficient numbers of people fail to have one or more of these needs met in the normal course of their lives, society must decide if it is to take responsibility for their well-being. If so, society must determine when and to what degree it will attempt to provide means for helping those people meet their needs. The more basic the need, the more likely it is that society will make some provision for meeting it. Human services for the hungry child are more likely to be supported than marital counseling for a middle-class couple—and marital counseling would gain more support than providing developmental or growth enhancing experiences to the "normal" or "healthy" person who wants to develop his or her potential more fully.

WHAT IS WELFARE?

In the literature on meeting human needs, the term *well-being* consistently appears. When needs are adequately met, people experience a sense of well-being, or a general satisfaction with their lives. An implicit goal of society is to facilitate the well-being of its members.

A dictionary definition expresses this same intent: "the good fortune, health, happiness, prosperity, etc., of a person, group or organization; well-being."[3] Social work has clearly accepted the role of promoting the well-being or welfare, in the sense of the above definition, of members of society and has placed particular emphasis on the most vulnerable members.

Not everyone interprets welfare in the same way. The way some commentators and politicians speak of people "on welfare" would lead one to believe that welfare is the means by which a large number of "lazy and immoral people" are ripping off tax dollars contributed by a handful of upstanding citizens. From a different perspective, some would say social welfare is a tool used by those in power to keep impoverished a group of poor, mostly minority females so they will be forced to do the menial work of society—yet not so impoverished that they will be moved to overthrow those in power.[4]

Society places different value judgments on the reasons people receive welfare services. To many people, it is acceptable for the farmer facing fluctuation in the price of crops to receive welfare in the form of price supports; for the small business owner to receive a government-subsidized loan; or even for the fallen savings and loan industry to be bailed out by the taxpayers. The well-being of farmers, entrepreneurs, and the savings and loan investors is considered important. It is somehow less important for the deserted mother and her children to be recipients of welfare in the form of food stamps. It is even more unacceptable for the alcoholic who cannot hold a job to receive welfare in the form of financial assistance, though the need is just as great as in many other troubled situations.

Mandell notes that "one's definition of social welfare depends partly upon one's conception of a society's responsibility to its citizens."[5] There are those who argue that each individual should be responsible for his or her own well-being. If that is not possible, at least the person's family should assume that responsibility, or in some cultures, a tribe, neighborhood, or community should assume that function. Historically, churches and synagogues assumed this backup function, and the residue from that involvement is still evident in the sponsorship of many human service programs by religious organizations. Others would argue that we live in a complex society in which people are highly interdependent and subject to difficulties that arise from malfunctions in the society itself (e.g., a continuing 5–7 percent minimum unemployment rate). Therefore, they argue, society must make provision for preventing or resolving difficulties that arise from this situation by providing human services. What, then, is welfare? In the broadest sense, welfare is the institutionalized expression of human concern for the well-being of individuals, families, groups, organizations, and communities.

SOCIAL INSTITUTIONS

Human needs must be met by the people in need themselves, their families and friends, or, at times, by others. When a society develops a formalized means of meeting these needs, it has created an *institution*. As the term is used here, an institution is "a formal, recognized, established and stabilized way of pursuing some activity in society."[6] Social institutions are the organized procedures societies create to meet the needs of people. Note that as the term is used here, institution *does not* refer to an organization or building where services are provided.

The primary social institution of U.S. society and all other societies is *the family*. Bierstedt notes that "the family . . . is a universal institution of society. There is no society anywhere on earth that does not have the institution of family: in all of them in all periods of history procreation has been institutionalized."[7] In most societies the family also performs the central functions of providing love and affection, safety, and facilitating child rearing. Relative to Maslow's hierarchy, the family provides a procedure for potentially meeting all the identified needs.

In the United States a second level of institutions exists for meeting specific needs. These institutions reflect the procedures adopted to help meet the needs that are high on Maslow's scale, or, in the case of religion, is central to the nation's belief system. At this level we find the *economic* institution that provides the system for exchange of goods and services, the *religion* institution that provides mechanisms for people to relate to the supernatural,[8] and the *public protection* institution that provides for defense of the nation as well as fire and police protection. Because of their importance in meeting the most basic human needs, these second-level institutions tend to receive priority over all other social institutions (except the family) in the law, public policy, and the allocation of resources.

The third level of institutions responds to some of Maslow's highest order needs, but relates more directly to those on the lower end of the scale. While addressing some survival and safety matters, these institutions emphasize procedures that are intended to improve the quality of life, that is, self-esteem and self-actualization. They are found in their most developed forms in the more advanced societies and include the *education* institution, for example, which is concerned with the transmission of knowledge, skills, and culture from one generation to another. Further, the maintenance of wellness, the rehabilitation of the handicapped, and the treatment of illness reflect the goals of the institution of *health.* Also, the *social welfare* institution, as we shall examine more fully in later parts of this chapter, initially emerged to meet basic survival needs, but more recently has broadened its scope to include problem solving and enhancement goals. A variety of other important but less central institutions such as *recreation, sports, arts and humanities, entertainment, environmental management,* et cetera also have emerged for the purpose of enhancing the quality of life.

In addition, a set of facilitative social institutions has been created to provide processes through which the other institutions operate. These facilitative institutions include *government,* which determines how decisions in the society will be made, *communication,* which involves patterns for transmitting important information, and, as U.S. society has become increasingly dependent on the movement of goods and people, *transportation.*

Since social institutions are created to meet certain needs of society, they can be expected to change as the society changes. For example, as industrialization altered the manner in which goods were produced, the structure of the family unit and its functions in the production of food and other goods also changed. The role of the extended family was diminished, and the nuclear family assumed a more central function. The ensuing stress on the nuclear family is well documented, and the negative fallout from this stress is reflected in the high incidence of divorce and family violence.

To achieve the goals of a social institution, a variety of programs, structures, and resources must be provided. These *programs* are the mechanisms through which the institution's purpose is carried out. Depending on the scope of an institution, a large number of programs may be required to achieve a goal. For example, within the education institution (and higher education in particular) a number of programs are required for any college or university to fulfill its role. Each student must complete both a general education and a specialized curriculum in his or her major field. To support that process of education, the school must have an admissions procedure, advising system, tutoring support, library, media resources, dormitories, bookstore, and faculty members. With all these programs, the student's education is not considered complete unless he or she engages in, or at least observes, various extracurricular programs such as plays, symposia, and sporting events that transmit aspects of this culture. A sample of the programs required to meet the goals of the social welfare institution are identified in Chapter 5.

Structures, too, must be created to provide vehicles for delivering the programs to people in need. Some form of association or organization is required at either the national, state, or local level to administer the program. Whereas an institution is an intangible process or procedure, an association is a tangible structure. It is a group of people who are organized to carry out a specific function. For example, a specific church is one expression of the institution of religion, while a human service agency is an association created to physically deliver social welfare programs. According to Bierstedt the important characteristics of associations are that they have "(1) a specific function or purpose, (2) associational norms, (3) associational statuses, (4) authority, (5) tests of membership, (6) property, and (7) a name or other identifying symbols."[9] In other words, associations are formal organizations. Chapter 6 examines in more detail associations that are settings for social work practice.

Finally, *resources* in the form of people, money, and various social provisions (e.g., food, housing, and clothing) are required for the associations to fully implement the established programs. To actually reach recipients of the social welfare programs, professionals and other staff members, as well as volunteers, provide direct and indirect services.

THE SOCIAL WELFARE INSTITUTION

The social welfare institution should be viewed as a supplement to, rather than a replacement for individual expressions of caring. There have always been informal efforts to meet needs through individual caring by family, friends, and other natural helpers. This natural helping, however, does not bring the resources or concerns of society to bear on the helping process. It is an individual as opposed to a society's institutionalized response.

The social welfare institution finds expression in the form of laws, policies, services, human service agencies, volunteers, and the variety of professions and other occupational groups that make it possible to help people meet their needs. Social work is one of the professions that helps to carry out the function of the social welfare institution. It is concerned with the welfare of people and with creating an environment that supports their growth and development. It addresses what Mills identifies as both "personal troubles" and "public issues."[10]

Development of the Social Welfare Institution

Colonial Times to the Great Depression.   The emergence of social work is closely related to the development of the social welfare institution. There was no place for social work or most other human service disciplines until society formalized its response to meeting human needs. Depending on the commitment society makes to meet social needs, the demand for social workers will rise and fall. Understanding the development of the social welfare institution helps one recognize the changing role of social work today.

Picture life in rural America as the land was plowed and the family worked together to tame the wilderness. Few have been spared watching at least a few episodes of *Little House on the Prairie* or *The Waltons* that present us with a Hollywood image of a pre-industrial society.

Although there were trials and tribulations in an agricultural society, the person with average intelligence and a willingness to work hard could usually succeed. Given an open frontier and liberal government policies for staking a claim to fertile land, an individual could readily acquire property to produce the necessities of life. Because the family was a strong institution and each member had sharply defined roles in support of efforts to conquer the land, people survived and, in time, prospered. The "American dream" could become a reality for most (unless one was of African, Asian, Mexican, or Native American background) in this simple agrarian society.

The family, however, was not alone or completely self-supporting in this adventure. For mutual protection, social interaction, and the opportunity to trade the goods they possessed, families would band together into loosely knit communities. Trade centers emerged as small towns; a market economy evolved; and merchants opened stores, bought and sold products, and extended credit to people until their products were ready for market.

These efforts to meet human needs can be characterized as *mutual aid.* Members of the extended family (i.e., grandparents, children, and other relatives) could be supported and were needed to work the farm or tend the store. Even the mentally or physically handicapped person could find meaningful ways to contribute to this simple and not too stressful environment. For the most part the family institution worked and the market economy, unencumbered by national and international trade conditions, also worked. When special problems arose, neighbors and the community helped. The barn that burned was quickly rebuilt; widows and orphans without extended families were cared for; and the sick were tended. People would share their products with needy friends and neighbors, knowing that the favor would be returned when conditions improved.

In this pre-industrial society, the quality of life depended on the "grace of God" and hard work. Society rarely needed to take responsibility for responding to unmet human needs; and when it did, the church often assumed that function. In short, the family, the church, and the market economy were the significant social institutions. Because people were acquainted with each other, services were highly individualized and personalized.

It is tempting to blame industrialization for the many problems that emerged in U.S. society in the 1800s and 1900s. Admittedly, industrialization is one important factor, but political, religious, international, and other factors also contributed to the pressures experienced by the family and market system. Nevertheless, industrialization did force a too-rapid change on society and exacerbated the problems of these institutions in adapting to serve human needs.

The movement from an agricultural society to an industrial society significantly affected the family and market system. People congregated in cities where there were jobs; the individual breadwinner rather than the family unit became the key to survival; and interactions with others were increasingly characterized by impersonality. Those with handicapping conditions had little opportunity for satisfying employment in the specialized technological work environment.

As people's needs were met less by the family and market system, society stepped in to provide for meeting those needs, and the social welfare institution emerged. Zald identifies the issues as follows:

> Modern society is an industrialized society, and the development of contemporary welfare institutions is directly linked to industrialization. First, as the level of industrialization increases, the over-all resources and standards of living increase. Thus, industrialization leads to higher minimum standards of human welfare. Higher minimum standards are reflected through the demands of potential recipients, professional groups, and the general public for greater welfare services. Second, as industrialization increases, many welfare functions that were previously handled by the family become the function of differentiated welfare institutions—"needs" that were previously met by the family, or not at all, become collective responsibilities. Third, as industrialization increases, the degree of societal interdependence and differentiation increases. On the one hand, welfare policies and programs become nationwide in scope. On the other hand, effective policies and programs must be adapted to the many types and categories of dependencies and needs created by the increased complexity of the social system.[11]

Industrialization began in Europe well in advance of the colonization of the United States. In England a series of laws were passed in the 1400s and 1500s that attempted to clarify the responsibility of the individual and the role of society in meeting human needs. These laws were drawn together into two significant pieces of legislation enacted by Parliament in 1601, the Statute of Charitable Uses and the Elizabethan Poor Law. The former became the basis on which U.S. philanthropy developed, and the latter was the basis for serving the poor.

The colonists had some respite from industrialization since they were first concerned with developing their agricultural base. Open land in the West slowed the process of urbanization and many of the related social problems. The immigrants who came to this country to escape government authority stressed the dignity of the individual, social equality, and equality of opportunity in their philosophy. They believed only those with a major defect could fail in this land of opportunity, and according to Puritan reasoning, those who failed must suffer from moral weakness. Thus, those in need of services were viewed as morally weak.

The Puritan view that people needing help were sinful was counterbalanced by the perception, derived from the French Enlightenment of the eighteenth century, that people are inherently good. The fallout from these conflicting viewpoints, as applied to the poor, resulted in a perception that there are two classes of people needing help from society: the worthy poor and the unworthy poor.

The worthy poor were viewed as good people who required help because they were afflicted by an ailment or were women or children left destitute by the death or desertion of the breadwinning husband and father. The unworthy poor were able-bodied yet in need because they were thought to have flaws in character. As late as 1818 John Griscom, reporting to the managers of the Society for the Prevention of Pauperism in the City of New York, identified the following as causes of poverty: "ignorance, idleness, intemperance in drinking, want of economy, imprudent and hasty marriages, lotteries, pawnbrokers, houses of ill fame, the numerous charitable institutions of the city, and war."[12] Most of the responsibility for being poor, according to this reasoning, rested with the poor people themselves.[13]

There were, of course, those who reflected a more sympathetic view of persons in need and attempted to reform the punitive and uncaring approaches to providing services or, more accurately, providing custodial care in the almshouses or prisons. As early as 1776 the Society for Alleviating the Miseries of Public Prisons was formed in Philadelphia, the same city where Thomas Bond and Benjamin Franklin had founded the first general hospital in the United States. Later Dorothea Dix visited and chronicled the deplorable conditions in prisons and almshouses. Her efforts stimulated the passage of a bill in the U.S. Congress to grant "public lands to states to assist in financing care of the insane."[14] The veto of this bill in 1854 by President Franklin Pierce established a position that was to dominate thinking in this field for the next three-quarters of a century—the federal government has no appropriate role in the social welfare institution.

Although some state and county government services emerged, the federal government did not become seriously involved in the social welfare institution until President Franklin D. Roosevelt's New Deal program in the mid-1930s. As late as December, 1930, President Herbert Hoover approved an appropriation of $45 million to feed livestock in Arkansas though he opposed the appropriation of an additional $25 million to feed the farmers who raised that livestock.[15] Although the provision of services through private philanthropy experienced considerable support during this period, private philanthropy alone could not weather the crisis created by the Great Depression of the 1930s. As Pumphrey and Pumphrey note:

> The depression of the thirties was an economic and social storm of such unprecedented proportions that established patterns had to be reconsidered. The Social Security Act represented an overriding of the Pierce Veto after the passage of eighty-one years. It was hailed by its supporters as a means of insuring sound democracy and as opening the door of opportunity for the social work profession to provide the leadership in a new era of humane, efficient, and constructive public welfare administration.[16]

Great Depression to the Present.   The Great Depression was also a great equalizer. People who had previously been successful in the market system suddenly required help. These were moral, able-bodied people who needed help. Could they be blamed for their condition? Or do other factors in a society create or contribute to the troubles that individuals experience? For a period of time U.S. society became more sensitive to people in need and increasingly came to recognize that indeed there are structural factors in modern society that are responsible for many social problems.

World War II rallied the people of the United States to a common cause and helped them recognize their interdependence. In such periods of potential disaster, each person must be counted on to contribute to the common good. Under these conditions the nation could ill afford a system that created "throwaway" people by failing to provide for their basic needs. World War II also served to stimulate the economy, and, after a period of recovery, the scope of the social welfare institution was permanently expanded.

The 1960s introduced a period of prosperity and unprecedented responsiveness to human needs. The Kennedy and Johnson administrations fostered the War on Poverty and Great Society programs, while the Human Rights Revolution was at its height. These activities focused public concern on the poor, minorities, women, the aged, the handicapped, and other population groups that had previously been largely ignored. Legislation protecting civil rights and creating massive social programs was passed; court decisions validated the new legislation, and social workers sprang to the foreground to provide needed services. Poverty rates, for example, dropped from 22.4 percent in 1959 to a low of 12.1 percent in 1969.[17]

The bloom on social concerns and social programs began to fade in the middle 1970s, and public apathy replaced public concern. A deteriorating economy was fueled by a growing conservatism, the U.S. trade balance began shifting to a negative position, and relationships with other countries that were strong as a result of the World War II began to erode. Military buildup was placed in direct competition for scarce resources with human services. By the 1980s the time was ripe for conservatives to attempt to dismantle the social programs that had developed over the last two decades. Echoing a political rhetoric incorporating the distrust of government that had characterized the philosophies of presidents Franklin Pierce and Herbert Hoover, mixed with punitive, moralistic views regarding the recipients of human services and a belief that a strong defense against external attack should be the Nation's highest priority, Ronald Reagan was swept into office in 1980.

High on the Reagan administration's agenda was the effort to reverse the growing federal role in the social welfare institution. Palmer and Sawhill's careful analysis of the goals of President Reagan's initial social agenda concludes:

> The president proposed to reduce annual spending on social programs by nearly $75 billion, about 17 percent, below prior policy levels by FY 1985. The deepest cuts (nearly 60 percent) were proposed for the smallest component of social spending—the myriad fixed-dollar grant programs that primarily fund the delivery of education, health, employment, and social services by state and local governments. Substantial cuts (28 percent) were also proposed for the somewhat larger category of benefit programs targeted on the low-income population, such as Food Stamps, Aid to Families with Dependent Children (AFDC), child nutrition,

housing assistance, and Medicaid, while more modest reductions (11 percent) were slated for the social insurance programs, such as Social Security, Medicare, and Unemployment Insurance, which account for about two-thirds of all social program spending.[18]

President Reagan's disdain for the broadened scope of the social welfare institution and the recipients of social welfare programs was evident in his popularized statement that the resources were not going "to the needy, but the greedy." His goal of cutting federal expenditures was aimed at restricting governmental participation and shifting the financial support for a contracted social welfare institution to the states and the private sector. Early in Reagan's first term there was only limited replacement of these federal revenues by other sources, but increasingly state and local governments, private organizations, and individuals all shared in partially filling the gap left by federal cutbacks.

In the following paragraphs Bawden and Palmer summarize the Reagan administration's success in implementing that agenda during his first term.

> The president clearly did seek to turn back the social policy clock, in some extreme cases (e.g., AFDC) to a pre–New Deal time. By and large, however, it was more recent history that sustained the most strenuous efforts at repeal. Given his way, the president would have eradicated most of the hallmarks of the Great Society and would have shrunk the social insurance programs to a scope more nearly approximating their New Deal origins. On the civil rights front the president would have scrapped the federal government's role as a "commanding general" in favor of something more like a reluctant sergeant; broad goals, quotas, and timetables would have been replaced by individual disciplinary action according to rather narrowly interpreted rules.
>
> As it turned out, Congress and the courts have been considerably moderating forces on the president's intentions. Congress acted to protect many of the Great Society programs and to hold together the bottom tier of the safety net. As a result, by and large, the most ineffective programs were deeply cut or eliminated, while the programs more generally acknowledged as effective were left unscathed or reduced only modestly. And, although the president had, as any president has, considerably more latitude in the civil rights area than in the social spending programs, Congress and the courts have provided a substantial check here, rejecting the administration's most ambitious efforts at narrowing the laws or their interpretation.[19]

With the election of Reagan's vice president, George Bush, to the presidency in 1988, the conservative philosophy of government was retained into the 1990s. Despite calling for "a gentler and kinder nation," George Bush's actions continued to reflect the harsh view of human service clients that characterized the 1980s.

ISSUES IN SOCIAL WELFARE

The commitment of a society to support the social welfare of its members is the first step toward responding to social needs. That commitment must then be translated into programs that respond to the needs that the society determines are appropriate to support. Making decisions about what needs, what type of response, and how many resources to commit creates several important issues. Since the social worker is responsible for implementing these programs, it is important for him or her to understand the issues. The manner in which they are resolved in relation to each program influences the ability of the social worker to respond to client needs.

Purpose of Programs

For some, the purpose of the social welfare institution is to facilitate the *socialization* of people to the norms and behaviors of society. Programs designed to help people develop the knowledge and skill to become full participating members of society are found, for example, in recreation programs and in the work of youth-serving agencies. Others expect social welfare to provide a *social control* function, by identifying and removing people from situations in which they are disruptive to society. These people can be found in mental hospitals and correctional institutions. Another view is that the social welfare institution has a *social integration* responsibility for helping people become more successful in interacting with the world around them. Counseling, therapy, rehabilitation, and other services are designed to achieve this purpose. Finally, some consider social welfare to have a *social change* purpose; that is, to express the conscience of society by stimulating changes that will enhance the overall quality of life. The multiple goals of the social welfare institutions at times confuse the society about its purpose.

Conceptions of Social Welfare Programs

The manner in which social programs are designed reflect differing philosophical views about who should be served and when services should be given. Russo and Willis identify the two dominant approaches as selective and universal.[20]

The *selective,* or residual, formulation of social programs is based on the premise that the proper sources for meeting a person's needs are the family and the market economy. If these sources fail to meet an individual's needs, social welfare services are brought into play to address that specific problem, on a temporary basis, until the person resolves the problem or the family and/or economic system begins to work properly. The social program following this philosophy would be designed in response to a particular problem, and the services would terminate as soon as a predetermined "normal" level of functioning is achieved. For example, social workers helping a couple improve their functioning as parents must determine that these clients are performing that role inadequately before the parents can be eligible for counseling or participation in a parenting class. Rather than approaching the task from one of enhancing the parents' abilities, the service must be viewed as solving a problem in their parenting, which carries the stigma of having failed as parents. Further, the selective approach requires that once the problem is resolved or, in the case of parenting, satisfactory parenting skills are developed, the client can no longer receive services, even if they could continue to benefit from additional assistance.

The selective approach to constructing human service programs has also been labled the *safety net* conception of social welfare. Like the safety net used in a circus, the net only comes into play after a person has fallen. It does not reflect efforts to prevent the fall, only to catch the fallen. Most of the social welfare programs in the United States reflect the selective philosophy. They are a conglomeration of social programs designed to meet the society's commitment to respond to emergency needs for those people who experience personal troubles and are unable to resolve those problems through the market or assistance from their families. These clients are, according to Romanyshyn, too often judged as "incompetent second-class members of society for whom second-class services may be provided."[2]

An alternate conception of human service programs is the *universal* (institutional or developmental) approach. This view recognizes that society has changed so much that traditional social institutions are no longer able to adequately meet the needs of all people. For example, technological advances may create unemployment because employees are not needed and not because there is either a malfunction of the economic institution or an inadequate or unwilling labor force. This conception, then, views the social welfare institution as one of society's first-line social institutions for meeting needs. Like the public utilities for water and electricity, these "social utilities" are available to all people who wish to make use of them. No "problem" needs to be defined if a parent wishes to place a child in day care, a young person wishes to join a scouting program, or a senior citizen wishes to take advantage of a senior center's lunch program. The client—in fact, all clients—may elect to participate in universal programs without the stigma of being defined as having failed.

The social welfare institution in the United States reflects both the selective and universal conceptions of social welfare. Frequently, within a single human service agency, there will be a confusing hodgepodge of programs embodying both philosophies. For example, a public welfare department administers selective services, such as financial assistance, yet carries responsibility for Medicare, a program based on the universal conception of social programs.

Local versus Federal Responsibility

There is continuing disagreement concerning the unit of society that is responsibility for social welfare. The view that unmet human needs signify the failure of the individual or "normal" need-meeting institutions assigns the responsibility for correcting those problems to the local level. This position argues that the family, private social agencies, community, or state should develop and finance human services. Its supporters contend the services are more personalized and attuned to the needs of people when they are developed locally. It is a perception that longs for a return to the conditions of a pre-industrial society.

Those supporting the other side of this issue seek a strong federal role in social welfare and argue the human needs to which the social welfare institution is prepared to respond are created, or at least intensified, by factors—such as chronic unemployment, the cost of energy to heat one's home, society's treatment of older people, or inflation and high interest rates—over which there is limited individual or local influence. Creating programs at a national level makes it possible to equalize the burden and the responsibility for taking corrective measures to help the people who experience these social problems. The disagreement over this issue has resulted in a complex system of services at all levels. Social workers have the responsibility for helping people find their way to services through this maze of programs.

Charity or Right to Service?

Another issue that is regularly confronted in the design of social programs is the right of clients to receive or refuse services. Historically, social services were viewed as charity—benevolent gifts that a righteous public bestowed on the worthy poor and begrudgingly provided for the not-so-worthy. The recipient is expected to be forever grateful for any help given through social programs; and the donors, as well as the persons providing the services, expect to be appreciated.

As the universal conception of social welfare became more accepted, the view of services as a right of the client emerged. Many clients have come to believe they are entitled to services and increasingly have organized or sought legal remedy to ensure they are provided to meet their needs. Groups advocating for the rights of the poor, the aged, the developmentally disabled, and the physically handicapped are found throughout the United States. When one's right to receive services becomes an issue, the question of one's right to refuse services must also be addressed.

Individualization of Service

Another issue that social workers and other professionals confront in delivering social programs is adapting services to meet individual needs. The policies and procedures that guide the delivery of human services are defined to respond to the typical person or group experiencing an unmet need. Thus, social programs are designed for a class of people who experience similar problems or needs for service. However, the circumstances of any one poor family, a specific battered wife, or any particular group of tenants of a slumlord will be in some ways unique. Effective service requires a degree of flexibility to make interpretations of these policies and procedures so they might be stretched to cover unique situations. Legislators, agency boards, and administrators must be aware of the importance of allowing for leeway in policy interpretation by the service providers. At the same time, service providers must avoid taking that flexibility as license to create their own eligibility requirements or service criteria.

Categories of Social Programs

It is useful to recognize that social programs can be divided into three distinct categories: social provisions, social services, and social action programs.

Social provisions are designed to meet the most fundamental needs of the population. These services can best be described as the tangible provisions given directly to persons with limited income. They include provisions that may be granted as either cash or in-kind benefits such as food, clothing, or housing.

Social provisions are the most costly programs in outlay of actual dollars. As the social welfare institution has evolved, the governmental agencies have assumed the primary responsibility for providing these services, and the private sector has taken the role of providing backup for those people who are missed by the public programs. Meals and lodging for transients and the homeless, emergency food programs, financial aid in response to crisis programs, shelters for battered wives, and many other human service programs are provided by voluntary social agencies. Yet, as Sosin found in his study of voluntary material aid programs, the basic social provision programs are too costly for the private sector.

> One anticipated finding is that government agencies are much more likely to deal with basic material needs. This is in keeping with the historical picture. Since the New Deal, the expectation has grown that material assistance is primarily a public activity.
>
> This expectation may have extended to emergency assistance, which is also more frequently provided in public than private agencies (although the differences are small). Homelessness and disaster problems are evenly distributed across public and private agencies. These results lead us to the possibility, as history suggests, that private agencies that provide emergency aid or continuing assistance still must face the issue of legitimating a service normally provided—and perhaps expected to be provided—by the public sector.[22]

What are the governmental social provisions? The list is extensive. A partial listing illustrates the broad array of such programs financed by the federal, state, and county governments. These social provision programs include: Aid to Families with Dependent Children (AFDC), Supplemental Security Income (SSI), Needy Veterans Pensions, General Assistance, Food Stamps, School Lunch, Nutrition for the Elderly, Low Income Housing Assistance, Low-rent Public Housing, Low-income Energy Assistance, and others. It is estimated that the programs mentioned above serve approximately 65,000,000 persons.[23] Thus, while some were recipients from more than one program, the programs nevertheless reached a substantial part of the U.S. population.

Social services are programs that are designed to help people resolve problems or enhance their social functioning. These personal services include, for example, family and child welfare, marriage and family counseling, social services for children and the aged, social care for the handicapped, and information and referral services. Unlike social provisions, social services are intangible services that help people change their social conditions.

Many social service programs are designed to contribute to the *socialization and development* of various groups of people. These services may be for children or adults, for healthy or disabled people, or even for persons not seeking to be helped. Kahn describes these services as having a goal of "socialization into communal values, transmittal of goals and motivation, and enhancement of personal development."[24] These services might be found in day care centers, scouting programs, parent education groups, YMCA or YMHA activities, senior citizen centers, and many other programs.

Other social services are designed to provide *therapy, help, rehabilitation, and social protection.* These services are delivered in many different settings and with a variety of clients. They may be short- or long-term services, provided in homes or in social agencies, and provided on an outpatient or inpatient basis. The goal is to help people resolve a variety of issues that interfere with their desired functioning or give guidance to people whose behavior interferes with the functioning of others. These services might be found in family service agencies, mental health centers, probation and parole offices, child welfare programs (including foster care and adoption), hospitals, schools, and agencies offering protective services for older people.

Finally, an important aspect of social services is facilitating *access to resources* that meet needs. A number of factors can make it difficult for people to use already existing social provisions and services. Usually, they must have transportation to the place where service is provided, so they may need help finding a way to get to the help. They may need help finding what agency offers the programs they need and, once there, may require help to get through the complex requirements of the agency to receive service. Finally, clients may face forms of discrimination because of their income, race or ethnicity, sex, age, or handicap, and, as a result, may need the support of a helping person to get the desired services. Access services are provided in many different agencies and may range from informal suggestions to advocating for a client. As Kahn notes, "access services may include information, advice, referral, complaints, case advocacy, class advocacy, and legal services, all on both individual and group bases."[25]

Social action approaches recognize that it is often inadequate just to help a person or group deal with an unjust world. Efforts must be made to create a more just and supportive environment. It is not enough to help a woman understand and even cope with a job that discriminates against her because of her sex. Although these activities are important, they do not resolve the basic problem, and they place the burden of change and adjustment on the victim. It is essential that social programs be created and maintained that can help clients change conditions causing problems or, by recognizing the accumulated experience of a number of clients, can provide leadership to broader efforts to eliminate these problems.

The problems that lead to social action programs stem from a variety of sources and require a range of change efforts. We may be concerned with something as basic and subtle as institutional racism, which has crept into the very fabric of our culture. Programs that are informational or consciousness-raising or that directly challenge the existing situation may help eliminate, or at least reduce, the impact of this problem. The problem may even be the agency itself. Do all people have equal access to the services? Does each client receive the services the agency has to offer or that the law requires? Is the agency open the proper hours to make services available to all potential clients? Are there physical barriers that make it difficult for blind or physically handicapped clients to use the services? Are the policies of the agency or the laws that create the programs fair and just, relative to those who will be served and to what services will be given? These and many other questions the helping person should raise require various forms of social action.

Social action requires an aggressive stance by the helping person, coupled with an understanding of change processes in communities and organizations. The efforts involved in social action include fact-finding, analysis of community needs, research, the dissemination and interpretation of information, organization, and other efforts to mobilize public understanding and support in behalf of some existing or proposed social program.

EXPENDITURES ON SOCIAL PROGRAMS

The causes of human need for which people depend on the social welfare institution may range from rat-infested housing to emotional upset over the loss of a loved one. To respond to these needs, a large number and variety of social programs have been created through laws passed by legislative bodies and through policies established by the boards of directors of voluntary social agencies. In the final analysis, however, the effectiveness of these social programs depends on their implementation through the social agencies and the competence of the staff.

Total Expenditures in the United States

Social programs are offered under the auspices or sponsorship of federal, state, and local governments, private human service agencies (both nonprofit and for-profit agencies), and through professionals engaged in private practice. A substantial amount of money is invested in these programs. Unfortunately, the reporting of expenditures lags several years behind the actual disbursement of funds, but it is nonetheless instructive to examine the money invested in human services in the United States. At last report, the combined expenditures for all levels of government and private philanthropy represented a substantial investment in human services, as depicted in Table 4–1. More than $863 billion was spent in 1987 on programs in health, education, and welfare. For those of us accustomed to dealing with money in $10- and $20-dollar increments, the billions of dollars invested in these services is sometimes difficult to appreciate. It is, perhaps, helpful to translate this into per-capita expenditures. In 1987 more than

TABLE 4–1   *Total Education, Health, and Human Service Expenditures, 1960–1987*

	1960	1970	1980	1987
Total expenditures (billions)	$57.1	$155.4	$510.7	$863.2
Federal, state, and local govt. expenditures (billions)	$52.3	$145.9	$492.8	$834.4
Percent GNP	12.1	21.0	19.8	18.4
Percent Total Govt. Outlay	38.4	48.2	56.5	53.5
Private philanthropy expenditures (billions)	$4.8	$7.9	$15.2	$28.8
Percent public expenditures	9.2	6.5	3.6	3.3

Source: US. Bureau of the Census, *Statistical Abstracts of the United States: 1990* (Washington, D.C.: The Bureau, 1990), pp. 350, 352, 372.

$3500 was spent through government and private philanthropy for the health, education, and social welfare needs for every person in the United States. With an average personal income of $13,123 per person in 1990,[26] people in the United States contributed 26.7 percent of their individual resources to these programs through taxes and voluntary donations.

The expenditures for social welfare programs between 1960 and 1987 reflect a substantial increase in the amount of money invested in social welfare, although the reduced buying power of the dollar accounts for part of the increase. When the share of the national wealth (i.e., the percentage of Gross National Product) spent on health, education, and human service programs is computed, it is evident that the substantial gains made through the Great Society programs in the 1960s were partially eroded by the more conservative political climate of the 1970s and 1980s. Yet a substantial investment remains.

The data on expenditures for health, education, and human service programs also reveal a considerably expanded government role in financing these programs in the past three decades. Table 4–1 indicates that of all expenditures made by federal, state, and local governments, the money spent on these programs increased from 38.4 percent of government outlay in 1960, to 56.5 percent in 1980—but declined to 53.5 percent in 1987. Despite the substantial amounts of money spent on national defense, roads and highways, servicing the national debt, and other governmental activities, these programs continue to consume more than one-half of all public expenditures.

Beginning in the 1960s a clear shift of responsibility for funding human service programs has emerged. Since that time, government or public funding has increased much more rapidly that the funds from the private sector. Public funds spent on these programs increased nearly sixteen-fold from 1960 to 1987, while voluntary contributions increased only six times the 1960 level. When computed as a percentage of governmental expenditures, private philanthropy declined from 9.2 percent in 1960 to 3.4 percent in 1987. Despite the conservative effort to "turn back the clock" on this matter, it is evident that the private sector cannot possibly fund the massive programs to meet human needs. Nonetheless, voluntary contributions of $28.8 billion to the well-being of people by individuals, business, and foundations is substantial. These funds have had an especially important influence on hospitals, schools, national health organizations, and thousands of smaller social agencies in local communities.

Federal Government Expenditures

To understand the choices the American people make (through their elected officials in federal government), it is instructive to examine the major categories of the national budget. One can also see changing priorities by comparing allocations over a period of time. As Table 4–2 shows, U.S. government outlays increased 48 percent between 1980 and 1989, or more than 5 percent each year. With the exception of Social Security and Medicare, which reflect interests represented by the powerful aging lobby in Washington, D.C., the largest relative increases during the 1980s were related to funding for national defense and paying interest on the national debt. The largest relative decreases that directly affect the human services have been in income security, veterans' benefits, employment and social services, and community and regional development programs.

It is evident from these data that the priorities of the United States shifted during the 1980s. Resources were taken from human service programs to support national defense and put off a tax increase, thus increasing the national debt. What was the impact of those reductions?

Public Sector Human Service Expenditures

Although the U.S. government classifies all health, education, and human service expenditures as social welfare outlays, each represents a different social institution in U.S. society. Placing all three social institutions under a single label can be misleading if one looks only at the total government expenditures (i.e., $834.4 billion) to achieve social welfare. To people who do not look more deeply into the services included as social welfare outlays it may appear that all of these funds are spent on the poor. In fact, as indicated in Table 4–3 almost 75 percent of these expenditures by federal, state, and local governments were related to two items: social insurance and education. Both of these are based on the universal conception of human services and are available to everyone. The social insurances include a variety of programs that are funded by worker and employer contributions (e.g., Social Security, worker's compensation, unemployment insurance), and education includes funds for instruction and school construction that few would view as "social welfare." If the social insurances and education programs are excluded from one's definition of social welfare, the total of $215.3 billion perhaps more accurately reflects the public's view of social welfare expenditures.

TABLE 4–2 *Total United States Government Outlays, 1980 and 1989*

	1980 $	1980 %	1989 $	1989 %	RELATIVE CHANGE 1980–1989 (%)
Total (billions)	$590.9	100.0	$1137.0	100.0	
National defense	134.0	22.7	298.3	26.2	+3.5
International affairs	12.7	2.2	10.7	.9	−1.3
Income security	86.6	14.6	136.9	12.0	−2.6
Health	23.2	3.9	49.8	4.4	−.5
Social Security and Medicare	150.6	25.5	319.1	28.1	+2.6
Veterans benefits and services	21.2	3.6	29.2	2.6	−1.0
Education, employment, & social services	31.8	5.4	36.4	3.2	−2.2
Commerce and housing credit	9.4	1.6	20.0	1.8	+.2
Transportation	21.3	3.6	28.0	2.5	−1.1
Natural resources and environment	13.9	2.4	16.5	1.5	−.9
Energy	10.2	1.7	4.1	.4	−1.3
Community & regional development	11.3	1.9	6.3	.6	−1.3
Agriculture	8.8	1.5	20.9	1.8	+.3
Net interest (on national debt)	52.5	8.9	165.7	14.6	+6.0
Science, space, & technology	5.8	1.0	12.6	1.1	+.1
General government[1]	13.0	.8	10.0	.9	+.1
Administration of justice	4.6	.8	9.4	.8	0.0

[1] Data base not comparable between 1980 and 1989.

Source: U.S. Bureau of the Census, *Statistical Abstracts of the United States: 1990* (Washington, D.C.: The Bureau, 1990), pp. 310–311.

When examining Table 4–3, note that from 1960 through 1987 the social insurances progressively took a larger share of government expenditures. As the Great Society programs began to be dismantled in the 1970s and particularly in the 1980s, the allocation to virtually all of the social programs that are supported by tax revenues declined in relation to the total social welfare expenditures.

If one looks at the government programs available only to persons with a limited income, that is, selective programs aimed at the poor, it is evident that

TABLE 4–3   *Federal, State, and Local Government Expenditures on Education, Health, and Social Welfare, 1960–1987*

	1960 $	1960 %	1970 $	1970 %	1980 $	1980 %	1987 $	1987 %
Total (billions)	52.3	100.0	145.9	100.0	492.8	100.0	834.9	100.0
Social insurance	19.3	36.9	54.7	37.5	229.8	46.6	415.0	49.7
Public aid	4.1	7.8	16.5	11.3	71.8	14.6	110.7	13.3
Health and medical	4.5	8.5	9.9	6.8	27.7	5.6	47.6	5.7
Veterans' programs	5.5	10.5	9.1	6.2	21.5	4.4	28.1	3.4
Education	17.6	33.7	50.8	34.9	121.1	24.6	204.5	24.5
Housing	.3	.5	.7	.5	7.2	1.5	13.6	1.6
Other social welfare	1.1	2.1	4.2	2.9	13.6	2.8	15.3	1.8

Source: U.S. Bureau of the Census, *Statistical Abstracts of the United States: 1990* (Washington, D.C.: The Bureau, 1990), p. 350.

the rising costs of medical care have taken the largest share of the increases during the 1980s. As the data in Table 4–4 indicate, expenditures on these programs increased overall by 51.7 percent between 1980 and 1987. However, the expenditures on medical care alone increased 88.5 percent, as compared to 35.4 percent for all other programs. One result of these choices has been an increase in poverty in the United States.

How is it determined if a person or family lives in poverty? Each year since 1959 the federal government has made an assessment of the annual cost for maintaining a minimal standard of living. A full-time worker at the new federal minimum wage ($3.80) earns $7904 before taxes and is therefore above the poverty level of $6280 for a single person. However, if that person has one or more dependents to support, his or her family falls below the poverty levels of $8420 for a family of two and $10,560 for a family of three.[27] Living at or near the poverty level is difficult for individuals and families. To live on that amount of income requires extremely careful control of expenditures and allows for few if any extras.

The following data, compiled by the U.S. Bureau of the Census, helps to identify some characteristics of poverty in the United States.[28] In 1987 more than 32.5 million people lived below the poverty line. It would have taken $4635 per family to bring all families up to the poverty line and $2576 for each unrelated individual who was not part of a family. One indicator used to reflect the amount of poverty in a country is its *poverty rate,* that is, the percentage of persons below the poverty line. In 1959 the poverty rate in the United States was a very high

TABLE 4–4   *Public Cash and Noncash Benefits for Persons with Limited Income, 1980 and 1987*

	1980		1987	
PROGRAM	$	%	$	%
Total (billions)	$104.6	100.0	$158.7	100.0
Medical care	$32.2	30.8	$60.7	38.3
Cash aid	29.4	28.1	42.5	26.7
Food benefits	13.6	13.0	21.0	13.2
Housing benefits	9.2	8.8	13.2	8.3
Education aid	5.2	5.0	10.2	6.4
Jobs and training	8.7	8.4	3.9	2.5
Social services	4.6	4.4	5.1	3.2
Energy assistance	1.7	1.6	2.1	1.3

Source: U.S. Bureau of the Census, *Statistical Abstracts of the United States: 1990* (Washington, D.C.: The Bureau, 1990), p. 353.

22.4 percent. The expanded social programs of the 1960s dropped that to 12.1 percent by 1969, but the rate again began to climb and in 1987 stood at 13.5 percent. Poverty does not fall evenly on the population. It falls most heavily on children. Although the poverty rate was 22.4 percent, 40 percent of the nation's poor were under age eighteen. Also, whereas the poverty rate for whites is 10.5 percent, blacks and Hispanics experienced 33.1 percent and 28.2 percent poverty rates respectively. Where families include a married couple—and the potential for two breadwinners—the poverty rate was 6.0 percent, as compared to male-headed households at 12.5 percent and female-headed households at a 34.3 percent poverty rate. In short, the choices made in the United States regarding its public or governmental expenditures have clearly placed the burden of poverty most heavily on minority, single-parent, female-headed households that include children under age eighteen.

Private Sector Social Welfare Expenditures

The alternative to government human service programs is for the private sector or private philanthropy to provide for human needs. In 1987, only 3.3 percent of the total expenditures in the United States on health, education, and welfare was provided by private philanthropy. Historically private contributions played the primary role in providing services, and those who hold a conservative philosophy of government argue for a return to that position—or at least a more even balance between the public and private sectors. For example, the position of the influential Business Roundtable (endorsed by the U.S. Chamber of Commerce and the National Association of Manufacturers) reflects the business community's opposition to the government's participation in the social welfare institution but at the same time recognizes the importance of human services. It calls for business and industry to increase their social responsibility by funding human service programs more generously:

> The principal alternative to private philanthropy is government funding, which is considered to be inherently less efficient in the distribution and control of funds for these purposes. The sources of government funds, it must be emphasized, are tax-paying individuals and business enterprise. As businessmen and individuals it is, therefore, in everyone's self-interest to support society through private social investments rather than through the complex and costly redistribution of tax dollars by government.[29]

Has the private sector increased its contribution to private charity as public funding has been reduced? Table 4–5 indicates that the increase in private philanthropy has been substantial during the past three decades. Gifts of over $114 billion make an important contribution to the society. However, if just the health, education, and human service contributions are considered, the contribution appears less substantial.

Although it is not possible to disaggregate the data in Table 4–5 to identify the sources of funds for each category of allocation, it is evident that the increases in private philanthropy did not come from business and industry. Business corporations gave 4.4 percent of the 1989 total, the same as in 1960. The major sources of charitable giving have not significantly changed their share of the contribution to private charity in the past three decades.

TABLE 4–5   *Total Private Philanthropy, 1960–1989*

	1960 $	1960 %	1970 $	1970 %	1980 $	1980 %	1989 $	1989 %
Total (billions)	$10.9	100.0	$20.9	100.0	$48.7	100.0	$114.7	100.0
Source								
Individuals	9.1	83.8	16.2	77.5	40.7	83.6	96.4	84.1
Foundations	.7	6.5	1.9	9.1	2.8	5.8	6.6	5.8
Businesses	.5	4.4	.8	3.8	2.4	4.8	5.0	4.4
Charitable bequests	.6	5.3	2.0	9.6	2.9	5.7	6.7	5.7
Allocation								
Religion	5.0	45.9	9.3	44.7	22.2	45.6	54.3	47.4
Education	1.7	15.7	3.3	15.7	6.9	14.1	10.7	9.3
Human services	1.6	14.9	2.9	13.9	4.9	10.1	11.4	9.9
Health & hospitals	1.4	12.5	3.4	16.4	6.7	13.7	10.0	8.8
Arts & humanities	.4	3.7	.7	3.2	3.1	6.5	7.5	6.5
Civic & public	.3	2.9	4.6	2.2	1.5	3.0	3.6	3.2
Other	5.0	4.6	9.3	4.5	3.5	7.1	17.2	14.9

Source: American Association of Fund Raising Counsel, *Giving USA, 1990* (New York: The Association, 1990), pp. 6–7.

The Reagan years represented the most direct assault on the human services since the 1930s. The effort was to not only reduce expenditures for human services but also to shift funding from the federal government to the states and the private sector. To some degree the Reagan administration was successful in reducing the federal contribution to human services, which had a substantial influence on the nonprofit social agencies, as many contract with government agencies to provide services for which they are reimbursed with public funds. Of the total revenues of these nonprofit organizations, it is estimated that 35 percent come from the federal government, 20 percent from private contributions, 5 to 10 percent from other levels of government, and the rest from fees and earned income.[30] Palmer and Sawhill summed up the impact of the Reagan administration on the voluntary human service agencies as follows:

> President Reagan hoped that reductions in taxes and domestic expenditures would restore the vitality of the voluntary sector. However, these reductions have adversely affected the finances of nonprofit organizations and thus their ability to provide services for two reasons. To begin with, lower tax rates raised the cost of charitable donations because the deductions permitted for this purpose were then worth less to the taxpayer.... (Second,) agencies established under the aegis of the Great Society and those focusing services on the poor were hit especially hard by the federal cutbacks. Unable to close the funding gap with sufficient private donations or with charges for services, many agencies had to reduce their activities, especially those engaged in housing development, legal services, social services, and employment and training.[31]

Although understanding the differences between the public and private sectors is useful when examining the human services and clearly is a part of the dominant political rhetoric, the movement of governmental agencies to purchase services from private for-profit and nonprofit agencies (see the section on privatization in Chapter 6) has blurred the distinction. Because any one source of funds may be unstable due to changing economic conditions and political climate, increasingly human service agencies prefer to depend on multiple sources of revenue to support their services. Typically the voluntary human service agency is funded by a mixture of client fees, donations from individuals and businesses, federated funding (e.g., United Way) allocations, and contracts to provide services to clients of governmental agencies. The administration of human service agencies has therefore become increasingly complex.

CONCLUDING COMMENT

Over the past half-century efforts to achieve the goals of the social welfare institution have yielded a rapidly increasing number of social programs at an escalating cost. In both the provision of tax dollars and voluntary contributions, the American people have increasingly recognized the need to provide both tangible goods and intangible services to the vulnerable members of the society.

The principal growth in human service programs was at the federal level, with the New Deal and Great Society programs dramatically changing the nature of the human services. The assumption of responsibility for the major social provision programs by the federal, state, and local governments has dwarfed the private sector in terms of dollars allocated to support these services. In fact, over the past three decades the share of the total education, health, and human service expenditures provided by private philanthropy has shrunk to only a small percentage of the total spent on these programs. Today it is unreasonable to think that sufficient resources from private contributors could ever be generated to meet the demand for social provisions; that is, income, housing, clothing, and food. The social service programs, however, have maintained strong support from the private sector. Also, with considerable financial contribution from government agencies through the purchase of services, private social agencies remain an essential part of the human service delivery system.

It is evident from the review of the funding patterns for human services presented in this chapter that political and economic forces can dramatically affect the ability of agents of the society—the social agencies and social workers—to meet the human service needs of the population. While financial investment in social programs is an important indicator of the Nation's willingness to support its more vulnerable members, it is also important to recognize that pouring more money into the existing services (important as that is) may not be the only means of improving our response to human needs. Miller notes, for example, that—

> Many social welfare policies were developed within social systems in which traditional one-earner nuclear families were the norm, and divorce and single parenthood the exceptions.... Proposed changes and additions to current policies and programs that would reflect the current life situations of families and individuals have been actively opposed as being "antifamily," too costly, not realistic, and whatnot. Few changes have been made and those that have been implemented ... may be called into question as to the extent to which they actually serve to meet social needs.[32]

If social work is to achieve its mission of social betterment, especially for the most vulnerable members of the society, it must have more adequate social programs to provide for people. The evidence indicates that the social programs in the United States have never been sufficient to meet the needs of the poor, the ill, the aged, and the handicapped. The efforts to reduce expenditures on these programs during the 1980s has particularly jeopardized our children. Social workers, then, face a dual challenge. They must search for new and more adequate human service programs and at the same time promote reform measures to eliminate the social conditions that oppress or limit human functioning.[33]

SUGGESTED READINGS

AXINN, JUNE, and STERN, MARK J. "Women and the Postindustrial Welfare State." *Social Work* 32 (July–August 1987): 282–288.

BERKOWITZ, EDWARD, and MCQUAID, KIM. *Creating the Welfare State: The Political Economy of Twentieth-Century Reform* 2nd ed. New York: Praeger, 1990.

BERNSTEIN, MERTON C., and BERNSTEIN, JOAN BRODSHAUG. *Social Security: The System that Works.* New York: Basic Books, 1988.

DAY, PHILLIS J. *A New History of Social Welfare.* Englewood Cliffs, N.J.: Prentice-Hall, 1989.

GILBERT, NEIL. "The Welfare State Adrift." *Social Work* 31 (July–August 1986): 251–256.

KAMERMAN, SHEILA B. "The New Mixed Economy of Welfare: Public and Private." *Social Work* 28 (January–February 1983): 5–10.

MORRIS, ROBERT. *Rethinking Social Welfare: Why Care for the Stranger?* New York: Longman, 1986.

PALMER, JOHN L., SMEEDING, TIMOTHY, and TORREY, BARBARA BOYLE, eds. *The Vulnerable.* Washington, D.C.: Urban Institute Press, 1988.

RICHAN, WILLARD C. *Beyond Altruism: Social Welfare Policy in American Society.* New York: Haworth Press, 1987.

SOSIN, MICHAEL. *Private Benefits: Material Assistance in the Private Sector.* Orlando, Fla.: Academic Press, 1986.

TRATTNER, WALTER I. *From Poor Law to Welfare State* 3rd ed. New York: Free Press, 1984.

ENDNOTES

1. John Romanyshyn, Victor Baez, and Bradford W. Sheafor, "Social Welfare, Organizational Structure, and Professionals" (Fort Collins, Colo: Colorado State University, 1976), videotape.
2. Abraham H. Maslow, *Motivation and Personality* (New York: Harper & Row, 1970), pp. 35–58.
3. *The Random House College Dictionary* rev. ed. (New York: Random House, 1975), p. 1493.
4. Gwendolyn C. Gilbert, "The Role of Social Work in Black Liberation, *The Black Scholar* (December 1974): 16–23.
5. Betty Reid Mandell, ed., *Welfare in America: Controlling the "Dangerous Classes"* (Englewood Cliffs, N.J.: Prentice-Hall, 1975), p. 3.
6. Robert Bierstedt, *The Social Order* 3rd ed. (New York: McGraw-Hill, 1979), p. 320.
7. Ibid., p. 324.
8. Bernard Berelson and Gary A. Steiner, *Human Behavior: An Inventory of Scientific Findings* (New York: Harcourt, Brace, & World, 1963), p. 384.
9. Bierstedt, p. 305.
10. C. Wright Mills, "Troubles and Issues," in Paul E. Weinberger, ed., *Perspectives on Social Welfare* 2nd ed. (New York: Macmillan, 1974), p. 31.
11. Mayer N. Zald, *Social Welfare Institutions: A Sociological Reader* (New York: John Wiley, 1965), pp. 21–22.
12. Ralph E. Pumphrey and Muriel W. Pumphrey, eds., *The Heritage of American Social Work* (New York: Columbia University Press, 1961), p. 60.
13. William Ryan, *Blaming the Victim* (New York: Vintage, 1971).
14. Robert H. Bremner, *American Philanthropy* (Chicago: University of Chicago Press, 1960), p. 191.
15. Harold L. Wilensky and Charles N. Lebeaux, *Industrial Society and Social Welfare* (New York: Free Press, 1965), p. 42.
16. Pumphrey and Pumphrey, pp. 432–433.
17. U.S. Bureau of the Census, *Poverty in the United States: 1987* (Washington, D.C.: The Bureau, 1989), p. 1.

18. John L. Palmer and Isabel V. Sawhill, eds., *The Reagan Record: An Assessment of America's Changing Domestic Priorities* (Washington, D.C.: Urban Institute Press, 1984), p. 13.
19. D. Lee Bawden and John L. Palmer, "Social Policy: Challenging the Welfare State," in Palmer and Sawhill, pp. 213–214.
20. Frances X. Russo and George Willis, *Human Services in America* (Englewood Cliffs, N.J.: Prentice-Hall, 1986), p. 7.
21. John Romanyshyn, *Social Welfare: Charity to Justice* (New York: Random House, 1971), p. 33.
22. Michael Sosin, *Private Benefits: Material Assistance in the Private Sector* (Orlando, Fla.: Academic Press, 1986), p. 37.
23. U.S. Bureau of Census, *Statistical Abstracts of the United States: 1987* (Washington, D.C.: U.S. Department of Labor, 1986), p. 343.
24. Alfred J. Kahn, *Social Policy and Social Services* (New York: Random House, 1973), p. 29.
25. Ibid., p. 31.
26. U.S. Bureau of the Census, *Statistical Abstracts of the U.S.: 1990* (Washington, D.C.: The Bureau, 1990), p. 456.
27. "Reading between the Numbers," *Hunger Action Forum* 3 (August 1990): 3.
28. U.S. Bureau of the Census, *Poverty in the United States,* pp. 1–4.
29. "The Business Roundtable Position on Corporate Philanthropy," issued March 26, 1981, by the Business Roundtable.
30. Palmer and Sawhill, p. 18.
31. Ibid., pp. 18–19; also see Lester M. Salamon, "Nonprofit Organizations: The Lost Opportunity," in Palmer and Sawhill, pp. 261–286.
32. Dorothy C. Miller, *Women and Social Welfare: A Feminist Analysis* (New York: Praeger, 1990), p. 2.
33. Armando Morales, "Beyond Traditional Conceptual Frameworks," *Social Work* 22 (September 1977): 387–393.

CHAPTER 5

Fields of Social Work Practice

One factor that makes social work different from many other professions is the opportunity to engage in helping people deal with a wide range of human problems without needing to obtain specialized professional credentials for each area of practice. During his or her lifetime, for example, a single social worker might organize and lead self-help groups in a hospital, deal with cases of abuse and neglect, develop release plans for persons in a correctional facility, plan demonstrations protesting racist or sexist injustices, arrange for foster homes and adoptions for children, secure nursing home placements for older people, supervise new social workers, and serve as executive director of a human service agency. Regardless of the type of work performed, the social worker always has the same fundamental purpose—namely, to draw on basic knowledge, values, and skills in order to help achieve desired change in order to improve the quality of life for the persons involved.

Although there are similarities in the tasks performed by social workers regardless of the practice setting, there are also unique aspects of their practice in each place of employment. The very nature of the social programs developed to address different social problems requires that social workers in different settings use specialized terminology and some specialized helping techniques. For example, the technical language and skills used by a social worker who is director of the local United Way should differ from those used by a social worker in the oncology unit of the local hospital. As social workers move from one setting to another, they must develop new competencies and adapt old ones to fit the practice needs. Social work provides a broad professional umbrella, and social workers must be flexible as they move among the various settings where they are sanctioned to practice.

What kind of human problems do social workers address? To examine the many areas where the perspective and abilities of the social worker are needed would require many pages of description. In fact, many of the more than 2000 pages of the *Encyclopedia of Social Work*[1] give general descriptions of social problems addressed by social workers and provide references to the most pertinent literature on the subject. The following list of fifty different social problems discussed in the *Encyclopedia* gives an indication of the range of issues social workers address:

Abortion	Housing
Adolescent pregnancy	Hunger and malnutrition
Adoption	Income maintenance
Aged	Infertility services
Alcohol use and abuse	Information and referral services
Child abuse and neglect	Juvenile offenders and delinquency
Child sexual abuse	Legal issues and services
Child welfare services	Literacy
Civil rights	Long-term care
Corrections	Loss and bereavement
Disabilities: Developmental	Mental health and illness
Disabilities: Physical	Patients' rights
Disasters and disaster aid	Poverty
Divorce and separation	Primary health care
Domestic violence	Prostitution
Drug use and abuse	Protective services for children
Emergency health services	Protective services for the aged
Family: One parent	Racial discrimination and inequality
Family: Stepfamilies	Refugees
Family and population planning	Runaways
Foster care for adults	Sex discrimination and inequality
Foster care for children	Sexual dysfunction
General and emergency assistance	Suicide
Group care for children	Unemployment and
Health planning	underemployment
Homelessness	Veterans and veterans' services[2]
Homosexuality	

The social programs designed to help people address these problems call for many different approaches to service delivery. As the helping profession with primary responsibility for helping connect people in need with the services in the community, social workers must have at least general knowledge of the full array of social programs. While detailed knowledge of each program and each human service agency may not be possible, the social worker should be familiar with all practice fields. With the help of directories of human service resources, and, in some communities, information and referral agencies, social workers are prepared to offer valuable assistance in locating specific sources of help.

The human service system is complex, and we cannot expect the layperson to successfully negotiate that system alone. The social worker is required to have considerable skill in matching people in need with resources. To reduce the client's sense of "getting the runaround" in securing services, and perhaps reduce the chance of the client becoming discouraged and not getting to needed help, the social worker must carefully check that the referral is to an appropriate resource. In addition, the professional at times may need to provide a variety of supports, such as encouragement, telephone numbers, names of individuals to contact, or even transportation to facilitate the client's getting to the correct resources.[3] Thus, the social worker must not only work within a single practice field but also be prepared to help clients negotiate services among practice fields.

This chapter identifies some of the features of the primary fields of social work practice to familiarize the beginning worker with the range of settings. The particular position of social work in each field of practice is also described briefly. *Field of social work practice* is a phrase used to describe a group of practice settings that deal with similar client problems. Each field may include a number of different agencies or other organized ways of providing services. For example, in any community, the social agencies concerned with crime and delinquency might include a juvenile court, a residential center or halfway house, a community corrections agency, a probation office for adult offenders, and/or a correctional facility where offenders are incarcerated. All work with people who have come to the attention of the legal system and would be considered part of the practice field of corrections. Although the fields discussed in the remainder of this chapter do not exhaust the full range where social workers might be employed, those identified suggest the great variety of settings in which the social worker is prepared to engage. One of this profession's strengths is the ability of its members to change employment from one practice field to another with only the need to adapt a part of one's knowledge and skills to the uniqueness of a new setting.

AGING

As industrialization increased, meaningful roles for older people decreased in our society. Because of improved medical care that extends life and inflation that reduces the buying power of savings and retirement funds, the elderly have become a large (more than 12% of the people in the United States) and vulnerable population. Most of the aging population leads active and productive lives. Only an estimated 5 percent of the 28.6 million persons over age sixty-five[4] live in long-term care facilities where they lose some of their independence, privacy, and autonomy. However, older people living in their own homes are more likely than the general population to experience problems with health (86% must manage one or more chronic illnesses); housing (an estimated 30% live in substandard housing); loneliness because of loss of mate, friends, and family members; and change of life style because of retirement and limited leisure-time activities.[5]

In their effort to enhance the quality of life, social workers provide services to older people, both those requiring support to remain in their own homes and those residing in long-term care facilities such as nursing homes and congregate-care centers. Teare, Sheafor, and Shank found that providing services to the aged population was the second largest practice area for baccalaureate-level social work graduates, with 16.8 percent reporting this as their primary area of social work. Only 3.6 percent of the MSW workers indicated this was their primary area of practice. A total of 11.6 percent of the baccalaureate social workers (as compared to 1.0% of the MSW social workers) were employed in nursing homes or hospice organizations, primarily serving aged patients and their families.[6] However, social workers are involved with the problems of older people in a number of other settings, including income maintenance, family services, hospitals, mental health centers, and senior recreation programs.

Supports for People in Their Own Homes

A number of programs are available to help older people remain in their own homes as long as doing so is a safe and satisfying experience. Social workers help older people make links to community programs that bring health care, meals, and homemaker services into their homes; provide transportation services; and offer day-care or recreation programs. Increasingly, when older people are faced with a terminal illness, social workers help them deal with their impending death through counseling or referral to a hospice program.

Supports for People in Long-Term Care Facilities

For many older people some form of long-term care in a nursing home or other group living facility becomes a necessity. Social workers frequently help the individual and/or family select the facility and make moving arrangements; some are even staff members of the facility.

While much attention in a long-term care facility is directed toward meeting the basic physical and medical needs of the residents, social workers in these facilities contribute to the quality of life for residents by helping them maintain contact with their families and friends when possible, to develop meaningful relationships with other people within the facility, and to engage in a variety of activities both within and outside the facility. They also facilitate access to other social services when needed and help residents secure arrangements that protect their personal rights and ensure quality care while living in the long-term care facility.

ALCOHOL AND SUBSTANCE ABUSE

In many practice settings the social worker is likely to work with people who are affected by problems of alcohol and substance abuse. Herrington, Jacobson, and Benzer indicate that between nine and twelve million individuals in the

United States are alcoholics or drug abusers and that each individual usually affects at least four other persons in some negative, unhealthy, or destructive manner.[7] The social implications of alcohol and substance abuse are significant as they are highly correlated with murders, suicides, accidents, health problems, and domestic violence.

In recent years social workers have increasingly found success in working with alcohol and substance abusers. Much of the credit for this success has come as social workers and other professionals have moved from viewing alcoholism not "as a moral weakness, requiring only a strong will and determination to 'reform,' "[8] toward viewing it as a disease. This has been beneficial not only for enlisting an alcoholic in his or her own recovery but also in approaching the problem from a sounder scientific basis.

Using current scientific understanding of these problems, Lawson and Lawson have identified three primary factors that should be considered in treating and preventing alcoholism and substance abuse. First, they recognize that physiological factors such as physical addiction, disease or physical disorders, medical problems, inherited risk, and/or mental disorders with physiological causes may contribute to the problem. Second, Lawson and Lawson identify several sociological factors, such as ethnic and cultural differences, family background, education, employment, and peer relationships as also related to alcoholism and substance abuse. Finally, they note that psychological factors, including social skills, emotional level, self-image, attitude toward life, defense mechanisms, mental obsessions, judgment, and decision making skills all can be contributors to this disease.[9] Growing understanding of these associated and interrelated factors has provided the helping professions with an opportunity to apply their knowledge and skills to helping clients to prevent and resolve their problems. Social work has a particularly important role, as the addictions inevitably have a significant affect on family, friends, co-workers and others who are in contact with the person experiencing the addiction. Both the person and the environment must be helped to change when this disease is addressed.

Only a relatively few social workers are employed in practice settings where alcohol and substance abuse are the primary areas of their practice. Teare, Sheafor, and Shank found that 3.3 percent of the baccalaureate social workers and 2.1 percent of the master's-level workers considered alcohol and substance abuse their primary practice area. These social workers were primarily employed in alcohol and drug treatment centers or engaged in private practice. However, 20.3 percent of the BSWs and 18.3 percent of the MSWs viewed this social problem as one of the three most prevalent problems involved in their practice.[10] These social workers were employed by virtually every type of social agency, from mental health centers and inpatient facilities to hospitals and schools.

CHILDREN AND YOUTH

Social workers have always been concerned about the well-being of children and youth. From work with the almshouses in the 1800s to work with street gangs today (see Chapter 15), social workers have devoted a major part of their effort to creating conditions that improve the quality of life for children. Today 18.8 percent of the baccalaureate-level social workers report work with children and youth as their primary practice area, the largest single practice area for BSWs, while 12.7 percent of the MSW workers are primarily involved in serving that population.[11]

Historically the need for services to children and youth emerged when U.S. society entrusted the social institution of the family with full responsibility for the care and nurturing of children. Law and custom mandated that other social institutions must not interfere with the rights and responsibilities of the family. It was assumed that parents would make choices that were in the best interest of both themselves and their children. For example, if parents thought it more important for children to work in industry or help with farm work than to attend school or have time for play, that was their decision. That authority, however, left children vulnerable. Through the years there has been legislation permitting other social institutions to intervene to protect children from some of the abuses that occurred within families. Today children and youth continue to be somewhat hidden within the family, with only limited protection and, at times, only minimal opportunity for experiences that stimulate healthy growth and development.

In most situations social workers seek to work with both the parents and children. Children can often be helped most if parents are assisted in obtaining needed resources and/or developing effective ways to raise their offspring. In addition, social workers have not only provided services directly to parents and children but have also actively promoted laws, programs, and public understanding of the needs of children and youth. Examples of some of the practice areas in which social workers serve children and youth follow.

Adoption and Services to Unmarried Parents

The adoption process begins with the expectant mother, usually unmarried, who faces the difficult decision of whether to keep her baby or place the child for adoption. A few of the factors to be considered in this decision include the mother's plans for the future such as continuing school or securing employment and child care, the attitudes of the mother's family about the pregnancy, the feelings of the father and the mother's relationship with him, and where the mother will live while pregnant and after the baby arrives. Social workers use both individual and group counseling to help women think carefully and sensitively about their decisions. They also, at times, offer counseling to the "unmarried fathers" to help them deal with this situation.

If the decision is made to place the child for adoption, the social worker must screen and select adoptive parents carefully. Matching parents and children is a difficult task that requires considerable knowledge and skill. To gain the best information possible on which to make these decisions, the social worker might conduct group orientation meetings and develop thorough social histories of the prospective adoptive parents. Detailed information on the child's background and even special interests of the natural mother for the child's future (religious affiliation, for example) become a part of the basis for final adoptive placement.

Although there is an abundance of prospective adoptive homes, recent trends making it more socially acceptable for single parents to raise children have reduced the supply of infants available for adoptive placement. However, it continues to be difficult to secure satisfactory adoptive homes for older children or those who are physically or mentally handicapped. An important function of the social worker is to recruit parents for these hard-to-place children.

Foster Care

At times children may need to be removed from their own homes, but it is not possible or desirable to permanently sever the relationship with their natural parents in order to place them for adoption. In these cases, temporary (sometimes long-term) foster care is required. The social worker must work with the parents, the child, and the courts to obtain a decision to remove a child from his or her own home and make a foster home placement. This process involves a careful assessment and a plan whereby the child can return home if conditions improve.

The social worker is also responsible for developing a pool of good quality foster homes. He or she must recruit, select, train, and monitor those families that are entrusted with the care of foster children. The placement of a child in a foster home often creates severe stress on the child, the natural parents, and the foster parents. Considerable practice skill by the social worker is required if he or she is to help resolve these problems.

Residential Care

At times the appropriate placement for a child is a residential care facility, that is, a group home or a residential treatment center. These facilities are most likely to be chosen when the child exhibits antisocial behavior or requires intensive treatment to change behaviors that may create problems for him or her or others.

In these situations one role of the social worker is to select an appropriate residential care facility, which involves working with the child, the family, and often the courts. In addition, other social workers are usually staff members of such a facility, providing care and treatment for the children who are placed there. They are especially involved in helping to maintain positive contact between the child and the family and in making plans for the child to return home when appropriate. The fact that these residential care facilities require licensing creates another role for the social worker—evaluating facilities for the purpose of licensing.

Support in Own Home

Much of the work with children and youth involves providing support services in order to keep children in their own homes. These support services can take the form of counseling or linking clients with outside resources.

Counseling may involve one-to-one consultation with a parent or child to resolve a particular problem with the child–parent relationship. It may also involve family consultation in which all the family members work with the social worker in an attempt to improve some aspect of their functioning. Family members may also participate in group counseling with other parents or children experiencing similar problems. The social worker guides the participants as they address the issues relevant to their problems.

In work with children and youth, the most common outside resources are day care and homemaker services. Day care centers provide a stimulating environment for children and relieve parents of the stress created by the child's continual presence in the home. The social worker must know the strengths and limitations of various day care centers and match children with appropriate resources. Homemaker services help parents learn homemaking skills and reduce the pressures of caring for the children and the household.

Protective Services

Some children are abused or neglected by one or both parents. Abuse, whether it is physical, sexual, or emotional, is an active mistreatment or exploitation of the child. Neglect is a more passive mistreatment of the child but can be just as damaging. It can take the form of inadequate food and shelter, unwholesome conditions, failure to have the child attend school, or inadequate provision of medical care.

The social worker, as an agent of society, seeks to protect the child without infringing on the rights of the parents. When a referral is received, the social worker must determine if the child is in immediate danger, assess the ability of the parents to resolve the problem, and make a judgment about the risks of working with the family while keeping the child in the home. If the child is removed from the home (with approval of the courts), the social worker continues to work with the family in an effort to eliminate the difficulties that led to the referral. This process may involve individual, family, or group counseling; the provision of support services; or education of family members in the areas of their incompetence.

Youth Services

Very early in U.S. history a number of human service programs were developed to provide educational and recreational opportunities for people of all social classes. These services were aimed at character-building among youth, with organizations such as the YMCA, YWCA, Boys and Girls Clubs, and various scouting groups developing. Later, with the growth of settlement houses, programs were broadened to serve other age groups. Although other disciplines also provide staff for these organizations, this field of practice continues to be a small but important area of social work.

Rooted in the universal or institutional philosophy of social program development, these services seek to enhance the growth and development of all interested participants, from the poor to the well-to-do. Through the use of such activities as crafts, sports, camping, friendship groups, drama, music, informal counseling, and other forms of group participation, the members are guided toward personal development. The role of the social worker might be to administer these agencies, to lead the group process, or to provide individual counseling.

With the exception of programs offered through local recreation departments and community education programs, these services are largely concentrated in the private human service organizations. Support from churches, United Way funding, foundation gifts, individual memberships, fees for service, and voluntary contributions provide the bulk of the financial support for these services.

COMMUNITY AND NEIGHBORHOOD SERVICES

The emphasis of social work on both the person and the environment makes the profession directly concerned with the communities in which people live. Beginning with both the Charity Organization Societies and the Settlement House Movement, social work clearly saw the need to coordinate multiple human services and change the structure and processes of communities to make them more responsive to the needs of people. Many of the social problems that people face (e.g., discrimination and unemployment) are at least partially created by the community and not by the individuals affected. Improving the environment is an important factor in improving the quality of life for all people.

In this discussion of community services as a field of social work practice, emphasis is placed on the different practice settings where social workers are employed full-time to help communities improve their functioning. It should be recognized, however, that all social workers have a responsibility as part of their professional commitment to engage in community change activities. Social action might be a responsibility of any social work position or conducted as a volunteer activity. Social agencies in almost any practice field occasionally create a position that is defined as a community change or social action job, but the primary settings where social workers focus on community services can be classified as community organization, community planning, and community development. Only about .5 percent of the BSWs and 1.5 percent of the MSW social workers are engaged in this form of practice as their primary practice area.

Community Organization

A traditional practice area for social work has been working within the network of human services to increase their effectiveness in meeting human needs. This activity involves the collection and analysis of data related to the delivery of services, matching that information with data on population distribution, securing funds to maintain and enhance the quality of services, coordinating the efforts to existing agencies, and educating the general public about these services. The principal agencies in which social workers are employed to do this type of work are community coordinating councils, United Way agencies, and other federations of agencies under the auspices of religious groups, such as the Jewish Welfare Federation.

Community Planning

A few social workers with specialized training join physical, economic, and health planners in the long-range planning of communities. This work requires the ability to apply planning technology in order to project and plan the growth and development of communities. The special contribution of the social worker is to analyze the needs for human services as towns, cities, or regions undergo change. These contributions might range from anticipating "boom-town" developments in energy-impacted areas of Colorado or Wyoming, to helping an urban ghetto plan for an increase in human service needs brought about by businesses moving to the suburbs, leaving the central city with an eroding tax base.

Community Development

Social work joins a number of disciplines in giving assistance to people in communities as they seek to improve conditions. This approach is based on a self-help philosophy that encourages members of the community to mobilize their resources in order to study their problems and seek solutions. In rural areas the social worker contributes to this "grass roots" approach by guiding the involved people toward use of a sound process that maximizes the participation of many concerned citizens. The social worker or other professional also serves as a resource for obtaining technical consultation in areas where there is not expertise among the community members. In urban areas this process, sometimes known as an "asphalt roots" approach, is used in helping neighborhoods or special population groups (such as the poor, minorities, or older people) work together to improve the quality of their lives.

CORRECTIONS AND CRIMINAL JUSTICE

Another small but important part of social work practice occurs in the area of corrections and criminal justice. Teare, Sheafor, and Shank found 2.7 percent of the BSWs and 1.3 percent of the MSWs working in courts, probation, and correctional facilities.[12] Social workers often find corrections a difficult field of practice because the structure of services is usually based on punishment and taking custody of the lives of offenders, which conflicts with many social work values and principles. Yet, because the problems clients experience in this field are basically those of social functioning, the social worker has valuable contributions to make to both clients and agencies. Together with other helping disciplines, social work has helped to introduce both a treatment and prevention philosophy into this practice area; however, finding solutions to the many problems that plague the corrections field will require continuing effort.

The corrections field embraces offenders from all aspects of society—youth and adults, males and females, rich and poor, members of dominant population groups and minorities, and even former White House aides and senators. As indicated in Chapter 11, the poor, especially minorities, however, are very much overrepresented. The social worker's involvement with the criminal justice system can begin at the time of arrest and terminate at the person's release. Some social workers serve as, or work with, juvenile officers in diversionary programs, where they provide crisis intervention or referral services at the time of arrest. These programs divert people from the criminal justice system and into more appropriate community services. Social workers also prepare social histories and make psychosocial assessments of individuals charged with crimes as part of the data a judge uses in making decisions about a case. If the person is placed on probation, a social worker might be the probation officer providing individual, family, or group counseling and helping the convicted person make changes in behavior that will satisfy the terms of probation and prevent additional problems from developing.

Social workers are also found in correctional facilities. In these facilities they provide counseling and serve as a link to the outside world, which encompasses the family, potential employers, and the community service network that will provide support to that person at the time of release. If parole is granted, a social worker might serve as the parole officer or work in a halfway house where the person may live prior to a completely independent re-entry to the community.

DISABILITIES, PHYSICAL AND INTELLECTUAL

It is estimated that 10.4 percent of the baccalaureate-level social workers and 3.9 percent of the master's-level workers are employed to serve mentally and physically disabled people and their families.[13] These disabilities include such conditions as mental retardation, visual and hearing impairment, communication disorders, learning disorders, and cerebral palsy, which affect not only the person's physical and intellectual functioning but also interaction with others, that is, social functioning. The special role of the social worker is in helping the estimated 3 percent of the U.S. population that is disabled and their families learn to live as successfully as possible in a society structured for the more fully functioning person. These disabilities are about equally divided between mental retardation, behavioral disorders, and sensory and/or physical disorders. Many handicapped persons experience more than one form of disability, with some experiencing the "dual diagnosis" of both emotional illness and a developmental disability.

What is a developmental disability? The term has evolved to include a rather broad range of handicapping conditions that affect the physical, social, and intellectual development of a person. The Developmental Disabilities Assistance and Bill of Rights Act (Public Law 95–602) provides the following definition of a developmental disability:

> . . . a severe chronic disability of a person which: a) is attributable to a mental or physical impairment or combination of mental or physical impairments; b) is manifested before the person attains age 22; c) is likely to continue indefinitely; d) results in substantial functional limitations in three or more of the following areas of major life activity, including self-care, receptive/expressive language, learning, mobility, self-direction, capacity for independent living, and economic self-sufficiency; and e) reflects the person's need for a combination and sequence of special, interdisciplinary, or generic care, treatment, or other services which are individually planned and coordinated.[14]

While the definition of a disabled person contained in PL 95–602 does not include all physically and intellectually handicapped people, it does encompass a large share of the most seriously disabled. In an effort to enhance the quality of life for all people, social workers serve clients who experience both mild and severe disabilities. To accomplish this goal, social workers help people find suitable living arrangements (either with their families or in community facilities), assist in the alleviation of problems associated with the disability, contribute to public education efforts about the causes and society's responses to these disabilities, and help individuals gain access to needed services.

EDUCATION AND TRAINING

Some social work practice does not involve directly serving clients, but rather prepares those who will be providing the services needed by individuals, families, groups, organizations, and communities. Some are employed by colleges and universities (education), while others provide training programs for volunteers or employees of human service organizations in order to enhance the quality of services being provided. Although a small number of baccalaureate-level social workers (2.2%) identify the provision of education and training as their primary employment function, this activity is performed by many graduate-level workers (7.0% of those holding master's and doctoral degrees).[15]

Education and training activities involve a wide range of skills. Much of the work involves classroom, workshop, or seminar formats for providing instruction. However, they also involve more individualized forms of instruction found in the direct observation and coaching of volunteers, students, professionals, or other staff members of social agencies. In particular, the communication skills and group interaction skills used in many aspects of social work practice have made social workers particularly effective in education and training activities.

FAMILY SERVICES

Approximately 13.5 percent of both the baccalaureate- and master's-level social workers report that their primary practice area involves providing family services. However, when asked to identify the three client needs for which they provide services, 38.7 percent of the BSW and 45.0 percent of the MSW social workers identified family functioning as an important part of their practice. It is clear that social work practice regarding family functioning exceeds help with any other single client need by a significant amount.[16]

Why are family services such a substantial part of social work practice? Changing marital arrangements, child rearing practices, and patterns of employment in the United States have placed considerable strain on the nuclear family. A growing number of single parent families, reconstituted families (often involving her children, his children, and their children), two breadwinner families, and gay/lesbian households, for example, has dramatically affected social structures that were established for the older family pattern of a mom, a dad, and two kids. Social workers have a key role in helping society address these changes and assisting individual families and households to adapt to these newer conditions or resolve problems associated with them. Three broad service areas capture the bulk of the activities in which social workers engage.

Family Counseling

Social work employs three approaches to family counseling in an effort to help the family adjust to its changing role and deal with the problems it experiences. The first is *family casework.* This approach emphasizes helping individual members of the family change their behaviors in order to make them more productive contributors to the family. It draws on techniques used in individual casework services that are strongly influenced by psychosocial treatment approaches and a problem-solving orientation.

A second approach is termed *family group work.* Recognizing that the family is a special form of a small group, it incorporates much of the theory of social work practice with groups. This approach emphasizes the process by which the family examines its relationships. The social worker helps family members work together to resolve their problems.

The third approach is *family therapy.* This approach seeks to change the structure of the family to make it more supportive of its members. The family, then, is regarded as a unit that can contribute to the well-being of its individual members and is encouraged to perform this function. As opposed to family casework and family group work, family therapy requires advanced skills and training to prepare properly for this therapeutic activity.

Family Life Education

In recent years an effort has been made to strengthen the family through activities that fall under the label of family life education. This social work practice activity recognizes that all families face certain kinds of stress and seeks to prevent family breakdown by educating the family members to cope with the anticipated problems. The Family Service Association of America (FSAA) has taken an active role in developing family life education programs. FSAA has described the goals of family life education as:

> to help group members to understand and anticipate the normal patterns and stresses of family and community living, and thus to improve interpersonal relationships and prevent or reduce situational crises.[17]

Simply stated, family life education provides education about individual and family living. It teaches about interpersonal, family, and sex relationships to help people have more satisfactory and fulfilling lives. Family life education is a preventive approach to human services that has the potential for reaching a large number of people.

Family Planning

Social workers have long been sensitive to the fact that both an unwanted child and his or her parents often experience problems. Adequately carrying out the responsibilities of raising a child is difficult under the best of circumstances, and an unwanted pregnancy makes it even more difficult. Most social workers contend that each child should have the right to begin life as a wanted person. Helping families to plan the number, spacing, and timing of the births of children to fit with their needs improves the chance of achieving the goal of bearing wanted children.

Family planning does not imply that there should be a minimum or maximum number of children in a family or that any specific birth control method should be used. Rather, from the social work perspective, the family is helped to make decisions about their patterns of reproduction in order to maximize the quality of life for both the child and other family members.

The social worker does not have medical training and cannot replace the important role of physicians and nurses in the physiological aspects of family planning. However, he or she must have a minimal understanding of human reproduction, contraception, and abortion to help families with the decisions they must make. Because the issue of family planning can arise in many counseling situations, social workers in hospitals, public welfare agencies, mental health clinics, family services, health departments, schools, Planned Parenthood clinics, and private practice must be prepared to help clients when the need for family planning decisions arise.

INCOME MAINTENANCE

Only 3.1 percent of the BSWs and 1.5 percent of the master's-level workers are employed in public assistance jobs. However, 15.0 percent of the baccalaureate-level and 7.0 percent of the MSW social workers report that they deal with financial issues as one of the three most frequent problems experienced by their clients.[18] Certainly it is important for all social workers to be knowledgeable about poverty and the several income maintenance programs that are available.

As indicated in Chapter 4, we tend to define poverty in terms of the amount of money available to a person or family. Social workers, however, have learned that poverty is a much more complex and insidious phenomenon. Data show that poverty is linked to such factors as health and housing, racism and sexism, old age and youth, single parent status, education and employment, and living in a rural, suburban, or urban environment. Experience indicates that financial assistance, at least at the levels U.S. society has been willing to make available, will not in itself break the cycle of poverty. The poor are perhaps the most vulnerable population group and are of primary concern to social workers.

Despite the many factors that contribute to poverty, lack of income is an unmet need that brings poor people to the attention of the social worker. A number of government-sponsored and voluntary social provision programs have been developed to provide assistance to, or reduce financial demands on, the poor. The two dominant areas of the income maintenance field are public assistance and social insurance programs, although there are other programs that serve this area of human need.

Public Welfare

From the time of the Charity Organization Societies to the present, social workers have been concerned with financial aid for the poor. The responsibility gradually moved from these private agencies to the states and, with the passage of the Social Security Act in 1935, to combined support at the local, state, and federal levels. Private income maintenance programs have almost disappeared.

Social workers have actively supported the development of adequate income maintenance programs and have led efforts to provide needed services. One major concern, in addition to the low levels of financial assistance, has been the requirement that clients pass a degrading means test before they can become eligible for public assistance. All social workers should be familiar with the four basic public assistance programs, since poor people use the services of almost every social agency.

The first public assistance program, *Aid to Families with Dependent Children* (AFDC), provides assistance to children in need through cash grants to the supporting parent or parents—usually the mother. To be eligible, according to the Social Security Act, children must have been deprived of parental care or support because of the death, continued absence from the home, or physical or mental incapacity of a parent. In about one-half of the states children of unemployed fathers are also eligible. These programs are administered by each state with funding from state and federal governments.

The second, the *food stamp program,* is designed to reduce the hunger that is surprisingly prevalent in our wealthy country. Food stamps are available to public assistance recipients and to some other low-income people. The stamps can be traded for groceries at most food markets. Social workers often have administrative responsibilities in food stamp programs, but the eligibility determination and distribution are usually carried out by paraprofessionals.

The third category of public assistance programs is *general assistance.* They are intended to temporarily meet the needs of people not eligible for other public assistance or social insurance programs. They vary widely from state to state because no federal funds are allocated for these programs. In most areas local governments begrudgingly and meagerly support these programs, which are largely utilized by able-bodied, unemployed people who have not succeeded in a job market that averages 5 to 8 percent unemployment.

Hospital and medical care for the poor are provided through the *Medicaid program* in an effort to minimize the financial impact of a serious illness. Medicaid pays the hospital and medical services of persons on welfare as well as the medically indigent. AFDC and Supplemental Security Income recipients, as well as some other poor people, are eligible to receive the benefits of this program. It is administered by the states but has substantial federal funding.

The fourth public assistance program, *Supplemental Security Income* (SSI), is administered by the federal government. This program is intended to provide a national minimum level of income for those people who were once called the "worthy poor" or the "truly needy." The aged, blind, and handicapped are eligible for this program. Most states supplement the federal dollars in order to make the level of support more adequate for the recipients.

Social Insurances

Social provisions that are funded through contributions to a specific program rather than through direct tax revenues are known as social insurance programs. These "universal" programs are funded by employee and employer contributions, and the benefits are made available at times when they are most needed. An eligibility test is not required to receive social insurance benefits.

The major social insurance program is *Old Age, Survivors, Disability, and Health Insurance* (OASDHI), better known as Social Security. This program makes benefits available to insured workers when they reach age sixty-five, to dependent spouses of these workers at age sixty-two, and to dependent children under age eighteen. It is intended to replace some of the income lost if a worker dies, becomes disabled, or retires. OASDHI has been under attack because of the manner in which it has been funded, but is now considered to be fiscally solvent well into the next century.

Medicare is a federal health insurance program directed at persons over age sixty-five, who are vulnerable to serious illnesses that can quickly deplete financial resources and place them permanently in need of public assistance. Medicare pays for hospital care, extended in-patient care, home health services, physicians' fees, and other health related services. If medical costs exceed these benefits, private health insurance or Medicaid can be used to fill the gaps.

Other social insurance programs include *Unemployment Insurance* and *Workman's Compensation Insurance.* The former provides temporary benefits to eligible persons who have lost their jobs, and the latter provides income and medical expenses to people who have been injured on their jobs.

Other Income Maintenance Programs

Cash and in-kind benefits are also available through a variety of private sources in local communities. Local churches and social agencies, such as the Salvation Army and American Red Cross, usually have small amounts of emergency support funds, and a number of other resources usually exist where the poor can obtain help with food, clothing, and shelter. These resources are so indigenous to local areas that local resources must be consulted to learn details. Social workers are familiar with these local sources of help, and frequently they are involved in their provision.

MEDICAL AND HEALTH CARE

Social workers have played a secondary role to physicians in health and medical settings since medical social work was initiated in the early 1900s. With increased understanding that illnesses can be caused or exacerbated by social factors, however, social work has gained a more central role in this field. Not only do a large part of the social workers report employment in hospitals (i.e., 13.8 percent of the BSWs and 20.9 percent of the MSWs), but next to work related to problems in family functioning and interpersonal relations, services regarding health-related problems are the highest client need area addressed by both baccalaureate- and master's-level social workers.[19]

A primary place for social work practice in this field is in hospitals. In these settings, for example, social workers address social and psychological factors that are either contributing causes of medical ailments or are side effects of a medical condition that must be dealt with to facilitate recovery and prevent occurrences of nonfunctional dependence. Social workers help to link patients, perhaps with changed levels of functioning due to a medical problem, with their environments by providing individual, group, and family counseling; serving as patient advocates; and working with self-help groups of patients experiencing similar medical or social problems. Social workers also might be engaged in counseling terminally ill patients and their families.

In addition social workers are involved in other health and medical care facilities besides hospitals. They work in public health clinics and private physicians' offices providing counseling and referral services to people who have sought medical treatment related to family planning, prenatal care, child growth and development, venereal disease, and physical disability, for example. They have also taken an active role in health maintenance and disease prevention programs in local communities. With the skyrocketing costs of medical care it is even more important that these efforts be continued by the social work profession.

MENTAL HEALTH AND ILLNESS

Social work has been involved in working with people who experience mental health problems since the early 1900s. Not surprisingly, social work has gradually become a dominant profession in this field, since serious problems in social functioning are often caused, or at least increased, by an emotional disturbance or mental illness. It is estimated that more than one-half of all professional mental health personnel are social workers. With an estimated 15 percent of the population experiencing emotional disturbance at any one time,[20] there is a high demand for social workers in this practice area. Social workers for whom mental health is the primary practice setting are for the most part MSW level workers. Mental health is the dominant practice area for master's-level social workers (28.3 percent), but ranks only fifth highest among the BSW workers, with 9.9 percent reporting mental health as their primary practice area.[21]

Mental health is defined as "a positive state of mental well-being in which individuals feel basically satisfied with themselves, their roles in life, and relationships with others."[22] The goal of achieving mental health is clearly compatible with the purpose of social work. The absence of mental health, mental illness, takes the form of a wide range of behaviors and is caused by multiple factors ranging from stressful situations to organic problems.

Social workers in mental health settings work with people experiencing these difficulties by treating those who can make changes to learn to cope with problems in their social functioning and, at the same time, changing environmental factors to promote better mental health or eliminate social conditions that have a negative impact on people. Some social workers (8.7 percent of the BSW workers and 18.9 percent of the MSWs) provide these services on an *out-patient* basis in a mental health center, sheltered workshop, or counseling center. They provide clinical or therapeutic services to individuals and families, or to small groups of clients. They may also work with a variety of organizations, such as schools or mass media, in an effort to create an environment that is conducive to the healthy growth and development of all people—both clients and the public.

A much smaller number of social workers (4.4 percent BSW workers and 3.7 percent MSW workers) provide mental health services on an *in-patient* basis in residential treatment centers and psychiatric hospitals. These services are given to people of all ages experiencing more severe problems requiring the full-time care and the structure available at a hospital or other living situation. In addition to providing a variety of treatment activities, these social workers serve as liaisons to the patient's world. A social worker might work to help the patient and family or friends maintain contact while the patient is hospitalized. He or she might also assess the impact of family, friends, employer, school, and so forth on the client's situation and offer assistance in helping these significant others change in ways that will benefit the client. Finally, when patients are ready to return to the community, social workers would become the key professional people helping them to make arrangements for returning to school or work, securing an appropriate living situation, connecting with supportive social service agencies, and developing and maintaining needed social relationships.

OCCUPATIONAL SOCIAL WORK

Social work has been practiced in business and industrial settings since the late 1800s. Social workers have been employed both by management and labor unions to offer services and provide consultation about the development of employee programs. In recent years there has been a rapid growth of interest in this area of social work practice. Although only about one-half of 1 percent of social workers are currently employed in occupational social work positions, as the practice field is becoming known, the potential to make valuable services available to the general population is enormous. Jorgensen indicates that 64 percent of the population over age 16, or nearly 104 million people, are in the labor force.[23] Like schools and hospitals, the workplace is an opportune place to identify social problems and provide needed services.

Although corporations are primarily interested in making a profit on the goods and services they produce, they are increasingly realizing worker productivity is closely related to the general welfare of the employees. The humanizing of big business has been a major theme in recent years. Efforts to resolve or prevent employee problems in social functioning are seen as simply good business. Occupational social workers are a support for the managers of the companies and a resource to the employees.

Shank and Jorve identify three models of social work practice in business and industry: the employee service model, the consumer service model, and the corporate social responsibility model.[24]

The *employee service model* of occupational social work focuses on activities that provide direct service to the employees of a business or industry. The social

worker using this model might develop and implement employee assistance programs and various supervisory training programs. In addition, the social worker
might provide counseling to individuals or families in relation to marital, family,
substance abuse, aging, health and retirement problems, offer referral to other
community agencies or self-help groups such as Alcoholics Anonymous, and consult with management on individual problems. Typical problems the social
worker might also address would be the identification of job-related factors such
as boredom or stress, an employee's desire to find resources to upgrade his or
her job skills, the need for preretirement planning, or a linkage to Workman's
Compensation or unemployment insurance programs.

The occupational social worker following the *consumer service model* might
serve as the company's representative to various consumer groups and focus on
identifying consumer needs and methods of meeting them. Typically found in
banks, public utilities, and government agencies, these social workers help to
provide liaison with consumer groups and social service agencies, develop outreach programs, and provide counseling to customers to meet unique needs.

The third model, the *corporate social responsibility model* of practice, places
the social worker in the role of assisting corporations and businesses to make a
commitment to the social and economic well-being of the communities in which
they are located. The social workers consult with management on their policies
concerning human resources, their donations to nonprofit organizations, and social legislation they may wish to support. In addition, social workers may administer health and welfare benefit programs for employees, represent the company in research and community development activities, and provide linkage
between social service, social policy, and corporate interests.

SCHOOLS

Seven percent of the MSW social workers and 2.1 percent of the BSW graduates
are employed in elementary and secondary schools.[25] Because education is compulsory, schools confront many social problems such as poverty, child abuse,
discrimination, developmental disabilities, and emotional disturbances. These
problems impact children and their ability to learn—the primary mission of education—and thus become of concern to school systems.

The traditional approach of social workers in schools has been to counsel
the child and confer with the family. They have depended on the cooperation
of teachers to make referrals when problems are evident and have had varying
degrees of effectiveness, depending on the willingness of teachers and school
systems to use them as a resource. Problems of truancy, suspected child abuse,
inadequate nutrition, substance abuse, parental neglect, and inappropriate behavior are often referred to the social worker.

Recently this practice field has undergone a marked change with the school
being approached as a primary setting where social problems should be identified

and addressed. Social workers have, under this approach, become more aggressive in their practice activities, serving as a link between school, family, and community. According to Costin, there are seven primary tasks one can expect to find the social worker performing in the schools today:

1. Facilitate the provision of direct educational and social services and provide direct social casework and group work services to selected pupils
2. Act as a pupil advocate, focusing upon the urgent needs of selected groups of pupils
3. Consult with school administrators to jointly identify major problems toward which a planned service approach will be aimed; aid in developing cooperative working relationships with community agencies; and assist in the formulation of school policy that directly affects the welfare of children and young persons
4. Consult with teachers about techniques for creating a climate in which children are freed and motivated to learn by interpreting social and cultural influences in the lives of pupils, facilitating the use of peers to help a troubled child, or assisting in managing relationships within a classroom
5. Organize parent and community groups to channel concerns about pupils and school and to improve school and community relations
6. Develop and maintain liaison between the school and critical fields of social work—child welfare, corrections, mental health, and legal services for the poor. Such liaison facilitates more effective community services for school children and their families, assists with planned change in the community's organizational pattern of social welfare programs and resources, and acts as a catalyst to change the pattern of the social structure
7. Provide leadership in the coordination of interdisciplinary skills among pupil services personnel, e.g., guidance counselors, psychologists, nurses, and attendance officers.[26]

These tasks clearly match the competencies one would find in the professional social worker.

CONCLUDING COMMENT

For the person considering a career in social work, it is important to have an understanding of the many different fields of practice open to the social worker. It is also important to recognize that the position of social work varies in these different fields; that not only affects the ability of the social worker to provide clients with services, but also influences the manner in which the social worker uses a part of his or her time. However, experience over time has demonstrated that social work has a viable role to perform in many different practice settings.

Two important points made earlier in this book are reinforced by this examination of selected social work practice fields. First, social work is indeed a profession of many faces. The variation in the type of human problems and social change activities in which social workers are involved is extensive. Social work deals with almost every facet of life and almost every element of the population.

Second, social work is unique among the helping professions because of its dual focus on the person and the environment. Social workers help people deal with the world around them in every field of practice. As a consequence, individuals are helped to relate more effectively to families; families are helped to deal with social agencies; social agencies are helped to relate more effectively with communities; and the cycle is completed as communities are helped to be more responsive to the needs of individuals.

The preparation received when obtaining a baccalaureate or master's degree in social work is intended to prepare one with the basic knowledge, values, and skills to engage in social work practice in any of these fields. The ability to transfer these competencies to several different settings gives the social worker considerable flexibility in selecting the setting where he or she will work. However, the social worker will need to acquire more in-depth knowledge about the uniqueness of each new setting and the specialized knowledge and skills that may be used in that particular field.

SUGGESTED READINGS

Aging

BRODY, ELAINE M., and BRODY, STANLEY J. "Aged: Services." *Encyclopedia of Social Work* 18th ed., vol. I, ed. Anne Minahan. Silver Spring, Md.: National Association of Social Workers, 1987, pp. 106–126.

BRUBAKER, ELLIE. *Working with the Elderly: A Social Systems Approach.* Newbury Park, Calif.: Sage, 1987.

DOBELSTEIN, ANDREW W. *Serving Older Adults: Policy, Programs, and Professional Activities.* Englewood Cliffs, N.J.: Prentice-Hall, 1985.

HANCOCK, BETSY LEDBETTER. *Social Work with Older People.* Englewood Cliffs, N.J.: Prentice-Hall, 1987.

ROFF, LUCINDA LEE, and ATHERTON, CHARLES R. *Promoting Successful Aging.* Chicago: Nelson-Hall, 1989.

SILVERSTONE, BARBARA, and HYMAN, HELEN KANDEL. *You and Your Aging Parent: A Family Guide to Emotional, Physical, & Financial Problems* 3rd ed. New York: Pantheon Books, 1989.

Alcohol and Substance Abuse

COOK, DAVID; FEWELL, CHRISTINE; and RIOLO, JOHN. *Social Work Treatment of Alcohol Problems.* New Brunswick, N.J.: Rutgers Center of Alcohol Treatment, 1983.

HERRINGTON, ROLAND E.; JACOBSON, GEORGE R.; and BENZER, DAVID G., eds. *Alcohol and Drug Abuse Handbook.* St. Louis, Mo.: Warren H. Green, 1987.

LAWSON, GARY W., and LAWSON, ANN W. *Alcoholism and Substance Abuse in Special Populations.* Rockville, Md.: Aspen Publishers, 1989.

WEGSCHIEDER-CRUSE, SHARON. *Another Chance: Hope and Health for the Alcoholic Family* 2nd ed. Palo Alto, Calif.: Science and Behavior Books, 1989.

Children and Youth

FELDMAN, RONALD A. "Youth Service Agencies." *Encyclopedia of Social Work* 18th ed., vol. II, ed. Anne Minahan. Silver Spring, Md.: National Association of Social Workers, 1987, pp. 901–907.

KADUSHIN, ALFRED, and MARTIN, JUDITH. *Child Welfare Services* 4th ed. New York: Macmillan, 1988.

LAIRD, JOAN, and HARTMAN, ANN, eds. *A Handbook of Child Welfare.* New York: Free Press, 1985.

LOAVENBRUCK, GRANT, and KEYS, PAUL. "Settlements and Neighborhood Centers." *Encyclopedia of Social Work* 18th ed., vol. II, ed. Anne Minahan. Silver Spring, Md.: National Association of Social Workers, 1987, pp. 556–561.

REID, KENNETH E. *From Character Building to Social Treatment: The History of Groups in Social Work.* Westport, Conn.: Greenwood Press, 1981.

Community and Neighborhood Services

BIEGEL, DAVID E. "Neighborhoods," *Encyclopedia of Social Work* 18th ed., vol. II, ed. Anne Minahan. Silver Spring, Md.: National Association of Social Workers, 1987, pp. 182–197.

BRILLIANT, ELEANOR L. "Community Planning and Community Problem Solving: Past, Present, and Future." *Social Service Review* 60 (December 1986): 568–589.

FELLIN, PHILLIP. *The Community and the Social Worker.* Itasca, Ill.: Peacock Publishing, 1987.

GILBERT, NEIL, and SPECHT, HARRY. "Social Planning and Community Organization." *Encyclopedia of Social Work* 18th ed., vol. II, ed. Anne Minahan. Silver Spring, Md.: National Association of Social Workers, 1987, pp. 602–619.

MARTINEZ-BRAWLEY, EMILIA E. *Perspectives on the Small Community: Humanistic Views for Practitioners.* Silver Spring, Md.: National Association of Social Workers, 1990.

ZANDER, ALVIN. *Effective Social Action by Community Groups.* San Francisco: Jossey-Bass, 1990.

Corrections and Criminal Justice

ASHFORD, JOSE B.; MACHT, MARY WIRTZ; and MYLYM, MELISSA. "Advocacy by Social Workers in a Public Defender's Office." *Social Work* 32 (May–June 1987): 199–203.

LONGRESS, JOHN F. "Juvenile Offenders and Delinquency," *Encyclopedia of Social Work* 18th ed., vol. II, ed. Anne Minahan. Silver Spring, Md.: National Association of Social Workers, 1987, pp. 21–27.

NETHERLAND, WARREN. "Corrections System: Adult," *Encyclopedia of Social Work* 18th ed., vol. I, ed. Anne Minahan. Silver Spring, Md.: National Association of Social Workers, 1987, pp. 351–360.

ROBERTS, ALBERT R. *Social Work in Juvenile and Criminal Justice Settings.* Springfield, Ill.: Charles C. Thomas, 1983.

Disabilities, Physical and Intellectual

BROWN, FREDDA, and HEHR, DONNA H. *Persons with Profound Disabilities: Issues and Practices.* Baltimore: Paul H. Brookes, 1989.

GARDNER, JAMES F., and CHAPMAN, MICHAEL S. *Program Issues in Developmental Disabilities: A Guide to Effective Habilitation and Active Treatment* 2nd ed. Baltimore: Paul H. Brookes, 1990.

McDonald-Wikler, Lynn. "Disabilities: Developmental." *Encyclopedia of Social Work* 18th ed., vol. I, ed. Anne Minahan. Silver Spring, Md.: National Association of Social Workers, 1987, pp. 422–434.

Stroud, Marion, and Sutton, Evelyn. *Expanding Options for Older Adults with Developmental Disabilities: A Practical Guide to Achieving Community Access.* Baltimore: Paul H. Brookes, 1988.

Turnbull, H. Rutherford, III; Turnbull, Ann P.; Bronicki, G. J.; Summers, Jean Ann; and Roeder-Gordon, Constance. *Disability and the Family: A Guide to Decisions for Adulthood.* Baltimore: Paul H. Brookes, 1989.

Whitman, Barbara J., and Pasquale, Accardo J. *When a Parent Is Mentally Retarded.* Baltimore: Paul H. Brookes, 1990.

Education and Training

Dedmon, Rachel. "Successful Social Work Educators Engaged in Practice." *Journal of Social Work Education* 25 (Spring–Summer 1989): 134–141.

Harrison, Dianne F.; Sowers-Hoag, Karen; and Postley, Brenda J. "Faculty Hiring in Social Work: Dilemmas for Educators or Job Candidates?" *Journal of Social Work Education* 25 (Spring–Summer 1989): 117–125.

Kendall, Katherine. "International Social Work Education." *Encyclopedia of Social Work* 18th ed., vol. I, ed. Anne Minahan. Silver Spring, Md.: National Association of Social Workers, 1987, pp. 987–996.

Latting, Jean Kantambu. "Identify the 'Isms': Enabling Social Work Students to Confront their Biases." *Journal of Social Work Education* 26 (Winter 1990): 36–44.

Family Services

Bush, Malcolm. *Families in Distress: Public, Private, and Civic Responses.* Berkeley, Calif.: University of California Press, 1988.

Chilman, Catherine S.; Nunnally, Elam W.; and Cox, Fred M. *Variant Family Forms: Families in Trouble Series* vol. 5. Beverly Hills, Calif.: Sage, 1988.

Erickson, A. Gerald. "Family Services." *Encyclopedia of Social Work* 18th ed., vol. I, ed. Anne Minahan. Silver Spring, Md.: National Association of Social Workers, 1987, pp. 589–593.

Johnson, Harriette C. "Emerging Concerns in Family Therapy." *Social Work* 31 (July–August 1986): 299–306.

Kaplan, Lisa. *Working with Multiproblem Families.* Lexington, Mass.: D. C. Heath, 1986.

McGoldrick, M.; Pierce, J.; and Giordano, Joseph, eds. *Ethnicity and Family Therapy.* New York: Guilford Press, 1982.

Star, Barbara. "Domestic Violence." *Encyclopedia of Social Work* 18th ed., vol. I, ed. Anne Minahan. Silver Spring, Md.: National Association of Social Workers, 1987, pp. 463–476.

Whittaker, James K.; Kinney, Jill; Tracy, Elizabeth M.; and Booth, Charlotte. *Reaching High-Risk Families: Intensive Family Preservation in Human Services.* New York: Aldine deGruyter, 1990.

Income Maintenance

Ginsberg, Leon H. *The Practice of Social Work in Public Welfare.* New York: Free Press, 1983.

Teare, Robert J. *Social Work Practice in a Public Welfare Setting: An Empirical Analysis.* New York: Praeger, 1981.

Wyers, Norman L. "Income Maintenance System." *Encyclopedia of Social Work* 18th ed., vol. I, ed. Anne Minahan. Silver Spring, Md.: National Association of Social Workers, 1987, pp. 888–898.

Yankey, John "Public Social Services." *Encyclopedia of Social Work* 18th ed., vol. II, ed. Anne Minahan. Silver Spring, Md.: National Association of Social Workers, 1987, pp. 417–426.

Medical and Health Care

Combs-Orne, Terri. *Social Work Practice in Maternal and Child Health.* New York: Springer, 1990.

Kerson, Toba Schwaber. *Social Work in Health Settings: Practice in Context.* New York: Haworth, 1989.

Leukefeld, Carl G. "Public Health Services." *Encyclopedia of Social Work* 18th ed., vol. II, ed. Anne Minahan. Silver Spring, Md.: National Association of Social Workers, 1987, pp. 409–417.

Miller, Rosalind S., and Rehr, Helen, eds. *Social Work Issues in Health Care.* Englewood Cliffs, N.J.: Prentice-Hall, 1983.

Rossen, Salie. "Hospital Social Work." *Encyclopedia of Social Work* 18th ed., vol. I, ed. Anne Minahan. Silver Spring, Md.: National Association of Social Workers, 1987, pp. 816–821.

Schopler, Janice H., and Galinsky, Maeda J. *Groups in Health Care Settings.* New York: Haworth, 1990.

Mental Health and Illness

Biegel, David E., and Naperstek, Arthur J. *Community Support Systems and Mental Health: Practice, Policy, and Research.* New York: Springer, 1982.

Callicutt, James W. "Mental Health Services." *Encyclopedia of Social Work* 18th ed., vol. II, ed. Anne Minahan. Silver Spring, Md.: National Association of Social Workers, 1987, pp. 125–135.

Callicutt, James W., and Lecca, P. J., eds. *Social Work and Mental Health.* New York: Free Press, 1983.

Sundel, Martin; Glasser, Paul; Sarri, Rosemary; and Vinter, Robert, eds. *Individual Change through Small Groups* 2nd ed. New York: Free Press, 1985.

Wasserman, Harry, and Danforth, Holly E. *The Human Bond: Support Groups and Mutual Aid.* New York: Springer, 1988.

Occupational Social Work

Akabas, Sheila H., and Kurzman, Paul A. *Work, Workers, and Work Organizations.* Englewood Cliffs, N.J.: Prentice-Hall, 1982.

Googins, Bradley, and Godfrey, Joline. *Occupational Social Work.* Englewood Cliffs, N.J.: Prentice-Hall, 1987.

Gould, Gary M., and Smith, Michael L., eds. *Social Work in the Workplace: Practice and Principles.* New York: Springer, 1988.

Kurzman, Paul A. "Industrial Social Work (Occupational Social Work)," *Encyclopedia of Social Work* 18th ed., vol. I, ed. Anne Minahan. Silver Spring, Md.: National Association of Social Workers, 1987, pp. 899–910.

Masi, Dale A. *Human Services in Industry.* Lexington, Mass.: Lexington Books, 1982.

Straussner, Shulamith Lala Ashenberg. *Occupational Social Work Today.* New York: Haworth, 1990.

Schools

ALLEN-MEARES, PAULA; WASHINGTON, ROBERT O.; and WELSH, BETTY L. *Social Work Services in Schools.* Englewood Cliffs, N.J.: Prentice-Hall, 1986.

CONSTABLE, ROBERT T., and FLYNN, JOHN P. *School Social Work: Practice and Research Perspectives.* Homewood, Ill.: Dorsey Press, 1982.

COSTIN, LELA B. "School Social Work." *Encyclopedia of Social Work* 18th ed., vol. II, ed. Anne Minahan. Silver Spring, Md.: National Association of Social Workers, 1987, pp. 538–545.

HANCOCK, BETSY LEDBETTER. *School Social Work.* Englewood Cliffs, N.J.: Prentice-Hall, 1982.

KONLE, CAROLYN. *Social Work Day to Day* 2nd ed. New York: Longman, 1989.

McNEELY, R. L., and BADAMI, MARY KENNY. "Interracial Communication in School Social Work." *Social Work* 29 (January–February 1984): 22–27.

ENDNOTES

1. Anne Minahan, ed., *Encyclopedia of Social Work* 18th ed. (Silver Spring, Md.: National Association of Social Workers, 1987).
2. Ibid., pp. xi–xiii.
3. Bradford W. Sheafor, Charles R. Horejsi, and Gloria A. Horejsi, *Techniques and Guidelines for Social Work Practice* (Boston: Allyn and Bacon, 1988), pp. 199–204.
4. Barbara Silverstone and Helen Kandel Hyman, *You and Your Aging Parent: A Family Guide to Emotional, Physical, & Financial Problems* (New York: Pantheon Books, 1989), p. 5.
5. Robert N. Butler and Myrna I. Lewis, *Aging and Mental Health* 3rd ed. (St. Louis, Mo.: C. V. Mosby, 1982), pp. 5–17.
6. Robert J. Teare, Bradford W. Sheafor, and Barbara W. Shank, "Similarities and Differences in BSW and MSW Social Workers." Paper presented at Baccalaureate Program Directors Workshop, Minneapolis, Minn., 1990).
7. Roland E. Herrington, George R. Jaconson, and David G. Benzer, eds., *Alcohol and Drug Abuse Handbook.* (St. Louis, Mo.: Warren H. Green, 1987), p. xiii.
8. David Cook, Christine Fewell, and John Riolo, eds., *Social Work Treatment of Alcohol Problems* (New Brunswick, N.J.: Rutgers School of Alcohol Studies), p. xiii.
9. Gary W. Lawson and Ann W. Lawson, *Alcoholism and Substance Abuse in Special Populations* (Rockville, Md.: Aspen Publishers, 1989), pp. 5–7.
10. Teare, Sheafor, and Shank.
11. Ibid.
12. Ibid.
13. Ibid.
14. Robert L. Schalock, *Services for Developmentally Disabled Adults* (Baltimore: University Park Press, 1982), p. 12.
15. Teare, Sheafor, and Shank.
16. Ibid.
17. National Commission of Family Life Education, "Family Life Programs: Principles, Plans, and Procedures," *Family Coordinator* 17 (July 1968): 211.
18. Teare, Sheafor, and Shank.
19. Ibid.
20. Milton G. Thackeray, Rex A. Skidmore, and O. William Farley, *Introduction to Mental Health: Field and Practice* (Englewood Cliffs, N.J.: Prentice-Hall, 1981), pp. 257–269.
21. Teare, Sheafor, and Shank.
22. Thackeray, Skidmore, and Farley, p. 8.

23. Lou Ann Jorgesen, "Social Services in Business and Industry," in Neil Gilbert and Harry Specht, eds., *Handbook for Social Services* (Englewood Cliffs, N.J.: Prentice-Hall, 1981), p. 337.
24. Barbara W. Shank and Beth K. Jorve, "Industrial Social Work: A New Arena for the BSW." Paper presented at the National Symposium of Social Workers, Washington, D.C., 1983, p. 14.
25. Teare, Sheafor, and Shank.
26. Lela B. Costin, "Social Work in the Schools," in Donald Brieland, Lela B. Costin, and Charles R. Atherton, eds., *Contemporary Social Work and Social Welfare* 2nd ed. (New York: McGraw-Hill, 1980), p. 247.

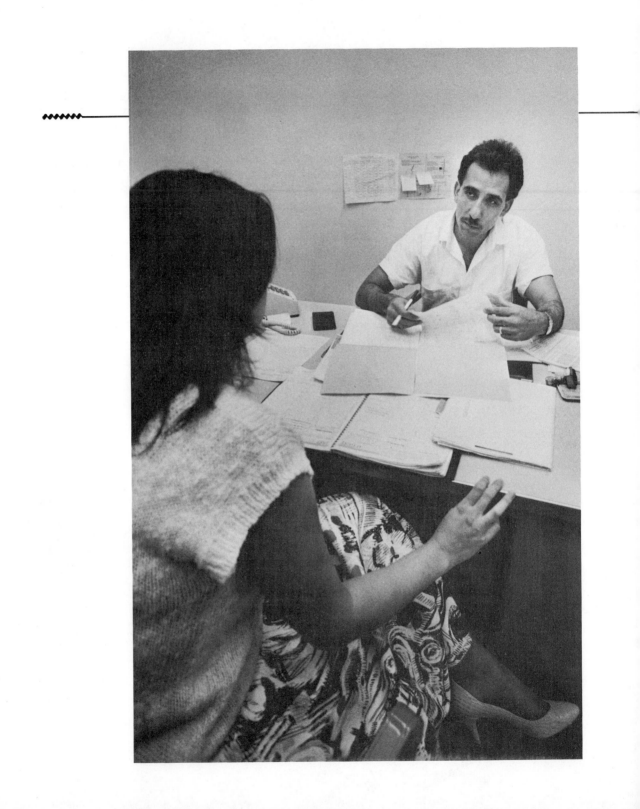

CHAPTER 6

Settings for Social Work Practice

Like nursing, teaching, and the clergy, social work practice emerged primarily within organizations and today, as in the past, most social workers are employed in some form of human service agency. Accreditation standards require that all students complete a substantial learning experience in a social agency, and the profession does not consider social workers ready for independent practice until they have completed a period of supervised work in an agency. Social work is clearly an agency-based profession, as opposed to medicine and law, which are essentially private practice or entrepreneurial professions.

In the last decade, however, social workers began making a shift in this pattern, and today an increasing number are employed in settings other than the traditional governmental and nonprofit voluntary social agencies. Many social workers are employed by for-profit organizations such as nursing homes, proprietary hospitals, and even large corporations. They can also be found conducting their own private practices or working in the clinical offices of other professionals. Perhaps more than at any other time in history, social workers must make a choice regarding the type of setting in which to practice.

This chapter identifies the four primary types of organizations where social work practice is conducted and examines special issues the social worker should consider when selecting either agency-based or private practice settings as their place of employment.

CHARACTERISTICS OF PRACTICE SETTINGS

When social programs are created to meet the needs of people, a decision must be made about how the program will be delivered to those in need. Whether the program is a direct benefit such as food stamps or a third-party payment such as Medicare, it must be provided through the auspices of some formal organization. These organizations, or associations, establish the necessary policies and supply the administrative structure to make the program available to recipients. When the organizations employ social workers to provide services or when the professionals have created their own organizations, that is, private practice, they are described as a practice *setting*.

The type of practice setting in which a social worker is employed partially determines who will be clients and the degree of flexibility possible in the manner in which clients are served. Thus, it is useful to examine the several types of organizations that serve as the settings for social work. Blau and Scott identify four unique types of organizations: mutual benefit, commonweal, service, and business.[1] Social workers can be found in all these forms of organizations, although the commonweal and service agencies are the predominant settings for social workers.

Mutual Benefit Organizations

Mutual benefit organizations are created when a group wishes to provide services for its own membership. Churches, labor unions, and civic clubs are examples of this type of organization. Although civic clubs and fraternal organizations such as Rotary, Soroptimist, Kiwanis, and various Masonic organizations support important human services programs ranging from research to sponsorship of Little League baseball teams, they rarely employ staff and are not considered a setting for social work practice.

Some religious groups have created programs staffed by social workers that are limited to the members of that denomination or faith. However, church-sponsored human service agencies that restrict their services to members are only a small part of the social programs supported by religious groups. Most human service programs that are sponsored by religious organizations (e.g., hospitals, children's institutions, homes for the aged, and family counseling agencies) serve the whole community and are considered nonprofit voluntary agencies— a different type of organization. Yet, there are some substantial human services provided by denominational groups exclusively for their members. The Jewish welfare system provides an illustration. Reid and Stimpson describe the rationale for limiting these services to members of the faith:

> They were more a response of Jewish communities to the special needs of their members than the work of Jewish religious institutions or rabbis.... This is not to say that Jewish welfare activities were completely secular in origin, since their initiators were often religious people acting on religious convictions who often viewed their work, particularly in settlements, as a way of drawing Jews closer to their faith. Another element in this emerging pattern was the cohesive character of Jewish communities, a cohesiveness engendered not only by common religious beliefs but by common ethnic roots and by the anti-Semitic posture of

the dominant Protestant culture. The Jews' desire to take care of their own reflected a merging of religious motives and community mindedness.[2]

Also, at the community level, some large churches or synagogues provide "in-house" social services primarily for their own members. These organizations sometimes employ social workers to provide counseling, referral, and youth-oriented services.

Labor unions represent another mutual aid setting where social workers might be found. Although relatively few social workers are employed by labor unions, they have expanded their social services in recent years. Unions historically have been successful in organizing workers who are underpaid and undervalued by management. Women are an expanding segment of the labor force, making it likely that social work jobs in labor unions will increase to meet their needs for services.

Like social workers employed in business and industry, the labor union setting presents an exceptional opportunity to intervene with people at the place they work, and therefore improve the likelihood of resolving problems before they reach a crisis level. Social workers in these settings typically help union members with such work-related problems as finding child care, dealing with family problems related to work schedules, and addressing stress created by changed family roles when both spouses are employed.

Commonweal Organizations (Public or Governmental Agencies)

Sosin accurately summarizes the emergence of the commonweal or public human service organizations during the past half century and identifies the central role they have played in protecting the poorest members of society:

> Since the New Deal reforms of the 1930s, public bureaucracies have greatly expanded their efforts to ameliorate individual economic distress. Government programs, while perhaps inadequate, now insure many of us against adversity arising from unemployment, illness, or old age. They also provide a financial cushion for many of the most needy families whose members cannot find work. Some have claimed that alternate strategies might have been more effective, but it is clear that the reductions in poverty that have occurred over the last two decades are largely a result of public transfer programs. Many even believe that the gap in the marketplace between the rich and poor is widening and that only governmental programs stand in the way of increasing inequality.[3]

Commonweal organizations are established and funded by the general public with the intent to perform services for the benefit of all people. The mandate is to provide the necessary services to preserve and protect the well-being of all people in the community. These agencies reflect city, county, state, and federal governmental efforts to respond to human needs and are created by law and limited by the provisions established in that law.

Government sponsored human service agencies are the principal type of organization that employs social workers. The 1982 NASW Membership Study found that 45.2 percent of all respondents were employed in this type of social agency,[4] and the 1987 NASW Salary Study reported average salaries in public agencies (including military, federal, state, and local organizations) ranging from $29,300 to $32,500.[5]

Most social programs that commonweal agencies offer are created by law makers in Washington, D.C., or a state capital. These policy makers are usually geographically distant from the clients and service providers alike and, too often, are unfamiliar with the issues that arise when these laws are implemented by local agencies. Social workers often find their practice in government agencies frustrating. There is inherent inflexibility in these settings because laws are difficult to change, budgeting and auditing systems are highly structured, cumbersome civil service or personnel systems are mandated, and coordination among the different governmental levels is difficult. Further, these organizations are subject to political manipulation, and financial support and program development can be significantly influenced by a changing political climate. Except through substantial political action efforts, those who must carry out these programs have limited opportunity to influence their structure and funding.

On the positive side, although sometimes client fees are required, public agencies are financed almost completely by taxes, and the regular flow of tax money offers some stability to the programs. Legislative bodies are authorized to levy taxes so human needs can be met, and in times of economic difficulty, when voluntary contributions may be reduced, the legislators have the power to tax and therefore maintain the services. Also, the larger amounts of money potentially available to public agencies allow for experimentation with various methods of service provision. Research and demonstration grants sponsored by government agencies have, in recent years, been the most significant factor in developing new and creative approaches to meeting human needs.

It should be recognized that the commonweal agencies provide services that meet the most basic human needs such as food, clothing, and shelter. It simply is not possible to adequately respond to the fundamental needs of the poor, homeless, disabled, aged, and others through voluntary and for-profit human services. Unless income is redistributed under government auspices and unless tax monies are used to create income maintenance programs, mental hospitals, prisons, and other vital human services, we cannot expect to improve the condition of the most vulnerable members of our society. Public agencies and the social workers they employ are absolutely essential to the success of the social welfare institution.

Service Organizations
(Private or Voluntary Agencies)

Private or voluntary social agencies are nongovernmental, nonprofit organizations that employ approximately 42 percent of the social workers.[6] Of all employment

settings, the private nonprofit sector had the lowest average salary level—
$26,100 reported in the 1987 NASW Salary Study.[7] Private agencies traditionally
have depended on voluntary individual and corporate contributions to support
their operation. Their sources of funds included gifts and bequests, door-to-door
solicitations, membership dues, fees for service, and participation in federated
campaigns such as United Way.

More recently, however, private agencies have begun receiving a substantial
share of their funding from governmental allocations. Private agencies receive
government funds through contracts to provide specific services, to conduct
research and demonstration projects, or to support their operation through rev
enue-sharing allocations. Government agencies have increasingly found this a
desirable arrangement because it has allowed them to bypass much of the rigidity
of the large bureaucratic organizations in favor of the more flexible private agency
structures. It is estimated that federal support now constitutes over 50 percent
of the total expenditures in many voluntary human service organizations.[8] Thus,
there is an evolving partnership between governmental and voluntary agencies
that involves an intermingling of public and private resources, making it difficult
to clearly distinguish one from the other. Nevertheless, the nonprofit agencies
are classified as private or voluntary because they operate with policies established by a governing board made up of volunteers, as opposed to public agencies,
which have elected officials who are responsible for making the basic policy
decisions.

Private agencies have, in most instances, the advantage of being small and
concerned with the provision of services locally. Thus, the board members have
the opportunity to become directly exposed to the agency and its method of
operation. In other words, there is an intimate relationship between governance
and service provision that is not usually possible in public agencies.

The boards of voluntary agencies theoretically have considerable flexibility
in developing policies to guide the operation of the agency. Yet, that flexibility
is increasingly constrained by external forces. For example, meeting the standards
established by a national organization such as the Child Welfare League of America
or the Family Service Association of America may impose some limitations on
agency functioning. Likewise, membership in a local United Way may also require
the sacrifice of some autonomy. While there are evident benefits to these affiliations, they also reduce agency discretion regarding programs and method of
operation. In addition, the relatively heavy dependence on voluntary contributions makes it quite possible that resources could be immediately impacted by
changing economic conditions, and in that event boards would have little ability
to avoid reducing services. Even when there are stable economic conditions,
unless a private agency is quite large there is rarely enough new money available
in any one year to allow for significant experimentation or change in services.
Thus, the voluntary sector, like the public sector, experiences constraints in
program innovation.

With the administrative complexity created by the multiple funding sources,
volunteer boards experience the difficult task of attempting to balance local needs

related to their own mission with the expectations of governmental agencies that contract for services. The frequent absence of both clients and clinical staff from the policy-making role exacerbates these problems. Agency boards, historically composed mostly of people who are influential in the community, have demonstrated that they can be effective in financial planning, public relations, and fund raising, but too often have been unable to become sufficiently aware of and responsive to client needs.

What is the importance of the voluntary sector in the provision of human services today? Sosin, in summarizing findings from his extensive study of material assistance programs sponsored by nonprofit human services organizations, concludes:

> Though the role of private agencies is limited, it is nevertheless significant. As the evidence suggests, private agencies exist in every community and save many from starvation and homelessness. Often they provide the only source of shelter to hundreds of thousands of people—some the victims of disaster, others facing a sudden loss of income or a change in family circumstances, still others chronically homeless for a number of reasons. Private food programs provide for many who would otherwise go hungry. General programs often cover utility payments, rent, and needs for furniture; side programs cover important health-related expenses; and single-mission agencies provide what they are organized to distribute, whether shoes or shelter. Although public programs may in theory meet the same needs, overlap is only theoretical owing to limited budgets; the private agencies indeed fill needs.[9]

Business Organizations (Entrepreneurial Social Work)

The major entrepreneurial setting where social workers are found is private or proprietary practice. As the most rapidly growing dimension of social work, this setting is characterized by its nonagency structure. Practice in this setting involves the use of a "process in which the values, knowledge, and skills of social work, acquired through sufficient education and experience, are used to deliver services autonomously to clients in exchange for mutually agreed payment."[10]

The term *private practice* is usually used to indicate a practice situation where a direct contract for the provision of clinical service is made between the worker and the clients. *Proprietary practice,* a term sometimes used interchangeably with private practice, refers to nonclinical activities such as consulting, conducting workshops or training programs, or contracting to perform research or other professional services for a fee. Proprietary practice most frequently involves a contract between the social worker and an organization, rather than with individual clients.

Barker has identified ten factors that characterize the private or proprietary practice of social work. He indicates that the practitioner in this setting

1. has the client (rather than an agency or organization) as the primary obligation;

2. determines who the client will be;
3. determines the techniques to be used;
4. determines practice professionally rather than bureaucratically;
5. receives a fee for service directly from or on behalf of the client;
6. has sufficient education as a social worker;
7. is sufficiently experienced;
8. adheres to social work values and standards;
9. is licensed or certified to engage in private practice if the jurisdiction has such regulations; and
10. is professionally responsible.[11]

The 1987 NASW study of social work salaries indicates that with a $31,100 average salary, self-employed private practitioners were among the highest paid social workers. These data also indicate that the highest one-fourth earned more than $45,000 that year, making it the setting with the greatest potential for earning a high income.[12]

Master's-level social workers have been rapidly moving into this mode of practice. Teare, Sheafor, and Shank found that although less than 1 percent of the BSW social workers were engaged in private practice, this field of practice is the fourth largest for MSWs, with 9.3 percent reporting private practice as their primary employment setting.[13] Although there are varying estimates of the number of social workers engaged in private practice, the best educated guess is that there are between 10,000 and 30,000 part-time private practitioners and from 4000 to 10,000 social workers in full-time private practice.[14] In recent years private and proprietary practice has unquestionably become a significant setting for social workers.

Another emerging entrepreneurial setting for social work is in *for-profit organizations.* During the past decade there has been a quiet but substantial transformation in the funding of human service programs. From the 1930s through the 1970s a pattern emerged in which legislative bodies allocated substantial funds for government agencies to provide services directly to clients. Therefore, a relatively large public sector developed. Later, that pattern shifted through purchase-of-service agreements with nonprofit agencies rather than governmental agencies providing these services themselves. A second, and perhaps even more dramatic, shift known as *privatization* is now occurring. Governmental agencies have begun to invest a substantial amount of their funds in the purchase of service from for-profit organizations that are owned and operated as any other business. In fact, many are owned and operated by large corporations.[15]

Because the commodity the for-profit human service organizations deliver is human services, they employ social workers. Data are not available to indicate the number of social workers involved in this practice setting, but the NASW Salary Study does indicate that those who responded in 1987 had an average salary of $29,000, or $1200 per year more than the average social worker.[16]

Several fields of practice have rapidly increased their reliance on these businesses to provide human services. For example, a national study of child welfare services found that proprietary firms were used as vendors for services by public welfare agencies to a greater degree than either nonprofit or other governmental agencies. The study revealed that government agencies purchased services from for-profit organizations that amounted to 51 percent of all residential treatment, 49 percent of institutional care, and 58 percent of the services provided in group homes.[17] To a lesser degree public agencies rely on contracts with proprietary organizations to provide day care, day treatment services, nursing home care, correctional facilities, and health care.

Why is the privatization of human services occurring at this time? Abramovitz analyzed the Reagan administration's rationale for fostering this dramatic shift in the pattern of funding human services in the 1980s:

> The (Reagan) administration's overall plan for promoting economic growth is based on directing larger amounts of capital into the private market and weakening the political power of groups whose social and economic demands have, since the 1930s, politicized the process of income distribution carried out through both government tax and spending programs and the process of trade union collective bargaining.
>
> Privatization channels public dollars into private hands, strengthens the two-class welfare state, and reproduces inequalities that the free market inevitably creates. In trying to serve the needs of both private providers and the poor, the welfare state has failed to modify the market in behalf of social justice, a goal reformers in earlier times had hoped government intervention in the economy would achieve.[18]

Social work, as well as medicine and other professions, is uneasy about the growing amount of for-profit practice. The trend toward the privatization of human services threatens to replace the service orientation of professions with the profit motive. Privatization risks making the bottom line the amount of return to the shareholder, rather than the quality of service to the client. When the shareholder is also the professional, serious ethical issues arise that can erode public trust in the professions. The ambivalence of many social workers regarding the growing privatization of human services is captured by Hasenfeld:

> The implications of the trend toward commercialization-privatization for the delivery of human services and quality of care are unclear at the present time. . . . The trend may increase consumer choice and improve efficiency. There is, however, concern that the commercialization of human services will inevitably substitute the profit motive for quality care and concern for the client's welfare. Organizations may select treatment technologies and establish service modalities that enhance their profitability but are not necessarily the most appropriate for or most responsive to the service needs of the population. Moreover, professional autonomy over practice may be seriously eroded as professional decisions become subject to corporate control. Finally, although the privatization of services increases consumer choice, the major beneficiaries of greater choice would not be the traditional clientele of the welfare state but consumers from middle and working classes to whom social welfare entitlements have been extended in recent years.[19]

ISSUES AFFECTING AGENCY-BASED PRACTICE

More than 90 percent of all experienced social workers and virtually every new social worker is employed in a mutual benefit, public, voluntary, or for-profit human service agency. Thus, when considering possible employment settings, most social workers must examine an agency to determine its relative compatibility with his or her personal and professional interests. The social worker should be knowledgeable about several factors that influence the manner in which a social worker is able to operate within the context of a social agency.

Accommodating Horizontal and Vertical Influences

Although some human service organizations are formed around a single field of practice and offer programs to meet a specific client need, the social workers employed in these agencies recognize they cannot operate in isolation from other agencies. Client needs are not necessarily experienced in the same way as social agencies identify their missions. As a member of the profession with primary responsibility for connecting individual clients, as well as social agencies, with the environment that affects them, social workers interact with a variety of human service organizations.

At the local level social workers often give leadership to efforts to coordinate the services provided to clients by the full array of social agencies in that community. This coordination requires that interagency networks, or *horizontal affiliations,* are developed among the agencies. The form of these horizontal networks may range from informal discussions among agency representatives regarding human service programs to the formal creation of councils of social agencies or human resources planning organizations that study the local service network, encourage efforts to fill gaps in the services, and facilitate cooperation among the agencies. The ability of a social worker to effectively perform his or her professional tasks is enhanced when there is a strong horizontal interagency network in a community and the social worker's employing agency supports his or her participation in these activities.

Social agencies and social workers are also influenced by *vertical affiliations,* that is, those organizations external to the community that have the authority to at least partially shape the services or operating procedures of a local agency. Voluntary agencies, for example, might affiliate as chapters or members of a national organization, which can immediately give the agency name recognition, provide the community with some assurance that at least minimum standards acceptable in that practice field are met, make staff development opportunities available through national meetings, and sometimes help secure financial resources. At the same time, these agencies give up some local autonomy as they are committed to operate within the guidelines of the national organization. Vertical affiliation with the American Red Cross, Boy or Girl Scouts of America, the

YWCA or YMCA, the American Heart Association, the Salvation Army, or the Family Service Association of America are all examples of such affiliations typical of private agencies. Further, many local voluntary agencies must meet state licensing requirements or other state standards if they are vendors of services to public agencies. This also limits their discretion.

Public agencies typically have more direct and formal relationships. A local governmental agency may be implementing programs that have been created and partially funded at the federal level, further defined and partially funded at the state level, and finally modified and also funded by county government. Thus, a county social services department, for example, is constrained by requirements imposed by federal, state, and county governments. Although these vertical affiliations add considerably to the complexity of tailoring service programs to local needs, they have the advantage of fostering greater equality in the benefits and services provided to people throughout a region and the Nation. In addition, vertical affiliation creates a larger geographic area for securing funds to support the services, making it possible to more adequately meet needs in a local or regional area that lacks its own resources.

Balancing Efficiency and Effectiveness

A fundamental goal of all human service agencies, whether they are public or private, is to use the scarce resources that are available to provide the most and best service possible. To achieve this goal agencies must operate both efficiently and effectively. An agency that leans too far in favoring one over the other ultimately creates problems for the staff members employed in that agency.

Efficiency represents the efforts of the agency to achieve the maximum output of services with a minimum input of resources. The goal of efficiency places the emphasis on the quantity of services provided and often attracts most of the attention of law makers, governing boards, and local media. Yet, quantity must be related to quality if an agency is to find a balance that represents the maximum level of service. The qualitative aspects of service are represented in an agency's *effectiveness,* or the degree to which the agency achieves its goals.

The governance of most social agencies has been dominated, in both the public and voluntary sectors, by "successful" people who have given leadership to thriving business and industrial enterprises. Their secret to success often was a strong bias toward efficiency; and, although some degree of effectiveness in producing goods was necessary, low cost-per-unit production was clearly the most valued goal. That orientation is especially evident in the for-profit human service organizations. Thus, the social worker considering agency employment should carefully examine the agency's effectiveness orientation lest the quality of his or her work be seriously compromised in favor of overemphasis on the goal of efficiency.

Accommodating the Professional Model

How can efficiency be attained in human service organizations? The successful managers from business and industry transferred the proven tools in their work to the human services. The primary tool was bureaucratic structure. And why not? Bureaucracy had worked to build automobiles and appliances at a fraction of the cost of handmade products. Weber created the clearest statement of bureaucratic theory. His "ideal-type" description of the characteristics of a bureaucratic organization was intended to reflect a pure, but extreme, statement of the characteristics of a bureaucracy:

1. Division of labor. Each person in the organization has a clearly defined and specialized assignment in the organization.
2. Hierarchy. Specific lines of authority exist in which every person in the administrative structure is not only responsible for his or her own assignments but is also responsible for the performance of subordinates.
3. Consistent System of Rules. Every task in the organization is governed by an explicit set of rules which specify the standards of performance and the relationships among tasks.
4. Spirit of Impersonality. Work is to be performed without favoritism or prejudice entering official decisions.
5. Employment Constitutes a Career. Persons are employed only on the basis of technical qualifications required by the organization, with rewards provided to encourage loyalty and offer opportunity for a career in that organization.[20]

With some modifications, when applied to the assembly line that produces automobiles in Detroit or toasters in New Jersey, bureaucratic principles led to a high degree of organizational efficiency. This model yielded good results when the product was made from standardized parts. In fact, the greater the standardization, the more effective the bureaucratic organization becomes. A person could quickly be trained to perform a very specific function, for example installing a fuel pump as an automobile passes on the assembly line. With a line supervisor to check for quality control and enforce the rules established for efficiency (the worker cannot be taking a break when the engine is there for a fuel pump), the trainee usually produced a good quality product. Under this system there could be no allowance for the worker's personal problems, nor could he or she be successfully assigned more responsible work simply because of friendship with the boss. Bureaucratic theory assumes that the rewards of seniority, salary increases, and promotion are sufficient to keep the successful employee satisfied with the organization.

As an ideal type, Weber's characteristics of a bureaucracy draw an extreme picture. These requirements are still present in successful businesses today, but in a considerably modified form. The people-oriented philosophy reflected by Peters and Waterman in their best selling book, *In Search of Excellence: Lessons from America's Best-Run Companies,*[21] reflect this emerging orientation. Nevertheless, important remnants of the bureaucratic approach are evident in virtually all organizations.

When leaders of industry attempted to apply these principles to the human service agencies with which they had contact, the social workers and other professionals responsible for providing services found that extensive bureaucratization created problems. The use of bureaucratic principles had the advantages of improving equity for clients and workers, facilitating more efficient operation, and enhancing public support of the agencies. At the same time, for at least two reasons, they were in conflict with the professional model of service provision.

First, in the provision of social services the parts (people) are constantly changing, and the product (human well-being) differs to some degree in each situation. It is simply not realistic to provide narrow technical training, to create highly specialized assignments, or to establish a strict system of rules for a staff that is helping clients or client groups deal with complex personal troubles or public issues. Because social work views special human qualities such as race, ethnicity, gender, and cultural background not only as a reality but also as a desirable feature in human behavior (see Part Four of this book), effective organizations must provide adequate flexibility and autonomy for staff members to be responsive to these individual and cultural differences.

Second, in Chapter 2 we examined the nature of professions and their characteristic methods of accomplishing their work. When the professional model is compared to the bureaucratic model, four inherent areas of conflict emerge. These conflicts have been identified by Scott as: (1) the professional's resistance to bureaucratic rules, (2) the professional's rejection of bureaucratic standards, (3) the professional's resistance to bureaucratic supervision, and (4) the professional's conditional loyalty to the bureaucratic organization.[22] These conflicts are present in varying degrees in any organization where the professional social worker is employed.

Bureaucratic rules present a constant dilemma for professionals. When a division of labor exists, each person provides only a part of the work for the agency. Procedures must then be set up that facilitate interaction among the workers to achieve the goals of the agency as a whole. With bureaucratic rules meetings must be held on time; workers must provide services within the established limits for their discipline; and paperwork must be completed for accountability purposes.

Bureaucratic standards also present difficulties for the professional. Often, the ideals acquired through professional education exceed the limits imposed on professional practice by agency policies and procedures. Agencies operate in the real world and are limited by laws, eligibility requirements, funds, available staff time, and the need to leave a trail of paperwork for accountability purposes. Workers employed in agencies that operate from a residual conception of social welfare are particularly aware of these problems, but such problems can also exist in developmentally oriented programs.

In bureaucratic systems, authority is assigned to a position. Conversely, professional authority is generated from competence as judged by one's peers. It is no wonder that professionals resist *bureaucratic supervision,* which is based on authority derived from a person's place in the organization. A professional is considered competent to perform his or her job without the requirement of someone always reviewing that performance. Because all practice cannot be supervised by direct observation, considerable paperwork is often generated so that supervisors can be aware of the activities of their staff.

Finally, professionals display a *conditional loyalty,* in contrast to a commitment to their organizations. Professionals are prepared with generic competencies that are transferable from one organization to another. A social worker, for example, can move from a welfare department to a juvenile court without additional educational preparation. The basic general skills developed through professional education are applicable with the addition of the specific knowledge required in each particular setting. This additional knowledge can be obtained through reviewing literature on the subject, through the supervisory process, and through continuing education courses and workshops. People wedded to a bureaucratic organization, however, do not have the same degree of flexibility and can experience job mobility only by moving up in the organization. Support of the organization may be given precedence over personal judgment; for social workers this priority would compromise services to clients.

Succeeding as a Social Worker in an Agency Structure

In many instances it is not sufficient for the social worker merely to be a passive employee who unquestioningly accepts and carries out the rules and regulations of the agency. The organization pressures one to conform. Staff members must perform certain tasks, provide an accounting of the work to a supervisor, complete the appropriate reporting forms, be on the job at the required time, and carry out the programs of the agency as designed by the policy makers and implemented by the administration. Promotions, salary increases, and even continued employment in the agency are often linked to one's conformity to the agency's rules and regulations. The successful agency-based social worker must be smart about organizational issues.

Clearly an employee is obligated to work within the legitimate requirements of his or her employer, and a social worker cannot ethically ignore the rules and regulations of the agency. Although it may be personally safe to rigidly conform to agency requirements, most rules and regulations provide some room for flexible interpretation if workers are creative in their approach. Some regulations, however, may not lend themselves to this flexibility and may, at times, seriously impede the work of the social worker. In this case the social worker should attempt to change these rules. Change, especially in large public agencies, takes considerable time and effort. The social worker who has attempted to bring about such change can identify with the adage, "The change agent must have the time sense of a geologist." With skill, patience, and perseverance, such change can be accomplished, and the attempt should be viewed as a professional responsibility of the social worker. There are times, however, when the social worker fails in an attempt to modify the agency's rules and either must learn to live with existing regulations or make the decision to seek employment elsewhere.

In addition to attempting to encourage the agency to adapt to his or her practice needs, the social worker must also attempt to adapt his or her practice to the agency. Pruger notes that in addition to their service function, social workers are also bureaucrats—distasteful as this term might be for many social workers—because one of their roles is to implement the policies and procedures of an agency.[23] Maintaining a reasonable balance between the goals of the service provider and those of the bureaucrat is a constant challenge for the social worker. Pruger suggests four tactics that can help the social worker be responsible to the agency and at the same time maximize the ability to provide services to clients.[24]

First, the worker must understand legitimate authority and organizational enforcement. Rules and regulations must be stated in general terms because they must cover an infinite variety of human situations. An important part of professional autonomy is concerned with the interpretation and application of agency regulations. Although clear limits to this discretion may be present, there is usually considerable latitude one can exercise before the agency will enforce disciplinary action. Within the guideline of responsible behavior, the social worker should seek to discover these discretionary limits in order to be of maximum service to the agency's clients.

Second, organizations present many demands that divert worker energy from the primary goal of serving clients. Demands for time in staff meetings, paperwork, evaluation processes, and many other activities are often frustrating for the service-oriented social worker. Moreover, organizations do a poor job of offering the person emotional support or recognition for accomplishment that, if expected by the worker, will surely drain energy from the service tasks. The social worker who builds supportive relationships with other employees can minimize the impact of this potential energy drain.

Third, an employee should seek to develop competencies needed by the organization. Rather than approaching the agency with a minimum personal investment, the social worker should make a special effort to help enhance the functioning of the agency. In addition to continuing professional development related to practice techniques, the social worker should develop needed organizational skills such as grant writing, computer programming, and budget planning. Such positive contributions help create a favorable climate for social work practice.

Finally, the social worker should keep in mind the goals of the agency and not yield unnecessarily to requirements established for administrative convenience. The use of professional judgment is always required, and regulations should constantly be reviewed to determine if they are viable for enhancing the work of the staff and the welfare of clients. Although challenging unproductive regulations may not help the social worker win popularity contests, this action is a valuable contribution to the organization's effectiveness.

In addition to the bureaucrat role required of a direct service provider, many agency-based social workers also assume administrative responsibilities in a human service agency. One important administrative role is that of supervising other social workers and agency staff members. Because they originally adhered to an apprenticeship approach to skill development,[25] social agencies have continued to depend heavily on supervision for monitoring and evaluating the work of practitioners and for helping them upgrade their competence. Increasingly, human service agencies have been emphasizing the educational aspects of supervision, but most have not yet abandoned the supervisory approach in favor of the consultation model that is a more appropriate form of support for professional practice. Consultation is based on seeking advice from the most competent person available and not necessarily from one's immediate supervisor. The effective social work supervisor, however, is able to combine both the supervisor and consultant roles in helping staff perform the services of the agency. The quality of supervision is one of the most important factors for the new social worker to look for when seeking a social work job.

Other social workers may assume executive or top administrative roles in a human service agency. Some fields of practice have developed career patterns for people in management positions where they receive extensive preparation for these roles. Master's degree programs in education and hospital administration, for example, specifically prepare graduates to administer schools and hospitals. Social agencies have not developed a parallel career line. Some human service organizations have enticed successful clinical social workers to move into administrative positions requiring them to make a transition from the role of service provider to administrator without additional educational preparation.[26] Too often a competent practitioner is converted to a marginal administrator. Other agencies have erred in the direction of seeking persons possessing a master's degree in business administration or in public administration, only to find that they were not appropriately sensitive to the unique organizational requirements for providing human services. This approach, too, has yielded marginal results and argues for social work developing administration specializations in MSW programs that provide a balanced understanding of organizational and professional needs.

The extent to which an agency supports the social worker in providing professional quality services and provides opportunity for career mobility is an important consideration when the new social worker is selecting a setting for employment.

Determining the Status of Social Work

One final factor to consider when selecting a place of employment is the centrality of social work to the mission of that particular setting. The status of social work in an agency influences the manner in which a social worker spends much of his or her time and affects the opportunity of clients to have the full benefit of the perspective that social work brings to the helping situation. When the policies and procedures of the organization are designed to maximize social work services, social workers can most effectively serve their clientele. However, in a practice setting where another discipline is dominant, social workers often spend considerable effort educating members of this discipline about the contributions social work can make to the agency's clientele.

In some practice settings social work is the *primary discipline.* The primary services provided call for social work expertise, most key jobs require social work training, and social workers hold the major administrative jobs. In practice fields such as child welfare, family services, and income maintenance social workers have traditionally been the primary discipline. In these settings other disciplines may be involved to provide specialized expertise or consultation, but the services are organized to maximize the contributions of the social worker.

In other practice settings the social worker is an *equal partner* along with members of one or more other disciplines. The services are organized to maximize interdisciplinary cooperation and a member of any of the disciplines might provide administrative leadership to the agency. The fields of aging, mental health and retardation, and community and neighborhood services are examples of practice fields that are shared by several disciplines.

In still other settings social work might provide supporting services to another profession. As the *secondary discipline* in these agencies social work is, in one sense, a guest of the primary discipline. The agency is organized to allow the primary discipline to work as effectively as possible and the needs of social work or other professions receive lower priority. The role of the social worker in a medical setting illustrates social work as a secondary discipline. Hospitals, a setting for medical practice, are geared to the needs of the physician. Social services are provided at the physician's referral and are organized so they do not compete with the schedule and work of the medical profession. A similar role would be assumed by the social worker in corrections, schools, and industrial settings.

Advantages of Agency-based Practice

Given the complexities of agency practice, why does social work continue to function as an agency-based profession? Why not adopt the private practice model of other successful professions? Most social workers recognize that agency-based practice offers several advantages.

First, it makes the services more visible and, therefore, more accessible to all persons in need. The existence of agencies in a community over time and the attendant publicity about their operations typically make both their programs and their locations familiar to all members of the community. As opposed to nonagency practice, which caters to those who can pay the full cost of services, the public and private human service agencies are more likely to have as clients the most vulnerable members of society. For the social worker committed to serving the part of the population experiencing the most serious social problems, agency practice is the only game in town.

Second, agencies survive because they have received the sanction, or approval, of the community for the services they provide. Clients approach the helping situation with a greater trust in the quality of services they will receive because of the commitment made by the agency and the oversight of its board and administrators. In private practice situations the client must place full trust in the individual practitioner to perform high quality practice.

Third, clients have the benefit of an extra layer of protection against possible misuse of professional authority in social agencies. Clients in any setting are protected by both the professional ethics of the professionals and, in many cases, the legal regulation or licensing of that practice. In agencies, however, they are also protected by the agency's selection of staff and ongoing monitoring of the quality of services.

Fourth, human service agencies tend to have a broad scope and often employ persons from several different professions, which provides clients with ready access to the competencies of multiple professions and gives the worker the opportunity for interdisciplinary practice activities. In addition, as opposed to the more limited service focus found in private practice, agencies typically offer a broad range of services, from direct practice to social action. Thus, they provide the social worker with the stimulation of engaging in a range of different practice activities and make it possible to change the focus of one's practice area or move into supervisory or management positions without changing employers.

Fifth, most agencies offer staff development opportunities that stimulate professional growth among workers. Characteristically, social agencies employ a large enough number of staff members that workers do not feel isolated and, in fact, typically carry out programs that contribute to the continued professional growth and development of other members. The rapidly changing knowledge and skill base of the helping professions makes continuing professional development important to the services the clients receive and adds to the intellectual stimulation of the staff.

Last, agencies have the ability to raise funds from the community, whether from taxes or voluntary contributions, and offer a stable salary to employees. Agencies do not face the risk of a fluctuating income experienced by persons in private or proprietary practice settings.

ISSUES IN PRIVATE OR PROPRIETARY PRACTICE

The principal alternative to agency-based practice for the social worker is private or proprietary practice. The remarkable expansion of this setting in the last decade is an important feature of social work today. While social work does not sanction entering private practice immediately on graduation from professional degree programs, it is useful for all social workers to be aware of the issues that surround this practice setting as they are having a profound influence on the social work profession.

Why is private practice gaining such popularity among social workers? From the vantage point of the social worker, private practice is attractive partially because of the greater opportunity for financial gain but more importantly for more freedom to exercise professional autonomy in the conduct of social work practice. The bureaucratic constraints of many human service agencies have placed such serious restrictions on the ability of social workers to effectively use their professional competencies for the benefit of clients that many have actively sought a different practice setting. In Barker's study of social workers in private practice, respondents identified the opportunity to "get away from the bureau-cratic constraints of agency employment" as the primary reason they entered private practice. Other reasons for leaving agency practice, as discovered by Barker, were that private practice offered greater flexibility in hours and practice activities, a desire to remain in direct practice without becoming subordinate to others in an administrative hierarchy, income considerations, a sense of greater challenge, and the opportunity to work with more motivated clients.[27]

Wallace indicates that a number of historical developments have come to-gether at this time that create a climate that makes private practice attractive to clients:

> A growing number of middle-class clients with a variety of personal and inter-personal problems believe that seeking professional consultation is a reasonable step to take. There is less stigma attached to obtaining help today, particularly when it is received from a practitioner who is not a psychiatrist. Moreover, the increasing professionalization of social workers, evidenced by such developments as granting the ACSW by the Academy of Certified Social Workers, the recent publication of registers of clinical social workers certified for independent prac-tice, legal registration and licensing of social workers, and publicly mandated or privately arranged vendorship, or third-party payments to workers, provides the rationale—and even the means to obtain payment—for private social work ser-vices. Finally, within the profession, private practice is not scorned as much as it once was by those who are not private practitioners.[28]

As a nonagency activity, private practice avoids many of the limitations that accrue from practice within a bureaucratic structure but also places greater re-sponsibility on the social worker to practice within the ethical guidelines of the profession. There is no oversight of private practice short of a complaint being filed with a licensing board or the local NASW chapter. NASW has rightfully been concerned about establishing guidelines that will identify for the public those social workers who have the requisite preparation and experience to conduct autonomous practice.

The Organization of Private Practice

The NASW definition of private practice is sufficiently broad to include social workers providing both private and proprietary practice. Clinical or direct service practice, however, is the dominant approach of private practitioners. In his study of private practice, Wallace found that the average for these social workers was "63 percent of private practice time in individual treatment, 19 percent devoted to work with marital couples, 8 percent to group therapy, 7 percent to family treatment, and 2 percent to joint interviews with clients other than married couples."[29] For the delivery of these clinical services, three organizational approaches are used.

In the first approach the social worker engages in multidisciplinary practice. In this arrangement the social worker participates with members of other disciplines (for example, psychiatry and psychology) to provide a *group practice* that can meet a broad range of client needs. The social worker is an equal partner with the other disciplines and, in fact, is a co-owner of the business.

In the second form of private practice, the social worker provides a *supportive practice* for a member of another profession. For example, some physicians are hiring social workers to help patients deal with personal problems that are related to specific illnesses. The social worker might also provide more general services in the physician's office such as educating expectant parents about child development, counseling families that need help with child rearing practices, or referring people to appropriate community resources for help with problems.

In the third form, social workers are the *sole owners* of their private practice. Sole ownership involves securing office space, hiring staff, advertising services, making contacts to acquire referrals, overseeing the determination and collection of fees, and all other factors related to the management of a small business. Like any other business private practice is a "sink or swim" proposition with no guarantee of income equivalent to expenses. The main problems for full-time private practitioners are generating sufficient referrals to be able to keep the business solvent, handling the business details including securing payment from third-party vendors, obtaining competent consultation, minimizing the inherent isolation and arranging for backup in managing crisis situations, and protecting against their vulnerable position if there should be malpractice charges.[30]

It is estimated that two to three times as many social workers are engaged in part-time as full-time private practice. Many of these social workers are employed by a social agency but maintain a small private practice as well. Kelley and Alexander identify four groups of social workers who elect to engage in part-time private practice[31]:

- Agency practitioners who welcome the independence and additional income,
- Social workers in supervisory or administrative positions who wish to maintain client contact and clinical skills,
- Educators who wish to have sufficient practice activity to remain sufficiently current with a practice to effectively teach clinical courses, and
- Social workers who are parents of young children and need to control their hours of work.

Part-time private practitioners experience many of the same problems as those in full-time practice. Kelley and Alexander's study of part-time private practitioners indicates that the most serious problems they face in getting a practice started are generating referrals and handling the practical business issues such as locating office space, securing financing, keeping records, and the like. Although these matters continue to be problems, they are somewhat transitional and become less consuming once a practice is established. Later, and particularly unique to the person in part-time private practice, time management problems become the most difficult part.[32]

Social workers in proprietary practice provide indirect services such as consultation. Consultation might be provided to another social worker or to a member of another helping profession concerning the handling of a case. For example, a social worker might consult with a lawyer about a divorce or child custody case. He or she might also be involved in working with a social agency—such as helping a nursing home with budgeting, administrative procedures, or program development.

Another form of indirect private practice involves the training of social workers or members of other disciplines in special skills. The increasing demand for experienced social workers to provide workshops, seminars, or other forms of training is contributing to the growing demand for proprietary practice.

Concerns Related to Private Practice

The private practice approach represents a substantial departure from social work's historical agency orientation. It has not been without controversy in the profession and has experienced problems in becoming accepted and appreciated in the general community. Four issues have emerged concerning this practice mode.

First, private clients do not have an agency monitoring system to provide protection against incompetence or abuses of the professional monopoly. Therefore, social work has been careful to specify more extensive education and experience as minimum preparation for the private practitioner than for the agency-based practitioner. The standards established by NASW call for completion of a master's degree in social work from an accredited school of social work, two years of full-time or 3000 hours of part-time practice experience, and successfully passing the examination required for membership in the Academy of Certified Social Workers (ACSW). To be listed in both the *National Registry of Health Care Providers in Clinical Social Work* and NASW's *Register of Clinical Social Workers,* a social worker is required to have completed at least two years of full-time, post-master's employment as a social worker.

Second, because many private practitioners work on a part-time basis, some agencies are concerned that private practice will detract from agency practice. They fear the social worker will place self-interest above the needs of the agency. A study of twenty voluntary agencies yielded the following common concerns about private practice:

1. That the worker will not do justice to his or her agency responsibilities because of the amount of time and energy that may go into private practice
2. That the worker may take clients from the agency or gain clients in the community who may otherwise have gone to the agency

3. That the staff person will become more his or her own agent instead of being an enabler for the agency
4. That the staff person may not meet the minimum standards set by the National Association of Social Workers for private practice.[33]

On the other side of this issue it is argued that private practice offers different professional stimulation than is found in agency practice and also provides a supplemental income to agency salaries that keeps workers satisfied with their agency employment. Some agencies even encourage social workers to engage in some part-time private practice by allowing them to use their agency offices in the evenings or by arranging schedules to allow a day off each week for this purpose. Such arrangements, however, are ripe for conflict of interest issues.

Third, some critics have accused private practitioners of "specializing in diseases of the rich" and diverting social work from its mission of serving the most vulnerable members of society. There is little argument that clinical private practice represents a deviation from social work's philanthropic roots. Barker states, "Undoubtedly, the major dilemma is that private practice services are less accessible to the very people who have historically been social work's traditional clientele—the disadvantaged."[34] Moreover, private practitioners have been accused of failing to perform the social action responsibilities of the profession. Borenzweig's study of agency and private practitioners did not refute that charge but found that agency practitioners were equally guilty of failing to be involved in social action.[35]

Finally, social workers in private practice have faced an uphill battle in gaining public sanction for their activity. Of particular concern to many clinical private practitioners has been the reluctance of health insurance companies and the federal government to recognize social workers as legitimate providers of services that can be reimbursed by insurance programs.

Advantages of Private or Proprietary Practice

There are also arguments in favor of social work's movement toward private and proprietary practice. First, in most human service agencies clients have little opportunity to exercise individual choice in regard to what professionals will provide services. Clients typically cannot select their individual social workers, nor can they fire them if unsatisfied with the services received. Clients exercise considerably more control in a private setting.

Second, from the social worker's perspective, the rules and regulations of agencies place constraints on the worker's ability to conduct a practice in the manner he or she believes would be most effective. Professional autonomy is inherently compromised. For example, agency-based social workers cannot choose their clients; are not completely free to determine the amount and type of service to be given; and are almost always supervised, at times by one who interferes with the professional judgment of the worker.

Third, agency salaries tend to be lower than for the private and proprietary practitioner. Further, as opposed to the market-driven income of the private practitioner that is at least theoretically based on competence, agency salaries are based to a greater degree on seniority and position within the agency.

Last, few agencies avoid the pitfalls that plague most bureaucratic organizations, in which workers find that a disproportionate share of their time is devoted to meetings and paperwork. The less elaborate mechanisms required for accountability in private practice free the worker of much of the less people-oriented activity found in agency practice.

For both clients and social workers, there are gains and losses from both agency and private practice. These factors influence the nature and quality of services provided as well as the social worker's satisfaction with his or her employment.

CONCLUDING COMMENT

Social work practice has permeated U.S. society to the extent that it occurs in every type of organization: mutual benefit, governmental, voluntary, and business. Although the roots of social work are in agency-based practice, where public concerns for people in need took the form of creating human service agencies, social work now is offered through both agency and private practice modes.

Most social workers continue to be employed in agency settings, and they must be able to work effectively within agency structures if they are to maximize their ability to serve clients. Understanding the principles on which agencies are organized and the problems social workers commonly experience in matching their professional orientation with agency requirements is therefore important to providing quality services.

An increasing number of social workers have entered private and proprietary practice to avoid some of the problems experienced by the agency-based practitioner and to increase potential income. However, private practice is certainly not trouble-free. Social work is beginning to address the important issues related to ensuring adequate preparation for the responsibilities of independent practice, lessening the quality of agency practice, moving away from the social work mission of focusing services on the poor and other vulnerable population groups, and gaining public sanction and client protection for this relatively new method of service delivery.

It appears at this point in history that the trend in social work is toward an increasing entrepreneurial approach to practice. However, it is clear that many critical social provisions and social services can never be made available in sufficient quantity through the mutual benefit and entrepreneurial human service organizations to meet the needs of the most vulnerable members of this society. Thus, it is reasonable to conclude that social work will continue to be primarily an agency-oriented profession and that social workers must continue to devote attention to means of making these organizations more responsive to the requirements for effective professional practice.

SUGGESTED READINGS

ABRAMOVITZ, MIMI. "The Privatization of the Welfare State: A Review." *Social Work* 31 (July–August, 1986): 257–264.

BARKER, ROBERT L. *Social Work in Private Practice: Principles, Issues, Dilemmas.* Washington, D.C.: National Association of Social Workers, 1983.

HAYNES, KAREN S. *Women Managers in Human Services.* New York: Springer, 1989.

MATORIN, SUSAN; ROSENBERG, BLANCA; LEVITT, MARLIN; and ROSENBLUM, SYLVIA. "Private Practice in Social Work: Readiness and Opportunity." *Social Casework* 68 (January 1987): 31–37.

OSTRANDER, SUSAN A. "Voluntary Social Service Agencies in the United States." *Social Service Review* 59 (September 1985): 435–452.

SALAMON, LESTER M., ed. *Beyond Privatization: The Tools of Government Action.* Washington, D.C.: Urban Institute Press, 1989.

SOSIN, MICHAEL. "Private Social Agencies: Auspices, Sources of Funds, and Problems Covered." *Social Work Research and Abstracts* 12 (Summer 1989): 21–27.

STOESZ, DAVID. "Corporate Welfare: The Third State of Welfare in the United States." *Social Work* 31 (July–August 1986): 245–249.

ENDNOTES

1. Peter M. Blau and Richard Scott, *Formal Organizations: A Comparative Approach* (San Francisco: Chandler, 1962), pp. 40–58.

2. William J. Reid and Peter K. Stimpson, "Sectarian Agencies," in Anne Minahan, ed., *Encyclopedia of Social Work* vol. II (Silver Spring, Md.: National Association of Social Workers, 1987), p. 548.

3. Michael Sosin, *Private Benefits: Material Assistance in the Private Sector* (Orlando, Fla.: Academic Press, 1986), p. 1.

4. National Association of Social Workers, "Membership Survey Shows Practice Shifts," *NASW News* 28 (November 1983): 6–7.

5. National Association of Social Workers, "First-Time Look at Members' Salaries Finds Their Average Income Is $27,800," *NASW News* 33 (January 1988): 18.

6. NASW, "Membership Survey," pp. 6–7.

7. NASW, "First-Time Look," p. 18.

8. Yeheskel Hasenfeld, "The Changing Context of Human Service Administration," *Social Work* 29 (November–December 1984): 526.

9. Sosin, p. 160.

10. Robert L. Barker, *The Social Work Dictionary* (Silver Spring, Md.: National Association of Social Workers, 1987), p. 125.

11. Robert L. Barker, *Social Work in Private Practice: Principles, Issues, Dilemmas* (Silver Spring, Md.: National Association of Social Workers, 1983), pp. 20–31.

12. NASW, "First-Time Look," p. 18.

13. Robert J. Teare, Bradford W. Sheafor, and Barbara W. Shank, "Similarities and Differences in BSW and MSW Social Workers." Paper presented at Baccalaureate Program Directors Workshop, Minneapolis, Minn., 1990).

14. Robert L. Barker, "Private and Proprietary Services," in Minahan, p. 326.

15. David Stoesz, "Corporate Welfare: The Third Stage of Welfare in the United States," *Social Work* 31 (July–August 1986): 245–249.

16. NASW, "First-Time Look," p. 18.

17. Catherine E. Born, "Proprietary Firms and Child Welfare Services: Patterns and Implications," *Child Welfare* 62 (March/April 1983): 112.
18. Mimi Abramovitz, "The Privatization of the Welfare State: A Review," *Social Work* 31 (July–August 1986): 257.
19. Hasenfeld, p. 256.
20. Peter M. Blau and Marshall W. Meyer, *Bureaucracy in Modern Society* 2nd ed. (New York: Random House, 1973), pp. 18–23.
21. Thomas J. Peters and Robert H. Waterman Jr., *In Search of Excellence: Lessons from America's Best-Run Companies* (New York: Harper & Row, 1982).
22. W. Richard Scott, "Professionals in Bureaucracies—Areas of Conflict," in Howard M. Vollmer and Donald L. Mills, eds., *Professionalization* (Englewood Cliffs, N.J.: Prentice-Hall, 1966), pp. 264–275.
23. Robert Pruger, "The Good Bureaucrat," *Social Work* 18 (July 1973): 26–27.
24. Ibid., pp. 28–32.
25. Aase George, "A History of Social Work Field Instruction: Apprenticeship to Instruction," in Bradford W. Sheafor and Lowell E. Jenkins, eds., *Quality Field Instruction in Social Work: Program Development and Maintenance* (New York: Longman, 1982), pp. 37–59.
26. Raymond Monsor Scurfield, "Clinician to Administrator: Difficult Role Transition?," *Social Work* 26 (November 1981): 495.
27. Robert Barker, "Private Practice Primer for Social Work," *NASW News* 28 (October 1983): 13.
28. Marquis Earl Wallace, "Private Practice: A Nationwide Study," *Social Work* 27 (May 1983): 262.
29. Ibid., p. 265.
30. Susan Matorin, Blanca Rosenberg, Marylin Levitt, and Sylvia Rosenblum, "Private Practice in Social Work: Readiness and Opportunity," *Social Casework* 68 (January 1987): 313–337.
31. Patricia Kelley and Paul Alexander, "Part-Time Private Practice: Practical and Ethical Considerations," *Social Work* 30 (May–June 1985): 254.
32. Ibid., p. 255.
33. Janice Proshaska, "Private Practice May Benefit Voluntary Agencies," *Social Casework* 59 (July 1978): 374.
34. Barker, "Private Practice Primer," p. 13.
35. Herman Borenzweig, "Agency vs. Private Practice: Similarities and Differences," *Social Work* 26 (May 1981): 243.

PART THREE

The Practice of Social Work

*T*he various activities that a social worker performs in carrying out his or her professional responsibilities constitute the *practice* of social work. In order to carry out the practice of social work effectively, however, the social worker must know *what* he or she is doing, *why* he or she is doing it, and of equal importance, *how* to do it. These three factors translate into the *knowledge* base of social work, the *value* base of social work, and the *skill* base of social work. The knowledge, value, and skill bases of social work provide the core ingredients and foundation of practice that guide the intervention activities of the social worker.

Chapter 7 discusses the basic knowledge a social worker should have. He or she must be well informed about how to help people deal with both their *internal* (psychological) and their *external* (significant others, groups, and neighborhood) environment. A case example provides an opportunity to examine the breadth and depth of knowledge the social worker needs just to be able to conduct a specific interview with a client.

Chapter 8 examines the value base of social work. The profession of social work is founded upon an adherence to certain values. These values include beliefs that humankind is inherently worthy, that people have a need to belong, and that all persons have responsibilities to themselves, their fellow human beings, and society. In addition, social workers also believe that society has a responsibility to help those less able to help themselves. Without values, the social work profession would lose its main purpose for being. Social work, in effect, would lose its professional uniqueness.

Chapter 9 focuses on the skill base of social work. In other words, what are the basic skills needed by the social worker as he or she begins to help people? *Skill* is ability to use knowledge effectively and readily in execution or performance. Seven basic skills for beginning practice are highlighted, namely, *basic helping* skills, *engagement* skills, *observation* skills, *communication* skills, *empathy* skills, *resistance intervention* skills, and *assessment* skills.

CHAPTER 7

The Knowledge Base of Social Work

To understand the many faces of social work in greater depth, some of the important parts of this profession must be isolated for closer scrutiny. The "Working Definition of Social Work Practice,"[1] which separates the knowledge, values, purpose, sanction, and methods or skills of social work, is used as a guide for this task. The primary emphasis, however, will be on the knowledge required of the social worker. The first six chapters of this book were concerned with purpose and sanction, which are prerequisites to practice activity. When engaged in practice, the social worker must relate simultaneously to the knowledge, value, and skill aspects of practice. In this way the profession resembles a three-ring circus: social work *skills* are the observable aspect of practice in the center ring, but important contributions are being made by *knowledge* and *values* in the side rings. In this chapter, the knowledge base of social work practice will be examined.

THE KNOWLEDGE BASE

If the social worker is to provide clients with competent service, he or she must be prepared with substantial knowledge. Although rigorously tested knowledge in the social and behavioral sciences is somewhat limited, the social worker should be familiar with what is available. The social worker should also know and be able to use the many theories and concepts relevant to practice. At a less scientific but equally important level, the social worker must develop individual practice knowledge based on experience in serving clients (*practice wisdom*) and also be sensitive to, and knowledgeable about, oneself—values, beliefs, and intuitions. The effective social worker, then, engages in *knowledge-guided practice*.

Knowledge may be generally defined as the "acquaintance with or theoretical or practical understanding of some branch of science, art, learning, or other area involving study, research, or practice, and the acquisition of skills."[2] All professions draw on a body of knowledge that serves as their basic foundation of practice. The knowledge is usually obtained from more research-oriented disciplines, and in some professions, such as law and medicine, it is accumulated over centuries. In addition to the historical knowledge, any *practitioner* should be aware of the body of knowledge related to his or her special area of practice.

A problem for social work, as well as for many other helping professions, is that a substantial number of social workers seem to have only a limited working conception of how to use knowledge in practice. Gordon suggests that they understand the development of skill much better than they do the pragmatic use of knowledge about a phenomenon in order to affect that phenomenon.[3] If one were to ask a social worker *what* he or she just did and *why* it was done that way, the answer would probably be verbalized with ease. One might say, for example, that an opportunity was created in the interview for Mr. James to cry so that he could vent his feelings. If asked to comment on the knowledge that guided that action, the social worker might describe reliance on a technique that had been observed and subsequently used in practice with good results (practice wisdom). Pursuing the matter further, if this social worker were asked to identify the concepts, propositions, and theory (knowledge base) that guides his or her practice, a reply might be more difficult. Although a major problem is the lack of much verified theory, Bartlett maintains that the social work profession has not been accustomed to looking directly and clearly at social work knowledge, as either a separate entity or a guide to practice.[4]

The social worker has been viewed as more a "doer" than a person engaged in knowledge-guided practice.[5] The low visibility and fragmentation of social work knowledge may also be the result of many social work educators' and staff supervisors' placing greater emphasis on the practitioner's awareness of *feelings* than on awareness of the generalizations on which action rests. The fact that social work has been slow in codifying its knowledge may be another major reason why the profession has only a limited foundation of tested knowledge.[6]

The social worker does not need to possess extensive knowledge in many fields, but it is important to be well versed in subjects related to helping people interact with the environment. Figure 7–1 helps draw some parameters around the specialized knowledge needed by the social worker.

SOCIAL WORK KNOWLEDGE: HISTORICAL OVERVIEW

For many years social workers have been attempting to systematize their knowledge. A milestone was the 1917 publication of Richmond's *Social Diagnosis,* the

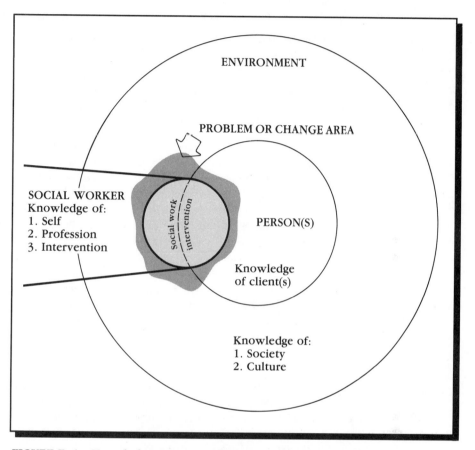

FIGURE 7–1   *Knowledge Components of Social Work Practice*

first significant effort toward organizing the knowledge base of one method of social work—social casework. The book systematically set forth an approach to the study and diagnosis of a client's problems and made explicit what have become basic tenets in casework, among them the need to *individualize* each client, the *reciprocity of relationship* between client and social worker, and the client's right to *self-determination.* Richmond established what a social worker ought to know, from the very general to the specific. Commenting on "what is true of everybody," Richmond stated:

> We all have a birthday and a place of birth, and have or had two parents, four grandparents, etc., with all that this implies by way of racial and national characteristics, of family inheritance and tradition, and probably of family environment. Our place of birth (assuming here and elsewhere the conditions of a mod-

ern civilization) was a house of some kind, and we have continued to live in this or in a series of other houses ever since. The characteristics of these houses, their neighborhood and atmosphere, have helped to make us what we are.[7]

Contrasting the general "what is true of everybody" to the specific in reference to ethnicity as a factor in working with a client, she commented:

> One of the social worker's difficulties with foreigners is that he does not understand their conventions any more than they do his, a knowledge of their history and of their old world environment is indispensable to the most helpful relations with them.[8]

If Richmond were alive today, she would support contemporary ethnic studies for social work students so they would have the knowledge enabling them to be more effective in helping clients from a variety of ethnic and racial backgrounds. Without minimizing the importance of ethnic, racial, and cultural factors in assessing clients either in Richmond's time or today (given the knowledge base of her era), she would have had difficulty in identifying alexithymia as a possible predisposing risk factor for a male substance abuse client—independent of race, ethnicity, or culture. *Alexithymia* refers to a specific disturbance in emotional processing that is manifested psychologically by difficulties in identifying and verbalizing feelings. It *may* have a biological etiology. This often results in dependency on drugs and/or alcohol to modulate and buffer feelings and emotions. In other words, the person buffers or acts out feelings rather than verbalizing his or her pain.[9] The point is that social workers have a responsibility to their clients to always be abreast of the most current knowledge available in their field of practice.

Another key historical event contributing to the knowledge base of social work was the 1929 Milford Conference, where a number of social work educators and social agency executives met to discuss issues related to social work practice. Porter Lee, a leader of the Milford Conference and director of the New York School of Social Work, promoted the idea that social casework should integrate the insights of psychology, psychiatry, political science, economics, and sociology. His synthesis of ideas from other fields into a new whole helped to formulate the *generic social casework theory* as expressed in the Milford Conference Report.[10] The report attempted to identify the generic components (those having common characteristics) in social casework practice, emphasizing that the *process* (procedure) in social casework and the knowledge base of the social worker should be basically the same for all practice settings.

Initial efforts toward developing a generic component of social work mainly concerned casework, and basic agreement was achieved about the major areas of content in social casework. However, substantial common ground was also discovered in knowledge content lists of casework, group work, and community organization.[11] Seeking a common core curriculum, social work educators proposed a "Basic Eight" curriculum to the American Association of Schools of Social Work in 1944.[12] The Basic Eight considered the following areas of particular importance to social work students: (1) social casework (generic and specialized); (2) social group work; (3) community organization; (4) social research and statistics; (5) social welfare administration; (6) public welfare and child welfare; (7) medical information; and (8) psychiatric information.

The goal of educators in social work during the 1940s was to help students develop competence in three major areas: (1) conceptual and perceptual understanding; (2) skills in methods, procedures, and processes; and (3) personal professional qualities.[13]

As late as 1955 Kahn criticized the curricula of graduate schools of social work for their emphasis on technical or how-to courses. He felt the curriculum structure alone did not clearly indicate what the social work profession considered its knowledge base. After analyzing a group of articles selected at random from social work periodicals, Kahn concluded that social work knowledge was at that time an amalgam of: (1) propositions borrowed from or markedly like those of psychiatry and some branches of psychology; (2) even fewer propositions borrowed from sociology and social anthropology and a scattering from other fields; (3) apparently original propositions about how to do certain things in casework, group work, and community organization; (4) methods, techniques, and attitudes clearly derived from the fields of administration, statistics, and social research; and (5) propositions about how to do things apparently derived from progressive education.[14]

In December, 1956, a definition of social work practice was prepared by a task force for the National Association of Social Workers (NASW). "The Working Definition of Social Work Practice" was published in *Social Work* in 1958 and spelled out the constellation of various components found in all professions, such as values, purpose, sanction, knowledge, and method. The particular content and configuration of this constellation in the definition, however, was seen as identifying social work practice and distinguishing it from the practice of other professions.[15] The knowledge component of the Working Definition views the social worker as typically guided by knowledge of:

1. Human development and behavior characterized by emphasis on the wholeness of the individual and the reciprocal influences of man and his total environment—human, social, economic, and cultural

2. The psychology of giving and taking help from another person or source outside the individual

3. Ways in which people communicate with one another and give outer expression to inner feelings, such as words, gestures, and activities

4. Group process and the effects of groups upon individuals and the reciprocal influence of the individual upon the group

5. The meaning and effect on the individual, groups, and community of cultural heritage including its religious beliefs, spiritual values, laws, and other social institutions

6. Relationships, i.e., the interactional processes between individuals, between individual and groups, and between group and group

7. The community, its internal processes, modes of development and change, its social services and resources

8. The social services, their structure, organization, and methods

9. Self, which enables the individual practitioner to be aware of and to take responsibility for his own emotions and attitudes as they affect his professional functions.[16]

As Heraclitus, an ancient Greek philosopher, said, "The same man never washes in the same river twice." Certainly the changeability of people, not to mention the environment, requires flexible application of knowledge. Since scientific knowledge of people is never final or absolute, the social worker is advised to take into account exceptions to existing generalizations and to be aware of, and ready to deal with, the spontaneous and unpredictable in human behavior.[17]

Boehm suggested in 1958 that social work had only fragments of practice theory, intermingled with incomplete knowledge of the nature of people, the nature of society, and their relationship. In assuming that social work practice was an art with a foundation of science and values, he perceived three types of knowledge in social work: (1) tested knowledge, (2) hypothetical knowledge, which required transformation into tested knowledge, and (3) assumptive knowledge (practice wisdom), which required transformation into hypothetical and then into tested knowledge. The practitioner uses all three types and assumes responsibility for knowing which type of knowledge is being used at any time and what degree of scientific certainty it carries.[18]

In 1959 Kadushin maintained that the literature detailing what the social worker needs to know, do, and feel was "almost embarrassingly rich."[19] He noted a certain repetitiveness in the materials, with "old friends" appearing many times. Although there were differences among statements regarding the required base of social work knowledge from one method to another, similarities in the listings may have been due to the *agreement of experts* rather than to a *detailed analysis of practice.* It appeared that there was a plea in the literature to study practice rather than to continue to use expert opinion as a basis for developing knowledge in social work.[20]

Kadushin was able to discern the origins of social work knowledge by building a framework separated into three major areas: social services, social work practice, and human growth and behavior. The *social service* area is concerned with the organization, administration, and operation of social welfare programs and services, the interrelationships of agencies, the historical development of such programs, and the nature of the human needs served by these programs.[21] *Social work practice* concerns the actual process of helping clients, the techniques of helping, the resources for helping, and appropriate attitudes for helping. *Human growth and behavior* is concerned with understanding the client in his or her problem situation, normal and deviant personality development and behavior, and the dynamics of individual and group behavior.[22]

Social work scholars and educators have seen the need become increasingly urgent for the building of additional social work knowledge. In 1962 following several years of discussion, the NASW Commission on Social Work Practice decided to have a "knowledge conference." A task force subsequently did initiate and give some beginning direction to the development of *social work knowledge* as an endeavor to strengthen the knowledge base of the profession.[23] The 117-page conference report was directed to the NASW Commission on Practice. One recommendation of particular interest was:

> That some means be established for systematically collecting and organizing so-cial work knowledge from the three sources so repeatedly emphasized at this conference, that is:
>
> a. Capturing and articulating what is known by practitioners but has not been sufficiently verbalized or communicated to the field at large and is not yet recognized substantively as part of social work's body of knowledge.
> b. Deriving clearer and more inclusive description of social work knowledge from social work literature.
> c. Supporting efforts to draw relevant knowledge from the social sciences and to develop this relevant knowledge in social work frames of reference.[24]

The conference concluded that the main sources of social work knowledge were the professional literature, relevant concepts from allied fields—especially the social sciences—and the wisdom of practitioners. A consultant at the con-ference suggested that social work must look more at its own substance for validation, knowledge, and theory-building; and in this process social work find-ings might contradict some theories in social science, thus demanding new testing by the social sciences.[25]

In attempting to identify the level of social work knowledge, Taber and Shap-iro conducted a content analysis of 124 social work articles published between 1920 and 1963. They tried to determine the nature and extent of the development of the social work knowledge base. When the data were classified as empirical or verifiable, trends over the forty-year period indicated a slight decrease in the proportion of empirical content, a dramatic increase in references to theories and concepts, and a sharp increase in the amount of verifiable material in each journal studied. Although they concluded that their findings did not show pro-gression toward a "relatively well-confirmed theory," the authors felt there was evidence of much potential for the development of knowledge and for more sophistication in the use of theory and facts.[26]

The search has continued for a firm knowledge base in social work. Perhaps the first step in more explicitly identifying the knowledge on which social work-ers rely is to formulate a clear conception of social work. The knowledge that is essential for social work practice could then be filtered out. Renewed activity to address the problem of identifying a clear concept of social work was stim-ulated in 1976 by the NASW at a conference on "Conceptual Frameworks for Social Work," held in Madison, Wisconsin, and reported on in a special issue of *Social Work* (September 1977). This effort was followed by the creation of a committee to work toward the development of a "Classification Scheme for Social Work Knowledge." This difficult task was finalized at a meeting in Chicago in May, 1979, and resulted in a second special issue of *Social Work* (January 1981) entitled "Conceptual Frameworks II."

A historical review indicates that to date there remains substantial disagreement as to what specifically constitutes social work knowledge. Burns suggests that social workers must function with a body of knowledge that is at best imprecise, at worst erroneous, and always inadequate and difficult to communicate.[27] The unusually broad boundaries of social work practice significantly contribute to this problem. The boundaries include all that is related to human behavior and could encompass all of society, including a range of conditions from health to pathology and a large selection of skills directed toward improved individual coping, institutional change, social policy and planning, and other areas as social workers enter new arenas of social issues and problems. "In effect," states Meyer, "it would seem that there are hardly any boundaries to the knowledge that is necessary for social workers to have just in order to get through a working day."[28]

ECOSYSTEMS MODEL: A WAY OF ORGANIZING SOCIAL WORK KNOWLEDGE

One way of organizing social work knowledge in assessing a practice situation, is through an ecosystems framework. The practice of social work involves a focus on the interaction between the person (or couple, family, group, organization, community, or larger societal structure) and the environment. The social work intervention focus might be directed at the person, environment, or both. The goal of the social worker is to enhance and restore the psychosocial functioning of persons or to change noxious social conditions that impede the mutually beneficial interaction between persons and their environment.[29]

Meyer maintains that for many years social work has been offering its well-honed methods only to those who could use them, instead of first finding out what was needed and then selecting the practice method from its interventive repertoire or inventing new methods. She believes the current social work methods framework maintains social work's denial of what needs to be done with regard to broader social problems. She therefore suggests an ecosystems orientation to practice, which involves the application of ecology (the study of the relationship between organisms and their environment) and general systems theory to professional practice tasks. This ecosystems perspective, according to Meyer, allows

> ... social workers to look at psychological phenomena, account for complex variables, assess the dynamic interplay of these variables, draw conceptual boundaries around the unit of attention or the case, and then generate ideas for interventions. At this point methodology enters in; for in any particular case—meaning a particular individual, family, group, institutional unit, or geographical area—any number of practice interventions might be needed.[30]

This ecosystems model of practice helps to promote social workers' understanding of the psychosocial problems experienced by actual or potential client populations, the incidence, prevalence, intensity and harmfulness of forces such as sexism, ageism, racism, and class discrimination, and the social environments (enhancing as well as noxious) in which people in need struggle to survive.

Bronfenbrenner originally developed an ecological model in 1977 utilizing four factors, such as individual, family, social structural and sociocultural, affecting human development.[31] Carlson in 1984 then adapted this model to the problem area of domestic violence. The model conceptualizes ecological space comprised of four different levels or systems, each of which is nested within the next.[32] This ecological framework, which can be called an ecosystems model, may be a helpful tool in analyzing from a micro to macro perspective the various factors impacting client population members. In addition to the minor modifications of two items—"sociocultural" to culture, and "social structural" to environmental-structural—as a means of more crisply delineating cultural from social or environmental-structural factors, the authors added a fifth-level factor for analysis, the historical.[33] Historical factors are particularly important for client populations as the historical origins of poverty, sexism, ageism, and racism, for example, continue to function today to "lock in" these groups in U.S. society. The ecosystems model is presented in Figure 7–2.

A social worker employing the ecosystems framework must comprehensively examine a practice situation from the five levels: individual, family, cultural, environmental-structural, and historical. First, at the *individual level,* the focus is on the biopsychological endowment each person possesses, including personality strengths, level of psychosocial development, cognition, perception, problem-solving skills, emotional temperament, habit formation, and communication and language skills. Additionally, it is important to be knowledgeable about the person's attitudes, values, cultural beliefs, life style, skills and abilities, educational/work performance, view of the world, and how he or she responds and copes with physical and psychological stress and problems. This represents only the highlights of factors at the individual level; the list is by no means exhaustive.

There are numerous growth and development life cycle theories, and modern theorists such as Bowlby, Erikson, Freud, and Rank, which are often used by helping health/mental health practitioners like social workers, to help guide understanding of human behavior. Actually, humankind has been developing theories concerning human behavior since Hippocrates, the Greek physician, originated the first classification of mental disorders in 400 B.C.![34] These theories *are,* in the final analysis, sets of concepts and ideas that have not yet been proven through rigorous scientific research. Perhaps they never will be, or are incapable of being "proven." Freud's *id, ego,* and *superego* concepts, conceived in 1923, for example, are not organic parts of the brain that can be seen, like the hypothalamus. Rather, the id, ego, and superego, each with its specific function, represent Freud's conceptualizations of a structural theory of the mind to explain personality and human behavior. Likewise, his theories pertaining to stages of psychosexual development (oral, anal, urethral, phallic, latency and genital stages)[35] are not factual truths "cast in stone"; rather, organized theoretical concepts that can be used in attempting to understand behavior. Caution must be

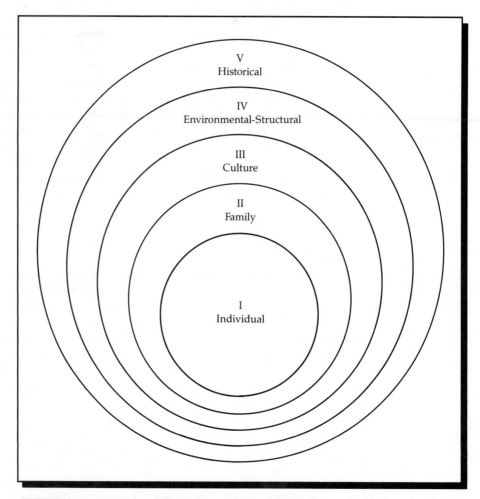

FIGURE 7–2   *Ecosystems Model for Analysis of Psychosocial Factors Impacting on Social Work Client Populations*

used in relying on Freud's concepts, as some communicate a sexist perspective; for example penis envy, the assumption that women prefer male genitals.[36]

For over thirty years, Erikson's eight-stage life cycle theory has been used extensively in the helping professions, particularly social work. Erikson, while accepting Freud's psychosexual development theories, nevertheless created a more extensive model which extended into adulthood and old age. He presented a succession of stages with a specific cycle of life tasks to master, with possible accompanying and cumulative consequences when a developmental task was not fulfilled satisfactorily. His eight stages and their accompanying tasks are[37]:

1. Oral stage: trust versus mistrust
2. Anal stage: autonomy versus shame and doubt
3. Genital stage: initiative versus guilt
4. Latency stage: industry versus inferiority
5. Adolescence stage: ego identity versus role confusion
6. Young adulthood stage: intimacy versus isolation
7. Adulthood stage: generativity versus stagnation
8. Maturity stage: ego integrity versus despair

Note that these theories are not universal, as most life cycle theoretical formulations are developed from white, middle-class clients, usually of European origin. Hence they may not have full applicability to all ethnic, racial, and cultural populations. Furthermore, theories developed by males, based on a few male patients, may include unconscious biases and hence lose some applicability to females.

Second, at the *family level,* the focus is on the nature of family life style, culture, organization, family, division of labor, sex role structure, and interactional dynamics. Even within a cultural context, each family is unique. It is therefore important to know its values, beliefs, emotional support capacity, affective style, tradition, rituals, overall strengths and vulnerabilities, and how it manages internal or external stress. The nature and quality of the spousal relationship and the depth of connectedness to children and extended family are other areas requiring examination.

Third, in civilizations cultures have evolved for survival purposes. Each culture develops behavioral responses influenced by the environment, historical and social processes incorporating specific structures such as language, food, kinship styles, religion, communications, norms, beliefs, and values. At the *cultural level* of the ecosystems model, therefore, the focus should be on understanding the cultural values, belief systems, and societal norms of the host culture, and in the case of minorities, their original culture. There may exist a conflict of cultures that in advanced form may result in mental-emotional impairment due to culture shock. The enhancing, nurturing aspects of the culture(s) should be noted as well as noxious elements such as sexism, class discrimination, ageism, and racism.

The fourth level of analysis involves *environmental-structural* factors and the positive or negative impact they have on client populations. Environmental-structural theories postulate that many of the problems of client populations are caused by the economic and social structure of U.S. society. Women, for example, are not poorer as a group than men because of biological or cultural inferiority. Rather, sexism is a U.S. male cultural value that is expressed and reinforced through the structure of economic, political, educational, and other social institutions. Ryan states that when U.S. white society looks at the poorly educated minority group child in the ghetto or *barrio* school, blame is placed on the parents (no books in the home), the child (impulse-ridden, nonverbal), minority culture (no value on education), or their socioeconomic status (i.e., they are socially and economically deprived and don't know any better). In pursuing this blaming-the-victim analysis, Ryan adds, no one remembers to ask questions about the collapsing buildings, old, torn textbooks, insensitive teachers, relentless segregation, callous administrators—in short, the environmental structure imposed on the person with its accompanying negative consequences.[38]

The fifth and final level of the ecosystems model concerns positive and noxious factors in the *historical experience* of the client population member(s). The historical roots and experience of female subordination by males, for example, will affect the nature and quality of the women's interaction with all agencies and their representatives. The male social worker may not be aware of his unconscious sexist behavior—the result of decades of conditioning—as he attempts to "help" female clients with their problems. Years of minority group oppression and exploitation, at times including genocide, lynching, and "police executions without trial," have left deep scars in minority group members and will affect the way they relate to human service agency representatives. Some elderly whites may recall very positive historical experiences, recalling how supportive and encouraging U.S. social institutions had been, only to become depressed and discouraged when abandoned by the government. In addition to knowing about the U.S. historical experience, it is also of value to know the historical experience of immigrants and the countries they came from.

To illustrate how the ecosystems model might work, the following case example is presented:

> José is a small, frail-looking fourteen-year-old Spanish-speaking only youngster brought into the community mental health center by his mother because he began to yell, cry, and scream and threw himself under a table at a public laundromat. The Anglo-American psychiatrist who saw José was able to speak some Spanish. José told the doctor that he was at the laundromat with his mother the day before and that he had seen a police car slowly pass by the laundromat. He insisted the police officer on the passenger side of the car pointed his machine gun at the laundromat. At that time, fearing for his life he threw himself under one of the tables and began screaming.
>
> The mother confirmed that a police car had passed the laundromat but stated that the officers merely passed and did not expose any firearms. Other symptoms José was exhibiting were fear to go to school (where he was failing), fear of leaving the house, nightmares (people trying to kill him), insomnia, fear of being arrested by immigration officials and deported, depression, agitation, and increasingly becoming more suspicious of people and irritable, especially at his mother, stepfather, and siblings. This progressively deteriorating behavior had been going on for about six months. The doctor concluded that José was at times incoherent, delusional, having visual hallucinations, and displaying behavior that was at times disorganized. This clinical picture was consistent with DSM III–R 298.80, Brief Reactive Psychosis. He was prescribed antipsychotic medication. He continued in treatment for two weeks but his symptoms did not subside. The medication was not having any effect. (Often medications not having effect may be the result of misdiagnosis.)
>
> A Hispanic bilingual-bicultural social work mental health consultant was asked to see José and his mother to make an assessment and treatment recommendation.

José was born in "Muy Lejos," a rural, agricultural village in El Salvador. His parents were both farm laborers, as were his grandparents. He was raised in a very traditional, religious, rural culture where sex roles, division of labor, and respect for the elderly, extended family, and authority figures were valued. When José was six, his father was suspected of being a guerrilla and was killed by right-wing government forces. Sensing her life was also in danger, José's mother left him with his grandparents and came to the United States without documents in order to obtain employment and then send for José and other relatives. José felt abandoned and cried on the phone whenever his mother was able to call him, which was once every three or four months. Frequently, José would have to join other villagers and escape into the hills, sometimes for several months. José saw many killings, including decapitated bodies placed in the village by the right-wing forces to intimidate villagers.

In the meantime his mother struggled for several years as a low-paid domestic and began to live with a documented Hispanic male. They had two children, two and four years younger than José. Finally, the mother was able to save enough money to send for José. He was brought to the United States by a secret, underground system some six months prior to the laundromat incident. Initially he was happy to be reunited with his mother, but then the symptoms began to surface.

José presents a difficult, complex case although in no way is his situation unique. Rather than presenting one clearly identified specific problem for the mental health practitioner to treat, as is often the case with many middle-class clients, José brings at least *five* major problems. They have to be prioritized in terms of severity and treated in a sequential manner. First of all, José is suffering acute *post-traumatic stress disorder symptoms* that have to be treated, including appropriately prescribed medication that will reduce his anxiety and fear, and permit him to sleep. Second, he is experiencing *culture shock,* having abruptly left an agrarian environment and then placed in a central area of Los Angeles. He doesn't understand the language or the requirements of school. He is being chased by urban gangs. Third, he is experiencing *separation anxiety,* having suddenly left his loving grandparents, who were really his substitute parents. It is also painful to separate from relatives, friends, and one's country, never knowing if one will return. Fourth, he harbors a significant amount of *unresolved anger* toward his mother, who he believes abandoned him at a critical point in his life. These unresolved issues are intensified at his current psychosocial developmental level, adolescence. Finally, young José is confronted with a *reconstituted family.* He has to learn to deal with a stepfather who is taking the place of his beloved father. He also has to learn to live with a ten- and twelve-year-old stepsister and stepbrother. In short, he is a complete outsider in *all* respects.

Following the treatment of the psychiatric symptoms, José then will have to work on cultural shock issues, separation anxiety, and unresolved matters related to his mother. At the appropriate time, family therapy should also be initiated to help them function more positively as a family unit. The social worker may also have to help José resolve school and community stress problems and link him up with community social-recreation programs.

In working with social work client population groups, once a sound knowledge base is established through the use of a conceptual tool such as the ecosystems model, the social worker has to intervene at both micro and macro intervention levels. In cases such as that of José, a detailed biological-psychological-sociological, cultural, and historical assessment has to be made in order to know what is needed, and more important, what has to be done. The case highlighted more micro intervention strategies than macro. Macro intervention approaches would have utilized the helping concepts of client advocacy, empowerment, social action, networking, and class action social work, which involves collaboration with the legal profession on behalf of oppressed, disadvantaged special populations. These approaches are spelled out in detail in Chapter 21.

FURTHER REFINEMENT OF NEEDED KNOWLEDGE

The ecosystems model can be a helpful tool in organizing macro-to-micro knowledge as a social worker tries to learn how to best help a client. Having the ecosystems model as a working framework for capturing social work knowledge, there can be further refinement and focusing of needed knowledge for practice. In this regard, borrowing concepts from Kadushin as to the knowledge he believes the social worker needs—especially those social workers affected by agency mission, policies, and practices—would be valuable. Kadushin stresses the importance of incorporating knowledge about a specific practice setting, a specific agency, a specific client (as seen in the ecosystems model but additionally in relationship to the agency), and a specific client contact.[39] The following case analysis can help to identify the general knowledge that a social worker needs as a basis for assessing any case and that which is specific to a field and setting or a particular client. It is also useful to distinguish between the knowledge required to understand the ecosystems with which the social work is concerned (i.e., individual, family, culture, environmental-structural, and historical), and the knowledge required to intervene effectively in the situation to help the client or clients change or engage in efforts to change the environment. This case centers on Josie Chavez, a Mexican American adolescent female who, due to habitual delinquency, is detained in a juvenile correctional facility. Josie's probation officer, Mr. Lopez, is a MSW-level social worker. The knowledge he uses in this case situation is organized according to the knowledge of a specific practice setting (corrections), knowledge about a specific agency (a twenty-four-hour female juvenile detention facility), knowledge of a specific client (a juvenile female offender), and knowledge about a specific contact (the initial interview).

Knowledge about a Specific Practice Field

This social worker is employed in the *corrections field* and must be acquainted with the goals, philosophy, and functions of the field in society. The worker needs to know that a function of corrections is punishment of the convicted offender. The types of punishment may be only those allowed by the law: imprisonment (deprivation of the right to liberty), fine (deprivation of property), and death and certain other punishments society that the United States accepts and imposes. The social worker must also be familiar with a common assumption in correctional philosophy, that the penal law and correctional treatment have two purposes: treatment of the offender and protection of the public. Another common assumption is that the treatment of the offender should be *individualized,* that is, appropriate for the particular offender.[40]

The social worker should also be familiar with criminological theories, which may be assembled into three main categories: (1) *biological and constitutional theory,* often called the *school of criminal biology,* which seeks the mainsprings of deviancy in the inherited physical and mental makeup of humans; (2) *psychogenic theory,* which traces antisocial character to faulty relationships within the family in the first few years of life; and (3) *sociological theory,* which maintains that the pressures and pulls of the social environment produce delinquent and criminal behavior.[41] Some theories, such as those emphasizing biological factors, date back to the early nineteenth century; while others, such as that propounded by Cloward and Ohlin, are quite recent. Cloward and Ohlin theorize that boys from urban slums gravitate to the delinquency subculture when they discover they do not have access to legitimate avenues of success.[42] Since our social worker is employed in a specific practice area—probation—he would obviously require more knowledge of that agency than of the parole or prison systems.

Knowledge about a Specific Agency

The probation department is responsible for probation services for adults and children as required or authorized by state or local laws. This agency is closely linked to the court but is not in the judicial branch of government; its services include the study, treatment, and supervision of probationers. Through this agency, society tries to provide corrective assistance to the individual in conflict with the law and to protect the community at the same time. Because it is not socially or economically feasible to imprison all offenders, probation seeks to rehabilitate persons convicted of crimes by returning them to society under supervision for a period of time.

The majority of offenders can be guided into a more constructive life without being removed from family, job, or community. The social worker should be familiar with the laws governing probation and the services provided by the probation department. Basic *field service* functions include investigation to help courts determine the proper sentencing of convicted persons and supervision of children and adults placed on probation by the courts. In addition to field service, the social worker must be familiar with other service functions of the department such as: (1) securing suitable living arrangements for nondelinquent juvenile court wards who are unable to remain in their own homes, (2) administering temporary detention facilities, and (3) providing *institutional* rehabilitation treatment facilities for juvenile delinquents who need treatment outside the home.

As can be seen, there are specialized subunits in the probation agency that require additional knowledge on the part of the social worker. The social worker in our case example is employed in a twenty-four-hour placement facility for thirteen- to seventeen-year-old girls. These girls have been made wards of the juvenile court and have been ordered "suitably placed" in the institution. The social worker learns that known psychotic girls are not admitted to the institution and that many girls placed there exhibit behavior or personality disorders.

Because these disorders are so prevalent in both juvenile delinquent and adult criminal institutions, they warrant extensive discussion. These disorders may range from those essentially neurotic, to behavior bordering on the socio-pathic. Given such a range of behavior, the social worker must have an accurate diagnostic formulation of the ward in order to work out an appropriate treatment plan. In other words the social worker must understand the *underlying causes* of the behavior problem (symptoms) the girls exhibit, such as running away, sex delinquency, incorrigibility, shoplifting, car theft, and assault.

Disruptive Behavior Disorders is a class of disorders described in the American Psychiatric Association's Diagnostic and Statistical Manual of Mental Disorders (commonly known as DSM III-R) as childhood and adolescent behavior that is socially disruptive and is often more distressing to others than to the persons with the disorders. The subclass of disruptive behavior disorders include *Attention-deficit Hyperactivity Disorder* (ADHD), *Oppositional Defiant Disorder,* and *Conduct Disorder.*

The essential features of ADHD, which begins before age seven, are developmentally inappropriate degrees of inattention, impulsiveness, and hyperactivity. Oppositional Defiant Disorder or Conduct Disorder may develop later in childhood in those with ADHD, and in those who develop Conduct Disorder, a significant number, according to DSM III-R, are found to have Antisocial Personality Disorder in adulthood.[43] In Conduct Disorder the essential feature is a persistent pattern of conduct in which persons violate the basic rights of others and major age-appropriate social norms or rules. This behavior typically presents itself in the home, school, with peers, and in the community. Physical aggression is common, and conduct problems are more serious than those seen in Oppositional Defiant Disorder. Early onset of Conduct Disorder in childhood is associated with greater risk of continuation into adolescent and adult life as Antisocial Personality Disorder.

In Oppositional Defiant Disorder there is a pattern of hostile, negative, and defiant behavior without the more serious violations of the basic rights of others that are seen in Conduct Disorder. Persons are more prone to argue, lose their tempers, defy rules, swear, and the like, rather than physically attack others as is found in Conduct Disorder. Practitioners do not know the course of this disorder, although in many cases it can evolve into Conduct or a Mood Disorder.[44]

The above three Disruptive Behavior Disorders may evolve into adolescent or adult Antisocial Personality Disorder. Conduct Disorder symptoms begin before age fifteen, and the first symptoms of Conduct Disorder in females who develop Antisocial Personality Disorder usually appear in puberty; in males the Conduct Disorder is generally obvious in childhood. The essential features of this disorder include a history of continual and chronic antisocial behavior in which persons violate the rights of others, persistence into adult life of a pattern of antisocial behavior that began before the age of fifteen, and failure to sustain good job performance over a period of several years (although this may not be evident in individuals who are self-employed or who have not been in a position to demonstrate this behavior, for example, students or housewives). The antisocial behavior is not due to either severe mental retardation, schizophrenia, or manic episodes.

Lying, stealing, fighting, truancy, and resisting authority are typical early childhood signs. In adolescence, unusually early or aggressive sexual behavior, excessive drinking, and use of illicit drugs are frequent. In adulthood, these kinds of behavior continue with the addition of the inabilities to sustain consistent work performance, function as a responsible parent, and accept social norms with respect to lawful behavior. After age thirty the more flagrant aspects may diminish, particularly sexual promiscuity, fighting, criminality, and vagrancy.

The diagnostic criteria for an Antisocial Personality Disorder (DSM III-R, classification 301.70) include[45]:

A. Current age at least eighteen
B. Evidence of Conduct Disorder with onset before age fifteen, as indicated by a history of *three* or more of the following:
   (1) was often truant
   (2) ran away from home overnight at least twice while living in parental or parental surrogate home (or once without returning)
   (3) often initiated physical fights
   (4) used a weapon in more than one fight
   (5) forced someone into sexual activity with him or her
   (6) was physically cruel to animals
   (7) was physically cruel to other people
   (8) deliberately destroyed others' property (other than by fire-setting)
   (9) deliberately engaged in fire-setting
   (10) often lied (other than to avoid physical or sexual abuse)
   (11) has stolen without confrontation of a victim on more than one occasion (including forgery)
   (12) has stolen with confrontation of a victim (e.g., mugging, purse-snatching, extortion, armed robbery)
C. A pattern of irresponsible and antisocial behavior since the age of fifteen, as indicated by at least *four* of the following:
   (1) is unable to sustain consistent work behavior, as indicated by any of the following (including similar behavior in academic settings if the person is a student):

(a) significant unemployment for six months or more within five years when expected to work and work was available

(b) repeated absences from work unexplained by illness in self or family

(c) abandonment of several jobs without realistic plans for others

(2) fails to conform to social norms with respect to lawful behavior, as indicated by repeatedly performing antisocial acts that are grounds for arrest (whether arrested or not), for example, destroying property, harassing others, stealing, pursuing an illegal occupation

(3) is irritable and aggressive, as indicated by repeated physical fights or assaults (not required by one's job or to defend someone or oneself), including spouse- or child-beating

(4) repeatedly fails to honor financial obligations, as indicated by defaulting on debts or failing to provide child support or support for other dependents on a regular basis

(5) fails to plan ahead, or is impulsive, as indicated by one or both of the following:

(a) traveling from place to place without a prearranged job or clear goal for the period of travel or clear idea about when the travel will terminate

(b) lack of a fixed address for a month or more

(6) has no regard for the truth, as indicated by repeated lying, use of aliases, or "conning" others for personal profit or pleasure

(7) is reckless regarding his or her own or others' personal safety, as indicated by driving while intoxicated, or recurrent speeding

(8) if a parent or guardian, lacks ability to function as a responsible parent, as indicated by one or more of the following:

(a) malnutrition of child

(b) child's illness resulting from lack of minimal hygiene

(c) failure to obtain medical care for a seriously ill child

(d) child's dependence on neighbors or nonresident relatives for food or shelter

(e) failure to arrange for a caretaker for young child when parent is away from home

(f) repeated squandering, on personal items, of money required for household necessities

(9) has never sustained a totally monogamous relationship for more than one year

(10) lacks remorse (feels justified in having hurt, mistreated, or stolen from another)

D. Occurrence of antisocial behavior not exclusively during the course of schizophrenia or manic episodes.

In addition to having a depth of knowledge concerning the major psychiatric diagnostic categories pertaining to delinquent adolescent clientele treated in the institution, in this instance, the social worker must also become familiar with the physical facilities, policies, and procedures of the program. At this particular detention facility, an Intake Committee composed of a consultant psychiatrist, intake social worker, and school principal meets regularly to discuss—

1. the kind of behavior expected from each girl and ways of dealing with it;
2. the setting of tentative goals for achievement during each girl's stay in the program;
3. selection of a treatment plan for each girl;
4. the best ways of working with each girl's family; and
5. the school program to be followed, whether academic, remedial, or activity.

The social worker must be knowledgeable about treatment plans and resources the institution offers. In this example the agency's treatment plan falls into three broad categories: individual, group, and family therapy. These modes of treatment are known as *direct social work practice,* that is, the social worker works directly with the individual, family, or group. Prior to proceeding with discussions about knowledge of a specific client and about a specific contact, brief descriptions of family therapy and group and individual treatment will be offered.

Family Therapy

Family therapy is one of the intervention approaches used by the agency. In considering family therapy, the social worker must recognize that the family is a key factor in the treatment process and that every effort should be made to involve the family actively in the treatment program. It therefore becomes important for the social worker to acquire knowledge about family dynamics and theory.

Family therapy has a sufficiently solid knowledge base to warrant it as a major mode of treatment. A survey of graduate schools of social work found that family therapy content was included in the required methods curricula in 90 percent of the responding schools. Eighty percent of respondents indicated that family therapy was a legitimate area of specialization in the curricula of graduate social work education.[46] Family therapy has many different therapeutic approaches, each with its own specific theoretical intervention base. Some family therapy approaches are spontaneous, using interpretations and uncovering techniques. Other approaches are carefully planned, and the outcome is documented. Some family therapists are method-oriented and others are problem-oriented, that is, they are more eclectic and change their method based on the problem. For some the focus can be on expressing emotions or changing family structure.

Depending on the problem and the family therapist's orientation, the focus of intervention may be the child in the family (individual), the child and a parent (dyad), the child and parents (triad), or the child, parents, and other family members. There are at least three core theories characteristic to most models of family therapy: *systems theory, family development theory,* and *structural theory.* The systems theory views the family as a system of interlocking forces that regulate the ways it and its members operate. The whole is greater than its parts, and the whole must be known if the parts are to be understood. Each part contributes to and is affected by the system. Any part that malfunctions for whatever reason affects the balance or equilibrium of the total system. An adolescent who acts out stealing a car, for example, might simply be reacting to stress caused by the impending divorce of his parents; that is, the system is in a state of disequilibrium.

Family development theory emphasizes the fact that all families are at various stages of development over time. Families change over the years as part of a natural process. Family developmental tasks, in large part, parallel and are intermeshed with individual life tasks. The place of each young person in the family, the meaning this has for the parents and siblings, and the success or difficulty with which the family copes and interacts heavily influence the development of children.[47] In the family life cycle there is a major shift in the hierarchial structure; that is, children shift from being cared for by their parents to being peers of parents to being caretakers of parents in their old age.[48] The family development literature reveals certain common stress points of which the family therapist should be aware. Briefly, they include: (1) marriage, when the young couple must separate from their families and develop new modes of communication and a new emotional alignment; (2) the birth of the first child, an event that creates family developmental problems as emotional alignments are shifted to include the child and parental roles are established; (3) the age when the child first begins to assert his or her autonomy; (4) the entrance of the child into school and related painful feelings of separation, both for the child and the parents; (5) the stormy adolescent years, with their conflict over dependency and independency, self-responsibility and interdependence, intimacy and privacy; (6) the leaving of the last child from home, an event that precipitates the new task of parents having to learn how to relate to one another as middle-aged persons; and (7) old age, with its attendant loss of work and physical and role changes between the parents and their children.[49]

Structural theory is concerned with factors of importance related to the family structure. Family structure can be described in terms of hierarchy based on power and status. Structural theorists maintain that problems develop when there is a confusion in a hierarchy or a violation of the rules innate in hierarchical organizations.[50] For example, if a father sides consistently with the teenage daughter against the mother, the child is breaching generation lines and so violating the norms and rules of hierarchical structures. This results in stress and problems in the family, between the parents and between the teenage daughter and mother. To intervene effectively, the family therapist conceptualizes the problem family as a system in disequilibrium, looks for developmental phase stressors and structural defects, and then, with the assistance of the family, attempts to correct these problems in order for the family to attain improved psychosocial functioning.

Group Treatment

Group treatment is another mode of intervention used to help girls at the agency. There appears to be some confusion about the terms *group treatment, group work,* and *group psychotherapy.* Group psychotherapy, in its most traditional form, is a form of treatment in which carefully selected emotionally ill persons are placed in a group, guided by a trained therapist, for the purpose of helping one another effect personality change.[51] It involves an "uncovering" procedure, the achievement of insight into unconscious motivations and other intrapsychic processes. Today there are different types of group psychotherapy, each with its own theoretical base and interventive mode. These include supportive group therapy, analytically oriented group therapy, psychoanalysis of groups, transactional group therapy, and behavioral group therapy.[52] Because all these types of group psychotherapy have as their primary goal being therapeutic or helpful, they are forms of *group treatment.*

   Group work is also helpful to people but is not usually referred to as group psychotherapy, since the primary goal is not to uncover unconscious material. Rather, the aim is to help people realize their potential for social functioning. This treatment helps people *through* groups.[53] For example, an acting-out, rebellious adolescent may learn to internalize controls by being in a social work group with peers who, through democratic values, processes, and activities, are learning to work together to accomplish goals.

   At the institution in our case example, two types of group treatment are offered:

1. Group work—a group composed of eight to ten girls whose chief focus is on activities to build responsibilities and better relationships between the girls and adults.
2. Group psychotherapy—a group of six to eight girls, led by a psychiatrist, clinical psychologist, or clinical social worker, whose primary emphasis is psychotherapy.

Individual Treatment

Individual treatment is the primary intervention approach used at the girls' institution. Individual treatment in social work involves the method of casework whereby help is given to individuals case by case, in order to resolve, alleviate, and prevent those problems that undermine the adequacy of their daily life functioning. It is a *method,* meaning the overall sum of procedures, and a *process,* identifying the separate parts and interlocking steps that in the whole constitute a method.[54] The social worker is concerned with the problem and the person who suffers it. Establishing a working relationship between the client and the social worker enhances the therapeutic problem-solving process. From the outset the social worker attempts to involve the client in active work on the problem. Active work involves talking about the problem, explaining possible causes and effects, expressing feelings, exploring wishes in regard to it, expressing reactions to the social worker's inputs about what seems possible, struggling with what to do next, and so on. In short, the client is helped to cope with his or her problem as far as age, mental and physical status, and current situation makes it possible.[55] To accomplish this, the social worker needs to know the client well.

Ethnic- and Culture-Sensitive Practice

In addition to a social work practitioner having a knowledge base and skills in family, group, and individual treatment, the social worker—in getting to know the client well—must also have some appreciation of the client's ethnic, cultural, and minority status variability in order to optimize therapeutic intervention. Over the last eight years three practice frameworks have evolved to attempt to accomplish this task.

The first framework was introduced by Devore and Schlesinger in 1981 and was referred to as *ethnic-sensitive social work practice.* Borrowing from sociological and psychological theories, ethnicity and social class issues were incorporated into social work practice assessment and intervention models. Ethnicity and social class were seen as affecting life's problems and influencing how they would be resolved. Because of a subordinate, minority group status, social work problem solving was seen as most effective with a micro and macro approach, that is, not only attempting to help the individual and/or the family, but also intervening on the larger societal stressors (e.g., unemployment, poverty) impacting on the client.[56]

The second framework, which could be called the *cultural awareness framework,* advocated by social worker Green in his 1982 publication *Cultural Awareness in the Human Services,* emphasizes an understanding of each group's cultural background. Special attention is given to the client's definition and understanding of a problem, how his or her language labels and categorizes a problem, what culturally community-based traditional resources have been utilized in the past dealing with such problems, and the client's cultural prescription for solving the problem.[57]

Being more specific in using a cultural awareness framework in treating black alcoholic families (and black families in general), Mary Lou Politi Ziter advises social workers to consider the following guidelines[58]:

1. Emphasis on the problem-solving process for resolving problems in both the white and black worlds
2. Appreciation by the family and the practitioner of recurrent behaviors that were functional adaptations when they were originally made for survival and that, although no longer helpful, have been continued through intergenerational identification
3. A dual perspective in assessment and treatment dictated by biculturalism
4. The family's control of its recovery and the recognition by members of that control

5. Emphasis on the larger social system that is necessitated by the victimization of black people in society
6. Self-assessment by the family of its functioning to check potential bias by the practitioner

A third conceptual framework developed by Lum in 1986 is called *ethnic minority social work practice.* This framework conceptualizes a systematic process-stage approach to minority practice, offers generic principles of practice universal to people of color, and supports them with examples from each of the major minority groups (Asians, blacks, Hispanics, American Indians). The framework is based on the notion that there are common themes pertaining to working with people of color, yet recognizing that each of the major minority groups has its own unique cultural history, socioeconomic problems, and treatment approaches. Lum refers to this emphasis as *cultural commonality* and *cultural specificity.*[59]

Lum defines minority social work practice as:

> ... the art and science of developing a helping relationship with an individual, family, group, and/or community whose distinctive physical/cultural characteristics and discriminatory experiences require approaches that are sensitive to ethnic and cultural environments.[60]

The reader can begin to appreciate that not only is there a significant volume of individual, family, and group treatment knowledge that the social worker must learn, but he or she must also be able to integrate this information with ethnic, cultural, and socioeconomic status factors. Chapter 10, *Social Work with Special Populations,* will go into more depth on these issues.

Knowledge about a Specific Client

Becoming increasingly specific, the social worker now needs to know something about the delinquent girl assigned to his caseload. The following admissions and intake evaluation report used as an example is a fairly typical one written by the intake probation officer. The social worker needs this background information prior to the first contact with the new probationer to be adequately prepared to provide competent services. The first contact with a social worker does not necessarily signify the time when treatment begins. Actually, treatment may begin at the point of intake, when the agency, through its intake worker, is attempting to establish a cooperative, positive working relationship with the client, to induct the client into the role of "clienthood," and to provide helping interventions appropriate to the intake situation.[61]

La Llorona School for Girls Admissions and Intake Evaluation Report

Name: Josie Chavez
Age: 15

Josie is a very attractive fifteen-year-old Mexican-American, Roman Catholic girl. She is very articulate and is well respected by her peers. She seems to be exceptionally bright and quite manipulative.

The Delinquency

The problem behavior includes: being beyond the control of her parents, truancy, battery, leaving home without permission, running away and inhaling glue. She is a ward of the court.

Family Constellation

The family includes the father, age 37; her mother, age 36; a half-sister, age 18; and six full brothers and sisters, ages 13, 12, 11, 10, 7, and 5. Josie is the oldest of the children. She feels that she is the only child who has "messed up," and said that the others are all doing well. However, the half-sister has been known to the Probation Department for being a runaway and for burglary. When this information was brought to the attention of Josie, she stated that it was such a long time ago and that her half-sister was only 12.

The family lives in a small, crowded, rented home in a poor white community. The father is presently employed as a roofer earning between $300 and $375 per week, of which $550 per month goes to rent. The parents are struggling to keep the family together on his income, and the mother has tried to supplement it by working. She has not worked in quite some time, however.

Josie's father was born in California and her mother in Texas. The half-sister was born out of wedlock, and although Josie's parents have lived together seventeen years they were married five years ago in Mexico.

The union has been stormy. There have been separations but never for long. Josie suggests that her mother and father are very dependent on each other and have a need to get together again. The mother claims that the trouble is caused by the father's drinking problem.

Last year Josie's mother was having trouble with the father and the girls, so she took the children to Texas. The girls gave her no trouble there, and they seemed happy. They supported themselves, picking potatoes and grapes. They would have liked to remain in Texas except that they ran out of money. As a result Josie's parents came to Venice to look for work. It was then that the father obtained employment as a roofer through an old friend. The children, in the meanwhile, were in Texas, living with Josie's paternal aunt. The aunt had six children of her own, but Josie liked living there. She feels that her aunt is very much like her and looks like her father. Her cousins did very little in the house, and it was her sisters who did most of the work. When Josie's parents came to pick up the children to take them back to Venice, Josie ran away because she wanted to stay in Texas, and she likes her aunt, who lets her do as she pleases. However, Josie stated that she wanted to go to a fair with some friends, and the friends left her at a park, where she had an appointment to meet a boy friend.

She stated that they did nothing but talk and walk around, and then he went home and she remained in the park. Then she discovered that it was very late, and she was afraid to go home. She fell asleep in the park and then turned herself in to the police. The case was then transferred to the Juvenile Court in Venice. Josie was never happy at home, and she hated school. She didn't like being disciplined by her parents, wouldn't listen to them, annoyed the other family members, and didn't get along with them. Her mother states that Josie could not understand the tremendous financial problems of the family and twice became very angry, when her mother couldn't buy her gym clothes and when she had a toothache and her mother could not afford to take her to the dentist right away.

Josie's parents state that they want her home, but they feel that they cannot control her at home. The father vacillates in his feelings about Josie. They are very confused about the reasons behind Josie's runaways and glue-sniffing and are very unsure of their methods of handling Josie—which alternate between extreme scoldings, sometimes physical punishment, and real overprotectiveness. They seem anxious for counseling and appear to be cooperative. They do not want Josie placed with relatives. Josie stated that she likes her grandfather and that he separated from her grandmother when her mother was about fifteen and since then has had about five wives. She is quite fond of some of them and very fond of his present wife. She likes this maternal grandfather and says that her maternal grandmother is very much like her own mother. She stated that she hates her grandmother because she makes remarks about her being like her father. Josie stated that she liked school in Texas, even though the school put her back a year because of technicalities related to the transfer.

Court Contact and Some Background on Problem Behavior

Josie first came to the attention of the Juvenile Court two years ago, when she was placed under court supervision for battery. She had come to "get" a girl at school, and scratched the registrar, who tried to take her to the office. The probation files show that Josie had been in frequent fights in school and was often truant. While on probation she was again arrested by the police for a second battery. She was counseled and released. Three months later Josie ran away from home and stayed away for nine days. She was to appear in court a week later, but her mother had moved all the children to Texas. The father appeared in court, however, and the matter was dismissed. The school reported on this occasion that Josie could not stand living in her home where there was so much fighting and noise. Josie's behavior at school had deteriorated, and she showed increasing lack of motivation and was often absent. She remarked that her mother and father were having terrible trouble with each other at home. Her next contact with the law was ten months later, when she again ran away from the paternal aunt's home where she was staying. She stated that she was afraid to go home because her parents would not understand why she was out so late, and so she turned herself in to the police. She appeared in the Texas Juvenile Court a month later and was declared a ward of the court under Section 601; then the matter was ordered transferred to Venice County (discussed above).

Josie was then released to her parents pending placement. However, Josie ran away again from her home a month later and stayed away until apprehended by her parents a week later at a cousin's home. Josie was found in an intoxicated condition along with five or six other girls, all of whom were quite drunk. The smell on the girls was not of liquor, but of glue. Josie explained that she was late for school in the morning, so she decided not to go and ran away. She had 90 cents in her pocket and decided to visit her friends in a nearby community, and because she wasn't happy at home, she decided to remain away "for good." Josie was detained in Juvenile Hall. At the court hearing a week later, the transfer of wardship from Texas was accepted by Venice County, an additional petition was filed by the police because of the glue sniffing, and suitable placement and a clinical study were ordered.

Clinical

Josie was seen by the psychologist, and the report states that she worked fairly well on the tests but seemed quite anxious, showed lack of controls, and although she functioned within the dull-normal range of intelligence (Beta IQ 88), her true potential is well within the bright-normal range and probably as high as superior. Essentially, she is an unhappy, depressed, immature, hedonistic youngster, whose sexual and self-identity are confused. She sees herself as bad, worthless, and guilty, and relatively impotent in terms of succeeding at anything in the world. The diagnostic impression: antisocial personality in formation.

The report states that she needs a highly structured, limit-setting situation in which she can begin to develop controls and psychotherapy to help her work through her deep feelings of rejection and hostility. Adequate stable female and male identification models are essential to her further development, particularly if her delinquentlike orientation is to be changed. She desperately needs socially acceptable success experiences (academics, peer group activities, etc.) if she is to internalize healthy values. Her personality and intellectual potentials are very rich but must be tapped before she solidifies an antisocial character structure.

Cottage Report

The cottage report describes Josie as being generally quiet and cooperative. She follows instructions, although she is occasionally slow in doing so. She is constantly being called on "too close" physical contact with other girls. When questioned, Josie was very vague and maintained that she is not involved in "chic-vot" (homosexual behavior). When confronted with staff's opinion that she was, she did not become hostile but merely denied it. When specific instances were mentioned, she said she was perhaps too much of a close friend and that she was by habit an affectionate person. She said she might consider curbing her physical contacting but that this was her "pride and joy." Josie is generally polite to staff, although she reacts violently on being called on physical contacting, expressing this by dirty looks and under-the-breath remarks. She admits she is very distrusting of staff but gives no reasons for this. She usually becomes very nervous when talking to staff. Josie appears to enjoy being seductive with everyone. She complies with instructions and appears to want people to think well of her, but she excuses her inappropriate behavior through rationalizations.

School Report

Josie is in the B-8 with academic deficiencies. She will complete the A-8 in summer school and enter the ninth grade in September. Her cumulative record indicates that she has always been an underachiever. The school report for Josie is generally negative at this point. Her behavior ranges from excessive talking, open hostility, and writing on desks, to showing open dislike for conformers or responsive students. Josie's best class is physical education, where she is earning a B. In her other classes, she is doing just enough to get by. She has been observed to sit with her back to the teacher, and thus far she has not really been reported to have any special interests in school. She gets along well with "acting-out" peers but can be easily irritated by the conformers. Josie plans to complete high school only. She is interested in nursing as a vocation.

Medical Report

The physician requested that a thorough urological checkup be made. At age 8 Josie suffered severe kidney infection that required hospitalization. There have been recurrences of this problem. Josie also suffers from severe menstrual cramps and has blacked out on occasion.

Intake Evaluation and Treatment Recommendation

At the intake evaluation Josie appeared guarded, aloof, and evasive. As usual, her dress was exceptionally neat (her skirt pleated). She had taken pains to arrange her hair very neatly. Josie warmed up momentarily on hearing herself described as a very beautiful child. She appeared to respond better whenever she was gently encouraged to provide the information as she saw it. Her sum total seemed the same, but it was a matter of how the conclusions were reached. Josie disagreed with many of the statements that appeared in her court report.

The majority of the staff felt that the prognosis for Josie was poor. Josie's intake probation officer felt that Josie was "workable" through peer-group pressure. Mrs. Garcia, a staff person who had worked very closely with Mexicans in Mexico for eleven years, felt that Josie was innately very Mexican and could be worked with on a warm one-to-one basis and especially through peer pressure. She suggested that Josie be assigned to Mr. Lopez, a social worker on the staff, who was of similar ethnic background. Because of this ethnic factor it was felt that Mr. Lopez would have an advantage in hastening a therapeutic working relationship with Josie and at the same time provide her with a consistent, warm, parental-authority figure that she desperately needed. The staff agreed and assigned the case to Mr. Lopez.

Knowledge about a Specific Contact

The social worker, Mr. Lopez, carefully studied Josie's file and was prepared for their first meeting, sometimes referred to as the *initial interview*. From knowledge obtained through literature and practice, he knew the first interview was very important in establishing a beginning working relationship with the client. He knew girls like Josie harbored much anger toward authority figures, especially men, and frequently tried to challenge, manipulate, and test adults to see if they could make them lose their temper. Success in this regard would confirm their feelings that adults could not be trusted, which in turn would create more anxiety. Josie's history revealed assaultive behavior (fight) as well as running-away (flight) behavior. Mr. Lopez's knowledge of therapeutic skills would take these factors into account in order to provide Josie the opportunity to establish a relationship. He set aside a period of time ranging from fifteen minutes to one hour for Josie, the length of the session depending on the amount of anxiety, anger, or emotional needs Josie would express during the interview. Mr. Lopez called Josie's cottage and asked that she be sent over to visit him. The following is the actual interview (names disguised) as reported by Mr. Lopez:

> Josie knocked on the door and I asked her to come into my office. She avoided looking at me and plopped herself into a chair by my desk. After a few moments of silence, she glared at me.
>
> "I'm Mr. Lopez, your new probation officer."
>
> "I know," she said, "you're a 'long-term' probation officer and keep your girls here a long time."
>
> "In part that might be true," I said. "Sometimes the girls are ready to go home in five or six months, and some are not ready until thirteen or fourteen months. It depends on the girl and her family."
>
> "Well, I don't want to see my parents. I *hate* them! They're always fighting."
>
> I didn't say anything, as I felt she was trying to see how I would react to her not wanting to see her parents. Furthermore, it would have been premature for me to enter into this sensitive area without the necessary foundation of a good relationship with Josie. After another moment of silence, Josie became anxious and said:
>
> "Just *how* long do I have to stay in this fucking place?"
>
> "I don't know, Josie. A lot depends on how hard you try to help yourself."
>
> "What do you mean? Just be a kiss-ass in school and do everything *you* tell me?"

"No. For one thing, I noticed that you were very angry at your parents. At some point, when *you* think you are ready, *we'll* invite them for a conference to see what is going on between you and your parents."

"I never want to see them again!" Josie screamed.

She began to get angrier and glared at me. She grabbed an ashtray and said:

"I'm going to throw this at you, you bastard!"

I calmly told her that if she would strike me, she would be hurting me and herself because she would be in even more trouble, and she would probably be placed in a more confining institution—the state school. In a gentle, supportive manner, I then handed her a box of Kleenex and told her to throw it at the door. She put down the ashtray and hurled the box at the door very hard. She left her seat and picked it up again and threw it against the door several times while cussing. Tears began to run down her cheeks. She sat down, sobbing, with her face in her hands. I got another box of Kleenex from my desk and leaned over and offered her some to blow her nose. It was a tangible gesture of help.

"Josie," I said, in a soft empathetic voice, "I *know* this is very painful for you. But I think you've made a *great* start."

She looked at me rather puzzled and asked sarcastically why I thought it was a "*great* start." I told her that she had shown judgment and control by not hurting me or herself and that this gave me a lot of confidence in her emotional strength.

"It proved to me that when you want to, you can make the right decisions!"

She seemed more controlled, pensive, and had stopped crying.

"Can I go now?" she asked.

I said she could leave if she wanted to. She stood up, and as she was walking out she asked:

"When can I see you again?"

"Tomorrow, or the next day," I said, "or next week, or the week after that. Whenever you say, as long as it's never more than an hour a day. In other words, let's work *together* on these things whenever *you* feel you want to."

"Can I see you tomorrow?"

"Yes, at 11:00 A.M."

"Goodbye 'Long Term,' " she said, smiling as she walked toward her cottage.

This was a brief, but very intense, powerful interview. It was an *initial interview* with a purpose—establishing a beginning relationship with an angry adolescent female probationer. A knowledge base from numerous sources prepared the social worker for that one interview. Knowledge alone, without the *skill,* however, would have accomplished little. Mr. Lopez was a skilled social worker whose practice was guided by a solid knowledge base.

CONCLUDING COMMENT

The effective social worker must engage in knowledge-guided practice. He or she must be well versed in subjects related to helping people interact with the environment. The social worker's knowledge base includes knowledge of self, the profession, practice intervention modalities, and the behavior of individuals, families, groups, the community, and society. It seems impossible for a social worker to master all the knowledge that can apply to social work practice.

Because of this seeming impossibility, an ecosystems model, evolving from the contributions of several scholars over the years and further refined by the authors in this text, was presented as a way of organizing social work knowledge from a micro (individual, family, culture) to a macro level (environmental-structural, historical) perspective. A case example demonstrated application of the ecosystems model.

A further focusing of the knowledge base finds the social worker needing to know also about the specific practice setting, specific agency, the specific client within the context of the agency, and knowledge about a specific client contact.

Within this comprehensive knowledge-focused framework involving both the ecosystems model and the more specific practice–agency–client contact, a detailed case example concerning an institutionalized delinquent girl demonstrated how the knowledge was used in a treatment setting.

SUGGESTED READINGS

BAER, BETTY L., and FEDERICO, RONALD. *Educating the Baccalaureate Social Worker* vol. I. Boston: Ballinger, 1978, pp. 186–223.

BARTLETT, HARRIETT. *The Common Base of Social Work Practice.* New York: National Association of Social Workers, 1970.

DORE, MARTHA M. "Functional Theory: Its History and Influence on Contemporary Social Work Practice." *Social Service Review* 64 (September 1990): 358–374.

GOLDSTEIN, EDA G. "Knowledge Base of Clinical Social Work." *Social Work* 25 (May 1980): 173–177.

GRAY, NORMA; ALTERMAN, TONI; and LITMAN, ELLEN. "Women's Issues in Psychotherapy: Training for Mental Health Professionals." *Women and Therapy* 7 (1988): 101–111.

GREEN, JAMES W. *Cultural Awareness in the Human Services.* Englewood Cliffs, N.J.: Prentice-Hall, 1982.

JACOBS, CAROLYN, and BOWLES, DORCAS D., eds. *Ethnicity and Race: Critical Concepts in Social Work.* Silver Spring, Md.: National Association of Social Workers, 1988.

KAPLAN, HAROLD I., and SADOCK, BANJAMIN, J., eds. *Synopsis of Psychiatry* 5th ed. Baltimore: Williams and Wilkins, 1988.

KUMABE, KAZUYE T.; NISHIDA, CHIKAE; and EPWORTH, DEAN H. *Bridging Ethnocultural Diversity in Social Work and Health.* Honolulu: U. of Hawaii School of Social Work, 1985.

LUM, DOMAN. *Social Work Practice and People of Color.* Monterey, Calif.: Brooks/Cole, 1986.

REID, WILLIAM J. "Mapping the Knowledge Base of Social Work." *Social Work* 26 (March 1981): 124–132.

ENDNOTES

1. Harriett M. Bartlett, "Toward Clarification and Improvement of Social Work Practice," *Social Work* 3 (April 1958): 5–7.
2. *Webster's Third New International Dictionary* (Springfield, Mass.: G. & C. Merriam, 1966), p. 1252.
3. William E. Gordon, "Toward a Social Work Frame of Reference," *Journal of Education for Social Work* 1 (Fall 1965): 23.
4. Harriett M. Bartlett, "The Place and Use of Knowledge in Social Work Practice," *Social Work* 9 (July 1964): 36.
5. Alfred J. Kahn, "The Nature of Social Work Knowledge," in Cora Kasius, cd., *New Directions in Social Work* (New York: Harper, 1954), p. 195.
6. Harry L. Lurie, ed., *Encyclopedia of Social Work* 15th issue (New York: National Association of Social Workers, 1965), p. 757.
7. Mary E. Richmond, *Social Diagnosis* (New York: Free Press, 1965), pp. 375–377.
8. Ibid., p. 73.
9. Graeme J. Taylor, James D. A. Parker, and R. Michael Bagby, "A Preliminary Investigation of Alexithymia in Men with Psychoactive Substance Dependence," *American Journal of Psychiatry* 147 (September 1990): 1228–1230.
10. Robert Morris, ed., *Encyclopedia of Social Work* 16th issue (New York: National Association of Social Workers, 1971), p. 752. For further information, see also *The Milford Conference Reports: Social Casework, Generic and Specific* (New York: American Association of Social Workers, 1929).
11. Kahn, p. 196.
12. Ibid. For further information, see also *American Association of Schools of Social Work, Recommendations and Report of the Work of the Curriculum Committee January 1943–January 1944* (New York: The Association, 1944).
13. Walter A. Friedlander, *Introduction to Social Welfare* (New York: Prentice-Hall, 1955), p. 626.
14. Kahn, p. 197.
15. Copyright © 1962, National Association of Social Workers, Inc. Reprinted with permission from Harriett M. Bartlett, "Toward Clarification and Improvement of Social Work Practice," *Social Work* 3 (April 1958): 3–9. See also William E. Gordon, "A Critique of the Working Definition," *Social Work* 7 (October 1962): 3–13.
16. Bartlett, "Clarification of Social Work Practice," pp. 6–7.
17. Ibid.
18. Werner W. Boehm, "The Nature of Social Work," *Social Work* 3 (April 1958): 11.
19. Alfred Kadushin, "The Knowledge Base of Social Work," in Alfred J. Kahn, ed., *Issues in American Social Work* (New York: Columbia University Press, 1959), p. 39.
20. Ibid., p. 42.
21. Ibid.
22. Ibid., p. 43.
23. *Building Social Work Knowledge, Report of a Conference* (New York: National Association of Social Workers, 1964), p. vi.
24. Ibid., p. 111.
25. Ibid., p. 114.
26. Merlin Taber and Iris Shapiro, "Social Work and Its Knowledge Base: A Content Analysis of the Periodical Literature," *Social Work* 10 (October 1965): 106.
27. Mary Burns, "Paths to Knowledge: Some Prospects and Problems," *Journal of Education for Social Work* 1 (Spring 1965): 13.
28. Carol H. Meyer, *Social Work Practice: A Response to the Urban Crisis* (New York: Free Press, 1970), p. 27.

29. Armando Morales, "Social Work with Third World People," *Social Work* 26 (January 1981): 45–51.
30. Carol H. Meyer, "What Directions for Direct Practice?," *Social Work* 24 (July 1979): 271.
31. Urie Bronfenbrenner, "Toward an Experimental Ecology of Human Development," *American Psychologist* 32 (1977): 513–551.
32. Bonnie E. Carlson, "Causes and Maintenance of Domestic Violence: An Ecological Analysis," *Social Review* 58 (December 1984): 569–587.
33. Nick Vaca, "The Mexican-American in the Social Sciences," Part II, *El Grito* VI (Fall 1970): 17–51.
34. Franz G. Alexander and Sheldon V. Selesnick, *The History of Psychiatry* (New York: Harper & Row, 1966), pp. 7–14.
35. Herbert I. Kaplan and Benjamin J. Sadock, eds., *Comprehensive Textbook of Psychiatry* 4th ed. (Baltimore: Williams & Wilkins, 1985), p. 360.
36. Julia B. Rauch, "Gender as a Factor in Practice," *Social Work* 23 (September 1978).
37. Erik E. Erikson, *Childhood and Society* (New York: W. W. Norton, 1959).
38. William Ryan, *Blaming the Victim* (New York: Pantheon Books, 1971), p. 4.
39. Kadushin, p. 44.
40. Sol Rubin, "Loss and Curtailment of Rights," in Leon Radzinowicz and Marvin E. Wolfgang, eds., *Crime and Justice* vol. 3 (New York: Basic Books, 1971), p. 25.
41. Walter C. Reckless, "A New Theory of Delinquency and Crime," in Ruth Shonle Cavan, ed., *Readings in Juvenile Delinquency* (New York: Lippincott, 1969), p. 165.
42. Richard A. Cloward and Lloyd E. Ohlin, *Delinquency and Opportunity* (Glencoe, Ill.: Free Press, 1960).
43. *DSM III-R—Diagnostic and Statistical Manual of Mental Disorders* 3rd ed. (Washington, D.C.: American Psychiatric Association, 1987), p. 51. Reprinted with permission from the *Diagnostic and Statistical Manual of Mental Disorders,* Revised. Copyright 1987 American Psychiatric Association.
44. Ibid., pp. 53–57.
45. Ibid., pp. 344–346.
46. Max Siporin, "Marriage and Family Therapy in Social Work," *Social Casework* 61 (January 1980): 11–21.
47. Francis H. Scherz, "Family Services: Family Therapy," in Robert Morris, ed., *Encyclopedia of Social Work* 16th issue, vol. 1 (New York: National Association of Social Workers, 1971), p. 402.
48. Jay Haley, "Family Therapy," in Alfred M. Freedman, Harold I. Kaplan, and Benjamin J. Sadock, eds., *Comprehensive Textbook of Psychiatry II* 2nd ed. (Baltimore: Williams and Wilkins, 1975), p. 1883.
49. Scherz, p. 400.
50. Haley, p. 1883.
51. Benjamin J. Sadock, "Group Psychotherapy," *Comprehensive Textbook,* p. 1850.
52. Ibid., p. 1852.
53. Emanuel Tropp, "Social Group Work: The Developmental Approach," *Encyclopedia of Social Work,* p. 1251.
54. Helen Harris Perlman, "Social Casework," in Neil Gilbert and Harry Specht, eds., *Handbook of the Social Services* (Englewood Cliffs: Prentice-Hall, 1981), pp. 434–451.
55. Ibid., p. 441.
56. Wynetta Devore and Elfrieda G. Schlesinger, *Ethnic-Sensitive Social Work Practice* (St. Louis, Mo.: C. V. Mosby, 1981).
57. James W. Green, *Cultural Awareness in the Human Services* (Englewood Cliffs: N.J.: Prentice-Hall, 1982).
58. Mary Lou Politi Ziter, "Culturally Sensitive Treatment of Black Alcoholic Families," *Social Work* 32 (March–April 1987): 132.

59. Doman Lum, *Social Work Practice and People of Color* (Monterey, Calif.: Brooks/ Cole, 1986), p. 66.

60. Ibid., p. 3.

61. Max Siporin, *Introduction to Social Work Practice* (New York: Macmillan, 1975), pp. 193–194.

Listen
Encouragements
Improved Listening Skills
1) Content-what
2) feeling
Observe
Rogers
1) Be prepared to listen
2) start listening immediately
3) Listen for something you can use
4) Eliminate distractions to improve
your listening environment
5) Concentrate on the message
instead of judging the Speaker
6) Listen for main ideas, principles, concepts
7) Identify & Evaluate
reasoning
8) Listen between lines
9) Hear the Speaker out
10) Do not relax and

CHAPTER 8

The Value Base of Social Work

If clients are to be helped to resolve social problems or enhance their levels of social functioning, social workers must bring the best knowledge available to bear on the situation. Knowledge, however, must be applied within the context of a judgment about what is good, proper, just, and humane. In other words, the use of knowledge must be conditioned by value considerations. A vivid illustration is the fact that through sheer knowledge the United States has built a nuclear arsenal capable of destroying life in all parts of the world. Because of the belief that life itself is precious, however, restraint has been used in the deployment of these weapons.

Values are the essential tools for selecting knowledge that is consistent with our beliefs about what we should be doing and how we should be doing it. We might reduce the number of children on the AFDC rolls by sterilizing all recipients, but social work's value of protecting individual choice prohibits such action. We could reduce homelessness by forcing homeless people into hospitals or prisons, but that is contrary to social work's commitment to helping people develop the ability to help themselves. We could perhaps even reduce the spread of AIDS by publishing the names of known AIDS carriers who use human services, but that would violate the social worker's commitment to protecting the confidential nature of information gained in helping relationships. The social worker, then, engages in value-guided as well as knowledge-guided practice.

THE NATURE OF VALUES

Unlike knowledge, which explains what is, values express what ought to be. Rokeach more precisely defines values as "a type of belief, centrally located in one's total belief system, about how one ought or ought not to behave, or about some end-state of existence worth or not worth attaining."[1] In short, values guide our thinking about how we should behave and what we want to accomplish.

Values, however, are much more than emotional reactions to situations or doing what feels right. Values are the fundamental criteria that lead us to thoughtful decisions. There is growing evidence that in most cases people act on the basis of their values. Kahle and Timmer thoroughly reviewed the research on the relationship between values and action and concluded that "both laboratory and survey studies have shown that values do indeed lead to commensurate behaviors."[2]

It is important to recognize that people do not always behave in a manner consistent with their values. Values guide decisions but do not dictate choices. People can and do make decisions contrary to their values. Such decisions might be made when other factors are given priority ("I know that I shouldn't have done that, but when will I ever get another chance like that?"), the person acts on emotion ("I was just so angry I hit her without thinking"), or when one fails to adequately think through and understand the value issues in a situation ("It just didn't occur to me that my quitting school would make my parents think that they have failed").

At other times a person may be forced to choose among values that are in conflict with one another. Who can avoid wrestling with a *value conflict* when confronted by a person on the street asking for a dollar to buy something to eat? We may value responding to people in need, but we may equally value encouraging people to use the organized system for receiving financial assistance that does not put the person into the degrading position of panhandling. The resultant decision represents a *value choice.*

Each person values a variety of things in life. Differences in the strength with which one holds any particular value and the priority a particular value will have among the whole constellation of that person's values, that is, the person's *value system,* is a part of what makes individuals unique. For example, for many people the most important value is feeling secure in their relationships with loved ones. For some, generating income is the driving force in their lives. For others, giving service or maintaining relationships dominates their value system. Still others attempt to maintain some balance among these values.

Dealing with values is particularly difficult for at least three reasons. First, values are such a central part of each person's thought processes that we often are not consciously aware of them and therefore are unable to identify their influence on our decisions. The social worker should constantly be alert to values in practice situations as these values may subtly influence the thoughts, feelings, attitudes, and behaviors of both the clients and the social worker.

Second, addressing values in the abstract may be quite different from approaching them in a real-life situation. Having the ability to identify and resolve value conflicts is an important skill for every person. We may feel that we have a pretty good understanding of the priorities in our own value system only to find that when applied to the realities of a series of actual events, these priorities are altered. Similarly, the social worker must recognize that clients may not act on the basis of value choices made in an interview when they are confronted with the unique situations that arise in the course of their daily lives.

Finally, values are problematic because of their dynamic quality. Priorities in our value system and the intensity with which we may hold a particular value can change over time. When we do not accomplish what we value, we can change our values or change our behaviors. In fact, we do both. Thus, various events, experiences, and even new information can lead us to adapt our system of values to more closely fit our reality.

THE PLACE OF VALUES IN SOCIAL WORK

Helping people to be clear about their individual values, that is, *values clarification,* and facilitating their understanding of how the particular set of values they hold influences their goals and decisions, is an important aspect of social work practice. At times clients also must be assisted in recognizing and understanding the values of others. Taking into consideration the values of family members, friends, employers, teachers, or others in that person's environment may be prerequisite to making appropriate and workable decisions. The matter becomes more complicated when social work practice involves more than one person, as it is likely that each will have a somewhat different value system. In that case the social worker may need to help resolve issues that stem from differences in values.

Further, the social worker must be concerned with his or her own values and control for their inappropriate intrusion into practice situations. Value choices that may be viable personally for the social worker may not coincide with the needs, wants, priorities, or realities the client experiences. Ultimately, the client must live with the decisions that are made, and they should be consistent with his or her own value system—not the value system of the social worker. Learning to suspend one's own values (i.e., *value suspension*) to keep the focus of helping on the client or client group is an important, yet difficult task for every social worker.

People are attracted to particular helping professions because they perceive that the work they do will be consistent with their personal values, and therefore the job will be satisfying. The way a profession views its role in society, the client groups it serves, the knowledge it selects as the basis for its practice, its requirements for ethical practice behavior, and so forth are all influenced by the profession's values. It is evident that a profession's values exert a significant influence on professional practice, and the person considering a career in any helping profession should carefully examine the value base of that profession.

Agency values and the values of the larger society also affect social work practice. Since professions receive their sanction from the society in general and their communities in particular, professions are constrained from too much departure from the values held by the general public. The result is an inherent conservatism or pressure toward maintenance of the existing structure.

With social work practice focused at the interface between person and environment, the social worker must be aware of several sets of values at the same time. This awareness should center on the client's values, but the social worker must also attend to the values of the social work profession, the employing agency, the community, and the larger society. Frankel identifies the complexity the social worker faces when attempting to be sensitive to the several sets of values that may influence a practice situation as follows:

> Undoubtedly, the tension between community sentiments and professional values is particularly acute in social work. The nature of the profession itself is such that the choices the professional worker must make between his professional values and the broader social values are more difficult and ambiguous. Social work's purpose is to guide and reinforce people's efforts to find and use their own powers. Unlike law or medicine, the social worker does not do the job for his client. In the end, the purpose is that the client should do the job. Thus, as a professional, the social worker has to make a special effort to enter into the perspectives and values of the nonprofessional.[3]

It is no wonder that social work has perhaps devoted more attention to values than has any other helping profession. McPheeters and Ryan criticize other human service professions for having given limited attention to the whole matter of values and attitudes, on the assumption that they are "value-free" professions—when, in fact, every behavior is influenced by some value orientation.[4] Although social work has not developed a sufficiently clear and adequately tested statement of its core values, it has been consistent throughout its development that values constitute a central dimension of practice. As early as the 1920s, for example, a series of meetings (the Milford Conference) were held in an effort to identify the commonalities in social work practice. The report of these meetings concluded that a philosophy of practice is required for the social worker and that there must be continued effort to identify and clarify the important value issues.[5]

SOCIAL VALUES IN AMERICAN SOCIETY

Values differ from needs. The latter refers to the basic biological or psychological urges of people, while values reflect what people want to get out of life and how this should be accomplished. Chapter 4, "Understanding the Social Welfare Institution," identified basic human needs, that is, survival, safety, belongingness, esteem, and self-actualization, and indicated that social institutions are fostered to help people meet these needs. The choice of what needs a society will attempt to meet depends on what it values. Thus, as a society's values change through time, so will the social needs it attempts to meet.

Clough suggests the single most uniform characteristic of all cultures is that they have basic values about what the "people want to get out of life, such as entry into heaven, freedom from want, the achieving of some masterpiece, control over their physical environment, and harmony in relation with their fellow beings."[6] He notes that the most predominant feature of Western society is the central place of the individual; that is, the society exists to help individuals lead satisfying and productive lives. The individual is the "masterpiece" of Western culture.

Like other parts of Western culture, the values that guide choices in U.S. society also center on the individual. The dominant social values in the United States have their roots in at least four different sources, all of which are concerned with the responsibilities of the individual toward self and society and/or the society's responsibility to the individual:

1. The Judeo-Christian doctrine with its concept of the integral worth of humans and their responsibilities for their neighbors;
2. The democratic ideals that emphasize the equality of all people and a person's right to "life, liberty, and the pursuit of happiness";
3. The Puritan ethic, which says that character is all, circumstances nothing, that the moral person is the one who works and is independent, and that pleasure is sinful;
4. The tenets of Social Darwinism, which emphasize that the fittest survive and the weak perish in a natural evolutionary process that produces the strong individual and society.[7]

It is evident that much of the disagreement in the United States over the provision of human services results from value conflicts inherent in the U.S. public's value system. Brill points out:

> Even the casual reader will see that a dichotomy exists within this value system. We hold that all men are equal, but he who does not work is less equal. . . . We hold that the individual life has worth, but that only the fit should survive. We believe that we are responsible for each other, but he who is dependent upon another for his living is of lesser worth.[8]

In carrying out the commitments of the social welfare institution to respond to human needs, the social worker becomes an intermediary between people in need and society's value judgments about what needs are to be met. As one cynic phrased it, the social worker stands "between the demanding recipient and the grudging donor." Therefore, the social worker must be particularly knowledgeable about the values that are dominant in U.S. society.

What is the constellation of values held by the U.S. population? Recognizing the importance of values, one is surprised that relatively little solid research has been conducted to determine the dominant values held by the U.S. public. A study that begins to remedy this problem is *Social Values and Social Change: Adaptation to Life in America,*[9] which drew on interviews with a carefully selected sample of noninstitutionalized adults selected from throughout the forty-eight contiguous states. This study asked 2264 respondents to judge which was the *most important* among eight fundamental values commonly held by the people of the United States. Recognizing the limitations of any attempt to represent the viewpoint of a nation based on a small sample of its population, one nevertheless finds it instructive to note the percentage of respondents who rated the following values as most important in their lives:

21.1%   *Self-respect:* looking within oneself for satisfaction in regard to achieving goals or taking pride in having done the "honorable or just thing."*

20.6%   *Security:* achieving a sense of freedom from danger or risk, i.e., achieving economic and existential security or feeling personally safe about being able to live comfortably in the future.

16.2%   *Warm relationships with others:* appreciating the significance of friendships or companionship in one's life. This value reflects more than just sociability; it also represents the importance of establishing and maintaining nurturing relationships.

11.4%   *Sense of accomplishment:* believing that the activities one sets out to complete are successfully done. The emphasis in this value is on the person feeling successful.

9.6%   *Self-fulfillment:* feeling that the accomplishments in one's life are personally satisfying or rewarding—that one's efforts are worthwhile. The person selecting this value feels good about what he or she has done or is doing.

8.8%   *Being well respected:* having others admire the manner in which a person acts or the status one has achieved. The well respected person is held in high esteem and looked up to by others.

7.9%   *Sense of belonging:* satisfying the need to be personally accepted by others and become a meaningful part of a group or collection of people. The person gains support from the group.

4.5%   *Fun-enjoyment-excitement:* wishing for an exciting, stimulating, active life that includes enjoyable and pleasurable activities.

When one is taking a global view of the most important values of the U.S. public, it is evident that the individual or personal orientation of Western culture also dominates the fundamental attitudes about what their goals in life should be and how these goals should be accomplished. The two values viewed as most important by the people interviewed in this study reflect the desire to feel good about oneself and feel personally secure for the future. These values reflect the self-oriented priorities in U.S. society. The interpersonal-oriented values, that is, warm relationships, being well respected, and having a sense of belonging, were rated as most important by less than one-third of the respondents.

---

* The descriptions of the individual values were not reported in the study. The authors of this book derived these statements from information reported in the study design and analysis of responses. The statements are included to give the reader a general understanding of intended meaning of each value item.

Although social workers provide a number of services that can help people accomplish self-oriented goals and are responsible for the delivery of social provisions that help people attain at least minimal levels of security, social workers' primary work centers on interpersonal behaviors. The value system of the U.S. public evident from these data perhaps helps one to understand the low priority given to many human service programs.

DOMINANT VALUES IN SELECTED POPULATION GROUPS

Since people vary in the values they consider most important, it is useful to identify value differences associated with various population groups—particularly those that are frequently the recipients of human services. Drawn from data reported in *Social Values and Social Change,* the value responses of selected population groups are summarized. The subtitle of the study, "Adaptation to Life in America," reveals an important point to recognize when one is drawing conclusions from these data. People adapt their value preferences to fit the reality of their lives. They do not place high priority on values they do not think they can realize.[10]

To highlight areas where a particular segment of the population reflected somewhat different value preferences from the total group of respondents, Tables 8–1 through 8–5 were prepared. When a particular category of respondent differed from the total by 15 percent or more (or 20 percent or more in the case of age) a plus (+) or minus (−) was recorded on the table indicating whether the respondents in that category were substantially above or below the norm.

Gender

As Table 8–1 indicates, men and women were similar in their selection of values regarding self-respect, security, self-fulfillment, and being respected. The differences confirmed the popular viewpoint that men tend to be more self-oriented and women more other-oriented. Women substantially exceed men in selecting warm relationships with others (18.5 percent to 13.1 percent) and sense of belonging (9.6 percent to 5.6 percent) as the most important values. Men, on the other hand, identified a sense of accomplishment or success (14.3 percent to 9.2 percent) and fun/enjoyment/excitement (6.9 percent to 2.7 percent) as the dominant value in their lives more frequently than women. Using warm relationships and sense of belonging to reflect interpersonal values, women exceed men 28.1 percent to 18.7 percent. At the same time, more than twice as many men as women selected the self-oriented values of accomplishment and fun/enjoyment/ excitement (23.9 percent to 11.9 percent).[11]

The influence that having a family has on a person's outlook is revealed by examining the responses of those who had children. Men with children tended to differ from those without children in several areas. Those with children placed

TABLE 8–1   *Primary Values (15 Percent or More from Average) by Gender*

	MALE	FEMALE
Self-respect		
Security		
Warm relationships with others	−	+
Sense of accomplishment	+	−
Self-fulfillment		
Being well respected		
Sense of belonging	−	+
Fun/excitement/enjoyment	+	−

Source: Susan Goff Timmer and Lynn R. Kahle, "Birthright Demographic Correlates of Values," in *Social Values and Social Change: Adaptation to Life in America,* Lynn R. Kahle, ed., (Praeger Publishers, New York, a division of Greenwood Press, Inc., 1983). Copyright © 1983 by Praeger Publishers. Used with permission.

the values of self-respect and security considerably higher than those without, while the latter group emphasized warm relationships with friends, self-fulfillment, and fun/enjoyment/excitement to a much greater degree. Similarly, women with children tended to value self-respect, security, and being well respected more than their counterparts who did not have children. Women without children gave much greater emphasis to the values of accomplishment, self-fulfillment, and fun/enjoyment/excitement than those who did have children.[12]

Age

The data suggest there is considerable similarity among men and women in various age groups. Table 8–2 represents the comparative data on three selected age groups: the youngest, oldest, and one middle-aged group. When compared to the norms of all persons of their sex, the middle-aged women differed from the men in that age group only in placing higher value on security and lower value on accomplishment. Older women were also less inclined to look for fun/enjoyment/excitement from life. Older men differed from older women by placing less value on warm relationships and having a sense of belonging but placed greater value on being respected. With these six exceptions, men and women in the three selected age groups deviated from overall average of their genders in exactly the same way.

Examination of the data for all age groups reveals that until a person reaches the late-20s or early-30s, self-respect and security do not take the dominant place in one's value system that they do later on. For both young adult males and

TABLE 8–2   *Primary Values (20 Percent or More from Average) by Age and Gender*

	Young Adult (21–24)	Middle Age (45–49)	Older (70 & Over)
Self-respect	−	+	
Security	−	+ (f)	+
Warm relationships with others	+		− (m)
Sense of accomplishment	+	− (f)	−
Self-fulfillment	+	−	−
Being well respected	−		+ (m)
Sense of belonging	−		− (m)
Fun/excitement/enjoyment	+	−	− (f)

Note: the designation for females (f) and males (m) identifies values where only persons of that gender deviated from the norm.

Source: Susan Goff Timmer and Lynn R. Kahle, "Birthright Demographic Correlates of Values," in *Social Values and Social Change: Adaptation to Life in America*, Lynn R. Kahle, ed., (Praeger Publishers, New York, a division of Greenwood Press, Inc., 1983). Copyright © 1983 by Praeger Publishers. Used with permission.

females, warm relationships with friends, a sense of accomplishment, self-fulfill-ment, and fun/enjoyment/excitement are the dominant values. The substantial differences in this young adult group from the total population are seen in the fact that they differ substantially from the norm on every value. To reflect the extent of this difference, it is instructive to analyze the two most dominant values: self-respect and security. For the sample as a whole, 41.3 percent of all women and 42.2 percent of the men selected one of these values as the most important. For the young adults, only 23.5 percent of the women and 20.6 percent of the men chose one of these as most important in their lives.[13]

For the 45 to 49 age group the importance of warm relationships with friends and companions, as well as giving priority to fun/enjoyment/excitement, was substantially lower than for the young adults. Achieving self-respect and security (for women) were much more prominent in their value systems. Achieving self-respect was identified as the most important value for 31.5 percent of the men and 32.6 percent of the women in this age group, compared to 21.7 percent and 20.6 percent, respectively, for the total population. For women in this age group achieving a sense of security was valued highly. More than one-fourth (26.1 percent) of the middle-aged women identified security as their number 1 value, while only one-fifth of all women considered this the most important.

For respondents age 70 and over, the desire for security, warm relationships with others, and being respected dominate the responses. The responses from those persons in the sample who were retired were similar. Nearly 65 percent of the retired persons in the sample listed one of these three values as most important to them.[14]

Race and Ethnicity

Some value differences existed among white, black, and Hispanic respondents. Due to the predominance of white people in the United States and, therefore, in the sample, one would not expect that Table 8–3 would reflect areas where the white respondents were substantially different from the total sample. White and black respondents were similar in their selection of self-respect as their most important value (21.1 percent and 21.3 percent, respectively), but only 16.3 percent of the Hispanic respondents identified this as the most important value. At the same time a much higher percentage of Hispanic respondents (14.3 percent) selected being respected by others than did the white (8.5 percent) or black (10.2 percent) persons who were interviewed.[16]

Perhaps the most dramatic and telling difference among any population groups in the study is in the value placed on security by minority group members. The white respondents selected this value as their first priority 18.8 percent of the time, while the black and Hispanic persons interviewed chose security as the most important value 33.6 percent and 30.6 percent, respectively. Kahle concludes that "black and Hispanic respondents worry far more about basic security than do their white counterparts." It is also of note that black and Hispanic respondents were considerably less likely than whites to value self-fulfillment (5.3 percent and 6.1 percent compared to 10.2 percent) and a sense of belonging (4.5 percent and 4.1 percent compared to 8.5 percent).[17] The effects of discrimination would appear to be reflected in these differences. Life is more insecure for blacks and Hispanics, and they often do not feel they are fully accepted into dominant society and therefore lack a sense of belonging. Their value preferences are adapted to that reality.

TABLE 8–3   *Primary Values (15 Percent or More from Average) by Race and Ethnicity*

	WHITE	BLACK	HISPANIC
Self-respect			−
Security		+	+
Warm relationships with others		−	
Sense of accomplishment			−
Self-fulfillment		−	−
Being well respected			+
Sense of belonging		−	−
Fun/excitement/enjoyment		−	

Source: Susan Goff Timmer and Lynn R. Kahle, "Birthright Demographic Correlates of Values," in *Social Values and Social Change: Adaptation to Life in America*, Lynn R. Kahle, ed., (Praeger Publishers, New York, a division of Greenwood Press, Inc., 1983). Copyright © 1983 by Praeger Publishers. Used with permission.

TABLE 8–4 *Primary Values (15 Percent or More from Average) by Educational Level*

	GRADE SCHOOL	HIGH SCHOOL	COLLEGE
Self-respect			
Security	+		−
Warm relationships with others			
Sense of accomplishment	−		+
Self-fulfillment	−		+
Being well respected	+		−
Sense of belonging	−	+	−
Fun/excitement/enjoyment			+

Source: Susan Goff Timmer and Lynn R. Kahle, "Ascribed and Attained Demographic Correlates of Values," in *Social Values and Social Change: Adaptation to Life in America,* Lynn R. Kahle, ed., (Praeger Publishers, New York, a division of Greenwood Press, Inc., 1983). Copyright © 1983 by Praeger Publishers. Used with permission.

Educational Level

Educational level, too, appears to affect one's value system. In Table 8–4 it is evident that persons with a grade school education are most concerned with security and being respected by others. More than 45 percent of the respondents at this level selected one of these two values as most important to them. Persons with a high school education were similar to the total group in all values except sense of belonging, which 11 percent considered the most important, compared to 6.8 percent of the grade school and 4 percent of the college graduates. The college educated respondents reflected considerably less concern with security (15.0 percent), being well respected (2.9 percent), and having a sense of belonging. College-educated persons exceeded the other groups in their value of a sense of accomplishment (15.7 percent), self-fulfillment (15.2 percent), and their desire for fun/enjoyment/excitement (5.7 percent).[18]

Income Level

While income is associated with gender, age, race or ethnicity, and educational level, the data from this study reflect some rather clear value differences among the low-, middle-, and upper-income groups. As Table 8–5 indicates, people at the lowest end of the income scale were much more likely to value security (26.7 percent) than those in the middle-income group selected for analysis and those in the highest-income group. They also placed substantially more emphasis on being well respected by others (16.2 percent). The respondents from the

TABLE 8–5 *Primary Values (15 Percent or More from Average) by Income Level*

	LOWEST	MIDDLE	HIGHEST
Self-respect		−	+
Security	+		
Warm relationships with others		+	−
Sense of accomplishment	−		+
Self-fulfillment	−		
Being well respected	+		−
Sense of belonging	−		
Fun/excitement/enjoyment			

Source: Susan Goff Timmer and Lynn R. Kahle, "Ascribed and Attained Demographic Correlates of Values" in *Social Values and Social Change: Adaptation to Life in America,* Lynn R. Kahle, ed., (Praeger Publishers, New York, a division of Greenwood Press, Inc., 1983). Copyright © 1983 by Praeger Publishers. Used with permission.

middle-income group placed greater priority on having a sense of belonging to a group. The highest-income group considered their own self-respect and experiencing a sense of accomplishment their most important values, while having warm friendships and being respected were of lesser importance.[19]

It is evident from the above data that people differ in their values, and these differences are affected by one's experience in society. Depending on where one is in the life cycle, whether he or she is employed, or even if one has children, for example, the priorities among values differ. Victims of the "isms," for example, ageism, sexism, or racism, reflect a particularly significant difference in values from the parts of the society that do not experience this discrimination. Those most likely to experience discrimination consistently place higher value on having security in their lives. When the members of a society fail to adequately protect against their fears about the future, these groups turn to a greater degree to intrapersonal values such as gaining respect from others, belonging, and having warm relationships with friends and companions.

Professionals

One final population group analyzed in Kahle's study of values is of interest to the social worker. The data make it clear that there are distinct differences in values among different groups of occupations. The professional category (see Table 8–6), which includes social work as well as other professions, valued security, being well respected, and experiencing a sense of belonging much less than did other groups. At the same time, they were substantially more likely to indicate that having a sense of accomplishment and fulfillment were the things

TABLE 8–6   *Primary Values of Professionals and Total Sample*

	Professionals	Total Sample
Self-respect	24.9%	21.1%
Security	11.8	20.6
Warm relationships with others	17.1	16.2
Sense of accomplishment	18.4	11.4
Self-fulfillment	16.7	9.6
Being well respected	2.9	8.8
Sense of belonging	4.5	7.9
Fun/excitement/enjoyment	3.7	4.5

Source: Susan Goff Timmer and Lynn R. Kahle, "Ascribed and Attained Demographic Correlates of Values" in *Social Values and Social Change: Adaptation to Life in America*, Lynn R. Kahle, ed., (Praeger Publishers, New York, a division of Greenwood Press, Inc., 1983). Copyright © 1983 by Praeger Publishers. Used with permission.

they valued most.[20] The data support the inference that professionals consider achieving personal satisfaction from their work the central feature in their experience, and that status issues such as income, being respected, and sensing acceptance from a group are of lesser importance.

VALUES HELD BY SOCIAL WORKERS

We have seen that the social worker must relate to the values of both the client or client group and the society. In order to avoid imposing personal values on the client or making inappropriate judgments about a client's values, the social worker must have a clear understanding of his or her own personal values. In addition the social worker must be fully aware of, and guided by, the fundamental values of the social work profession.

What, then, are the values commonly held by social workers? The International Federation of Social Workers, an organization comprising fifty-six professional membership associations including the National Association of Social Workers (NASW), has devoted considerable effort to identifying values and ethical behaviors appropriate for all social workers. Although social work is significantly affected by the culture in which its practice occurs, the International Federation of Social Workers has been successful at transcending the cultural differences of the many nations to develop a code of ethical behavior applicable to the whole of social work practice. The preamble of that Code concisely summarizes the most fundamental values of this profession:

Social work originates from humanitarian ideals and democratic philosophy and has universal application to meet human needs arising from personal-societal interactions and to develop human potential. Professional social workers are dedicated to service for the welfare and self-realization of human beings; to the disciplined use of scientific knowledge regarding human and societal behavior; to the development of resources to meet individual, group, national and international needs and aspirations; and to the achievement of social justice.[21]

As a part of NASW's effort to establish a classification scheme for the different practice levels (see Chapter 3, "Entry to the Social Work Profession"), the committee developing this scheme found it useful to identify the basic values that are central to social work practice at any level. As a result ten values were identified in the guidelines for the classification of social work practice.[22] When this report was adopted by the board of directors, the following values statements became an NASW-sanctioned expression of the basic U.S. social work values:

1. *Commitment to the primary importance of the individual in society.* In this value statement social work reaffirms its commitment to the most basic cultural value in Western society—the primacy of the individual. Social work accepts the position that the individual is the center of practice and that every person is of inherent worth because of his or her humanness. Sheafor, Horejsi, and Horejsi, for example, contend that "the primary activity of the social worker is to help people change; it is not intended to punish or condemn. Therefore, it is necessary to accept clients as valued people simply because of their humanity and to avoid making judgments of worth based on personal or dominant societal values."[23] The social worker need not approve of what a person does but must value that person as an important member of society. Each client should be treated with dignity.

Commitment to the centrality of the individual has also led social workers to recognize that each person is unique and that practice activities must be tailored to that person's or group's uniqueness. Such individualization permits the worker to determine where and how to intervene in each helping situation, while at the same time communicating respect for the people being served.

2. *Commitment to social change to meet socially recognized needs.* Giving primacy to the individual does not minimize the commitment of the social worker to achieve social change. Rather, it suggests that the social worker recognizes that the outcome of change activities in the larger society must ultimately benefit individuals.

As discussed in Chapter 4, social work evolved as the primary profession responsible for helping society fulfill its commitment to meet the social needs of people, that is, to operationalize the social welfare institution. The obligation of social work is not only to deliver social provisions and social services to people in need, but also value serving as instruments of social change as a means of allowing each person to realize his or her fullest potential.

Social workers, then, are committed to the belief that the society has a responsibility to provide resources and services to help people avoid such problems as hunger, insufficient education, discrimination, illness without care, and inadequate housing. While social workers accept the primacy of the individual, they also hold the society responsible for meeting social needs. Social workers serve both the person and the environment in responding to social needs.

3. *Commitment to social justice and the economic, physical, and mental well-being of all in society.* The obligation of social workers is to attempt to improve the quality of all people's lives. Social workers believe that social justice must be achieved if each person is to have the opportunity to develop his or her unique potential and, therefore, make his or her maximum contribution to society. Thus, social workers believe that each person should have the right to participate in molding the social institutions and the decision-making processes in U.S. society so that the programs, policies, and procedures are responsive to the needs and conditions of all.

Of course, when needs are competing in a diverse society and when resources are limited, choices must be made. Not every person can have all needs met. When they are making choices, the values held by social workers emphasize the importance of responding to the needs of the most vulnerable members of the society. Typically, these vulnerable people are children, the aged, minority group members, the handicapped, women, and others who have been victims of institutionalized discrimination. Social workers are committed to assuring that social justice is achieved for these persons, individually and as a population group.

4. *Respect and appreciation for individual and group differences.* Social workers recognize that there are common needs, goals, aspirations, and wants that are held by all people. In some ways we are all alike. However, social workers also recognize that in other ways each individual's life experience and capacities make him or her different from others. Where some may fear differences or resist working with people who are not like themselves, social workers value and respect uniqueness. They believe that the quality of life is enriched by different cultural patterns, different beliefs, and different forms of activity. As opposed to efforts to assimilate persons who are in some way different from the general population, social workers value a pluralistic society that can accommodate a range of beliefs, behaviors, languages, and customs.

The title of this book, *Social Work: A Profession of Many Faces,* is intended to suggest that social work not only includes people of many backgrounds performing a wide variety of human services but that social workers also provide services to people from virtually all backgrounds and walks of life. The chapters in Part Four, "Special Populations and Concerns in Social Work," elaborate on some of these differences and their impact on social work practice.

5. *Commitment to developing clients' ability to help themselves.* If clients are to change their social conditions, their actions that contributed to the conditions must ultimately change. Unlike medicine, where an injection may solve a patient's problem, social change requires that the people affected become personally engaged in the change process and actively work to create the desired change. Underpinning social work practice, then, must be the social worker's

belief that each person has an inherent capacity and drive that can result in desirable change.

Social workers do not view people as static or unchanging, nor is anyone assumed to be unable to engage in activities that may produce a more satisfying and rewarding life. Rather, social workers view people as adaptable. Although there are conditions that some people face that cannot be changed, the people themselves or the world around them can be helped to adapt to these conditions. For example, the terminally ill patient cannot be made well, the blind child cannot be made to see, and the severely retarded person cannot be made self-sustaining. Yet in each case the person involved can be helped to adjust to these conditions, and the person's environment can be adapted to more adequately accommodate special needs. Within the individual's or group's capacities, the social worker places high value on helping people take responsibility for their own decisions and actions.

6. *Willingness to transmit knowledge and skills to others.* Since the social worker cannot change the client, perhaps the most important function performed by the social worker in helping clients accomplish the change they desire is to effectively guide the change process. A significant part of this guidance involves helping clients understand the situation they experience from both a personal perspective and the perspectives of others, as well as helping them develop the skills to resolve their problems.

Effective helping avoids making clients dependent on the helpers and prepares them to address other issues that arise in their lives. Thus, it is important that social workers assist clients to identify their strengths that can be mobilized for solving the immediate problem and to help them learn how to use these strengths in solving problems that may arise in the future.

A second application of this value concerns the commitment of professionals to share knowledge with colleagues. Knowledge or skills developed by a social worker are not to be kept secret or limited to clients who work only with that social worker. Rather, the social worker is obligated to transmit this information to other social workers so that they might bring the best knowledge and skill possible to their clients.

7. *Willingness to keep personal feelings and needs separate from professional relationships.* It is important for the social worker to recognize that the focus of practice must be maintained on the client—not the social worker. Because social workers care about the people they work with, it is easy to become overidentified with clients' lives or even to develop personal relationships with them. If that happens, the client loses the benefit of an objective helper, the social worker can be placed in a compromising position, and the quality of the helping process is diminished because the relationship has changed from professional to personal.

As opposed to the many personal relationships that each person has throughout life, professional relationships require that a degree of professional objectivity be maintained. If a social worker becomes too closely identified with a client, the ability to stand back from the situation and view it from a neutral position is minimized. Sheafor, Horejsi, and Horejsi identify the importance of maintaining an appropriate degree of personal distance from clients:

> By the time most clients come into contact with a professional helper, they have usually attempted to resolve the situation themselves—by either personally working through the situation or getting assistance from family, friends, or other natural helpers. Often, these helping efforts are thwarted by high levels of emotion that preclude clear understanding and response to the situation. As opposed to the natural helper, the professional adds a new dimension to the client or client group by operating with a degree of emotional neutrality.

> Maintaining this neutrality without appearing unconcerned or uncaring is a delicate balancing act for the social worker. The worker who becomes too identified with the client's situation can lose perspective and objectivity.[24]

8. *Respect for the confidentiality of relationship with clients.* Although it is rare that the social worker can guarantee "absolute confidentiality" to a client, social work values achieving the maximum possible protection of information received in working with clients. The very nature of a helping relationship suggests that there is sensitive information that must be shared between the person being helped and the helper. For example, the social worker must learn the reasons a client has been fired from a job, why a developmentally disabled patient has failed in a community group home placement, what keeps a homeless person from being able to secure resources to pay rent, why an alcoholic has not been able to stop drinking, or the reasons a couple involved in marriage counseling has not been able to solve problems without fighting, and the like. In each case, some information typically passes between client and worker that could potentially be emotionally or economically damaging if it is inappropriately revealed to other parties. Social workers consider it of critical importance to respect the privacy of this communication.

9. *Willingness to persist in efforts on behalf of clients despite frustration.* The situations that require social work intervention typically do not develop quickly and usually cannot be resolved readily. Recognizing the frustration that social workers experience when change is slow to occur, they have come to value tenacity in addressing both individual problems and the problems that affect groups of people, organizations, communities, and the society in general.

When providing direct services, a social worker may become frustrated with a client who at a given time is unable or unwilling to engage in activities the social worker believes would improve the situation. Or, when advocating on behalf of a client with another agency to provide needed services, the social worker may also experience frustration when the client is denied service or is placed on a waiting list. Advocacy for classes of clients or in relation to broad social issues can also prove quite frustrating. If delay tactics or the length of the change process is extended, the social worker may understandably become discouraged. Social workers must be persistent.

10. *Commitment to a high standard of personal and professional conduct.*
The final value on the NASW list directs the worker to use the highest ethical
standards in his or her practice. It suggests that the worker must conduct professional activities in a manner that protects the interests of the public, the agency,
the clients, and the social worker.

This value has been operationalized in the form of the social work Code of
Ethics, which is perhaps the single most important unifying element among social
workers. Loewenberg and Dolgoff identify the following four functions served
by the Code of Ethics:

1. Provide practitioners with guidance when faced by practice dilemmas that
   include ethical issues
2. Provide clients and prospective clients who have no way of assessing a professional's integrity and competence with protection against incompetence and
   charlatanism
3. Regulate the behavior of practitioners and their relations with clients, colleagues, practitioners from other professions, employer (if employed), and the
   community
4. Provide supervisors, consultants, and other professionals with a basis for ap-
   praising and evaluating practitioner activities.[25]

To join NASW, the social worker must sign a statement agreeing to abide by
the ethical standards contained in the Code of Ethics. Negative sanctions against
a member may be applied if the code is violated. To protect against misuse of
negative sanctions, NASW has created an elaborate procedure for hearing grievances, at both the local or chapter and national levels. The following are examples
of three cases in which, after completing extensive review procedures, the NASW
Board imposed sanctions for breaking the Code of Ethics:

> (Worker X was) found to have violated three sections of the code by exploiting
> relationships with clients for personal advantage, engaging in relationships with
> clients that conflicted with their interests and making sexual overtures to clients.

> (Worker Y was) found to have violated code provisions that prohibit misrepre-
> sentation, call for professional discretion and impartiality, bar exploitation of
> relationships with clients for personal advantage, and prohibit relationships with
> clients that conflict with their interests.

> (Worker Z [incarcerated in prison for a criminal offense] was) found to have
> violated the sections of the code that call for high standards of personal conduct,
> professional integrity and impartiality, and protection and enhancement of dig-
> nity and integrity of the profession.[26]

It is evident that social work does not take its Code of Ethics lightly. Every
social worker should be thoroughly familiar with its contents (See Box 8–1 at
the end of this chapter). It is not only the basis on which negative sanctions
might be imposed against a social worker by NASW, but more importantly, it
provides a very helpful guide to practice that protects the interests of clients,
agencies, the profession, and the communities in which social workers practice.

VALUES AND ETHICS IN SOCIAL WORK PRACTICE

How do values and ethics express themselves in the day-to-day practice of the social worker? R. Huws Jones, a prominent British social work educator, once stated that, "A man's values are like his kidneys; he rarely knows he has any until they are upset."[27] For most social workers engaged in practice, the more theoretical or abstract discussion of values is not a daily event. It is only when value dilemmas or ethical issues are experienced in working with clients that these matters take on full significance.

However, social workers regularly must address practical matters of values and ethics in their daily practice activities. Hokenstad notes that "half of professional decision making requires ethical rather than scientific judgment. . . . Such judgment requires the capability to make moral precepts operational in specific situations and calls for tolerance of ambiguity in some cases and the ability to resolve conflicts between principles in others."[28] It is through consideration of a case example describing a social worker in action that the reader may be able to extend his or her more applied understanding of social work values.

In her book *Never Too Old,* Twente presented an excellent case illustration of a social worker providing service to an aged widower who was unsuccessfully attempting to establish a new life with his son and his son's family.[29] In the following excerpt from this case, some values issues become evident.

> When Miss Jones visits Mr. Brandon, Sr., he at first seems determined not to enter into any kind of a discussion. He answers with a curt "no" or "yes" or "hmmm." Some reference to an old chair in which he sits brings forth the comment that it belonged to "mom and me." It was bought secondhand when they "set up housekeeping."
>
> "How long ago was that?" asks Miss Jones.
>
> "Fifty-one years last February," Mr. Brandon is struggling with tears.
>
> "It must be hard to go on without her," comments Miss Jones quietly. Mr. Brandon nods. There is a sob. Miss Jones rises, walks to the bedtable and looks closely at a photograph. "Is this she?"
>
> "Yes," Miss Jones sits down again. There is a silence. "There never was a better wife or mother than she." Miss Jones nods sympathetically. "Is the other picture on the table of your granddaughter?" she asks. "There seems to be a resemblance."
>
> "There is," responds Mr. Brandon, and for the first time his face lights up. "She is like my wife, Peggy is. Sometimes she comes into my room and asks me questions. All kinds of fool questions. She'll say, 'Grandpa, how did you meet grandma?' or 'What did you do when you took her out?' or 'Did you and grandma dance at parties?' And when I'll say, 'Yes, but not the kind of dances you kids dance,' she'll get up and do some funny turns and say, 'Was it like this, Grandpa?' I tell her, 'No. We waltzed and sometimes I jigged.' 'Show me, Grandpa,' she says. And I get up, but these stiff hips of mine won't move like they ought to." Then he becomes silent again.

The gentle probing of Miss Jones in this part of the case allows her to understand some of the things that Mr. Brandon values, such as the satisfaction from the warm relationship he had with his wife and the joy he gets from his granddaughter. The social worker reflects her value of the worth of Mr. Brandon and treats him with dignity by listening carefully and showing interest in his experiences and feelings. He is important not because of his charm or good looks, but because of his humanness. The case continues.

"You aren't very happy here, are you?"

The next comments come like the rush of water through a broken dam. "No, I'm not happy. How can I be? I am just an old man in everybody's way. Oh, perhaps that is not quite true of Peggy. She likes to visit me, I think. But she has many friends. You know how popular young girls are. Tom is a good son. He works hard, and sometimes he comes in to talk to me. But I can tell he would rather read about sports or look at TV."

"How about Tom Junior?" prods Miss Jones.

"Oh, young Tom is like all young fellers. He is so busy going off on hikes and playing ball and the likes, he doesn't know I exist. I have his room. That should not be. The boy needs his own room to keep things like rocks and frogs and snakes." Again, there is that impish expression. Now there can be no mistaking it. "Margaret doesn't like them things in the house, and she's put her foot down about bringing them alive into the basement. She says she has to do the washing down there and she doesn't want the critters around her feet."

"You don't get along too well with Margaret," said Miss Jones.

"Oh, Margaret's all right. She is just too persnickity. When I first came I said, 'Now, Margaret, you let me do the dishes.' She said it would be hard for me to get them clean because I don't see so well. Well, I washed them, and then I saw her wash them over again. I don't see so bad, but I could see what she did." Then, after a short pause, "I am just in the way. I am an old farmer, and I am what I am. Margaret doesn't like the way I eat. When they had fancy company, she said to me, 'Grandpa, would you prefer to eat in your own room? I can fix your dinner on the card table.' I knew the score. She just didn't want me."

In this passage Mr. Brandon reflects his loss of a sense of self-respect. He views himself as an unimportant old man who doesn't suit the tastes of his daughter-in-law and is a burden for the rest of the family. Like many older people, he feels that he is of little use in a society that values work and productivity. While his life may have been fulfilling before and there was a real sense of achievement when he was managing the farm, life was hollow for Mr. Brandon now. Miss Jones communicates genuine concern about his well-being and seeks to understand the roots of the problem. The story goes on:

After a while Miss Jones asks him if he knows anyone in town besides Tom and his family. "No, all of my friends are out in the country, what is left of them. I can't go out there and they can't come in. Too far."

"And how about church?" asks Miss Jones.

"Mom and I always went to the Methodist Church. Tom and Margaret go to the Christian. Disciples of Christ, they call it. That was Margaret's church. Tom had to be 'ducked' before he could belong." Mr. Brandon does not want to be baptized again. "Once is enough." And he doesn't know anybody. So he stays at home and listens to the radio. Anyhow, his stiff hips can't do those steps very well. "Did you ever like fishing or hunting?" asks Miss Jones. "No, you know, where we lived there was no water for miles around. And as to hunting, there are jackrabbits and prairie dogs, but I was never one to shoot except to protect the crops."

"When you and your wife had company on Sunday afternoons, what did you men do?" Miss Jones continues her questions.

"Oh, we talked politics and things like that, and looked at crops; and sometimes we played horseshoe," replies Mr. Brandon. "Horseshoe was fun, then, but with these hips, it's out of the question." "How about Sunday afternoons in the winter?" Miss Jones is not giving up.

"Well, we played checkers and dominoes and sometimes Flinch."

"Did you enjoy that?" asks Miss Jones.

"Yes." His face brightens. "Hank Brown and I used to play checkers. We played to win. Maggie, that was my wife, and Elizabeth, Hank's wife, had to remind us that the stock had to be fed and we had to go home."

"Would you care to play checkers now, that is, if there were someone to play with you?"

"No. Anyhow, there's nobody to play with."

"There is a Center on Elm Street and retired men get together for checkers and cards. They seem to have fun."

Here Miss Jones moves the conversation to understand better the uniqueness of Mr. Brandon. Although he faces problems experienced by other old people, Mr. Brandon is a unique individual with his own interests and abilities. Miss Jones responds to his need to belong and searches for interests that match community resources which would provide him with an opportunity to make new friends. She knows that men in Mr. Brandon's age group especially need to have warm relationships with a group of friends. Miss Jones reflects the belief that people can change in a new environment and that Mr. Brandon could once again enter the mainstream of life. She is persistent and does not let his despair frustrate her efforts to help find a solution.

Mr. Brandon shakes his head. "I've heard about the Center but it does not appeal to me. Anyhow, I won't be in town very long. I overheard Tom and Margaret discuss me. They want me to go into a home." He seems resigned.

"And do you want to go?" Miss Jones keeps on digging.

"Hell, no. But what can an old man like me do? I don't want to stay where I am not wanted. Not me."

"I am not sure that you are not wanted," says Miss Jones. "Why don't you talk it over with Tom and Margaret and tell them how you feel?"

"I couldn't do that," says Mr. Brandon. "Anyhow, what's the use? I shouldn't have blabbered so much to you. I wasn't going to, and then I went and did it anyhow."

"Do you want me to talk to Tom and Margaret and perhaps with Peggy and young Tom present, too?" asks Miss Jones.

"What would Peggy and Young Tom have to do with it?" He is almost shouting. "They are not responsible for me. Not them young kids."

"No, they aren't, but they are a part of the family and they know whether they want you to stay or to leave. I think Peggy, especially, would hate to see you go to a home."

"Well, I'm going and that is that." Mr. Brandon is trembling. "Like I told you, I am not going to be in anybody's way."

"Do you want me to tell you about the homes nearby?" asks Miss Jones.

The answer sounds something like assent. Miss Jones lists the four different kinds of institutions in the county and briefly describes each one. Mr. Brandon is silent. After a while he says, "You sure know about all these things, don't you?"

"It's my business to know," says Miss Jones.

There is another pause. This time it is a long one. "Does Tom know about all of this, I mean all of these homes?"

"Yes," replies Miss Jones, "I told them when they came in to see me."

"And they want me to go?"

"Only Tom and Margaret and Peggy and Tom Junior can answer that," says Miss Jones. "I do think they would like to see you happier than you have been here."

"Well, I would be! A damn sight happier!" Then, in quite another voice, "Can family visit you in those places? I mean, can young kids come too?"

"Yes, they can, especially during visiting hours."

"What do you have to do with all of this?" he then asks.

"Really very little, Mr. Brandon. We do give information when it is wanted and needed, and sometimes we help with the finances. Most of all we are interested in trying to help families find the best solutions in situations like yours. Tom and Margaret told us they were concerned about you. They know you are lonely and unhappy. They thought a home might be a solution and they asked for information."

"Did they also ask you to come and talk with me?" Mr. Brandon is shouting again.

"Yes, but they understood that I would not try to persuade you to go to a home or do anything else you don't want to do. I think this is up to you and your family."

"And that includes Peggy and Tom Junior?"

"To me it would seem so."

Soon after that, Mr. Brandon comments, "Well, I've got something to think about."

We find Miss Jones reflecting the social work value of helping the clients help themselves. She recognizes that people must be permitted to determine what is best for them and take responsibility for these decisions. Miss Jones is also aware that Mr. Brandon said some things he would not want her to report back to Tom and Margaret. She reinforces the confidentiality of their conversation by asking if he wants her to talk with the family about his views. Yet she refuses to be drawn into the role of an interpreter for the family and, instead, helps them come together to talk about the problems and possible solutions. The final decision, however, is left to them. Although frustrated at times, she continues to pursue working with the family until a satisfactory solution is achieved.

CONCLUDING COMMENT

One cannot understand social work without being sensitive to values. Values represent a highly individual and personal view that must be constantly examined during practice.

The social worker must be aware of the value system of the client or client group and the values held by society that impinge upon the client. Research reported in the chapter identifies the dominant values in U.S. society that form the context in which social programs are formulated and social workers and their clients engage in the helping process. These values, however, are not held equally by all people and client groups can be expected to vary in the intensity with which they hold particular values.

The social worker must be especially cognizant of his or her personal values, lest they intrude into the helping process. Certainly it would be unrealistic to expect, or even desire, that the helping process occur in a value-free environment. Yet the social worker must attempt to avoid imposing personal values inappropriately on the client or client groups. In order to practice social work, one must be prepared to accept and understand people who hold values that are different from their own.

The social worker also must be guided by the values of the social work profession, including the Code of Ethics. These particular values are not held exclusively by social workers; other professions hold many of them. There is also evidence that people involved in the helping professions hold values that are somewhat different from the general population.[30] It further appears that social workers may reflect some differing values from the other helping professions, particularly those that support social work's dual focus on the person and society. Abbott, for example, found areas of significant difference in the values held by social workers, physicians, nurses, teachers, psychologists, and business people. Of these groups, psychologist were most like social workers in their beliefs.[31]

In many ways values or beliefs about how things ought to be or how people ought to behave are the cornerstone of social work. It does not take long in many practice situations to recognize that the knowledge available may be insufficient to guide practice. Moreover, the skills required to be helpful to clients in a specific situation may exceed the competence of the worker. In such an event, the social worker who falls back on the values of the profession cannot go far wrong in guiding the helping process. Thus, in addition to serving as guidelines for the selection of knowledge and skills for practice, social work values serve as a safety valve for client protection.

BOX 8–1

THE NASW CODE OF ETHICS

Preamble

This code is intended to serve as a guide to the everyday conduct of members of the social work profession and as a basis for the adjudication of issues in standards expressed or implied in this code. It represents standards of ethical behavior for social workers in professional relationships with those served, with colleagues, with employers, with other individuals and professions, and with the community and society as a whole. It also embodies standards of ethical behavior governing individual conduct to the extent that such conduct is associated with an individual's status and identity as a social worker.

This code is based on the fundamental values of the social work profession that include the worth, dignity, and uniqueness of all persons as well as their rights and opportunities. It is also based on the nature of social work, which fosters conditions that promote these values.

In subscribing to and abiding by this code, the social worker is expected to view ethical responsibility in as inclusive a context as each situation demands and within which ethical judgment is required. The social worker is expected to take into consideration all the principles in this code that have a bearing upon any situation in which ethical judgment is to be exercised and professional intervention or conduct is planned. The course of action that the social worker chooses is expected to be consistent with the spirit as well as the letter of this code.

In itself, this code does not represent a set of rules that will prescribe all the behaviors of social workers in all the complexities of professional life. Rather, it offers general principles to guide conduct, and the judicious appraisal of conduct, in situations that have ethical implications. It provides the basis for making judgments about ethical actions before and after they occur. Frequently, the particular situation determines the ethical principles that apply and the manner of their application. In such cases, not only the particular ethical principles are taken into immediate consideration, but also the entire code and its spirit. Specific applications of ethical principles must be judged within the context in which they are being considered. Ethical behavior in a given situation must satisfy not only the judgment of the individual social worker, but also the judgment of an unbiased jury of professional peers.

This code should not be used as an instrument to deprive any social worker of the opportunity or freedom to practice with complete professional integrity: nor should any disciplinary action be taken on the basis of this code without maximum provision for safeguarding the rights of the social worker affected.

The ethical behavior of social workers results not from edict, but from a personal commitment of the individual. This code is offered to affirm the will and zeal of all social workers to be ethical and to act ethically in all that they do as social workers.

BOX 8–1 (Continued)

The following codified ethical principles should guide social workers in the various roles and relationships and at the various levels of responsibility in which they function professionally. These principles also serve as a basis for the adjudication by the National Association of Social Workers of issues in ethics.

In subscribing to this code, social workers are required to cooperate in its implementation and abide by any disciplinary rulings based on it. They should also take adequate measures to discourage, prevent, expose, and correct the unethical conduct of colleagues. Finally, social workers should be equally ready to defend and assist colleagues unjustly charged with unethical conduct.

I. The Social Worker's Conduct and Comportment as a Social Worker

A. Propriety—The social worker should maintain high standards of personal conduct in the capacity or identity as social worker.
   1. The private conduct of the social worker is a personal matter to the same degree as is any other person's, except when such conduct compromises the fulfillment of professional responsibilities.
   2. The social worker should not participate in, condone, or be associated with dishonesty, fraud, deceit, or misrepresentation.
   3. The social worker should distinguish clearly between statements and actions made as a private individual and as a representative of the social work profession or an organization or group.
B. Competence and Professional Development—The social worker should strive to become and remain proficient in professional practice and the performance of professional functions.
   1. The social worker should accept responsibility or employment only on the basis of existing competence or the intention to acquire the necessary competence.
   2. The social worker should not misrepresent professional qualifications, education, experience, or affiliations.
C. Service—The social worker should regard as primary the service obligation of the social work profession.
   1. The social worker should retain responsibility for the quality and extent of the service that that individual assumes, assigns, or performs.
   2. The social worker should act to prevent practices that are inhumane or discriminatory against any person or group of persons.
D. Integrity—The social worker should act in accordance with the highest standards of professional integrity and impartiality.
   1. The social worker should be alert to and resist the influences and pressures that interfere with the exercise of professional discretion and impartial judgment required for the performance of professional functions.
   2. The social worker should not exploit professional relationships for personal gain.

BOX 8–1 (Continued)

E. Scholarship and Research—The social worker engaged in study and research should be guided by the conventions of scholarly inquiry.

1. The social worker engaged in research should consider carefully its possible consequences for human beings.
2. The social worker engaged in research should ascertain that the consent of participants in the research is voluntary and informed, without any implied deprivation or penalty for refusal to participate and with due regard for participants' privacy and dignity.
3. The social worker engaged in research should protect participants from unwarranted physical or mental discomfort, distress, harm, danger, or deprivation.
4. The social worker who engages in the evaluation of services or cases should discuss them only for professional purposes and only with persons directly and professionally concerned with them.
5. Information obtained about participants in research should be treated as confidential.
6. The social worker should take credit only for work actually done in connection with scholarly and research endeavors and credit contributions made by others.

II. The Social Worker's Ethical Responsibility to Clients

F. Primacy of Clients' Interests—The social worker's primary responsibility is to clients.

1. The social worker should serve clients with devotion, loyalty, determination, and the maximum application of professional skill and competence.
2. The social worker should not exploit relationships with clients for personal advantage or solicit the clients of one's agency for private practice.
3. The social worker should not practice, condone, facilitate, or collaborate with any form of discrimination on the basis of race, color, sex, sexual orientation, age, religion, national origin, marital status, political belief, mental or physical handicap, or any other preference or personal characteristic, condition, or status.
4. The social worker should avoid relationships or commitments that conflict with the interests of clients.
5. The social worker should under no circumstances engage in sexual activities with clients.
6. The social worker should provide clients with accurate and complete information regarding the extent and nature of the services available to them.
7. The social worker should apprise clients of their risks, rights, opportunities, and obligations associated with social service to them.
8. The social worker should seek advice and counsel of colleagues and supervisors whenever such consultation is in the best interest of clients.
9. The social worker should terminate service to clients, and professional relationships with them, when such service and relationships are no longer required or no longer serve the clients' needs or interests.

BOX 8–1 (Continued)

10. The social worker should withdraw services precipitously only under unusual circumstances, giving careful consideration to all factors in the situation and taking care to minimize possible adverse effects.
11. The social worker who anticipates the termination or interruption of service to clients should notify clients promptly and seek the transfer, referral, or continuation of service in relation to the clients' needs and preferences.

G. Rights and Prerogatives of Clients—The social worker should make every effort to foster maximum self-determination on the part of clients.
   1. When the social worker must act on behalf of a client who has been adjudged legally incompetent, the social worker should safeguard the interests and rights of that client.
   2. When another individual has been legally authorized to act in behalf of a client, the social worker should deal with that person always with the client's best interest in mind.
   3. The social worker should not engage in any action that violates or diminishes the civil or legal rights of clients.

H. Confidentiality and Privacy—The social worker should respect the privacy of clients and hold in confidence all information obtained in the course of professional service.
   1. The social worker should share with others confidences revealed by clients, without their consent, only for compelling professional reasons.
   2. The social worker should inform clients fully about the limits of confidentiality in a given situation, the purposes for which information is obtained, and how it may be used.
   3. The social worker should afford clients reasonable access to any official social work records concerning them.
   4. When providing clients with access to records, the social worker should take due care to protect the confidences of others contained in those records.
   5. The social worker should obtain informed consent of clients before taping, recording, or permitting third party observation of their activities.

I. Fees—When setting fees, the social worker should ensure that they are fair, reasonable, considerate, and commensurate with the service performed and with due regard for the clients' ability to pay.
   1. The social worker should not divide a fee or accept or give anything of value for receiving or making a referral.

III. The Social Worker's Ethical Responsibility to Colleagues

J. Respect, Fairness, and Courtesy—The social worker should treat colleagues with respect, courtesy, fairness, and good faith.
   1. The social worker should cooperate with colleagues to promote professional interests and concerns.
   2. The social worker should respect confidences shared by colleagues in the course of their professional relationships and transactions.
   3. The social worker should create and maintain conditions of practice that facilitate ethical and competent professional performance by colleagues.

BOX 8–1 (Continued)

4. The social worker should treat with respect, and represent accurately and fairly, the qualifications, views, and findings of colleagues and use appropriate channels to express judgments on these matters.
5. The social worker who replaces or is replaced by a colleague in professional practice should act with consideration for the interest, character, and reputation of that colleague.
6. The social worker should not exploit a dispute between a colleague and employers to obtain a position or otherwise advance the social worker's interest.
7. The social worker should seek arbitration or mediation when conflicts with colleagues require resolution for compelling professional reasons.
8. The social worker should extend to colleagues of other professions the same respect and cooperation that is extended to social work colleagues.
9. The social worker who serves as an employer, supervisor, or mentor to colleagues should make orderly and explicit arrangements regarding the conditions of their continuing professional relationship.
10. The social worker who has the responsibility for employing and evaluating the performance of other staff members should fulfill such responsibility in a fair, considerate, and equitable manner, on the basis of clearly enunciated criteria.
11. The social worker who has the responsibility for evaluating the performance of employees, supervisors, or students should share evaluations with them.

K. Dealing with Colleagues' Clients—The social worker has the responsibility to relate to the clients of colleagues with full professional consideration.
1. The social worker should not solicit the clients of colleagues.
2. The social worker should not assume professional responsibility for the clients of another agency or a colleague without appropriate communication with that agency or colleague.
3. The social worker who serves the clients of colleagues during a temporary absence or emergency should serve those clients with the same consideration as that afforded any client.

IV. The Social Worker's Ethical Responsibility to Employers and Employing Organizations

L. Commitment to Employing Organization—The social worker should adhere to commitments made to the employing organization.
1. The social worker should work to improve the employing agency's policies and procedures and the efficiency and effectiveness of its services.
2. The social worker should not accept employment or arrange student field placements in an organization which is currently under public sanction by NASW for violating personnel standards or imposing limitations on or penalties for professional actions on behalf of clients.

BOX 8–1 (Continued)

3. The social worker should act to prevent and eliminate discrimination in the employing organization's work assignments and its employment policies and practice.
4. The social worker should use with scrupulous regard, and only for the purpose for which they are intended, the resources of the employing organization.

V. The Social Worker's Ethical Responsibility to the Social Work Profession

M. Maintaining the Integrity of the Profession—The social worker should uphold and advance the values, ethics, knowledge, and mission of the profession.
  1. The social worker should protect and enhance the dignity and integrity of the profession and should be responsible and vigorous in discussion and criticism of the profession.
  2. The social worker should take action through appropriate channels against unethical conduct by any other member of the profession.
  3. The social worker should act to prevent the unauthorized and unqualified practice of social work.
  4. The social worker should make no misrepresentation in advertising as to qualifications, competence, service, or results to be achieved.
N. Community Service—The social worker should assist the profession in making social services available to the general public.
  1. The social worker should contribute time and professional expertise to activities that promote respect for the utility, the integrity, and the competence of the social work profession.
  2. The social worker should support the formulation, development, enactment, and implementation of social policies of concern to the profession.
O. Development of Knowledge—The social worker should take responsibility for identifying, developing, and fully utilizing knowledge for professional practice.
  1. The social worker should base practice upon recognized knowledge relevant to social work.
  2. The social worker should critically examine, and keep current with, emerging knowledge relevant to social work.
  3. The social worker should contribute to the knowledge base of social work and share research knowledge and practice wisdom with colleagues.

VI. The Social Worker's Ethical Responsibility to Society

P. Promoting the General Welfare—The social worker should promote the general welfare of society.
  1. The social worker should act to prevent and eliminate discrimination against any person or group on the basis of race, color, sex, sexual orientation, age, religion, national origin, marital status, political belief, mental or physical handicap, or any other preference or personal characteristic, condition, or status.

BOX 8–1 (Continued)

2. The social worker should act to ensure that all persons have access to the resources, services and opportunities which they require.
3. The social worker should act to expand choice and opportunity for all persons, with special regard for disadvantaged or oppressed groups and persons.
4. The social worker should promote conditions that encourage respect for the diversity of cultures which constitute American society.
5. The social worker should provide appropriate professional services in public emergencies.
6. The social worker should advocate changes in policy and legislation to improve social conditions and to promote social justice.
7. The social worker should encourage informed participation by the public in shaping social policies and institutions.

Source: Copyright © 1980, National Association of Social Workers, Inc. Reprinted with permission from *NASW News* 25, No. 1 (January 1980): 24–25.

SUGGESTED READINGS

ABBOTT, ANN A. *Professional Choices: Values at Work.* Silver Spring, Md.: National Association of Social Workers, 1988.

GOLDSTEIN, HOWARD. "The Neglected Moral Link in Social Work Practice." *Social Work* 32 (May–June 1987): 179–180.

LEIBY, JAMES. "Moral Foundations of Social Welfare and Social Work: A Historical View." *Social Work* 30 (July–August 1985): 323–330.

LEVY, CHARLES S. *Social Work Ethics.* New York: Human Services Press, 1976.

LOEWENBERG, FRANK, and DOLGOFF, RALPH. *Ethical Decisions for Social Work Practice* 3rd ed. Itasca, Ill.: F. E. Peacock, 1988.

MORAN, JAMES. "Social Work Education and Students' Humanistic Attitudes." *Journal of Social Work Education* 25 (Winter 1989): 3–12.

REAMER, FREDERIC G. "Ethics Committees in Social Work." *Social Work* 32 (May–June 1987): 188–192.

WALSH, JOSEPH A. "Burnout and Values in the Social Service Profession." *Social Casework* 68 (May 1987): 279–283.

WELLS, CAROLYN CRESSY, with MASCH, M. KATHLEEN. *Social Work Ethics Day to Day: Guidelines for Professional Practice.* New York: Longman, 1986.

ENDNOTES

1. Milton Rokeach, *Beliefs, Values, and Attitudes: A Theory of Organization and Change* (San Francisco: Jossey-Bass, 1968), p. 124.
2. Lynn R. Kahle and Susan Goff Timmer, "A Theory and a Method for Studying Values," in *Social Values and Social Change: Adaptation to Life in America,* Lynn R. Kahle, ed. (Praeger Publishers, New York, a division of Greenwood Press, Inc., 1983), p. 52. Copyright © 1983 by Praeger Publishers. Used with permission.

3. Charles Frankel, "Social Values and Professional Values," *Journal of Education for Social Work* 5 (Spring 1969): 35.
4. Harold L. McPheeters and Robert M. Ryan, *A Core of Competence for Baccalaureate Social Welfare and Curricular Implications* (Atlanta: Southern Regional Education Board, 1971), pp. 74–75.
5. American Association of Social Workers, *Social Case Work: Generic and Specific: A Report of the Milford Conference,"* reprint (Washington, D.C.: National Association of Social Workers, 1974), p. 28.
6. Shepard B. Clough, *Basic Values of Western Civilization* (New York: Columbia University Press, 1960), p. 5.
7. Naomi I. Brill, *Working with People: The Helping Process* 4th ed. (New York: Longman, 1990), p. 29.
8. Ibid., p. 12.
9. Kahle, *Social Values and Social Change.*
10. Kahle and Timmer, pp. 47–51.
11. Susan Goff Timmer and Lynn R. Kahle, "Birthright Demographic Correlates of Values," in *Social Values and Social Change: Adaptation to Life in America,* Lynn R. Kahle, ed. (Praeger Publishers, New York, a division of Greenwood Press, Inc., 1983), p. 76. Copyright © 1983 by Praeger Publishers. Used with permission.
12. Debra C. Eisert, "Marriage and Parenting," in *Social Values and Social Change: Adaptation to Life in America,* Lynn R. Kahle, ed. (Praeger Publishers, New York, a division of Greenwood Press, Inc., 1983), pp. 149–150. Copyright © 1983 by Praeger Publishers. Used with permission.
13. Timmer and Kahle, pp. 84–85.
14. Ibid.
15. Kathleen J. Pottick, "Work and Leisure," in *Social Values and Social Change: Adaptation to Life in America,* Lynn R. Kahle, ed. (Praeger Publishers, New York, a division of Greenwood Press, Inc., 1983), p. 52. Copyright © 1983 by Praeger Publishers. Used with permission.
16. Timmer and Kahle, p. 94.
17. Ibid., p. 95.
18. Susan Goff Timmer and Lynn R. Kahle, "Ascribed and Attained Demographic Correlates of Values," in *Social Values and Social Change: Adaptation to Life in America,* Lynn R. Kahle, ed. (Praeger Publishers, New York, a division of Greenwood Press, Inc., 1983), p. 106. Copyright © 1983 by Praeger Publishers. Used with permission.
19. Ibid., p. 108.
20. Ibid., p. 110.
21. Chauncy A. Alexander, "An International Code of Ethics for the Professional Social Worker, mimeo. (Washington, D.C.: National Association of Social Workers, 1975), p. 2.
22. National Association of Social Workers, *NASW Standards for the Classification of Social Work Practice, Policy Statement 4* (Silver Spring, Md.: The Association, September 1981), p. 18.
23. Bradford W. Sheafor, Charles R. Horejsi, and Gloria A. Horejsi, *Techniques and Guidelines for Social Work Practice* (Boston: Allyn and Bacon, 1988), p. 59.
24. Ibid., p. 56.
25. Frank Loewenberg and Ralph Dolgoff," *Ethical Decisions for Social Work Practice* 2nd ed. (Itasca, Ill.: F. E. Peacock, 1985), p. 23.
26. "Board Imposes Sanctions," *NASW News* 35 (April 1990): 10.
27. R. Huws Jones, "Social Values and Social Work Education," in Katherine A. Kendall, ed., *Social Work Values in an Age of Discontent* (New York: Council on Social Work Education, 1970).
28. M. C. Hokenstad, "Teaching Practitioners Ethical Judgment," *NASW News* 32 (October 1987): 4.

29. Esther E. Twente, *Never Too Old: The Aged in Community Life* (San Francisco: Jossey-Bass, 1970), pp. 151–158.

30. Bradford W. Sheafor, "The Effects of Board Members on Staff of Community Mental Health Centers: A Study of the Relationship of Their Values to Job Satisfaction," *Journal of Social Welfare* 3 (Spring 1976): 75–82; and Arthur W. Combs et al., *Florida Studies in the Helping Professions,* University of Florida Social Science Monograph 37 (Gainesville: University of Florida Press, 1969).

31. Ann A. Abbott, *Professional Choices: Values at Work* (Silver Spring, Md.: National Association of Social Workers, 1988), pp. 74–75.

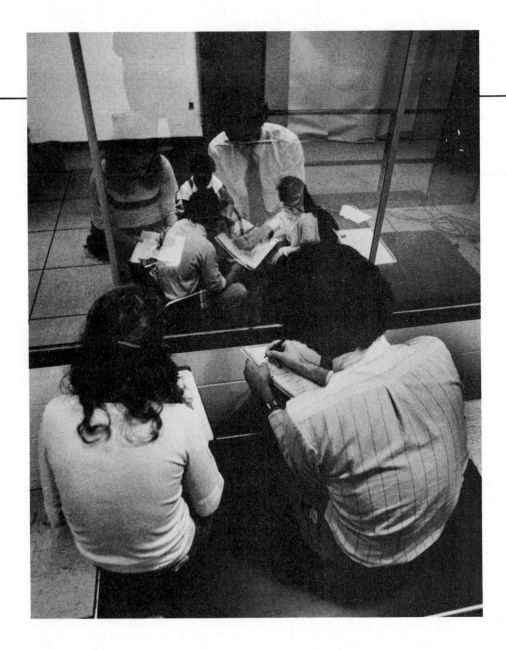

CHAPTER 9

The Skill Base of Social Work

Among the many definitions of social work are several that appropriately describe it as both an art and a science. Certainly there is an artful part of social work practice that relates to the natural abilities and personality traits of the social worker. Inherent ability is especially apparent in the skills of some social workers. Undoubtedly, some people possess special qualities that make them good natural helpers. However, many skills required for practice have a knowledge base and can be learned. The social worker's batting average is, of course, improved when he or she demonstrates both natural abilities and professionally developed skills.

To be effective the social worker must have the capacity to use a wide repertoire of techniques. The skill of social work requires both the appropriate selection of techniques for a particular situation and the ability to use the techniques effectively. Selection of particular techniques must be based on a conscious effort to use the best available knowledge and to screen that knowledge carefully to be sure it is compatible with social work values. In a sense, values become a filter between the available knowledge and the skills used by the social worker in providing services. Once appropriate knowledge and values have been given full consideration, the practice skill of the social worker comes into play (see Figure 9–1).

THE NATURE OF SKILL

When one has an opportunity to observe a social worker in practice, his or her skill is readily apparent. *Skill* may be defined as the "ability to use knowledge effectively and readily in execution or performance."[1] The term is used somewhat

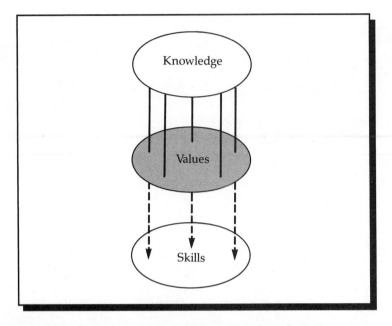

FIGURE 9–1   *Factors Underpinning Social Work Skill*

differently in other fields. In industry a person is regarded as skilled when he or she is qualified to carry out trade or craft work involving knowledge, judgment, accuracy, and manual deftness, usually acquired through extensive training. In *motor* or *manual skills,* the overt action forms an essential part of the activity. Psychologists use the concept of *mental skills,* in which the overt actions play a more incidental part, giving expression to a skill rather than forming an essential part of it.[2] In social work, on the other hand, overt actions are rarely observed as part of the mental skills of the social worker in a helping role, except, for example, when a worker uses recreational activities in working with a group.

A major distinction between professional and nonprofessional occupations is the possession of skill and knowledge generally not available to the public. Many nonprofessional occupations involve skill—in many cases greater than that of professions. A major distinction between the two, however, rests on a *body of knowledge* organized into a system that can be called a body of theory. The acquisition of skill in professions, therefore, depends on the mastery of the underlying body of theory, which, in turn, demands education and training of a high order.[3]

Unlike many professionals, the social worker does not bring many tangible resources to the helping situation. The social worker brings primarily a body of knowledge, a set of values, and a repertoire of skills from which the most promising helping approach or intervention is selected. Unlike the physician, for ex-

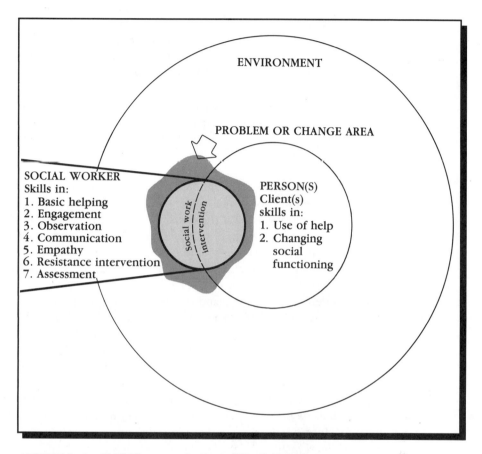

FIGURE 9–2   *Skill Elements in Social Work Practice*

ample, who can administer medication that will "cure" a patient's illness, the social worker can only help a client or clients improve their social functioning. Central to this task is the development and maintenance of a mutually trusting, satisfying, and productive relationship between client(s) and social worker. Some professionals offer their skills "to" the client, but the social worker uses skills "with" the client. As Figure 9–2 suggests, the successful helping process not only requires the skill of the social worker but also the skill of the client in using the available help and in changing his or her social functioning.

SKILL IN SOCIAL WORK

Boehm suggests that professional skill is expressed in the activities of the social worker. It constitutes the social worker's artistic creation resulting from three internal processes: (1) conscious selection of knowledge pertinent to the professional task at hand, (2) fusion of this knowledge with social work values, and (3) expression of this synthesis in *professionally relevant activity.*[4] What constitutes professionally relevant activity, however, does not seem explicit and allows room for subjective interpretation. As Boehm states:

> Social work should and does adopt what may often be unpopular positions. In the light of its own selection and interpretation of certain values which other sections of society may view differently, social work may also serve as the conscience of society.[5]

Demonstrating social work skills in a professionally relevant activity seems to leave determination of that activity with the agency and the social work profession. The implication is that the social worker's activity needs to be "sanctioned." But would not the sanction of the client also be of paramount importance? In this view the social worker would be using skills in *client-relevant activity;* the activity would be determined by client needs. Yet, agency and social work sanction do not have to be a condition of intervention if the activity takes place independent of the agency and the profession. For example, a social worker in private practice who treats a police brutality victim in emotional crisis and who then helps similar victims organize in the community to protest against such police practices is using social work skills to help people in need who sanction this intervention. This intervention may or may not be sanctioned by the profession, but it is still social work practice.

Given the foregoing discussion, we propose the following definition of social work skill. *Social work skill is the social worker's capacity to set in motion, in a relationship with the client (individual, group, community), guided psychosocial interventive processes of change based on social work values and knowledge in a specific situation relevant to the client. The change that begins to occur as the result of this skilled intervention is effected with the greatest degree of consideration for the client and by the use of the strengths and capacity of the client.*

The social worker's skill is expressed within the framework of one or more social work methods. As an orderly, systematic mode of procedure common to a discipline, practice, or range of disciplines and practices, the term *method* in social work traditionally encompasses social casework, social group work, and community organization, but increasingly relates to a generic practice method.[6] The social work method is the responsible, conscious, skilled, disciplined use of self in a relationship with an individual or group. It includes systematic observation and assessment of the client and formulation of an appropriate plan of action. Implicit in this process, according to William Gordon, is a continuing evaluation of the nature of the relationship between the social worker and the client and of its effect on both the participant individual or group and the social worker.

TECHNIQUES AND SOCIAL WORK SKILLS

Techniques, that is, instruments or specific procedures and operations used in a given discipline, are incorporated in the use of the social work method. Gordon lists some of the techniques that may be applied in different combinations by social workers: support, clarification, information giving, interpretation, development of insight, differentiation of the social worker from the individual or group, identification with agency function, creation and use of structure, use of activities and projects, provision of positive experiences, teaching, stimulation of group interaction, limit setting, utilization of available social resources, effecting change in immediate environmental forces operating on the individual or groups, and synthesis.[7]

Competence in social work practice lies in developing skill in the use of the social work method and its associated techniques. Skill entails the ability to help a particular client or clients in such a way that they clearly understand the social worker's role and intention and are able to participate in the process of solving their problems or enhancing their social functioning. In further defining social work skills, Gordon adds:

> Setting the stage, the strict observation of confidentiality, encouragement, stimulation or participation, empathy, and objectivity are means of facilitating communication. The individual social worker always makes his *own* creative contribution in the application of social work method to any setting or activity.[8]

THE SKILL-LEARNING PROCESS

It is impossible for any one social worker to learn all skills of practice. Social casework, for example, has a distinct repertoire of skills, based on either the "functional approach," the "problem-solving approach," or the "psychosocial approach" to intervention.[9] The social group worker is also faced with a wide range of skills to learn, depending on which interventive mode is selected for practice. There are, for example, the "developmental approach," the "interactionist approach," and the "preventive and rehabilitative approach."[10] In community organization the crucial elements of practice and the field's boundaries and content are very much in flux.[11] Several problem-solving models are difficult to define because of overlap in purpose and method among the various community organization, development, and planning approaches.[12] Because of the lack of definition, learning community organization practice skills is therefore even more difficult than learning the skills of casework and group work.

Social work's many faces cover a wide variety of social phenomena and practice interventions, each requiring special skills. It should be pointed out that although certain aspects of practice call for specialization, there are still many skills more generic in nature. Bartlett maintains that the idea of a *common base*—

one whose elements are applied together in practice but vary according to the particular characteristics of the practice—brings together the concepts of generic and specific, of basic and specialized.[13]

Setting aside for a moment the social worker's task of learning generic and specialized skills for practice, we turn to the more basic issue of *how* the social worker learns a particular skill. It is not difficult, for example, to tell a social work student or worker to develop skills in interviewing. However, simply assigning a book on interviewing skills will not guarantee that the necessary skills will be learned.

An adult who sets out to acquire a new skill usually begins with a communicable program of instruction. Another person communicates or demonstrates what the learner is supposed to do. But just having the written or oral strategy is not enough to acquire certain skills. For example, almost no one—including physicists, engineers, and bicycle manufacturers—can communicate how to keep your balance when you ride a bicycle. "Turn your handle bars in the direction you are falling," the teacher says, and the student accepts blindly, not quite understanding, then or later, why this method works. Some teachers may not impart any instructions at all but run alongside the bicycle, holding it up until the learner gets the feel and the idea. Skills, particularly mental skills, are uniquely taught and learned. Given verbal and written instructions about skills, when forming a plan to guide their actions, people find for themselves the essential elements of the skill. Finding these elements is basically a test of the adequacy of the strategy. Once a strategy has been developed, alternative modes of action become possible. The person now understands the specific job he or she has to do and has acquired the necessary skill to get it done.[14]

Techniques, which are refinements of skill, should not be rigid, particularly as they pertain to mental skills applied in helping human beings:

> There are so many knotty problems with which they [social workers] deal, so many stubbornly closed doors that will not yield to their opening devices, that they look eagerly for some keys, be they words or actions, which will prove to be open-sesames. *But the more individualized and creative a process is, the more skill eludes being captured* and held in the small snares of prefabricated kinds of behavior, and the paradox is that the less susceptible skill is to being caught, and mastered by ready-made formulas, the more anxiously are formulas sought. "What should I say when . . . ?" "What does one do if . . . ?" "How do you get a client to . . . ?" These are the questions caseworkers typically bring to supervisors, to psychiatric consultants, or to their peers, seeking for *the* manner, *the* word, that will break the impasse.[15]

Thus, we view social work practice as a science—that is, the systematic application of knowledge and skill in effecting a desired result, combined with the art each social worker develops in the unique selection and application of appropriate techniques and skills. From practice experience every social worker develops special ways of saying and doing what his or her knowledge and values determine will most effectively achieve the client's goals.

BASIC SKILLS FOR BEGINNING PRACTICE

Social workers in the human services must have at their disposal a wide repertoire of knowledge, skills, techniques, and strategies to attain goals with people. In application of knowledge and skills, values are inseparable from any step in the process, for without values the social worker may be a technician rather than a value-directed human services professional.[16]

Built on a foundation of knowledge and values, the element of skill in social work has two preliminary applications: to select the method or methods to use— or not to use—and to act accordingly.[17] An experienced practitioner knows, for example, that it is rarely helpful—and often counterproductive—to encourage a grossly psychotic individual to elaborate on his or her hallucinations. Instead, the skillful social worker carefully directs the patient to a more realistic level of functioning by asking the patient simple, clear, concrete questions. The skillful, appropriate selection and application of a method in this case appears rather uncomplicated; but a great deal of preparation is needed.

There is a gradation of skill attainment from a low to a high level of sophistication among social work practitioners. The advanced social worker is expected to have more interventive skills than the basic social worker. But what are the appropriate skill expectations of the social work student? Traditionally, social service agencies serving as field placements have provided the major opportunity for skill learning, and in most educational programs field experience coincides with a practice course. Effective and efficient learning is likely when classroom and field faculty work together in identifying common objectives and in integrating learning activities.

Loewenberg and Dolgoff maintain, however, that students should develop elementary skills, such as interviewing, *before* they come to the field-work placement agency.[18] They provide several ideas and suggestions as to what should be included in basic skills for beginning practice. This section, with various modifications, relies on their contributions. The following skill areas, with accompanying key concepts, will be highlighted as recommended basic skills for beginning practice: (1) basic helping skills; (2) engagement skills; (3) observation skills; (4) communication skills; (5) empathy skills; (6) resistance intervention skills; and (7) social work assessment skills. Each person learns and applies helping skills in his or her own way. Skills mechanically learned and applied will be perceived by clients as false and superficial and will only interfere with the helping process.

Basic Helping Skills

Helping people is a planned, purposeful process that involves a helping worker. The student needs to develop perceptive skills in order to look at familiar things with new eyes, to identify people who need help and conditions that need changing. For example, the neighborhood bully whom everyone dislikes may be acting out feelings of inadequacy in response to brutal treatment by his or her parents. The task is to look for the cause of the behavior.

Helping people is a purposeful response to individual needs, group and community requirements, and societal conditions. The helper's relationship with the person receiving help varies and depends on the problem or condition; the helping strategy selected; characteristics of the individual, family, or group asking for help; and characteristics of other elements of the system.

The helper–receiver relationship need not always be a direct relationship. For example, the bed-wetting problem of a five-year-old might be resolved in a specific case by helping the parents feel less anxious about being parents rather than by focusing only on the child.

Developing relationships is an essential helping skill. For a helper to have a positive effect on another person, a good relationship is fundamental. In the process of helping people, social workers must develop working relationships within a bureaucratic organization, with other bureaucratic organizations, and with other professional helpers.

Using oneself appropriately and purposefully is an important skill. Social workers have to work both independently and as members of a team. A related factor is understanding the meaning of supervision and consultation and using that assistance effectively. The skill to organize one's work effectively benefits the client both directly and indirectly.

Some basic principles in the helping process are accepting others as they are, treating people as individuals, maintaining one's own integrity, respecting a person's right to self-determination, and working with people at *their* pace.

In developing one's basic helping skills, one must continue to learn. Opportunities for further education must be cultivated. Professional journals, books, institutes, and workshops can be rich sources of learning. And, in addition to learning from colleagues, one can learn from clients.

Engagement Skills

The process of effectively involving individuals, families, or groups in a helping situation requires the purposeful use of self. In attempting to achieve this, the goals, purposes, role, and position of the worker must be made explicit to the person needing help. Likewise, the goals, purposes, role, and position of the person needing help have to be made clear. For example, a wife asking a family services worker to make her alcoholic husband "behave" must understand that the worker can only invite the husband to join a discussion of her concerns. He, in turn, might share his concerns about his wife. The worker's role then might assume a more supportive, neutral, facilitative, conciliatory posture, depending upon the new merged goals and purposes evolving from discussions.

Role and status factors impinge on the helping process. Engagement skills have to consider stratification factors, knowledge of subcultures, deviant groups, reference groups, ethnic minority groups, and differing value systems and life styles. Ignoring these factors can make it difficult to establish working relationships with people from these groups. If, for example, a worker were to try to impose a heterosexual value system on a gay client who is attempting to work through separation feelings after abandonment by his lover, it would probably not be too long before the client would disengage himself from the helping relationship.

Context and structure also affect the engagement process. Factors such as the time, setting, and structure of the interview may enhance or impede the engagement process. The time and setting should be chosen for the convenience of the person being helped. Distractions and inconveniences should be minimized to afford worker and client maximum attention and concentration. The availability of the worker may also affect the engagement process. If it is difficult to contact the worker, the engagement process suffers.

There are specific phases in the engagement process. Usually it is fairly easy to establish a working relationship with persons who initiated the contact for help. They are often precise in defining their problems and are motivated to work on them. When the contact is initiated by the social agency or by a third party such as the church or police, it is usually more difficult to establish a good working relationship, since these people may not want help. In such cases, the engagement process is enhanced when the worker is able to establish clearly what his or her role and responsibilities will be. The client's rights, responsibilities, and options should also be spelled out. Once the initial working relationship is established and client resistance is at a minimum, the engagement process may be strengthened, and the potential contribution of the worker becomes more obvious to the client. The importance of developing skills in understanding and managing *resistance* will be discussed later in this chapter.

It is in the middle phase that the worker can more efficiently and effectively help individuals, families, and groups identify and define problem areas and can develop and implement intervention action strategies. The ending phase of the engagement process is concerned with the delicate process of termination. Depending on the nature and depth of the relationship between the worker and the individual, family, or group, careful planning of the termination process can result in a positive separation.

Elimination of negative attitudes helps the engagement process. Workers with punitive and judgmental attitudes have difficulty establishing a helpful relationship with clients. Scolding a client who is late for an appointment may only evoke resentment. Criticizing a welfare mother because she occasionally goes to night clubs rather than to church will likewise place the client on the defensive and will make it difficult for her to trust the worker. Holding unrealistic expectations for clients may initially motivate and excite them; but, when they are unable to achieve these goals, frustration, guilt, and even anger toward the worker may result. Subsequent attempts to engage the client in other efforts may prove fruitless. Unwarranted promises by the worker may also contribute to the client's frustration and may make the engagement process more difficult. In short eliminating the negatives and striving to be open, honest, nonjudgmental, realistic, and dependable will enhance the engagement process. Basic guidelines include patience, understanding, and acceptance of different values and life styles.

Observation Skills

People see only what they are socially conditioned to look for. During the lifetime conditioning process, a person absorbs countless biases—conscious and unconscious. In learning observation skills, therefore, a fundamental goal is for social workers to become more aware of the particular biases that color their perception of others. Of course, it is doubtful that pure, objective perception is ever possible.

Observation is more than just "seeing." Obviously, the worker observes what the client says. The worker should also note what the client does *not* say, such as significant gaps in a story. For example, a married man in the first few sessions may talk about how frustrated he feels on the job. His not mentioning significant people in his life, such as his family, is important to note. The worker should also notice physical appearance, that is, bodily tensions, flushing, perspiration, trembling, excitability, and looks of dejection, because these factors supplement—and at times may even contradict—an impression given by the client's words. The mother who smilingly complains that her acting-out teenage son is "growing up to be just like his father" may not be aware of her ambivalent feelings about her son. Observation of the client's physical behavior can often provide clues to deeper motivations.

An observation involves a choice of what to see. The worker must continually decide what should be observed, because it is never possible to observe everything. In family therapy, for example, if the worker observes only the verbose mother who is attempting to dominate and control the family with her talking, the result may be that the mother also dominates the social worker. However, if the worker observes the other family members and then shares his or her observations with the family that some members appear angry, bored, or "turned off" by the mother's talking, this statement may immediately encourage responses that will confirm or reject the initial observations. In this respect, the helper's observation is not passive but always goal-directed.

The observer's presence influences the person or behavior observed. Even the most passive observer will affect the individual or group being observed. If, for example, a client is told that she is going to be observed through a two-way mirror during an interview, her behavior will be affected in some way. A worker's raised eyebrow or skeptical look in response to an exaggeration by the client may cause the client to become angry, threatened, or embarrassed. Such subtle but powerful confrontations by the observer can best take place after a good relationship has been established, when the worker knows the client well and has sufficient basis for questioning certain information. The observer has to be conscious that his or her reactions do not necessarily lead the client into discussing approved client behavior.

Communication Skills

Communication—that is, the exchange of information between people—is the basic ingredient in helping people. It is the social worker's chief tool. The client has to be able to tell the worker what is troubling him or her, and the worker has to let the client know he or she understands what is said. Through the reciprocal process of communication and understanding, the client is then in the best position to transform new information into new behavior.

An individual or group can accept a communication only when the communication is understood. If the communication is not understood, it will be disregarded. The most obvious example is a client who communicates in a different language from the worker's. Interpreters improve the situation somewhat, but injecting a third party increases the chances for distortion. Communication should also be compatible with the client's life style and general interests. Often, words used by one group of people are not understood by another. For example, a worker might comment, "It apparently was a traumatic episode that caused you some anxiety." The client might reply, "Oh, no, man. I was scared shitless and uptight!" The worker should use clear, nontechnical words: "You were probably scared and nervous."

Nonverbal behavior can also be significant communication. A handshake, facial expression, mode of eye contact, bodily posture, yawning, and other nonverbal behavior can communicate valuable information about the client to the skilled observer. These behaviors often communicate feelings that the client is unable to say in words. Emotional pain may render one speechless. Tears may communicate pain, in which case the worker can respond empathetically: "I guess it hurts you so much that it's hard to talk about it." In family treatment, children often sit by their favorite parent; increased social distance in seating arrangements may indicate the less preferred members of the family. The distance and postures that clients assume in their interviews with the worker also indicate the amount of acceptance or rejection they feel toward the worker.

Interviewing involves listening, interpreting, and questioning. Garrett once said that interviewing is an art and that everyone engages in interviewing. While the social worker is interviewing a client, the client is also interviewing the worker! The social worker, however, is a professional interviewer whose skilled technique is accompanied by theoretical knowledge, appropriate values, and by conscious study of his or her own practice. "The obvious fact about interviewing," states Garrett, "is that it involves communication between two people. It might be called professional conversation."[19]

Listening is a fundamental task of interviewing. A good interviewer is a good listener. A good listener does not merely listen passively but is sincerely interested in, and concentrating on, what is being said. Occasional brief, relevant comments or questions give the client the feeling that the listener wants to and does understand to a great degree what the client is trying to say. Listening to silences may occasionally be embarrassing, but one should not be too quick to fill them with comments or further questions. Silences must be respected because the client may be searching for words to communicate something difficult or painful. The listener must be sensitive to the client's needs and feelings and must recognize when so many areas are being opened up that neither the interviewer nor the client can handle them all at once.

The process of *interpretation* should be continuous in communication between the social worker and the individual or group. In achieving as fully as possible an understanding of the client's problem, the worker has to interpret constantly the meanings (conscious and unconscious) of the client's behavior and words. The social worker should, in effect, develop a "third ear" tuned to deeper interpretations of what the client is saying. Initially, the worker should make interpretations only for herself or himself, not for the client. These initial interpretations are hypotheses to be tested and either rejected or retained, pending further confirmation. "Flexibility, the ability to change our hypothesis with the appearance of new evidence," notes Garrett, "is a trait well worth cultivating."[20]

Generally, interpreting case material for clients is not as productive as helping clients to arrive at their own interpretations and conclusions at their own pace. On occasion the worker can, however, help the client make connections. In order to do this, at least three conditions have to exist: (1) a good working relationship, (2) good timing, and (3) indications that the material is already near a level of awareness or consciousness. The following case, involving incest between a father and his oldest daughter, age fourteen, highlights these three factors. The daughter, who is being seen individually, is not in the interview. It is the third interview with the father and mother.

> *Father:* My wife is very hard to live with. She's always nagging that I'm always laying around the house doing nothing.
>
> *Mother:* That's true. He had his auto accident three years ago, and I know he'll never regain the complete use of his leg—but he can at least do some things around the house. He's like one of the kids. I constantly have to yell at all of them.
>
> *Father:* Yep! That's true (laughing).
>
> *Worker:* That must have been quite a responsibility you assumed following your husband's accident. Were there ever times when you yelled at or scolded Tricia (fourteen-year-old daughter) and your husband?
>
> *Mother:* Yes. Many times. Why, they used to sneak off together in the car and he would buy her things. It made me jealous. When they'd get back, I'd really scold them!
>
> *Father:* See what I mean? She really can be a bitch. You can't blame me for wanting to get out of the house.
>
> *Worker:* It sounds as if your husband *adopted* or was *placed* in the role of a peer or boyfriend to Tricia since the accident.
>
> *Father:* (Smiling.)

Mother: I guess I was behaving like a mother to him, too. I really think that's what happened. Maybe I pushed him into it.

Father: (Father didn't say anything but looked at mother very seriously and in thought.)

Questioning is another component in communication that is an important skill for social workers to develop. What you ask is what you get! Accusatory, tricky, abrupt, interrogation-type questions are counterproductive in social work interviews because they place the client on the defensive. The manner and tone in which questions are asked will often determine whether or not the question will be answered. Again, good timing, appropriateness, and a good relationship with the client enhance the questioning process.

Usually, questions that are leading and open-ended are more productive than questions that can be answered with a simple yes or no. Open-ended questions stimulate the client to elaborate on the story. Questions should evolve smoothly and not interrupt the comfortable pace of the client. Charging ahead of the client with questions may result in confusion for the client and in valuable information missed for the worker. Garrett suggests that a good general rule is to ask questions for only two purposes: to obtain needed information or to direct the client's conversation from fruitless to fruitful channels.[21]

Empathy Skills

The term *empathy* has been defined as the "imaginative projection of one's own consciousness into another being."[22] Empathy may be viewed as both a cognitive and affective process and as a complex skill containing three components: (1) the ability to distinguish among and label the thoughts and feelings of another, (2) the ability to take mentally the role of another, as in role taking, and (3) the ability to become emotionally responsive to another's feelings.[23] The ability to empathize enhances the helping relationship between the social worker and the client.

The social worker must be willing to enter into the emotional experience of the client. The verbal and nonverbal feeling cues that manifest themselves in the client's internal state are perceived by the social worker in an open, receptive, passive manner. Keefe states:

> Clients evoke physiological and emotional responses in the worker. When unfettered by complex cognitive processes, such as premature diagnosing, the worker sorts his or her own unique responses to the client from the feelings shared with the client. The worker then provides accurate verbal feedback to the client regarding his or her understanding and feelings. These several behaviors, feelings and thoughts comprise empathy.[24]

For example, Mr. Bolton, an elderly man in his mid-seventies who lives alone, who suffers from high blood pressure, and who was recently robbed by three young men, tells the social worker about his fear of leaving his apartment. He feels very depressed and lonely. After listening intently and empathetically to Mr. Bolton's story, the social worker says:

> It must be very, very difficult to be somewhat limited because of your high blood pressure, getting older, and then being assaulted and robbed. I can really understand how you feel and why you are afraid to leave your apartment. It is the only place you feel safe. However, isolating yourself can contribute to your feelings of loneliness. We've got to figure out how you can leave your apartment safely and begin to reach out and establish new social relationships.

The social worker, in effect, placed himself emotionally and psychologically in Mr. Bolton's situation and felt the physical security of the apartment but also its confining and socially isolating aspects. Even though the social worker did not change Mr. Bolton's situation, the fact that he verbalized what Mr. Bolton was feeling made the elderly man feel that at least one person in the world understood what he was experiencing. Mr. Bolton did not feel he was alone—he felt supported. Furthermore the worker's statement, *"We've* got to figure out how you can leave your apartment safely," reinforced Mr. Bolton's feelings that he indeed was not alone and that *together* they would find a solution to the problem.

Research has demonstrated that when one's suffering and dilemma is sensed by another person, it is perceived as empathic by the client.[25] Because of this empathy, the client will share more about himself or herself. This additional disclosure of feelings and personal discussion by the client builds more trust into the client/social worker relationship and facilitates problem solving in the treatment process.[26] Moreover, being empathetic makes the social worker more cognizant of the client and his or her social context.

Resistance Intervention Skills

Hartman and Reynolds state that the resistant client is the Achilles heel of social workers and that guilt, anger, and frustration may often lead to professional distancing by social workers toward resistant clients.[27] Resistance is the act of opposing, or retarding or slowing down a particular force. Freud perceived resistance in *all* cases and believed that the role of the therapist was to combat these resistances as part of therapy.[28] For social work, *resistance* may be defined as the conscious or unconscious efforts by client populations (individuals, couples, families, groups, communities) to resist improving their psychosocial functioning, which could be of benefit to themselves and/or society. Resistance by those being helped is perhaps present in most cases, if not in all cases as Freud would have us believe, or at some or several points in the helping process. It is almost always there. Social workers especially need to develop skills in identifying resistance and should be aware of the many different faces and manifestations that resistance assumes in the variety of practice situations (individual, couple, family, group, community). The factors of race, ethnicity, culture, sex, socioeconomic class, and involuntary client status, make the identification and management of resistant behavior even more difficult. Being late for an appointment, for example, might not necessarily indicate resistance, but rather financial difficulty in obtaining transportation, a baby sitter, or a cultural value not placing as much emphasis on punctuality as does the social worker. Social workers need to develop skills in effectively dealing with resistance as they progress in the helping process or else they may lose clients.

Resistance can take various forms. Examples of client resistance may include defensiveness, lying, silence, "no shows," being late, not paying, arguing, excessive affect, arriving intoxicated, forgetting, monopolizing and attempting to control the interview, making flirtatious comments, and not completing assignments. The list is endless. The bottom line is that resistance exists, it opposes treatment/help, it is aggressive, and it is counterproductive to the client. The resistance exhibited by *involuntary* clients (persons who are not seeking help) would presumably be different than voluntary clients, with more conscious than unconscious resistance being evident in the former. Table 9–1 compares voluntary with involuntary clients, highlighting manifestations and dynamics of resistance working against being helped.

Although the examples of client resistance in the table involve *individuals,* resistance is also often present as one works with marital couples, families, non-family groups, committees, and neighborhoods. In individuals, couples, families, and therapy groups, unconscious motivations to resist treatment and help can be expected more frequently than in committees, neighborhoods, and other large bodies, whose resistant behavior would be quite conscious.

One exception to totally conscious resistance can be seen in the collective, preconscious behavior of a large community group blocking out another from full participation in society through the use of institutional racism. Morales defined the *collective preconscious* as "the simultaneity, uniformity, or similarity

TABLE 9–1   *Examples of Client Resistance*

VOLUNTARY CLIENT			INVOLUNTARY CLIENT		
1. I want help with this problem,	*but*	It's frightening to explore what is underneath.	1. I don't want help with any problems,	*and*	I really don't have a problem anyway.
2. I'm seeing how I've been into denial. There can be possible solutions,	*but*	I'm so used to my problems.... Do I really want to change?	2. I'm not to blame for being on welfare. It's the system.	*and*	The system has to change. I'm not coming back.

of a response to a stimulus perceived on a preconscious level among many members of a group or society," which includes "some of the beliefs and sentiments common to many members of society including white racism," which is seen as existing on a preconscious level. The collective preconscious acts in concert toward outgroups with its actions emanating from beliefs, norms, and values including racism, which is an American value acquired through the acculturation process of formal and informal education.[29]

Groups clinging to conscious, preconscious, and unconscious racist or other oppressive beliefs often acted on and implemented through policy, may not be motivated to be "helped" since they would not see their beliefs and behavior (discriminatory policies) as harmful or self-destructive. They might see social work efforts toward a more equitable society as harmful to them, as they would lose their position of resource advantage and dominance. Social work values would indicate that forces such as racism, sexism, and class discrimination, *are* harmful to society, as they prevent all citizens from maximizing their potential to contribute to the common good. Confronting resistance at the macro level is perhaps one of social work's biggest challenges and may require macro-level intervention efforts such as social action, neighborhood and community organization, developing new policies and legislation, and *class action social work* (social work collaboration with the legal profession in behalf of oppressed people, discussed in Chapter 21) to effect change. In this respect, social workers are *consciously* working against client encountered resistance. There may be occasions, however, when social workers themselves unknowingly or unconsciously work against treatment or a positive outcome. They, much like their clients, can also—for any number of conscious or unconscious reasons—sabotage the helping process. Hence, social workers must also learn to develop skills to not only identify and manage resistance in clients but also in *themselves.* The concepts of transference and countertransference can assist in this endeavor.

Freud is credited with being the first to identify the tendency for patients to respond to their therapists as if they were someone else. He called this *transference.*[30] Since then, the concept of transference has been going through an evolution related to the types of patients or clients coming to the attention of mental health practitioners. The nature and varied presentations of our clients' problems cause us to modify and further refine our working concepts. For example, in modern general psychiatry transference is perceived as a loose designation for all aspects of the patient's feelings and behavior toward the psychiatrist. It also includes rational and adaptive aspects and irrational distortions arising from unconscious strivings. Transference can be positive, as in the idealization of the therapist, or negative, where the therapist is seen as manipulative and untrustworthy. In both instances these are reflections of the client's need to repeat old, unresolved conflicts that originated in childhood.[31]

Social workers need to modify and adapt this concept so it can have more relevance and applicability to the many faces and variety of life experiences of clients coming to the profession's attention. The authors therefore propose the following social work definition of *transference* as the conscious, preconscious, or unconscious displacement and projection of positive or negative attitudes and feelings on the identified helping person (social worker, therapist, counselor) by a voluntary or involuntary client, which are based in large part on early childhood experiences with parents, family members, and/or significant surrogates and later reinforced by transactions with subsequent authority figures, therapists, agencies and institutions. Such a definition makes it possible to include persons who since infancy were raised in institutions by various surrogate parent and authority figures. It is theorized that the nature of such experiences (positive or negative) will get played out or acted out, consciously or unconsciously, in the client–worker relationship. In those instances where an involuntary client is being "forced" into treatment, transference resistance can be expected to significantly thwart the helping process. What would be the reaction of a social worker confronting such a client? The concept of *countertransference* may give important clues. Countertransference is generally defined as the psychological process (mostly unconscious) in which a therapist is transferring, projecting, or displacing his or her feelings, attitudes, or emotions on a client, usually in response to "something" in the client.

Countertransference was posited by Freud five years after transference, and he saw it as emanating from the therapist as the result of the patient's influence on the therapist's unconscious feelings. The therapist, not unlike the patient, may in the countertransference state, react in frustration and deploy defensive behavior.[32] Kaplan and Sadock maintain that countertransference has components of which the therapist is unaware, that is, is partly unconscious, but that the therapist ought to be aware of countertransference issues that may interfere with the ability to be objective. They believe there are some groups of patients with whom a particular therapist does not work well and that the experienced clinician, recognizing this fact, will refer these patients to a colleague.[33]

Should therapists refer clients if they suspect the possibility of countertransference and thereby continue to avoid their own "blind spots"? Or should they try to understand the possible motivations for liking or disliking the client to the point where it is harmful or counterproductive for the client and the practitioner? As is the case with client transference, there are many clues to countertransference that may interfere with the helping process. Students, particularly, should develop their skills in identifying countertransference behavior, conscious or unconscious. The following are a few examples of clues:

1. Not wanting case assignments of clients who are of the same ethnic, racial, cultural, age, sex, or religious background
2. Feeling bored and unstimulated by certain clients
3. Appearing late or forgetting an appointment with a client
4. Often feeling affectionate or having sexual feelings toward a client
5. Not liking a client and not knowing why

These examples highlight countertransference behavior as it might involve worker–client interactions occurring primarily in a clinical context, or therapeutic setting. The examples could have included similar countertransference responses not only to individual clients but also to couples, families, or therapy groups. And for social work practice this concept could also be expanded to apply to other client populations such as community groups and neighborhoods.

Countertransference toward a community group or neighborhood is not currently reported in the literature, but this does not mean that these feelings and attitudes do not exist. For example, a social worker who was assaulted by members of an adolescent gang as a junior high student might twenty years later as a social worker have conscious or unconscious feelings and attitudes (fear, anger, anxiety, revenge) toward a client who is a gang member. Countertransference feelings may also be aroused in the social worker when he or she is assigned to work with a gang group or an inner-city area where there are gangs. An example of countertransference in a positive context would be a social worker consciously or unconsciously trying to impose a debating team program on a group of adolescents because he or she had such an exciting time as a member of a debating team in high school. In any of these examples, the social worker is not being objective, as old significant life experiences are interfering with his or her ability to effectively serve clients. In sum, a social worker countertransference is treating clients as if *they* were someone else. For social work practice application, then, *countertransference* may be defined as the unconscious, preconscious, or conscious displacement and projection of positive and/or negative attitudes and feelings by a social worker toward an individual, couple, family, group, neighborhood, or other community group with whom he or she is in a professional relationship. These feelings and attitudes had their origin in childhood or other significant psychosocial experiences later in life, and they currently interfere with the social worker's objectivity in the helping process.

The literature concerning patient or client resistance and transference is far more extensive than that for clinician resistance and countertransference. Because of all the years of academic and supervised clinical practice experience and preparation requiring discipline and professional responsibility, it can be concluded that the ego strength and maturity of social workers and other helping practitioners is significantly greater than that of their clientele. The ego strength and emotional maturity of clients would range, on a continuum, from weak to strong. Table 9–2 shows two examples of transference–countertransference transactions between a client and her or his social worker, highlighting the thoughts, feelings, and attitudes of the participants. The client statements are verbalized, but the social workers' countertransference responses are *not.*

For effective practice, even licensed social work practitioners may need occasional consultations when they have a hint of possible positive or negative bias toward a client that may indicate countertransference. There is no *one* way of handling resistance with clients who are not cooperating with the helping process since there are so many treatment theories and different disciplines with practitioners with varied levels of experience. A guiding principle should be that the intervention should be within the context of the theoretical framework employed by the practitioner, his or her experience level, and most important, the nature of the client's problems, ego strength, and maturity. The resistance encountered

TABLE 9–2   *Examples of Transference-Countertransference Resistance*

Voluntary Client Transference	Social Worker Counter-Transference	Involuntary Client Transference	Social Worker Counter-Transference
I've been very depressed, and last month I made my third suicide attempt. I see no reason to live. I can pay whatever you charge.	These cases bother me—often hopeless. Nothing seems to work, even medications. They depress me and make me feel anxious and helpless. Whom can I refer to?	It's a waste of time coming here. Just get off my case and I'll be fine. Put me back in the institution, I don't care. But I'm not coming back.	It's a waste of time for me too, and it won't bother me if you don't come back. You're violent, a loser, and I fear you. I wish I was in private practice so I could select all my cases.

with a psychotic hallucinating client who will not take his medication, for example, would be handled differently than that of a husband who keeps forgetting to do his communication exercise with his wife prior to attending a marital counseling session, or that of a welfare applicant who keeps forgetting the baby's birth certificate that can assist the worker in identifying the father.

Hartman and Reynolds developed a client resistance intervention approach they call *CIA,* that is, *C*onfrontation, *I*nterpretation, and *A*lliance. In exploring the underlying theory related to this intervention, Hartman and Reynolds explain, "Attachment theory is the theoretical foundation for the CIA paradigm. Attachment, in its primitive form during infancy, is the result of a cyclical process: A stressor or need arises that, in turn, produces tension. As the tension increases, rage mounts until it is expressed. When a caregiver responds to the expressed need, relaxation results."[34] The repetition of this tension–relaxation cycle is seen as creating trust, which is the building block of attachment.

In this three-stage framework, the social worker is faced with client resistance, for various reasons and assuming any number of forms. The underlying overt or covert affect is presumed to be anger. The client is seen as being in control, maintaining equilibrium through the deployment of defense mechanisms protecting him or her from progress and development, that is, in resistance. Seeing this resistance stance, the social worker then deliberately activates attachment behavior or longing in the client by creating a crisis through confrontation. The crisis in turn creates anxiety, fear of loss, and/or anger in the client, which then precipitates old patterns of attachment behavior within the client. The client next perceives strength in the social worker as the result of the confrontation, then feels cared for as the worker moves from confrontation to alliance. The alliance stage produces a relaxation response in the client, which leads to trust and hence a more therapeutic climate.

The CIA model is operationalized in the following case example:

Ms. C., age 21, was referred for therapy by the court because of a drug problem which resulted in the foster placement of her only child, age 4. A drug program helped her to become drug-free, but she needed additional in-depth treatment to understand the reasons for her underlying depression. The social worker inquired why she had missed her last two appointments.

Ms. C. flared up angrily, loudly stating that she was really busy with several errands, and it had slipped her mind, and furthermore that she did not have money to call, and besides she had misplaced the worker's phone number. The worker responded firmly, with good eye contact, stating that they had made an agreement to meet at a regular time for an initial three-month period but that already in the first month she was reverting to old, unreliable patterns and had missed two appointments. The worker wondered if she really wanted to take responsibility for getting her baby home.

Ms. C. seemed surprised and unprepared for this encounter, as previous therapists had usually assumed a rather indirect, passive approach with her. The worker then quickly moved from the brief confrontation to interpretation by asking, "Are there times you feel simply overwhelmed with all the responsibilities of a young mother living alone, sometimes depressed, and fearing you might be tempted to start using drugs and lose the baby again?"

The worker leaned closer to Ms. C., who by now was crying, and stated in a soft, supporting tone (moving into the alliance stage), "It's not going to be easy, but what *is* going to be different this time is that you *are* drug-free and I will be in your corner to help and emotionally support you as you need it. Ms. C. nodded "yes" as she smiled through her tears.

Skilled judgment has to be exercised in applying the CIA model, as confrontation may provoke excessive anger in some weak ego-strength, immature, low-functioning clients. The model may be more appropriate with higher ego-functioning clientele. Skilled intervention in the management of resistance thus must be appropriate to the personality strength of the client.

The second type of intervention approach in dealing with resistance is especially geared to involuntary clients and operates from a theoretical base borrowed from physics. According to Bertrand Russell, power, like energy, continually passes from any one of its forms into any other[35]; in other words, is transferable in direction. For example, Milner tells the story of how once he was accidentally locked in a room with a violent, psychotic patient. The patient began to strangle the therapist (application of power), and the therapist resisted the patient's expression of power. Then, for some unknown reason (perhaps intuition) Milner decided not to resist the patient's power and became limp. The patient then released him.[36] Can it be that power flowing in one direction, when confronted with power flowing in the opposite direction, will result in friction and resistance? And that power, when meeting resistance that is then neutralized, will return to the original form?

Consider the following summarized case reported by Morales in which the transfer of power had a therapeutic impact on a client. The client was a fifteen-year-old girl in a girls' twenty-four-hour correctional institution. For several months she kept demanding release from the institution, stating that she was not going to participate in individual or family therapy. Morales states,

> One day, as she was screaming that she wanted to leave, I handed her the keys (transfer of power) to the backyard gate. She responded in shock. "Where will I go? What will I do? How will I be able to eat? Who will take care of me?" she asked. I remained silent and shrugged my shoulders. She asked me what would happen to me if she left. I told her that probably I would get fired. She seemed overwhelmed with this power as she looked at the keys. She tearfully returned the keys, stating that she did not feel she was ready to leave the institution. There was a therapeutic breakthrough with the patient, which greatly minimized her resistance and allowed her to complete the program successfully.[37]

Note that this cannot be done in all cases. Obviously, certain factors have to be considered to minimize risks to the client and the social worker, such as the skill of the worker and knowledge of the client's capacities. Too much power may overwhelm some clients and have an iatrogenic effect. Whether we like it or not, clients have the power to decide if they want to be our clients and cooperate with being helped.

It is extremely important that involuntary clients participate in a process in which they are given the power or authority to decide whether they wish to become voluntary clients. This is based on the clinical assumption that a person who voluntarily participates in treatment derives more from it than a person who has treatment imposed on him or her. How might this be done? Morales states that when accepting an involuntary-client referral (from a probation or parole officer or welfare worker), he makes it clear he will not share information (respecting client confidentiality) with them about the client without permission, unless it pertains to a potentially suicidal or homicidal situation involving the client. This is also told to the client. Another condition of acceptance of the referral is that the client can terminate at *any point* of treatment without negative sanctions, even in the first interview. This information is also communicated to the client. During the first interview, there is an effort to elicit a contract from the client for at least two, four, or six visits, after which the client can either terminate or renegotiate treatment following evaluation of the initial sessions. The client is also left with the power to decide what he or she wishes to discuss and not discuss in treatment. It is, after all, for *the client's* benefit. Having a "say-so" in the session makes clients feel they are in control and may lessen fears and anxieties about participation.

The following case[38] illustrates how the concept of power was applied with a psychotic, violent person (with weak ego strength) who had been resisting treatment:

The (Involuntary) Client

Cali is a 21-year-old schizophrenic who called himself a "sniffomaniac." He was a parolee of bright intelligence, the second oldest in a family of six siblings (two sisters and three brothers). He had no memory of his father and, during the last two years since his release from a state institution, where he had been placed for armed robbery, had lived either with his mother and stepfather or his girl-friend and her mother.

Case Background

His childhood was extremely chaotic, with frequent fighting throughout school. He began stealing at the age of 7 and became involved in gang activities at about age 9. He was placed in foster homes beginning at the age of 10 for incorrigibility and truancy but ran away from all of them and was then placed in a boys' home on three different occasions. He was sent to probation camps from the age of 13 to 17 and then to the state youth corrections system until age 20. Between periods of institutionalization, he had multiple arrests ranging from assault with knives, pipes, and guns to purse snatching, armed robbery, and physical assaults. Commenting on his behavior, he stated, "I just want to hurt people, especially if they want to hurt me." Cali was involved in numerous gang fights and had scars of gunshot wounds in both legs and stab wounds in his back. Cali had been a chronic "sniffer" since about age 8. He made one wrist-cutting suicide attempt about two years before but was unable to recall the reason. He admitted to global homicidal thoughts but had no intent or specific plan.

Transforming the Involuntary Client into a Voluntary One

While in county and state confinement over the last five years, Cali had been diagnosed as schizophrenic, hospitalized on three occasions in psychiatric units and provided with psychiatric medication. He was a difficult treatment case and was on parole from the State. Cali was very paranoid and cunning and argued that since the social worker was being paid to see him, he should also be paid to see the social worker. The worker recommended to the parole office director that he should receive $10. each week immediately after he had spent a minimum of thirty minutes with the therapist. Cali kept practically all of his weekly 9 A.M. appointments over a fifteen-month period, until his successful discharge from parole.

Joint Treatment Plan

The treatment plan for Cali, which he approved, included the following:

1. The provision of emotional support over a period of many months during his gradual and eventual withdrawal from paint sniffing
2. The involvement of his girlfriend in conjoint sessions as a means of minimizing conflict in their relationship
3. The eliciting of his cooperation in applying for a psychiatric disability pension, which he eventually received
4. The assistance of the development of a more compassionate perception of Cali as a psychiatrically disabled person rather than as a criminal by the parole staff. Their changed perception had a reciprocal effect on Cali: he became friendlier to the staff and began to enjoy visiting the parole program.

5. The increase in socialization between Cali and the parole officer, such as the parole officer's taking him shopping, to entertainment events, and to lunch and dinner.

When Cali demanded to be paid for his time like the social worker, he actually was asking for a share of the power and an opportunity to be treated equally. He felt that his time was also valuable. He wanted to be a partner in a transaction that was supposed to benefit him. The sharing of power transformed him into a voluntary client. The agency director felt that Cali was going to use the money to support his "habit", and no doubt he initially did. At times he came to sessions intoxicated, but because of an earlier agreement he was not seen and not paid on these occasions. Initially the behavioral reinforcement (reward) of being paid was a motivating factor in his "cooperating" with treatment, but after a trusting relationship had been established he also liked to visit his "shrink." After termination of parole, he returned voluntarily some months later for some more sessions—without being paid to participate.

Social Work Assessment Skills

Having developed the basics of helping, engagement, observation, communication, empathy, and resistance intervention skills, the next task is to develop basic social work assessment skills in order to have a conceptual framework for helping people with their difficulties. In its purest form, assessment is simply the basis for a plan of action. In social work it is the assessment of the person-in-environment complex out of which develops a plan for intervention. It includes those activities in the selection and interpretation of information relevant to treatment. The goal is to define the areas for intervention and delineate the types of intervention strategies and treatment goals.[39]

Monkman and Allen-Meares present a social work assessment model called TIE (the *T*ransactions between *I*ndividuals and *E*nvironments). This framework, developed by Monkman, maps the domain of social work assessment, intervention, and outcome. This framework also has other uses in outcome research and for organizing values, knowledge, and skills in practice settings. Using an ecological perspective, the TIE Framework centers on the transactions and interface between persons and the environment. In theory the worker can be more effective in the intervention when he or she has assessed fully each side of the interface between person and environment.[40]

On the *person* side of the interface, the social worker focuses on the coping behaviors (cognitive, behavioral, affective) of the person, which include: (1) *surviving;* (2) *affiliating;* and (3) *growing and achieving.* Surviving-coping behaviors are defined by Monkman and Allen-Meares as those behaviors that enable the person to obtain and use resources and make it possible to continue life or activity. Affiliating-coping behaviors are the behaviors that enable the person to relate to other persons and institutions in the environment satisfactorily; that is, the capacity to develop and maintain close personal relationships as well as relate to resources and structures (institutions). Growing-and-achieving coping behaviors are the behaviors that enable the person to pursue intellectual and social activities valuable to the self as well as others.[41]

On the environment side of the interface of the framework is the "Quality of Impinging Environments." This is defined as those positive and negative qualities and characteristics of the situation with which the person (client) is in direct contact. The three major components of this environment include: (1) *resources* (people, organizations, or institutions that can be helpful); (2) *expectations* (roles, tasks); and (3) *laws and policies* (binding customs, rules, policies governing individual behaviors).

The task of the social worker, then, is to help people and their environments form a better match so that persons can live a more enriched and productive life, hence also improving the environment. In short, the social worker intervenes with the goal of bringing about a more positive outcome for both the person and the environment. The following case will serve as an example for incorporating the TIE Assessment Framework:

Case Illustration

Mark, an only child, is a bright, fourteen-year-old middle-class Anglo youngster residing in an affluent West Coast suburban area. He was referred to a community drug treatment program by the school because he was caught using cocaine with a few male peers on two occasions. His parents had been divorced three years and had joint custody of Mark. Although the parents were only a few miles from each other, Mark "bounced" back and forth living with his parents, depending on each of his parents' business and social commitments. Mark admitted using cocaine about three times per week and getting "loaded" on marijuana, "coke" and alcohol on weekends. He began experimenting with marijuana at age 11, when his parents were divorcing. Six months later, his maternal grandmother, who often took care of him on weekends, suddenly died of a heart attack.

Mark's parents were college graduates. His father, a realtor and former 1960s "flower child," admitted that he on occasion would smoke marijuana in his son's presence. The mother, a department store manager, divorced the father because he had been involved in several affairs over most of the years they had been married. The parents tended to minimize Mark's drug use, but they did acknowledge that his school performance had been deteriorating for a few years.

The focus of the TIE Framework begins by identifying the critical players and elements in the case: Mark, the mother, the father, the deceased grandmother, *and* the transactions between and among them and the environment. The drug-treatment social worker begins with Mark, since he is having the most difficulty functioning. There are certain questions that the worker has to ask to assist in the assessment, outlined as follows:

Mark's Transactions

What are the transactions between and among Mark and his mother, Mark and his father, Mark and his late grandmother? What are Mark's transactions with the school, peers at school, peers at home, and drug life style? What are his transactions with the drug program? What are his social and recreational resources and expectations?

Mother's Transactions

What are the transactions between and among the mother and Mark, the mother and the father, the mother and the late grandmother? What are the transactions between the mother and her employment, social life (new relationship?), and relatives? What are her psychosocial strengths and housing, recreational, and economic resources? Does her current life style and structure involve a place for Mark? What are her expectations concerning Mark?

Father's Transactions

What are the transactions between and among the father and Mark, the father and mother, the father and late grandmother? What are the transactions between the father and his employment, social life (new relationship?), and relatives? What are his psychosocial strengths and housing, recreational, and economic resources? Does the father's life style and structure permit a place for Mark? What are the father's expectations concerning Mark?

Late Grandmother's Transactions

What were the transactions between and among the grandmother and Mark, his mother, and father? What emotional and economic resources did she provide Mark and the parents? Did the grandmother's life style and structure provide a place for Mark? What were her expectations concerning Mark?

Even though the grandmother was not living, her loss was still having a significant emotional impact on Mark's life. Among life's most stressful, critical life events for adolescents is the loss of a parent through death; second, losing a parent through divorce. In Mark's case, he lost his parents through divorce and six months later he lost his grandmother, indeed two very traumatic life events.

Table 9–3 assists in the identification of critical elements, the focus of change efforts, and the areas in which the results of the change efforts are found.[42]

The TIE Framework reveals that a significant amount of positive change occurred in Mark's case. Other cases may exhibit more or less change. Sometimes negative trends can be seen, which then call for different, more effective intervention strategies. Changes that are often related as change in one category may affect change in others. For example, as Mark vented his unresolved feelings about his grandmother, he felt less depressed and hence had less need of drugs. His health improved, and he went out for sports. As he began to feel psychologically better, he had much less need to use drugs, which improved his health; this motivated him to do better in school. Soon he was drug-free.

TABLE 9–3   *TIE Assessment and Evaluation Outcome Framework*

Coping Behaviors	Quality of Impinging Environment
Surviving	**Informal Resources**
Assessment: Mark's school work is poor. He has a substance abuse problem.	*Assessment:* Housing is inconsistent for Mark. Receives minimal affection and care from his parents.
Outcome: Mark is in a drug treatment program. School work is improving.	*Outcome:* The parents are providing Mark more consistent housing and involving him more in their lives.
Affiliating	**Societal Resources**
Assessment: Mark's relationship to his parents is strained—Mark still misses the grandmother.	*Assessment:* Drug treatment and tutoring program are needed for Mark. Family therapy is indicated.
Outcome: Mark's relationship with his parents is improving. He is working through his loss of the grandmother.	*Outcome:* Mark is attending a drug treatment program and receiving tutoring. Mark and his parents are in family therapy.
Information and Skills	**Formal Resources**
Assessment: The parents did not know where to obtain family therapy or a tutor for Mark.	*Assessment:* Some local business firms provide recreational outings for youths.
Outcome: The parents learned about family therapy services from the drug program. At the parents' request, the school obtained a tutor for Mark.	*Outcome:* Mark is participating regularly in business-sponsored recreational activities. He is developing new, positive friends.
Growth and Achievement	**Expectations**
Assessment: Mark has poor academic achievement and frequent truancy. His health has deteriorated due to late-evening life style and drugs.	*Assessment:* Neither parent wanted to assume responsibility for Mark.
Outcome: Mark has stopped drugs. Has gone out for the cross-country team. With tutoring, grades are improving. Is working as a box boy on weekends.	*Outcome:* Both parents have now given Mark priority in their lives. Parents are giving Mark much more attention and assisting him with some of his homework.
Coping Pattern	**Policies and Procedures**
Assessment: Mark's behavioral pattern toward school was irresponsible, as was his life with illegal drugs. Drugs were in part dulling his psychological pain related to parental rejection and the loss of the grandmother.	*Assessment:* The school had the option of sending Mark to juvenile court for his substance abuse and truancy.
Outcome: Mark is planning to graduate from high school and go to junior college. He is coping better with the loss of the grandmother. He feels less angry toward his parents.	*Outcome:* School policies permitted a diversion-program referral for Mark's drug problem. The school decided to allow Mark to improve his school performance.

CONCLUDING COMMENT

Social work skill is defined as the social worker's capacity to set in motion with a client interventive processes of change based on social work values and knowledge in a situation relevant to the client. Competence in social work practice lies in developing skill in the use of social work methods and social work techniques for intervention into problem situations.

The dynamic process in learning skills is complex and difficult to communicate. Mental skills are uniquely taught and learned. Given written and oral instructions about skills and given time, individuals may develop the skill themselves when they form a plan to guide their actions; yet they will fully maximize these skills only with experience. By viewing social work practice as an art, each practitioner will develop a configuration of techniques and skills that reflects his or her own style.

Seven areas and related key concepts were highlighted as recommended basic skills for beginning social work practice: *basic helping skills, engagement skills, observation skills, communication skills, empathy skills, resistance intervention skills,* and *social work assessment skills.* The new worker needs to develop perceptive skills in order to look at familiar things with new eyes, to identify people who need help and conditions that need to be changed. In developing engagement skills, the process of effectively involving individuals, families, or groups in a helping situation requires the purposeful use of self. Factors such as the time, setting, and structure of the interview may enhance or impede the engagement process. The engagement process includes beginning, middle, and ending phases. In learning observation skills, social workers must become aware of particular biases that distort their perception of others. Observation is more than just seeing; the observer chooses what to see. Equally important are communication skills. Clients can accept a communication only when they understand it. Various suggestions, supported by brief case examples, were provided for developing skill in some components of communication (listening, interpreting, and questioning). Empathy is both a cognitive and an affective process, a complex skill that can be learned in order to help people. The ability to enter into the emotional experience of the client enhances the therapeutic relationship. The omnipresent resistance, with its accompanying transference and countertransference dynamics, surfaces in practically all helping situations involving social work practitioners. Developing skills in the knowledge of its various conscious and unconscious manifestations and skills in its management results in more effective social work practice. Finally, developing client assessment skills involving the application of a conceptual scheme, such as the TIE Framework, helps the social worker maintain a clearer focus on the transactions and interface between persons and the environment.

SUGGESTED READINGS

BRILL, NAOMI I. *Working with People: The Helping Process* 4th ed. New York: Longman, 1990.

CHESTANG, LEON, "Competencies and Knowledge in Clinical Social Work: A Dual Perspective." In *Toward a Definition of Clinical Social Work,* Patricia Ewalt, ed. Denver: NASW Invitational Forum of Clinical Social Work, June 1979.

CONNAWAY, RONDA S., and GENTRY, MARTHA E. *Social Work Practice.* Englewood Cliffs, N.J.: Prentice-Hall, 1988.

FRANKENSTEIN, RENATE. "Agency and Client Resistance." *Social Casework* 63 (January 1982).

GARRETT, ANNETTE. *Interviewing: Its Principles and Methods* New York: Family Service Association of America, 1972.

GITTERMAN, ALEX. "Uses of Resistance: A Transactional View. *Social Work* 28 (March–April 1983).

HARTMAN, CARL, and REYNOLDS, DIANE. "Resistant Clients: Confrontation, Interpretation, and Alliance." *Social Casework* 68 (April 1987).

HASENFELD, YEHESKEL. "Power in Social Work Practice." *Social Service Review* 61 (September 1987).

HEPWORTH, DEAN H., and LARSEN, JO ANN. *Direct Social Work Practice: Theory and Skills* 3rd ed. Homewood, Ill.: Dorsey Press, 1990.

HEUS, MICHAEL, and PINCUS, ALLEN. *The Creative Generalist: A Guide to Social Work Practice.* Barneveld, Wis.: Micamar Publishing, 1986.

MONKMAN, MARJORIE, "A National Study of Outcome Objectives in Social Work Practice: Person and Environment." Unpublished paper, University of Illinois, Urbana.

MONKMAN, MARJORIE, and ALLEN-MEARES, PAULA. "The TIE Framework: A Conceptual Map for Social Work Assessment," *Arete* 10 (Spring 1985), University of South Carolina: 42.

MORALES, ARMANDO. "Clinical Social Work with Special Populations." In *Toward a Definition of Clinical Social Work,* Patricia Ewalt, ed. Denver: NASW Invitational Forum of Clinical Social Work, June 1979.

PIERSON, ARTHUR. "Social Work Techniques with the Poor." *Social Casework* 51 (October 1970): 481–485.

SHEAFOR, BRADFORD W., HOREJSI, CHARLES R., and HOREJSI, GLORIA A. *Techniques and Guidelines for Social Work Practice.* Boston: Allyn and Bacon, 1988.

SOLOMON, BARBARA BRYANT. *Black Empowerment: Social Work in Oppressed Communities.* New York: Columbia University Press, 1976.

WHITTAKER, JAMES, and TRACY, ELIZABETH. *Social Treatment* 2nd ed. New York: Adeline DeGruyter, 1989.

ENDNOTES

1. *Webster's Third New International Dictionary* (Springfield, Mass.: G. & C. Merriam, 1966), p. 2133.
2. A. T. Welford, "On the Nature of Skill," in David Legge, ed., *Skills* (Baltimore: Penguin Books, 1970), pp. 21–22.
3. Brian J. Heraud, *Sociology and Social Work* (New York: Pergamon Press, 1970), p. 223.
4. Werner W. Boehm, "The Nature of Social Work," *Social Work* 3 (April 1958): 11.
5. Ibid.
6. William E. Gordon, "A Critique of the Working Definition," *Social Work* 7 (October 1962): 7.
7. Ibid., p. 8.
8. Ibid. Italics (ours) call attention to the fact that the way a social worker applies skills is a unique phenomenon, an "artistic creation."
9. See Ruth Smalley, "Social Casework: The Functional Approach"; Helen Harris Perlman, "Social Casework: The Problem-Solving Approach"; and Florence Hollis, "Social Case-

work: The Psychological Approach," in Robert Morris, ed., *Encyclopedia of Social Work* 16th issue (New York: National Association of Social Workers, 1971), pp. 1195–1225.

10. See Emanuel Tropp, "Social Group Work: The Developmental Approach"; William Schwartz, "Social Group Work: The Interactionist Approach"; and Charles D. Garvin and Paul H. Glasser, "Social Group Work: The Preventive and Rehabilitative Approach," in *Encyclopedia of Social Work,* pp. 1246–1272.

11. Robert Perlman, "Social Planning and Community Organization: Approaches," in Robert Morris, p. 1338.

12. Ibid., p. 1339; Robert Perlman and Arnold Gurin, *Community Organization and Social Planning* (New York: John Wiley, 1972), pp. 52–89; Alfred J. Kahn, *Theory and Practice of Social Planning* (New York: Russell Sage Foundation, 1969), pp. 60–129; and Bradford W. Sheator, "The Community Adjustment Process from a System Perspective," *Journal of Social Welfare* 1 (April 1974): 37–44.

13. Harriett M. Bartlett, *The Common Base of Social Work Practice* (New York: National Association of Social Workers, 1970), p. 195.

14. Legge, pp. 237–248.

15. Helen Harris Perlman, *Social Casework: A Problem-Solving Process* (Chicago: University of Chicago Press, 1957), pp. 157–158 (emphasis ours).

16. Frank Loewenberg and Ralph Dolgoff, *Teaching of Practice Skills in Undergraduate Programs in Social Welfare and Other Helping Services* (New York: Council on Social Work Education, 1971), p. 6.

17. Herbert Bisno, "A Theoretical Framework for Teaching Social Work Methods and Skills," in Lester J. Glick, ed., *Undergraduate Social Work Education for Practice: A Report on Curriculum Content and Issues* vol. I (Washington, D.C.: U.S. Government Printing Office, 1971), p. 248.

18. Loewenberg and Dolgoff, pp. 60–67.

19. Annette Garrett, *Interviewing: Its Principles and Methods* (New York: Family Service Association of America, 1972), p. 5. Ms. Garrett's book, first published in 1942, has been translated into nineteen foreign languages. A true classic in the social work literature, it is an unparalleled resource for learning about interviewing.

20. Ibid., p. 61.

21. Ibid., p. 48.

22. *Webster's New Collegiate Dictionary* (Springfield, Mass.: G. & C. Merriam, 1950), p. 269.

23. Norma D. Feshbach, "Empathy in Children: Some Theoretical and Empirical Considerations," *Counseling Psychologist* 5 (1975): 25–30.

24. Thomas Keefe, "Empathy Skill and Critical Consciousness," *Social Casework* 61 (September 1980): 388–389. Reprinted with permission of the Family Service Association of America.

25. Wilbur Wright, "Counselor Dogmatism, Willingness to Disclose, and Client's Empathy Ratings," *Journal of Counseling Psychology* 22 (September 1975): 390–394.

26. Tamar Plitt Halpern, "Degree of Client Disclosure as a Function of Past Disclosure, Counselor Disclosure, and Counselor Facilitativeness," *Journal of Counseling* 24 (January 1977): 41–47.

27. Carl Hartman and Diane Reynolds, "Resistant Clients: Confrontation, Interpretation, and Alliance," *Social Casework* 68 (April 1987): 205–213.

28. Sigmund Freud, *Beyond the Pleasure Principle,* 1920 Standard Edition of the Complete Works of Sigmund Freud vol. 18 (London: Hogarth Press, 1955), pp. 3–64.

29. Armando Morales, "The Collective Preconscious and Racism," *Social Casework* 52 (May 1971): 285–293.

30. Karl Menninger, *Theory of Psychoanalytic Technique* (New York: Harper & Row, 1958), pp. 79–80.

31. Harold I. Kaplan and Benjamin J. Sadock, eds., *Synopsis of Psychiatry* 5th ed. (Baltimore: Williams and Wilkins, 1988), p. 466.
32. Menninger, p. 87.
33. Kaplan and Sadock, p. 467.
34. Hartman and Reynolds, pp. 205–213.
35. Bertrand Russell, *Power: A New Social Analysis* (New York: W. W. Norton, 1938).
36. Personal communication by Professor John Milner during a lecture, University of Southern California School of Social Work, 1961.
37. Armando Morales, "The Mexican-American Gang Member: Evaluation and Treatment," in Rosina Becerra, Marvin Karno, and Javier Escobar, eds., *Mental Health and Hispanic Americans* (New York: Grune and Stratton, 1982), pp. 139–155.
38. For additional literature concerning work with involuntary clients, see Leon Chestang, "Competences and Knowledge in Clinical Social Work," and Armando Morales, "Clinical Social Work with Special Populations," in *Toward a Definition of Clinical Social Work,* Patricia Ewalt, ed. (Denver: NASW Invitational Forum of Clinical Social Work, June 1979). This case is a shorter, modified version of a case appearing in "Clinical Social Work with Special Populations" by Morales.
39. Srinika Jayaratne and Rona Levy, *Empirical Clinical Practice* (New York: Columbia Press, 1979), p. 17.
40. Marjorie Monkman and Paula Allen-Meares, "The TIE Framework: A Conceptual Map for Social Work Assessment," *Areté* 10 (Spring 1985), The University of South Carolina: 42. Also see Marjorie Monkman, "A National Study of Outcome Objectives in Social Work Practice: Person and Environment," unpublished paper, School of Social Work, University of Illinois, Urbana.
41. Ibid, p. 42.
42. Ibid, p. 47–48.

PART FOUR

Special Populations and Concerns in Social Work

*P*art One provided an overview of social work: its domain and practice, its emergence, and entry into the profession. Part Two examined social welfare institutions, fields of social work practice, and agency and private practice in social work. Part Three dealt with the knowledge, values, and skill requirements of the social worker. The prospective social worker may now feel that all that is needed to enter the "waiting arms" of the community is superhuman energy and altruism. However, much like the new physician, who discovers with frustration that his or her impoverished patients cannot afford the medications prescribed, or the rookie police officer who wishes to fight crime in a poor community only to become the most hated person in the neighborhood, the social worker may become discouraged in the effort to help people with their problems.

To avoid such discouragement, the student has to be prepared with additional knowledge, values, and skills. The purposes of Part Four, therefore, are (1) to expose the potential social work practitioner to various ideological concerns and issues that may be confronted in poor and rural communities, particularly in ethnic minority communities throughout the United States; (2) to help the student distinguish the impact of various forces at work in poor communities, such as social welfare, social services, social agency bureaucracies, social workers, sexism, racism, homophobia, ageism, and class discrimination; and (3) to help the student develop a perception of the knowledge and skills needed for working in specific minority communities and better understand the cultural and value systems found in some ethnic and rural communities.

It was stated in Chapter 4 that social welfare represents society's formal effort, independent of the family and private enterprise, to maintain or improve the economic conditions, health care, or interpersonal competence of some or all parts of the population. Social agencies such as welfare and probation departments are organizations established to carry out the social welfare functions in a specific region of a state. Briefly restated, social work was seen as the professional activity of helping individuals, groups, or communities to enhance or restore their capacity for social functioning and for creating societal conditions favorable to that goal. Social workers are persons employed by social agencies to carry out professional social work activities within the framework of policies, rules, ethics, and regulations of social welfare, the social agency, and the social work profession.

These distinctions must constantly be kept in mind when one is reading the following chapters because social work and social workers are often blamed for conditions that are neither of their making nor within their control. Some of these critical voices have already had an impressive impact on minority communities and among social workers.

Chapter 10, "Social Work Practice with Special Populations," is a chapter developed by Armando T. Morales to serve as both an informational and demographic needs assessment and conceptual foundation for Part Four. A definition of special populations is provided, which includes persons such as children, women, the elderly, and minorities who have unique needs. The new, emerging special population groups include the growing numbers of homeless people in the United States, police brutality victims and persons suffering from and dying from AIDS. For centuries the world has feared the poor, reminding many in society that "There, but for the grace of God, go I." AIDS victims today are seen in many ways as history's dreaded "lepers" of society, and there are occasional cries for quarantine of this population. All these special populations share second-class status in society and suffer the consequences of sexism, ageism, racism, homophobia, and classism. The ecosystems model developed in Chapter 7 can assist social workers in assessing the psychosocial needs of special populations.

In working with special population clients, a generalist practice approach would seem preferable, considering the specialized issues, problems, and range of needs. A gen-eralist practitioner would examine the various aspects of a situation needing intervention using an assessment scheme such as the ecosystems framework, then apply the knowledge, values, and skills to initiate service and/or to obtain appropriate resources or specialized expertise. Generalist practice, therefore, involves both the capacity to take a comprehensive view of a practice situation and having the necessary knowledge and skills to intervene at multiple levels and in a broad range of client concerns. Numerous rich case examples employing the generalist practice mode are evident in the following ten chapters on special populations.

Chapter 11, "Social Work Practice with Women," an original work by Diane Kravetz, deals with the increasing health and mental health problems impacting women as a result of sexism, classism, and ethnic-racial discrimination. Women are impoverished in greater numbers than men, constitute the majority among older Americans, and are the fastest growing group of people with AIDS. Very large numbers of women continue to be victims of physical, psychological, and sexual abuse, often caused by members of their own families. Kravetz calls for social workers to eliminate sexism within the profession as it impacts female clients and workers. She presents rich case examples.

Chapter 12, "Social Work Practice with Lesbians and Gays," by George A. Appleby and Jeane W. Anastas, another original, very educational piece for this volume, painstakingly defines the complex, often confused and misused term *homosexuality*. They provide unique insights involving micro practice with lesbian and gay individuals, couples, parents, and older homosexuals.

Chapter 13, "Social Work Practice with the Elderly," by Manuel R. Miranda and Armando T. Morales, is another original, commissioned chapter for the volume. The authors describe the elderly as one of the

neediest of all social work practice populations as they constitute the fastest growing
subgroup in the nation and will represent 25
percent of the total population by 2040. Because of ageism, a changing economic structure "pushes out" the elderly despite still
being able to perform in the job market and
places many of them in positions of economic
vulnerability, frequently made worse by the
loss of spouse, inflation, and increasing physical frailty over the years. Currently, as many
as four million people are affected by Alzheimer's disease, and it is estimated that unless a
cure is found, fourteen million persons will
suffer from the disease by the year 2050. Miranda and Morales present a unique micro-to-
macro level case that highlights transference
and countertransference dynamics as a social
worker attempts to help an elderly couple.

Chapter 14, "Practice in Rural America:
The Appalachian Experience," by Bradford W.
Sheafor and Robert G. Lewis, is a response to
readers of previous editions and practitioners
in the field wanting more exposure in the literature of a neglected special population in
the United States, the rural poor. The case example describes the millions of poor people
in need of social services in rural Appalachia.
They often have the same needs and problems
as urban clients, but because they are so isolated, rural people also encounter numerous
barriers in the delivery of services. These populations have been ignored for many years,
and it is the intention of the authors that in
some way social work practitioners will develop a greater interest in serving them.

Chapter 15, "Urban Gang Violence: A Psychosocial Crisis" was written by Armando T.
Morales, a former gang group worker, probation officer, and currently a state parole
mental health consultant. Inner city areas in
many parts of the Nation are in crisis, with
gang violence and homicide reaching astounding rates, resulting in thousands of young
males being killed each year (600 deaths per

100,000 as compared to AIDS, which is 190
deaths per 100,000 population). Gang homicide is indeed a human problem of epidemic
proportions. The quality of life for these victims and family survivors should definitely become a health and mental health concern and
a priority practice area for social work. Social
work's body of knowledge dealing with gangs
dates from the 1930s, 1940s, and 1950s, and
an appeal is made to update and upgrade the
profession's micro and macro practice intervention skills to deal more effectively with this
growing problem.

Ethnic and racial minorities have been and
continue to be overrepresented among the
underclass. A racist might state, for example,
that black minorities are overrepresented
among the poor because they are somehow
inherently or biologically inferior to whites,
who generally continue to have a significantly
higher standard of living. Either minorities are
inferior (a racist perspective), or white racism
has prevented their natural equality with
whites from asserting itself during their more
than 100 to 300 years in the United States.
Those who deny that overt racism and institutional subordination are essentially responsible for the current lower status of minorities
are implying that minorities are biologically
or inherently inferior.

Chapter 16, "The Impact of Macro Systems on Puerto Rican Families," by Emelicia
Mizio, highlights the importance of understanding the cultural heritage of Puerto Ricans
and the degree of each family's identification
with Puerto Rican or Anglo culture. Mizio suggests that the Puerto Rican family has to be
permitted to utilize its own strength, draw on
its humanitarian values, and support both kin
and the Puerto Rican community at large.

Chapter 17, by John Red Horse, pertains
to the "Cultural Evolution of American Indian
Families." Contrary to popular stereotypic belief and social learning from movies and television, American Indians are actually a very

heterogenous population, representing almost 500 tribes and speaking 149 different languages, with 24 percent of all American Indians using their native language. Red Horse discusses several aspects of American Indian life styles, culturally determined family systems, and combinations of behavior.

In Chapter 18, "Practice with Asian Americans," author Man Keung Ho continues with his "state-of-the-art" original chapter, which replaced his classic piece published in 1976 and made its first appearance in this book in 1977. Dr. Ho provides excellent demographic and cultural information that assists the reader in discerning the great heterogeneity found among the Asian-American population (Chinese, Filipino, Japanese, Korean, Vietnamese, Cambodian, Samoan, and Guamanian). He describes therapy models developed by different Asian cultures, such as *Morita* therapy, *Maikan* therapy, and *Ho'oponopono* (Hawaiian family therapy). Without knowledge of these therapies, social work practitioners may unwittingly cause problems for themselves or the Asian clients they are attempting to help.

Chapter 19, "Social Work with Mexican Americans," an original chapter by Armando T. Morales and Ramon Salcido, points out that the Mexican American population is also a very heterogeneous one, one of the most diverse groups in the United States. Similar to the American Indian population, it is one of the oldest groups in the United States, but because of continuing migration, it is also one of the newest. Mexican Americans number

about 12.1 million, with some experts estimating the number closer to 15 million when Mexicans without documentation are included. The median age is 23.5, compared to 31.9 for the overall population. And whereas 11 percent of the general population is over sixty-five years old, only 4 percent of Mexican Americans are in this age group. This dramatic preponderance of youth translates into different human service needs compared to the general population. And their general state of political powerlessness makes it difficult for Mexican Americans to persuade human service institutions to become more responsive to these needs.

Chapter 20, "Social Work with Afro-Americans," by Barbara Bryant Solomon, helps social workers understand this large population. Afro-Americans, numbering 31 million persons in the United States, are a very heterogeneous group, with more than half residing in central cities throughout the United States. The author maintains that racism and discrimination, rather than the process of urbanization, contribute to the creation of an underclass among some Afro-Americans. Solomon encourages social workers to learn to know Afro-Americans better by becoming actively involved in the educational, political, and cultural life of blacks. In helping Afro-Americans, Solomon suggests the intervention strategy of empowerment, which encourages the social worker to engage in activities with clients that will help reduce the psychosocial powerlessness caused by society.

Chapter 10

Social Work Practice with Special Populations

Armando T. Morales

PREFATORY COMMENT

"Social Work Practice with Special Populations" is a chapter developed to serve both as an informational and demographic needs assessment profile for Part Four. Special population members such as women, children, the elderly, and minorities continue to share second-class status in the United States. In recent times economic forces and a frightening virus have produced two new, growing special population groups, respectively the homeless and AIDS (acquired immune deficiency syndrome) patients, who also suffer social stigma and are generally denied the kinds of economic resources and medical treatment and research they need to function in society in a humane, comfortable manner.

The practice skills of social workers are being challenged by special population groups and in beginning to meet this challenge, the evolving ecosystems model, presented in Chapter 7, assists the social worker in obtaining a comprehensive analysis of a specific case for micro or macro intervention.

The concept of human diversity appears in the literature from time to time and refers to persons who are perceived as members of diverse groups such as women, the elderly, and racial and ethnic minorities. Some recipients of the label, however, reject the label and do not feel they should be perceived as "diverse" persons, or as members of "diverse groups" in U.S. society. Although the intent of the concept is positive—a means of assisting practitioners in the helping profession to develop skills in recognizing and accepting differences in needs, communication, relationships and life styles—the term ironically seems to create divisiveness. Inherent in the word diverse *is a divisive rather than an integrative quality.*

Beginning with the first edition of this volume, the authors preferred to substitute the term special populations. *In the definition of* special, *according to Webster's Third New International Dictionary, there is something "additional to the regular." In the context of human behavior, all humans have certain universal needs, but in addition to these needs, some people have special needs beyond what might normally already be applicable or available to others. Within this conceptual definition, special populations such as the elderly, the homeless, children, women, lesbians and gays, police brutality victims, AIDS patients, and minorities bring unique needs and circumstances that must be recognized when the social worker serves these persons. A year after the authors began using the term* special populations, *the President's Commission on Mental Health produced their definition, which was similar, defining special populations as:*

> *Americans who are characterized by (1) uniqueness and diversity in terms of race, ethnic origin, sex, and physical status and (2) by de facto second class status in American Society.[1]*

The President's Commission added that special-population groups are both at times overrepresented in the statistics on mental health and inappropriately served by the current mental health system in the United States. Women, for example, are overrepresented in the mental health system and suffer the stresses of second-class status. Children, minorities, and the elderly are very underserved in human service systems, based on their needs, and also suffer the psychosocial consequences of second-class status. Citing what it referred to as a well-documented national scandal, the President's Commission reported that, whereas middle-class nonminority children with behavior problems receive appropriate mental health services in voluntary clinical settings, minority children are more likely to be processed by the police and juvenile courts for the same behavioral problems.[2] Those persons being tracked into the juvenile and adult criminal justice systems may also be included in the definition of a special population, in which there is a marked overrepresentation of minorities.

SOCIETALLY INDUCED STRESSORS AFFECTING SPECIAL POPULATIONS

In attempting to help persons who are from the special populations groups, as previously defined, the social worker needs to understand what forces are at work to keep these groups in a disadvantaged, second-class position in society. The biopsychosocial experience of living as a second-class-status person is quite stressful, often resulting in non-health-related premature death (accidents, suicide, homicide), poor physical and mental health, chronic substance abuse, and repeated voluntary and involuntary institutionalization. The forces or stressors that keep many special population members from realizing their full potential to contribute to society include sexism, homophobia, ageism, racism, and class discrimination. These factors are also directly correlated with and contribute to poverty.

Are women and racial minorities overrepresented among the poor because they are in some way inherently or biologically inferior to men and whites? Either women and minorities are inferior—women biologically and emotionally inferior to men; minorities biologically inferior to whites, a sexist and racist perspective—or sexism and racism have restricted women and minorities from functioning to their optimal capacity. The crippling effects of sexism and racism are being expressed through the structural fabric of U.S. society. Those who deny the existence of sexism and racism are in effect implying that women and minorities *are* biologically and inherently inferior. Beyond identifying sexism, racism, and ageism as factors that contribute to the poverty of special populations, one must also understand the *functions* these factors fulfill in U.S. society, hence their persistence. Sexism and ageism, like racism, provide definite benefits to those who dominate. These factors yield significant psychological, political, and economic advantages to the predominantly white middle and upper classes in U.S. society.[3] For example, men of all classes generally have a psychological need to feel superior to women. Whites representing all socioeconomic levels generally have a psychological need to feel superior to minorities. Younger persons of all ethnic-racial groups and classes generally are threatened by the aging process and have a need to feel superior to, and ignore and discriminate against, the elderly. Those receiving the benefits will fight very hard to maintain their advantaged, superior position. Perhaps it is the economic benefits derived from discrimination against women, minorities, and the elderly that function most strongly and effectively to perpetuate this massive U.S. problem, which keeps many living in a state of poverty.

The origin of these discriminatory attitudes may be traced to England in the 18th century, as reflected in the political economy writings of Adam Smith and Thomas Malthus. England was in the midst of an industrial revolution that found the government catering to the interests of big business. The poor were economically exploited and further impoverished, but this did not seem to concern the middle class as they had developed the rationale of *laissez faire*—the doctrine of free enterprise unrestricted by government intervention. Out of unrestricted competition, in theory, the strong would survive and society would benefit— the "trickle down" theory of the 18th century. In *The Wealth of Nations,* Adam Smith argued that one of the roles of government was the defense of the rich against the poor. He saw public assistance for the poor as an artificial and "evil" arrangement in which they consumed money that could have been used for wages. "Unearned subsistence" (welfare), according to Smith, simply furthered human misery.[4]

Malthus, in his *Essay on Population,* believed populations would always outrun food supplies. War, pestilence, and famine were therefore seen by Malthus as positive checks on the growth of populations. These theories were absorbed into Social Darwinism as advocated by Englishman Herbert Spencer (1820–

1903). Extending lower-life biological theories to humans, he originated the concept of "survival of the fittest." Spencer opposed all state welfare assistance to the poor because he felt they were unfit and should be eliminated. He stated:

> The whole effort of nature is to get rid of such, to clear the world of them, and make room for the better. If they are sufficiently complete to live, they do live. If they are not sufficiently complete to live, they die, and it is best they should die.[5]

Spencer's doctrines had significant impact on U.S. thought and many of his ideas were adopted.[6]

In the Social Darwinistic militant stage, society is organized chiefly for survival, bristling with military weapons, training its people for warfare, relying more on an autocratic state, submerging the individual, and imposing a vast amount of compulsory cooperation.[7] In pointing out the U.S.'s priorities, NASW reported in 1970 that over 66 percent of the U.S. annual budget of $200 billion went for military purposes, with 34 percent for all other governmental expenditures including health, education, welfare, agriculture, national resources, pollution, post offices, roads, and foreign relations. More specifically, the United States was spending $480 per person for war and $14 per person for health.[8] An upward trend in military spending began in 1979, followed by a rapid increase, from $176 billion to $254 billion in 1985. This represented the most sustained military buildup in the Nation's history.[9] During fiscal year 1989/90, the budget for military spending increased to $315 billion, but with the increasing freedom and democracy in communist nations in eastern Europe a $24 billion reduction was planned for fiscal year 1990/91. However, Saddam Hussein's invasion of Kuwait in the summer of 1990, leading to President Bush's deployment of over 200,000 U.S. troops to the area, resulted instead in only an $18 billion reduction by the House. As this book went to press, U.S. troop presence in the Persian Gulf was costing American taxpayers an unanticipated $1 billion per month, with estimates between $17 and $86 billion.[10] And in fact, once the war ended in February, 1991, a countermovement by the armed forces, supported by many elected officials in Washington, began advocating for a slowdown in the planned military cuts. Apparently the wrong lesson was learned from the brief, one-sided war, and that is that rather than advocating for a more assertive United Nations world peace-keeping capability, hence permitting U.S. military cutbacks—and increased domestic spending—the Desert Storm victory is being used to maintain a military posture and reinforce the role of the United States as the world's policeman.

According to Powell and Powell, poverty is the most severely disabling condition in childhood, handicapping 9 million white children and 6 million minority-group children in the United States. The Powells point out that White House Conferences on Children, held each decade over the last seventy years, have been laudable in their ideals but short on action and accomplishment, particularly for minorities.[11] There has been a significant drop in infant mortality in the United States during the twentieth century, but the mortality rate for minority infants is triple that for white infants. The maternal mortality rate is four times higher for minority mothers than for white mothers. Another disturbing fact is that the combined perinatal and maternal mortality rates have actually increased for minorities relative to whites. In considering the five leading causes of death in ages 1 to 14 (accidents, congenital malformations, malignant diseases, influenza, and pneumonia), the rates for minority children have been consistently higher (often twice as high) than for white children over the last forty years.[12] Poverty is indeed a stressor that can and *does* kill.

In September, 1990, President Bush joined thirty-four presidents, twenty-seven prime ministers, a king, a grand duke and a cardinal at a historic United Nations World Summit for Children. These world leaders discussed the plight of 150 million children under five suffering malnutrition, 30 million living in the streets, and 7 million driven from their homes by famine and war. Perhaps indicative of the *value* of children in the United States, thousands of American babies are born prematurely and underweight; and along with Iran, Iraq, and Bangladesh the United States is one of only four countries in the world that still allow execution of juvenile offenders.[13]

THE SPECIAL POPULATIONS

Based on the definition of *special populations* established by the President's Commission on Mental Health, children, women, the elderly, gays and lesbians, and minorities could be included. Each suffers the effects of a second-class status in society. Since infants and children have already been commented on, the following discussion will involve mainly women, the elderly, minorities, AIDS patients (physical status), and the homeless, which include many special population members. (An extensive discussion of lesbians and gays as a special population group is presented in Chapter 12.)

Women

Considering that females number 51.4 percent of the population in the United States, they are by far the largest special population group, with whites comprising 92.5 million, blacks 13.7 million, Hispanics 7.3 million, and "other races" 2.8 million. The median age for white women is 32.9, compared to 26.1 for blacks and 23.8 for Hispanics.[14]

Women share not only the debilitating effects of economic exploitation and inequality, but also the traumatic experiences of physical and sexual abuse. Although it is generally believed that wife abuse primarily occurs among the poor, current research indicates that this is not true. Wife abuse cuts across ethnic, racial, and socioeconomic class boundaries.[15] Approximately 50 percent of *all* adult women, according to Walker, will be battered at some time in their lives, and it is estimated that 24 million women have been beaten at least once by men they live with in an intimate relationship.[16] A national sample of U.S. families revealed that up to 60 percent of all marriages contain some violence.[17] Domestic violence, if not checked, may escalate in frequency and intensity and result in homicide. One quarter of all homicides in the nation involve close family members, and in over half of these one spouse killed the other, with wives being the victims in 52 percent of the cases and the perpetrators in the other 49 percent.[18] In California approximately one-third of all female homicide victims were killed by their husbands.[19] In Kansas City spousal homicides accounted for 40 percent of all homicides in one year, and in 50 percent of these cases police had been called five times or more within a two-year period prior to the murder.[20] Like poverty, sexism in its most advanced form can kill and, also like poverty, there are many warning signs prior to the actual occurrence.

Rape is another major form of sexist abuse that, according to Federal Bureau of Investigation statistics, is reported once every ten minutes in the United States.[21] Abarbanel states that not every rape is reported and that the ratio is 1 to 3.5 between victims who do report the crime and those who do not. She adds that with a population of over 100 million females in the Nation, it is reasonable to assume that at least 250,000 of these will be raped in a year. If the rate remains constant, the likelihood that a female will be raped at some time during her life is one in 15![22] In addition to physical injury, the rape victim is injured psychologically. She is terrorized by her total loss of control, the assault on her integrity, sense of security, and personal identity. Rape produces acute post-traumatic stress disorder symptoms that may become chronic without prompt intervention. It causes a social disruption in a woman's life, her primary relationship, and the life of her family.[23]

The underlying causes of physical and sexual abuse of women by men share similar dynamics, but also have some differences. One prominant theory of wife abuse argues that it occurs because of the sexist structure and traditions of Western society. The norms and values in U.S. society define women as unequal and subordinate to men. These sexist norms and values permeate the entire society and are accepted by the majority of persons. The oppressive economic structure that constrains women's opportunities and legal traditions (e.g., women not permitted to vote until 1920, 144 years after men), which confirm a second-class status for women, are evidence of the sexist structure of the United States. Acting on the clear message that they are the ruling sex and acting out their various frustrations, men batter women.[24] A second major contrasting theory is proposed by Gelles, who maintains that all family violence is behavior that is learned in the family of origin. He sees the family as society's primary socializing institution, teaching the norms, values, and techniques of violence as well as other things. He adds that family violence is a response to stress that originates in the social structure of Western society. He sees the stresses of poverty, unemployment, and unmet role expectations leading to frustration and ultimately to violence. Gelles believes because structural stresses affect the lower classes to a greater extent, family violence also occurs there more frequently.[25] Previously quoted data concerning the prevalence of female physical abuse do not support this theory.

Theoretical explanations concerning sexual abuse of women have victim precipitation as a core concept; that is, the women's behavior is claimed to cause assault. Freud's libido and unconscious-motivation theories explain rape as the result of conscious and unconscious sexual desires of women, or as emanating from the rapist's feelings of penis inadequacy and castration anxiety rooted in anxious relations with mothers, wives, and girlfriends.[26] Some theorists see "situational contingencies" as being a cause of rape, with culture and social structure establishing the preconditions. Again, however, the victim is blamed, for dressing too seductively, going to singles' bars, hitchhiking, or going out alone at night.[27]

Another theory, based on gender-role socialization, explains the cause of female sexual assault as males learning that masculinity means domination, and that rape is the ultimate act of men's domination over women. The male is stereotypically seen as a natural sexual predator.[28] Within the theoretical context of a radical feminist perspective, according to Andersen and Renzetti, the sexual assault of women by men is a phenomenon related to women's lack of political and economic autonomy.[29] Drawing on crosscultural data, Sanday demonstrates that male violence against women is not universal; rather, it is related to the social inequality of women and general interpersonal violence in a society.[30] Considering the severe inequality women suffer in the United States, coupled with the fact that the United States ranks *first* in violence among the seventeen Western democracies, it should not be surprising to observe the magnitude of physical and sexual abuse directed at women.[31] A sexist, violent country places this special population at great risk; and it should be a top priority for social work.

The Elderly

Large numbers of people over sixty-five in the United States are a fairly recent phenomenon. Persons over sixty-five numbered only 3.1 million in 1900 (4 percent); today they number more than 25 million persons, or 11.2 percent of the population. Estimates are that by the year 2000 they will number more than 31 million (12.2 percent), and by 2030, 55 million (18.3 percent). These projections are based on the assumption that there will be no major biomedical breakthroughs significantly extending the life expectancy of the middle-aged and elderly. Thus not only will there be a proportionately larger elderly population in the future, but the median age of the elderly will also be higher. For example, in 1980, 40 percent of elderly persons were seventy-five years of age or older. By the year 2000, 49 percent of the aged will be over seventy-five.[32]

The elderly are the most vulnerable special population group with respect to physical health, mental health, income, and housing status. They are often victimized and suffer the stresses of ageism, class discrimination, sexism, poverty, and racism. The income levels of the elderly are substantially less than those of younger persons, and the incidence of poverty is significantly higher.[33] Many aged poor become poor only after reaching old age, losing half to two-thirds of their total income from loss of wages and retirement.[34] Women outnumber men among the elderly population, numbering approximately 60 percent of the total. Elderly women, as a group, are poorer than elderly men, and less often employed. The black elderly profile (median family income $5,177, compared to $8,676 for whites) caps a lifetime of limited economic rewards, as earnings for blacks of all ages are below the levels of their white peers.[35] Elderly Hispanics also have much higher rates of poverty than their white counterparts.[36] The minority elderly are at higher risk than whites as a result of their pervasive poverty; compounded by problems of access to services because of institutional racism barriers, and even more so for those Hispanics who speak primarily Spanish. Normally funds through Title XX of the Social Security Act flow to states based on need indicators such as percentage of a state's poor elderly population and percent of minority elderly population. Tragically, however, the greater the percentage of elderly minorities in a state's population, the larger has been the corresponding decrease in the elderly poor's share of Title XX funds.[37]

Only 5 percent of the elderly reside in nursing homes and other long-term institutions. Almost 76 percent of elderly men lived with their wives; 7 percent with children or other relatives. Women are far worse off. Only 38 percent live with their husbands; another 19 percent live with children or other relatives. The likelihood of living alone increases significantly with age at the same time that the aging process increases the need to be functionally dependent.[38]

The health problems of the elderly are quite different than those of younger persons. Whereas accidents are the leading cause of death among persons under forty-five, accidents are only the seventh leading cause of death in the elderly. The leading killers of older persons are heart disease, cancer, and stroke. The likelihood of dying from stroke, influenza, pneumonia, and arteriosclerosis all increase significantly as persons live to be sixty-five and older. A national health survey of the elderly found that 90 percent of persons over sixty-five had at least one chronic condition, and many had multiple chronic illnesses. The most commonly reported chronic health conditions were arthritis at 44 percent, hypertension at 39 percent, hearing loss at 28 percent, and heart ailments at 27 percent.[39] Because of poor health the elderly account for a third more physician visits than the population as a whole, and they use three times as many hospital days.[40] The rates of psychosis and organic mental disorders rise with advancing age. There is a high reported correlation between physical and mental illness, and the linkage is highest between physical and organic mental impairment.[41]

In a profit-making capitalist system, the nonproductive, including the elderly, are simply "dead weight" and are often treated as such. Government sometimes provides them with as few resources as it can, in order to invest more in defense or more profitable projects. This attitude is illustrated by Dr. Eileen M. Gardner, an appointee to the Reagan administration's Department of Education, who in testimony before the Senate Appropriations Committee's Health and Human Services subcommittee, stated that handicapped children were draining badly needed resources from the normal school population. The Secretary of Education asked for her resignation.[42] The U.S. population, according to Butler, suffers from a personal and institutionalized prejudice against the elderly, which he attributes to a primitive dread of aging.[43] That was written in 1977. It may be even more true in today's age of narcissism, beautiful bodies, and the worship of the young. Perhaps ageism and its persistence has at its core thanatophobia—the fear of death. It is ironic that people in the United States worship youth and are looking desperately for ways to prolong life, while at the same time largely neglecting the elderly, those whose lives have been extended.

In addition to institutional neglect, increasing numbers of the elderly are suffering physical abuse. Ira Reiss reports that 4 percent of the elderly population (one million persons) are abused by their children, and the abuse increases as the numbers of elderly grow.[44] The types of abuse include physical assault, verbal harrassment, malnutrition, theft or financial mismanagement, unreasonable confinement, over-sedation, sexual abuse, threats, withholding of medication or required aids (false teeth, glasses, hearing aids), neglect, humiliation, and violation of legal rights. The victim is usually over seventy-five, with significant physical or mental impairment.[45] Much more research is needed to understand the incidence and prevalence of a significant and growing social problem among the elderly.

It should come as no surprise that the elderly lead the Nation in suicide. In 1980 the suicide rate for fifteen- to twenty-four-year-olds was 11.9 percent per 100,000; and for persons over sixty-five, 17.7 percent. This pattern has existed since 1900. Women are a low-risk group for suicide at all ages—especially in old age—while men are generally a high-risk group, especially in old age.[46] Whereas the elderly comprised 11.3 percent of the population in 1980, they accounted for 16.9 percent of the suicides. White males are at highest risk for suicide, as are those persons over seventy-five. Other high-risk elderly groups include the widowed, those who have experienced recent losses, those with chronic physical pain, and those who have undergone status changes such as retirement, with loss of income status, roles, and independence. In contrast, minority group suicide peaks in young adulthood and declines significantly in old age.[47] It appears that whites (mostly males) kill themselves when they become old and have lost their income, status, role, and independence, and minorities (mostly males) more often kill themselves at a young age in their losing struggle to obtain income, status, role, and independence. In other words, racism kills some minorities on the way up, and ageism kills some whites on the way down.

Minorities

Next to women, the second-largest population group in the United States are the ethnic-racial minorities, sometimes referred to as "third-world" people. This group, numbering over 40 million people, does not include white ethnics, who now have a higher educational and income status than Anglo-American Protestants.[48] Minorities are well represented in all the special population groups, but in *addition* to suffering the same stresses of sexism, AIDS, homelessness, ageism, poverty, and class discrimination, their condition is compounded by racism.[49] Racism is the assumption and belief of inherent, biological racial superiority, or the purity and superiority of certain races and consequent discrimination against others. Racism is any attitude, action, or institutional structure (institutional racism) that subordinates a person or group because of color. While *race* and *color* refer to two different types of human characteristics, in the United States it is the visibility of skin color and other physical traits associated with particular skin colors that mark specific persons as targets for subordination by members of the white majority.[50] This will be seen clearly in Chapter 22 in which Section 287.1 (c) of the Operating Instructions of the U.S. Immigration and Naturalization Service is cited, identifying "foreign cultural characteristics" as one of the "articulable factors" or reasons officers may use to stop and question a person suspected of being in the United States illegally. No doubt officers must internalize, consciously and unconsciously, subjective criteria as to who appears foreign and who does not. Those who are not considered "white" by whites include ethnic-racial groups such as blacks, Chinese, Vietnamese, Mexican Americans, Cubans, Puerto Ricans, Central and South Americans, Japanese, and American Indians. Some minority group members are actually Caucasian or "white" (e.g., Mexican Americans) and may even want to be identified as such, but they will still be rejected by whites unless they are able to "pass" on the basis of fair skin and light-colored hair and eyes.[51] The following discussion will focus on the larger minority groups in the United States such as American Indians, Asian Americans, blacks, and Hispanics. The ecosystems framework highlighting each group's demographic profile, health and mental status, and special social problem areas is utilized. Chapters 11 through 20 will deal more specifically with social work practice intervention strategies concerning each of these minority groups.

In April, 1985, Mae Chee Castillo, a seventy-two-year-old volunteer aide Navajo woman, was publicly honored, in person, at the White House by President Ronald Reagan for having rescued ten children from a burning bus. Instead of verbalizing her appreciation for the recognition being offered to her by the President, she told the President her people needed schools, hospitals, housing for the elderly, and other facilities. She added:

> We need to continue the current level of economic benefits such as Social Security since many, many Native American elderly depend on this support for their only source of income. We need funds for these services that I have mentioned because, in Indian country, there is little or no private sector. I ask for your support, Mr. President.[52]

The President replied:

> Most of those things that you were talking about here, those problems come under what we have called the *safety net* and which we intend to continue and, even in our battles to lower the deficit, these things will not be done away with or reduced.[53]

The old Navajo woman tried to give a White House aide a woven basket and rug for the President, but they were rejected and she was ushered out "very quickly."[54] Those few moments of interaction between two elderly people symbolize the history of the relationship between American Indians and whites in positions of power. Responding to poverty and powerlessness imposed by whites, the American Indian practically has to beg for mercy and justice, even offering gifts of peace, kindness, and good faith. As has been the traditional response for well over a hundred years, both the request for help, the gifts, and American Indians themselves are rejected.

Due to changing definitions of the term *American Indian* by the U.S. Bureau of the Census, it is difficult to obtain an accurate appraisal of the size of this population in the United States. When American Indians, Alaskan Natives, and Aleuts are all included, Indians numbered 827,000 persons in 1975, a 51 percent increase over the 1960 Census.[55] American Indians may be found in most states, although their highest concentration is in California, Oklahoma, Arizona, New Mexico, and North Carolina. Within the last ten years, the American Indian population in California has tripled. American Indians are a very heterogeneous group, comprised of approximately 481 tribal groups, many with unique norms, culture, and language. Half of all American Indians belong to nine tribes, with the largest tribal group being the Navajo, numbering 140,000.[56] About half of all Indians live in urban areas; the other half reside in rural areas or reservations. Urban Indians are generally older than rural or reservation Indians. In Utah, for example, median Indian age is 15.6, compared to 26.4 in New York.[57]

American Indians, like many persons of Mexican descent, are different from other minority groups in that they are *not* immigrants. The immigrants were the Anglo-Americans who conquered the Indians on their land. Also like Mexican Americans, Indians fought several battles with the U.S. Army before finally being defeated. Anglo-American resentment toward Indians goes back many years and is expressed both overtly and in subtle, destructive ways. For example, in the late eighteenth century California Indians numbered about 250,000. By 1900 California's Indian population was down to 10,000 due to "peaceful" attrition by European civilization and its attendant diseases, dehumanizing and decimating conditions, warfare, slave-like treatment, and genocide by whites.[58]

Racism toward Indians has been expressed in the lack of a comprehensive, progressive federal policy over a period of many years, a lack that has severely hampered Indians' ability to move forward in the United States. Their health is very poor, educational achievement dismal, and many live in extreme poverty, both on and off the reservations. Although Indians governed themselves for centuries until the "white man" invaded their territories, they were not permitted to vote until 1924, when they were finally declared citizens of the United States. In 1934 the Indian Reorganization Act was passed, which permitted tribal self-government.[59] Another landmark occurred in 1955, when the Indian Health Service was established under the U.S. Public Health Service rather than the Bureau of Indian Affairs. The Indian Civil Rights Act, which was passed in 1968, required due process in tribal courts and right to legal counsel, but no appropriations were provided to exercise these rights. In 1975 the Indian Self Determination and Education Act (P.L. 93–638) was passed, which permitted tribes to contract with the Bureau of Indian Affairs and the Indian Health Services for services, with

funding from these sources. Another very important piece of legislation and tragically, very late, was the passage of the Indian Child Welfare Act in 1978. It
established minimum standards for state custody proceedings affecting Indian
children, with the jurisdiction of child welfare matters returned to the tribes.
Funds ($5.5 million) were appropriated by Congress in 1979 for services to
strengthen families and serve children.[60] This represented a little over $5 for
each American Indian in the United States. A greater commitment is needed in
order to make any significant impact. The Indian Child Welfare Act, however,
established the legal foundation that permits Indians to have greater authority in
attempting to keep and enhance the lives of children within the tribal environment. It also provides Indians a unique opportunity to try to maintain their culture.[61]

During one historical period, all school-age American Indian children were
required to attend federal boarding schools. Even today, according to Blanchard
and Barsh, it is difficult to find an Indian whose parent, grandparent, or other
close relative did not attend boarding school.[62] A 1977 survey by the Association
on American Indian Affairs reported that 25 to 35 percent of all Indian children
are separated from their families and placed in foster homes, adoptive homes, or
institutions.[63] Such practices can only have the result of destroying the family
unit. Byler concludes that federal assimilation policies cause the Indian family to
break up, with a loss of self-esteem in the parents, cultural disorientation in the
children, and loss of identity, resulting in school failure, suicide, alcohol abuse,
and alcoholism.[64]

Alcoholism is a significant problem in the American Indian community, and
stereotypes have been created about the Indians' attraction to alcohol. Alcohol
abuse is simply a symptom of the inhuman social conditions (historical and contemporary) in which the Indian has been forced to live. Child abuse and neglect
exist in the Indian community, where alcohol plays a role in about half the cases,
as it does in most child abuse. Some Indian parents themselves have suffered
abuse and neglect in their lives, according to Metcalf, but their parents should
not be blamed. Rather, it is the disruption in Indian families caused by Anglo-
American institutions that is the underlying cause. As Anglo institutions en-
croached more and more on Indian family life, the effects on Indian children
became more and more disruptive.[65]

The term *Asian Americans* commonly refers to Chinese, Koreans, Japanese,
Vietnamese, Thais, and Pacific Island persons (Hawaiians, Guamanians, Filipinos,
and Samoans). Asian Americans, hereafter referred to as *Asians,* are, like Indians
and Hispanics, a very heterogeneous group, each with its own unique language,
history, culture, religion, and appearance. They share immigration and assimilation stresses, historical and current economic exploitation, and the consequences of racism.[66] Largely drawn by the U.S. demand for manual labor, Asians
immigrated to the United States during several different periods, with the greatest
number of Chinese arriving between 1850 and 1882; Japanese from 1880 to 1924;
and most Filipinos in the 1920s and again in the mid-1960s. Various discriminatory
laws and legislation controlling the flow of Asian immigrants—at times restricting

admission of Asian women—created a severe sex imbalance that led to serious personal, social, and community-life consequences for many Asian immigrant males. For over 100 years, Murase states, Asian Americans have been the victims of "humiliating, repressive, and vicious acts of racism."[67] Murase documents numerous examples of legislative racism directed at Asians, a few of which will be highlighted, such as California's 1850 Foreign Miners' Tax directed at Chinese miners, the 1882 federal law prohibiting Chinese from becoming naturalized, the massacre and lynching of Chinese in Wyoming (1885) and Idaho (1888), segregated schools for Chinese and Japanese in California (1860, 1906); prohibition of racial intermarriage in California (1906); and the anti-alien land law prohibiting property purchases in California (1913).[68] One of the most brutal acts of U.S. racism directed specifically at Asian Americans occurred in 1942, when President Franklin D. Roosevelt, who held the racist belief "once a Jap always a Jap," signed an order forcibly uprooting more than 110,000 innocent Japanese Americans in three West coast states and placing them in so-called relocation centers. They were in fact concentration camps (as opposed to the genocide camps in Hitler's Germany). The Japanese Americans, both alien and citizens, young and old, rich and poor, were sent to ten concentration camps, to live in barracks, surrounded by barbed wire, with armed guards, in largely barren areas in the interior of the United States, from California to Arkansas.[69] They suffered poverty, deprivation, loss of property, and were left with lifelong emotional scars.[70] According to Sata, the imprisonment experience caused a cultural erosion of established roles and functions within the family unit, while the establishment of English as a primary mode of communication both emancipated and deprived Japanese Americans of the stabilizing influence of traditional family life.[71] Their culture was raped. Today, roughly half a century after their U.S. concentration-camp experience, many emotionally traumatic residues continue to exist for Japanese Americans.

One of the newest Asian immigrant groups to enter the United States, the Vietnamese, present a host of very serious cultural, economic, and psychosocial problems requiring immediate, comprehensive intervention. Vietnamese came to the United States in two separate groups at two different times. The first group was comprised of about 20,000 students, permanent residents, and war brides who came prior to the fall of Saigon in April, 1975. The second group consisted of over 140,000 adults and children who fled their homeland during and after the fall of Saigon. In their struggle to escape from Vietnam, many died on their way to the United States. Le states succinctly that for the Vietnamese refugee, all the forces of disaster such as war, death, injury, loss of home, possessions, and family memorabilia are joined with the crushing losses of country, culture, language, tradition, and history, "endlessly inflicting painful memories down to the lowest trivia of life."[72]

The current mental health problems and needs of the Vietnamese are many. Like other minority groups in the United States, they are confronted with white racism, a foreign culture, a confusing and complicated economic, social, and political system, and ignorance about their rights and obligations. Perhaps the greatest handicap is language, the tool they require in order to negotiate on the most basic level. At best Vietnamese refugees symbolize the United State's painful, ambivalent sacrifice in a "no win" war, and at worst Vietnamese are scapegoats, blamed for that war and the loss of thousands of U.S. soldiers.

Unemployment among Vietnamese is high, partially due to the language barrier. Many Vietnamese veterans were trained only for war and are without vocational skills. They feel frustrated, resentful, and angry, feelings that are often turned inward, resulting in depression. Vietnamese women feel even more isolated and alienated from U.S. society and cannot even communicate with their English-speaking neighbors. They have large families, suffer poverty, and reside in high-crime areas in the cities. Their children also suffer severe psychological problems related to their experiences and psychosocial development level. Many are still experiencing war-related, post-traumatic stress disorder symptoms; some are suffering culture shock manifested in various speech problems, and many adolescents experience a severe identity crisis. All these problems are exacerbated by unstable home situations, governed by parents who are also experiencing major emotional difficulties.[73] In short, the mental health situation of Vietnamese is critical and, according to Le, "may soon become disastrous."[74] He calls for immediate, positive intervention. Will the future of the Vietnamese parallel that of blacks, who lost their African culture and language, yet were and are still barred from entering the U.S. mainstream? The Vietnamese, like other war refugees such as Central Americans, present a real challenge to the social work profession.

Blacks, sometimes referred to as Afro-Americans and African Americans (not of Hispanic origin), constitute the largest minority group in the Nation, with a population numbering 31 million persons. Fifty-four percent live in the South, but 76 percent live in cities, with 57 percent residing in the central city.[75] The median family income gap between Afro-Americans and whites continues to grow, with Afro-Americans in 1988 earning a median income of $18,500, compared to $35,953 for whites.[76] The number of poor Afro-American families was as high in 1980 as in 1970, while the number of poor white families decreased.[77] Like other minorities, Afro-Americans are a very heterogeneous group, with the majority being productive members of society. However, their overrepresentation among the poor, as the result of institutional racism in U.S. society, places many of them under severe stress, creating an affected and at-risk, highly vulnerable group. They remain far behind whites in almost every social, health, and economic measurement.

Blacks have been the most brutalized minority group in the United States ever since their transport to the North American continent as slaves almost 375 years ago. Billingsley once noted that black families have shown an amazing ability to survive in the face of impossible conditions.[78] The centuries-old African tradition, based on ritual, custom, and law, of maintaining family ties wherever and whenever possible, has survived an enormous traumatization as "subhuman" slaves whose family members were sold as market commodities.[79] Today approximately two-thirds of African American families are nuclear, comprised of mother, father, and children. They are economically heterogeneous, with about

40 percent of Afro-American families in the middle class, 10 percent in the upper class, and about 50 percent in the lower class. Twenty-five percent of the lower class are classified as nonworking poor, and it is this group that receives the most attention from the media, the academic community, law enforcement, and social work, and reinforces white prejudice, racism, and discrimination toward blacks.[80] The vast majority of African Americans have experienced the effects of white racism in one form or another, whether overt or covert. According to the National Center for Health Statistics, black babies born in Detroit today are dying at twice the national rate, 22.1 per 1,000 live births compared to 10.6. Low birth weight is the primary cause of death. This is caused in turn by social and economic problems, such as the poor maternal diet, inadequate education on the need for prenatal care, lack of access to proper care, smoking, alcohol, and drug abuse. A city health official remarked, "Infant mortality is the medical expression of a social problem. The problem is poverty—poverty of resources."[81]

Based on actual mental health needs, blacks underutilize mental health services. Those who have entered the mental health system face discrimination and tend to be treated less often as outpatients, more often with drugs, and less often with one-to-one modalities. They tend to drop out earlier in the treatment process. Many blacks who go to mental health agencies have been referred by agents of social control. Solomon maintains that Afro-Americans experience the same mental health problems as those occurring in all groups in U.S. society, such as schizophrenia, depression, adjustment reactions, and so on. However, the *cause* of those problems may be different. Feelings related to low self-esteem and powerlessness may play a greater etiological role with Afro-Americans than with whites experiencing the same problems, according to Solomon. Other problems, such as dysfunctional male–female relationships, may be unique to Afro-Americans, created by a combination of the slavery experience, subsequent employment practices, the current feminist movement, and the ratio of Afro-American men to women.[82]

Large-scale wars such as World War II, the Korean War, and the Vietnam War, in conjunction with a contemporary volunteer U.S. army comprised of 50 percent minorities, a continuing overrepresentation of Afro-Americans in juvenile and adult detention facilities, high homicide and suicide rates, and police homicides of blacks, have significantly reduced the availability and ratio of young black males in relation to black females. For example, Sherman points out that there is an extremely disproportionate number of police "executions" of blacks without trial. Official national statistics revealed that in 1975, blacks comprised 46 percent of people killed by police, while constituting only 11.5 percent of the population. Similarly, the national death rate from police homicide of black males over ten years of age in a recent ten-year period was ten times higher than the rate for white males.[83] Hispanic males are also at high risk with respect to police homicide; in Chicago, for example, a death rate of 4.5 per 100,000, compared to 2.67 per 100,000 for blacks and .34 per 100,000 for whites. The killing of blacks and Hispanics by police was far out of proportion to their felony crime rate.[84] The discussion of the incarceration of Afro-Americans will be combined with that of Hispanics, following a demographic description of the Hispanic population.

In 1970 there were nine million Hispanics in the United States; by March, 1987, the Bureau of the Census reported 18.7 million Hispanics. In 1987 Hispanics of Mexican descent numbered 11.7 million (62 percent), Puerto Ricans 2.2 million, Central and South Americans 2.1 million, Cubans 1 million, and other Hispanics 1.5 million. Not included in these population figures were an estimated six million undocumented aliens, mostly from Mexico.[85] Demographers predicted that by 1990 Hispanics would be the Nation's largest minority, comprising half the population of California, a third of Texas; and a majority of the population in three states by the year 2000.[86]* Over 50 percent of all Hispanics reside in California (31 percent) and Texas (20 percent), followed by New York (11 percent), Florida (6 percent), Illinois (4 percent), Arizona, Colorado, and New Mexico (9 percent), and the remainder of the United States (18 percent). Hispanics are (1) largely urban dwellers, with 84 percent residing in metropolitan areas, (2) a youthful population, with a median age of 23.5 years (vs. 31.9 for the overall population), (3) low in educational achievement, with 58 percent being high school graduates (vs. 88 percent for non-Hispanics), and (4) generally poor, with a median income of $21,921 (vs. $35,953 for non-Hispanic whites).[87]

Perhaps the most significant aspect of Hispanic cultural heritage is the Spanish language, as over 80 percent of Hispanics report Spanish as their primary language.[88] Many Hispanics suffer the effects of poverty to a much greater extent than the general population. Low income, unemployment, underemployment, and undereducation, discrimination, racism, prejudice, poor housing, and cultural-linguistic barriers, according to the President's Commission on Mental Health, have been compounded by the low quality and quantity of mental health services available to Hispanics. These conditions have placed undue stress on Hispanics, with serious consequences as evidenced by the increased prevalence of alcoholism and substance abuse,[89] juvenile delinquency and gangs,[90] and an over-representation of adults in jails and prisons.[91]

The largest minority groups in the United States, Afro-Americans and Hispanics are also increasingly high-risk groups as their numbers continue to escalate dramatically in all aspects of the juvenile and adult criminal justice system. Currently, on any given day there are approximately 2.4 million persons under public correctional supervision in the United States (jails, 210,000; prisons, 412,000; adult parole, 220,400; adult probation, 1,118,100; juvenile detention, 12,300; juvenile training school, 25,000; juvenile camps and ranches, 4,860; juvenile probation, 328,900; juvenile parole, 53,300). There are 622,000 incarcerated adults and 42,300 juveniles housed in public juvenile correctional facilities. About seven million jail bookings occur per year. By the end of 1983, the U.S. Bureau of Justice Statistics reported 438,830 adults confined in state and federal prisons, indicating

---

* The demographers' predictions will have to await the official results of the 1990 U.S. Census, which were not yet available at the time of this edition.

that the Nation's prison population had doubled during the last decade and had become the largest in U.S. history.[92] Ninety-six percent of this prison population were males, and 48 percent were black, far exceeding their proportion in the general population. The statistics for Hispanic males were not consistently available, yet experts believe prison incarceration rates for Hispanics are higher than for white males.[93]

The state and federal prison incarceration rate has been steadily increasing over the last sixty years, from 79 per 100,000 persons in 1925, to 98 per 100,000 in 1945, to 108 in 1965, to 111 in 1975, and 179 per 100,000 in 1983. The U.S. Government Accounting Office projected that by 1990, the U.S. prison population would be 566,170, an all-time high incarceration rate of 227 per 100,000.[94] This in fact turned out to be an underestimate. The last federal and state prison population count as of December 31, 1989, was 703,687, of which 39,689 were women.[95]

States have identified four factors related to prison population growth. The first is demographic, as certain age, sex, and racial-ethnic groups in the general population have higher arrest rates and imprisonment than others. A self-fulfilling prophecy is often at work here, in that poor minorities are *believed* to be more criminal and are under greater police surveillance, hence are more likely to be arrested. Given the increasing numbers of minorities in the Nation and their low median age, the percentage of minorities in prison is going to become greater.

Crime rates are the second factor related to incarceration rates, but this is a widely debated issue with no clear answers. Historically there is an inverse relationship between crime rates and incarceration; that is, as crime rates increase, fewer persons fall under correctional supervision, and conversely, the prison population grows as crime rates decline.[96]

A third factor, which is really more of a theory, suggests that imprisonment is strongly related to economic conditions, more specifically to rates of unemployment and poverty levels. Those supporting this view cite the high rate of unemployment among minority youth and the disproportionate number of incarcerated minorities. This view is strongly challenged by Austin and Krisberg, who point out that from 1978 to 1983 the unemployment rate increased dramatically for minorities, yet the crime rate held steady and later even declined while the prison population increased during the same period.[97]

The final factor related to imprisonment rates concerns changes in criminal justice policies, such as determinate sentences, mandatory sentencing legislation, and increasing penalties and prison terms—in short, "get tough" approaches. The general public, police, and legislators want to "crack down" hard on crime but, as will be seen, they are very selective about whom they decide to punish more severely. Usually it is minorities.

Rarely do social scientists examine prejudice, racism, and class discrimination in the criminal justice system (police, prosecutors, judges, correctional facilities, probation, parole) as factors that may play a significant role in determining who is incarcerated. For example, the U.S. Department of Justice funded the SHODI (Serious Habitual Offenders—Drug Involved) program to identify "serious" offenders and ensure they receive "stiff" sentences. Almost 25 percent of SHODIs had never appeared in court (no convictions), and in one city 83 percent of SHODIs were minority youths. In comparing a middle-class white and lower-class Hispanic community of similar size and very similar juvenile crime rates in Los Angeles, Morales found that Hispanic youths were twenty-three times more likely to be arrested for loitering offenses than non-Hispanic white youths.[98]

Policies and attitudes toward juvenile crime and minorities differ from state to state. In a selection of four large states with large urban areas and large minority populations, the collective attitudes of policy makers are dramatically transformed into incarceration rates, shown in Table 10–1.[99] California does not have juvenile delinquents ten times more criminal than New York. Rather, the incarceration rates reflect the *attitudes* of the criminal justice system. California has 10 percent of the nation's ten to nineteen year-old juvenile population, yet 30 percent of the nation's juvenile detention admissions occurred in California (138,000 out of 451,000).[100] California is #1 in this regard.

The California Attorney General reported in 1984 that juvenile crime had dropped by 41.2 percent between 1974 and 1983, but that the number of youths committed to local and state detention centers had increased by 11 percent.[101] In California in 1983 the percentage of non-Hispanic white juveniles ages 10 to 19 was 61.1 percent; Hispanic, 24 percent; black, 9.6 percent; and other, 5.3 percent. Non-Hispanic white juveniles were involved in 44 percent (50,000 offenses) of felony arrests that year, compared to 27.6 percent (31,000 offenses) for Hispanics and 25.3 percent (28,500 offenses) for blacks. Thirty-three percent of non-Hispanic white arrests were for violent offenses, compared to 27 percent for Hispanics and 36 percent for blacks.[102] It is interesting to note that even though non-Hispanic whites committed the most felonies (44 percent), the percentage committed (first commitment) to the California Youth Authority was 27.7 percent, a 16.3 percent drop. On the other hand, there was a 4.5 percent increase of CYA commitments of Hispanics (up to 32.1 percent) based on their percentage of felonies (27.6 percent), and a significant 13 percent increase of CYA commitments for blacks (up to 38.1 percent) in light of their felony percentage (25.3 percent). Since blacks and non-Hispanic whites had similar felony

TABLE 10–1 *Juvenile Incarceration Rates of Selected States*

State	Major City	Admission to Detention (per 100,000)	Admission to Training School (per 100,000)
New York	New York (42% minority)	455	38
Illinois	Chicago (57% minority)	871	114
Michigan	Detroit (67% minority)	1300	53
California	Los Angeles (52% minority)	4400	447

offense rates, one would have expected similar first time CYA commitments. The CYA institution juvenile inmate population reflects the same ethnic-racial percentages as first-time commitments: 73 percent minorities and 27 percent non-Hispanic whites.[103] It is obvious that the *public* juvenile justice system resists the penetration of white youths, while easily admitting minority youths in disproportionate numbers. However, the *private* juvenile justice system (private, nongovernment-administered training schools, ranches, camps, halfway houses, and group homes) resists the penetration of minorities (only 25 percent blacks and 7 percent Hispanics) and admits 65 to 70 percent whites.[104] The third system to which juvenile delinquents may be tracked is called the "hidden" juvenile justice system, located in private psychiatric hospitals, with a 95 percent population of affluent white adolescents. A triple standard of justice therefore exists for juvenile delinquents.

Commenting on a similar discriminatory phenomenon in the adult criminal justice system, Petersilia states:

> Critics of the criminal justice system view the arrest and imprisonment of blacks and other minorities as evidence of racial discrimination. Although the laws governing the system contain no racial bias, these critics claim that where the system allows discretion to criminal justice officials in handling offenders, discrimination can, and often does, enter in. They argue that blacks, for example, who make up 12 percent of the national population, could not possibly commit 48 percent of the crimes—but that is exactly what their arrest and imprisonment rates imply.[105]

Significant sentencing disparities exist between crime rates and imprisonment. For example, blacks account for 30 percent of the arrests for larceny in the Nation, yet are 51 percent of those imprisoned for larceny. Petersilia concludes that a great deal of discretion by all aspects of the criminal justice system leads to discrimination. Petersilia further adds that an astonishing 51 percent of black males residing in large cities are arrested, at least once during their lives, for an index crime (murder, rape, robbery, assault, burglary, larceny/theft, auto theft, and arson), compared to only 14 percent of white males. Blacks are six times (18 percent to 3 percent) more likely than whites to serve time in a correctional facility, either as juveniles or adults.[106] A similar pattern seems to be emerging for Hispanics. Since half of black males and a very significant number of Hispanic males are coming to the attention of the juvenile and adult criminal justice system, it would seem mandatory that social workers know something about the interactional dynamics of these systems with minorities in order to make an accurate assessment of the client(s) and be more effective. An additional law enforcement stressor affecting Hispanics involves contact with the patrol officers of the U.S. Immigration and Naturalization Service. A detailed account of the psychiatric symptoms produced by INS interrogations among Hispanics *suspected* of being undocumented is reported in Chapter 21.

Normally, when migrating from one country to another, a certain amount of immigration and acculturation stress is experienced by the migrant. The degree of the stress, however, will in part be related to the economic and social resources available to the migrant, how similar or different the new culture is, and the perception and receptiveness of the immigrant by the new country. The United States will be much more receptive to a Russian ballerina defecting to the United States to escape what she considers an oppressive Soviet government, than to a Guatemalan who entered the United States illegally to escape Central American right-wing death squads. Politics and racism, therefore, will affect the nurturing or negative reaction the United States will have toward the new immigrant. Many Hispanics legally and illegally entering the United States as political or economic refugees do experience migration and acculturation stress, and fear being apprehended and deported by INS officials, with possible execution on return home, or assassination in the United States by compatriots of a rival political party, or abrupt separation from wives and children.

It is estimated that the number of undocumented persons residing in the United States entering from the Canadian and Mexican borders ranges from two to ten million.[107] The majority appear to be economic refugees. In recent years, however, greater numbers of political refugees—mostly from Central America—are entering the United States. The Legal Aid Office of the Archdiocese of San Salvador reported that during the first ten months of 1983, 4113 civilians were killed by the security forces, the army, and right-wing death squads. Sixty-seven were killed by guerrillas.[108] Guatemalan refugees report that the army's anti-guerrilla campaign in rural Guatemala has resulted in genocide, kidnappings, burning of residences, and torture.[109] The U.S. government usually resists acknowledging that many apprehended, undocumented Hispanics are political refugees, perhaps due in part to the fact that the United States supports some of the Central and South American right-wing political groups. Those documented and undocumented Hispanics suffering migration and acculturation stress (including culture shock), fear of apprehension, and post-traumatic stress disorders related to war, civil conflict, and torture, require psychotherapeutic intervention, yet find it difficult to obtain these services due to a lack of financial or insurance resources to pay for them. They are also handicapped by their legal status and by the scarcity of bilingual-bicultural mental health practitioners. Consider the Los Angeles mental health staffing situation, for example, where Hispanics number 2.5 million persons, or 33 percent of the population. The number of bilingual-bicultural mental health practitioners is shown in Table 10–2.[110] Regardless of legal or economic status, Spanish-speaking Hispanics find it difficult to obtain bilingual therapists, since approximately 75 percent of mental health practitioners are English-speaking, non-Hispanic whites, and the majority of Hispanics are Spanish-speaking. The situation is also difficult for other minorities, and Los Angeles now has a population comprised of 60 percent minorities. This presents a real challenge to federal, state, and local mental health planners and professional schools.

The Homeless

The economic gap between the haves and the have-nots is at the widest point since government began monitoring this factor over forty years ago. Brown points

TABLE 10–2   *Mental Health Discipline by Ethnicity in Los Angeles County (LA County Population, 7.5 Million; Hispanics, 2.5 Million (33%)*

DISCIPLINE	TOTAL	HISPANICS	% HISPANICS
Child psychiatrists	61	1	2%
Psychiatric nurses	46	3	7%
Ph.D. psychologists	153	5	3%
Nurses, R.N.	226	9	4%
Psychiatrists	233	11	5%
MSWs	451	44	10%

Source: Data taken from Floyd H. Martinez, "Mental Health Manpower Survey for Los Angeles County Department of Mental Health," September, 1983, p. 4. The survey included all Short-Doyle and Short-Doyle Medi-Cal providers in the country, representing 3959 employees of mental health facilities.

out that the last time unemployment was at current levels, in 1977, the United States had 24 million people living in poverty. Today the rate is 2 percent higher, with 32 million people living in poverty. In 1985 the media reported that 20 million U.S. persons were going hungry and that the problem was getting worse. A year later then-President Reagan defended his administration, stating that hungry people were simply too ignorant to know where to obtain food.[111] Brown issued a warning:

> America has changed greatly during this decade. We are a nation that has millions more who are hungry. Millions more who are without homes in which to raise families. Millions more who are poor. We are a country where economic disparity has reached a record high. America is at a crossroads.[112]

One of the symptoms of poverty is people not having the financial resources to obtain housing. In 1984 the U.S. Department of Housing and Urban Development described the homeless as belonging to three major categories: (1) those who encountered economic problems such as unemployment; (2) the chronically disabled; and (3) those in personal crises (divorce, domestic violence, or health problems).[113] In these categories may be found people evicted from their residences due to lack of funds, former state hospital patients, substance abusers, runaway youths, the unemployed, and families. Twenty percent of the nation's homeless are homeless families.[114]

Since then, a more heterogeneous group has been emerging, comprised of even more families, young people, minorities, and women. A survey of the homeless in thirteen U.S. cities by the U.S. Conference of Mayors revealed the following ethnic pattern: 51.9 percent black; 33.3 percent non-Hispanic white; and 14.8 percent Hispanic, Native, and Asian American. Another survey, covering sixteen cities and involving 42,539 cases, showed that 51 percent of clients receiving services were minority (blacks, 40 percent; Hispanics, 11 percent). In three large cities, New York, St. Louis, and Los Angeles, 65 percent of the homeless were racial or ethnic minorities. In Chicago 69 percent of survey-respondent homeless were minority.[115] A significantly greater number (75 percent) of minority group homeless were permanent residents of the districts they were interviewed in, compared to non-Hispanic white homeless persons (60 percent). It appears that homelessness for minorities may be related more to economic factors than it is for non-Hispanic white homeless persons. For example, in Ohio black respondents were less likely than non-Hispanic whites to have had income from earnings in "the last month," and nearly 20 percent had never had a job. The conclusion was that blacks suffered more than whites from unemployment, even when blacks had more education and better preparation for employment.[116] It would appear that in addition to racism and economic hardship, immigration stress, being non-English-speaking and having illegal status would be contributing factors to homelessness in Hispanic groups.

First et al. point out that social work as a profession has a critical role, yet to be played, in designing, documenting, and testing policy approaches to alleviating minority group homelessness. He adds that some persons are simply unemployed, some are mentally ill, and others are not or have never been linked to traditional social support systems.[117]

Zeroing in on the psychiatric aspects of homelessness, Gelberg et al. studied 529 homeless adults who had used in-patient and out-patient mental health services. They found that many of the homeless subjects had an overwhelming set of social, mental health, criminal, alcohol, and drug problems. The greatest number of problems was found in those homeless who had a previous psychiatric hospitalization.[118] The findings reported in these various studies indicate that the homeless population is rather heterogeneous, with diverse needs, and hence requires different psychosocial strategies of intervention.

Current findings by Whitman et al. in 1990 concerning the impact of homelessness on a new homeless population—children—revealed certain psychosocial developmental defects. A battery of psychological tests measuring cognitive, language, and emotional status indicated that homelessness has a significant cognitive and language development impact on children, with language being more severely affected. Although the tests lacked precision in detecting emotional pathology in the children, in general intelligence they tested in the mentally retarded or borderline range at *three times* the expected rate.[119] Federal reductions in all human service programs, beginning with the eight-year Reagan administration and now followed by President Bush, continue to exacerbate poverty and homelessness in America, with over two million currently homeless, of which 100,000 are children.[120]

AIDS Patients

Persons diagnosed with AIDS (acquired immune deficiency syndrome) eventually die of this disease; a cure has not yet been found. According to the U.S. Centers for Disease Control after six years of studying 54,723 AIDS cases, there are only

three ways the disease is transmitted in the United States: through blood con-
tamination, sexual contact, and birth by an infected mother.[121] More than 81,000
AIDS cases had been reported by 133 countries to the World Health Organization
by February, 1988, twice the number that reported the year before. The United
States had the most cases with a little over 54,000, up from 31,000 cases the year
before.[122] The likelihood of suicide among AIDS patients far exceeds that of
persons suffering from other major illnesses, including cancer. The risk of suicide
among U.S. men with AIDS is sixty-six times higher than in the general population.

An AIDS study (March 1988) in Los Angeles County predicted that as many
as 340,000 people in the country would be infected by the AIDS virus by 1991,
with 16,000 to 23,000 of those infected actually dying. The health department
reported that there had been 4354 confirmed cases of AIDS as of January 31,
1987, which included 2722 who died of the virus. The persons considered at
highest risk are homosexual males and intravenous drug users.[123] Hispanics, who
comprise 7 percent of the U.S. population, represented nearly 14 percent of the
54,000 AIDS cases in the United States at that time.

By the end of 1989, AIDS cases in the United States exceeded 100,000, with
an estimated projected increase to 300,000 or 400,000 in 1992. In addition there
were 1.5 million Americans infected with HIV (human immunodeficiency virus)
at the end of 1989.[124] There continues to be a great deal of social stigma associated
with AIDS since initially there were an overwhelming number of homosexual
men who contracted the disease. Today, AIDS is afflicting many poor, black, and
Hispanic heterosexual intravenous (IV) drug users, their sexual partners, and
their children.[125] In Chapter 12 of this text, "Social Work Practice with Lesbians
and Gays," Appleby and Anastas state that initial public perception of AIDS as a
"gay plague," resulting in apathy, is slowly changing. Gays and lesbians are taking
a proactive stand by combining their political energy and assuming leadership
of the Nation's efforts by organizing local, state, and national self-help efforts
directed at developing services, advocating in behalf of patients, and lobbying
for additional research and treatment funds and protective legislation.

The medical-treatment aspect of AIDS appears hopeless, as a cure is yet to
be found. The psychiatric and clinical intervention aspects with persons suffering
from AIDS are also very difficult for the patient as well as the therapist. It is
usually very difficult to work with people who have a terminal illness. It becomes
even more difficult when working with patients who are stigmatized by the public
and by many mental health professionals. Some hospitals are beginning to set up
support groups for staff who work with AIDS patients.[126]

Psychiatrist Francisco Fernandez states that both anxiety disorders and
depression are prevalent in AIDS patients. Usually these disorders can be treated
with psychiatric medications along with psychotherapy. But subtle to more serious organic mental disturbances accompanying AIDS (found in 80 percent of
cases) make medication treatment complicated because of central-nervous-sys-
tem side effects such as Parkinsonism, hypotension, sedation, and confusion. Fernandez adds that few AIDS patients respond even moderately to antidepressant
medication.[127]

Navia, Jordan, and Price found in their study of AIDS patients that 66 percent suffered from progressive dementia with apathy, social withdrawal, and emotional blunting being the most common initial behavioral symptoms.[128] Stephen Buckingham and Wilfred Van Gorp identified specific social work intervention strategies when they were working with AIDS patients with related dementia. Treatment intervention assistance can be in the following areas[129]:

1. Problem solving with everyday concerns and difficulties
2. Estate planning
3. Decreasing the level of hypochondriacal preoccupation
4. Guidance in designing adequate structure and limits for activities of daily living
5. Assisting with family conflict

The AIDS problem certainly is a challenge for the medical and mental health professions. AIDS patients and their helpers are currently overwhelmed by this problem. It was included as a special population issue since it is increasingly becoming a great societal concern. Social workers need to learn more about this topic.

Police Brutality Victims

On March 3, 1991, a citizen's videotape graphically captured an assault by four or five Los Angeles Police Department officers on an unresisting African-American motorist, Rodney King, suspected of being under the influence of drugs or alcohol. The beating involved approximately fifty-six blows with police batons. The event was witnessed by at least fifteen other officers, who did not interfere in the assault. The videotape was shown nationwide several times per day for almost two weeks. Four of the officers were charged with felony assault. Daryl Gates, Chief of Police for the city of Los Angeles, resisting local and national demands to resign, maintained that the beating was an aberration.[130]

Police brutality can be defined as the use of unnecessary force by one or more law-enforcement officials toward a citizen or group of citizens, resulting in minor, moderate, or severe physical injury, up to and even including death. *Psychological* police brutality can be defined as verbal insults, implied threats, apparent ability to inflict physical harm, and/or intimidation by police toward citizens but with no actual physical harm. Other terms describing this behavior are police misconduct, police malpractice, and police abuse. Depending on the seriousness of the alleged misconduct, such acts may be prosecuted in local or state courts as misdemeanor or felony offenses, or in federal court as federal offenses. The principal federal criminal statutes with relevance to police misconduct are U.S. Code Section 1983 of Title 42 and U.S. Code Sections 241 and 242 of Title 18, the latter of which prohibit the deprivation of any rights, privileges, or immunities secured or protected by the Constitution or laws of the United States on account of an inhabitant being an alien or by reason of color or race.

Rodney King is filing a $56 million civil suit against the Los Angeles Police Department; $1 million for each blow against him. In 1990, numerous police brutality victims sued the LAPD, and all together they were paid $10.5 million. One victim, who received a $265,000 judgment, was an eighteen-year-old white youth who was dragged from his car and beaten severely, causing permanent ear damage.[131] Similarly, in 1989, 151 police brutality lawsuits were filed against the Los Angeles County Sheriff's Department. In fact, over a three-year period ending September, 1989, the Sheriff's Department cost the County of Los Angeles $8.5 million in major settlements and jury awards to police brutality victims.[132] Some of the victims were not compensated directly, as they had been killed by law enforcement; it was their families who received the awards. The victims represented all racial and ethnic groups, but with an overrepresentation of poor minorities. The American Civil Liberties Union maintains that, in Los Angeles alone, three to five citizens each day are abused by law enforcement. Note that police brutality in Los Angeles may only be the "tip of the iceberg." Consider the following:

In February, 1991, five New York City police officers were indicted on murder charges for the suffocation of a twenty-one-year-old Hispanic male suspected of auto theft. The officers were accused of having kicked, hit, and choked Federico Pereira while he lay face down. In June, 1989, an African American county sheriff in Memphis, Tennessee, was accused of choking to death Michael Gates, 28, an African American drug suspect. In Minneapolis, *Time* reported in April, 1991, a large group of community demonstrators protested the shooting of Tycel Nelson, age 17; and at the University of Massachusetts in Boston, at a police and communities conference, numerous African-American youths complained about how scary and demeaning it was to be stopped by the police.

Social work has a rich history of providing advocacy and other social services to victims of police brutality. Brutality was not an uncommon experience for recent immigrants settling in large cities in the 1910s, '20s, and '30s. Jane Addams, the founder of Hull House, fought against police malpractice and eventually became a founding member of the American Civil Liberties Union. The Abbott sisters, both respected social workers of that era, were part of Herbert Hoover's National Commission on Law Observance and Enforcement and its *1931 Report on Crime and the Foreign Born.* This investigating commission uncovered numerous instances of injustice in the courts being visited on Mexicans in the United States. In addition, Mexican and Polish immigrants, in particular, often received brutal treatment at the hands of police.[133]

Since the days of Addams and the Abbots, however, the social work profession has assumed a passive, dormant stance toward citizen abuse by law enforcement. In fact, with the increasing "clinicalization" of the profession, it has become the role of social workers to work with the police on a referral, diagnostic-and-treatment-services basis, rather than being advocates for clients who have been assaulted by the police. As stated by Morales in 1977, "This is not to say that poor people do not need social services when they are arrested, but rather that they are being denied assistance in an area of need (police–community conflict) that is far greater today than it was in the 1930s."[134]

Police brutality is a human rights as well as a civil rights violation. Such beating and choking are not unlike physical and psychological torture. Severe beatings stopping short of death may cause not only permanent physical impairment, but also permanent or chronic psychological pain known as post-traumatic stress disorder. Family members, and particularly children, witnessing these brutal assaults on their loved ones likewise may be permanently traumatized. Early, prompt intervention and treatment, both physical and psychological, are definitely essential in reducing the course of decompensation.

Most police brutality victims are powerless and poor. The values of the social work profession, expressed in its code of ethics which was cited earlier in this volume; that is, "The social worker should act to prevent practices that are inhumane or discriminatory against any person or groups of persons," make it mandatory for the profession to make this a practice priority. Successful macro-level class-action social work intervention in behalf of poor people being persecuted by law-enforcement officials is discussed in Chapter 21 of this text.

CONCLUDING COMMENT

Special populations are persons such as women, lesbians and gays, the elderly, AIDS patients, the homeless, and minorities, who have unique needs and circumstances that must be recognized when the social worker attempts to provide services to these persons. Special population members are not only unique, because of sex, age, race, sexual preference or ethnicity, but alike in that they also share second-class status in U.S. society. They are indeed a high-risk group because of their status in society.

The crippling effects of sexism, ageism, police brutality, homophobia, and racism, as expressed through the structural fabric of U.S. society, were analyzed not only as to intensity and prevalence but also with respect to the basic causes and functions of these stresses. Understanding the historical origin of these attitudes assists the social worker in understanding their expression as modern dynamics.

An examination of overall trends and demographics involving special population problems and needs shows that matters are becoming worse, especially given the attitudes of the previous and current administrations toward human services programs. The income gap between men and women continues to widen, AIDS continues to spread, the elderly are finding a greater economic and health struggle as they get older, homophobia transformed into "gay bashing" continues, there are more homeless, and minorities, especially blacks and Hispanics, are being directed into the juvenile and adult criminal justice system in even greater and more disproportionate numbers. Police brutality is beginning to receive the nation's "spotlight." Will social work respond to these victims?

The practice skills of the social work profession are being challenged as never before by special population needs. The ecosystems model, presented in Chapter 7, may prove valuable in assisting the social worker in obtaining a comprehensive analysis of any special populations case. Following analysis, micro- and macro-level interventions can then be attempted. The special populations chapters in Part Four will follow this format.

Minahan perhaps said it best when reminding social workers about their professional values and commitment to help oppressed people:

> Social workers can help people cope with their situations and increase their competence, but the very nature of the problems that oppressed people face are linked to the discrimination and exploitation they face in their environment. Social workers can work to make organizations and societal institutions responsive. Social workers can help people obtain resources. Social workers can work to influence social and environmental policy. Social workers pursue all these activities in social service organizations, in schools, in health and mental health facilities, in criminal justice institutions, in services designed for people with special problems or age characteristics, and in different geographic areas. In all these activities, social workers must value and respond humanely and helpfully to diverse populations and help others to do the same.[136]

SUGGESTED READINGS

ALLEN, C., and BROTMAN, H. *Chartbook on Aging in America* (Washington D.C.: White House Conference on Aging, 1981).

"Our Crowded Prisons," *The Annals of the American Academy of Political and Social Science* 478 (March 1985).

BECERRA, ROSINA M.; KARNO, MARVIN; and ESCOBAR, JAVIER I., eds. *Mental Health and Hispanic Americans: Clinical Perspectives.* New York: Grune & Stratton, 1982.

BILLINGSLEY, ANDREW. *Black Families in White America.* Englewood Cliffs, N.J.: Prentice-Hall, 1968.

BUCKINGHAM, STEPHEN L., and VAN GORP, WILFRED G. "Essential Knowledge about AIDS Dementia." *Social Work* 33 (March–April 1988) 112–115.

COHEN, B. E., and BURT, M. R. "The Homeless: Chemical Dependency and Mental Health Problems." *Social Work Research and Abstracts* 26 (March 1990).

DANE, B. O. "New Beginnings for AIDS Patients." *Social Casework* 70 (May 1989).

DELORIA, VINE, JR. "Native Americans: The American Indian Today." *The Annals of the American Academy of Political and Social Science* 454 (March 1981): 139–149.

GELBERG, LILLIAN; LINN, LAWRENCE S.; and LEAKE, BARBARA D. "Mental Health, Alcohol and Drug Abuse, and Criminal History among Homeless Adults," *The American Journal of Psychiatry* 145 (February 1988): 191–196.

MCINTOSH, JOHN L. "Suicide among the Elderly: Levels and Trends." *American Journal of Orthopsychiatry* 55 (April 1985): 288–293.

MARTIN, DEL. *Battered Wives.* New York: Pocket Books, 1977.

MORALES, ARMANDO. *Ando Sangrando (I Am Bleeding): A Study of Mexican American-Police Conflict* (La Puente, Calif.: Perspective Publications, 1972).

MORALES, ARMANDO. "The Collective Preconscious and Racism." *Social Casework* 52 (May 1971): 285–293.

MORALES, ARMANDO. "Social Work with Third-World People." *Social Work* 26 (January 1981): 45–51.

POWELL, GLORIA JOHNSON; YAMAMOTO, JOE; ROMERO ANNELISA; and MORALES, ARMANDO, eds. *The Psychosocial Development of Minority Group Children.* New York: Brunner/Mazel, 1983.

President's Commission on Mental Health. *Mental Health in America: 1978 vol. III.* Washington, D.C.: U.S. Government Printing Office, 1978.

SHERMAN, LAWRENCE W. *"Execution without Trial: Police Homicide and the Constitution." Vanderbilt Law Review* 33 (January 1980): 71–100.

SHERNOFF, M. "Why Every Social Worker Should Be Challenged by AIDS." *Social Work* 35 (January 1990).

Social Work 33 (May–June 1988). Special Issue on Social Work and AIDS.

Social Work 34 (November 1989). Special Issue on Homelessness.

Social Work 21 (November 1976). Special Issue on Women.

VLADEK, BRUCE C., and FIRMAN, JAMES P. "The Aging of the Population and Health Services." *The Annals of the American Academy of Political and Social Science* 468 (July 1983): 132–148.

WALKER, LENORE E. *The Battered Woman.* New York: Harper & Row, 1979.

ENDNOTES

1. President's Commission on Mental Health, *Mental Health in America: 1978* vol. III (Washington, D.C.: U.S. Government Printing Office, 1978), p. 731.
2. President's Commission on Mental Health, vol. III, Appendix, p. 646.
3. The U.S. Commission on Civil Rights, *Racism in America and How to Combat It* (Washington, D.C.: U.S. Government Printing Office, 1970), p. 19.
4. Blanch D. Coll, *Perspectives in Public Welfare* (Washington, D.C.: U.S. Department of Health, Education, and Welfare, 1969), p. 9.
5. Richard Hofstadter, *Social Darwinism in American Thought* (Boston: Beacon Press, 1944), p. 41.
6. Ibid., p. 50.
7. Ibid., p. 42.
8. "The Crisis Is Mounting," Special Report, National Association of Social Workers, Los Angeles Area Chapter, 1970.
9. *U.S. News and World Report,* April 15, 1985, p. 25.
10. *Newsweek,* February 4, 1991, p. 65.
11. Gloria Johnson Powell and Rodney N. Powell, "Epilogue: Poverty—The Greatest and Severest Handicapping Condition in Childhood," in Gloria Johnson Powell, Joe Yamamoto, Annelisa Romero, and Armando Morales, eds., *The Psychosocial Development of Minority Group Children* (New York: Brunner/Mazel, 1983), p. 579.
12. Ibid., p. 577.
13. "Suffer the Little Children," *Time,* October 8, 1990.
14. Carmen De Navas and Edward Fernandez, "Condition of Hispanic Women Today," U.S. Department of Commerce, Bureau of the Census, July 27, 1984.
15. Del Martin, *Battered Wives* (New York: Pocket Books, 1977), pp. 10–42.
16. Lenore E. Walker, *The Battered Woman* (New York: Harper & Row, 1979).
17. Murray A. Straus, "Social Stress and Marital Violence in a National Sample of American Families," *Annals of New York Academy of Sciences* 347 (1980): 229–250.
18. Anna F. Kuhl, "A Preliminary Profile of Abusing Men," a paper presented at the Annual Meeting of the Academy for Criminal Justice Sciences, Philadelphia, 1980.

19. Commission on Crime Control and Violence Prevention, *Ounces of Prevention: Toward an Understanding of the Causes of Violence,* 1982 Final Report to the People of California, monograph, Sacramento, California, p. 33.

20. Martin, p. 14.

21. Clarence Kelley, *Uniform Crime Reports for the United States* (Washington, D.C.: U.S. Government Printing Office, 1974).

22. Gail Abarbanel, "Helping Victims of Rape," *Social Work* 21 (November 1976): 478.

23. Ibid.

24. Roger Petersen, "Social Class, Social Learning, and Wife Abuse," *Social Service Review* 54 (September 1980): 399.

25. Richard J. Gelles, *The Violent Home* (Beverly Hills, Calif.: Sage Publications 1972), pp. 183–190.

26. Mary Valentich and James Gripton, "Ideological Perspectives on the Sexual Assault of Women," *Social Service Review* 58 (September 1984): 451.

27. Lorne Gibson, Rick Linden, and Stuart Johnson, "A Situational Theory of Rape," *Canadian Journal of Criminology* 22 (1980): 51–65.

28. Susan Brownmiller, *Against Our Will* (New York: Simon and Schuster, 1975).

29. Margaret L. Andersen and Claire Renzetti, "Rape Crisis, Counseling, and the Culture of Individualism," *Contemporary Crisis* 4 (1980): 331–332.

30. Peggy Reeves Sanday, *Female Power and Male Dominance: On the Origins of Sexual Inequality* (Cambridge: Cambridge University Press, 1981).

31. Hugh Davis Graham and Ted Robert Gurr, *Violence in America: Historical and Comparative Perspectives* (New York: Bantam Books, 1969), p. 799.

32. Bruce C. Vladeck and James P. Firman, "The Aging of the Population and Health Services," *The Annals of the American Academy of Political and Social Science* 468 (July 1983): 133.

33. Ibid., p. 137.

34. Elaine M. Brody, "Aging," in John B. Turner, ed., *Encyclopedia of Social Work Seventeenth Issue* vol. I (Washington, D.C.: National Association of Social Workers, 1977), p. 57.

35. Lawrence S. Root and John E. Tropman, "Income Sources of the Elderly," *Social Service Review* 58 (September 1984): 390, 393.

36. C. Allen and H. Brotman, eds., *Chartbook on Aging in America* (Washington, D.C.: White House Conference on Aging, 1981), p. 57.

37. Gary M. Nelson, "How States Distribute Title XX Funds to the Elderly Poor," *Social Work Research and Abstracts* 19 (Summer 1983): 5, 7.

38. Vladeck and Firman, p. 138.

39. Allen and Brotman, pp. 78–80.

40. Allen and Brotman, p. 17.

41. Brody, p. 57.

42. *Los Angeles Times,* April 21, 1985, Part IV, p. 5.

43. Robert N. Butler, "Geriatric Medicine," *New York State Journal of Medicine* 77 (August 1977): 1471.

44. Ira Reiss, *Family Systems in America* 3rd ed. (New York: Holt, Rinehart and Winston, 1980).

45. R. Douglass, "A Study of Maltreatment of the Elderly and Other Vulnerable Adults," Institute of Gerontology and School of Public Health (Ann Arbor: University of Michigan, 1980).

46. John L. McIntosh, "Suicide among the Elderly: Levels and Trends," *American Journal of Orthopsychiatry* 55 (April 1985): 289.

47. Ibid., p. 291.

48. Armando Morales, "Social Work with Third-World People," *Social Work* 26 (January 1981): 45.

49. Armando Morales, "The Collective Preconscious and Racism," *Social Casework* 52 (May 1971): 285–293.

50. U.S. Commission on Civil Rights, *Racism in America,* p. 5.

51. Ibid.

52. *Los Angeles Times,* April 27, 1985, Part I, p. 12.

53. Ibid.

54. Ibid.

55. J. S. Passel, "Provisional Evaluation of the 1970 Census Count of American Indians," *Demography* 13 (1976): 397–409.

56. U.S. Department of Health, Education, and Welfare, Office of Health Research, Statistics, and Technology, *Health United States: 1979,* No. 80–1232 (Washington D.C.: U.S. Government Printing Office, 1980); also see Armando Morales, "Social Work with Third World People," p. 45.

57. Vine Deloria, Jr., "Native Americans: The American Indian Today," *The Annals of the American Academy of Political and Social Science* 454 (March 1981): 140, 141.

58. Roger Daniels and Harry H. L. Kitano, *American Racism: Exploration of the Nature of Prejudice* (Englewood Cliffs, N.J.: Prentice-Hall, 1970), pp. 29–33.

59. Deloria, p. 146.

60. Ronald S. Fischler, "Protecting American Indian Children," *Social Work* 25 (September 1980): 342, 347.

61. Evelyn Lance Blanchard and Russel Lawrence Barsh, "What Is Best for Tribal Children? A Response to Fischler," *Social Work* 25 (September 1980): 350, 354.

62. Ibid., p. 352.

63. James Abourezk, "The Role of the Federal Government: A Congressional View," in Steven Unger, ed., *The Destruction of American Indian Families* (New York: Association on American Indian Affairs, 1977), p. 12.

64. William Byler, "The Destruction of American Indian Families," in Steven Unger, p. 1.

65. Anne Metcalf, *A Model for Treatment in a Native American Family Service Center* (Seattle: School of Social Work, University of Washington, 1978), pp. 4–6.

66. Kenji Murase, "Minorities: Asian Americans," in John B. Turner, ed., *Encyclopedia of Social Work Seventeenth Issue* vol. 2 (Washington, D.C.: National Association of Social Workers, 1977), p. 953.

67. Ibid.

68. Ibid.

69. Daniels and Kitano, p. 62.

70. Powell et al., p. 240.

71. Lindbergh S. Sata, "Mental Health Issues of Japanese American Children," in Powell et al., p. 366.

72. Daniel D. Le, "Mental Health and Vietnamese Children," in Powell et al., p. 373.

73. Ibid., pp. 378, 379.

74. Ibid., p. 383.

75. "Blacks and Hispanics in the United States," Data Track 6 (Washington, D.C. American Council of Life Insurance, 1979), p. 5.

76. U.S. Bureau of the Census, *Marital Status and Living Arrangements: March 1988* Current Population Reports Series P-20, No. 433 (Washington, D.C.: U.S. Government Printing Office, 1989), p. 42.

77. U.S. Bureau of the Census, *Characteristics of Populations Below Poverty Line,* Current Population Reports Series P-60, No. 130 (Washington, D.C.: U.S. Government Printing Office, 1979).

78. Andrew Billingsley, *Black Families in White America* (Englewood Cliffs, N.J.: Prentice-Hall, 1968), p. 71.

79. Barbara Ann Bass, Gail Elizabeth Wyatt, and Gloria Johnson Powell, eds., *The Afro-American Family: Assessment, Treatment, and Research Issues* (New York: Grune & Stratton, 1982), p. 10.

80. Ibid., pp. 10, 11.

81. *Los Angeles Times,* April 28, 1985, Part I, p. 4.

82. Barbara Bryant Solomon, "The Delivery of Mental Health Services to Afro-American Individuals and Families: Translating Theory into Practice," in Bass et al., pp. 165, 166.

83. Lawrence W. Sherman, "Execution without Trial: Police Homicide and the Constitution," *Vanderbilt Law Review* 33 (January 1980): 95, 96.

84. Armando Morales, "Police Deadly Force: Government-Sanctioned Execution of Hispanics," paper presented at National Council of La Raza Symposium on Crime and Justice for Hispanics, Racine, Wisconsin, June 28–30, 1979, p. 6.

85. "The Hispanic Population in the United States: March 1986 and 1987 (Advance Report)," U.S. Department of Commerce, *Bureau of the Census,* Series P-20, No. 416, issued August 1987, p. 5.

86. *Business Week,* June 23, 1980, p. 86.

87. U.S. Bureau of the Census, *Marital Status and Living Arrangements,* p. 42.

88. "Report of the Special Populations Subpanel on Mental Health of Hispanic Americans," *The President's Commission on Mental Health vol. III, Appendix* (Washington, D.C.: U.S. Government Printing Office, 1978), p. 905.

89. Armando Morales, "Substance Abuse and Mexican American Youth: An Overview," *Journal of Drug Issues* 14 (Spring 1984): 297–311.

90. Armando Morales, "The Mexican American Gang Member: Evaluation and Treatment," in Rosina M. Becerra, Marvin Karno, and Javier I. Escobar, eds., *Mental Health and Hispanic Americans: Clinical Perspectives* (New York: Grune & Stratton, 1982), pp. 139–155.

91. Armando Morales, "Institutional Racism in Mental Health and Criminal Justice," *Social Casework* 59 (July 1978): 387–395.

92. *Prisoners in 1983,* Bureau of Justice Statistics Bulletin (Washington, D.C.: Department of Justice, BJS, 1984), App. A.

93. James Austin and Barry Krisberg, "Incarceration in the United States: The Extent and Future of the Problem," *The Annals of the American Academy of Political and Social Science* 478 (March 1985): 24.

94. *Federal, District of Columbia, and States Future Prison and Correctional Institution Populations and Capacities, GAO/GGD-84-56* (Gaithersburg, Md.: U.S. Government Accounting Office, 1984).

95. George Church, "The View from Behind Bars," *Time,* vol. 136, no. 19, 1990.

96. Austin and Krisberg, p. 25.

97. Ibid., p. 26.

98. Armando Morales, Yvonne Ferguson, and Paul Munford, "The Juvenile Justice System and Minorities," in Powell et al., pp. 458–460.

99. Barry Krisberg and Ira Schwartz, "Rethinking Juvenile Justice," *Crime and Delinquency* (July 1983): 346–349.

100. Ibid., p. 351.

101. *Sacramento Chronicle,* September 26, 1984, p. 1.

102. "Arrests in California and First Commitments to the Youth Authority by Race/Ethnicity," Department of the Youth Authority, State of California, February 1985, p. 7; also see "Ethnic Groups in Correctional Facilities, 1983," statistics, California Youth Authority, #586IHY-1, 1983.

103. "A Comparison of Characteristics of Youth Authority Wards in Institutions and on Parole, 1974–1983," November 1983, Department of the Youth Authority, State of California, p. 9.

104. "United States Private Juvenile Correctional Facilities 1-Day Counts, 1983," U.S. Bureau of the Census, Children in Custody Series.

105. Joan Petersilia, "Racial Disparities in the Criminal Justice System," June 1983, Rand Corporation, Santa Monica, Calif., pp. v, xii.

106. Lawrence A. Greenfeld, "Measuring the Application and Use of Punishment," National Institute of Justice, Washington, D.C., November 1981.

107. Tom Morganthau, "Closing the Door," *Newsweek,* June 25, 1984, p. 19.

108. Ed Griffin, "Reagan Runs into the Religious Left," *In These Times,* April 11–17, 1984, p. 11.

109. "Social Work in the Sanctuary Movement for Central American Refugees," *Social Work* 30 (February 1985): 74, 75.

110. Floyd H. Martinez, "Mental Health Manpower Survey for Los Angeles County Department of Mental Health," September, 1983, p. 4. The survey included all Short-Doyle and Medi-Cal providers in the country, representing 3959 employees of mental health facilities.

111. J. Larry Brown, "Domestic Hunger Is No Accident," *Social Work* 33 (March–April 1988).

112. Ibid, p. 100.

113. "A Report to the Secretary on the Homeless and Emergency Shelters," U.S. Department of Housing and Urban Development, Office of Policy Development and Research, May 1984.

114. Ellen L. Bassuk, Lenore Rubin, and Alison S. Lauriat, "Characteristics of Sheltered Homeless Families," *American Journal of Public Health* (September 1986): 1097–1101.

115. Richard J. First, Dee Roth, and Bobbie Darden Arewa, "Homelessness: Understanding the Dimensions of the Problem for Minorities," *Social Work* 33 (March–April, 1988): 120.

116. Ibid., p. 122.

117. Ibid., p. 123.

118. Lillian Gelberg, Lawrence S. Linn, and Barbara D. Leake, "Mental Health, Alcohol and Drug Use, and Criminal History Among Homeless Adults," *The American Journal of Psychiatry* 145 (February 1988): 191–196.

119. Barbara Y. Whitman, Pasquale Accardo, Mary Boyert, and Rita Kendagor, "Homelessness and Cognitive Performance in Children: A Possible Link," *Social Work* 35 (November 1990): 516.

120. Children's Defense Fund, *Children 1990: A Report Card, Briefing Book, and Action Primer* (Washington, D.C.: The Fund, 1990).

121. *Los Angeles Times,* Part II, March 4, 1988, p. 8.

122. Ibid.

123. *Los Angeles Times,* Part I, March 19, 1988, p. 30.

124. Michael Shernoff, "Why Every Social Worker Should Be Challenged by AIDS," *Social Work* 35 (January 1990): 5.

125. Barbara Oberhofer Dane, "New Beginnings for AIDS Patients," *Social Casework* 70 (May 1989): 305.

126. Kathleen Moriarty and Teddye Clayton, "Highlights of the 39th Institute on Hospital and Community Psychiatry," *Hospital and Community Psychiatry* 39 (February 1988): 131.

127. Ibid.

128. B. A. Navia, B. D. Jordan, and R. W. Price, "The AIDS Dementia Complex: Clinical Features," *Annals of Neurology* 19 (June 1986): 517–524.

129. Stephen L. Buckingham and Wilfred G. Van Gorp, "Essential Knowledge about AIDS Dementia," *Social Work* 33 (March–April 1988): 112–115.

130. Richard Lacayo, "Law and Disorder," *Time,* April 1, 1991, pp. 18–21.

131. Lacayo, p. 21.

132. *Los Angeles Times,* Sunday, May 27, 1990, p. 1.

133. National Commission on Law Observance and Enforcement, *Report on Crime and the Foreign Born* (Washington, D.C.: United States Government, 1931), p. 229.

134. Armando Morales, "Beyond Traditional Conceptual Frameworks," *Social Work* 22 (September 1977): 388. Also see Albert R. Roberts, "Police Social Workers: A History," *Social Work* 21 (July 1976): 298.
136. Anne Minahan, "Social Workers and Oppressed People," *Social Work* 26 (May 1981): 184.

Chapter 11

Social Work Practice with Women

Diane Kravetz

PREFATORY COMMENT

Diane Kravetz, former Dean of the School of Social Work at the University of Wisconsin at Madison, was commissioned to write this chapter pertaining to social work practice with women. Doctor Kravetz enjoys national respect for her scholarly work on women. She cautions that even though they live longer than men, women are the fastest growing group of persons with AIDS, representing 10 percent of all reported cases. As a special population group, large numbers of females of all ages suffer significant cases of physical, psychological, and sexual abuse, mostly by perpetrators known to them.

Kravetz calls for the elimination of sexism in the social work profession. One of the first steps in working toward this goal is to learn about the manifestations of this dynamic in the profession. This chapter will make a major contribution to that goal.

Since the 1970s, social workers have identified and worked to eliminate discrimination and gender bias in social work education and practice. They have incorporated the expanding scholarship on women into the knowledge base of the profession and have developed services and interventions that are more responsive to the unique concerns of women clients. However, it remains true that the personal and social problems of women clients (as well as all other women) are inextricably linked to gender inequality and institutionalized sexism. Social workers need to continue to identify the ways in which sexism pervades practice, to understand the cultural and social context of women's problems, and to develop strategies that can meaningfully change women's lives.

The special needs and concerns of women are relevant for every field of practice, social problem area, and level of intervention. Women's issues can be identified for female clients of every age, ethnic and racial group, and class. Correspondingly, for every women's issue, differences can be identified by age, class, ethnicity or race, and sexual orientation.

The first section of this chapter, current demographics, provides some basic facts about women's lives in the United States today. Then, using the ecosystems model of practice as the framework for analysis, the chapter reviews the personal, social, and economic problems of women and presents the principles and methods of practice that provide the foundation for effective and ethical social work practice with women.

CURRENT DEMOGRAPHICS[1]

Over the past three decades, there have been dramatic changes in the composition of the family and women's participation in the work force (see Table 11–1). In 1987, 56 percent of women sixteen years old and over were in the civilian labor force, compared to 43 percent in 1970 and 38 percent in 1960.

In married-couple families, which represent only 58 percent of all households, women's employment reflects not only changing social attitudes but also the economic necessity of two incomes. In 1987, the median income for a dual-earner family ($40,939) was significantly higher than the median income for married-couple families in which the wife was not in the paid labor force ($26,652). Working wives decrease the poverty rate of married couples by 35 percent among whites, 39 percent among blacks, and 26 percent among Hispanics.[2]

The major change in the composition of families has been the substantial increase in the number of families headed by women. In 1987, 16 percent of families were maintained by women, whereas in 1960 only 10 percent were. The proportion of families maintained by women differs greatly among black (42 percent), Hispanic (23 percent), and white (13 percent) families.

The most significant factor in the increase in families maintained by women has been the increase in out-of-wedlock births. From 1970 to 1987, the proportion of one-parent families headed by never-married women increased from 7 to 28 percent. Among blacks, births to unmarried women represented 38 percent of births in 1970 and 61 percent in 1986. Among whites, the rates of birth to unmarried women almost tripled between 1970 and 1986, increasing from 6 to 16 percent. In 1985, teenagers accounted for one-third of births to unmarried black and unmarried white women.[3]

The increase in female-headed families has been caused also by increasing rates of divorce. From 1970 to 1987, divorce rates more than doubled, and the proportion of one-parent families consisting of divorced women and children increased from 29 to 36 percent.

TABLE 11–1   *Selected Socioeconomic Characteristics of Women and Men in the United States, 1987 (percentages)*

Characteristics	Women	Men
Proportion of adult population	52.0	48.0
Persons 65 years and over (percent of total population)	14.2	10.2
Marital status		
Single	18.6	25.3
Married	60.5	65.5
Widowed	12.1	2.5
Divorced	8.7	6.7
Education (persons 25 years old and over)		
Less than a high school degree	24.7	24.0
Completed high school	41.6	35.4
1–3 years of college	17.1	17.1
4 years of college or more	16.5	23.6
Participation in civilian labor force	56.0	76.2
Proportion of women and men in selected occupations		
Managers and administrators	37.9	62.1
Professionals	50.1	49.9
Dentists	8.9	91.1
Engineers	6.9	93.1
Lawyers and judges	19.7	80.3
Librarians	85.6	14.4
Mathematical and computer scientists	34.1	65.9
Physicians	19.5	80.5
Registered nurses	95.1	4.9
Social workers	65.6	34.4
Teachers, college and university	37.1	62.9
Teachers, except college and university	73.6	26.4
Cashiers	83.0	17.0
Secretaries	99.1	0.9
Private households (child care workers, cleaners, servants)	96.3	3.7
Median income of householders ($)	14,600	31,534
Married—spouse present	34,847	34,782
Married—spouse absent	10,517	19,496
Widowed	10,209	13,424
Divorced	17,597	24,005
Never-married	15,759	21,493

Source: U.S. Bureau of the Census, *Statistical Abstract of the United States: 1989* 109th ed. (Washington, D.C.: The Bureau, 1989).

With divorce, most women experience drastic declines in their standard of living and income. A 1985 study found that one year after divorce women's standard of living had decreased by 73 percent, whereas men's had increased by 43 percent.[4] Divorced women's financial problems are compounded by inadequate or unpaid child support. Only 61 percent of single mothers are awarded child support by the courts; further, over half the women who are awarded child support fail to receive the full amount. More than a quarter receive nothing.[5]

Nearly two-thirds (63 percent) of female family heads work full or part time.[6] Predictably, female householders have lower median incomes than either male householders or married-couple families. In 1987, in families with children, female householders had a median income of $10,551, as compared to $20,967 for male householders and $36,366 for married couples. Also, women are more likely than men to have part-time or temporary jobs for which there is no health insurance coverage.

Highly limited employment options and social norms that assign women primary responsibility for children are largely responsible for the so-called feminization of poverty. In 1987, over one-third (35 percent) of female-headed families were poor, a rate almost six times that of married-couple families (6 percent) and over three times that of single male-headed families (11 percent). The rate of poverty for single males was 13 percent; for single females, 19 percent.[7] Members of minority female-headed families are particularly at risk for poverty. In 1987, more than half of single-parent families maintained by black and Hispanic women were poor, compared to over one-fourth of those maintained by white women.[8]

Women constitute the majority of older Americans. In 1986, there were 100 women for every 68 men among people aged sixty-five and older. Among persons born in 1970, white females can expect to live to about seventy-six and white males to about sixty-eight. Females of color born that same year can expect to live to about sixty-nine, and men of color to about sixty-one.[9]

In 1987, for persons sixty-five years old and older, more men (77 percent) than women (41 percent) were married; more women (49 percent) than men (14 percent) were widowed. More elderly women (41 percent) than elderly men (16 percent) were living alone. These differences are due to women's greater longevity and the fact that widowed or divorced men are more likely to remarry.

Because of their relatively low incomes and greater likelihood of being widowed, older women have higher rates of poverty than do older men. Over the decade of 1969 to 1979, 35 percent of elderly women (ages 66–75) were in poverty at least once, compared with 20 percent of men in this same age group.[10] In 1986, nearly 36 percent of all black elderly women were poor, as were 13 percent of elderly white women. Many older women lack adequate health care, since Medicare provides little coverage for long-term care and nursing home care, the two services that women use more than men.[11]

Health and Mental Health Risk Factors

As noted, in the United States, women live longer than men. But also, women more than men experience infections and respiratory diseases and chronic conditions such as arthritis, osteoporosis, and diseases of the urinary system, as well as deaths due to childbearing, abortion, and breast cancer.[12] The proportion of women who smoke is now approaching that of men. And although men are more likely than women to be heavy drinkers, women are more likely than men to use and abuse prescription drugs.[13]

There are significant differences in the health status of black and white women. Black women's death rates from diabetes and homicide are more than double those of white women. For black women, the mortality rates from complications of pregnancy and childbirth are more than four times those for whites. White women have higher mortality rates than black women from accidents, lung cancer, and suicide.[14]

Women are the fastest growing group of people with AIDS, with the number of reported cases among women increasing from 59 in 1981 to 2476 in 1988, or just over 10 percent of all reported cases. The risk of AIDS in black and Hispanic women is 13.2 and 8.1 times that in white women.[15] The Centers for Disease Control estimate that there are fifty to eighty times as many women infected with HIV as there are women with cases of AIDS. Many of these women have no symptoms and are unaware that they are capable of infecting others. The women at greatest risk are intravenous drug users, the sexual partners of male intravenous drug users and bisexual men, and prostitutes. Many are poorly educated and unemployed. Women of childbearing age (ages 13–39) account for four out of five of all female AIDS cases, and it is estimated that half of the babies born to HIV-infected mothers may be infected with the AIDS virus.[16]

Finally, large numbers of women are victims of physical, psychological, and sexual abuse, often by members of their own families. Violence toward women is wide-ranging and includes child sexual assault, wife abuse, rape, and sexual harassment. Victims are subjected to physical injuries, unwanted pregnancies, and sexually transmitted diseases; victimization also has severe and prolonged negative effects on women's emotional health.[17]

Estimates suggest that one-third to one-half of all marriages involve some physical abuse of the wife, including pushing, slapping, punching, choking, sexual assault, or assault with weapons. According to the 1985 FBI Uniform Crime Report, 30 percent of female homicide victims were killed by their husbands or boyfriends. Between 1978 and 1982, 2.1 million women were victims of domestic violence at least once during an average twelve-month period.[18]

In 1987, there were 91,110 reported rapes or attempted rapes, a figure that does not include marital rapes and is unlikely to include most date rapes.[19] Reported rates of childhood sexual abuse in clinical populations are as high as 70 percent for women. In studies of nonclinical populations, approximately 20 to 30 percent of adult women report experiences of childhood sexual abuse.[20]

These figures significantly underrepresent the actual rates of female victimization. A 1984 study found that only 10 percent of rape cases, 6 percent of extrafamilial child sexual abuse cases, and 2 percent of incestuous child sexual abuse cases were reported to the police.[21] Most women are reluctant to report their abuses due to shame, guilt, and obstacles created by the legal, health, and social service systems. Traditional legal procedures and sexist attitudes toward

women and female children have led to the dismissal of many cases of child
sexual abuse and rape.

ECOSYSTEMS PERSPECTIVE

The ecosystems model can provide a framework for understanding the beliefs,
norms, institutional arrangements, and social roles that define and maintain
women as a subordinate social group. Each of the five interconnected levels of
the ecosystems model (historical factors, environmental-structural factors, culture, family, and individual) are discussed below in relation to the social and
psychosocial problems of women.

The historical experience of women is best understood in terms of changing
gender roles in the family and changes in women's social and economic circumstances. Therefore, historical factors are incorporated into the sections on the
family and environmental-structural factors.

Cultural Factors

Cultural ideology about women shapes women's reality and maintains female
subordination by men. Gender stereotyping, gender bias, and discrimination
based on sex all reflect and promote negative cultural beliefs about women and
their "appropriate" status in society. Women are defined as innately and inevitably
different from and inferior to men. This androcentric view is supported by socially
constructed definitions of woman as biologically destined to be dependent, nur-
turant, and domestic. The social, economic, and political arrangements that
emerge from these cultural assumptions give males authority over females and
formal power over public policies and practices.

American Indian, Asian American, black, Hispanic, and white women represent distinct cultural groups, each having specific and different problems, issues,
and concerns. Within each of these groups, women's experience differs by class,
and for some groups, by nationality or tribe. However, some generalizations can
be made. Within every cultural group, female and male experience differs significantly, with women in each group having problems related to gender inequality within their own group and in society at large. For women of color, issues
related to gender must be understood in terms of the overwhelming influence
of racism and ethnic prejudice as well.

For lesbian women, oppression stems from sexism, homophobia, and heterosexism (heterosexism being a belief system that values heterosexuality as
superior to and more natural than homosexuality). Misconceptions about and
prejudice against lesbians are extensions of cultural myths and biases concerning
traditional female roles and female sexuality. Lesbianism involves a life style and
subculture in which women function relatively independently of men. Thus lesbianism challenges cultural mandates that women seek personal fulfillment and

economic security through heterosexual bonding. Heterosexism is, then, a major aspect of male-dominated culture, for it functions to maintain traditional power relationships between women and men. Homophobia and fear of being labeled homosexual serve to keep both women and men within the confines of traditional gender roles.

Environmental-Structural Factors

Women's personal concerns, experiences, and problems are inextricably linked to the subordinate social, economic, and legal status of women as a group. Institutional sexism in education, law, and employment reinforces damaging views of women, creates role conflicts for women, and limits women's real and perceived options for personal growth and economic security. Although there is evidence of gender-role changes for women of every class and ethnic or racial group, all institutional arenas continue to be pervaded by male-centered values and discriminatory policies and practices.

Women's Education.   The development of free, public elementary education by the mid-nineteenth century and public high schools by the end of the nineteenth century provided women with equal access to education. However, resistance to women in higher education remained firm. In 1920, a time when less than 8 percent of young people went to college, twice as many men as women received Bachelor's or Master's degrees, and five times more earned doctorates.[22]

Due to social norms, structural barriers (including policies barring married women from employment and opposition from male professionals), and difficulties in combining family and career roles, many college-educated women chose to remain single in order to pursue their careers. These women provided leadership in the teaching profession, developed the professions of social work and home economics, established women's colleges and all-female medical schools, and became leaders in the first wave of the feminist movement.[23]

In 1987, the median number of school years completed was slightly higher for white women (12.6 years) than for black (12.4 years) and Hispanic (12.0 years) women. More white women (43 percent) graduated from high school than did black (38 percent) and Hispanic (30 percent) women. Similarly, more white women (17 percent) completed four years or more of college than did black (10 percent) and Hispanic (8 percent) women.

By 1987, women received half of the Bachelor's and Master's degrees awarded. However, women still received a smaller proportion (35 percent) of doctorate degrees, and they continued to be underrepresented in fields such as agriculture, business, computer science, dentistry, economics, engineering, law, medicine, and the physical sciences. Women earned the majority of the Master's and doctoral degrees awarded in fields such as education, English, fine arts, foreign languages, home economics, and social work.[24]

Women in the Labor Force.   In pre-industrial American society, the workplace and the family were not separate entities. Although divisions of labor by gender were present, the basic economic roles of women and men were the same; that is, the production of goods and services to meet the needs of the family.

With industrialization, women's and men's spheres became separate and differentially valued, especially in urban areas. During the nineteenth century, paid work outside of the home was viewed as masculine, was valued as contributing to the larger social good, and was predominantly performed by males. Work inside the home which produced goods and services for the benefit of the family was defined as a woman's responsibility. It was not viewed as contributing to the public good, and, as unpaid labor, was no longer considered productive work.

As part of these changing social values, women became viewed as responsible primarily for providing a comfortable and nurturing environment for husbands and children, with their worth being defined in terms of how well they met the needs of their families. They became economically dependent on their husbands and psychologically dependent on being successful wives and mothers.

The ideology that defined women only in terms of their domestic roles was reinforced by social norms defining paid work as deviant for married women of all classes. The pervasive power of this ideology ensured that most women in the paid labor force were single. Until the middle of the twentieth century, most female workers were young, single, and primarily from white working-class, immigrant, and black families; they worked in factories, as servants and waitresses, as clerical workers and secretaries, and in retail sales. Women with postsecondary education became teachers, librarians, settlement house workers, and nurses. When economically feasible, married women of all racial and ethnic groups dropped out of the labor force.

However, some married women have always been part of the paid labor force. In the nineteenth and early twentieth centuries, employment was common for married black women, most of whom still lived in the South. In 1890, for example, one-quarter of black wives and two-thirds of the large number of black widows worked, usually as field hands or domestic servants. Also at that time, paid work was common for married immigrant women in the textile-manufacturing towns of New England.[25] By 1920, 43 percent of black females over the age of fifteen were employed, whether married or not, generally as domestic servants.[26] By World War II, although only 12 percent of white married women were paid workers, almost 25 percent of black married women were.[27]

A series of changing social conditions made employment socially acceptable and necessary for women, including middle-class married white women. These include: (1) "labor-saving" devices in the home; (2) recruitment of female labor during the World Wars and expanded employment opportunities, post–World War II, in "pink-collar" work (clerical work and sales); (3) increased economic need for two-income families; (4) increased educational opportunities for women; (5) a rising divorce rate and increasing numbers of female-headed households; (6) women's increased control of reproduction; (7) new antidiscrimination laws in education and employment; and (8) changing views of gender roles. These factors decreased barriers to female employment and increased women's opportunities and desire to enter the paid labor force.[28] The result has been a dramatic increase in the labor force participation of women. From 1960 to 1987, the percentage of the female population in the labor force increased from 38 to 56 percent, with rates for white women and women of color now similar (56 percent for white women, 58 percent for black women, 52 percent for Hispanic women).

These increases are mostly due to increases in labor force participation among married women. In 1987, 56 percent of married women were paid workers, compared with 32 percent in 1960. Single, divorced, and widowed women also increased their rates of participation. From 1960 to 1987, single women's participation rate increased from 44 to 65 percent, while the rate for previously married women grew from 37 to 43 percent.

In 1950, about 28 percent of all women with school-aged children were in the labor force. Ten years later, the rate was almost 40 percent; by 1970 it was nearly 50 percent; and by 1980 it was 60 percent. In 1988, almost 73 percent of married mothers of school-aged children and 57 percent of married mothers of children under six years old were in the work force.[29] Unlike women who were born prior to World War II, these women have tended to postpone marriage and children, have fewer children, have a longer prematernity history of employment, and remain in the work force after the births of their children.

Even with substantial gains in education and training, gender inequality still characterizes women's experiences in the labor force. On average, women's earnings in 1987 were $14,600; men's were $31,534. Women with college degrees earn less than men who have only graduated from high school. In the professions and white-collar and blue-collar jobs, women continue to hold a disproportionate share of the lower status, lower paying jobs.

For many women, paid work does not provide adequate monetary compensation or personal satisfaction. Sexual harassment reminds working women of their subordinate status and often causes them to quit jobs or seek transfers. Further, women's unpaid labor in their homes, on farms, and in their communities still is not included in cultural concepts of "work" and is not compensated by private pensions or social security.

Women's Legal Rights.   Changes in women's roles and status are reflected in the legal system as well. Historically, women had few rights; they were viewed as the property of their fathers or husbands and in need of a man's protection. Unmarried women were viewed as deviants or exceptions and did not challenge legal definitions of women's rights and roles. The assumptions of the appropriateness and legitimacy of male control and dominance rendered invisible the needs of married women and their children to be protected from their "protectors."

The right to vote was extended to women only seventy years ago. Other major legal changes have occurred only within the past few decades. For example, Title VII of the 1964 Civil Rights Act bars sex discrimination in hiring, firing, promotions, and working conditions. Women now have the right to equal pay for equal work through the 1963 Equal Pay Act. Equal access and participation in education are covered by Title IX of the Educational Amendments of 1972. Abortions became legalized through the *Roe* v. *Wade* decision in 1973, though legal decisions since then have greatly restricted access to abortion for many women. Only in the past decade has there been some degree of reform in the laws and policies governing the treatment of rape victims, battered women, and victims of childhood sexual abuse.

The Family

Major shifts have occurred in women's marital and parental roles. Beginning with women born in the 1940s, there has been a significant shift toward marrying at a later age, delaying childbearing, and having fewer children. For example, women born in 1930 to 1934 had an average of 3.4 children; women born in 1950 to 1954 had an average of 2.2 children.

Changing gender roles, increased education and labor force participation, and wider availability of contraception and abortion have contributed to women's delay of childbearing. In 1970, about 36 percent of women had their first child before they were twenty; another 46 percent had their first child when they were twenty to twenty-four years old. Only 4 percent of first births were among women over thirty. In 1987, at the birth of their first child, about 23 percent of women were under twenty, 33 percent were twenty to twenty-four, and 16 percent were thirty and older. In 1985, there were 1,588,600 legal abortions, with rates highest among adolescents, women over forty, and unmarried women.[30]

By the 1980s, more heterosexual couples were choosing to remain unmarried and/or childless, and more women were part of nontraditional, "alternative" families (e.g., single parents, lesbian mothers, and lesbian couples with or without children). The "traditional" family—an employed husband, a wife who is not in the labor force, and children—represented only 14 percent of American families in 1985. Most common (40 percent) was the dual-earner family, with both husband and wife in the labor force (with or without children). Married couples with the husband employed, the wife not in the labor force, and no children were 9 percent of the total. Families headed by a single parent, married couples with only the wife in the labor force, and unemployed spouses accounted for 37 percent of families.[31]

For most women, family responsibilities are willingly assumed and personally rewarding. However, traditional gender-role divisions in the family have a debilitating effect on women due to their loss of autonomy, the low social value placed on wife and mother roles, and the unstructured, invisible, and isolating aspects of these roles.[32] Moreover, after divorce or the death of their husbands, women who have devoted themselves full time to their families often find that survivor benefits or alimony payments, if any, are inadequate; that they are living near or in poverty; and that they have inadequate medical care, housing, and health insurance.[33]

Due to their increased participation in the labor force, higher levels of education, and changing social values, many women are more autonomous, independent, and have more egalitarian family structures. However, women continue to be responsible for household tasks and meeting the needs of husbands, children, and older relatives.[34] Taking care of young children and providing long-term care for the elderly are stressful and time-consuming and have damaging consequences for women's paid work, social lives, marital relationships, and mental health. Women assume these family responsibilities with no financial compensation, little recognition, and few public supports. Moreover, leaving the labor force at various times in order to care for children and/or elderly family members places women at a disadvantage in competing for jobs and reduces their earnings and retirement benefits.[35]

For every racial and ethnic group, women's roles in the family are shaped by the unique cultural values and traditions and the specific historical, social, and economic circumstances of each group. For women of color, family life has also been profoundly influenced by the effects of prejudice, discrimination, and poverty.[36]

Racism has placed extraordinary burdens on blacks, including poor housing, education, and health care; high rates of unemployment and limited job opportunities; and racial violence. Nonetheless, black women have managed to create and maintain strong family and community networks. Because of their long-standing participation in the paid labor force, black women are less tied to stereotypic female roles and behaviors and view paid work as compatible with family roles.[37]

In the lives of Hispanic women, patriarchal family, community, and religious systems have a pervasive effect. The *machismo* norm promotes female passivity and frequent childbearing, discouraging education and employment for women. Powerlessness is reinforced for those Hispanic women who do work, for they are often isolated by language barriers and in low status, low paying jobs as migrant farm laborers, factory workers, and clerical and service workers.[38]

Traditionally, Asian American women have also held compliant and submissive roles within their families and communities. The experiences and goals of independent, career-oriented Asian American women are in conflict with traditional cultural expectations that women be unassuming, reserved, and highly family-oriented. Asian American women in the work force are concentrated in low wage jobs, despite the fact that they tend to be relatively well educated.[39]

American Indians are the most economically depressed and least acculturated minority; and American Indian women earn less and are less acculturated than men. Although American Indian culture is not patriarchal, American Indian women's prestige and influence have decreased, due to federal policies and practices that gave decision-making power and other rights, minimal as they were, only to American Indian men. Being in the center of family life, American Indian women deal with all the stresses of their families, including poor living conditions, educational problems, and poor health, including high rates of infant mortality and alcoholism.[40]

The Individual

The Women's Movement and the increasing participation of women in the labor force have had a dramatic impact on the behaviors, roles, and opportunities of women. Women are becoming increasingly autonomous, psychologically and economically. Female and male role socialization is becoming more flexible and nontraditional, especially for members of the middle class. However, the dysfunctional consequences for women of traditional gender roles and gender inequality remain.

Social inequality, social powerlessness, and social dependency translate for women into personal submissiveness, low self-esteem, and a focus on caring for and nurturing others. Negative cultural beliefs about women continue to be transmitted through gender-role socialization and internalized by women, to the detriment of their psychological health and personal growth. Confining social roles and limited options in education and employment continue to reinforce women's sense of powerlessness and personal devaluation.

The relationship between gender inequality and women's psychological problems is most clearly evidenced in the differences in rates of depression in women and men. For whites as well as racial minorities, women consistently have higher rates of depression than do men. The factors most commonly identified as influencing women's greater susceptibility to depression include their subordinate social and economic status, female socialization, and women's family roles, especially the role of mother.[41] Conversely, paid work has significant physical and mental health benefits for women. Employed middle- and working-class women have more life satisfaction, higher self-esteem, fewer health problems, and less psychological distress and depression than their nonemployed counterparts.[42]

For many women, gender inequality results in "legal and economic helplessness, dependency on others, chronically low self-esteem, low aspiration, and ultimately, clinical depression."[43] Many women also have "learned helplessness"; that is, they have learned that goal-directed, competent behavior is not expected of them and will not be rewarded with support, encouragement, equal pay, or equal rights. As noted by Greenspan, "The major ingredients of depression—the feelings of hopelessness, helplessness, worthlessness, futility, and suppressed rage—are the affective components of the objective social condition of female powerlessness in male society.... *Feeling* helpless is in some sense a rational adaptation to the social fact of *being* powerless."[44]

There is a high rate of mental health problems among low income women, with low income single mothers particularly at risk. Social and economic stresses contribute to low income women's heightened risk of distress and disorder. They are more likely to experience crime and violence, the illness or death of children, and the imprisonment of husbands; and to suffer from chronic life conditions such as inadequate housing, dangerous neighborhoods, and financial insecurities.[45]

Racism and ethnic prejudice exacerbate the health and mental health problems of women of color. They are subjected to stresses created by white ethnocentrism and discrimination based on race and sex, and often suffer the debilitating consequences of poverty as well. Also, many of these women experience difficulties as they attempt to reconcile their cultural values and traditions with the demands of white society. In addition, problems associated with the immigration process often lead to psychological distress.[46]

Lesbianism has often been viewed as psychopathological, an arrest of normal sexual development, an outgrowth of poor family relationships, and a sign of emotional immaturity. However, current research consistently demonstrates that lesbian women are at least as healthy as nonlesbian women. Nonetheless, as victims of heterosexism, lesbians have some problems in common with one another, including the stresses associated with "coming out" and difficulties stemming from discrimination in housing, employment, and child custody.[47]

Finally, victimization creates profound emotional difficulties for many women. Many victims of rape, childhood sexual abuse, and wife abuse experience high levels of depression, fear and anxiety, shame, social and sexual withdrawal, and low self-esteem. Sexual assault victims are at a higher risk for developing major psychiatric disorders, including affective disorders, substance abuse disorders, and anxiety disorders. Moreover, fear of victimization severely constrains the behavior of women as a group and undermines their psychological well-being.[48]

INTERVENTION STRATEGIES

For every level of intervention, social workers can use the ecosystems model to frame their understanding of how sexism affects the psychosocial problems experienced by women and the social conditions that enhance or restrict their lives. Social workers must analyze and evaluate the personal, social, and economic consequences of gender inequality in order to determine appropriate goals, targets of change, and interventions with women clients.[49]

Social workers also must understand the ways in which sexism influences social work practice with women. Mainstream services and treatments for women are often adjustment-oriented, or aim to help women to understand, accept, and adjust to traditional roles and norms. Social workers continue to rely on theories and research that (1) uncritically mirror social myths and stereotypes about women; (2) use the experiences of men as the standard against which the experiences of women are judged; (3) value "male" behaviors and roles over "female" ones; and (4) use female biology to explain women's feelings and behavior.

To counter the pervasive influence of incomplete, inaccurate, or biased information about women, it is essential that social workers be knowledgeable about current research on gender differences, gender roles, differences in the socialization and life experiences of women and men, and the nature of institutionalized inequality and female oppression. Social workers also need to understand the effects of sexism on their own beliefs, values, expectations, and behavior. They need to identify the range of ways gender bias can influence every phase of the planned-change process.

Further, social workers must recognize that female experience differs by class, race, ethnicity, and sexual orientation but that generalizations cannot be made for all women of color, all white women, all lesbians, or all poor women. Social workers need to understand the cultural heritages of minorities and the unique aspects of women's lives within their own cultural groups. Social workers need to understand the influence of homophobia and heterosexism on all women and become knowledgeable about the unique experiences of lesbians and the nature of the lesbian subculture.

In social work practice, issues related to female socialization, gender inequality, and sexism will be of varying significance, depending on the specific problem or issue. In every situation and for every client, the social worker needs to evaluate (1) the relationships between traditional gender roles and gender inequality and the presenting problem; (2) the ways in which gender bias affects the established knowledge base about that problem and contaminates traditional services and treatments; (3) the new and corrective knowledge that has emerged; and (4) the range of methods and approaches that have been developed to deal with the gender-related aspects of the presenting problem.

For example, work on the cause, course, and treatment of chronic mental illness has practically ignored gender-related issues. Yet, it is apparent that there are important sex differences in the course and treatment of the chronically mentally ill; further, additional attention should be focused on understanding chronically mentally ill women in terms of their marital and family roles, sexuality, and experiences with sexual violence and exploitation.[50]

Similarly, in dealing with substance abuse among women, social workers need to be knowledgeable about the patterns and experiences that differentially characterize women's use and abuse of alcohol and other drugs and that lead to different consequences of chemical dependency for women and men. They need to be aware that male-dominated and male-centered organizations, treatments, and services have served as barriers to women's seeking and obtaining help, and that alternate programs and treatments have been developed to meet the needs of women with alcohol and/or drug problems.[51]

Micro Practice with Women

To help women deal with problems in psychosocial functioning, social workers use a range of micro-level interventions. They may choose to work with the individual woman or may place the woman in a group with others with similar problems and issues; they may meet with her alone, with her partner, and/or with her entire family. For each level of intervention, there is specialized knowledge about women and women's issues that needs to be incorporated into every phase of the planned change process.

In the assessment phase, a social worker needs to evaluate women's functioning at home, at work, and in the community in terms of existing gender-role norms and discriminatory practices. Although the immediate target of change is the woman and/or her family, there must be ongoing recognition of the ways in which a woman's personal problems are shaped by her social, economic, and legal circumstances. Social workers must be realistic about the many ways in which discriminatory employment practices, sex-biased community attitudes, and restrictive family roles create barriers and place limits on women's options for change. The effects of racism, heterosexism, classism, and ageism must also be actively taken into account.

To work effectively with female clients, social workers need to accept a wide range of behaviors and roles as appropriate and beneficial. Nonsexist social workers use a nonbiased perspective and knowledge base to assess the experiences and problems of clients; to make judgments about the biological, psychological, and/or social factors that have influenced clients' problems; and to ensure that goals are not based on outmoded stereotypes.

Understanding the full range of factors that shape women's lives, a social worker can extend the range of solutions and life changes to be considered and select interventive strategies that will help clients reach their goals. Social workers should incorporate knowledge concerning female oppression and gender-role socialization in the same manner that they incorporate knowledge concerning all other aspects of clients' problems and situations: selectively and sensitively, taking into account the values, needs, concerns, and goals of their clients.

With an awareness that women's lack of social power can generate passivity and dependence, workers should include female empowerment as a central goal. This can be accomplished by sharing resources, power, and responsibility with clients. Interventive strategies consistent with these principles include appropriate self-disclosure by the worker, having the client take an active part in goal-setting and outcome evaluation, making the worker's own values explicit, and emphasizing the client's strengths and assets. Such strategies minimize clients' dependency on the worker, increase the likelihood that clients feel free to reject the values and approaches of the worker, and concretely demonstrate the belief that women are capable of being autonomous and in control of their own lives.

As with all oppressed groups, it is empowering for women to understand the influence of social factors on their personal lives. Social workers can incorporate gender-role analyses into their work with women to encourage clients to evaluate the ways in which social roles, norms, and structural realities limit female autonomy and choice. Through this process, women can come to understand how, by internalizing cultural values about women, they sometimes act as co-conspirators in their own oppression.

All-women groups can be used to deemphasize the authority of the social worker and help members share and understand the experiences that have influenced them as women. Such groups facilitate the respect and trust of women for one another and help them to develop a sense of solidarity with women as a group. Finally, workers can encourage their clients to participate in social action on their own behalf. It is growth-producing for women to engage in social actions designed to change those conditions at work and in their community that most directly have negative effects on their lives.

The essential aspects of effective work with women include the ability to incorporate a nonsexist knowledge base and value system into every aspect of practice. This is true for both female and male social workers. However, it is essential that workers recognize that, in some circumstances and with some women, a nonsexist female worker is preferable. Female social workers serve as role models for their clients and can avoid the male–female interactions that reinforce women's passivity and powerlessness. Being female increases the worker's ability to empathize with clients and to understand and share experiences related to being female in a male-dominated society.

In their practice, male social workers must develop ways to ensure that traditional male–female power relationships and interactive strategies do not characterize their work with women clients. They need to recognize that there are limitations in their ability to empathize with women and serve as role models, and that the male worker–female client combination reinforces cultural views that women are dependent on male authority.

In working with groups, workers must be aware of the intersection of gender issues with group dynamics. This includes recognition of the differences between mixed groups and all-female groups in stages of group development, goals and structure, leadership, interpersonal relations, and communication patterns.[52] Workers should be aware of the ways in which groups have been especially useful in work with women with common issues; for example, with substance abusing women, women with eating disorders, lesbian mothers, unwed teenage mothers, women of color, and low-income women.[53]

In working with couples and families, social workers need to be knowledgeable about the wide range of family forms and how gender inequality influences family dynamics, division of labor, decision-making, and power relationships. Idealization of the family and motherhood has obscured the negative consequences of the traditional family for women, including economic vulnerability, depression, isolation, and psychological and physical abuse.

Work with families must take into account the social, economic, and political realities that shape family roles and relationships, and conversely, how women's roles and responsibilities in their families support or constrain their participation in public life. In working with families, social workers can provide support and direction to help mothers and their female children become more assertive and self-directed. They can help clients challenge gender-role stereotypes in the family, examine more flexible and nontraditional roles, and equalize power.[54]

In establishing goals, in planning interventive strategies, and in evaluating outcome, workers and clients must recognize that some changes *will* increase women's self-esteem, feelings of autonomy, and social functioning, but at the same time produce new stresses and conflicts. Presenting a self-image and behaviors that deviate from traditional roles and norms may incur difficulties for women. Some relationships may become more satisfying, but others are likely to become more stressful. Parents, spouse, children, friends, relatives, and co-workers may be ambivalent, if not hostile, toward a woman's desire to make nontraditional changes in her life. Also, because of sexism in education and employment as well as in other social institutions, women may not be able to fully or easily achieve the changes they desire. Assessment and evaluation must focus, therefore, on whether women are behaving in a self-directing, autonomous manner and whether their behavior is the result of a conscious understanding of available options and a deliberate weighing of costs and benefits.[55]

Macro Practice with Women

Meaningful change for women requires that social workers work with clients to provide more resources and to change services and policies in their local communities, states, and nation. This includes working for the provision of adequate and affordable housing, child care, and educational opportunities; increasing employment opportunities and financial and legal assistance; and developing programs and policies that are responsive to women's needs and protect them from victimization in the community, the workplace, and their homes.

The principles and methods that are incorporated into nonsexist micro practice are also used in nonsexist approaches to macro practice. Empowerment of women and the development of responsive policies and services require that workers emphasize client participation, egalitarian relationships, and collaborative decision-making and that they reduce the power and status differences between themselves and their clients.

At the macro level, workers' tasks include assessing the impact of sexism, heterosexism, racism, and poverty on female clients; analyzing the unmet service needs of women and their children; evaluating the presence of bias in the design and delivery of existing services; and developing and/or modifying programs and services to meet the special needs of women. Neighborhood organizing, community development, and social action provide a range of methods that workers can apply to provide and/or improve local resources for women. Social planning, program development, and policy analysis engage higher level political processes and public education efforts on behalf of women.[56]

Social workers can utilize their planning skills to systematically identify the problems of women in their communities; to identify goals, objectives, and the resources that will need to be mobilized; and to design, implement, and evaluate new and alternative programs. Skills in conducting needs assessments are particularly valuable for identifying the unmet needs of women in a community and modifying priorities in service delivery patterns. Workers' knowledge of patterns of power and influence within the community and their skills in community education and advocacy are especially important for mobilizing support and gaining sanction for new programs and services for women.

Empowering women includes helping them to gain the power to control their own lives. Community organization skills can be used to help women build and maintain their own groups, organizations, and agencies. Social workers can help women to translate their concerns into specific objectives and goals; to develop their organizational and leadership skills; to increase the resources available to the group; and to identify and evaluate strategies which will help them to reach their goals. Workers' knowledge of funding and resource development can be particularly valuable to such groups.[57]

In community and organizational practice, as in micro practice, there are some circumstances in which a female social worker is likely to be more effective than a male. For example, in the areas of physical abuse, child sexual abuse, and teen pregnancy, a female social worker is likely to be trusted more. Women workers' experience as women, and often as mothers, helps them identify women's needs and concerns and may enhance their credibility. Also, women community organizers, planners, and administrators can work with female client systems without the power–status differential that is inherent when men work with women.[58]

For female social workers, macro practice requires recognition that the workers themselves are likely to be influenced by the sexism pervading both the systems in which they work and those they want to influence. Administration and community organization are viewed as male domains and rely primarily on male models. Further, the policies, programs, and services that are targets of change are most likely controlled and administered by men. Women who enter these domains as workers or who attempt to change them on behalf of their clients often encounter gender-role stereotyping, devaluation, exclusion, suspicion, prejudice, sexual harassment, and discrimination.[59]

Micro Practice with a Battered Woman

The following case illustrates the ways in which women's problems involve social, economic, and legal factors; role socialization; and interpersonal and psychological distress and dysfunction. It demonstrates how micro practice can be used to improve the lives of battered women.

Background

Tracy was brought to the shelter for battered women from the emergency room of the local hospital. She had been severely beaten by her husband, who had also threatened to kill her. She had two black eyes, two broken ribs, severely bruised legs and arms, and a broken finger on her left hand. According to Tracy, her husband pulled the phone from the wall when she tried to call the police; it was then that she sustained the black eyes. Fortunately, a cousin came by for an unexpected visit, at which time Tracy's husband fled the house. The cousin drove Tracy and her three-year-old daughter, Jane, to the hospital.

Impact on the Family System

Jane had witnessed her mother's physical and emotional abuse, on this occasion and on other occasions. The child was very upset and visibly terrorized that her father would come back, hurt her mother again, and take her away, as he had threatened to do.

When Tracy and her daughter came to the shelter, the taxi fare was paid by the shelter. Tracy's husband had taken her purse when he fled from the house. The only possessions Tracy and her daughter had with them were the clothes that they had on. Tracy was still in serious pain from her injuries. Jane was crying off and on, asking, "Is Daddy going to come here and find us?" Despite her own pain and needs, Tracy attended to her daughter's fears. She held the child, which was painful due to her bruises and broken ribs, and comforted her.

Initial Client Contact and Engagement

When she met with the social worker, Tracy expressed much concern about whether or not this was really the right thing to do. She was angry, confused, and very worried about how she would manage for herself and her child. The worker reassured Tracy that all her feelings were natural, and in fact, common to many of the women when they first came to the shelter. The worker emphasized that the shelter would provide Tracy with safety and security; no decisions about other services or goals would be made until Tracy was ready. The worker's goals were to communicate her caring and her willingness to help; to reduce the fears and anxiety associated with being in this new situation; and to assure Tracy of safety and confidentiality.

The worker explained that she would be meeting with Tracy and that Jane would have her own social worker and be part of the children's play group at the shelter.

Identifying Needs and Obtaining Resources

At their second meeting later that same day, the worker began to collect information about Tracy's situation and needs for service. Tracy was severely depressed and on antidepressants. Following their session, the worker contacted Tracy's psychiatrist to coordinate services. She also began to work with the county social service department to obtain financial assistance for Tracy's medical and psychiatric care. The worker told Tracy about the range of resources and services available at the shelter and in the community.

Providing Support

Throughout the first week, the worker assured Tracy that she would not be critical of her nor pressure her in any way. The worker looked for every opportunity to validate Tracy's feelings and to give her positive feedback. She let Tracy know that she understood and empathized with Tracy's many conflicting and confusing feelings about her husband and her current situation.

Promoting Client Self-Determination

The worker explained that her role was to help Tracy make decisions about her life, not to make decisions for her. Tracy would need to decide what she wanted to do and what would be in her best interests. The worker emphasized that she would support, encourage, and advocate for Tracy throughout, but that it was Tracy's right and responsibility to make her own decisions.

Empathy and Empowerment

Tracy told the worker that she was very confused, that she trusted the worker, and that she would like the worker to develop a plan for her to leave her husband. The worker reassured Tracy that she appreciated her trust and that she understood her anxiety, but that Tracy would be able to determine her own needs and set her own goals, with the worker's help. Not taking over at this point, although this was the request of the client, began the process of empowering Tracy to take control of her own life.

Working through Resistance Expressed as Ambivalence

At their next few meetings, Tracy discussed her ambivalence about leaving her husband. The worker listened in a nondirective and supportive fashion. Also, she asked specific questions to collect information on the patterns of abuse; she helped Tracy begin to think about the various aspects of the problem and to identify her strengths and the ways in which she had coped and survived. A primary goal was to provide a supportive atmosphere in which Tracy could ventilate her anxieties, fears, shame, and anger, as well as sort out the love she felt for her husband.

Identifying and Building on Strengths

The worker was committed to helping Tracy explore her options without encouraging her to go in any one particular direction. The worker needed to support Tracy's discussion of the positive parts of her family life and her warm feelings for her husband without implying that she should stay with him. On the other hand, the worker needed to encourage Tracy to explore leaving her husband without implicitly suggesting that she should. She wanted Tracy to know that she would be there for her, regardless of the specific decisions she made.

Resistance Expressed as Fear of Changing

Tracy had difficulty expressing any anger toward her husband. She blamed herself for provoking his anger. She was afraid of him but also felt he worked hard and deserved her sympathy and understanding. She said that sometimes he was very loving, that he often apologized for hitting her, begged for her forgiveness, and promised to change. He swore he loved her and could not live without her.

Tracy said that for years she believed he was trying to change and that she could find some way to prevent his attacks by keeping everything just the way he liked. Finally she realized she was unable to do this. No matter how hard she tried, he found things that bothered him about the house, about her, and about their child. Tracy was very upset that she had failed as a wife and mother. She could not imagine not being married, and she did not know how she could cope on her own, especially with a toddler.

Counteracting Low Self-Esteem

The worker tried to refocus Tracy's feelings of self-blame and shame; instead of getting angry at herself, it was important that Tracy begin to focus on her anger toward her husband. She wanted Tracy to discover that she could deal with her anger, that she would not be rejected for her anger, and that anger can turn into positive energy for problem-solving and self-protection. Also, she helped Tracy focus on her own needs and feelings. This was very difficult for Tracy, since she had only thought about predicting and meeting her husband's needs for many years.

Facilitating Empowerment through Group Support

The worker also encouraged Tracy to join the shelter's counselor-facilitated support group. Here, Tracy was able to see that she was not alone. She saw the ways that other women were able to come to terms with their abuse; she heard from women who had begun to work with lawyers and to find housing; and she began to see some commonalties between her experiences and those of other battered women. The group helped her to feel more optimistic about her own ability to change and to become more assertive. She felt less isolated and received support for her attempts to help other women deal with their issues.

Enhancing Self-Esteem through Validation

Tracy particularly liked group discussions about how they had been raised as females and brought up to expect that a happy marriage was a certainty and their most important goal. Sometimes they brought in magazines or discussed TV programs in terms of how women were portrayed. They described the pressures they felt from family to remain married no matter what. Tracy felt increasingly free to talk and express her own opinions, since she felt support and acceptance from the other members of the group. She became active in helping think through problems and possible alternatives for herself and other group members. The support group provided Tracy with opportunities to share experiences, overcome her social isolation and lack of female friendships, and find hope and strength by seeing the successes of others.

Transforming Feelings into Action

In their individual sessions, the worker progressed from encouraging Tracy to express her feelings and helping her to clarify emotions, to encouraging Tracy to take steps to improve her situation. The worker reassured Tracy that she was not to blame. She was neither the instigator of the abuse nor a willing participant; she was not responsible for her husband's violence. She helped Tracy believe she had the right to be safe and that no one had the right to abuse her.

Developing Client Insight

The worker also wanted Tracy to recognize that, with new information and options, she was responsible for protecting herself and her child. The worker helped Tracy to understand the dynamics of wife abuse and the ways in which social factors contributed to her abuse. In discussing social factors and common patterns of domestic violence, it was important that the worker not reinforce Tracy's feelings of helplessness. Instead, by understanding these social factors, Tracy was expected to take increased responsibility for the choices she made, thereby gaining a sense of personal power.

As part of their discussion, the worker presented factual information about the effects of violence on women and their children, Tracy's legal rights and options, and the difficulties in starting over. With Tracy, the worker explored intrapsychic factors *and* societal norms and roles, not to reinforce her view of herself as a victim but to help her understand that she had the power to change important aspects of her life.

Planning for Change

In considering Tracy's leaving her husband, they discussed her needs for housing, employment, child care, and improved parenting skills, as well as financial aid to cover transportation, medical and psychiatric expenses, and legal assistance. Tracy did decide to leave her husband, although she was worried about her actual ability to do so. As Tracy set her goals, she and the worker outlined the steps that would be necessary, including Tracy's spending time with workers in other agencies.

The worker had a wide range of possible resources, but needed to tailor these to meet Tracy's specific needs. In many ways, Tracy was like many battered women and knowing these commonalities helped the worker predict what services would be necessary. However, Tracy was also a unique individual, and the worker wanted to make sure that she didn't stereotype Tracy as a-battered-woman-leaving-her-husband. The intervention had to be *individualized.*

Macro Practice on Behalf of Battered Women

Macro social work practice finds the social worker providing services on behalf of people, as opposed to micro practice in which the worker provides a direct service on a face-to-face basis with an identified client. In macro practice, the worker attempts to make social and legal institutions such as organizations, neighborhoods, and communities, responsive to the needs of clients. Macro practice may also involve developing or changing policies, regulations, and laws to help people. This can be seen in the following macro case.

Defining the Problem and Need

Shelter staff had already established community education programs with business leaders and church groups, and they had recruited volunteers to assist with the twenty-four-hour crisis line. However, several problems were constantly confronting the staff and their clients. All the workers at the shelter were frustrated with the ineffectiveness of restraining orders. Also, they increasingly saw ties between domestic violence and substance abuse, but their programs could not deal with the substance abuse, and the alcohol and drug programs did not address the battering. Finally, and most frustrating, they knew that therapists in their community continued to help battered women "resolve their conflicting feelings about their marriage and become more satisfied wives and mothers." These therapists, in assuming a traditional stance, were defining women's depression as the primary problem, seeing the depression as a symptom of the "neurotic conflicts that interfered with the woman's capacity to nurture and care for others" rather than seeing it evolving from the abuses they were suffering.

Developing Strategies

The shelter workers decided to pursue a range of different strategies to address these specific problems. First, they wanted to gain more cooperation from the legal, law enforcement, social service, and medical systems in the community. Several workers began to meet with the police to explore their willingness to participate in a series of workshops on battered women. The goals of these workshops were to improve police officers' knowledge about and attitudes toward woman abuse and to try to improve the enforcement of restraining orders. The long-range goal was to involve other systems in such educational programs as well.

Networking

Second, they decided to hold a meeting for alcohol and drug abuse counselors and social service providers to begin to assess the dual problems of substance abuse and battering in the community. They were particularly interested in improving cooperation between agencies that worked with battered women and those that worked with substance abuse.

Community Education

Third, they decided to ask to speak at meetings of therapists and counselors in the community, to describe the shelter's services and provide information about the social and economic aspects of woman abuse. They would speak with some of the shelter residents to see if they were willing to come to these meetings to speak about their experiences with traditional therapists, counselors, and social workers.

Needs Assessment Survey

Finally, to gain a fuller perspective on service delivery problems, they decided to conduct a survey to assess the obstacles women encountered in receiving adequate services. The survey would be distributed to clients and former clients, shelter staff, and workers in other agencies encountering battered women. The survey would ask clients and workers to provide information about clients' interactions with medical, legal, and social service systems in the community. The workers would also be asked to assess agency policies and procedures in terms of whether they facilitated or impeded effective work with battered women.

Getting Results

Providing counseling and advocacy helped individual battered women change their lives. Also, working with individual battered women helped the staff to identify inadequate or nonexistent services and the ways in which various helping systems were exacerbating or reducing the problems of battered women. The staff's work in community education and in changing the policies and procedures of other agencies helped the individual battered women who came to the shelter and ultimately would improve the circumstances of all women in their community.

EMERGING ISSUES AND TRENDS

By some measures, women's economic and social condition has dramatically improved over the past three decades, partially due to the efforts of the Women's Movement. In fact, until the Reagan era, public policy and law at all levels of government had become significantly less oppressive; there was considerably less public support for traditional familial and gender ideology. Since the election of Reagan in 1980, however, there has been a concerted effort to reverse this trend.[60]

Throughout the 1980s, legislation and policies on affirmative action, abortion rights, discrimination in education and employment, and AFDC narrowed women's rights and options. We are far from achieving equality for women. More than ever, women who are not attached to men are poorer than those who are, and women of color are poorer than white women. Health care is inaccessible to many families and elderly women due to their lack of health insurance, including Medicaid. Most employed women continue to be in sex-segregated, low-wage clerical, sales, and service jobs. Compared with men, women continue to have less independence and fewer resources.

Social workers possess the knowledge and skills to assume a major role in improving the social circumstances of women. Working with women individually, in groups, and with their families, social workers can empower them to become more autonomous, assertive, and self-affirming. They can help women reverse the debilitating effects of traditional socialization and gain more control over their own lives.

Social workers should not minimize the significance of helping women to make changes in their own feelings, attitudes, everyday behaviors, and relationships. Women's oppression is supported by internalized cultural views that devalue them and legitimate their powerlessness and victimization. By helping women to alter these internalized views and change their behaviors in nontraditional ways, social workers can challenge one of the most basic ways that oppression is maintained. When the nature of personal change conflicts with the dominant values of society, personal change becomes political and holds broad social and political implications.

The profession of social work has a major role to play in the design and implementation of social policies, programs, and services. The feminization of poverty will continue to dominate the focus of social welfare policies and programs. Increases in the rates of divorce and out-of-wedlock pregnancies, sex segregation and discrimination in the labor force, and the lack of federal family-support policies will maintain women's disadvantaged status. Our challenge is to find ways to support the needs of employed women and at the same time create alternate approaches to support childrearing and caregiving.

Social policies directed at reducing the feminization of poverty include (1) promoting equality in the labor force; (2) providing additional economic supports for parents, especially single parents, including increasing the availability of low-priced housing and housing subsidies; and (3) disseminating information about sexuality and contraception to reduce the rates of teenage motherhood.[61] Welfare reform includes providing job training and education for women, but must also ensure services and supports for children so that women can attend school and enter the work force with the confidence that their children are safe and cared for.

For the benefit of all women, social workers should actively work for changes in social policies, including (1) passage of the Equal Rights Amendment and other federal policies that will ensure equal opportunity and pay equity; (2) increasing the availability and affordability of child care, including employer-sponsored child care programs; (3) broadening employment options to include flextime, job-sharing, and parental leave to help families meet both family and work responsibilities; (4) enforcement of child support and alimony payments; and (5) improving women's health care, including working to maintain women's right to abortion, advocating for federal funding of family planning services and abortion, and preventing the further spread of AIDS to women and children.

Most important, social workers need to eliminate sexism within the profession as it impacts on the lives of female clients and workers. Services and programs need to be evaluated to eliminate the presence of sexism as well as racism, class bias, and heterosexism. Social workers must be knowledgeable about the relationships between female subordination, women's problems, and social work services. They must proactively work to eliminate gender inequality in schools of social work and in social work agencies and organizations. Until these conditions are met, we cannot presume that we have the theoretical, empirical, and ethical base for our practice with women. To develop meaningful and non-oppressive policies, services, programs, and interventions for women, social workers must work to eliminate stereotyping and discrimination for clients and women social workers as well.

SUGGESTED READINGS

AMARO, H. and RUSSO, N., EDS. *Psychology of Women Quarterly: Special Issue on Hispanic Women and Mental Health* 11 (December 1987).

BRANDWEIN, R. "Women in Macro Practice." In A. Minahan, ed., *Encyclopedia of Social Work* vol. 2. Silver Spring, Md.: National Association of Social Workers, 1987: 881–892.

BURDEN, D., and GOTTLIEB, N., EDS. *The Women Client: Providing Human Services in a Changing World* New York: Tavistock, 1987.

DIEHM, C., and ROSS, M. "Battered Women." In S. Rix, ed., *The American Woman 1988–89* New York: W. W. Norton, 1988: 292–302.

DOMINELLI, L., and McLEOD, E. *Feminist Social Work.* New York: New York University Press, 1989.

FIMBRES, M. "The Chicana in Transition." In A. Weick and S. Vandiver, eds. *Women, Power, and Change* Washington, D.C.: National Association of Social Workers 1981: 89–95.

GOLDBERG, G., and KREMEN, E. "The Feminization of Poverty: Only in America? *Social Policy* (Spring 1987): 3–14.

HANMER, J., and STATHAM, D. *Women and Social Work: Towards a Woman-Centered Practice.* Chicago, Ill.: Lyceum Books, 1989.

RODGERS-ROSE, L., ED. *The Black Woman* Beverly Hills, Calif.: Sage Publications, 1980.

RYAN, A. "Asian American Women: A Historical and Cultural Perspective." In A. Weick and S. Vandiver, eds., *Women, Power, and Change.* Washington, D.C.: National Association of Social Workers, 1981, pp. 78–88.

SAPIRO, V. *Women in American Society: An Introduction to Women's Studies* Mountain View, Calif.: Mayfield Publishing, 1990, p. 381.

TRUE, R. "The Profile of Asian American Women." In S. Cox, ed., *Female Psychology: The Emerging Self.* New York: St. Martin's Press, 1981, pp. 124–135.

WILKINSON, D. "Afro-American Women and Their Families." *Marriage and Family Review* 7 (Fall/Winter 1984): 125–142.

ENDNOTES

1. Unless stated otherwise, all figures presented in this chapter are taken from U.S. Bureau of the Census, *Statistical Abstract of the United States: 1989* (Washington, D.C.: The Bureau, 1989).

2. R. Blank, "Women's Paid Work, Household Income, and Household Well-Being," in S. Rix, ed., *The American Woman 1988–89* (New York: W. W. Norton, 1988), pp. 123–161.

3. Rix, p. 357.

4. L. Weitzman, *The Divorce Revolution* (New York: Free Press, 1985).

5. C. Harrison, "A Richer Life: A Reflection on the Women's Movement," in S. Rix, p. 74.

6. Rix, p. 376.

7. P. Popple and L. Leighninger, *Social Work, Social Welfare, and American Society* (Boston: Allyn and Bacon, 1990), p. 177.

8. V. Sapiro, *Women in American Society: An Introduction to Women's Studies* (Mountain View, Calif.: Mayfield, 1990), p. 381.

9. Ibid., pp. 18–19.

10. T. Smeeding, "Economic Status of the Elderly," in R. Binstock and L. George, eds., *Handbook of Aging and the Social Sciences* (San Diego, Calif.: Academic Press, 1990), p. 370.

11. K. Davis, "Women and Health Care," in S. Rix, pp. 162–204.

12. Ibid.; J. Albino and L. Tedesco, "Women's Health Issues," in A. Rickel, M. Gerrard, and I. Iscoe, eds., *Social and Psychological Problems of Women: Prevention and Crisis Intervention* (New York: Hemisphere Publishing, 1984), pp. 157–172.

13. L. Biener, "Gender Differences in the Use of Substances for Coping," in R. Barnett, L. Biener, and G. Baruch, eds., *Gender and Stress* (New York: Free Press, 1987), pp. 330–349.

14. Davis, pp. 162–204.
15. R. Selik, K. Castro, and M. Pappaioanou, "Racial/Ethnic Differences in the Risk of AIDS in the United States," *American Journal of Public Health* 78 (December 1988): 1539–1545.
16. G. Weissman, "Women and AIDS," in Rix, pp. 286–291; D. Richardson, "AIDS Education and Women: Sexual and Reproductive Issues," in P. Aggleton, P. Davies, and G. Hart, eds., *AIDS: Individual, Cultural, and Policy Dimensions* (New York: Falmer Press, 1990), pp. 169–179.
17. S. Martin, "Sexual Harassment: The Link between Gender Stratification, Sexuality, and Women's Economic Status," in J. Freeman, ed., *Women: A Feminist Perspective* (Palo Alto, Calif.: Mayfield Publishing, 1984), pp. 54–69; S. Nolen-Hoeksema, *Sex Differences in Depression* (Stanford, Calif.: Stanford University Press, 1990), pp. 77–104.
18. C. Diehm and M. Ross, "Battered Women," in Rix, pp. 292–302.
19. Sapiro, p. 278.
20. J. Briere and L. Zaidi, "Sexual Abuse Histories and Sequelae in Female Psychiatric Emergency Room Patients," *American Journal of Psychiatry* 146 (December 1989): 1602–1606.
21. D. Russell, *Sexual Exploitation: Rape, Child Sexual Abuse, and Workplace Harassment* (Newbury Park, Calif.: Sage Publications, 1984).
22. M. Ferree and B. Hess, *Controversy and Coalition: The New Feminist Movement* (Boston: Twayne, 1985), p. 6.
23. Hunter College Women's Studies Collective, *Women's Realities, Women's Choices* (New York: Oxford University Press, 1983), pp. 397–437; and Sapiro, pp. 95–120.
24. Sapiro, p. 21.
25. F. Blau, "Women in the Labor Force: An Overview," in Freeman, p. 300.
26. Ferree and Hess, p. 2.
27. J. Lipman-Blumen, *Gender Roles and Power* (Englewood Cliffs, N.J.: Prentice-Hall, 1984), pp. 159–160.
28. For reviews of women's changing participation in the paid labor force, see Blau; Hunter College Women's Studies Collective, pp. 479–530; Lipman-Blumen, pp. 155–175; Sapiro, pp. 344–386.
29. Sapiro, p. 328.
30. Ibid., pp. 308–343.
31. Rix, p. 374.
32. C. Travis, *Women and Health Psychology* (Hillsdale, N.J.: Lawrence Erlbaum Associates, 1988), pp. 31–53; Nolen-Hoeksema, pp. 77–104.
33. N. Hooyman and R. Ryan, "Women as Caregivers of the Elderly: Catch-22 Dilemmas," in J. Figueira-McDonough and R. Sarri, eds., *The Trapped Woman: Catch-22 in Deviance and Control* (Newbury Park, Calif.: Sage Publications, 1987), pp. 143–171.
34. Blank, pp. 123–161.
35. Hooyman and Ryan, pp. 143–171; N. Chappell, "Aging and Social Care," in R. Binstock and L. George, eds., *Handbook of Aging and the Social Sciences* (San Diego, Calif.: Academic Press, 1990), pp. 438–454.
36. For discussion of the structure of the family in various racial and ethnic groups, see E. Almquist, "Race and Ethnicity in the Lives of Minority Women," in Freeman, pp. 423–453; M. McGoldrick, N. Garcia-Preto, P. Hines, and E. Lee, "Ethnicity and Women," in M. McGoldrick, C. Anderson, and F. Walsh, eds., *Women in Families: A Framework for Family Therapy* (New York: W. W. Norton, 1989), pp. 169–199; C. Mindel, R. Habenstein, and R. Wright Jr., eds., *Ethnic Families in America: Patterns and Variations* (New York: Elsevier, 1988).
37. L. Rodgers-Rose, ed., *The Black Woman* (Beverly Hills, Calif.: Sage Publications, 1980); D. Wilkinson, "Afro-American Women and Their Families," *Marriage and Family Review* 7 (Fall–Winter 1984): 125–142.

38. H. Amaro and N. Russo, eds., *Psychology of Women Quarterly: Special Issue on His-panic Women and Mental Health* 11 (December 1987); M. Fimbres, "The Chicana in Transition," in A. Weick and S. Vandiver, eds., *Women, Power, and Change* (Washington, D.C.: National Association of Social Workers, 1981), pp. 89–95.

39. R. True, "The Profile of Asian American Women," in S. Cox, ed., *Female Psychology: The Emerging Self* (New York: St. Martin's Press, 1981), pp. 124–135; A. Ryan, "Asian American Women: A Historical and Cultural Perspective," in Weick and Vandiver, pp. 78–88.

40. E. Blanchard, "Observations on Social Work with American Indian Women," in Weick and Vandiver, pp. 96–103; S. Verble, ed. *Words of Today's American Indian Women: OHOYO MAKACHI* (Wichita Falls, Tx.: Ohoyo Resource Center, 1981).

41. R. Barnett and G. Baruch, "Social Roles, Gender, and Psychological Distress," in Barnett, Biener, and Baruch, pp. 122–143; J. Marecek, "Engendering Disorder: The Social Context of Women's Mental Health," in M. Gibbs, J. Lachenmeyer, and J. Segal, *Community Psychology* (New York: Gardner Press, in press); Nolen-Hoeksema, pp. 77–104; Travis pp. 31–53.

42. Barnett and Baruch, pp. 122–143; E. Sales and I. Frieze, "Women and Work: Implications for Mental Health," in L. Walker, ed., *Women and Mental Health Policy* (Beverly Hills, Calif.: Sage Publications, 1984), pp. 229–246.

43. G. Klerman and M. Weissman, "Depressions among Women: Their Nature and Causes," in M. Guttentag, S. Salasin, and D. Belle, eds., *The Mental Health of Women* (New York: Academic Press, 1980), p. 79.

44. M. Greenspan, *A New Approach to Women and Therapy* (New York: McGraw-Hill, 1983), p. 193.

45. D. Belle, "Inequality and Mental Health: Low Income and Minority Women," in Walker, pp. 135–150; N. Goldman and R. Ravid, "Community Surveys: Sex Differences in Mental Illness," in Guttentag, Salasin, and Belle, pp. 31–55.

46. E. Almquist, "Race and Ethnicity in the Lives of Minority Women," in Freeman, pp. 423–453; O. Espin, "Psychological Impact of Migration on Latinas," *Psychology of Women Quarterly* 11 (December 1987): 489–503; E. Olmedo and D. Parron, "Mental Health of Minority Women: Some Special Issues," *Professional Psychology* 12 (February 1981): 103–111; D. Wilkinson, "Minority Women: Social-Cultural Issues," in A. Brodsky and R. Hare-Mustin, eds., *Women and Psychotherapy* (New York: Guilford Press, 1980), pp. 285–304.

47. J. Cummerton, "Homophobia and Social Work Practice with Lesbians," in Weick and Vandiver, pp. 104–113; H. Hidalgo, T. Peterson, and N. Woodman, eds., *Lesbian and Gay Issues: A Resource Manual for Social Workers* (Silver Spring, Md.: National Association of Social Workers, 1985); D. Martin and P. Lyon, "Lesbian Women and Mental Health Policy," in Walker, pp. 151–179.

48. R. Janoff-Bulman and I. Frieze, "The Role of Gender in Reactions to Criminal Victimization," in Barnett, Biener, and Baruch, pp. 159–184; Nolen-Hoeksema, pp. 77–104; C. Sheffield, "Sexual Terrorism: The Social Control of Women," in B. Hess and M. Ferree, *Analyzing Gender: A Handbook of Social Science Research* (Newbury Park, Calif.: Sage Publications, 1987), pp. 171–189.

49. For more detailed discussions of social work practice with women, see D. Burden and N. Gottlieb, eds., *The Woman Client: Providing Human Services in a Changing World* (New York: Tavistock, 1987); L. Dominelli and E. McLeod, *Feminist Social Work* (New York: New York University Press, 1989); J. Hanmer and D. Statham, *Women and Social Work: Toward a Woman-Centered Practice* (Chicago, Ill.: Lyceum Books, 1989); E. Norman and A. Mancuso, *Women's Issues and Social Work Practice* (Itasca, Ill.: F. E. Peacock, 1980); N. Van Den Bergh and L. Cooper, eds., *Feminist Visions for Social Work* (Silver Spring, Md.: National Association of Social Workers, 1986); Weick and Vandiver.

50. M. A. Test and S. Berlin, "Issues of Special Concern to Chronically Mentally Ill Women," *Professional Psychology* 12 (February 1981): 136–145.

51. J. Sobeck and M. Kilbey, "Etiology and Treatment of Alcoholism among Women," in Travis, pp. 109–131.

52. L. Walker, "Women's Groups Are Different," in C. Brody, ed., *Women's Therapy Groups* (New York: Springer, 1987), pp. 3–12.

53. J. Lee, ed., *Group Work with the Poor and Oppressed* (New York: Haworth Press, 1989); B. Reed and C. Garvin, eds., *Social Work with Groups: Special Issue on Group Work with Women/Group Work with Men: An Overview of Gender Issues in Social Groupwork Practice* 6 (Fall–Winter 1983).

54. L. Braverman, ed., *A Guide to Feminist Family Therapy* (New York: Harrington Park Press, 1988); R. Hare-Mustin, "A Feminist Approach to Family Therapy," in E. Howell and M. Bayes, eds., *Women and Mental Health* (New York: Basic Books, 1981), pp. 553–571.

55. M. Klein, "Feminist Concepts of Therapy Outcome," *Psychotherapy: Theory, Research and Practice* 13 (Spring 1976): 89–95.

56. R. Brandwein, "Toward Androgyny in Community and Organizational Practice," in Weick and Vandiver, pp. 158–170; C. Ellsworth, N. Hooyman, R. Ruff, S. Stam, and J. Tucker, "Toward a Feminist Model of Planning for and with Women," in Weick and Vandiver, pp. 146–157; N. Hooyman, "Redefining Models of Power and Administration Styles," *Social Development Issues* 2 (Winter 1978): 46–54.

57. S. Reinharz, "Women as Competent Community Builders: The Other Side of the Coin," in Rickel, Gerrard, and Iscoe, pp. 19–43; D. Masi, *Organizing for Women: Issues, Strategies, and Services* (Lexington, Mass.: Lexington Books, 1981).

58. R. Brandwein, "Women and Community Organization," in Burden and Gottlieb, pp. 111–125.

59. R. Brandwein, "Women in Macro Practice," in A. Minahan, ed., *Encyclopedia of Social Work* vol. 2 (Silver Spring, Md.: National Association of Social Workers, 1987), pp. 881–892; R. Chernesky, "Women Administrators in Social Work," in Norman and Mancuso, pp. 241–262; M. Weil, "Women in Administration: Curriculum and Strategies," in Burden and Gottlieb, pp. 92–110.

60. V. Sapiro, "The Women's Movement, Politics, and Policy in the Reagan Era," in D. Dahlerup, ed., *The New Women's Movement* (Newbury Park, Calif.: Sage Publications, 1986), pp. 122–139.

61. G. Goldberg and E. Kremen, "The Feminization of Poverty: Only in America?," *Social Policy* (Spring 1987): 3–14.

CHAPTER 12

Social Work Practice with Lesbians and Gays

George A. Appleby and Jeane W. Anastas

PREFATORY COMMENT

A social work intern assigned to a street outreach unit of an AIDS service organization developed a relationship with several under-age male and female prostitutes. Her specific task was to help them adopt safe-sex and clean needle-use behaviors. After she established a level of trust, she hoped to connect them with a range of other services they might need. The intern was concerned because she knew that to survive economically these under-age street people were selling their bodies with little regard for the dangers of HIV infection or the sexually transmitted diseases running rampant in the community. As a social worker, she is committed to helping her clients find more healthful alternatives to their lives on the streets. She came to realize that a significant number of her clients were lesbian or gay youth who had been kicked out of their homes or who had run away because of parental reactions to their gayness. She remembered that the reaction of the parents was called homophobia, *or the irrational fear and hatred of those who are sexually oriented towards persons of the same sex. It often gives rise to a range of discriminatory practices. As she got to know each individual, she was struck by the recurring themes of coming painfully to the recognition of their sexual orientation, family rejection, hostility of peers and friends, verbal and physical abuse, and the resulting confused, angry, and fearful feelings that increased their self-doubt. Homophobia and discrimination often give rise to "internalized oppression," which creates problems with self-esteem and self-image for homosexuals.*

Our intern, like all good social workers, attempted to formulate an assessment and intervention plan based on her knowledge of the clients' life situations. Unfortunately, she was unable to recall any required readings re-

lated to this topic, nor did she remember an in-depth discussion about lesbians or gays in her social work classes. She did recollect, however, that once someone in class said that "faggots and dykes" should not be allowed to work with children because what they did was sinful and would have a bad influence on the development of those in their care. The professor did not say much, and the subject was dropped. She thought this seemed consistent with a NASW workshop she had attended, where the presenter confirmed the high level of homophobia among social work students and faculty.[1]

However, this intern knew that the NASW Code of Ethics encouraged her to further the cause of social justice by promoting and defending the rights of persons suffering injustice and oppression. Gays and lesbians certainly met this requirement. She recalled that the Code was translated into NASW policy statements that prescribed the practice behavior of members; thus social workers are enjoined to view discrimination and prejudice directed against any minority as adverse to the mental health of the affected minority, as well as a detriment to society. Furthermore, social workers are urged to work to combat discriminatory employment practices and any other form of discrimination that imposes something less than equal status on gay or lesbian individuals. NASW, she recalled, affirmed the right of all persons to define and express their own sexuality. All persons are to be encouraged to develop their individual potential to the fullest extent possible.

Our budding Jane Addams, while highly motivated to act ethically and to give the most effective help, had no idea where to start. She, after some thought, decided to ask her supervisor for assistance. Her supervisor had received her MSW over a decade ago and knew little herself. She suggested that the intern do a literature review on this topic and that she start with reading this text.

CURRENT DEMOGRAPHICS

An understanding of the lesbian and gay population in the United States must begin with a presentation of the current demographic picture. There is a significant gap in our knowledge because scholars, like the general public, have been affected by the societal myths and taboos surrounding homosexuality. Thus they have often avoided the objective analysis of this aspect of human functioning entirely. When the topic has been studied at all, its science has often been limited by moral and social doctrines, seldom debated, about the ways humans ought to behave.[2] Twenty years ago public discussion of homosexuality was minimal, very little research existed, and available studies were usually limited to the investigation of individuals who sought treatment or to change their sexual orientation; thus they were not helpful in understanding the vast majority of homosexuals, who are not in treatment.[3] Gonsiorek documents that there exists, even today, a process of selective attention in the study of homosexuality which continues to limit our knowledge.[4]

Because oppression has resulted in the invisibility of gays and lesbians as a whole until recently, and because it is hard to define and describe an invisible population, much of the data we have about the homosexual population today are inferred from small survey research and ethnographic studies. Developing representative samples of lesbian and gays populations for research is notoriously difficult.[5] The data we do have suggest, however, that there is greater similarity than difference between gay and straight people.

Defining Homosexuality

Because of the myths and lack of knowledge that have surrounded this topic, it is especially important that we discuss who is and who is not homosexual. The following vignettes can help to highlight the difficulties in defining homosexuality in a way everyone can agree on.

A young PhD candidate has a crush on her professor. She manufactures numerous ways to be near her. Is she a lesbian? An army captain is discharged from the service for having sexual relations with an enlisted man. Is he gay? Two adolescents boys masturbate one another to orgasm. Are they homosexual? While having sexual intercourse with her husband, a woman frequently fantasizes about having sexual relations with other women. She has never had actual sexual contact with another woman. What is her sexual orientation? Because human sexuality occurs on a spectrum of feelings, ideas, and behavior, the answers to these questions are not so easy.

Categorization can lead to understanding—or to stereotyping. For example, if a woman is labeled a lesbian, it may be assumed that she will date women, be involved in many tempestuous short-term relationships, wear pants, play sports, raise dogs, and drive a truck. Likewise, if a person is a gay male, then he may be assumed to be very promiscuous, be overly concerned about his body and youth, obsess about fashion and style, frequently flick his wrists, and become a hairdresser or nurse. These are common stereotypes, but in reality attributes such as these (even if true) are seldom so predictable or clear. Zastrow warns that a stereotype, or a fixed mental image of a group frequently applied to all its members, is often unflattering and fails to take individual differences into account.[6]

Despite these dangers, the task of understanding any phenomenon starts with naming and defining. Shively and DeCecco help to clarify the controversy over who is and who is not a homosexual. They warn that various behaviors and life styles have been confused with sexual orientation. They distinguish among social sex role (the way society expects you to act according to your sex), gender identity (whether you consider yourself female or male), and gender role (whether you act so as to be taken as a male or female).[7] Each of these often confuses the issue of being gay or lesbian.

Moses and Hawkins suggest we view sexual orientation as an individual's preference for partners of the same sex, opposite sex, or both sexes for sexual and affectional relations. The desire to share affection or become life partners plays a significant role, as does sexual attraction, in the determination of sexual orientation.[8] A lesbian or a gay male, then, is one who is attracted primarily to someone of the same sex to satisfy sexual, sexual fantasy, and affectional needs. Those oriented toward both sexes would be termed bisexual.

This, then, is our definition. Unlike the more traditional definitions, three aspects are included: (1) sexual behavior, (2) sexual fantasy, and (3) affectional preference. This definition is compatible with most contemporary thinkers.[9]

The term *life style* has been confused with the definition of homosexuality. The term is used more appropriately to describe certain forms of lesbian and gay social and cultural expression, not fundamental sexual orientation. However, Friedman adds personal identity and social role to the dimensions of homosexuality discussed above, and notes that the various parts of the definition may be either congruent or incongruent in any one individual.[10]

Also problematic is the term *sexual preference,* widely used until recently. Research findings indicate that homosexual feelings are a basic part of the individual's psyche rather than something that are consciously chosen. Thus the more appropriate term is *sexual orientation.*

Terminology has been changing along with definitions. The term *homosexual,* once the most common, is now sometimes rejected because it denotes a category first imposed from a medically-oriented, heterosexual perspective. *Gay* is now the most common popular term for people who define themselves as homosexual, in contrast to the term *straight,* used to describe heterosexuals. While *gay* is used to describe both men and women, many homosexual women prefer to call themselves *lesbians.* These newer terms reflect the stance that lesbians and gay men will no longer allow the heterosexual majority to name and define them.[11]

Given the complexities of terminology and definition just described, it is essential to be sensitive to language. Ask clients or colleagues what they mean when you are uncertain of how homosexuality is being defined or of how they are defining themselves. Such a question will be interpreted more often as a demonstration of respect and concern for feelings than as ignorance.

It is important to remember that most heterosexuals often view the lesbian or gay male only in terms of sexuality and not other aspects of his or her personality or experience. As social workers it is vital that we go beyond this definitional process to fully understand the complexity and richness of being gay.

Social Characteristics

Lesbians and gay men live in every area of the United States, but they appear to be found in larger numbers in urban areas where there is anonymity and relative tolerance for diversity. They are represented in all occupations and socioeconomic groups. They are white, black, Hispanic, Southeast Asian, and American Indian. They probably reflect the same demographic proportions as found in the general population; impressionistic data, however, point to higher levels of education and disposable income than are found in the general population.

Gay men and lesbians live alone, with a lover of the same sex, with children, friends, or other family members. Some live with a spouse—many in the lesbian and gay communities believe that a large percentage of homosexuals are married and thus closeted from families and friends. Many lesbian and gay men form heterosexual relationships for a significant portion of their lives. Sometimes these relationships are exclusive, and other times they allow for multiple and bisexual attachment. Much of what is known about the social and family situations of lesbians and gays is anecdotal, reported by observers who have had limited access to homosexual lives. Some of these studies have been sympathetic and partially informed, while others have only served to perpetuate stereotyping and discrimination. Although there are limits to our knowledge base, failure to acknowledge the variety of gays' and lesbians' social situations only adds to the marginalization of their lives.

Population Size

The size of the homosexual population varies depending on what is observed. According to the definition one uses, homosexuals represent the first, second, or third most common minority in the United States today. Kinsey and his associates indicated that the amount of homosexual activity was greater than previously suspected.[12] Gebhard and Johnson have updated their figures. However, most of the statistics report behavior and not the other elements of a homosexual identity.[13]

Bell and Weinberg estimate that 10 percent of the population is homosexual.[14] This means that there are over 25 million gay men and lesbians in this country. This percentage, while commonly reported throughout the literature, is considered quite conservative by most. A 1977 Gallup poll reported a widely held belief that homosexuals represent more than 20 percent of the population. Woodman suspects that the proportion of lesbians could be greater than reported because the lives of lesbians are so hidden due to concerns about child care and custody.[15] As for men, Kinsey, Pomeroy, and Martin report that 13 percent of males had predominantly homosexual orientations for at least three years between the ages of sixteen and fifty-five, 25 percent of males had more than incidental homosexual experience for at least three years between the ages of sixteen and fifty-five, and 37 percent of males had at least some overt homosexual experience to the point of orgasm.[16] If we were to consider the typical size of an individual's network of family, friends, work colleagues, and others, these data suggest that everyone has a close relationship with someone who is lesbian or gay, whether or not they are aware of it.

Whatever the true numbers, it is important to recognize that there are a breadth of lifestyles and a number of subpopulations within the group, many of which overlap. Any community will have different social networks based on age, class, ethnicity, race, sex, and special interests. Hidalgo warns that class differences and racism do divide lesbian and gay communities.[17] Some observers suggest, however, that there is a greater commitment to democratic structures and an integration of subgroups than is commonly seen in heterosexual communities. This may be true because the need for affiliation is met in a group of similarly oriented people who share the common experience of oppression. Social networks crossing conventional group boundaries may be necessary to ensure a degree of group survival in a hostile environment. This same phenomenon has been noted among other minority groups.

However, racial and ethnic factors do have an impact on associations. Black and Hispanic gays, for both economic and cultural reasons, often maintain residence with or near their families, unlike many white gays, who establish homes away from relatives, often in one of the larger urban areas. This has an impact on the amount and intensity of association with other gays. Smith suggests that self-identification is another factor in determining the level of association of blacks with the gay community: "Gay whites are people who identify first as being gay and who usually live outside the closet in predominantly White gay communities. . . . Black gays, on the other hand, view our racial heritage as primary and frequently live 'bisexual front lives' within Black neighborhoods."[18] While there are no empirical data on the subject, the observation has been made that identification is equally important in other racial and ethnic groups.

Carballo-Dieguez notes that religion and folk beliefs strongly influence the Hispanic culture. Conservative and traditional values are barriers to an open gay life style.[19] Of the various religions, fundamentalists and Baptists seem likely to condemn homosexuality, and blacks, as Mays and Cochran point out, hold membership predominantly in these denominations.[20] Newby would concur with the importance of social structure, values, and religion on the public expression of sexual orientation in the black community and proposes that this may explain the higher rate of bisexuality and lower percentage of gay exclusivity than is found among whites.[21] Thus black and Latino gays are a double minority, often stigmatized by both the minority of color and gay communities.

ECOSYSTEMS FRAMEWORK

Social work addresses the interaction between the person and the environment. The goal of practice is to enhance and restore the psychosocial functioning of persons, or to change the oppressive or destructive social conditions that negatively affect the interaction between persons and their environments. The ecosystems model of practice, the framework of this text, consists of five interconnected domains or levels: (1) historical, (2) environmental-structural, (3) cultural, (4) family, and (5) individual. The lives and social conditions of lesbians and gay men are now assessed in relation to each of these domains.

Historical Factors

The ecosystems model is concerned with the positive and noxious factors in the historical experience of members of the population of interest. The history of minority group oppression and exploitation has already been noted. It has taken form in religion, culture, law, and social sanction. American society, strongly influenced by interpretations of Judeo-Christian moral codes, is one of the most homophobic. While change is in fact taking place in each of these areas, not one of these social structures could be characterized as nurturing. At best, they are benign.

The Stonewall "riot" in 1969, in which a group of gays resisted and protested against police harassment and brutality at a gay bar in New York, is usually regarded as the birth of the Gay Liberation Movement. Since that time, lesbian and gay individuals have become increasingly visible in our society. They are fighting for equal protection under our laws and for access to quality health and social care. Social workers have been at the forefront of these struggles, serving as advocates for this minority group. The profession asserts that homosexuals are entitled to the same rights, liberties, lack of harassment, and protections as are other citizens. The right of the individual to privacy and freedom from government regulation should be extended to all sexual orientations.

While this stand is progressive and consistent with the values of our profession, as well as with the ethical pronouncements of other health, legal, and mental health professions, it is not the position of the public in general. Unfortunately, widespread legal and social discrimination against lesbians and gays is the current political reality. Legal rights are denied lesbians and gay men in relation to same-sex couple marriages; custody of children and provision of foster and adoptive care; rights of inheritance and decision-making as biological next-of-kin; housing, employment, and employee benefits; immigration and naturalization; and military service.

Religious groups have been in the forefront of opposition to homosexuality. However, not all religions oppose it. Biblical interpretations vary widely, with advocates of both sides quoting scriptures as their defense. Presently, each of the major Judeo-Christian denominations has begun to recognize the spiritual and civil rights needs of their gay and lesbian members. The Metropolitan Community Church, a nondenominational group founded to minister to homosexuals, has over one hundred member churches throughout the country.

While some members of the gay community choose to remain invisible in an attempt to isolate themselves from the effects of oppression, others have committed themselves to action and self-realization. Many lesbians and gays recognized the community's potential political clout in the 1960s, as they became aware of their size as a minority group and their significance as a voting bloc. This led to the enormous growth of gay political organizations on local and national levels in the 1970s and 1980s. Currently, lesbian and gay civil rights issues, including partnership rights, foster-parenting protections, custody rights, and access to all available health care and treatment options, especially in relation to the AIDS epidemic, are being addressed at both the state and local levels. For example, gay activists have helped to bring about a general reassessment of federal ethical guidelines in medical treatment and research in order to bring potentially

life-saving treatments to patients sooner than in the past. The visibility and influence of the lesbian and gay minority will continue to grow.

In identifying history as a relevant dimension of the ecosystems model, it is
important to recognize the subjective experiences of the gay and lesbian. Historical factors may be less important to the individual than a positive self-image
today. Others may find in the knowledge of their collective history a source of
pain, anger, or pride. The history of gays and lesbians and their treatment is an
extensive topic best handled with additional reading (see Suggested Readings).

Environmental-Structural Factors

Homophobia is probably the most relevant environmental or structural issue
affecting lesbians and gays, and this chapter has already described some of the
ways in which homophobia has been institutionalized as a barrier in this society.
This dynamic, compounded with sexism and racism, has generated additional
barriers to the healthy development and well-being of lesbians and gays. The
impact of these environmental-structural factors gives a specific social form to
homosexuals. Paul and Weinrich identified three such factors: social invisibility,
social diversity, and social and personal differentiation.[22] The great majority of
homosexuals, including openly gay men and lesbians, are not easily identifiable.
There are as many kinds of gays as there are kinds of straights.[23] Finally, the ways
in which people adapt to having a gay orientation vary according to the relative
tolerance or hostility of the immediate social environment.

Social invisibility makes it possible for the general public to be ignorant of
diversity as it really exists. One result has been widely held inaccurate stereotypes. One such example would be the assumed connection between male heterosexuality and involvement in sports. Garner and Smith reported significantly
higher rates of homosexual activity in several samples of athletes than had been
previously found.[24] The current passion among some gay men for bodybuilding
and athletic club membership also serves to challenge this stereotype.

Homosexuals have always been the victims of homicides, gay bashing, and
extortion because of religious sanctions and legal discrimination. The social acceptance of homophobia, racism, and sexism in our society serves only to exacerbate hate. And the incidence of hate, violence, and harassment have increased
significantly as a result of the AIDS epidemic.[25] This oppression has had a significant impact on the health and mental health status of lesbians and gay men.[26]
High rates of suicide, drug abuse, and alcoholism have been reported, as well as
a range of psychosomatic illnesses.

The National Survey of Lesbian Health,[27] polling almost 2000 lesbians, reported that the most common health problem experienced was depression or
sadness. Other stress-related illnesses (ulcers and weight problems) were reported by significant percentages. More than half the sample reported that they
had been too nervous to cope with ordinary responsibilities sometime during
the year. Twenty-one percent had suicidal thoughts, and eighteen percent had
actually made a suicide attempt. Three-fourths of those surveyed were in coun-

seling. The mental health symptoms reported appear similar to those of other high stress groups.

Although gays and lesbians are sometimes victimized because of their sexual orientation, lesbian women also suffer abuse as women. Thirty-seven percent of the Bradford and Ryan sample reported that they had been harshly beaten or otherwise physically abused at some time in their lives. Twenty-one percent had been raped or sexually attacked as children; 15 percent as adults. Almost all the perpetrators were male. Adult attacks were comparable for all races, but one third of blacks, compared to one fifth of whites, were raped as children. As in other studies of physical and sexual abuse, white women were less likely to report this event. Approximately the same percentages are reported among nongay women.

Over half the sample had been verbally attacked for being gay. Eight percent had been physically attacked for this reason, while 13 percent had lost their jobs because they were gay. Although for methodological reasons generalization to all lesbians cannot be made, the data do suggest an interaction among the effects of discrimination, physical and sexual abuse, and substance abuse. The study also offered support for the positive effects of social acceptance and integration of lesbian identity. Comparable large scale surveys of gay men have not been reported.

Institutional homophobia and discrimination, with their resultant pressure toward social invisibility, have each been connected to higher incidence of social and health problems among lesbians and gay men. The structural-environmental factors addressed here are not exhaustive, and the experiences and adaptations of gay and lesbian individuals to these challenges are diverse. The literature related to minority groups will be relevant to your understanding of the gay experience in American society.

Culture

Popular images often suggest that gay and lesbian people are involved with a specific subculture or life style. As a result, gays and lesbians may be thought to be readily identifiable by styles of dress or behavior, or to be invested only in activities or institutions designated as exclusively gay and/or lesbian. However, lesbians and gays are in fact an invisible minority, only some of whom choose to make themselves and their interests visible individually and collectively in the gay and/or lesbian community and subculture.

As a stigmatized group, many gay and lesbian people do welcome and seek out places, occasions, and activities where they can enjoy the company of others clearly identified in that context as lesbian or gay as well. In some areas, especially in large cities, a gay and lesbian community or subculture exists which consists of those gathering places—restaurants, bars, bookstores, and other businesses seeking a gay and/or lesbian clientele—and those social service, health, political, arts, and media organizations dedicated to engaging and serving the lesbian and gay populations.

Access to such gay- or lesbian-identified institutions and organizations is often very important for individuals who have affirmed, are exploring, or are consolidating a gay or lesbian identity. People who live in rural or small communities far removed from these centers of activity may thus be disadvantaged in making connections with others like themselves, in developing ways to receive affirmation for significant parts of their lives, or in finding help or support in coping with homophobia.

Contact with the gay/lesbian subculture, however, will quickly dispel any notion that gay and lesbian people are similar to each other in appearance or life style beyond the sexual orientation that they share. Diversity within the identifiable lesbian and gay community is as great as among heterosexuals as a group. As in any other social group, these differences can be a source of tension, which may disappoint those looking to "the community" for an ideal way of life to emulate; or for a conflict-free environment as they work on developing their own identities or seek refuge from the discrimination from the community at large. The relationship between the individual and the community can thus be either a mutually enhancing or a conflicted one. Many lesbians and gays, however, draw essential support and affirmation from the subculture.

Just as gay and lesbian people are often seen almost exclusively as sexualized beings because their minority status is defined by their sexual orientation, lesbian and gay organizations, institutions, and events are often seen as devoted only to sexual ends. In fact, the institutions within the gay and lesbian subculture provide essential social, informational, health, economic and political resources for the population of gays and lesbians as a whole. While providing a safe place for dating and socializing is indeed a function of some parts of the subculture, homosexual organizations are no more inherently sexual than heterosexual ones.

In addition, many gay and lesbian people do not participate in the identifiable gay and lesbian subculture even when it is available to them. Their political, social, and recreational pursuits may not be related to their sexual orientation at all, and their social and emotional supports may come exclusively from friends and/or family. Sometimes this choice may stem from a wish to remain private or "closeted" in their sexual orientation out of fear; at other times it may result from a choice to give other dimensions of their lives and identity priority. Thus the degree of an individual's involvement with the gay or lesbian subculture is itself a dimension of diversity among lesbians and gays.

The concept of *biculturality* has recently been used to describe the socialization processes that lesbians and gays undergo.[28] Acceptance of a gay or lesbian identity means adopting new norms and values and being rejected by and/or rejecting old standards. Dating and coupling, definitions of family, celebrations and ritual participation, both secular and religious, and political and social interests are all affected by sexual orientation. For lesbians and gay men of ethnic- and racial-minority background, the cultural issues are even more complex.

This concept of a homosexual culture is viewed as controversial by some, because intergenerational transmission of this culture and socialization into it does not ordinarily take place in the family of origin, as it does in cultures as defined in other contexts. In fact, gay and lesbian individuals are usually first socialized into majority, heterosexual culture. However, applying the concept of culture to gay and lesbian ways of life highlights the inclusiveness of a lesbian or gay identity, the shared experiences of gay and lesbian people over time and across societies, and the diversity of gays and lesbians on other dimensions such as race, class, and gender. The related notion of biculturality points out that gays and lesbians live to differing degrees in multiple worlds, with the attendant opportunities and stresses of negotiation and boundary maintenance.[29]

Family Factors

The ecosystems model of practice helps the practitioner understand the potential strengths and barriers to psychosocial functioning resulting from family life. The family is the primary institution responsible for social adaptation in our society. It provides its members with emotional, financial, and social support. The family is an institution cherished by all but rarely examined from an analytical point of view.

Lesbians and gay men have been categorized by society as people without families, uninterested in creating families, and threatening to family life. Despite this perception, the fact is that at least two million lesbians and gay men are parents of minor children.[30] Large numbers of the homosexual population live in long-term, committed, coupled relationships.[31] Achtenberg notes that discriminatory treatment, misunderstanding, and prejudices often pose social and legal barriers to the recognition and protection of families created by lesbians and gay men.[32]

Many gays credit their family of origin as the source of their emotional support and strength as well as their positive belief and value system. Yet for other gays and lesbians, the family is a source of interpersonal tension and conflict, hardly the basis for self-acceptance or a healthy adjustment to a hostile society. Many gays credit their "chosen family"—family of design consisting of lover and friends—as the buffer that has had the greatest impact on their adaptation.

It is important that a social worker have a framework to understand families in relation to practice and to incorporate new knowledge as it develops. Labeling theory, a sociological approach to understanding family, may prove most productive for the social work practitioner because it introduces an unambiguous distinction between homosexual behaviors and feelings, and stigma. Stigma itself, once it has become a part of culture, has certain predictable consequences. Hammersmith suggests these include stereotypic interpretations of behavior; social rejection, distancing, and discrimination; "passing" and altered self-concept; development of a special subculture; and "secondary deviation."[33] Each of these is discussed as it affects the families of lesbians and gays.

The gay or lesbian, his or her parents, and the spouses and children of a homosexual person are all confronted daily with this stereotyping and social rejection. The images of homosexuality are all negative: the "sinner," the "drag queen," the "child molester," the "diesel dyke." By the time one reaches adulthood, the association (not necessarily conscious) between homosexuality and the stereotype is formed. These dehumanizing stereotypes are perpetuated by the peer group, the mass media, and cultural tradition. The individual may feel pressure to establish distance from homosexuality. Few people, then, are socially prepared to deal with this issue when it arises.

"Passing" is a second consequence of stigma. Anyone who does not fit the stereotype can "pass," while those who meet the stereotyped expectations become visible. An individual may come to recognize his or her homosexual orientation without realistic models of what this means. The reaction may be, "I'm the only person in the world like this"; or "I'm not like them, thank God." Parents, other family members, and friends are likely to avoid or deny disclosure when their loved one does not fit the stereotype. Gay youth are reared in heterosexual families, peer groups, and educational institutions. Thus gay youth grow up learning the same stereotypes and negative judgments as their straight peers, threatening the sense of self. Because "passing" is so pervasive, gay youth are deprived of positive role models or the preparation for dealing with homosexuality. Sustaining self-esteem and a sense of identity becomes problematic at best.

Rejection is the fourth consequence of stigma, which produces distancing between those with the stigma and those without. Disclosure can become a critical issue within the family. The homosexual child may lose the sense of authenticity characteristic of family relationships if he or she keeps the secret, or face rejection if he or she seeks understanding and emotional support by disclosing the homosexuality. This potential alienation from the family is one way in which the homosexual minority is different from other minority groups, who generally can count on support within the family in the face of stress from the outside world. This same dynamic will be true with friends and work colleagues. Bell, Weinberg, and Hammersmith note that secrecy brings about a different sort of distancing, offering the example of a gay person who appears outwardly popular and well liked by the group yet feels alienated and isolated.[34]

The development of a subculture, a separate space that allows a sense of community and naturalness, is the fifth consequence of stigma. The subculture may be an opportunity to develop a special kinship with fellow victims of stigma. The stronger the disapproval by the majority culture, the more attractive a subculture as a source of mutual support.

The final consequence identified by Hammersmith is that of the self-fulfilling prophecy or secondary deviance. This means that features of the stereotype may be embraced in protest or defiance or for lack of support for more normative styles of life. "Camp" and "leather" are stereotypic styles reflecting theatrical and humorous responses to society's arbitrary distinctions between masculine and feminine cultures. This poking of fun at gender roles by flouting them is often seen by nongays as confirmation of their worst stereotypic fears.

So far this discussion has focused on the dynamics of stigma because of its relevance to our understanding of the impact of family on lesbians and gays. Primary attention has been given to the family of origin, but stigma must also be appreciated for its impact on the family of design.

Forming Families: Myths and Realities.   The fact that lesbians and gays may be parents like other adults is important to remember. Some gays and lesbians are or have been heterosexually married and may have become fathers or mothers in that context. Because divorcing women are still more likely than men to seek and be granted custody of children, many lesbians and a few gay men may continue the active rearing of their children following a divorce. The new reproductive technologies, especially alternate insemination, have opened up the possibility of child bearing for all younger lesbians. Many, both single and in couples, are electing to bear and/or rear children. Finally, many gay men and lesbian women, single and in couples, are choosing to be foster and/or adoptive parents. Social workers in medical and child welfare settings increasingly find themselves dealing with lesbian clients as they give birth, and with gay and lesbian clients seeking adoptive or foster children or who come for help with the vicissitudes of parenting.

Numerous studies have been made of children being reared by lesbians to determine what effects on development there may be. Because artificial insemination and access to adoption by gays are relatively new phenomena, the studies to date have generally compared children of divorced lesbian mothers to those of divorced women who are not lesbians. Taken together, the studies have consistently shown that gay men and lesbians who parent do not differ in child rearing practices or life style from other parents and that the children of lesbian mothers and gay men have no more problems in adjustment or development than do others.[35] There is no evidence of gender-role confusion or higher rates of gay or lesbian orientation among them, as had initially been hypothesized. In fact, there is some evidence that children of lesbians have a greater appreciation for diversity of all kinds and value tolerance more highly than others, having seen first-hand the toll that prejudice like homophobia can take.

The concern that a child who grows up with a homosexual parent will develop a gay orientation appears to be a widely held myth. The assumption that children develop their sexual orientation by emulating their parents is false. Remember that the vast majority of homosexuals were raised by heterosexual parents.[36]

Another myth is that children who grow up with a gay or lesbian parent are at risk of molestation or abuse by either the parent or the parent's friends. However, research on the sexual abuse of children shows that the offenders are, in disproportionate numbers, heterosexual men.[37]

It is also a common assumption that children in the custody of a lesbian or gay parent will be harmed by social stigma. But Kirkpatrick and Hitchens state that there are no clinical reports of stigma or unusual emotional problems in these children.[38]

There is a vast literature on family applicable to this discussion, but it is beyond the scope of this chapter, which has focused on how stigmatizing processes may affect families and especially on some myths often applied to them. The practitioner must also realize that the coping and adaptational qualities of gay people in families are also tempered by economics, ethnicity, race, and class identity. These are issues are addressed in detail in family studies. The reader is encouraged to explore the resources listed in the Suggested Readings for additional information on this topic.

Individual Factors

Much of the theorizing of the nineteenth century viewed homosexuality as either willful sin or a biologically determined illness. It was commonly believed that homosexuals were another sex, different from both male and female. At the beginning of this century, however, Freud postulated that bisexuality is inherent in all people. Early experiences and ensuing personality development then were thought to determine which individuals were homosexual, heterosexual, or bisexual as adults. Beginning with the pioneering work of Kinsey, researchers have come to view sexual orientation as a continuum, from those who are exclusively homosexual to those who are exclusively heterosexual. Most people fall somewhere in between.

The study of why people become gay usually starts with an exhaustive review of biological theories focusing on genetic and hormonal factors, and psychoanalytic and behavioral theories addressing pathology and dysfunction. The conclusions of these studies are seldom supported by the data presented (if any). Recent research, however, notes that the attempt to identify etiological factors has a long history, but with close inspection one must conclude that no specific genetic, intrapsychic, or interpersonal causative factors can be generalized to the lesbian and gay population.[39] Therefore, the information to follow will select insights on individual development that have value for practice intervention.

One way to improve our understanding or our definition of gayness is to correct the myths and inaccuracies surrounding homosexuality. One myth, which represents the popular version of an outmoded psychoanalytic explanation of homosexuality, is that male homosexuality represents a fear or hatred of women. (The reverse is also sometimes said of lesbian women.) This myth has led to ineffective treatment based on the assumption that gay men can be converted to heterosexuality simply by having sexual experiences with women. This simplistic view is contradicted by the large proportion of gay men who have had or continue to have heterosexual experiences but retain a positive gay identity.

Another myth is that gay people are compulsively sexual. The Kinsey Institute's estimates of gay sexual activity are probably overstated. Like straights, most gays spend most of their time doing things other than looking for sex or having it. Since 1981, the AIDS epidemic has struck a large number of gay and bisexual men. The widespread awareness in the gay community that the virus believed to cause AIDS is transmitted through unprotected sex (i.e., without condoms) has led to significant changes in sexual practices and thus a dramatic reduction in sexually transmitted disease and the rate of AIDS infection among gay men.

Finally, while lesbians and gay men may often be accused of flaunting their sexuality, in fact most conceal their sexual orientation at least part of the time. Stigma and the consequences of discrimination in many areas of daily living are convincing reasons for concealment.[40] Berger suggests that because lesbians and gay men are generally indistinguishable from other men and women, public attitudes are formed on the basis of those who are most open about their sexual orientation.[41] Heterosexuals apply a double standard to same-sex and opposite-sex behavior, in that public displays of affection between a man and a woman are taken for granted while even holding hands in public is considered flaunting when it occurs between two women or two men.

Identity Formation.   Sexual orientation may change over time. A woman who is primarily homosexual in early adulthood may become more heterosexual in later life or vice versa. In his study of older gay men, Berger found that it is not uncommon for a man with an essentially heterosexual orientation in early adulthood to develop predominately homosexual interests in middle age.[42] These observations lead us to the view that homosexuality is an identity formation process occurring over time. This formulation has much promise for social work assessment and intervention.

Berger proposed a model wherein homosexual identity results when a person completes three tasks that are independent of one another. The first in this process is the sexual encounter; that is, physical contact of a sexual nature with someone of the same sex. Second is the social reaction; that is, the process of labeling the individual by others as homosexual. The last component in this model is the identity task; that is, the individual experiences identity confusion, the discomfort felt between a same-sex experience and a heterosexual self-image, and works to come to terms with this in some way.[43]

This identity develops over time as the individual begins to label him- or herself as lesbian or gay. This labeling process entails decisions related to managing the new identity with family, friends, and peers and colleagues, and incorporating the norms and attitudes of the new reference group. The ultimate tasks in this process are adaptation and self-acceptance.

Viewing homosexuality as the result of an identity-formation process has important implications for social work intervention. First of all, and most important, there is no empirical justification for the belief that homosexuality, in and of itself, is a psychiatric illness or a result of poor psychological adjustment. Practitioners who continue to advocate illness models are ignorant, irresponsible, or both.[44]

Social Stress and Social Supports.   Like Berger, other theorists have adopted an interactionist perspective to examine the intricate linkage between social life and personal experience. Human beings cannot escape the influence of social position and social expectation on their development and self-perception. Bradford and Ryan note that "those who are discriminated against or who expect to face discrimination if their 'condition' were to become known are different from those who do not occupy stigmatized or 'deviant' social positions. The connection between living on the margins of society and the impact of this upon daily life and an adequate sense of psychosocial security" is yet to be fully documented. However, we do know that lesbians and gay men always live with this tension.[45]

Discrimination often results in being barred from participation in the community institutions that sustain other members of society, thus the options for social connections are limited. Legally sanctioned ties such as marriage and family relations are seldom available. Lesbians and gay men must either create their own systems, or live in relative isolation from sympathetic others. Since lack of adequate social connection can have a significant impact on health, it is reasonable to assume that gays are vulnerable to a type of stress not normally experienced by straights.

This stress and lack of support may result in higher rates of alcoholism among lesbians and gays. Gay bars are one of the few legitimate places where gay men and lesbians can meet to socialize. Drinking can also provide emotional insulation from homophobic or racist attitudes.[46] Anderson and Henderson estimate that one third of lesbians are alcoholics. Legal, health, and social service agencies have tended to focus on sexual orientation as the cause of this phenomenon, despite evidence that lesbians do not differ in psychosocial functioning from heterosexual women. Lesbians of color, like their male counterparts, have a higher incidence of alcoholism than straights.[47]

Brooks emphasizes the importance of social support networks for lesbians and gay men. These are relationships with significant others, developed as a result of sharing a history of common experience through which people create environments of caring and support for each other.[48] While recognizing that the importance of supportive interactions among people is not new, Bradford notes that research evidence of social supports' helping people in health crises is recent. Maintenance of good health is related to the number of people in a social network.[49] Alcalay adds that the number of contacts, the frequency and intensity of contacts, as well as the presence of family and friends within the network are all related to health.[50] In other words, friends can be "good medicine."

Bradford and Ryan have synthesized the research related to social support and crisis in relation to lesbian health. They conclude that supports encourage preventive behavior, provide needed resources, increase a sense of personal control over one's environment, and reduce the social marginality of one's minority status. Supports are buffers against the distress of traumatic life events. Lesbians and gay men without sufficient supports are especially vulnerable to commonplace stressors as well as the monumental stress related to minority status.[51] It is within the context of stress, social marginality, and minority status that the impact of a hostile, discriminatory environment should be understood. This approach to understanding developmental issues focuses our attention on life adaptations and thus is consistent with the ecosystems perspective.

The social-psychological concepts presented here can be useful in reconceptualizing ideas about the development and adaptability of homosexuals. They offer alternate explanations for some of the same processes described in common folk beliefs and older illness models. These theories also explain how labeling,

stereotyping, and prejudice can shape and determine the perceptions and behaviors of gay and straight individuals.

MACRO PRACTICE WITH LESBIANS AND GAYS

Macro practice is associated with a set of values that guide the methods used.
The values are justice, independence and freedom, community life, self-determination, and change. Justice must be accessible to all on an equal basis; it must
be impartially applied. Social conditions must be just. People want to feel a sense
of self-importance and have a real ability to make decisions to affect their own
lives, not be manipulated by an impersonal bureaucracy. Independence and freedom are needed to experiment, reflect, and change. People generally want to
create their own community to have a chance to experience support and a feeling
of belonging, to have greater power over their lives, and to find ways of resolving
problems. On the other hand, when people are isolated they may become victims
of exploitation and alienation, and feel powerless, vulnerable, and unimportant.
People want a chance to affect their own future; to make choices. A sense of
accomplishment comes from engaging in action, not from being acted on. Products of change are all around us, and it is these that feed our sense of optimism.

Direct and Indirect Macro Practice

Case Example

The social work intern introduced at the beginning of this chapter was concerned
about the well-being of a group of gay and lesbian "runaway" and "throwaway"
youth who were surviving on the streets through prostitution. (**Initial Problem**)
She recognized that this behavior placed them at risk for AIDS, STDs, violence,
and exploitation. (**Professional Consultation**) She sought the assistance of her
supervisor, who in turn discussed the issue with the agency director. (**Legitimize
the Problem**) The director suggested that the worker call together a group of
prominent lesbian and gay community leaders who would help define the problem. The director, a lesbian active in an array of civil rights issues, offered to
make the initial contact to confirm interest and commitment. (**Use High Status
Individuals to Move an Issue**) In this situation the director, recognizing the
stigma of being "out," decided to check with these leaders first before advancing
their name for the project.

(**Worker Set the Tone and Sought Commitment**) The worker presented her
observations at the first meeting of twelve activists. The group was appalled and
motivated to act. (**Redefinition of the Problem, Community Action Goals
Set**) After a great deal of discussion, they agreed that protective and supportive
services were unavailable to these youth because of their sexual orientation.
(**Organizational Development**) Various members assented to take on assign-

ments so as to move the objectives of the group. (**Assessments**) A lawyer chose to review the statutes (**Advocacy**) related to this problem. A social worker and a psychiatrist agreed to research the psychosocial needs and programs identified for this population. (**Community Assessment and Education**) The minister of the M.C.C. church and the director of the Women's Center committed to canvasing their members to gauge support for becoming involved in youth work. (**Client Problem Definition**) Our intern decided to explore the perceptions of youth related to the problem and its solution. (**Expand Constituency and Work Group**) Each person decided to tap an additional potential member for this working task force.

(**Leadership Identification and Group Composition**) The task force increased in size to thirty members, representing the broadest racial, occupational, and class cross-section of lesbians and gay men. (**Consensus Seeking**) Numerous meetings were held to refine the problem statement and to develop a course of action. (**Compromise and Group Dynamics**) This was no easy task for the worker, since interests and working styles were so varied. A lesbian and a gay man, both well-respected leaders, were elected to chair the group. (**Leadership and Planning**) Through their sensitive leadership, the defined need was broadened to include lesbians and gay men from the metropolitan area who might use a full range of social, educational, health, and mental health services. (**Self-Help**) The needs of all gay youth would be addressed. (**Priority Setting and Strategy**) The specific requirements of the original population would be dealt with while working on other organizational issue and in time would be incorporated into the activities of the (**Structure**) new Lesbian and Gay Community Service Center (L&GCSC). (**Provide Internal Structure for Community Group**) The worker helped to form a series of working groups, to identify leaders, and to offer staff support for their activities. (**Client Commitment and Activity**) Several of the youth agreed to be involved (**Negotiation**) but were emphatic that their situation not be ignored but be given top priority. The first task to be completed was the organization of a shelter with support services for lesbian and gay street youth. (**Negotiation and Lobbying**) This was accomplished through legal challenge of the Department of Child Welfare, who were accused of not meeting the statutorily mandated needs of children who required protection. (**Organizational Development**) Start-up money and operational funds were funneled through L&GCSC to support the program.

(**Organizational Stability**) The task force eventually reconstituted into a legal board of directors with a paid director, a structure for programs and services, and a cadre of volunteers and members. (**Project Termination**) On graduation the intern was asked to be a member of the board.

Building Coalitions and Supporting Legislation

Organizations who advocate for the rights of homosexuals, such as the American Civil Liberties Union, Lambda Legal Defense, and the National Gay and Lesbian Task Force, just like the health and mental health professional associations like NASW, have lobbied with clear objectives. Their position is that homosexuals are entitled to the same rights, liberties, lack of harassment, and protections as are other citizens.

The right of individual privacy free from government regulation should extend to sexual conduct of consenting adults. Criminalization of homosexual acts is a violation of the right of individual privacy. Criminal statutes proscribing adult homosexual behavior create an environment of oppression arising from fear of prosecution and provide the means of blackmail. Such statutes are most reprehensible when linked to enforcement by entrapment. These laws perpetuate discrimination against homosexuals. Finally, discrimination on the basis of homosexuality violates an individual's right of privacy and denies the person equal protection of the law.[52]

Achtenberg reminds us that to favor lesbian and gay rights or to support an end to discrimination must mean to deplore the ways in which society undermines the formation, preservation, and protection of the lesbian and gay family.[53] Gay rights must also include support for custody and visitation statutes that ensure strict neutrality with regard to the sexual orientation of the parent. Advocacy for adoption and foster parenting laws and administrative practices that are strictly neutral should become a related activity. Joint adoptions by same-sex couples should be permitted when it is in a child's best interests and when the parent–child relationship has been cemented. Laws permitting delegation of personal and health care duties to nonrelatives should be created, as well as provision for fair determination of the guardian or conservator for an ill person. The same sentiment should inform the laws of intestate succession. Equity, not sexual orientation or marital status, should become the value undergirding the distribution of work-related and governmental benefits.

Legislation embodying the above principles should be the goal of the profession. Passage of such legislation on state or national levels requires building coalitions of like-minded civil rights advocacy groups and extensive public education. Social workers are skilled in problem identification and resolution through organization building and strategy development. These are the needed skills if environments are to be supportive of positive gay identity development and no longer barriers to healthful functioning and psychosocial adaptation.

MICRO PRACTICE WITH LESBIANS AND GAYS

Most micro practice with lesbians and gays does not come to the attention of the social worker identified as such. The friend or roommate who brought the heart attack victim to the hospital and seeks to visit him or her in the intensive care unit; the parent of the first-grader with a visual impairment who meets with the school social worker to discuss the child's adjustment to school; the middle-aged woman attending a support group for those caring for elderly parents with Alzheimer's disease; the adolescent referred to the mental health center because he or she is feeling depressed or suicidal—any of these may be a client who is lesbian or gay.

Failure to consider that a client may be gay or lesbian is the most common mistake made by workers in situations like the ones described above. Despite stereotypes, most lesbian and gay clients are not visually identifiable as such, and many may not identify themselves as gay or lesbian at first, especially when the problem for which they are seeking assistance may not have much to do with sexual orientation.[54] However, the social worker is unlikely to get a full enough picture of the client's situation in order to be helpful without keeping an open mind to the possibility of a gay or lesbian identity.

In dealing with a situation where the sexual orientation of the client is unknown, having an attitude and using language that conveys an openness to both a heterosexual or a homosexual possibility are critically important. If the assumption of heterosexuality is made, as it usually is, or if it is assumed that the client's most important family ties are only biological ones, it can be actively, if unwittingly, painful and alienating to the client seeking help. Exploring the situation with an open mind to whatever identity the client chooses to convey will be both more comfortable for the client and more fruitful for the worker who genuinely wishes to understand the client's reality.

Effective work with lesbians and gay men requires what Hall has termed a dual focus: "The practitioner must be able to see the ways in which the client's presenting problem is both affected by and separate from her sexual orientation."[55] Damage to self-esteem resulting from oppression and stigmatization must always be considered, but at the same time the client probably occupies roles, works on developmental tasks, and experiences feelings in which being gay or lesbian is incidental. For example, the teenage prostitutes our intern met through her work at the AIDS service organization must deal with the rejection they experienced from families because they were gay or lesbian. At the same time, these teens have the same developmental needs for the support and approval of adults and peers that others do and would be seeking a way to separate and differentiate themselves from their families even if rejection based on their sexual orientation had not occurred. Thus, a worker counseling any of them might expect to hear both a longing for the love and approval of their parents, despite their rejecting behavior, and a simultaneous longing to be completely free of parental restraint or control.

Attitudes about homosexuality in the helping professions as a whole have been changing markedly since the 1970s. Thus, both worker and client may be affected by the residue of outmoded psychological theory that until recently viewed homosexuality as pathology in and of itself. Hall points out that the worker's feelings, attitudes, and level of comfort with a gay or lesbian life style or orientation must be examined; they require self-exploration over time.[56] It is the homophobia gay and lesbian individuals may encounter that is likely to be a problem, not the homosexuality itself. Rather than seeking causes or explanations for homosexuality, this perspective leads the social worker to explore and help the client to overcome the obstacles, internalized or external, that may stand in the way of healthy functioning as a gay or lesbian person.

Psychological and psychoanalytic theory have given more attention to male than female homosexuality over the years. The most thorough discussion of psychoanalytic theory and male homosexuality to appear in recent years posits that there are twelve possible sexual orientations resulting from of the resolution of the Oedipus complex; six of them are homosexual and six heterosexual.[57] Thus from a contemporary psychoanalytic standpoint there are many varieties of both heterosexual and homosexual functioning, and homosexual or heterosexual object choices are not viewed in themselves as healthy or unhealthy. Nevertheless, studies suggest that negative attitudes toward homosexuality and homosexual clients persist among some social workers and social work students.[58] Such attitudes create barriers that keep gays and lesbians from seeking or receiving effective mental health services in times of need.

When homosexuality was viewed as pathological, it was assumed that some critical experiences early in life produced an outcome, same-sex object choice, which was thought to be immutable without psychological treatment. Not only has it proven very difficult to identify any experiential or developmental "causes" or antecedents of homosexuality with any confidence,[59] but the treatment of homosexual people in psychological distress was usually distorted to mean treatment of the homosexuality itself.[60]

On the one hand, adult developmental theory now tells us that the personality and life course is not "cast in stone" in childhood. On the other hand, close study of the sexual practices of both heterosexual and homosexual people and attention to the life histories of gay and lesbian people suggest that sexual practices and self-identification may change over time. To self-identified gay or lesbian individuals, however, the homosexual identity may feel immutable, essential, and core to their sense of themselves as persons. Psychological treatment is thus focused on addressing whatever distress a self-identified gay or lesbian person may be experiencing, rather than on the sexual orientation itself.[61]

Contemporary theory emerging from research and clinical work with gays and lesbians, then, suggests that the developmental pathways to a gay or lesbian identity are numerous. Homosexual identity is no longer assumed to be pathological. The task of the social worker is to understand and accept the varieties of gay and lesbian identity and experience that exist and to assist the lesbian or gay client to deal with any problems that may accompany or simply coexist with his or her particular sexual orientation.

Common Problems

As with other minority groups, the oppression that may be visited on gay and lesbian people because of their sexual orientation can be destructive to individual self-esteem and well-being. At early stages of the coming-out process, many people actively resist acknowledging, even to themselves, that they are sexually attracted to or active with others of their own gender. This resistance is often the product of negative attitudes toward homosexuality they themselves have absorbed, as everyone does, from the society as a whole; or of negative reactions they fear from significant others such as parents, children, friends, associates, or authority figures such as teachers, coaches, or religious leaders. It is essential that the social work services gays and lesbians receive be free of the homophobia that would add to or reinforce these fears and attitudes.

The process of coming out can be a time of intense personal crisis as well as joyful self-discovery. Feelings of acute anxiety or depression may occur; and behavior problems such as excessive use of substances or other forms of acting out can develop or intensify. Professional help may be sought or recommended, and the responses of the social worker to such an individual in crisis, who may or may not initially identify coming out as an issue, are critically important to the client's comfort and progress toward a more comfortable self-definition and self-acceptance.

CASE EXAMPLE

Lynn, who was seventeen and a high school senior, was referred to a social worker for counseling following a brief psychiatric hospitalization. She had been admitted to the hospital after friends of hers, becoming alarmed, reported to her parents that she had ingested a number of pills and was "acting funny." This episode was viewed as a suicidal gesture by both the young woman and her parents. It followed a period of several months during which arguments between the girl and her parents had been growing in frequency and intensity. The arguments were over such issues as Lynn's style of dress, her social activities, her "lack of respect" for her parents, and the fact that she had stopped attending church with the family.

Lynn was the youngest of three children and the only one still living at home. Her father owned his own small business and worked long hours; her mother worked as a nurse. Both parents were fundamentalist Christians, and their recreational activities, which were few, were centered on the church. The family lived in a suburban community on the outskirts of a large metropolitan area in the Northeast.

From the beginning of counseling, Lynn announced firmly that she was a lesbian, and she always appeared for her appointments dressed in tight blue jeans, studded leather jacket, and black boots. Her manner appeared angry and "tough," and the image she cultivated was that of the stereotype of the "dyke." Lynn had also told her parents she was a lesbian. Her father was extremely rejecting of homosexuality, which he regarded as sinful; her mother was slightly more sympathetic. Because she had also spoken openly about her sexual orientation in the hospital, Lynn had been referred to a worker who was also a lesbian, although Lynn was not aware of that fact.

Starting with what Lynn had said was important about herself, the worker began exploring Lynn's sexual orientation and what it meant to her. Lynn had begun heterosexual dating at fifteen and had enjoyed a relationship with a boy she liked very much. However, as time went on she realized she experienced her relationship with him as a "good friend" and not as a "boyfriend" like her friends did. About this time, she also became aware of her attraction to other young women. She had her first sexual experience with a woman at sixteen, which she described as her coming out. After this point, for her "there was no going back."

The worker began exploring what being gay meant to Lynn. It turned out that Lynn knew only two other lesbians, both "tough kids" from her home town. The worker then asked Lynn if she would be interested in making contact with an organization for lesbian and gay youth in the city, where Lynn began to meet a much more varied and congenial group of peers and where she could begin to talk about the pain of isolation and disapproval she was experiencing at school and at home. She also used the group to talk about her plans for college and her worries about what it would be like to be identified as a lesbian on campus.

As Lynn gained social support from the group and a sense of personal support and acceptance from her social worker in their meetings, her appearance and style of dress began to change somewhat. She also began tentatively to share with her worker some painful feelings she had about being gay, especially her parents' reactions to her and the religious beliefs she still heard from them that regarded her orientation as a sin. Lynn's presentation changed from angry and tough to depressed and vulnerable as she struggled to understand the painful feelings she was dealing with. During this stage, the worker was glad she had not shared information about her own sexual orientation with Lynn, who had never asked about it, thinking that doing so might have made it harder for Lynn to feel comfortable talking about the negative side of her feelings about her own homosexuality.

The more Lynn talked about her experiences in the family, however, the more it became clear that Lynn's parents had been distant from her in other ways for quite some time. It also became clear that her low self-esteem went back to early childhood. Lynn's father was quite rigid in his beliefs and standards and was rarely home because of his work; her mother was alcoholic and thus not reliably available to Lynn. Lynn increasingly expressed interest in understanding things in her family that had been going on long before her sexual orientation became an issue. In order to deal with these issues and to help prepare Lynn to leave home, Lynn and her parents were referred for family therapy as well.

Lynn continued in counseling until the time came for her to leave for college. Although she continued to suffer some periods of depression, no further suicidal gestures were made, and the conflict at home was somewhat reduced. When she left, Lynn was able to imagine herself meeting others at college who might share both her sexual orientation and some of her other interests as well.

This case illustrates the importance of attending to a range of issues in working with a gay or lesbian client. Clearly, comfort with the client's homosexuality and understanding the homophobic reactions of others was essential to working with this case. This comfort must encompass both the positive and negative feelings a client will most likely experience in coming out. Second, the typical developmental issues and concerns of the age or stage of development must be considered as well. Here the anxiety of an impending separation as Lynn "grew up" and went off to school was upsetting to parent and child alike. Third, it was important to be aware of the problems and vulnerabilities of both the individual and the family as they met the challenges of coming out and their life stage transitions. Finally, the role of social supports and ways to reduce isolation for lesbians and gays—lesbian and gay youth in particular—cannot be overestimated. Lynn's contact with peers provided validation for her sexual orientation and role models for the many ways in which people incorporate and express a gay or lesbian identity.

Working with Couples

Because the norms and privileges associated with marriage have not been extended to gay and lesbian couples, living together as a permanently committed couple is not as universal a style of life and not the unquestioned ideal among as many gay and lesbian people as nongays. Nevertheless, many lesbians and gays seek to develop long-term, committed couple relationships. These relationships can have as much meaning and emotional significance to the partners as marriage does to heterosexual pairs. However, these relationships face some special challenges others may not have to confront, and the social worker must consider these when working with gay and/or lesbian couples.

Dating and coupling behavior is often what exposes gays and lesbians to their greatest risk from homophobia. It is not simply walking down the street alone but wanting to walk down the street holding a partner's hand that most often produces panic in the individual or fear of abuse from others. Going to a bar or expressing affection to a lover in public may in fact even precipitate a gay-bashing attack. With the incidence of such violence on the rise, gay and lesbian relationships are sometimes actually as well as metaphorically under assault.

Entering into a relationship may be what causes an individual to acknowledge openly for the first time to self and others a gay or lesbian identity, precipitating potential crisis in family, social, and work relationships. The process of negotiating a new identity as lesbian or gay may be a large part of the couple relationship for one or both partners and may place considerable stress on it.

The lack of formal and informal social sanction for the relationship is a source of strain for all gay and lesbian couples. Even if the relationship is one between partners whose lesbian or gay identity has long been established, the lack of validation of the relationship itself can produce a range of reactions, including sorrow and anger, at times that would otherwise be marked by joy. Holidays, for example, may find the partners separated as they fulfill commitments to families that may not welcome them together. Rituals of courtship and commitment may be lacking entirely or may be limited to the context of the gay community. Family and friends who are prepared to be generally supportive of the individual may react negatively to any steps taken by the couple to make the relationship public or legally sanctioned. Socializing in work or other contexts in which a husband or wife may be automatically included will leave gay and lesbian couples to decide whether to ask for the recognition and inclusion of a partner, or to give up validation of the relationship and the opportunity to be together in order to feel more private or more safe.

As a result of these stresses and complications, a gay or lesbian couple may become quite isolated. Opportunities for the couple, as a unit, to be in the company of others and to get the feedback that such socializing normally offers may be quite limited. Partners can easily become totally or exclusively dependent on each other for emotional support. Unusual patterns of behavior within the relationship can then come to seem quite normal. Access to the gay or lesbian community can offer isolated couples or partners resources for socializing, self-help, and support in an affirming and nonjudgmental atmosphere.

In the face of these strains, gay and lesbian couples have invented customs and rituals to sustain themselves and have adapted available supports to their own needs. Small groups of couples or friends may celebrate holidays together as faithfully as many families do. Some alternate churches celebrate the vows of gay and lesbian couples, and some couples have chosen to invent their own spiritual or secular celebrations of commitment. Anniversaries are often carefully observed, although the date chosen is usually that of some significant event signifying involvement other than marriage.

Without the mechanisms of legal marriage, couples may enter into joint financial ventures and arrangements, including home ownership; may write wills to benefit one another; and may seek devices such as a durable power of attorney or a living will to give to one another the right to make medical decisions and other legal arrangements on each other's behalf, as married couples can. In the absence of such an instrument as a will, next of kin, who may be estranged, can dispossess a lover of long standing in the event of a death, which can be a significant worry to one or both partners. Laws governing such arrangements and the limits on their use differ from state to state, and people may need assistance in finding information about resources for developing these supports in their own area.

Because these are same-sex couples, sex roles usually do not define the patterns within gay and lesbian couples to the extent they may among mixed-sex couples. In the absence of more common norms, patterns of work-sharing and relating may be more egalitarian, or they may follow some reciprocal pattern invented by the participants. As in all couples, rigid and inflexible roles may come to feel burdensome or stifling to one partner or the other, or both may be unaware of the habits that have developed. As with heterosexual couples, what couples do and what they say they do about roles and work-sharing may not be the same.[62] The role of the worker, then, is to explore the wishes and feelings of both members of the couple and to help them design whatever arrangement for living seems most comfortable.

While sexuality does not define the lives or adjustment of gay and lesbian people any more than it does for heterosexuals, problems in sexual functioning can affect gay and lesbian relationships. Some of these may relate to social pressures, as partners who must suppress the expression of love and attachment outside the home may have difficulty in expressing tenderness and sexuality spontaneously and comfortably at home as well. Patterns of sexual behavior are often quite different in gay and lesbian couples. On average, lesbian couples often experience low levels of sexual activity after the first few years, and most are monogamous. Although ideologies about monogamy differ among lesbians, an affair often seems to precede the break-up of a relationship. Gay couples, on average, enjoy higher levels of sexual activity for longer and have often been stably nonmonogamous. For gay couples, sexual behavior within and outside the couple relationship has been changing because of the AIDS epidemic, and the new patterns emerging may call for new adjustments. What is important, of course, is to assist each gay or lesbian couple in achieving open communication, mutually satisfying sexual expression, and acceptable negotiation of any differences that may exist between the partners in the context of their emotional relationship.

Despite the supports that lesbian and gay couples attempt to provide for themselves, there is some evidence that these relationships may fail more often than marriages do. This fact is often attributed to the strains of homophobia and the lack of official supports and sanctions for such couples. For example, one recent study found a correlation between being open about one's sexual identity with significant others, although not distant others, and relationship satisfaction among lesbians and gays.[63] By implication, pressures to "pass" even with close associates and isolation from supportive others are hard on couples. Because there are no comprehensive data on gay and lesbian relationships to compare with official divorce statistics, any real basis for comparing the stability of gay or lesbian relationships to heterosexual ones is unavailable. It is common, however, for the break-up of a couple relationship to precipitate a crisis, when a gay or lesbian person may seek help, and the experience of loss of a significant relationship is a piece of personal history for many, if not most, lesbians and gays.

Working with Gay and Lesbian Parents

There are some special issues lesbian and gay parents and their children must deal with that the practitioner must be prepared to respond to. Divorced parents and their children often worry that the other biological parent (or even a grandparent) may seek custody, claiming that the custodial parent is unfit simply because of sexual orientation. These fears can have profound effects on how the family represents and conducts itself, both outside and inside the home.

Given the pervasiveness of homophobia, the children of lesbians and gays are also likely to be questioned, teased, or discriminated against too, and parents must help them find ways to talk about and deal with these experiences. Older children, adolescents in particular, are likely to be bothered by such incidents and may elect to try to handle them on their own. Each gay or lesbian family must be helped to acknowledge these potential or actual problems and talk together about how to deal with them.

Each gay or lesbian parent must decide how to talk with the children about his or her identity. Children too young to understand much about sex understand clearly about love; a gay or lesbian identity may best be explained in terms of loving other men or women and by differentiating love between adults from the love of an adult for a child. Sex need not be the center of the discussion, any more than it would be if a heterosexual parent were talking about his or her relationship with another parent or lover. In addition, because children identify so strongly with parents, they do need to hear that they will not necessarily grow up to be gay or lesbian just because a parent is gay or lesbian. Most of all, the parent must try to help the child ask any questions or express any fears he or she may have. The meaning of the parent's lesbian or gay identity is not a topic that can be dealt with once and set aside; rather it must be revisited and reinterpreted as children grow older and their questions change.

In gay and lesbian families with children, the definition of the role of the parent who did not bear or legally adopt the child is usually an issue for the partners. What to call the "other mommy" or the "other daddy" may be a unique challenge, and the lack of language reflects the normlessness that gay and lesbian families face. In other ways, however, the issues of how child care, housework, and employment responsibilities will be managed and shared may differ little from what heterosexual couples who become parents go through. The issues for blended families in which each partner brings offspring into the relationship may be similar as well. Asking the family about the role of each parent and how each is named and defined will validate both partners and reveal much about how the family has organized and represented itself at home and in the wider world of the extended family, the school, the workplace, and the community at large.[64]

Working with Older Lesbians and Gays

Lesbians and gays are an invisible minority in general, and older gay and lesbian people may feel invisible both in the gay and lesbian community and among older people. Ageism keeps them marginal to the gay community; homophobia keeps them marginal to elder service agencies and programs. Research has shown that stereotypes of the older lesbian or gay man as isolated, depressed, and unfulfilled are untrue; health, access to needed material resources, and social contacts that reduce loneliness all contribute to life satisfaction among older gays and lesbians, just as they do among the nongay elderly.[65]

Today's older gays and lesbians came of age in the pre–Stonewall era, and most had to come to terms with their sexual identity at a time when homophobia was even more widespread and overt than it is today. Professional mental health services were then more likely to be a source of stress than of support to lesbians and gays. Some elders may only have discovered or affirmed their gay or lesbian identity later in life, but they may still carry with them residues of the attitudes that were pervasive in their younger years.

Despite these obstacles, older lesbians and gays of today have much to offer the community. Their life stories are often tales of survival and affirmation that can instruct and inspire their younger counterparts.[66] Life review is often useful to the elderly, whose task is to consolidate a sense of the meaning of their individual lives and to understand them in the context of the historical events that have framed them. Because of the oppression they have confronted and survived, gay and lesbian elders may wish to share their stories with younger gays and lesbians as well as with family and nongay friends.

The common challenges of aging—retirement, ill health, the death of a lover or close friends—affects older gays and lesbians as well. Although many have strong social support systems, the majority will not have children to turn to when meeting these crises. Those who are sick, who care for a sick or disabled partner, or who are bereaved may find that access to the support services available to other older people in similar circumstances is not so easy for them. How can gay or lesbian partners provide for each other in retirement, illness, or after death? Will the hospital, nursing home, physician, or nurse give the gay or lesbian partner the same consideration and access to the patient a husband or wife would get? Will the widows' or widowers' group or the caregivers' support group accept a gay or lesbian member? Will the gay or lesbian elder feel comfortable in reaching out for the support that is needed?

EMERGING ISSUES AND TRENDS

The future of social work practice with gays and lesbians will build on the advances in understanding gained in the recent past and outlined in this chapter. There are some emerging issues and trends we know about today that will take the practice of social work in new directions in the years to come.

Gay and Lesbian Professionals

Many social workers are themselves lesbian or gay, some being openly identified to their colleagues as such, others not. Thus, the professional social worker must consider lesbian and gay issues in relation not only to clients and the community but also to professional relationships with students, supervisees, peers, and employers. As the Gay Liberation Movement and the professions come of age, the number of openly gay- or lesbian-identified professionals is likely to grow.

Whether or not to "come out" when seeking employment or once on the job is a major dilemma that every gay and lesbian social worker must face. Fear of losing one's job is widespread and a major factor affecting the decisions of gays and lesbians to remain closeted on their own or a partner's behalf.[67] Although documented instances of such discrimination are scant except in the military, few states have civil rights legislation explicitly protecting gays and lesbians from discrimination in hiring and other aspects of employment. Despite the provisions of the NASW Code of Ethics, few social work agencies and institutions have antidiscrimination policies of their own that explicitly mention sexual orientation, and most schools of social work also lack such protections. Workers who retain their jobs may experience social and/or professional isolation, mild harassment, or especially close scrutiny of their performance on the job.[68] For example, a recent survey of supervisors at one school of social work's field placement agencies suggested that the responses to a social work intern's "coming out" on placement might be quite variable.[69]

Providing training to all staff and support to those working with clients who are lesbian, gay, or from families with gay or lesbian members are ways both to legitimate the issues and to remove pressure from identified gay or lesbian staff to be the resident experts. Such practices are not just affirming for staff; they are therapeutic for clients as well, some of whom may be dealing with issues of sexual orientation themselves.

Many lesbian and gay professionals are very careful to ensure variety in their caseloads and work. They may do so both to protect themselves and their clients from identification by association, to enable themselves to pursue other interests, or simply to enhance their own growth and development as professionals. Others choose to specialize in serving gay and lesbian clients, both because of a commitment to serving others like themselves and because they prefer work in which openness about their lesbian or gay identity is safe, expected, and valued.

The profession, through its associations (e.g., NASW, Societies for Clinical Social Work, Association of Black Social Workers, as well as other ethnic and specialty groups) has begun to respond to minority group pressure by increasing membership education, establishing state level lesbian and gay caucuses, and sanctioning agencies who discriminate. Many more social agencies, such as child and family services and mental health clinics, have broadened their mission to serve this population. The Council on Social Work Education will in time add lesbian and gay content to the required human diversity curriculum standards and sanction those programs who continue to discriminate against lesbian and gay students, staff, and faculty. The profession has responded to similar changes in cultural ideology in the past and will continue to do so in the future.

Impact of AIDS

AIDS is our nation's number one public health crisis, and the effects of this epidemic will remain with us for many years to come. Although they are no longer the fastest growing group affected, gay men have been hardest hit by this disease. Approximately 60 percent of the total cases (150,000 in 1990) involve gay men, and over 50 percent of those diagnosed have died. It is estimated that there are perhaps 10 times as many cases of persons who are chronically ill with an HIV-related infection and 50 times as many cases of persons who are seropositive with the virus but asymptomatic. Initial perceptions of AIDS as a "gay plague" and the feelings of impunity and apathy of the general public are slowly changing. It is still difficult, however, for the public to accept that AIDS is caused by a virus, not by homosexuality itself. Lesbians have been identified as at least risk, but many of them have become active in the fight to provide adequate care for its victims.

A *Time* magazine article stated that "There is, in fact, no parallel to the anguish now being endured by America's gay men, who live in every town and city in the U.S. and total ... the combined population of all eight Mountain States."[70]

Gay men and lesbians have experienced the death of lovers, friends, and associates in staggering numbers, and, given the numbers of those infected but not yet ill, this experience will no doubt continue until a cure is found. Many have not had the opportunity to process these multiple losses. There is a pervasive sense of mourning and depression in the homosexual community which affects many aspects of life, including sexuality, and a real risk exists of reverting to more negative attitudes about homosexuality, among gays and lesbians themselves as well as among straights. This backlash has resulted in some bitterness and despair in the gay community, and fear that hard-earned gains and increased acceptance may slip away in the face of AIDS. These concerns are justified, according to Douglas, Kalman, & Kalman, whose survey of health professionals concluded that a disturbingly high percentage acknowledged more negative, hostile feelings toward gays since AIDS, and as a result AIDS patients received inferior care while hospitalized.[71]

For many homosexuals, the stresses of being different in a nonaccepting, nonunderstanding society are intensified by the AIDS health crisis. The irrational fear of AIDS, exacerbated by contradictory information along with the actual threat, has resulted in a population of "worried well."[72] These are persons at risk of AIDS because of past or present sexual activity or intravenous (IV) drug use but without a known exposure to the virus, and those who have tested HIV-positive but have not developed symptoms. Quadland and Shattls suggest that it is extremely important for mental health and other health professionals to clearly convey the message that homosexuality and sexual behavior did not cause AIDS and not allow society to blame the victims of this tragedy.[73] Without a significant effort to expand affirming mental health services, the emotional needs of gays and lesbians will continue to be met primarily through organized self-help groups.

In response to the epidemic, gays and lesbians combined their political energy and skill and assumed leadership of the Nation's efforts by organizing local, state, and national self-help efforts, developing services, advocating for patients, lobbying for expanded research and treatment funds, and pressing for protective legislation. Most local AIDS service organizations were founded by gays and continue to be influenced by gays.[74] However, in recent years there has been concerted effort to move AIDS planning, education, and service into the mainstream of health and welfare programs. This is happening as more health care providers accept their professional responsibility for the epidemic and as the profile of those infected changes from primarily white gay and bisexual men to black and Latino IV drug users, their sexual partners, and their babies. Presently the fastest growing categories of victims are minority women and their children. Because this process of mainstreaming services is quite slow and requires considerable experience, lesbians and gay men will continue to provide leadership and financial support in this effort.

Toward the Future

In the last decade, a revolution has taken place in gay people's perception of themselves. The notion of homosexuality as an individual illness has been discredited, replaced with a political definition which posits that to be gay is to be a member of an oppressed minority, similar in many ways to racial and ethnic minorities.[75] In response to oppression, lesbians and gays have organized to reinforce this new self-view and to press for civil rights that are currently denied. The future political agenda of lesbian and gay communities will include state and national activity around each of the following issues: (1) civil rights (e.g., the repeal of state sodomy laws, passage of antidiscrimination statutes, and legal recognition of relationships); (2) violence/hate crimes (e.g., protections against gay-bashing, harassment and abuse related to racism and sexism); (3) substance abuse (e.g., increased awareness of, access to, and the development of lesbian- and gay-sensitive drug and alcohol services); (4) health care (e.g., ensuring access to and the quality of gay-sensitive services, sexually transmitted disease and AIDS care, reproductive rights, new reproductive technologies such as alternative insemination, and women's health equity); (5) mental health service based on life style–affirming models; (6) community, family, and social life (e.g., custody, child, and foster care rights); (7) youth services (e.g., education, support services, and legal protections); and (8) elder care (e.g., expansion of services to reflect the increase in numbers and the different life histories and expectations of the elders of the future).

Social visibility will become the norm. Social acceptance and integration will be illusory in some sectors of society while a reality in others. Social work professionals are in a position to have an influence on many of the issues facing lesbians and gays today and in the future: civil rights, access to health and reproductive services, child custody, and adoption and foster care, to name but a few. We will all be challenged to use that influence for the good.

SUGGESTED READINGS

BELL, A. P., and WEINBERG, M. S. *Homosexualities: A Study of Diversity among Men and Women.* New York: Simon and Schuster, 1978.

BELL, A. P., WEINBERG, M. S., and HAMMERSMITH, S. K. *Sexual Preference: Its Development in Men and Women.* Bloomington: Indiana University Press, 1981.

BERGER, R. M. "Homosexuality: Gay Men." In *Encyclopedia of Social Work* 18th ed., ed. A. Minahan. Silver Spring, Md.: National Association of Social Workers, 1987.

BERGER, R. M. *Gay and Gray: The Older Homosexual Man.* Boston: Alyson Press, 1984.

BERGER, R. M. "What Is a Homosexual?: A Definitional Model," *Social Work* 28 (2), (1983): 132–135.

BOSWELL, J. *Christianity, Social Tolerance, and Homosexuality.* Chicago: University of Chicago Press, 1980.

BROOKS, V. *Minority Stress and Lesbian Women.* Lexington, Mass.: D.C. Heath, 1981.

CLARK, D. *Loving Someone Gay: A Gay Therapist's Guide for Gays and People Who Care about Them.* Millbrae, Calif.: Celestial Arts, 1977.

COLEMAN, E. *Integrated Identity for Gay Men and Lesbians: Psychotherapeutic Approaches for Emotional Well-being,* ed. E. Coleman. New York: Harrington Park Press, 1988.

Council on Social Work Education. *An Annotated Bibliography of Lesbian and Gay Readings.* Washington, D.C.: The Council, 1983.

CRAWFORD, S. "Lesbian Families: Psychosocial Stress and the Family-Building Process." In *Lesbian Psychologies: Explorations and Challenges,* ed. Boston Lesbian Psychologies Collective. Urbana: University of Illinois Press, 1986.

GONSIOREK, J. C. *Homosexuality and Psychotherapy: A Practitioner's Handbook of Affirmative Models,* ed. J. C. Gonsiorek. New York: Haworth Press, 1982.

HIDALGO, H. "Third World." In *Lesbian and Gay Issues: A Resource Manual for Social Workers,* ed. H. Hidalgo, T. Peterson, and N. J. Woodman. Silver Spring, Md.: National Association of Social Workers, 1985, pp. 14–16.

ISAY, R. A. *Being Homosexual: Gay Men and Their Development.* New York: Farrar, Strauss, & Giroux, 1989.

MENDOLA, M. *A New Look at Gay Couples.* New York: Crown, 1980.

MOSES, A. E., and HAWKINS, R. O. *Counseling Lesbian Women and Gay Men: A Life-Issue Approach.* St. Louis, Mo.: C.V. Mosby, 1982.

PAUL, W., WEINRICH, J. D., GONSIOREK, J. C., and HOTVEDT, M. E., eds. *Homosexuality: Social, Psychological, and Biological Issues.* Beverly Hills, Calif.: Sage Publications, 1982.

TRIPP, C. A. *The Homosexual Matrix.* New York: McGraw-Hill, 1975.

WOODMAN, N. J. "Homosexuality: Lesbian Women." In *Encyclopedia of Social Work* 18th ed., ed. A. Minahan. Silver Spring, Md.: National Association of Social Workers, 1987.

ENDNOTES

1. A. P. Weiner, "Racist, Sexist, and Homophobic Attitudes among Undergraduate Social Work Students and the Effects on Assessments of Client Vignettes," unpublished doctoral dissertation (New Brunswick, N.J.: Rutgers University, 1989); also see G. Appleby, "Hearing: Gay Bashing and Harassment," unpublished conference proceedings (San Francisco: NASW Annual Program Meeting, 1989).

2. W. Paul and J. D. Weinrich, "Introduction," in *Homosexuality: Social, Psychological, and Biological Issues,* ed. W. Paul and J. D. Weinrich (Beverly Hills, Calif.: Sage Publications, 1982).

3. I. Bieber, H. J. Dain, P. R. Dince, M. G. Drellich, H. Grand, R. H. Gundlach, M. W. Dremer, A. H. Rifkin, C. B. Wilbur, and T. B. Bieber, *Homosexuality: A Psychoanalytic Study* (New York: Basic Books, 1962).

4. J. C. Gonsiorek, "Psychological Adjustment and Homosexuality," in *Catalog of Selected Documents in Psychology,* 7(2), 45, MS. 1478 (Arlington, Va.: American Psychological Association, 1977).

5. A. P. Bell and M. S. Weinberg, *Homosexualities: A Study of Diversity among Men and Women* (New York: Simon and Schuster, 1978).

6. C. Zastrow, "Sexual Preference," *Human Behavior in the Social Environment* (Homewood, Ill.: Dorsey Press, 1989).

7. M. G. Shively and J. P. DeCecco, "Components of Sexual Identity," *Journal of Homosexuality* 3 (1977): 41–48.

8. A. E. Moses and R. O. Hawkins, *Counseling Lesbian Women and Gay Men: A Life-Issue Approach* (St. Louis, Mo.: C. V. Mosby, 1982), pp. 43–44.

9. J. C. Gonsiorek, *Homosexuality and Psychotherapy: A Practitioners' Handbook of Affirmative Models,* ed. J. C. Gonsiorek (New York: Haworth Press, 1982).

10. R. C. Friedman, *Male Homosexuality: A Contemporary Psychoanalytic Perspective* (New Haven, Conn.: Yale University Press, 1988).

11. S. F. Morin and E. M. Garkinkle, "Male Homophobia," *Journal of Social Issues,* 34(1) (1978): 29–47.

12. A. C. Kinsey, W. B. Pomeroy, and C. E. Martin, *Sexual Behavior in the Human Male* (Philadelphia: W. B. Saunders, 1948); also see A. C. Kinsey and P. H. Gebhard, *Sexual Behavior in the Human Female* (Philadelphia: W. B. Saunders, 1973).

13. P. H. Gebhard, "Incidence of Overt Homosexuality in the United States and Western Europe," in NIMH Task Force on Homosexuality: Final Report and Background Papers, ed. J. M. Livingood, DHEW Publication No. (HSM) 72–9116 (Rockville, Md.: National Institute of Mental Health, 1972); also see P. H. Gebhard and A. B. Johnson, "The Kinsey Data: Marginal Tabulations of the 1938–1963 Interviews Conducted by the Institute for Sex Research (Philadelphia: W. B. Saunders, 1979).

14. Bell and Weinberg.

15. N. J. Woodman, "Homosexuality: Lesbian Women," in *Encyclopedia of Social Work* 18th ed., ed. A. Minahan (Silver Spring, Md.: National Association of Social Workers, 1987); V. Brooks, *Minority Stress and Lesbian Women* (Lexington, Mass.: D.C. Heath, 1981).

16. Kinsey et al., pp. 650–651.

17. H. Hidalgo, "Third World," in *Lesbian and Gay Issues: A Resource Manual for Social Workers,* ed. H. Hidalgo, T. Peterson, and N. J. Woodman (Silver Spring, Md.: National Association of Social Workers, 1985), pp. 14–16.

18. M. C. Smith, "By the Year 2000," in *In the Life: A Black Gay Anthology,* ed. J. Beam (Boston: Alyson Press, 1986), p. 226.

19. A. Carballo-Dieguez, "Hispanic Culture, Gay Male Culture, and AIDS: Counseling Implications," *Journal of Counseling and Development,* 9/10 (68) (1989): 26–30.

20. V. M. Mays and S. D. Cochran, "Black Gay and Bisexual Men Coping with More Than Just A Disease," *Focus* 4(1) (1988): 1–3.

21. J. H. Newby, "The Effects of Cultural Beliefs and Values on AIDS Prevention and Treatment in the Black Community," a paper presented at the Annual Program Meeting of the National Association of Social Workers, San Francisco, October, 1989.

22. W. Paul and J. D. Weinrich, "Whom and What We Study: Definition and Scope of Sexual Orientation," in *Homosexuality,* pp. 26–27.

23. A. P. Bell, M. S. Weinberg, and S. K. Hammersmith, *Sexual Preference: Its Development in Men and Women* (Bloomington: Indiana University Press, 1981).

24. B. Garner and R. W. Smith, "Are There Really Any Gay Male Athletes? An Empirical Survey," *Journal of Sex Research* 13 (1977): 22–34.

25. National Association of Social Workers, National Committee on Lesbian and Gay Issues, unpublished Annual Report, August, 1990 (Silver Spring, Md.: The Association, 1990).

26. J. Bradford and C. Ryan, *The National Lesbian Health Care Survey* (Washington, D.C.: National Lesbian and Gay Health Foundation, 1988); also see M. Shernoff and W. A. Scott, *The Sourcebook on Lesbian/Gay Health Care* 2nd ed. (Washington, D.C.: National Lesbian and Gay Health Foundation, 1988).

27. Bradford and Ryan.

28. C. A. Lukes and H. Land, "Biculturality and Homosexuality," *Social Work* 35 (1990): 155–161.

29. Ibid.

30. N. Hunter and N. Polikoff, "Custody Rights of Lesbian Mothers: Legal Theory and Litigation Strategy," *Buffalo Law Review* 25 (1976): 691–733.

31. M. Mendola, *A New Look at Gay Couples* (New York: Crown, 1980); also see D. McWhirter and A. Mattison, *The Male Couple: How Relationships Develop* (Englewood Cliffs, N.J.: Prentice-Hall, 1984).

32. R. Achtenberg, "Preserving and Protecting the Families of Lesbians and Gay Men," in *The Sourcebook on Lesbian/Gay Health Care.*

33. S. K. Hammersmith, "A Sociological Approach to Counseling Homosexual Clients and Their Families," in *Integrated Identity for Gay Men and Lesbians: Psychotherapeutic Approaches for Emotional Well-being,* ed. E. Coleman (New York: Harrington Park Press, 1988), pp. 174–179.

34. Bell, Weinberg, and Hammersmith; Hammersmith, p. 177.
35. M. Kirkpatrick, K. Smith, and R. Roy, "Lesbian Mothers and Their Children: A Comparative Study," *American Journal of Orthopsychiatry* 51 (1981): 545–551; also see B. Miller, "Gay Fathers and Their Children," *The Family Coordinator* 28 (1979): 544–552; F. Bozett, "Gay Fathers: Evaluation of the Gay Father Identity," *American Journal of Psychiatry* 51(3) (1978): 173–179; R. Green, "Thirty-five Children Raised by Homosexual or Transsexual Parents," *American Journal of Psychiatry* (1978): 135; B. Hoeffer, "Children's Acquisition of Sex-Role Behavior in Lesbian Mother Families," *American Journal of Orthopsychiatry,* 51(3) (1981); S. Golombok, "Children in Lesbian and Single Parent Households: Psychosexual and Psychiatric Appraisal," *Journal of Child Psychology and Applied Discipline* 24 (1983); E. F. Levy, "Lesbian Mothers' Coping Characteristics: An Exploration of Social, Psychological, and Family Coping Resources," unpublished doctoral dissertation (Madison: University of Wisconsin, 1983).
36. Kirkpatrick, Smith, and Roy.
37. R. M. Berger, "Homosexuality: Gay Men," in *Encyclopedia of Social Work.*
38. S. Susoeff, "Assessing Children's Best Interests When a Parent Is Gay or Lesbian: Toward a Rational Custody Standard," *UCLA Law Review* 32(4) (April 1985); M. Kirkpatrick and D. Hitchens, "Lesbian Mothers/Gay Fathers," in *Emerging Issues in Child Psychiatry and the Law* (New York: Brunner & Mazel, 1985).
39. Woodman.
40. M. S. Weinberg and C. J. Williams, *Male Homosexuals: Their Problems and Adaptations* (New York: Oxford University Press, 1974).
41. Berger.
42. Ibid.
43. R. M. Berger, "What Is a Homosexual?: A Definitional Model," *Social Work* 28(2) (1983): 132–135.
44. E. Coleman, ed., *Integrated Identity for Gay Men and Lesbians: Psychotherapeutic Approaches for Emotional Well-Being* (New York: Harrington Park Press, 1988), p. 19.
45. Bradford and Ryan, p. 4.
46. L. Icard and D. M. Traunstein, "Black Gay Alcoholic Men: Their Culture and Treatment," *Social Casework* 68(5) (1987): 267–272.
47. S. C. Anderson and D. C. Henderson, "Working with Lesbian Alcoholics," *Social Work* 30(6) (1985): 518–525.
48. Brooks.
49. J. B. Bradford, "Reactions of Gay Men to AIDS: A Survey of Self-Reported Change," unpublished doctoral dissertation (Virginia Commonwealth University, 1986).
50. R. Alcalay, "Health and Social Support Networks: A Case for Improving Communication," *Social Networks* 5 (1983): 71–88.
51. Bradford and Ryan, pp. 3–5.
52. M. Coles and W. Rubenstein, "Rights of Gays and Lesbians," paper presented at the Biennial Conference at the University of Wisconsin, Madison, June 15–18, 1987.
53. Achtenberg, p. 244.
54. M. Hall, "Lesbian Families: Cultural and Clinical Issues," *Social Work* 23 (1978): 380–385.
55. Hall, p. 380.
56. Ibid.
57. K. Lewes, The Psychoanalytic Theory of Male Homosexuality (New York: Simon and Schuster, 1988).
58. A. Rosenthal, "Heterosexism and Clinical Assessment," *Smith College Studies in Social Work* 52(2) (1982): 145–159.
59. A. P. Bell and M. S. Weinberg, *Homosexualities: A Study of Diversity among Men and Women* (New York: Simon and Schuster, 1978).

60. J. Krajeski, "Psychotherapy with Gay Men and Lesbians: A History of Controversy," in *Contemporary Perspectives on Psychotherapy with Lesbians and Gay Men,* ed. T. S. Stein and C. J. Cohen (New York: Plenum, 1986).

61. C. Golden, "Diversity and Variability in Women's Sexual Identities," in *Lesbian Psychologies.*

62. A. Hochschild, *The Second Shift* (New York: Viking Press, 1989).

63. R. M. Berger, "Passing: Impact on the Quality of Same-Sex Couple Relationships" *Social Work* 35(4) (1990): 328–332.

64. S. Crawford, "Lesbian Families: Psychosocial Stress and the Family-Building Process," in *Lesbian Psychologies.*

65. R. M. Berger, "Realities of Gay and Lesbian Aging," *Social Work* 29(1) (1984): 57–62; also see M. Kehoe, "Lesbians over Sixty Speak for Themselves," *Journal of Homosexuality* 16(3/4) (1988): 1–78.

66. M. Adelman, *Long Time Passing: Lives of Older Lesbians,* ed. M. Adelman (Boston: Alyson Publications, 1986).

67. M. P. Levine and R. Leonard, "Discrimination against Lesbians in the Work Force," *Signs: Journal of Women in Culture and Society* 9(4) (1984): 700–710.

68. J. Rabin, K. Keefe, and M. Burton, "Enhancing Services for Sexual-Minority Clients: A Community Mental Health Approach," *Social Work* 31(4) (1986): 292–298.

69. K. Lewes, *The Psychoanalytic Theory of Male Homosexuality* (New York: Simon and Schuster, 1988).

70. "AIDS: A Growing Threat," *Time,* August 12, 1985, pp. 40–47.

71. C. Douglas, C. Kalman, and T. Kalman, "Homophobia among Physicians and Nurses: An Empirical Study," *Hospital-Community Psychiatry* 36 (1985): 1309–1311.

72. K. J. Harowski, "The Worried Well: Maximizing Coping in the Face of AIDS," in Coleman.

73. M. C. Quadland and W. D. Sattls, "AIDS, Sexuality, and Sexual Control," in Coleman.

74. G. A. Appleby, "What Social Workers Can Do," in *You Can Do Something about AIDS,* ed. S. Alyson (Boston: The Stop AIDS Project, 1989).

75. W. Paul, "Social and Cultural Issues," in *Homosexuality: Social, Psychological, and Biological Issues.*

Chapter 13

Social Work Practice with the Elderly

Manuel R. Miranda and Armando T. Morales

PREFATORY COMMENT

This is the most recent, "state-of-the-art" scholarly essay in the field on social work practice with the elderly. It was developed by Manuel R. Miranda, psychologist and former UCLA social work faculty member and now Assistant Director for Interdisciplinary Research, National Institute on Aging; and Armando T. Morales, Chief of the Clinical Social Work Department of the Neuropsychiatric Institute, School of Medicine, UCLA. They report dramatic demographic changes in the U.S. population, with projections that by the year 2030 the proportion of young persons and elderly will be equal.

Unless a cure is found for Alzheimer's disease by the year 2050, 14 million people will be affected, resulting in $88 billion per year in health-care costs. This figure does not measure the emotional costs which will be borne by their families. In addition, the mental health needs of the elderly are increasing, with recent research indicating up to 28 million Americans over 65 suffering from some form of mental illness. On the positive side, because of improved nutrition and health care, the elderly are living longer than ever before, with average life expectancy in 2020 estimated at 82 years for women and 74.2 for men.

Social work can play a significant psychosocial role in assisting this major population group. A case example involving an elderly couple demonstrates how micro- and macro-level practice can benefit elderly clients.

One of the most needy populations within the social work practice spectrum is that of the elderly. The fact that they represent the most rapidly increasing subgroup in the United States demands immediate attention to present as well future policy developments in relation to social service delivery systems.

In the last two decades, those sixty-five and older increased by 56 percent, while the under-sixty-five population grew by only 19 percent. The increase in the older population is expected to continue into the future. The U.S. Bureau of the Census (1984) projections estimate that the elderly will comprise from 20 to 25 percent of the total population in 2040.[1] In addition, the proportion of those aged seventy-five to eighty-four and eighty-five and over is expected to increase significantly. The U.S. Bureau of the Census (1984) estimates that in the year 2040, over 19 percent of elderly persons will be aged eighty-five or older, whereas only 9 percent of the elderly population was 85 or older in 1980. The implications of these projected growth rates will have an enormous impact on the field of social work. Issues of health care, housing, social security, and older-worker programs will generate a rapid expansion of programs and services specifically developed for the elderly.

GENERAL POPULATION FIGURES

The rapid increase in the number and proportion of older persons is reflected in the 1986 population estimates prepared by the U.S. Census Bureau (Table 13–1). As of 1986, there were 51.4 million Americans age fifty-five or older, and 29.2 million who were at least sixty-five. These two figures represent 21 percent and 12 percent of the population respectively. In reference to growth rate, it should be noted that at the beginning of this century, less than 10 percent of Americans were fifty-five or older; only 4 percent were sixty-five and above.

Life expectancies for men and women in the United States between 1900 and 1980, and the most recent projections by the Census Bureau for future increases, are presented in Figure 13–1. It is predicted that by the year 2020,

TABLE 13–1   *Distribution of the Population by Age Groups: 1986*

Age Group	Number (in thousands)	Percent
All ages	241,596	100
0 to 54	190,193	79
55 to 64	22,230	9
65 to 74	17,325	7
75 to 84	9,051	4
85-plus	2,796	1
55-plus	51,403	21
65-plus	29,173	12

Source: U.S. Bureau of the Census, "Estimates of the Population of the United States, by Age, Sex, and Race: 1980–1986," *Current Population Reports* Series P–25, No. 1000 (February 1987).

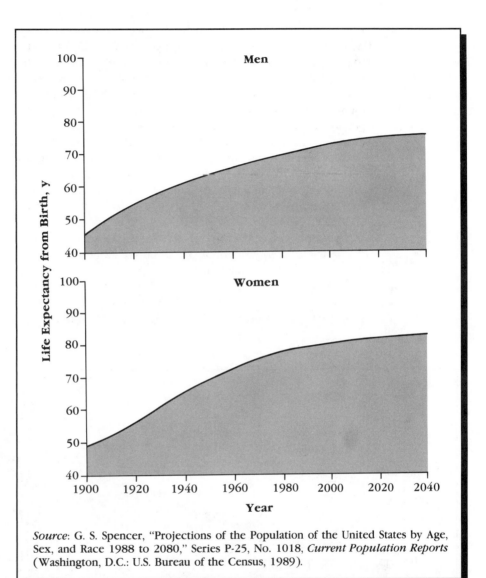

Source: G. S. Spencer, "Projections of the Population of the United States by Age, Sex, and Race 1988 to 2080," Series P-25, No. 1018, *Current Population Reports* (Washington, D.C.: U.S. Bureau of the Census, 1989).

FIGURE 13–1 *Life Expectancy for Men and Women from 1900 to 2040. From 1900 to 1980, the line represents actual life expectancy at birth. Projections are based on middle- (series 14) mortality assumptions from the U.S. Bureau of the Census.*

the average life expectancy will be 82.0 for women and 74.2 for men. By the year 2040, it is predicted that the average life expectancy will rise to 83.1 for women and 75.0 for men. This projected increase in life expectancy will raise the median age of the U.S. population from thirty-three in 1990, to thirty-six by the year 2000 and forty-two by the year 2040. Between 1985 and 2050, the total U.S. population is projected to increase by a third, while the fifty-five-plus population is expected to more than double (Figure 13–2). This shift in the proportion of elderly to young represents one of the most dramatic incidences of changing age distribution in the United States (Figure 13–3). In 1900, 4 percent of the population was age sixty-five and over, while young persons birth to seventeen years of age made up 40 percent of the population. By 1980, the proportion of sixty-five-plus persons had increased to 11 percent, whereas those birth to seventeen had decreased to 28 percent.

U.S. Census Bureau projections suggest that by the year 2030 the proportion of young persons and elderly will be approximately equal, those falling within the first seventeen years of life representing 22 percent and the elderly equaling 21 percent of the population.

The eighty-five-plus population is one of the fastest growing groups in the country. Figure 13–4 illustrates the growth of this population in relation to projected growth in the under-fifty-five population and that of three other age

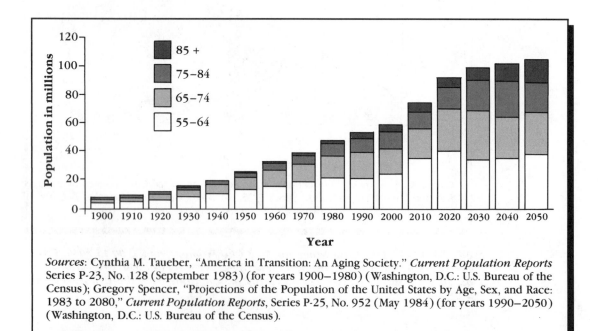

Sources: Cynthia M. Taueber, "America in Transition: An Aging Society." *Current Population Reports* Series P-23, No. 128 (September 1983) (for years 1900–1980) (Washington, D.C.: U.S. Bureau of the Census); Gregory Spencer, "Projections of the Population of the United States by Age, Sex, and Race: 1983 to 2080," *Current Population Reports*, Series P-25, No. 952 (May 1984) (for years 1990–2050) (Washington, D.C.: U.S. Bureau of the Census).

FIGURE 13–2   *Population 55 Years and Over by Age: 1900–2050*

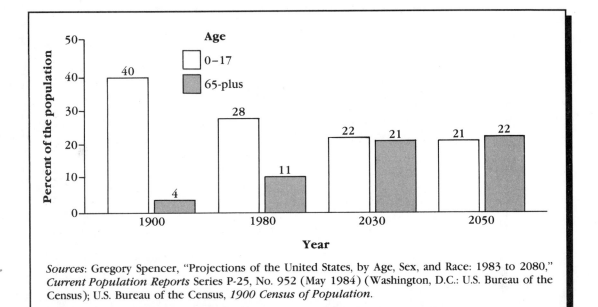

FIGURE 13–3   *Actual and Projected Distribution of Children and Elderly in the Population:*
1900–2050

groups. The eighty-five-plus group is expected to nearly quadruple between 1980 and 2030, and to be seven times as large in 2050 as in 1980. The implications of this increase in the number of individuals living past eighty-five years of age possess special significances for social workers, since it is this age group most susceptible to health problems and physical frailty. The issues of long-term care in the home setting and nursing home care represent some of our most pressing social welfare concerns.

Sex Ratios

Elderly women outnumber men three to two, a change from 1930 when they were about equal in number. In 1986 there were about 5.6 million more elderly women than elderly men. The difference between the number of men and women grows with advancing age (Figure 13–5). At ages sixty-five to sixty-nine, there were eighty-three men for every one hundred women. Among those eighty-five and older, there were only forty men for every one hundred women. Because women are more likely than men to survive to the oldest ages, the health, social, and economic problems of the oldest old are primarily the problems of women. This fact requires a significant shift in our existing social service systems if the growing need of these elderly women are to be met.

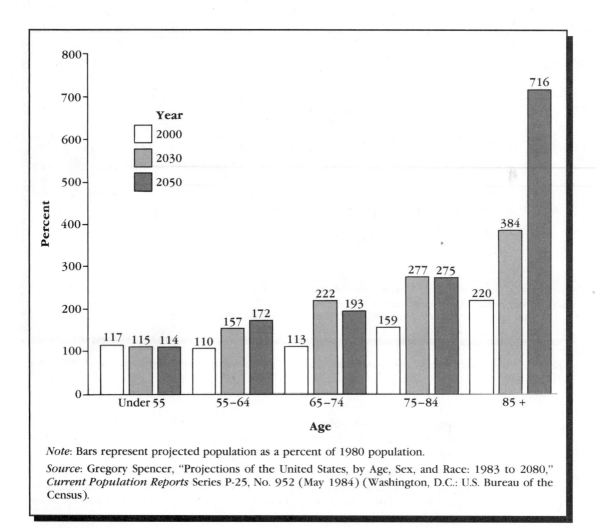

Note: Bars represent projected population as a percent of 1980 population.

Source: Gregory Spencer, "Projections of the United States, by Age, Sex, and Race: 1983 to 2080," *Current Population Reports* Series P-25, No. 952 (May 1984) (Washington, D.C.: U.S. Bureau of the Census).

FIGURE 13–4   *Projected Growth in Population, by Age Group: 1980–2050 (1980 = 100%)*

Racial and Ethnic Diversity

Although the nonwhite and Hispanic populations represent a smaller percentage of the elderly population than the white population, we can expect to see more racial and ethnic diversity among our elders in the coming years (Figure 13–6). In a 1990 projection of all those sixty-five years of age and over, 28.3 million are white; 2.6 million are black; 603,000 are other races; and 1.1 million are of Hispanic origin.[2] A 1980 census analysis indicated that there were 222,000 elderly

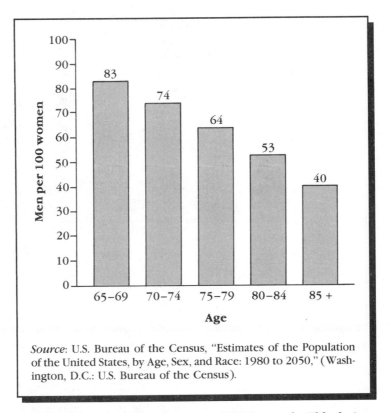

Source: U.S. Bureau of the Census, "Estimates of the Population of the United States, by Age, Sex, and Race: 1980 to 2050," (Washington, D.C.: U.S. Bureau of the Census).

FIGURE 13–5   *Number of Men per 100 Women by Elderly Age Group: 1986*

Asians and Pacific Islanders, and about 80,000 elderly American Indians, Eskimos, and Aleuts, out of a total 26 million elderly.[3]

Of the 69 million elderly projected for 2050, nearly 10 million would be black, an increase from 8 to 14 percent; 5 million would be persons of races other than white or black, an increase from 2 to 7 percent; and 8 million would be Hispanic, an increase from less than 4 percent to nearly 12 percent.[4] In essence, the minority portion of the elderly population is expected to grow rapidly, from 14 percent in 1985 to 33 percent in 2050.

Income and Assets

In general, the income level of older Americans is significantly lower than for younger adults. For the most part, this is due to retirement from the work force, with limited replacement of lost wages through Social Security and pension ben-

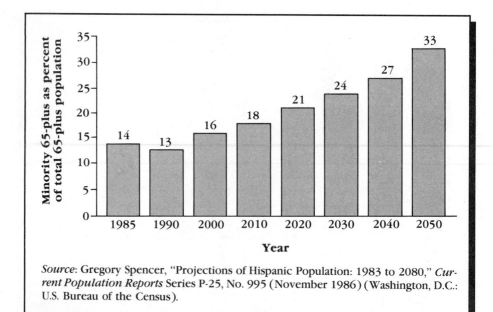

FIGURE 13–6   *Growth of the Minority Elderly Population: 1985–2050*

efits. Many elderly individuals are unable to find employment due to age discrimination in the workplace, or they are encumbered with physical disabilities preventing them from working. As a consequence, many older individuals are placed in a position of economic vulnerability frequently heightened by inflation, loss of a spouse, and increasing frailty.

While the overall economic picture for the elderly is, in general, less than satisfactory, it would be a mistake to perceive them as a homogenous group. Income differs greatly as a result of such variables as age, sex, race, living arrangements, educational attainment, and work history. Some of the elderly have considerable assets and high income levels, others have very little.

A review of simple statistical averages conceals the fact that a high percentage of the elderly have incomes below or just above the poverty level. Table 13–2 provides a straightforward comparison of those under sixty-five versus those sixty-five and over. As the table demonstrates, in 1986 the median income of families with household heads aged sixty-five and older was about 62 percent of the median income of families with household heads aged twenty-five to sixty-four. The median income of elderly individuals not living in families was about 46 percent of that for nonelderly individuals.

In recent years, there has been a changing perception of the poverty status of the elderly. Whereas one-third of all elderly had incomes below the poverty

TABLE 13–2 *Median Income of Older and Younger Families and Unrelated Individuals: 1986*

FAMILY TYPE AND AGE OF HEAD	MEDIAN INCOME
Families:	
Head 25 to 64	$32,368
Head 65 and over	19,932
Unrelated individuals:	
25 to 64	16,880
65 and over	7,731

Source. U.S. Bureau of the Census, "Money Income and Poverty Status of Families and Persons in the United States: 1986," *Current Population Reports* Series P–60, No. 157 (July 1987).

line in the 1960s, 12.2 percent of individuals sixty-five years and older were considered to be such in 1987. However, there are differences in poverty rates among the various subgroups of the elderly. Poverty increases with age, and the rates are considerably higher for the oldest old (Figure 13–7).

The 1987 poverty rates were higher for elderly blacks (31.0 percent) and Hispanics (22.5 percent) than for whites (10.7 percent). In terms of sex differences, the poverty rates are greater for elderly women than elderly men, irrespective of race or ethnicity (Table 13–3).

Educational Background

As illustrated in Table 13–4, level of education is inversely proportional to age. This trend has lessened somewhat over the past thirty years, and the decrease is expected to continue in the future. Between 1970 and 1986, the median level of education among older individuals rose from 8.7 years to 11.8 years. It is expected that with the beginning of the twenty-first century, the median level of education completed by those sixty-five years and older will be 12.4 years, relative to 12.8 for individuals twenty-five years and older.[5]

While there are no significant sex differences in educational level within the elderly population, there are considerable differences among whites, blacks, and Hispanics. Less than 20 percent of older blacks and Hispanics had completed high school in 1986, with the median level of education equivalent to an 8th grade education. For elderly whites, a little more than half had completed high school or beyond, whereas less than 20 percent of elderly minorities had done so. Approximately 21 percent of older whites had completed at least one year of college, relative to 8 percent of elderly blacks and 7 percent of elderly Hispanics.

While the elderly are reflecting higher educational levels as new cohorts enter the sixty-five-and-above bracket, the present situation seriously limits their

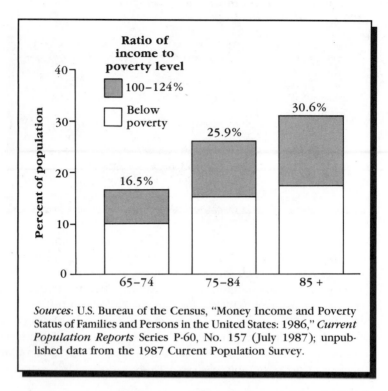

FIGURE 13–7 *Older Persons below and near Poverty Level by Age: 1986*

ability to compete for employment in the modern technological world. Alternate educational opportunities, such as extension programs at local educational institutions as well as government-sponsored vocational rehabilitation programs, are greatly needed. The role of social work in assisting the elderly to re-enter employment or remain productively employed is a challenge to the profession.

Health Status and Needs

Advancing medical interventions and preventative programs have markedly improved the health status of our elderly population. The average individual sixty-five and older generally perceives him- or herself to be in good health. In fact, 70 percent of individuals included in the 1986 Health Interview Survey conducted by the National Center for Health Statistics rated their health excellent, very good, or good relative to others their age.[6] However, given that most chronic diseases and disabilities occur in the later decades of life, the increasing aging of our population is likely to have a substantial impact on the need for medical

TABLE 13–3   *Number and Percent of Elderly below Poverty by Race, Hispanic Origin, Sex, and Living Arrangement: 1986*

| | LIVING ARRANGEMENTS OF PERSONS BELOW POVERTY LEVEL | | | | | |
| | NUMBER (THOUSANDS) | | | PERCENT | | |
RACE AND HISPANIC ORIGIN	IN FAMILIES	UNRELATED INDIVIDUALS	TOTAL	IN FAMILIES	UNRELATED INDIVIDUALS	TOTAL
White:						
Male	420	304	724	4.9	16.7	6.9
Female	442	1,523	1,965	5.3	23.7	13.3
Total	862	1,827	2,689	5.1	22.1	10.7
Black:						
Male	129	97	226	18.7	39.8	24.2
Female	144	352	496	17.8	59.8	35.5
Total	273	449	722	18.2	53.9	31.0
Hispanic[1]:						
Male	49	24	73	15.1	(B)	18.8
Female	44	87	131	12.2	55.1	25.2
Total	93	111	204	13.6	50.2	22.5
All races:						
Male	566	412	978	6.0	19.6	8.5
Female	599	1,899	2,498	6.4	26.8	15.2
Total	1,166	2,311	3,477	6.2	25.2	12.4

[1] Hispanic persons may be of any race.

(B) Percentage not shown if base population is less than 75,000.

Sources: U.S. Bureau of the Census, "Money Income and Poverty Status of Families and Persons in the United States: 1986," *Current Population Reports* Series P–60, No. 157 (July 1987); unpublished data from the March 1987 Current Population Survey.

services, long-term care, and social services. Of the 11 percent of the gross national product spent on health in 1984, one-third of the expenditures for personal health care were for older individuals.[7] The significant increase in the number of elderly individuals in the population, presently as well into the distant future, will require a substantial allotment of medical, economic, and social resources to meet their needs.

Maintenance of the quality of life for our older citizens will become an increasingly vital issue for the health and social welfare professions. Existing governmental programs such as Medicare and Medicaid are presently experiencing difficulties in covering out-patient as well as in-patient expenses. There is currently no long-term care provision in Medicare for either nursing home care or in-the-home assistance. Only those elderly individuals "spending down" to poverty are eligible for long-term nursing home care supported by Medicaid—a frightening prospect for the vast majority of our elderly.

TABLE 13–4 *Selected Measures of Educational Attainment by Age Group, Sex, Race, and Hispanic Origin: March, 1986*

Measure of Educational Attainment and Age	Total	SEX		RACE AND HISPANIC ORIGIN		
		Male	Female	White	Black	Hispanic Origin[1]
Median years of school completed:						
25 plus	12.6	12.7	12.6	12.7	12.3	11.7
65 plus	11.8	11.7	11.9	12.1	8.3	7.2
65–74	12.1	12.1	12.1	12.2	8.7	7.8
75 plus	10.1	9.6	10.4	10.5	7.4	6.2
Percent with at least a high school education:						
25 plus	74.7	75.1	74.4	76.2	62.3	48.5
65 plus	49.3	48.9	49.5	51.8	22.3	19.2
65–74	54.6	54.1	54.9	57.3	26.9	23.4
75 plus	40.7	38.8	41.8	43.1	14.4	12.0
Percent with one or more years of college:						
25 plus	36.3	40.2	32.8	37.1	26.7	20.1
65 plus	19.5	21.9	17.8	20.5	8.2	6.6
65–74	20.6	23.3	18.4	21.6	10.4	7.7
75 plus	17.7	19.3	16.9	18.8	4.5	4.5

[1] People of Hispanic origin may be of any race.

Source: U.S. Bureau of the Census, unpublished data from the March 1986 Current Population Survey.

As for the major health problems afflicting the elderly, heart disease leads all other conditions in both cause of death and utilization of health care services. As Figure 13–8 illustrates, heart disease, cancer, and stroke taken together are responsible for better than 75 percent of all deaths among the elderly. All three of these physical problems frequently lead to chronic conditions requiring long-term care.

Alzheimer's disease and other forms of dementia are major and rapidly grow-ing public health problems in the United States. Based on findings in a recent study, it is estimated that as many as 4 million people in the United States are suffering from Alzheimer's disease, with half of those age eighty-five and older thought to be afflicted.[9] Unless a prevention or cure is discovered, as many as 14 million individuals in the United States may suffer from Alzheimer's disease by the year 2050. In 1990 the cost of caring for victims of Alzheimer's disease was thought to exceed $88 billion per year. The economic and emotional impacts on the family and care providers of Alzheimer's patients are devastating.

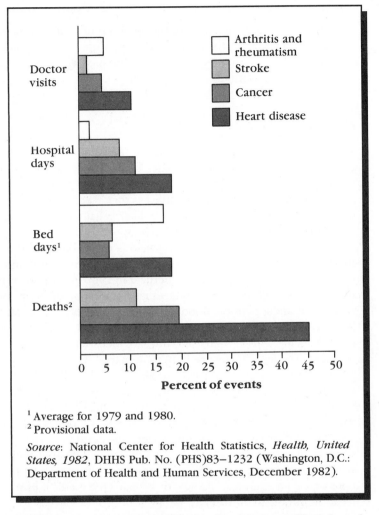

FIGURE 13–8   *Proportion of Medical Events Caused by Selected Conditions for Persons Age 65 and Older: 1980*

The elderly are more likely than younger age groups to be afflicted with multiple health problems, thus creating a synergistic effect in increasing their degree of emotional despair. This problem is particularly acute in nursing home settings, which have increasingly become the dumping ground for our mentally ill elderly.[10] The degree of mental illness coupled with the virtual absence of significant mental health treatment in nursing homes represents one of the most neglected problems in the field of mental health services in this country.

ECOSYSTEMS MODEL ANALYSIS

Any reasonable understanding of the aging process may be obtained through an interactional process providing multivariate input into the analysis of the phenomenon. The ecosystems model provides such an analytical scheme and will thus serve as the outline for this section.

Historical Factors

The diseases of the aged, the quality of their lives, their ability and willingness to care for themselves, their capacity to cope with stress—all these are shaped not only by individual histories, such as heredity and early family life, but also by the society in which the aged lived as they were growing up. What were work conditions like? What was family life like? What social services were provided? Were there economic calamities, such as a severe depression?

Certainly, the milieu of today's aged is quite different from that of the aged in 1900. There were fewer aged then, both in absolute numbers and as a percentage of the total population: 4 percent in 1900 (3 million) versus 12.0 percent in 1986 (29 million). Work was usually a lifetime affair in 1900, with formal retirement and a pension an oddity. Today, work is more a stage of life, one that is increasingly entered at an older age and left at a younger one. One pension (Social Security) is now usual, with two pensions per retiree becoming more frequent. The aged today are better educated.

Less quantifiable changes have also occurred. The belief that the aged are the fittest survivors and the mystique of old age as a time when cares are gone were shattered early in the 20th century as the realities of the lives of many of the aged became more widely known. Desperate poverty was often the reward of a lifetime of labor, since there were no pensions and no room for elderly workers in an increasingly efficiency-conscious industrial society. Illnesses often went untreated, because the aged could not afford to pay, because illness was considered inevitable in old age, or because the medical profession preferred to treat the problems of younger people.

In the early 20th century, with public support perceived as charity, with poorhouses and homes for the aged usually perceived as nothing more than warehouses for the unfit and the dying, with steady employment uncertain, and often with parents and older children all working, the family was essential for survival. Grandparents, parents, and children assumed various roles in assuring the integrity and well-being of the family. The elderly maintained their property rights, in part as insurance that they would always be cared for. There was no clear distinction between family life and work, no formal retirement age.

The elderly today reflect different experiences. Various centrifugal forces on the family—social legislation giving individuals more independence and greater mobility; more emphasis within the family on raising children and more mothers working outside the home—have distorted the traditional interdependencies between the elderly and their children and grandchildren. The Great Depression left its economic and psychological scars. A lifetime of relatively low earnings now shows up as relatively low pensions for many of the elderly. And life expectancies for men and women have changed; today most elderly women are likely to be widows.

Any effort to understand and deal with the problems of the aged must include these and other elements of their background. Similarly, social work interventions intended to help shape future policies and strengthen current ones must consider changes now occurring in U.S. society. The family today is radically different from what it was thirty-five years ago, and there is evidence of further forces for change. For example, single-parent families have become a significant phenomenon. The number of adults per household (including those with no children) dropped in 1986, to an average of two. The proportion of families living with a relative such as a grandparent (extended families) has dropped appreciably in the last forty years, and the majority of mothers now work or seek work outside the home when their children reach school age.

These facts are being interpreted by some students of family life as symptomatic of a long-term decline in relationships between parents and children—parents more involved in work or community activities, and children placed in group settings, formal and informal. Whatever the interpretation, what will be the effects of these changes on people, both parents and children, as they age? How will they as elderly adults cope with stresses, with chronic illness? What problems will they have that are not evident now among the elderly?

The needs and demands of the future aged will be different from those of today, but we are uncertain of what those differences will be. Many of the future aged will be better educated. Their Social Security pensions, increasingly supplemented by a second pension, should enable them to sustain a tolerable standard of living, although paradoxically the gap between their employment earnings and their pensions may be greater than it is for many of today's aged.

All in all, an understanding of the terrain in which the aged have lived and are living is needed if the field of social work is to perform its task of providing information and insights needed by society to optimally serve its current and future aged.

Environmental-Structural Factors

How do the elderly maintain themselves? Elderly widows and couples? Urban and rural elderly? Well-to-do, suburban white and poor, inner-city black? What perceptions do different groups of the elderly have of their lives—of health, of their status in society, of their links to younger people? How are these perceptions formed, and what do they imply about the services needed by the aged? How do these perceptions square with their needs as seen by others? How does this pattern of life prepare the individual for retirement, for the change in income, and often in status that may accompany it? How does the individual who has worked for thirty or forty years find new values to replace economic ones?

Infusing these and other questions pertaining to the aged in society are attitudes toward the aged and aging—attitudes held by the aged themselves and by the younger population. Prejudice against the aged—ageism—is displayed in several ways: (1) in our obsession with youth (although that may wane as the average age continues to rise); (2) in the emphasis by the media on extraordinary achievements of the aged, rather than on their ordinary, often satisfying lives; and (3) in the poor general understanding of the values of old age.

Anthropologists have found that the aged are regarded differently in different cultures. Gerontocracies seem to be the norm in traditional, preliterate folk societies. Urbanization, industrialization, and increased mobility may have been among the elements reducing the significance of gerontocracies and lowering the regard for old age. Continued cross-cultural research should further illuminate these elements, which are disputed. The point is that views of the aged widely held in Western societies, including the notion that the old are useless, are not shared by other societies. Bias against the old is not inevitable; rather, it is shaped by various, only partly known, forces.

One important element affecting the Western attitude toward the elderly and becoming old is the economic valuation of human worth: how much money a person makes, how big his or her house is, how much money his or her material possessions cost. In retirement, income drops markedly for most Americans, and there may be the false perception that with retirement one's income is no longer determined by work, but by pension policies. Such changes in level and source of income may result in a loss of esteem among the elderly.

In addition to ageism and the potential loss of status as a result of reduced income with retirement, the elderly generally face a number of additional stresses during the later years of life. As stated by Butler and Lewis, "The elderly are confronted by multiple losses, which may occur simultaneously: death of a partner, older friends, colleagues, relatives; decline of physical health and coming to personal terms with death; loss of status, prestige, and participation in society; and for large numbers of the older population, additional burdens of marginal living standards."[11]

The process of aging, even in the absence of health problems or loss, can be acutely distressing. Confusion and uncertainty confront the elderly as they attempt to deal with the variety of changes accompanying the aging process. Some of these changes occur slowly, such as physical appearance and social status, whereas others occur much more dramatically, such as catastrophic health problems or forced retirement. The process of aging should be visualized as a continuous stream of changes occurring within an environmental-structural setting that more or less dictates how the changes will affect the elderly. The increasing unpredictability and loss of physical and/or mental control accompanying aging, plus the inevitability of death, contribute to making this life stage one of considerable difficulty.

The sensitivity of one's environment in responding to the multitude of physical, economic, and social needs accompanying old age symbolizes its valuation of its elderly population. The diseases of the aged, the quality of their lives, their ability and willingness to care for themselves, their capacity to cope with stress—all these are shaped not only by individual histories, such as heredity and early family life, but also the environmental-structural setting in which the elderly live. This setting must provide the acceptance needed in structuring effective policies, planning effectively for the future, enabling both society and the elderly to make optimum use of available resources, and, above all, enriching the lives of the elderly.

Culture

The question as to whether an elderly culture exists remains unclear in the social science literature. Comparability to other minorities, such as ethnic or racial subgroups, as well as other age groups (e.g., teenagers), are seen by some researchers as inappropriate and lacking in clarity as to the special role of the aged in our society:

> The aged do not share a distinct and separate culture; membership in the group defined as "aged" is not exclusive and permanent, but awaits all members of our society who live long enough. As a result, age is a less distinguishing group characteristic than others such as sex, occupation, social class, and the like. True, many aged persons possess distinctive physical characteristics. But even here there is a broad spectrum, and these "stigmata" do not normally justify differential and discriminatory treatment by others.[12]

With the rapid increase in the number of individuals sixty-five years of age and older, as well as the dramatic rise in their percentage of the general population, the social and political visibility of the elderly has never been higher. A multitude of professional, political, economic, and social organizations representing the elderly have developed over the past twenty years, forcing an increased focus on both social-service and political action. However, evidence as to whether the elderly can be thought of as a separate and distinct culture remains equivocal at best. The tremendous heterogeneity among our elderly (e.g., race, ethnicity, economic status, health, sex, education level, and geographic location) makes it quite difficult to think of them as an age-segregated subculture. But they do reside within the context of an American culture that values and practices ageism, with its accompanying social, economic, and psychological consequences.

It would seem more appropriate to think of the elderly as a group with many common concerns related to their physical, social, and economic status; and that our social service delivery systems should become more cognizant of these needs in developing effective intervention modalities. The fact that the elderly are often economically vulnerable and beset with health and social problems are factors associated with the aging process, as opposed to cultural organization or process. The concept of a distinct subpopulation, however, does assist in the organization and development of social policy, planning, and service delivery.

Family Issues

With the increased aging of our society, separate generations of children, parents, and grandparents will share such experiences of adulthood as work, parenthood, and even retirement. Altered mortality and fertility patterns have resulted in the development of a new atmosphere for the building and maintenance of family relations. The fact that contemporary parents and children will spend a greater proportion of their lives together as adults than ever before in history speaks directly to the opportunity to form deep bonds of rapport and empathy. In addition, with reduced fertility rates, there are fewer individuals within the family network, thus affording the opportunity for not only a more extensive intergenerational network but a more intensive one as well.

As a result of the reduction in fertility and mortality, our society is currently confronted with a situation in which, for the first time in history, the average married couple has more parents than children.[13] With a significant reduction in the number of childbearing years, as well as a reduction in the number of years between the first- and last-born child, generation demarcations have become clearer. For most women, the active years of child-raising are over by the time they become grandmothers. And with the extension of life, grandparents are now living independently of their children for twenty-five years or more. The implications of this are not totally clear, but serving as some familial stabilizing force due to their experience, wisdom, and economic resources is a distinct possibility.

The elderly are frequently portrayed as a frail and dependent group who create a drain on our national resources and are a strain on family care-giving. There is no doubt that the oldest-old, those eighty-five and above, are in greater need of medical assistance and long-term care. Meeting the physical and social needs of our rapidly growing oldest-old represents one of the major social welfare concerns of the future. However, there are a vast number of our elderly who are healthy, independent, and willing to contribute to the enhancement of their families' well-being. In fact, available research indicates that the elderly in industrialized societies tend to give more economic assistance than they receive.[14]

The ability of the elderly to serve as a "safety-valve" within the family network can express itself in a variety of ways. They could serve as arbitrators between their children and grandchildren, specifically assisting grandchildren to understand parental responsibilities, as well as give economic back-up during the usual family problems of home ownership, educational expenses for children and grandchildren, and unexpected financial burdens. With the increasing number of separations, divorces, and single-parent households, grandparents are frequently called on to serve as stress-buffers for their children, as well as serving as substitute parents for their grandchildren.

Clearly, the changing roles of the elderly in family life include an increasing degree of multigenerational networking, with more distinct lines between the generations due to decreased mortality and fertility. The opportunities for more extensive and intensive bonding within families in an aging population could provide the basis for the strengthened interdependency necessary for meeting an individual's needs in the eighth and ninth decades of the life cycle.

Individual Issues

Self-concept among the aged has shown some interesting change throughout history. In pre-industrial eras, the elderly generally enjoyed revered status, although their numbers were much smaller than is the case today. With the advent of the industrial and post-industrial eras, however, the value placed on accumulated historical knowledge and experience has given way to innovation, creativity, and productivity. At this point the elderly were increasingly perceived as outdated, a burden on society's overall economic development. Over time, more and more employers developed strategies to remove older individuals from the work force with early retirement incentives or outright dismissal. As a consequence, the perception of growing old frequently implied being unproductive, not retrainable, and physically incapable. Many of the elderly accepted these negative stereotypes, thus creating a diminished sense of self-worth and low motivation to continue to engage society in a meaningful manner.

With the aging of our population, these negative stereotypes are beginning to change. What it means to be sixty-five and older in today's aging society differs significantly from what it meant in earlier periods. The majority of those over sixty-five today are healthy, youthful in outlook, and willing to remain actively involved in the world of work, family, and community affairs. Clearly, the elderly in contemporary society are redefining the concept of being old, particularly as it applies to societal norms of age-appropriate behavior. Old age in an aging society should be seen as a fluid concept, defined by the traits and abilities of each generation as it becomes older, not determined by past expectations and norms.

With better health and independence in the later stages of life, becoming sixty-five does not have to begin a period of withdrawal and decline. On the contrary, this period of the life cycle should represent the opportunity for renewal, with the development of new skills and goals for leading a productive life. Being productive does not necessarily imply working full time. Many of today's elderly seek part-time employment and/or full- or part-time volunteer work. With the aging of our society, never before has there been such a need to keep our older individuals actively involved in our general welfare. Likewise, with the lengthening of their lives, the elderly in turn need more than ever to remain meaningfully engaged in productive activity. The development of such opportunities in our society will greatly contribute to a continuing sense of self-worth and overall health among our elderly citizens.

INTERVENTION STRATEGIES WITH THE ELDERLY

The ecosystem model provides an excellent framework for the development of both macro and micro practice with the elderly. The inclusion of a multivariate set of factors representing the internal as well as external influences on the elderly client provides the necessary guide in structuring an effective intervention strategy. In addition, the profession of social work, with its values and interactional approach, is ideally suited to effectively serve our elderly population. With the variety of changes and needs confronting the elderly client (e.g., financial stability, acute and long-term health care needs, adequate housing, loss of a spouse and other family members, etc.), a profession such as social work, with its focus on making changes in the sociostructural environment as well as within the individual, provides the necessary practice base for effectively developing intervention strategies.

As a field of practice, the profession of social work has enjoyed a longer period of involvement with the elderly than other practice professions.[15] However, social work, as is the case with other practice professions, is frequently guilty of ageism. Butler has defined *ageism* as a "process of systematic stereotyping of and discrimination against people because they are old, just as racism and sexism accomplish this with skin color and gender. Old people are categorized as senile, rigid in thought and manner, old-fashioned in morality and skills."[16] The categorization of all elderly by a simple set of stereotypes leads to their exclusion from the more advanced techniques of social, mental, and physical health interventions. The perception of their lack of psychological abilities and skills has generally left them excluded from both public and private mental health settings.[17] The great diversity among our elderly in terms of health, income, and educational, occupational, and familial status should immediately disallow any simplistic perception of who they are and what can be done for them. Although their health status may be more vulnerable, the elderly are more often than not very much as they were during earlier periods of their life cycle. To think of them as diminished representatives of their former selves results in two failures: one's effectiveness as a social work practitioner; and meeting the needs of a worthy elderly client.

In general, the development of any intervention strategy for the elderly, whether macro or micro, should have as its basic objectives (1) the promotion of independence to the maximum degree possible; (2) assistance in obtaining the necessary resources for the maintenance of a good quality of life; (3) facilitating effective interaction between the elderly and others in their environment; and (4) influencing the development of social policy enhancing their lives. As noted by Cantor, "Basic to the concept of social care is the notion that assistance is provided as a means of augmenting individual competency and mastery of the environment, rather than increasing dependency."[18] With these premises in mind, mental health services for the elderly will be discussed, accompanied by an example of a macro and micro intervention.

MENTAL HEALTH AND THE ELDERLY

While the problem of mental illness occurs in all age groups, America's elderly represent one of our more seriously afflicted populations. Recent studies suggest that between 15 and 25 percent of the 28 million Americans over the age of sixty-five suffer from some form of mental illness.[19] As many as 7 million elderly Americans may be in need of mental health services, a figure that would be considered epidemic in any other health context. The factors responsible for the high degree of emotional disruption among the elderly are multiple, but the increasing degree of alienation from significant societal responsibility, fragmented family support systems due to loss of spouse and mobility of children, and declining physical health and/or the demands of caring for a chronically ill spouse contribute to increased feelings of alienation and hopelessness. Depression, for instance, is a major problem whose seriousness cannot be overestimated, especially in light of the fact that elderly men over the age of seventy-five display one of the highest suicide rates of all age categories. Alcohol abuse is increasing in its degree of severity among the elderly, as is the misuse of prescription drugs. All of these represent reactions to feelings of severe stress and alienation. The elderly are also more likely than younger age groups to be afflicted with multiple health problems, thus creating a synergistic effect in increasing their degree of emotional despair. This problem is particularly acute in nursing home settings, which have increasingly become the dumping ground for many of our mentally ill elderly, as an alternative to state institutionalization.[20] The degree of mental illness, coupled with the virtual absence of significant mental health treatment in nursing homes, represents one of the most neglected problems in the field of mental health services in this country.

Unfortunately, the lack of mental health services to the elderly is not limited to nursing home settings. The elderly, while comprising 12 percent of the American population, represent only 6 percent of all persons served by community mental health centers, and only 2 percent of those served by private therapists.[21] The underrepresentation of the elderly among recipients of mental health services, in both the public and private sectors, directly reflects the lack of sensitivity within the mental health system to the mental health problems and needs of our elderly population.

Existing mental health service delivery systems have generally failed to recognize the diverse nature of our elderly population. The depressed elderly female living alone, the severely stressed and overwhelmed elderly male attempting to care for his Alzheimer's-afflicted wife, the economically deprived elderly couple forced to live with their children represent a few examples of the multitude of life-stress situations the elderly confront. Increased vulnerability in the health, economic, and social areas of life would seem to justify the expectation that the elderly would be among the most active utilizers of existing mental health services. The fact that they do not use these services speaks directly to the various impediments preventing effective access.

Traditionally, ageism has prevented many mental health professionals from servicing the elderly, in the belief that therapeutic efforts with older people are likely to be difficult or unproductive. The focus on younger clients, both at the professional practice level and in the training setting, has prevented an understanding of and sensitivity to the special needs of the elderly client. Unfortunately, reversal of this trend is frequently confounded by the elderly themselves. Long-standing negative stereotypes of the mentally ill and "snakepit" institutions frequently prevent the current cohort of elderly from seeking needed services. The end result is that many of them are reluctant to admit to emotional problems and tend to recategorize the situation as either a moral problem, thus seeking assistance from the church, or as a physical problem, resulting in visits to a physician.

A number of practical barriers contribute to the limited access of the elderly to receiving mental health services. Misinformation, coupled with the lack of even the most basic knowledge about the availability of mental health services, contribute to the underutilization problem. Even the healthy, more mobile elderly are frequently discouraged from seeking mental health services due to poor service locations and/or settings lacking environmental sensitivity (e.g., not employing "seniors" in key staff positions) in helping the elderly to seek assistance. In addition, many of the elderly are intimidated by the often-confusing regulations and paperwork imposed by federal and state programs. The fragmentation of the service delivery system, encompassing the processing of each case only as part of a treatment plan and its accompanying red tape, provides a strong disincentive to continue treatment.

The lack of mental health services specifically for the elderly is particularly problematic. Recent research demonstrates that participation by the elderly in community mental health center programs could more than double if there were services specially designed for the elderly and staffed with trained mental health professionals.[22] Unfortunately, the consolidation of federal support of mental health services into a block grant, as mandated by the Omnibus Budget Reconciliation Act of 1981, has resulted in a dramatic decrease in funding. As of 1985, nearly 40 percent of the community mental health centers surveyed reported reductions in service delivery to older persons.[23] Almost half of these centers lacked staff with special training in geriatric mental health, and a similar number reported having no specialized services for the elderly.

The health care system in this country must be strengthened and restructured so as to encourage the improved delivery of desperately needed mental health services to our nation's elderly. These services should include a variety of support systems for both the elderly and their families and caregivers. Mechanisms are needed to ensure not only that elderly persons and their families have access to the full range of needed services, but that these services be appropriately modified to meet the special needs of the various elderly populations. While admittedly a difficult task, current research demonstrates that increased cooperation between federally funded area agencies on aging and community-based mental health centers has dramatically improved service utilization rates, even among our most difficult-to-reach elderly.[24] Coordination and cooperation among agencies whose responsibilities involve successful aging, health, and mental health must be ensured if the elderly with mental health needs are to be served adequately.

Micro Practice with the Elderly

What follows is a case example of social work practice with elderly clients. It highlights the special nature of the elderly's problems, which at times require a different intervention response from social workers than would be so with younger clients.

Background

Mr. and Mrs. Soto, age seventy-five and seventy-three respectively, are an elderly Mexican American couple living in a lower-income Hispanic section of El Paso, Texas. Mr. Soto, who had six years of formal education, came to the United States as an immigrant laborer in his early twenties. He eventually settled in El Paso as a laborer with the Southern Pacific Railroad. Mrs. Soto, who also had six years of formal education, was raised as an orphan in Northern Mexico and immigrated to Los Angeles with an older sister in her late teens. The couple met in El Paso, married, and raised two sons and a daughter. The eldest son was killed in Vietnam, leaving the second-born daughter and the younger son.

Strained Family Relationships

While the Sotos had a close and caring relationship, their children experienced severe difficulties with the acculturation process. Their daughter became pregnant in her middle teens, dropped out of high school, and eventually married. Their son was heavily involved in gang activities as a youth and was in and out of the penal system. The son "grew out" of gang activities and now is supporting a wife and three children as a mechanic in a local El Paso auto shop. As a result of the children's problems during their earlier years, the relationship between Mr. Soto and his children is seriously strained. The son feels particularly rejected by his father, believing that he always favored the eldest son who was killed in Vietnam. In the early years, Mrs. Soto frequently attempted to intervene on behalf of her adolescent children, but was generally forced to accept Mr. Soto's negative perception of his children's behavior and life style. Mr. Soto has not spoken with his daughter in over five years, and only rarely visits his son on holidays or special occasions. Mrs. Soto has maintained telephone contact with both of her children.

Cultural Factors

Although Mr. and Mrs. Soto are bilingual, they have always felt more comfortable speaking Spanish. Since Mr. Soto's retirement seven years ago, the couple has spoken Spanish almost exclusively. Neither has been actively involved in the political or social life of the community. They have been content during their married life to regularly attend the local Catholic church, as well as annual cultural events marking significant Mexican holidays. Both have always been actively involved in their garden on weekends, being proud of their skills. On retirement, Mr. Soto also began spending a couple of afternoons during the week at a social club developed for retirees (mostly Hispanic) by the Southern Pacific railroad.

Health Crisis Changing Traditional Roles

Mrs. Soto's activities mainly consisted of taking care of her husband, talking to her children and grandchildren on the telephone, maintaining her garden, and attending church on the weekends. Over a five-year period, Mrs. Soto's visits to the local comprehensive health clinic became more frequent, since she suffered from osteoporosis and had fractured her hip in a fall six months before. Following two months of hospitalization, she was released to be cared for at home by her husband.

After fifty-one years of marriage, Mr. Soto was now placed in the position of being the caregiver instead of the care receiver. While at first assuring his wife and hospital staff that he could manage her care on his own, Mrs. Soto's minimal healing and limited mobility began to overwhelm him. He began to feel guilty about his anger at her dependency and too proud to accept his estranged daughter's request that she be allowed to help out. Mr. Soto's son was having severe difficulties meeting his own family's needs and wasn't sure how to approach his father to offer whatever help he could give. Mr. Soto was not particularly good in providing clarity to his son as to now he could assist anyway.

Physical and Emotional Decompensation

As the months passed and his wife's condition was not improving, Mr. Soto became withdrawn and depressed. Mrs. Soto had regressed to the point of requiring her husband's assistance in bathing and toilet needs. He found these activities particularly distasteful and became increasingly impatient with his wife's requests. Sensing her husband's discomfort and feeling increasingly guilty about her dependency, Mrs. Soto attempted to take care of her own toilet needs and fell, refracturing her hip. She was immediately rehospitalized, with a prognosis of long-term nursing home care. She went home temporarily, awaiting Mr. Soto's decision.

Limited Resources

The hospital social worker informed Mr. Soto that nursing home care would cost approximately $28,000 per year. Considering that Mr. Soto's total yearly income from his railroad pension and Social Security came to approximately $22,000 per year, placing his wife in a private nursing home was out of the question. Since Mr. Soto, a homeowner, was not sufficiently impoverished to qualify for Medicaid, his only alternatives were to attempt to care for his wife in their home again, or spend down to the poverty level required to qualify for Medicaid. Neither of Mr. Soto's children were in a position to help financially. With their Medicare eligibility quickly reaching its limits, Mr. Soto became increasingly despondent. He stopped answering his telephone. Following a telephone call from the hospital social worker, Mr. Soto's son went to his father's home to find him in a deeply depressed state and cognitively disoriented. He kept mentioning that there was no hope and that both he and his wife would be better off dead, as they were now useless and of no benefit to society. "Ni para que vivir," Mr. Soto remarked. Hearing this frightened the son, who the following day called his old parole officer asking for advice. The parole officer referred the son to the local community mental health program.

The Initial Plea for Help

The son phoned the El Paso Community Mental Health Center (EPCMHC) and spoke to the intake worker, who in turn referred him to Ms. Lewis, a twenty-seven year old Anglo social worker. The son explained his father's situation and the fact that he wanted to die. Ms. Lewis explained that she did not speak Spanish and asked if the father spoke English. She was assured that the father spoke English but was more fluent in Spanish. Because the only Spanish-speaking therapist at the EPCMHC was already overextended with Spanish-speaking clients, and because of the urgency of the case, Ms. Lewis decided to accept the case herself. Ms. Lewis asked the son to have his father call for an appointment.

Client, Worker, Intervention Model, and Agency Resistance

The following day the son reported to Ms. Lewis that he had talked to his father but that his father did not want to see Ms. Lewis because he was not crazy. Ms. Lewis did not want to see the father unless he was motivated for help. The son was very worried about his parents and pleaded with Ms. Lewis to visit his father at home. Ms. Lewis thought to herself that this would be counterproductive, might stimulate transference, and might be considered overidentifying with the client. Furthermore, the agency frowned on home visits. The son by now was near tears and was pleading for Ms. Lewis's help. Finally Ms. Lewis stated that she would make an exception to visit the father at home, if he agreed to join her for the visit. Sighing with relief, the son agreed.

Visiting the Involuntary Client

The son and Ms. Lewis arrived at the home unannounced, and the father seemed annoyed and made a comment in Spanish to the son. The son appeared to be pleading with the father. The mother's voice from the bedroom inquired as to what was going on. The son replied that he had asked Ms. Lewis to come over to see if she could be of some help. Mrs. Soto invited Ms. Lewis to the bedroom, and at this point the father criticized the son's bad manners and asked him to prepare coffee and Mexican bread for their guest. Mr. Soto observed how well Mrs. Soto and Ms. Lewis were interacting and began to smile, seeing how responsive his wife was. Ms. Lewis then involved the husband in the conversation and remarked in a supportive, concerned way that their life had certainly changed since Mr. Soto's retirement and Mrs. Soto's physical injuries. The son was standing at the door listening, prompting the father to reestablish his position of authority by asking his adult son not to listen in on "grown-up conversations." The son smiled and thanked Ms. Lewis for visiting the parents, adding that he had to return to work.

Transforming the Involuntary Client to a Voluntary Client

Ms. Lewis did not want to stay long, as she did not want to impose on the Sotos. She excused herself, stating she had to return to the office. Mrs. Soto stated she enjoyed the visit and hoped she would return. Mr. Soto offered to walk Ms. Lewis to her car, commenting on how much she had helped his wife and made her smile again. Ms. Lewis said she noticed that he also had been smiling at times and wondered whether he sometimes felt lonely, isolated, unsupported, and over-whelmed with all of his responsibilities. He nodded in agreement. Ms. Lewis, handing her card to Mr. Soto, stated that if he wanted to talk more about these matters, he could phone her. He looked at the card, replied that he was not crazy, and said he had heard they saw "locos" at her clinic. Ms. Lewis stated that they did see a few people who needed medication to help them think more clearly, but that the majority of people were just like him and everybody else—struggling with problems of daily living.

Engagement Phase

A few days later Mr. Soto phoned for an appointment to see Ms. Lewis. Although he kept his first appointment, he was a little nervous and mostly spoke about his wife and *her* problems. He did not want his wife to know he was visiting Ms. Lewis. In the initial interviews Ms. Lewis assumed a tactful, supportive approach, not wanting to frighten or embarrass Mr. Soto. She observed him to be depressed and asked whether there were times when he just wanted to give up and run away. He became serious as his eyes reddened, stating firmly that he never would run away from anything, as a man always faces his responsibilities. The following week Mr. Soto stated that he wondered if not wanting to live, or wanting to die, was a form of running away. Ms. Lewis explored this further and made a deter-mination that Mr. Soto had suicidal thoughts, but was not suicidal, as he did not have a specific plan or give indications of a major depression. Ms. Lewis assured Mr. Soto that his depression was in response to his wife's physical condition. He denied this, stating that it was due "to other things," but would not elaborate, adding that she just would not understand.

Transference and Countertransference

The following week Ms. Lewis explored what he had meant about "other things." He became annoyed, stating that she was too young to know, probably not mar-ried, and that this was something related to men and she could not help. Ms. Lewis became defensive, stating that she was not too young, was married, had children, and knew something about male impotence. Mr. Soto was not familiar with the word *impotence.* Ms. Lewis, red-faced and in a clumsy manner, tried to explain what impotence was, using her index finger to demonstrate. Mr. Soto burst out laughing, stating that it had *never* happened to him, and that young Ms. Lewis looked funny explaining this to a man with sixty-three years of sexual experience. Ms. Lewis became aware of her embarrassment, anger, and anxiety and recalled how once her own father had tried to speak with her about sex when she was a young adolescent. She also became aware of the fact that she was perhaps stereotyping Mr. Soto as an old man who had lost his sexual ability and desire.

Culture versus Situation

This brief emotional confrontation "broke the ice," as Ms. Lewis by now was also laughing, pointing to her finger. She then said, "Really, tell me what is happening." Mr. Soto stated that he had always had a big sexual appetite but that since the injuries of his wife, she was not able to meet his sexual needs. He stated that he had taken younger women that he was meeting at the retirement club out for sex. Initially he enjoyed this, but then he began feeling guilty because it was against his religious and cultural beliefs. He was feeling unfaithful to his wife, who was ill. The more he did this, the worse he felt, and he was unable to face her. Ms. Lewis initially thought that Mr. Soto's "fooling around" was simply a Latin cultural requirement for males, but then realized that Mr. Soto was an honorable, religious man who was ashamed of his unfaithfulness. Ms. Lewis reminded him about how she had once raised the concept of "running away" from problems and asked if this wasn't an example of that. He seemed puzzled and replied that it could be seen that way. She also asked whether being overwhelmed with financial and caring responsibilities for his wife, "a person might not want to live." He acknowledged that possibility but argued that taking one's life was more of a *solution* to a problem than running away. Ms. Lewis did not want to argue the point; she left him with his dignity and a sense of control over his life.

Client Involvement in Planning

At the sixth session Ms. Lewis inquired about Mr. Soto's response to their meetings, and he commented that he found them helpful and that even though she was young and inexperienced in life, she had made him think about things in a different manner. He hadn't been "fooling around," but his desire for sex was building, he remarked with the wink of an eye. Prior to her medical condition, Mrs. Soto had been fulfilling his sexual desires. Ms. Lewis commented that with his and his wife's permission, she could speak to her physician about any possible limitations she might have. Mr. Soto thanked her for this, stating that he would just feel too uncomfortable discussing this with his wife, as he did not want to hurt her. Furthermore, he did not think he could talk to the physician because "they all use such big words." Ms. Lewis inquired if Mr. Soto wanted to continue with their weekly problem-solving meetings. He stated that they had been helpful to him but wondered how they could be more helpful to his wife, especially not knowing what to do if he couldn't take care of her at home. "I just don't understand it all. All these people and agencies talk so much about what they're going to do for my wife, but nothing gets done. That's when I feel down and useless." Ms. Lewis agreed that at times it became very complicated, but at the next meeting, *together* they would try and figure what had to be done.

Macro Practice with the Elderly

Identifying Resources

Prior to her next meeting with Mr. Soto, Ms. Lewis set up a consultation with an EPCMHC social work colleague who was in charge of a senior citizens' daycare program. On hearing of Mr. Soto's situation, the colleague informed Ms. Lewis of the services provided by the El Paso Area Agency on Aging (AAA), as mandated by the National Older Americans Act. Ms. Lewis was pleasantly surprised to learn that in addition to neighborhood senior citizen centers providing midday meals, AAAs were capable of arranging homemaker support programs at the neighborhood Senior Citizens' Center. In addition, Ms. Lewis was informed that a national senior citizens' organization had recently set up a demonstration project in El Paso to provide special health services for the elderly Hispanic population.

Sharing Information with the Client

Following further information-gathering on available support programs for the elderly population, Ms. Lewis scheduled her next meeting with Mr. Soto. The meeting proved to be a real "eye opener" for Mr. Soto. He was delighted to learn that he could receive assistance, in the home, in meeting his wife's daily-living activities as well as special transportation to assure that she was able to keep her medical appointments. Of particular interest to Mr. Soto was Ms. Lewis's description of the special health demonstration projects being set up for the Hispanic elderly. These projects contained a physical rehabilitation program directed at reducing frailty among the elderly as well as increasing their independence. Mr. Soto inquired as to his wife's ability to benefit from such a service and was informed that she was a prime candidate, since one of the major goals of the rehabilitation program was building muscle mass and bone density. The prospect of reversing his wife's current state of dependency to that of increased mobility, physical strength, and independence brought a smile to Mr. Soto's face. Perhaps he really could have his wife back as he knew her prior to her hip fractures.

Toward Culturally Sensitive Practice

Ms. Lewis informed Mr. Soto that the rehabilitative process would take some time, but with the assistance of the in-home support services, daily meal, and transportation provided by the El Paso AAA, Mrs. Soto had a good chance of resuming her normal activities. Mr. Soto acknowledged his gratitude for such assistance but pondered his existing sexual needs and lack of social outlets, since he refused to return to the Southern Pacific social club due to his sense of guilt. Ms. Lewis mentioned that her agency sponsored a senior citizen day care program that included a weekly support group for senior citizens undergoing emotional stress. Mr. Soto inquired as to the composition of the group and was informed that it consisted of mostly white, elderly females, with an occasional Hispanic. This disturbed him, and he relayed his disappointment to Ms. Lewis as to her agency's lack of cultural sensitivity in not sponsoring a support group for elderly Hispanics with problems similar to his. Ms. Lewis gave careful consideration to Mr. Soto's concerns and then asked what *they* should do about the problem.

Building on Family Strengths

Following several more individual sessions between Mr. Soto and Ms. Lewis, it was decided that Ms. Lewis would contact the national senior citizens' organization sponsoring the rehabilitation program in which Mrs. Soto was participating, to inquire about helping with the problem. It was quickly discovered that although the rehabilitation project had been developed as a basic medical intervention strategy, they had received numerous requests for greater involvement of the healthy spouse in his or her mate's rehabilitation. A quick survey noted that approximately 70 percent of the patients were females, thus providing a cadre of Hispanic men who could be recruited to participate in a support group.

The sponsoring organization quickly agreed to participate in organizing a support group and asked Ms. Lewis to assist them.

Client Involvement in Treatment Planning

In further conversations with Mr. Soto, Ms. Lewis inquired as to whether he felt the support group should be all male or a mix of males and females. Ms. Lewis argued that a mixture of males and females would help the two sexes appreciate the differences and similarities in their problems as well as how to resolve these problems. Mr. Soto argued that it would be culturally inappropriate to have Hispanic men and women openly discussing their sexual problems and opted for an all-male group.

Group Support

Mr. Soto entered an all-male, English-speaking seniors' support group comprised of non-Hispanic whites and a few Hispanics. He was relatively quiet during the first few sessions, but at the third session he announced that he thought he had entered a sex therapy group but they had not been discussing sex. Mr. Green, the social work leader of the group, asked if he felt he had a sexual problem. Mr. Soto replied that he had, in that he had "desires" and his ill wife was unable to fulfill his needs. One of the "old timers," Mr. Gonzalez, who had been in the group about a year, commented to Mr. Soto that a few members in the group had had a similar problem and solved it by having visits as needed with "Manuela." "Where do I find Manuela?" Mr. Soto innocently asked. "In either your right or left hand," whispered a laughing Mr. Gonzales. As the group laughed, Mr. Soto joined in, adding "Oh, *that* Manuela. I had forgotten about her!"

A Different Ending

In the following months, Mr. Soto felt increasingly supported and enjoyed "his group." He had now terminated with Ms. Lewis. Contributing to his improved morale was also the gradual but steady improvement of Mrs. Soto's health. It was hard for Mr. Soto to believe that just four months previously he had been thinking of taking his *and* his wife's lives!

EMERGING ISSUES AND TRENDS

With the aging of our population, increasing concern for the maintenance of the quality of life among our elderly will continue to be one of our major societal goals. The extension of life and the compression of the morbidity period serve as ideal objectives in assuring that our elderly citizens lead full, productive, and satisfying lives, with minimal dependency and physical and mental deterioration prior to death.

There are those who believe that with emerging patterns of physical and psychological health behavior and more widespread preventive medicine, the total proportion of elderly living in states of dependency will significantly decrease, thus lessening the need for both informal and formal care.[25] Others paint a much more negative picture, with widespread assumptions of a serious shortage in our ability to meet the health care needs of our elderly in the near and distant future.[26] While the truth may lie somewhere in between, we can be assured that our present as well as future elderly citizens will be major utilizers of our public and private health, economic, and social welfare resources.

Solutions to the problems that will confront our service delivery system must represent a combination of economic and social change, from both the public and private sectors. The following macro-level recommendations represent those issues most pertinent to the field of social work and should be evaluated in that context.

Economic Improvements

The problem of economic deprivation among our elderly can generally be traced back to their employment histories prior to age sixty-five. Income inequality during their working life translates into income inequity in retirement. The vast majority of those elderly who have labored in low-income occupations with minimal or no benefits will generally end up with inadequate retirement benefits and savings. Efforts to change this situation must be directed at existing federal programs. The Social Security program must be modified to provide increased benefits for those elderly individuals having worked many years at minimum wage levels or experienced extended periods of unemployment. As the Social Security Trust Fund becomes increasingly solvent, this should become possible. Infusion of additional general revenues into Social Security would provide the rest of the resources for the implementation of such a program.

The Supplemental Security Income (SSI) program represents the federal government's intention to provide a safety net of income support for the poorest and most vulnerable of our older, blind, and disabled citizens. However, this program only brings needy individuals up to 75 percent of the poverty level and currently reaches only one-half of those who are eligible. Many potentially eligible recipients of SSI fail to apply for the benefits, due to the complexity of the forms and lack of publicity of its existence. In addition, SSI has an asset eligibility test, the cutoff for which has been cut in half by inflation since 1974. And there is an additional problem for those minority elderly unable to read, write, or speak English, since they must provide their own interpreter at the local SSA office.

Clearly, SSI revision is a must if we are to reduce the increasing percentage of our elderly living in poverty. The fact that minority elderly are six times more likely to be on SSI than white elderly provides a solid rationale for improving the benefits.

As a third recommendation, legislative action to increase the minimum wage level would significantly assist those individuals currently working in these types of positions, as are many within our minority populations. The current minimum wage provides only 73.6 percent of the projected poverty level for a family of three; and there are currently 8 million individuals working at minimum wage or less. A disproportionate percentage of these are minorities. Improved income levels for individuals in these positions will have a direct impact on their future Social Security benefits.

Housing Improvements

The family and all its associated responsibilities are among the most treasured experiences for the elderly. Proximity to family members is significant in urban as well as rural settings. Proximity is particularly sought out by the elderly as they strive to maintain intergenerational continuity with their children and grand-children. Thus housing is of critical importance in affording the elderly the opportunity to remain in the community, near their families.

Existing federal housing programs have created barriers to the maintenance of extended family relationships. Low-income housing projects are generally located away from minority communities, with occupancy limited to an elderly couple or single person. Housing assistance in the form of vouchers requires searching for apartment units that are difficult to find, frequently unaffordable, and again located outside the community.

Clearly, significant modification of our national housing policies must be undertaken if we are to meet the needs of those elderly most in need of this form of assistance.

The first general goal on an improved national housing policy for the elderly is freedom of choice. They must have the opportunity to choose the type of housing and living environment that best reflect their preferences and needs. Thus some elderly may prefer to stay in their own homes as long as possible, while others may prefer some type of group quarters. Likewise some elderly prefer living in neighborhoods relatively balanced in age composition, while others prefer age-segregated retirement communities. The goal of freedom of choice means that a one-dimensional housing policy emphasizing only a few choices is unacceptable.

A second general goal, clearly related to freedom of choice, is that housing policy should be designed to preserve or sustain independent living situations as long as possible. There is considerable agreement that those elderly who prefer to remain in their own homes should be allowed to do so, and that public programs sustaining independent or noninstitutional living should be made available. This particular recommendation has great relevance for our minority elderly, since it provides the opportunity to maintain intergenerational relationships and cultural continuity. This suggests that more attention be paid to services and support facilitating independent-living status.

A third goal provides for adequate housing assistance and services. These could take the form of direct financial or income support through housing allowances, or income supplements enabling the elderly to secure the type of housing best meeting their needs, while staying within their limited financial resources. Housing counseling programs for the elderly enable them to select the most appropriate living arrangements to maintain intergenerational continuity. In addition, service programs providing homemaker services, home repairs, home-delivered meals, and special transportation increase the ability of the elderly to maintain independent or semi-independent existence within their communities.

Effective housing assistance for the minority elderly must incorporate a multifaceted and flexible set of policies and programs. Freedom of choice, coupled with effective support services, will greatly prolong the ability of minority elderly to remain in their communities, continuing the intergenerational dialogue so critically important to their cultural identity. Current housing policies limiting choices will only continue to fragment minority families. Future legislation must appropriate resources for the development of creative alternatives and maintenance of aging "in place."

Enhancing Health: The Need for Continuing Care

The elderly's ability to obtain adequate health care services is frequently reduced by their low-income levels and lack of health insurance. The relationship between income, the cost of care, and access/utilization of services is complex and not well understood. As the cost of health-related services continues to rise, people of limited financial means will obviously be disadvantaged. Among the elderly, women, minorities, and those living alone are particularly vulnerable; their limited social support systems are unable to compensate for inadequate economic resources. Providers of continuing care services favoring self-paying clients find the elderly among the least attractive potential clients. Medicare and Medicaid are limited in the extent to which they cover continuing care services—particularly those delivered outside nursing homes, where the vast majority of the elderly reside.

Medicare is primarily designed to cover hospital care for acute illnesses. While this program has benefitted the elderly in meeting acute care needs, its lack of coverage for chronic care is a significant limitation. Medicare coverage for the low-income elderly is expensive. As a result of the rising costs of co-insurance rates and deductibles, the elderly are paying more for health care now than before the enactment of Medicare. By 1988, the hospital deductible alone had increased 252 percent in real dollars since the enactment of Medicare in 1966.

Much has been written about the fragmented nature of continuing-care service in the community. Poorer, less-educated and less-informed elderly are victimized the most by this fragmentation. They are bounced from one provider system to another, each with its own (often conflicting) eligibility criteria. Recently there has been a significant promotion of case management to reduce the existing barriers and fragmentation in elderly health services. Case management can be of help to the elderly, but only to the extent that they can access the services. The elderly need to be educated in case management as an effective tool in receiving services; and such services need to be developed in communities where the elderly reside. For case managers, a full understanding of the sources of continuing care, both formal and informal, within the community is a must. Case managers also need to fully understand those cultural factors influencing preferences for care arrangements within elderly minority populations.

Lack of cultural sensitivity in the design and delivery of services has a negative impact on the retention of minority elderly clients after they enter the service system. Use of appropriate language, traditional leisure activities, ethnically familiar foods, and acknowledgement and celebration of cultural holidays are examples of enhancements of the quality of life in continuing-care facilities for ethnic-minority elderly. Attention to these factors in the delivery of services to the home, adult day care center, and nursing home would significantly improve the participation of the ethnic minority elderly in these programs.

While improvements in the development and delivery of continuing-care service to the elderly are greatly needed, in reality the vast majority of continuing care in the community will be provided by the informal support system. More information is needed on the care-giving capacity and resources within the extended family. This will obviously vary with economic status and family size, but we need a comprehensive picture of these informal systems and their major contributors.

Care-givers, in particular, need information, referral, economic assistance, and respite. The middle-aged woman, most likely the primary care-provider for her elderly parents or in-laws, struggles to meet the needs of her own children, and sometimes those of her grandchildren as well. Her lack of economic resources to independently handle all these care-giving responsibilities forces her to use an already overutilized, informal support system. The development of an effective home care system providing nursing care assistance and home helper activities holds the greatest promise for assisting the dependent elderly.

Legislative efforts to renew a long-term care home services bill must begin immediately. We must continue pushing for better Medicare coverage of continuing care services offered outside the institutional setting. In addition, there should be a sliding scale applied to Medicare deductibles and co-payments, reducing current negative effects on service utilization by the low-income elderly.

Intermediate-care facilities, skilled nursing homes, and home care services are absent or significantly underdeveloped in ethnic minority communities. Needs assessments and feasibility studies should be initiated at local levels to plan service development. Technical assistance should be granted to businesses and professional and social organizations wishing to fill service voids. Contributions from public and private sources should fund such enterprises.

The development of effective health and welfare policies enhancing the quality of life among our elderly citizens must focus on economic stability, housing, and health care. Universal access to health resources is a goal not only for the elderly, but for the population as a whole. As this country moves to assist the most dependent segments of our society (e.g., the elderly, children, handicapped), all citizens in turn benefit. This country cannot afford to think of fragmented subpopulations separately from each other, but must conceive of an intergenerational partnership providing the resources, time, and caring to assure that those most in need receive the appropriate assistance.

SUGGESTED READINGS

Bass, S. A., Kutza, E. A., and Torres-Gil, F. M., eds. *Diversity in Aging: Challenges Facing Planners and Policymakers in the 1990s.* Ill.: Scott, Foresman and Co., 1990.

Binstock, R. H., and George, L. K., eds. *Handbook of Aging and the Social Sciences* 3rd ed. San Diego, Calif.: Academic Press, 1990.

Butler, R. N. *Why Survive? Being Old in America.* New York: Harper & Row, 1975.

Callahan, D. *Setting Limits: Medical Goals in an Aging Society.* New York: Simon & Schuster, 1987.

Commonwealth Fund Commission on Elderly People Living Alone. "Old, Alone, and Poor: Overview and Recommendations." April 16, 1987.

Dobelstein, W., and Johnson, A. B. *Serving Older Adults: Policy, Programs, and Professional Activities.* Englewood Cliffs, N.J.: Prentice-Hall, 1985.

Litvak, E. *Helping the Elderly: The Complementary Roles of Informal Networks and Formal Systems.* New York: Guilford Press, 1985.

McNeely, R., and Colen, J. *Aging in Minority Groups.* Beverly Hills, Calif.: Sage Publications, 1983.

Neugarten, B. L., and Neugarten, D. A. "Age in the Aging Society." *Daedalus* 115 (1986): 31–49.

Ony, M. G., and Bond, K., eds. *Aging and Health Care: Social Service and Policy Perspectives.* London: Routledge & Kegan Paul, 1989.

Pifer, A., and Bronte, L., eds. *Our Aging Society: Paradox and Promise.* New York: Norton, 1986.

Ward, R. *The Aging Experience* 2nd ed. New York: Harper & Row, 1984.

ENDNOTES

1. U.S. Bureau of the Census, "Projections of the Population of the United States by Age, Sex, and Race: 1988 to 2080," *Current Population Reports,* Series P-25, No. 952 (Washington, D.C.: The Bureau, 1984).

2. Spencer, G. "Projections of the Population of the United States by Age, Sex, and Race: 1988 to 2080," *Current Population Reports.* Series P-25, No. 1018 (Washington, D.C.: The Bureau, 1989).

3. U.S. Bureau of the Census, "1980 Census of Population," *General Social and Economic Characteristics,* PC80–1–9, U.S. Summary (Washington, D.C.: U.S. Government Printing Office, December 1983), Table 120.

4. U.S. Bureau of the Census, "Projections of the Population of the United States by Age, Sex, and Race: 1988 to 2080" *Current Population Reports,* Series P–60, No. 163 (Washington, D.C.: U.S. Government Printing Office, 1989), Table 2.

5. U.S. Bureau of the Census, "Demographic and Socioeconomic Aspects of Aging in the United States," *Current Population Reports,* Series P-23, No. 138 (Washington, D.C.: U.S. Government Printing Office, 1984).

6. National Center for Health Statistics, "Current Estimates from the National Health Interview Survey, United States, 1986." Vital and Health Statistics Series 10, No. 164 (October 1987).

7. Davis, K., "Aging and the Health Care System: Economic and Structural Issues," *Daedalus* 115 (1986): 217–246.

8. Flemming, A. S., Rickards, L. D., Santos, J. F., and West, P. R., "Report on a Survey of Community Mental Health Centers" vol. 3 (Washington, D.C.: Action Committee to Implement the Mental Health Recommendations of the 1981 White House Conference on Aging, 1986).

9. Evans, D. A., Funkenstein, H. H., Albert, M. S., et al., "Prevalence of Alzheimer's Disease in a Community Population of Older Persons: Higher than Previously Reported," *JAMA* 261 (1989): 2552–2556.

10. Harper, M., and Lebowitz, B., eds., *Mental Illness in Nursing Homes: Agenda for Research*, No. ADM 86-1459 (Washington, D.C.: U.S. Government Printing Office, 1986).

11. Butler, R. N., and Lewis, M. I., *Aging and Mental Health* 2nd ed. (St. Louis, Mo.: C.V. Mosby 1977), p. 34.

12. Streib, G. F., "Are the Aged a Minority Group?," in B. L. Newgarten, ed., *Middle Age and Aging* (Chicago: University of Chicago Press), pp. 46–47.

13. Preston, S. H., "Children and the Elderly in the U.S.," *Scientific American* (December 1984): 44–49.

14. Hill, R., and Foote, N., *Family Development in Three Generations* (Cambridge, Mass.: Scheukman, 1970).

15. Lowy, L. *Social Work with the Aging* 2nd ed. (New York: Longman, 1985).

16. Butler, R. N., *Why Survive? Being Old in America* (New York: Harper & Row), p. 12.

17. MacDonald, D. I., *ADAMHA Testimony before the U.S. House of Representatives Committee on Appropriations, Subcommittee on Labor–Health and Human Services Education* (Washington, D.C.: *Congressional Record*, 1987).

18. Cantor, M. H., "Social Care: Family and Community Support Systems," *The Annals*, 503 (May 1989): 100.

19. Flemming et al.

20. Harper and Lebowitz.

21. Flemming et al.

22. MacDonald.

23. Flemming et al.

24. Light, E., Lebowitz, B. D., and Bailey, F., "CMHCs and Elderly Services: An Analysis of Direct and Indirect Services and Service Delivery Sites," *Community Mental Health Journal* 22 (1986): 294–302.

25. MacDonald.

26. Flemming et al.

CHAPTER 14

Social Work Practice in Rural Areas: The Appalachian Experience

Bradford W. Sheafor and Robert G. Lewis

PREFATORY COMMENT

One of the many faces of social work finds social workers serving the residents of the rural areas of the United States. The U.S. Bureau of the Census estimates that in 1990 there were 56,390,000 people, or 22.9 percent of the population, living in nonmetropolitan areas. Nearly 17 percent of these people (9,529,910) live below the poverty line, and many more experience serious social problems that confront both rural and urban dwellers. Rural people, however, often find it difficult to obtain professional help to deal with these problems due to limited availability of services in rural areas; human service delivery systems require clients to obtain services in urban areas or small cities. Sheafor and Lewis illustrate aspects of the uniqueness of rural social work using Appalachia as a case example.

In recent years rural areas of the United States have undergone dramatic change, profoundly affecting the basic social institutions of rural life. The rise of corporate farming and timber harvesting, depletion of mineral reserves and the discovery of new energy resources in isolated areas, substantial fluctuations in the farm economy, often rapid expansion and contraction of ski, fishing, and other recreational-oriented areas, and the conversion of rural towns into bedroom communities for urban dwellers have dramatically changed the lives of rural people. Economic and population change in rural areas have often meant an increase in social problems experienced by rural people and rural communities. The incidence of poverty, poor health care, and lack of adequate housing plaguing rural America has been at least equal to urban areas, although comparable human services have not reached rural residents.

If social workers are to respond to the special needs prevalent among the rural U.S. population, appropriate knowledge and practice competencies will be required. Social workers in rural areas should be aware that, like other special population groups, rural people have much in common. They usually share a dependence on the land, they tend to be more religious than urban dwellers, and they are reluctant to make use of professional helpers and human service programs.[1] They also tend to be more independent and conservative in their attitudes about social problems, and resisting of governmental interventions to resolve them. In addition, in most rural communities the people have the experience of living in an environment undergoing such rapid social change that existing social institutions cannot adequately adapt. The ensuing social problems require human service programs and human service professionals that are aware of these special needs.

The initial part of this chapter presents an overview of the changes in the rural United States and the special problems in service delivery experienced by social workers who serve rural people. Rural areas, however, are not all alike. Martinez-Brawley has clearly identified that the social problems experienced in rural areas and the intensity with which they are felt by the population varies from region to region.[2] The final part of the chapter examines the unique dimensions of rural social work practice in one geographic area of the United States, Appalachia. Appalachia includes all the state of West Virginia and parts of twelve other states extending 1300 miles from New York to Mississippi. Although this region includes several large urban centers, nearly one-half of the Appalachian population is considered rural, and a unique culture has developed among the rural residents of this region. Thus it makes a useful case example.

CHARACTERISTICS OF THE RURAL UNITED STATES

Rural life has played a gradually diminishing role in U.S. society. Until the 20th century, the United States was primarily rural, and its social institutions were organized around rural life. As the open lands in the West were settled and the frontier closed, as the Industrial Revolution increasingly required large numbers of people in concentrated geographic areas in order to manufacture needed products, and as the rapid population increase in the United States ballooned the sizes of its cities, rural life dropped from the mainstream of public interest. The emphasis of evolving social policies in the United States turned to problems in urban life, and the rural areas were largely neglected in the formulation of social programs and the allocation of resources.

The ability to describe rural life is partially hampered by the difficulty in finding agreement on a definition of *rural.* In the early periods of U.S. history, the isolation rural people experienced made it sufficient to define rural areas in terms of the number of people who lived in a given geographic area where they bought and sold goods, attended churches and schools, and had most of their social interaction. The population-based definition of the U.S. Bureau of the Census, which defined those sparsely populated areas with 2500 people or less as *rural,* was sufficient. However, as timber was cleared, mines closed, farms mechanized, and employment for more and more rural people available only in urban centers, and as urbanites moved to rural areas in search of "the good life" and cities annexed large amounts or rural land without subsequent housing or industrial development, the line between urban and rural became blurred. Beginning in 1980, census data reported on the rural United States population included all people *except* those living in a "central city or core, together with contiguous and closely settled territory, that combined have a total population of 50,000."[3] That is, the U.S. Bureau of the Census moved from viewing *rural* as small isolated areas to considering *all* nonmetropolitan areas (i.e., unincorporated rural areas, rural areas proximate to metropolitan areas, and towns as large as 40,000 population) as rural.

Many experts believe that somewhere between the two definitions is a more accurate population maximum for considering an area rural, but that other factors should also be considered. Waltman, for example, notes that, "The word *rural* means more than a numerical population limit. It connotes a way of and an outlook on life characterized by a closeness to nature, slower pace of living, and a somewhat conservative life-style that values tradition, independence and self-reliance, and privacy."[4] DuBord further suggests that an additional characteristic of rural communities is that they are primarily dependent on occupations tied to the land.[5]

Factors to consider, then, when attempting to understand rural people and rural life are the land, the economy, the people, and the communities.

The Land

Rural life is directly linked to the land and to nature. The primary land uses in rural areas have been for agriculture, mining and energy development, timber, fishing, recreation, and absorbing urban sprawl. The urban population has depended on farmers and ranchers to provide their food supplies. They have also expected rural communities to incorporate the often dramatically different population groups that may suddenly arrive to set up oil rigs, extract minerals, or fish or ski during relatively short periods of the year. Similarly, rural people are expected to give up farmland to housing developments and to integrate new residents into their social structures.

One byproduct of the dependence on the land and nature for earning a living is always living with a degree of risk. A wet planting or harvest season, an early frost, a hail storm, a forest fire, the presence of pollutants in a lake, a mine shaft cave-in, or even the price of a barrel of oil in the Middle East can dramatically affect life for the rural population. For these reasons, religion[6] and fatalism are inherent parts of rural culture, and a certain amount of emotional stress is ever-present in rural life.

The Economy

The rural economy is intertwined with the land. Changing employment patterns in agriculture and the extractive occupations (e.g., timber, mining) affect the rural economy, as do changes in land use patterns. For example, the primary rural occupations, agriculture and the retail trades that support it, are currently experiencing rapid change due to mechanization and the large capital investments required for farming, as well as the increased amount of land required to profitably maintain a commercial farm or ranch. Between 1930 and 1980 the number of farms in the United States declined from 6.5 million to 2.5 million, and the number of farmers dropped from 30.5 million to 6.6 million.[7] Similarly, reports of boom-and-bust conditions in the Rocky Mountain West and virtually every other rural area of the United States document dramatic changes in ownership, management, and demand for differing occupational skills. Inevitably, these changes impact the employment patterns, the economy, and the quality of life of the rural communities.

While the social structures in rural communities were once able to accommodate the gradual changes that occurred, the rapid development of corporate agriculture, changing national and international price structures, enhanced transportation systems surrounding metropolitan areas, and expanding or contracting tourism have strained the economic institutions in the rural United States. Social workers can play an important role in not only helping individuals and families to deal with the personal impact of these economic changes, but also aiding rural communities as a whole in anticipating and planning for such change.

The People

People typically select rural life because their livelihood is bound to the land, they prefer what they consider the qualitative aspects of rural living over urban life, or they are trapped there, by lack of resources and skills or family situations requiring their presence. For whatever reasons, a substantial number of people have elected to reside in rural areas. The U.S. Bureau of the Census reports that in 1988 56.4 million people, or 22.9 percent of the population in the United States, lived in nonmetropolitan areas.[8] Rural families were slightly smaller and, on average, older than urban families[9] and experienced a higher poverty rate (16.9%) than did metropolitan families (12.5%).[10] It is noteworthy, however, that families living in cities, per se, had a poverty rate of 18.6 percent, but that was offset by the 8.5 percent poverty rate among suburban families reported in the same "metropolitan" category.[11]

Rural areas have population characteristics that differ from urban areas. Rural people are more likely than their urban counterparts to be male, married, disabled, unemployed, and have a lower annual income. They also have fewer breadwinners in their households, are less likely to be members of minority groups (except for Native Americans), are typically less educated, are less likely to be part of the labor force (particularly females), and are less frequently foreign-born than is the case in the urban population.[12]

Historically, rural people have been exceptionally family-oriented. The demands of farm life required that all able family members help with preparing and tilling the land, planting and harvesting the crops, and maintaining the equipment and farm. The extended family, therefore, was an important part of rural life, and there was usually some meaningful work that could be done by people of all ages—even those with physical and intellectual handicaps. Rural culture was family-centered.

The reality of rural family life today is that economic conditions have forced millions of families to leave agriculture, and the characteristics of rural families are now much more similar to urban families. Rural families now include their share of single-parent families, dual-employment families, and families living in poverty. They, too, experience rising rates of substance abuse, divorce, family violence, and adolescent pregnancies.[13] Despite these similarities to urban families, the culture of rural life continues to maintain the family as a central social institution, and many social activities and social programs are designed around the family.

Religion plays a particularly important part in the lives of rural people. Studies of rural and urban populations indicate that rural people are more religiously oriented than their urban counterparts. Meystedt summarizes the findings of several such studies:

> In comparison to urban populations, rural people are more likely to rate themselves as "very" or "fairly" religious and to a greater extent feel that religion can answer "all or most of today's problems." In other dimensions, such as Bible reading, they also exceed urbanites; rural people are resisting the nationwide downward trend in church attendance. Nearly 75 percent of persons in rural areas profess "a great deal" or "quite a lot" of respect for and confidence in the church and organized religion.[14]

In addition to worship, instruction, and other activities of religious expression, churches have a central place in rural life because of the various social functions such as dinners, group meetings, and youth activities they sponsor.

The more conservative political positions held by the people of rural America are documented by Glenn and Hill in their analysis of a series of Gallup polls conducted in the mid-1970s. These data indicate that people living in communities of less than 50,000 population differed from people living in larger communities on many political and social issues. For example, they tended to be more opposed to abortion, premarital sex, the Equal Rights Amendment, female presidential candidates, amnesty for draft evaders, the registration of firearms, and re-establishing diplomatic ties with Cuba than persons living in urban areas.[15]

The people of rural areas, then, differ from the urban population in the central role played by the family and religion in their lives. Further, they tend to be more conservative politically than their urban counterparts and often elect to suffer from social problems rather than seek help from human service agencies or professional care-givers. The rural population has an especially strong dedication to the earth and the land, making foreclosure or the necessity for an elderly person to sell the farm and move to a town or nursing home, for example, an event that has significant emotional as well as economic implications.

Finally, rural culture places great value on friendships, interpersonal communication, and helping acquaintances in need. The pace of life tends to be slower than in urban areas, there is time for more leisurely interpersonal interactions, and perhaps the strongest natural helping networks in the United States exist in rural communities. At the same time, sparse population creates high visibility, making it difficult for a person or family to maintain the level of privacy that urban people expect. Family history colors the perception of the individual, few matters remain secret for any length of time, and gossip serves as an effective social control mechanism. Rural people, then, reflect a mix of attitudes that can best be characterized as "conservative, provincial, traditional, primary relationships, informal decision-making process, sense of independence and self-reliance, wholesome, simple, natural, and folksy."[16]

The Communities

Rural America cannot be fully appreciated without recognizing the importance of communities in enhancing the quality of life for the people. Rural towns serve as important centers of business, trade, education, religion, and interpersonal interaction. The relative isolation experienced by many rural people makes community activities especially important. These activities tend to center around schools (especially school sports), churches, retail stores, and outlets where necessary equipment or products grown and produced are bought and sold (e.g., the local coop, grain elevator, or farm implement store).

Several types of rural communities can be identified—including the farm/ ranch trade center, the mining/energy/timber company town, the tourist center, and the bedroom community for a metropolitan area. Each type of community faces unique problems, but all are undergoing rapid transition and experience difficulty in maintaining appropriate decision-making structures that can address these problems. Rural towns have traditionally exercised a considerable degree of internal control and have been tenacious in maintaining the power to decide community issues. That power was usually located in a few influential, but accessible, members of the community. Increasingly, community issues have been decided by the often "invisible" representatives of corporations that control the economy of rural towns and by state and national governmental bodies that construct guidelines or make decisions that affect the schools, roads, and other public programs. Local control in rural communities has clearly been diminished.

The development of extensive highway systems has reduced the geographic isolation of rural inhabitants. Increasingly, trade is conducted in urban centers some distance from the rural community, which erodes the ability of local merchants to succeed in business and for the community to perform its traditional role as the center of economic and social activity. The pressure to "buy local" takes on great significance in rural communities.

SOCIAL WELFARE IN RURAL AREAS

An extensive array of human services have emerged in recent years. Access to these services in times of need has become an expectation of every person in the United States—rich or poor, majority or minority, urban or rural. Advancing technology has increased the complexity of providing these services and has encouraged the professions that deliver them to become more and more specialized. At the same time, the major programs developed to respond to the social welfare needs of the U.S. population have characteristically been designed in an urban mode, where it is assumed that people can readily see helping professionals in their offices. For persons residing in rural areas, where the population is insufficient to support even a limited number of highly specialized, full-time human service providers, that service delivery approach restricts the ability of rural people to obtain professional help.

Two factors work against rural inhabitants gaining access to professional services. First, rural people are reluctant to seek professional help for personal problems. In a study conducted in Iowa and Pennsylvania by Martinez-Brawley and Blundall, farm families identified the following obstacles they perceived in using social services, in rank-order: concerns about families' reputations in the community; lack of understanding about what services do and how they work; grew up with the idea of not reaching for help from social agencies; lack of money; feeling that one must bear one's problems; fear of being perceived as lazy or incapable of taking care of oneself; feeling that no one has real answers to life's problems; fear of being perceived as mentally ill; distrust of workers who get paid to do the job; fear of social workers; and pride.[17] Second, the human service delivery system often makes services inaccessible to rural people. The financial burden and time required to simply reach a social agency is too often placed on the person needing the service. It is simply too costly and time consuming for many potential recipients of services to travel great distances to reach the providers; thus many do not receive needed services. Their health and social problems go unattended—or family and friends, that is, natural helpers, address the matter as best they can.

Human services in rural areas are typically provided through governmental agencies, on a county or regional basis, by public welfare departments, community mental health centers, the criminal justice system, nursing homes, hospitals and public health care agencies, and schools. Private or voluntary services are not plentiful in rural areas and, when they are offered, are typically provided through churches and youth-oriented programs such as 4-H and scouting.

Although serious social problems pervade much of rural America, communities that experience rapid growth and the infusion of a new population group into an established area often experience a dramatic increase in problems requiring professional services. Bachrach cites the following example:

In one Colorado boom town the population increased by 43 percent between 1973 and 1976. Over the same time period there were parallel—but strikingly disportionate—increases in selected reported social problems for that community: respectively, a 130 percent increase in reported child neglect and abuse, a 222 percent increase in crimes against property, a 352 percent increase in family disturbances, a 623 percent increase in substance abuse, and a dramatic 900 percent in crimes against persons.[18]

Another common source of rapid change for rural areas is rural towns becoming bedroom communities for urban areas. Often an idealized view of rural life attracts the urban family, who hopes the wholesome rural environment will solve their problems; they commute many miles each day in order to raise their children in a rural environment. One rural school superintendent reported that when a large, ten-acre-per-home-site land development was created in his school district, he found that children from this area represented 5 percent of the school population, required 15 percent of bussing funds, involved 85 percent of the school-attendance problems, and used more than half of the pupil personnel resources.[19] The animosity typically felt by the traditional rural dweller toward the new breed of rural commuter is captured by Bryan and McClaughry:

> The new exploiters tire of driving thirty miles an hour on country roads, so they have them straightened and drive forty. They came to grow their own vegetables, discovered that weeds pull hard, and now demand a new grocery store on the village green. . . . These are the people who believed the Dogpatch stereotype of the rural dweller and who, from either ignorance or arrogance, came to the country and expected to know at once how to live there competently and happily, forgetting that water freezes in the winter and dogs like to kill ducks.[20]

Research into the provision of human services in rural areas suggests that there are no significant differences in the social problems addressed or the manner in which practice is conducted.[21] The most substantial difference is in the delivery of services. The solution to this problem appears to lie in taking programs to the people and adopting practice approaches incorporating as fully as possible the rural orientation toward self-help and mutual aid. Innovative delivery mechanisms, such as establishing personal support networks, "circuit riding" professionals, mobile human service agencies, and maintaining office hours in rural schools or churches one day or evening per week, are examples of efforts to develop more appropriate means of serving rural populations.

IMPLICATIONS FOR SOCIAL WORK PRACTICE IN RURAL AREAS

Given the uniqueness of rural life and the particular problems experienced in delivering human services, the social worker in a rural area must have special competencies. Often he or she is the only (or one of a very few) professional in a community. Wide-ranging knowledge and skill is required to improve conditions for both individuals and communities. Specialization is a luxury that sparsely populated rural areas simply cannot support. The "all-purpose" rural social worker must be innovative, resourceful, self-motivating, and able to function with minimal supervision.

Employing agencies must also recognize that rural practice requires more than just transporting urban social workers to rural areas. Rural social workers cannot work exclusively at either practice extreme—that is, "deep-dish" therapy or social policy analysis. Needed practice skills will most likely focus on the middle range of social work activities, such as generalized counseling with individuals and families, building support networks and accessing natural helpers, and facilitating the efforts of communities to engage in self-help to prevent or resolve their problems. Agencies must select and/or prepare their staff members for the breadth of rural practice. The fact that substantial differences in the tasks performed by urban and rural social workers do not appear to exist may suggest an unresponsiveness by social work education and agency staff development programs to the unique requirements for social work practice in rural areas.[22]

The practice model most generally accepted as appropriate for rural practice is labeled *generalist.*[23] The generalist perspective requires that the social worker approach practice without a bias as to which intervention approach(es) would be most appropriate until the situation is carefully examined. As reported by Sheafor and Landon in the *Encyclopedia of Social Work,* "Generalist practice requires that the social worker examine the various facets of a situation that need intervention and apply the knowledge, values, and skills either to initiate service or to secure appropriate specialized expertise. Thus generalist practice involves both the capacity to take a wide view of the practice situation and the necessary abilities to intervene at multiple levels and in a range of situations."[24] (See Chapter 1 for a more complete discussion of the generalist approach to social work practice.)

In social work education, preparation for generalist social work practice is required by the accreditation standards for all baccalaureate (BSW) social work education programs[25] and is frequently offered in the first stages of Master's (MSW) programs. Advanced generalist preparation is available in a growing number of MSW programs, which view the generalist approach as desirable for both rural and urban social work practitioners. A national study of BSW social workers suggests that the generalist preparation of graduates has been well received by rural social agencies. Whereas 22.9 percent of the U.S. population resides in communities of 40,000 or less people, 43.9 percent of BSW graduates reported they were employed in human service agencies serving communities of 40,000 or less, and 38 percent of those social workers served communities of 10,000 or less.[26]

The generalist social worker practicing in a rural area might accurately be viewed as a "utility" worker. Like the utility infielder on a baseball team, he or she must be prepared to enter virtually any practice situation with at least beginning competence at intervention at both the micro and macro practice levels.

Micro Practice in Rural Areas

At the micro or direct-practice level, rural social workers provide face-to-face services to clients, as would any other social worker. However, the social worker must be especially alert to the fact that because of the strong value placed on self-reliance, rural clients may be resistant to counseling services and reluctant to accept tangible assistance, that is, social provisions. When combined with the traditional dependence on friends, family, or other natural helpers, the professional helper is truly a "resource of last resort," and the problems presented tend to be severe. Due to the high visibility of people and the likelihood of interaction between worker and client in other activities in rural communities, it is essential that the client understand the special nature of professional relationships and that the social worker provide protections to maximize confidentiality regarding the practice activity.[27]

The generalist worker must be prepared to offer a wide range of services but must also be cautious not to slip into the trap of believing he or she has the tools to solve all problems. There are times when specialized service is in the best interest of the client and referral to existing services within the community or in urban areas is essential. The task of becoming knowledgeable about the available resources in the region for the many problems the rural social worker confronts is an onerous, but essential, activity. Once appropriate resources are identified, considerable care and skill are required to complete a successful referral. While many people view referral as a relatively simple task, it is actually a very complex procedure and many attempted referrals end in failure.

Another direct practice activity that is compatible with the orientation of rural people involves engaging clients in self-help groups and supporting the use of natural helping networks to meet their less complicated needs. This activity is especially important, both because the culture supports care-giving by friends and families and because professional service providers have limited time to devote to any single practice situation. The challenge for the social worker is to determine which situations are appropriate for this type of intervention and to mobilize the appropriate natural helpers to perform this service.

Macro Practice in Rural Areas

While all social workers are expected to engage in both direct and indirect service activity, the rural worker should be prepared to devote a substantial part of his or her time to indirect or macro practice activity. The central place of community life in rural areas suggests the importance of providing community-centered, rather than problem- or case-centered, services.

Existing social organizations such as churches, schools, and local government agencies are important resources for collaboration by the rural social worker. To effectively use these resources to solve or prevent social problems in the community, the worker must be skilled at needs assessment, social policy analysis, small town politics, and able to work intimately with community leadership. It is important for the worker to be able to accurately assess the local decision-making structure and effectively interpret the needs of the residents to these people. The opportunity for face-to-face contact to influence these decision makers, or even become one of the key decision makers, is especially possible once the social worker is well established in a rural community.

Efforts to advocate for client services need not stop with the local community. The rural social worker has a particularly good opportunity to interpret the community's needs and to lobby directly with county and state legislators who represent that district. To work at these levels, the social worker needs to be competent in program and practice research, social policy development, community planning activities, and influencing the legislative process.

Social work practice in rural areas, then, requires knowledge of the special issues that face rural people, a generalist perspective for practice, and skills for working with people at both the micro and macro levels. Regional differences, too, affect practice in various parts of the United States. The Appalachian region illustrates a rural area with some unique characteristics and needs.

RURAL SOCIAL WORK PRACTICE IN APPALACHIA

The remainder of this chapter examines some of the unique factors that would affect a social worker practicing in Appalachia, a large and primarily rural region of the United States. The case of Mary illustrates a social worker's need to understand Appalachia as a context for social work practice with a young woman from that region.

> Mary, a twenty-two-year-old, unmarried community college student, grew up in a coalfield county in central Appalachia. Mary became pregnant while attending college, and a college counselor urged her to visit with the caseworker who staffs the county welfare department's satellite center three days each week. The social worker interviewed Mary when she first requested care and recorded the following information.

> Mary, the oldest of four siblings, is a bright young woman who is committed to completing her college degree. She is a first-generation college student who feels that she will let herself down if she does not move ahead with her education at this time. Mary's mother has no marketable employment skills, her father is disabled because he contracted Black Lung Disease from his years in the coal mines, and her youngest sister has a chronic health problem that constantly drains the family's financial resources. For generations the family lived below the poverty level, and Mary sees college as her way out of poverty. Mary's family belongs to a fundamentalist church in their community, and Mary fears her out-of-wedlock pregnancy has caused her family disappointment and embarrassment.

To adequately understand Mary's situation, the worker needed to be familiar with several unique characteristics of Appalachia, the context in which service was to be provided to Mary. Some of the general knowledge the social worker should have about this region of the United States is included in the following paragraphs.

Characteristics of Appalachia

Appalachian is a term that has become accepted during the past thirty years for identifying residents of a large, primarily rural region of the United States. Prior to that time, terms frequently used to describe the Appalachian people were *mountaineers, Southern mountain people, highlanders,* and *hillbillies.* Although those terms are sometimes used today, the common identification of the people is with the Appalachian Mountain chain that extends from Maine to Georgia. There is no doubt the lives of people who live in or near the Appalachian Mountains are shaped by the climate, topography, and minerals contained in those mountains.

Stereotyping by the mass media has contributed significantly to the region's negative image. At the same time, media attention has made the U.S. public aware of the problems experienced by the Appalachian people, which contributed to the creation of massive economic development projects in the region. Although poverty was nationwide during the Great Depression of the 1930s, excessive problems associated with poverty in Appalachia drew considerable public attention at the time. As a result, Congress created the Tennessee Valley Authority (TVA), with the intent of assisting a large depressed area to become economically viable. The construction of hydroelectric dams resulted in flood control, improved navigation of the rivers, and electricity for parts of seven states in the Tennessee Valley.

In the 1960s publicity surrounding Lyndon Johnson's War on Poverty again focused attention on Appalachia. Extreme poverty in the region, along with the associated problems of poor health, illiteracy, substandard housing, and so forth, were depicted in the media as the plight of most Appalachians. Public knowledge of the conditions in this region helped to generate support for passage of the Economic Opportunity Act in 1964.

The Appalachian Regional Redevelopment Act, passed the following year, focused entirely on the needs of the region, and the Appalachian Regional Commission (ARC) was immediately created to implement the provisions of the act. Hundreds of federal programs resulting from the 1964 and 1965 legislation inundated the region for the next two decades. Although duplication, lack of coordination, mismanagement, and questionable priorities hampered the effectiveness of these efforts, much was accomplished. More than $5 billion has been spent by the ARC since its inception, with most aimed at improving the infrastructure. For example, the construction of over 1900 miles of new highways, vocational–technical schools, hospitals, clinics, airports, and public service systems has placed many sections of the region in an improved competitive position in the national marketplace.

Some sections of the region, especially those that are dependent on coal mining and associated industries, continue to experience extremely high rates of unemployment, poverty, poor health, illiteracy, and other social problems. Although Appalachia is now closer to the national average in terms of education, health care, income, and the like than before these federal programs were initiated, the region is still somewhat below the rest of the country on most important indicators of social well-being. Also, the ARC has experienced severe reductions in funding for more than a decade, and continuing economic development efforts are not likely to be underwritten or heavily subsidized by the federal government.

Because of the uniquenesses of rural Appalachia, social workers who serve the residents of that region must have an understanding of the background and cultural traits of the Appalachian people. This is equally important for the social workers who serve the large Appalachian population that has migrated to cities—both within Appalachia and in the surrounding areas—known as *urban mountaineers.*

The Land.   A map of the eastern United States (Figure 14–1) shows the enormous land area of the Appalachian region. Although its boundaries have been redefined several times during this century, the current boundaries contain 194,871 square miles[28]—an area comparable in size to Central America. The ARC has defined three subregions: the Northern, Central, and Southern. The Northern subregion is the most populous and urbanized. The Central subregion is the smallest, most rural, and experiences the highest degree of poverty and isolation. The Southern subregion is developing a modern infrastructure and experiencing the highest level of industrial diversification and expansion.[29]

In contemporary rural Appalachia, the uses of the land and the close relationship between the people and the land is similar to other parts of the rural United States. Yet notable differences exist. Although the steep mountain slopes and narrow valleys, which are prone to flooding, have prohibited extensive commercial agricultural development, the land is central to the way of life for the Appalachian people. The extractive industries (especially coal mining and gas production), timber harvesting, and tourism and recreation dominate the economy. Each depends on the land and is subject to the risks of depleted resources, changing demand, and fluctuating price structures throughout the world.

Family farms are generally small and continue to shrink as each generation has fewer acres to subdivide among heirs. Consequently, there are many part-time farmers whose primary employment is in another occupation, often in larger communities. Some part-time farmers live and work during the week outside the region and return to work the family farm on weekends, placing strain on family life.

The largest landholder in Appalachia is the federal government, which has acquired more than 14 million acres of timber land. As government property, the land does not generate property taxes for the states and municipalities of the region. However, much of the land is now federal parks and forests, which has increased tourism and recreation in the region.

FIGURE 14–1 *Appalachia and the Appalachian Subregions*

The extraction of minerals from the land draws many corporations into the life of Appalachia. Coal mining is the primary extractive industry and extends throughout the Central and much of the Northern subregions, but the mining of iron ore, aluminum, and other metals is also extensive. Few of the local people, however, own mineral rights or mineral land, which are possessed by absentee corporate owners, resulting in little return to the local economy.[30] The quality of life for a large segment of the Appalachian population has been further complicated by the political power of these corporate owners. They have effectively prevented tax and regulatory laws from adequately addressing critical problems such as mine safety, Black Lung Disease, unemployment, water pollution, destruction of surface land, and other harmful factors associated with the extractive industries.

The Economy.   The economic history of Appalachia is intertwined with the land and its outside ownership. First came the timber barons, who purchased hundreds of thousands of acres of prime virgin timber at only a fraction of their true value. Next came the large corporations, which bought mineral rights and land at prices substantially below their real value. Then the railroads were built, with government subsidies in order to have a means to transport timber, coal, and other extracted natural resources to national markets, as well as to distribution points for international markets. Finally, the tourism and recreation industry emerged as another central feature of the economy. However, problems associated with tourism, such as seasonal employment, low wages, and high property taxes, undermine a stable economic base for many local residents.

The fact is that economic prosperity has been achieved by many non-Appalachian corporations through exploitation of the landowners. Caudill effectively drew public attention to this in his popular book, *Night Comes to the Cumberlands:*

> We have seen that the mountaineer sold his great trees for a consideration little
> more than nominal, but if his timber brought him a small financial reward, his
> minerals were virtually given away. The going price in the early years was fifty
> cents an acre ... and a seam of coal five feet thick produced a minimum of five
> thousand tons per acre! Where more than one seam was mined, a single acre
> sometimes yielded fifteen or twenty thousand tons! ... For this vast mineral
> wealth the mountaineer in most instances received a single half-dollar.[31]

Chronic economic problems have persisted due to the lack of a diversified industrial economy. Although improvements have been realized in some areas during the past twenty-five years, the region has suffered historically from boom and bust periods associated with the extractive industries. As the price of oil changes on the international market, or as modernized mining methods reduce the labor force, poverty increases because viable alternative sources of employment are limited or nonexistent in parts of the region. For many the only alternative is long-term unemployment—or migration to urban areas, without the assurance of employment there. The skills required for the mining, steel, and textile industries do not readily transfer to other jobs, except in manufacturing. Attracting large manufacturers to an area, however, requires modern highways and other transportation systems that are not currently present in the mountainous areas of Appalachia. Much of the Central subregion and some counties in other subregions are even more economically distressed than they were in the 1980s. The unemployment and poverty rates in Appalachia continue to range well above national averages.[32]

All rural Appalachia should not be viewed as economically depressed or under the control of multinational conglomerates. Although the economic situation in the coalfields and steel industry is dismal, many other areas are economically healthy and closely resemble the affluent circumstances elsewhere in the United States. One example is the Southern subregion, which has a variety of favorable geographical features, including the Piedmont and Coastal Plains areas, which are in a good location to serve large national markets. Recent industrial development in these areas has involved the utilization of modern technology and innovations not possible in some of the more isolated industrial areas.

The People.   The 20,638,000 people who reside in Appalachia constitute nearly 9 percent of the population of the United States. Although hundreds of small towns and cities and some larger cities (e.g., Pittsburgh, Pennsylvania; Roanoke, Virginia; Knoxville, Tennessee; and Birmingham, Alabama) dot the landscape, 45.5 percent of the region's population is rural—nearly double the national percentage.[33]

The majority of people are of Anglo-Saxon extraction and descendants of several generations of Appalachians. The region has a negligible foreign-born population and a small black one (concentrated mostly in urban areas) that constitute 8 percent of the total.[34]

Contrary to some portrayals of Appalachia, as a region characterized by a homogeneous culture, there is enormous social, economic, and cultural diversity there. A social worker in Appalachia should be aware that numerous subcultures exist. Even the most rural families today are increasingly less isolated and insulated from the outside world. They are made aware of mainstream culture through regular exposure to the mass media, especially television. Also, today's money-oriented society, unlike the former trade-oriented economy, makes it necessary for people to interface with social systems and institutions in mainstream America. Lewis accurately characterizes rural Appalachian people as being bicultural, since most learn and practice mainstream and mountain culture simultaneously.[35] This bicultural perspective is also observable, to some extent, among middle-class, urban Appalachians, since most have roots in the rural areas.

The mass media have provided the people of the United States with regular doses of distorted images of the region and its people. Most stereotypes are centered on a few perceived character or behavioral traits such as laziness, ignorance, uncleanliness, immorality, violence, and passivity. Television programs that have been the most stereotypical include "The Beverly Hillbillies," the "Dukes of Hazzard," "Green Acres," "Gomer Pyle," and "Hee Haw." Comic strips like "Snuffy Smith" and "L'il Abner" have also contributed their share of mythical descriptions of Appalachian life. Among the many movies that have stereotyped the Appalachian people, few can surpass "Deliverance." Stereotypes usually have some basis in fact, but accuracy is soon lost through distortion and exaggeration, which is then generalized to include a whole region, race, or class of people.

The prevalent cultural values ascribed to Appalachians had their origins in the early frontier-agrarian society. These values include strong family ties, individualism and self-reliance, traditionalism, fatalism, and religious fundamentalism. They are an outgrowth of the harsh realities of survival in the rugged mountains and hollows of the eighteenth, nineteenth, and early part of the twentieth centuries. Historically families were self-contained social units, with each household living its own life independent of other families in the hollow. Family members were dependent on one another for survival, and opportunities for activities outside the nuclear or extended family were severely restricted. Until fairly recently three-generation households were not unusual, and much of the out-migration from the region during the past three decades has included moving the nuclear family as well as extended-family members. Today the extended family is no longer the usual family constellation. The typical rural Appalachian family, as in urban areas, is the nuclear family consisting of husband, wife, and dependent children. Also, it is now much less common for adult children to remain in the same locality as their parents; most must relocate in order to find employment.

Even with the out-migration of rural Appalachian families (a trend, incidentally, that has recently been reversed), the attachment to extended family members has not been lost. Visiting and other social relationships are regular occurrences, even among distant relatives. It is typical for migrated families to maintain frequent contacts with family members "back home," and many make weekend trips several times each year for this purpose. Family members nearby and from great distances gather quickly when there is serious illness or death in the family. Naturally, family relationships have changed as Appalachia has changed, but there is strong evidence that rural Appalachian families continue to be among the most closely knit families in the United States.

Another characteristic of the people in the rural areas of Appalachia is the importance of the family surname. Individuals are evaluated, and even judged, to a large extent, on the reputation of their family, which may be considered more important than one's accomplishments or lack thereof. This is an advantage to some and a detriment to others. A person whose family is held in low esteem may not be able to overcome the stigma, even through educational achievement and material success. On the other hand, a person from one of the "good" families generally maintains a positive status, even if little is achieved on his or her own merits.

Individualism and self-reliance were traits necessary for survival on the frontier, and these qualities served the frontier family well. However, the ability to exercise these traits is increasingly restricted in today's expanding industrial economy. Jones notes that, with the change to an industrial economy, the Appalachian lost autonomy and "became a captive of circumstances. But the belief in independence and self-reliance is still there, whether or not the mountaineer is truly independent and self-reliant."[36]

Traditionalism has characterized the Appalachians for generations. It was easier and safer to hold on to the "old ways" than to adapt to a changing society. That characteristic, too, may be passing; many Appalachians have demonstrated their desire and capacity to be progressive and participate in the emerging industrial economy.

Fatalism is intertwined with religion and internalized primarily by the poor and oppressed. It is viewed as an adjustive or survival technique of the powerless.

For those who endure deprivation and hardship on a daily basis, it is comforting to have something to sustain them. The black Delta sharecropper, the white mountain tenant farmer, and the chronically unemployed and dispossessed believe, with good reason, that their living conditions will never improve and thus are comforted by religious fatalism. One hears statements in rural Appalachia like, "This is God's will," "God will not put more on you than you can take," and "Blessed are the poor. ..." Present life is devalued, and there is an expectation of receiving rewards in heaven.

Today there is a mixed pattern of traditional religious groups and local sects. Most rural Appalachians adhere to fundamentalism, which includes a belief in the literal interpretation of the Bible and results in selection of churches that reflect this view. One cannot understand the Appalachian without first understanding his or her religion. Religious beliefs and practices permeate every facet of life.

Finally, additional strong values among Appalachians are neighborliness and hospitality, personalism, love of place, modesty and being oneself, sense of beauty, sense of humor, and patriotism. Jones interprets the values held by the Appalachian people as primarily positive, but also recognizes that some of them are counterproductive:

> Our fatalistic religious attitudes often cause us to adopt a "What will be, will be" approach to social problems. Our "Original Sin" orientation inhibits us from trying to change the nature or practices of people. Our individualism keeps us from getting involved, from creating a sense of community and cooperation and causes us to shy away from those who want to involve us in social causes. Our love of place, sometimes, keeps us in places where there is no hope of creating decent lives.[37]

The Communities.   The social worker employed in Appalachia must recognize that the typical communities in that region are small towns and even smaller villages and hamlets. The changing economy has created distressed conditions for many towns that traditionally were dependent on agriculture and coal-mining. Many once-vibrant towns have become little more than ghost towns. In the 1950s coal camps and company-owned towns began to decline, and by the end of the following decade most had disappeared. Dilapidated company houses were either dismantled by the company, or abandoned. Houses that were in good condition or could be repaired were sold, generally to retirees who could afford the purchase price of a few hundred dollars. The more moderate-sized towns, especially those accessible by interstate and other major highways, have experienced industrial growth that created a healthier economy. At the same time, small towns previously serving as trade centers for people who lived in isolated areas were adversely affected by the expanded highway system that allowed people to make their purchases in larger trade centers. Many middle-class Appalachians take periodic shopping trips to urban areas or shopping centers that have emerged on the fringes, even though the centers may be as far as fifty to one hundred miles away. This trend has changed the "local flavor" of businesses in rural Appalachia.

Many small grocery stores and merchandise stores, for example, that used to be scattered through the remote areas, no longer exist. The few business establishments left in the small "crossroads" communities are primarily self-service establishments serving a motoring public. The discontinuation of many post offices in very small localities has also affected the role of the community as a gathering place for residents of the area. The social activities of "loafing" and visiting with neighbors in the stores and post offices have practically ceased, and the important role of communities as social centers has diminished.

School consolidation has also affected community life. Many rural parents feel intimidated by contact with larger, consolidated schools and find that they do not represent a meaningful place for social interaction because of the many people with whom they have not traditionally been engaged in face-to-face interaction. Many rural children, too, do not adjust to large, consolidated schools because of their perceived social and cultural inferiorities, as measured against more affluent "town kids." Consequently, neither parents nor children involve themselves in school-related activities, and the school drop-out rate, already high, increases as schools perform a less important role in rural Appalachian life. However, churches and church-centered social events continue to be important in rural communities. Churches have been the most stable institutions in rural Appalachia and continue to perform a central social function as well as religious ones.

In sum, in the past the daily activities of rural families took place in the community of their residence. With few exceptions, people worked, shopped, worshipped, and attended school within walking distance or a short commuting distance from home. This changed with the abandonment of family farms, the disappearance of coal camps, school consolidation, and greater mobility. Now many workers commute many miles each day to reach their jobs, shop outside their local community, and send their children by school bus or other means to a consolidated school. These societal changes have lessened the Appalachian's sense of community identity and cohesiveness. The decreasing isolation and increasing interaction with mainstream society is causing many rural communities to lose their central role in the lives of their people.

SOCIAL WELFARE IN RURAL APPALACHIA

To illustrate the functioning of the human service delivery system in Appalachia, we return to the case of Mary as she deals with her out-of-wedlock pregnancy.

> It was evident that Mary was going to need a variety of services. In addition to prenatal care, she would require financial assistance if she was to remain in school and complete her AA degree. She also would need help as she made her decision about whether to place the baby for adoption when it was born. Finally, she would need support as she interacted with her parents and community when the out-of-wedlock pregnancy became known.

For the social worker, knowledge of the human service delivery system in rural Appalachia and the resources available to help Mary was essential to helping her through this difficult period in her life.

Social welfare in rural Appalachia includes restrictive service delivery modes and other barriers to effective human service provision. The major differences in the utilization of human services in Appalachia, compared to other parts of the United States, lie in the severity of the communities' inability to finance adequate services and outreach efforts, as well as the reluctance of many potential recipients to seek out and utilize the services that are available. As the Manpower Education and Training Project's Rural Task Force of the Southern Regional Education Board pointed out,

> Problems of rural areas tend to be more like problems of underdeveloped countries; that is, basic public services and the necessities are lacking. Services related to sustaining life will have priority (i.e., food, shelter, health, transportation, etc.) over social services focused on the quality of life.[38]

This characterization of rural problems and services does not apply universally, but it accurately reflects the difficulty a social worker in rural Appalachia often experiences in locating services for clients.

Not only do localities have a tax base insufficient to support even a limited number of highly specialized full-time human service providers, but they are often unable to either recruit or support an adequate number of service providers with desired qualifications. For example, positions designed for social workers are often held by persons whose educational background is not in social work; their clients too often do not receive service of adequate quality. This is not unique to Appalachia, but in vast areas of the region it is virtually impossible to recruit professionals who are not native to the localities—and few qualified natives are available.

Cultural factors such as independence and self-reliance are thought to influence Appalachians more than any other group of people. The kinship group generally does what it can to take care of its own, and outside help is usually sought only as a last resort. Therefore, social agencies are constantly dealing with crisis situations. In addition, the topography of the region causes enormous transportation problems for consumers of services. Although this is generally the situation throughout rural America, much of Appalachia is especially hampered by travel requirements. Many recipients must depend on neighbors or other individuals for transportation, and even the cost of gasoline places an additional burden on extremely limited budgets. Also, out-migration consists mostly of the young and healthy and has left many areas with a disproportionate share of elderly, for whom travel to receive services may be a virtual impossibility.

One alternative is to take the services to the clients. Service delivery in some agencies is primarily through home visits, but the travel time required for service creates a costly and inefficient system for the agencies and workers. Travel time often exceeds the time available for professional contacts with recipients of service.

The public welfare department is the major service agency and generally the only source of financial assistance, except for those eligible for Supplemental Security Income (SSI). Mental health centers have been slow in locating in the more rural areas, and many have only satellite centers staffed part-time as extensions of urban mental health agencies. Also, the staff of the rural centers too often simply transfer their urban approaches to practice to the rural areas.

Nursing homes and hospitals are generally overburdened with indigent patients, and the support services that would enable many of these patients to remain in their own homes or with relatives seldom exist. The problems of the aged are magnified in Appalachia because of the vulnerability of a large, aged population.

Limited private or voluntary services are provided by churches and other benevolent groups on a selective basis. One frequently hears the statement "God helps those who help themselves," so those organizations working through churches tend to provide assistance only to those considered "deserving." This problem is compounded by the fact that rural Appalachians are reluctant to contribute to "worthy causes" that have unknown beneficiaries. Thus few private human service agencies exist in rural Appalachia. However, on a personal level, individuals and small groups are characteristically generous in sharing their limited resources with others.

The attitudes of Appalachians toward social welfare are heavily influenced by cultural beliefs in the importance of independence, self-reliance, and religious fatalism. However, these views have been modified during major economic downturns that resulted in massive unemployment. In the Eastern Kentucky coalfields in the 1950s and early 1960s, the rapid decline in the coal industry created special hardships for the unemployed middle-aged miner, who was less likely to find employment outside the industry and less able and willing to leave the area. Therefore, the only way for the family to survive was to qualify for public assistance based on disability of the wage earner. Caudill reports that many became "symptom hunters" in order to convince physicians they were "sick enough to draw." They complained of a wide range of ailments, and many could point to scars on arms, legs, and chest—mementos of old mining accidents—to support their claims. Above all, they complained of having "bad nerves."[39] Nooe discovered similar behavior among mental patients in rural Appalachia, noting that often among unemployed coal miners being judged mentally ill was preferable to being labeled lazy, enabling them to maintain some dignity and justify receiving financial assistance to support their families.[40]

The solutions to service delivery problems in Appalachia approximate those considered desirable for other rural areas. Circuit-riding has been a mainstay of public welfare departments. Circuit riders conduct initial as well as follow-up services in locations other than the main offices. Due to funding limitations and the occasional need for technical diagnostic equipment, it is not feasible for all human service providers to make home visits, and serious attention should be given to the establishment of mobile units as well as permanent substations of social agencies. Some agencies have been innovative in scheduling nontraditional office hours, but there is an increasing need for more flexibility in this regard.

The problems of transportation cannot be seriously reduced without changes in agency policies, and proposals for such changes have often been rejected because funding for these programs would create additional tax burdens for the towns and counties.

Micro Practice in Appalachia

The rural social worker must be prepared to address both individual troubles and social problems existing within a community or region. At the individual, couple, or family (micro) level, the social worker must provide services to directly benefit the client and/or help the client gain access to helping services that might be available:

> The caseworker from the county welfare department soon found that Mary was eligible for food stamps and helped to arrange for this financial aid, which would assist her in maintaining a diet sufficiently nutritious for the baby.
>
> In the course of her interviews with the social worker, Mary revealed that when she first discovered she was pregnant she considered suicide. Rejecting that option, she went to her counselor at the college to explore the possibility of obtaining an abortion. It was that counselor who referred Mary to the agency. As they worked together, the social worker helped Mary to carefully examine her beliefs related to abortion, and Mary decided to carry the baby to term. Mary and the caseworker then initiated a contract to explore her decision about keeping the child or placing it for adoption after birth.
>
> The worker also arranged for Mary to have an appointment every Wednesday morning, when the mobile clinic from the county health department was in town. Mary was told that the clinic opened at 8 A.M. and that she could appear when it was convenient, as the clinic's policy was to take patients on a first-come-first-served basis. Mary indicated she would be there promptly at 8 A.M. because she had a 10:00 class and was determined to not to let this pregnancy interfere with her college education. Her family had put their faith in her, and she did not want to let them down any more than she already had.

Like Mary's social worker, most professional service providers in rural Appalachia serve lower-class or working-class clients, whose cultural values may be different from their own. It is imperative that the professional helpers understand and appreciate the clients' culture as being different—not deficient—and develop innovative service approaches and tools appropriate for this population. Although his remarks were not directed specifically toward practice with Appalachians, Kadushin accurately captured this perspective:

> Good interviewing in a contact with a client who differs from the interviewer in some significant characteristics requires more than a knowledge of the culture and life-style of the interviewee. It also requires an adaptation of interview techniques—pace of interview, activity level, choice of appropriate vocabulary, modification of nonverbal approaches—to be in tune with the needs of the interviewee.[41]

The rural Appalachian places great value on personal relationships and is dismayed by persons perceived as cold, methodical, or indifferent. During the first contact with a human services agency, the Appalachian can be expected to be cautious, suspicious, and highly anxious. It is essential that the worker demonstrate empathy, unconditional acceptance, and warm personal regard for the client. Otherwise, the person is likely to withdraw from the situation, regardless of the severity of need. Although the professional relationship is essential in social work practice regardless of the clientele served, it takes more effort and time to develop this with the Appalachian client, especially if the worker is viewed as an outsider.

The Appalachian client is not impressed by professional qualifications and credentials. However, "who" the worker is is likely to be of great concern. For example, one's belief in God, friendliness, and a familiar name or location will expedite the client–worker relationship. Most clients will continue to see a professional they like, even if the person is not fully competent. For example, one elderly Appalachian woman nearly died from improper care by her physician. After being rushed to the city hospital and surviving, she returned to her regular doctor for follow-up treatment. Her rationale was that she considered him a nice person because he spoke to her at the grocery store, was friendly, and had a nice family that attended church regularly. She did not consider returning to the physician who had saved her life.

Use of language and communication skills are also important considerations for the social worker. The uneducated, rural Appalachian has a very limited vocabulary and usually a slow pattern of speech. Communication may be deliberate, passive, and unexpressive, and there may be difficulty in responding to open-ended questions until the client feels comfortable with the social worker. Particular localisms, colloquialisms, and maxims may be unique to this subculture, and the social worker should be prepared to seek clarification when necessary. For example, one client of a native Appalachian social worker expressed concern about her son-in-law, indicating several times that he had a "white liver." Probing by the social worker revealed that she considered the son-in-law to be oversexed. Since language is not always understood, even by native social workers, it can present especially difficult communication problems for the outsider.

It is also very difficult for the rural Appalachian to understand the need for the extensive documentation often required when receiving services. Too, Appalachians typically expect immediate results when they do request service; thus long-term interventions are less likely to be successful with Appalachians than with other clients.

It is important to note that social workers also work with Appalachians who have migrated to non-Appalachian cities. Many of these former Appalachians have enjoyed upward mobility and assimilated into the mainstream of city culture. However, tens of thousands could be described more accurately as "urban mountaineers," and many interface with the social welfare system. Therefore, social workers need to understand and relate to these individuals in a manner that is sensitive to their cultural uniqueness.

The generalist perspective to social work practice is critical to the worker serving Appalachian people. In addition to providing services that meet client needs, the social worker often serves as a broker in assisting with arrangements and advocating on behalf of clients. The client is usually fearful about entering another unknown situation when a referral has been made, and the social worker should be especially careful to "pave the way" by helping with logistical factors such as transportation and appointment scheduling. The worker also needs to prepare the client very carefully to actually utilize the services, providing as much information as possible in order to reduce his or her anxiety. Whenever possible the social worker should try to make use of the natural helping networks in the community. These resources are especially important because of the underdevelopment of human services and the people's preference for being in an environment with family and friends.

The essence of micro practice with rural Appalachians was succinctly summarized by Humphrey:

> If agency workers are to help mountain people they must understand what their clients' words and actions are actually trying to convey to them. It is then that services may be offered in ways people can accept. Their place, their families and their religion all are parts of a very intricate culture which must be respected and taken seriously. The social worker must first come to know the person before he or she can help him.[42]

Macro Practice in Appalachia

When referrals are made, it is important for the social worker to follow-up, to be sure that the services are actually received by clients. When clients experience problems obtaining needed services the generalist social worker, who is equally prepared to intervene with both the person and the environment, may need to help the client find ways to change the human service delivery system:

> During one interview, the social worker at the county welfare department's satellite center asked Mary about the prenatal care she was receiving from the health department's mobile clinic. Mary reported that she arrived each week before 8 A.M., hoping her check-up would be completed in time to attend her first class of the day at 10 A.M. However, Mary so far was not able to be finished in time to attend that class. She saw her options as foregoing prenatal care, or possibly failing her class.

> The worker, sensitive to Mary's goal not to let the pregnancy keep her from progressing with her college education, suggested that she and Mary might discuss this matter with the director of the health department. Mary was reluctant to get involved, but later indicated she knew two other girls who were having the same problem and wondered if it would be OK if they, too, went to the county seat to discuss this problem. The meeting was set for the following week.

> The director of the health department declared that he did not have the authority to change any policies established by the state health department for the op-

eration of mobile clinics. Unwilling to accept this defeat, the social worker and three girls decided to seek help from area legislators and ultimately succeeded in getting a resolution passed by the state legislature calling for greater flexibility in the manner in which services were made available. By then, however, the process could not be concluded in time to resolve Mary's dilemma. She continued her weekly check-ups but failed her 10 A.M. science class. Nevertheless, she was hopeful she had helped others to avoid such situations in the future.

Since rural communities rarely have full-time social work specialists at the macro level, efforts to effect change for groups and communities are crucial. The task of involving poor Appalachians in activities that might improve their conditions is especially difficult. Much of the social life of the rural Appalachian centers around reference groups (e.g., family, a close circle of friends, church groups, and neighbors) that provide comfort and security, but also discourage them from engaging in change efforts unless the rest of the reference group is involved. Weller identified the power of the reference group for Appalachian people as follows:

> Let everyone who works in the Appalachian South take cognizance of the power of these reference groups, which stand at the very center of the mountaineer's life. To step out of the group would mean loss of identity. To stand out in the group or to try to change the group from within is practically impossible, for one would quickly be ostracized. Any outsider who tries to change the reference group is very likely to find himself rejected by it.[43]

Although many changes have been realized through group efforts, the impetus and leadership have generally been provided by persons not strongly entrenched in the references groups. The social worker must find ways to creatively engage reference-group support for social change efforts.

In order to facilitate change at the community level, the social worker must become an accepted member of the community to some degree. The circuit rider, who lives elsewhere and comes into the community only periodically to fulfill his or her professional role, is unlikely to be successful in stimulating community change. The same holds true for the outsider, who comes into the community for a temporary period in an effort to effect change. This was forcefully demonstrated by President Johnson's War on Poverty programs, which brought thousands of "saviors" from outside the region. They were community action program workers, VISTA volunteers, Appalachian volunteers, and others whose motives were benevolent but whose actions reflected considerable naiveté. The local power structure and established social agencies were often ignored, thus ostracizing potentially strong allies.

The social worker involved in community change in rural Appalachia faces a dilemma. The community power structure may at times be the target of change, yet the support of these influential community members is imperative if one is to be successful in achieving the desired change. The worker must be patient, as community changes are likely to evolve only over a long period of time. People often hold steadfastly to established community values and institutions, and are not amenable to rapid change. Social action approaches and techniques found to be effective in urban areas must be evaluated carefully for their appropriateness in a rural context. For example, efforts to mobilize one segment of the community to boycott business establishments, or withhold rent from "slumlords," may prove disastrous in small, tightly knit communities. Individuals may be willing to protest on a person-to-person basis, but they are not likely to participate in collective, organized efforts. A sense of powerlessness, fear of retribution, and reluctance to become involved in either small or large group efforts generally preclude aggressive social action as an effective means to change communities and organizations in rural Appalachia.

To be successful at community change, then, social structures and organizations that are indigenous to the people must be utilized to the fullest, and the worker must have a thorough knowledge of the power structures and invisible influences that affect decision-making. Local governing bodies are powerful, and many have real or implied obligations to outside corporate owners. Therefore, the social worker must constantly walk the thin line of garnering political support for needed changes while maintaining a productive relationship with the power structure. Some very sensitive areas relate to health and environmental concerns, where this balance is particularly difficult to maintain. For example, occupational hazards and industrial pollution generally cannot be dealt with effectively at the local level because of the locality's overdependence on a particular industry. However, changes that take place at the state and national levels relieve the localities of possible blame and retribution. It is essential for the social worker, then, to develop and maintain close relationships with area legislators at all levels, with the goal and ability to influence legislative processes for community improvements.

CONCLUDING COMMENT

Changes in rural areas have placed nearly one-fourth of the population of the United States into a category of special population that requires some adaptations to social work practice. A new practice specialization based on the generalist perspective is emerging, which is helping to address the uniqueness of practice in rural America.[44] The definition of rural social work included in the *The Social Work Dictionary* captures the essential elements that make this specialization unique. Rural practice is defined as:

> Social work practice oriented to helping people who have unique problems and needs arising out of living in agricultural or sparsely populated areas or small towns. These people face most of the same problems and needs as do urban clients; in addition, however, they often encounter difficulties because of limited services and "resource systems," less acceptance of any variations from the social norms prevalent in the area, and fewer educational and economic opportunities.[45]

It is important for social workers who intend to practice in rural areas to recognize that it is not sufficient to simply transfer an urban perspective to a rural environment. Effective rural social work requires understanding the specific culture (e.g., Appalachian culture), rural people, and the unique role rural communities play in the lives of the people. It involves working with both clients and communities that is, perhaps, best served by the generalist practice perspective. And it involves tolerance for professional isolation, a more conservative political climate, resistance to professional services, and dependence on natural helping systems.

When entering a rural community, the social worker should be prepared for the fact that he or she will be viewed as an outsider. While perhaps extreme, it is said that one is not accepted into a rural community until a family member is buried there. One must *earn* a place through evidence of a willingness to behave within community norms such as working hard, not displaying wealth, supporting local establishments, attending church and school functions, and, above all, being friendly.

Due to the isolation professionals experience in rural practice, employing agencies must make special efforts to help the social workers regularly experience professional stimulation and development through conference and workshop attendance. In addition, innovative approaches, such as televised staff development programming and teleconference consultation services, are needed to support rural practice.

The uniquenesses discussed in the description of rural Appalachians and their influence on social work practice in this chapter can help one to appreciate the importance of adapting to the special characteristics of any client(s) being served. Not all Appalachians are alike, and not all rural people are alike. Yet, there are many similar issues that rural social workers need to address. The National Association of Social Workers' public policy statement "Social Work in Rural Areas" points out some actions that would address these issues. Social work plays an important role by (1) advocating for the empowerment of people in rural areas; (2) influencing public policies at all levels of government and the reorientation of the service delivery systems in rural areas; (3) supporting rural social work educators in their attempts to incorporate rural content into curricula of schools of social work; (4) continuing to work for broadly based legislation or health care, transportation, employment, and housing for rural America; (5) developing further expertise and becoming more involved in issues related to the ownership and retention of land; and (6) refining social work's position regarding rural development.[46]

SUGGESTED READINGS

ARNOW, HARRIET SIMPSON. *The Dollmaker.* Lexington: University Press of Kentucky, 1985.
COLLIER, KEN. *Social Work with Rural Peoples: Theory and Practice.* Vancouver, Canada: New Star Books, 1984.

FARLEY, O. WILLIAM, GRIFFITHS, KENNETH A., SKIDMORE, REX A., and THACKERAY, MILTON G. *Rural Social Work Practice.* New York: Free Press, 1982.

GAVENTA, JOHN. "Poverty of Abundance Revisited," *Appalachian Journal* 15 (Fall 1987): 24–33.

JOHNSON, H. WAYNE. *Rural Human Services.* Itasca, Ill.: F. E. Peacock, 1980.

MARTINEZ-BRAWLEY, EMILIA E. *Perspectives on the Rural Community: Humanistic Views for Practitioners.* Silver Spring, Md.: National Association of Social Workers, 1990.

MARTINEZ-BRAWLEY, EMILIA E. "Rural Social Work." In Anne Minahan, ed., *Encyclopedia of Social Work* 18th ed. vol. 2. Silver Spring, Md.: National Association of Social Workers, 1987, pp. 521–537.

MARTINEZ-BRAWLEY, EMILIA E. *Seven Decades of Rural Social Work.* New York: Praeger, 1980.

TURNER, WILLIAM H., and CABBELL, EDWARD J., eds. *Blacks in Appalachia.* Lexington: University Press of Kentucky, 1985.

WATERFIELD, LARRY W. *Conflict and Crisis in Rural America.* New York: Praeger, 1986.

WATKINS, JULIE M., and WATKINS, DENNIS A. *Social Policy and the Rural Setting.* New York: Springer, 1984.

WHISNANT, DAVID E. *Modernizing the Mountaineer.* Boone, N.C.: Appalachian Consortium Press, 1980.

ENDNOTES

1. Emilia E. Martinez-Brawley and Joan Blundall, "Farm Families' Preferences toward the Personal Services," *Social Work* 34 (November 1989): 513.
2. Emilia E. Martinez-Brawley, "Social Work and the Rural Crisis: Is Education Responding?," *Journal of Social Work Education* 24 (Fall 1988): 255–257.
3. U.S. Bureau of the Census, *Statistical Abstracts of the U.S., 1987* 107th ed. (Washington, D.C.: The Bureau, 1987), pp. 3–4.
4. Gretchen H. Waltman, "Main Street Revisited: Social Work Practice in Rural Areas," *Social Casework* 66 (October 1986): 467.
5. Richard A. DuBord, "The Rural Minority in an Urban Society: Content for Social Work Education," Salt Lake City: unpublished paper (University of Utah, 1979), p. 9, cited in O. William Farley, Kenneth A. Griffiths, Rex A. Skidmore, and Milton G. Thackeray, *Rural Social Work Practice* (New York: Free Press, 1982), pp. 6–7.
6. Diana M. Meysted, "Religion and the Rural Population: Implications for Social Work," *Social Casework* 64 (April 1984): 219–226.
7. Larry W. Waterfield, *Conflict and Crisis in Rural America* (New York: Prager, 1986), p. 5.
8. U.S. Bureau of the Census, *Statistical Abstracts of the U.S., 1990* 110th ed. (Washington, D.C.: The Bureau, 1990), p. 28.
9. U.S. Bureau of the Census, *Household and Family Characteristics: March 1988* (Washington, D.C.: The Bureau, 1988), p. 29.
10. U.S. Bureau of the Census, *Poverty in the United States: 1987* (Washington, D.C.: The Bureau, 1987), pp. 1–4.
11. Ibid.
12. U.S. Bureau of the Census, *1980 Census of the Population: Characteristics of the Population* vol. 1, part 1 (Washington, D.C.: U.S. Department of Commerce, 1983), tables 1, 18, 37, 40, 72, 73, 106, and 109.
13. Raymond T. Coward and William M. Smith Jr., "Families in Rural Society," in Don A. Dillman and Daryl J. Hobbs, eds., *Rural Society in the U.S.: Issues for the 1980s* (Boulder, Col.: Westview, 1978), pp. 77–78.

14. Meystedt, pp. 219–220.

15. Norval D. Glenn and Lester Hill Jr., "Rural–Urban Differences in Attitudes and Behavior in the United States," in Richard D. Rodefield, Jan Flora, Donald Voth, Isao Fujimoto, and Jim Converse, eds., *Change in Rural America: Causes, Consequences, and Alternatives* (St. Louis, Mo.: C. V. Mosby, 1978), p. 356.

16. DuBord, p. 9.

17. Martinez-Brawley and Blundall, p. 519.

18. Leona L. Bachrach, "A Sociological Perspective," in L. Ralph Jones and Richard R. Parlour, eds., *Psychiatric Services for Underserved Rural Populations* (New York: Brunner/Mazel, 1985), p. 6.

19. Farley et al., p. 231.

20. Frank Bryan and John McClaughry, *Vermont Papers: Recreating Democracy on a Human Scale* (Chelsea, Vt.: Chelsea Green, 1989), p. 49; also, Chapter 6 ("The Rural–Urban Wars") in Waterfield, presents a useful series of case examples where rural and urban perspectives are in conflict.

21. Louise C. Johnson, "Human Service Delivery Patterns in Nonmetropolitan Communities," in H. Wayne Johnson, ed., *Rural Human Services: A Book of Readings* (Itasca, Ill.: F. E. Peacock, 1980), p. 65; John F. O'Neill and William Horner, "Nourishing People and Communities through the Lean Years," in G. Michael Jacobsen, ed., *Selected Papers of the Seventh National Institute on Social Work in Rural Areas* (Iowa City: University of Iowa Printing Service, 1983), pp. 138–151; and Reginald O. York, Roy T. Denton, and James R. Moran, "Rural and Urban Social Work Practice: Is There a Difference?," *Social Casework* 69 (April 1989): 201–209.

22. Martinez-Brawley, pp. 251–265; and Gretchen H. Waltman, "New Options in Continuing Education: Professional Development for Rural Social Workers," *Human Services in the Rural Environment* 13 (Winter 1990): 16–20.

23. Ken Collier, *Social Work with Rural Peoples: Theory and Practice* (Vancouver, Canada: New Star, 1984), pp. 58–65; Johnson, *Rural Human Services*, pp. 143–148; and Jo Anne Mermelstein and Paul Sundet, "Social Work Education for Rural Program Development," in Leon H. Ginsberg, ed., *Social Work in Rural Communities* (New York: Council on Social Work Education, 1976), pp. 15–16.

24. Bradford W. Sheafor and Pamela S. Landon, "Generalist Perspective," in Anne Minahan, ed., *Encyclopedia of Social Work* 18th ed., vol. 1 (Silver Spring, Md.: National Association of Social Workers, 1987), p. 664.

25. Council on Social Work Education, "Curriculum Policy Statement," *Handbook of Accreditation Standards and Procedures* (Washington, D.C.: The Council, 1984), p. 126.

26. Robert J. Teare, Barbara W. Shank, and Bradford W. Sheafor, "Career Patterns of BSW Social Workers," unpublished paper (Fort Collins: Colorado State University, 1990).

27. Barbara Lou Fenby, "Social Work in a Rural Setting," *Social Work* 23 (March 1978): 162–163.

28. "The New Appalachian Subregions and Their Development Strategies," *Appalachia, Journal of the Appalachian Regional Commission* 8 (August–September 1974): 10–27.

29. Ibid., p. 27.

30. Appalachian Land-Ownership Task Force, "Alliance Releases Land Ownership Study Findings: Land Task Force Urges Community Response," in Bruce Ergood and Bruce E. Kuhre, eds., *Appalachia's Social Context Past and Present* 2nd ed. (Dubuque, Ia.: Kendall/Hunt, 1983), p. 173.

31. Harry M. Caudill, *Night Comes to the Cumberlands: A Biography of a Depressed Area* (Boston: Little, Brown, 1963), p. 75.

32. "Appalachia in Distress," *Johnson City Press* (September 13, 1990): 17.

33. Jerome Pickard, "A New County Classification System," *Appalachia* 21 (Summer 1988): 24.

34. Wilber Hayden Jr., "Blacks: An Invisible Institution in Appalachia?," paper presented at the Eighth Annual Appalachian Studies Conference (Bera, Kentucky, March 30, 1985), p. 2.
35. Helen Lewis, "Fatalism or the Coal Industry?" in Frank S. Riddel, ed., *Appalachia: Its People, Heritage, and Problems* (Dubuque, Iowa: Kendall/Hunt, 1974), pp. 224–225.
36. Loyal Jones, "Appalachian Values," *Twigs* magazine 10 (Fall 1973): 85.
37. Ibid., p. 93.
38. Southern Regional Education Board, Manpower Education and Training Project Rural Task Force, "Educational Assumptions for Rural Social Work," Ginsberg, p. 41.
39. Caudill, pp. 279–281.
40. Roger M. Nooe, "A Clinical Model for Rural Practice," in Ronald K. Green and Stephen A. Webster, eds., *Social Work in Rural Areas: Preparation and Practice* (Knoxville: University of Tennessee School of Social Work, 1977), p. 355.
41. Alfred Kadushin, *The Social Work Interview* (New York: Columbia University Press, 1983), pp. 303–304.
42. Ibid., p. 17.
43. Jack E. Weller, *Yesterday's People* (Lexington: University Press of Kentucky, 1965), p. 59.
44. Emilia E. Martinez-Brawley, "Beyond Cracker-Barrel Images: The Rural Social Work Specialty," *Social Casework* 66 (February 1986): 101–107.
45. Robert L. Barker, *The Social Work Dictionary* (Silver Spring, Md.: National Association of Social Workers, 1987), p. 142.
46. National Association of Social Workers, *Compilation of Public Social Policy Statements* (Silver Spring, Md.: The Association, 1985), pp. 186–187.

CHAPTER 15

Urban Gang Violence: A Psychosocial Crisis

Armando T. Morales

PREFATORY COMMENT

The philosophical spirit of this textbook (originally published in 1977) is to provide readers timely, relevant, scholarly material to not only reflect social work's past and current status concerning particular problem areas, but also shed light on new problem areas requiring the profession's attention. To maintain this spirit, the authors include a chapter dealing with an urban psychosocial crisis that is resulting in the premature death of thousands of adolescent and young adults across the Nation from gang homicide.

Violent urban gangs, therefore, are in social work's practice environment, contributing to social disorganization and dysfunction. Youth gangs and their violent behavior are a symptom of the community telling the world their needs are not being met by the family, neighborhood, and various social institutions and the social work profession. These youths have the same rights to service as other clients. In addition to highlighting epidemiological data about homicide in general as well as it involves gangs, social work intervention strategies are suggested for work with individual gang members, families, gang groups, and the community.

Violence in the United States has become one of the most pervasive issues of our time and U.S. ambivalence about violence is historic.[1] In recent years the profession of social work increasingly has been focusing on some aspects of the violence problem, primarily domestic violence (family, spousal, and child abuse) and suicide. The most recent issue of the *Encyclopedia of Social Work,* for example, devotes entire chapters to these topics.[2]

If all ages are included, suicide is the tenth leading cause of death in the United States and is viewed as a public health concern. Because of its person-in-situation perspective and the presence from time to time of suicidal clients in mental health and social service agencies, the profession of social work has adopted this high-risk population as one of its practice targets.[3]

A comparable cause of death in the United States is homicide, which historically has been a matter of concern for law enforcement, criminologists, sociologists, and more recently, the health profession. *Homicide* is defined as death due to injuries purposefully inflicted by another person or persons, not including deaths caused by law enforcement officers or legal execution by the federal or state government. Aside from occasional, brief epidemiological (incidence and prevalence) data related to forensic populations, suicide, or domestic violence, this subject is by and large ignored in the social work literature. As is the case with suicide clientele, many social workers deal daily with people suffering the effects of social, psychological, economic, and political oppression and dehumanization, who eventually become homicide perpetrators or victims. Hopps argues that social workers are in the best position to articulate the relationship of micro- to macro-psychosocial forces to violence and contribute recommendations for positive change. Offering a challenge to social work, Hopps asks: "If we in the social work profession don't, who will?"[4] This chapter will attempt to provide an in-depth look at one dimension of the problem, specifically, urban youth gang violence and homicide.

During the Great Depression in the late 1920s and 1930s, in urban areas such as Chicago social workers armed with social group work skills were deployed from settlement houses to work directly with youth gangs. Social workers also made their presence known as gang group workers in Los Angeles following massive violent confrontations between U.S. servicemen and Hispanic gang youths in the early 1940s. These intergroup conflicts were called the *Zoot Suit Riots.* Working with gangs in various parts of the country continued to be an area of practice interest for social work in the 1950s and into the 1960s with the federally funded Office of Economic Opportunity teen post programs. In those early days, noted Wilson, social work was painfully aware of the deprivation of people and never lost sight of the fact that institutional change was a prerequisite to the actual relief of suffering.[5]

Since the 1960s there has been a growing public apathy toward the poor in the United States, particularly the immense needs of inner city youth. Group work, anchored in social work's longstanding values of social reform and concern for oppressed people, dwindled as a practice interest, increasingly replaced by a shift to the clinical, intrapsychic functioning of individuals and families.[6] Fox points out that the quality of life in U.S. cities has continued to decline and that social workers have paid little attention to the urban youth gang, symptomatic of what is feared most concerning the consequences of human and environmental neglect.[7] Fox's 1985 social work article dealing with urban youth gangs was only one of four articles appearing in a social work journal from 1984 and 1991, perhaps confirming that gangs are no longer a social work practice interest.[8] The "gang" label has a negative connotation and has been applied to what is generally considered a unique lower-class phenomenon. Rarely are middle-class adolescent groups referred to as *gangs,* irrespective of the similarity of their criminal behavior to their lower-economic-class counterparts. For example, the white, middle-class youths involved in the killing of a black in 1986 at Howard Beach in New York were not referred to as a *gang.* The author therefore, proposes the following definition:

> A *gang* is a peer group of persons in a lower, middle, or upper-class community who participate in activities that are either harmful to themselves and/or others in society.[9]

Urban gangs are viewed as a growing health and mental health crisis; their antisocial behavior is resulting in thousands of homicides and assaults each year, and their involvement with drugs, as both consumers and dealers, is causing untold human destruction in central city communities, particularly as it concerns poor families. At a recent public hearing conducted by the California State Task Force on Youth Gang Violence, a victimized parent who lost two sons stated:

> When I lost my second son I was depressed and in shock. I couldn't believe that this happened to me, not twice. After this, I thought I was the only mother who had lost two sons. Since then, I have met other mothers who have lost a couple of sons to gang violence.[10]

Gangs are not a unique U.S. phenomenon; most countries have them. In Japan they are called *Mambos,* in Germany, *Halbstarke,* in Italy, *Vitelloni,* in South Africa, *Tsotsio,* in France, *Blousons Noir,* and in England, *Teddys.*[11]

THE HISTORY OF GANGS

There is no doubt that gangs have been with us since the beginning of civilization, but the concept of gangs was first reported in the literature by a former gang member, St. Augustine (A.D. 354–430), over 1600 years ago. His father was described as a pagan who lived a "loose life," and his mother, whom he loved greatly, was a pious Christian who had difficulty controlling St. Augustine during his adolescent years. In his book *Confessions,* he demonstrates an astute understanding of the psychology of adolescent gangs, with his discovery that committing a crime in the company of others enhanced the gratifications derived from it. Through his autobiographical psychoanalytical method, he discovered that actions are determined by more than a single motive, stating:

> I loved then in it also the company of the accomplices with whom I did it . . . for had I then loved the pears I stole and wished to enjoy them I might have done it alone, had the bare commission of the theft sufficed to attain my pleasure; nor needed I have inflamed the itching of my desires by the excitement of ac-

complices. But since my pleasure was not in those pears, it was in the offense itself, which the company of fellow-sinners occasioned.[12]

The first youth gangs in the United States made their appearance in the national turf-oriented atmosphere of "manifest destiny"—the rationale for the forceful take-over of the Mexican-owned Southwest—in the mid-1800s. These gangs did much more than steal pears from neighbors and were first seen in Philadelphia in the 1840s. They evolved from volunteer fire companies. Volunteer fire companies provided status and recognition to young, white, lower-class adult males, who were competitive with other companies in trying to be first in extinguishing a fire. The intense competition at times developed into physical conflict, and even killing when a company extinguished a fire on a rival company's "turf." The tough firemen—the Super Bowl heroes of the era—were the idols of neighborhood adolescents, who looked upon them with awe. These "groupies," who likewise identified with the company's turf, also engaged in physical fights with rival fire company youth groups. These early gangs had names such as the *Rats,* the *Bouncers,* and the *Skinners.* With graffiti they defaced walls, fences, and buildings, similar to what gangs do today in urban areas. The Philadelphia *Public Ledger,* on August 13, 1846, described them as being "armed to the teeth with slug shots, pistols, and knives." The biggest provocation to violence was the intrusion of rival gangs into their turf.[13]

During this pre–Civil War period, intense conflict was also seen in New York among white adolescent and young adult gangs forcibly attempting to establish dominance over a particular neighborhood. Asbury writes in *The Gangs of New York:*

> The greatest gang conflicts of the early nineteenth century were fought by these groups (the Bowery Boys and the Dead Rabbits). . . . Sometimes the battles raged for two or three days without cessation, while the streets of the gang area were barricaded with carts and paving stones, and the gangsters blazed away at each other with musket and pistol, or engaged in close work with knives, brickbats, bludgeons, teeth, and fists.[14]

Police were reluctant to and did not intervene in this gang conflict, which at times lasted two or three days. Gangs comprised of latency-age children eight-to twelve-years-of-age, such as the Little Plug Uglies or the Little Daybreak Boys, were almost as ferocious as the older gang members, whose name they adopted and crimes they tried hard to imitate.

Such intense, prolonged conflict is not seen today among gangs. Rather, one of the most frequent violent gang crimes committed today is the "drive-by" shooting, made possible by automobiles. A gang will seek out a home, vehicles, or "hang-outs" of a rival gang and, using an assortment of weapons including automatics, drive by and shoot randomly. As in the nineteenth century, there are instances in which innocent people are accidentally wounded and/or killed. Police officer Perrera, of Fresno, California, commenting on citizens being victimized by gangs, stated:

> We had a recent murder where an innocent woman and her 3-year-old were killed during a drug deal. The juveniles that pulled the trigger will do time in the Youth Authority until they're 25 years old, then they'll be back on the streets again.[15]

It would be difficult to document whether the nineteenth-century gangs were more lethal than contemporary urban gangs, as homicide statistics were not uniformly recorded at that time.

THE PREVALENCE OF GANGS

It is possible, however, to compare the number of gangs in the early 1900s with the number of gangs in some cities today. The most comprehensive study of gangs was undertaken by Frederick M. Thrasher in Chicago between 1919 and 1927. In his book *The Gang: A Study of 1313 Gangs in Chicago,* he found that the gangs comprised various ethnic and racial groups, which included Polish, Italian, Irish, Anglo-American, Jewish, Slavic, Bohemian, German, Swedish, Lithuanian, Chinese, black, and Mexican youths. Three hundred and fifty-one of these gangs contained "mixed nationalities"; the other 962 gangs comprised a single ethnic or racial group. The Polish, numbering 16.4 percent of the population, had the most gangs, 148, followed by the Italian, 99, Irish, 75, and black, 63. Membership in gangs and conflict between gangs were related more to turf than to racial or nationality factors. A "fair-minded" thirteen-year-old Lithuanian gang leader once remarked, "I never ask what nationality he is. A Jew or nigger can be a pal of mine if he's a good fellow."[16] It is interesting to note that by and large, the *white* ethnics described above have faced fewer barriers in the road to assimilation than the Asians, blacks, and Hispanics, who still have gangs in Chicago seventy-one years later.

As far as can be determined, to date there has not been a solid, data-based gathering of information comparable to Thrasher's classic work, as to the numbers of gangs currently in large cities. It is generally agreed that the County of Los Angeles has the most youth gangs in the nation, with estimates ranging from 300 gangs and 30,000 members, to 500 gangs with 50,000 members.[17] Even the larger figures fall significantly short of Chicago's 1313 gangs in the 1920s. In that period Chicago had approximately 65 gangs per 100,000 population, compared to 7 gangs per 100,000 for Los Angeles in 1987. In other words, Chicago had a ratio of gangs per population nine times greater than Los Angeles! In Los Angeles, where minorities represented 54 percent of the population, Hispanics being the largest minority group at 2.4 million, two-thirds of all gangs were composed of Hispanics, followed by blacks, non-Hispanic whites, and Asians.

Ewing reports that in 1988 Chicago had 12,000 youths belonging to approximately 125 gangs, significantly less than Thrasher's 1313 gangs in the 1920s in the same city. Los Angeles, on the other hand, apparently has not peaked in the prevalence of gangs, as in 1988 authorities reported 600 youth gangs with 70,000 members.[18] By October, 1990, Captain Gott of the L.A. County Sheriff's Department stated during public hearings on mental illness in America that Los Angeles had approximately 900 gangs with 100,000 members.

THEORIES OF GANGS

Five theoretical perspectives explaining the causes of gangs will be examined. The first theory is similar to Thrasher's classic description of gangs in the 1920s, in which gangs are seen as a natural progression from, and the consequence of, a youth's search for excitement in a frustrating and limiting environment. They are usually a result of a general breakdown of social controls, and characterized by persons with few social ties, such as immigrants, the mentally ill, and the destitute, and a corresponding lack of parental control over the young.[19]

A second casual factor has been proposed by anthropologist Miller, who studied lower-class gangs in Boston. He describes gang members as males who usually were reared in a female-dominated household, and consequently in adolescence, the gang, he says, "provided the first real opportunity to learn essential aspects of the male role in the context of peers facing similar problems of sex role identification."[20] This theory does not account for the fact that even though 68 percent of black and 67 percent of Hispanic poor families were headed by a woman, according to a 1983 U.S. Commission on Civil Rights report, approximately 95 percent of the youths were *not* gang members or delinquents.[21]

A third perspective is suggested by social scientists such as Cohen, Cloward, and Ohlin. They maintain that the gang is the collective solution of young, lower-class males to a situation of stress, where opportunities for the attainment of wealth and/or status through legitimate channels are blocked. In response, the gang develops a subculture or *contra-culture.* The gang, therefore, must be explained in terms of social conditions in which lower-class youths are placed by the dominant society.[22] This would account for the continued existence of minority group gangs in Chicago since 1918 and the general absence of white ethnic gangs. In other words, minority youth are far more likely to be blocked from having equal access to resources in society. However, this theory does not explain the growing number of white, middle-class gangs in some parts of the country, such as Stoners and Skinheads, which will be discussed later.

A fourth perspective is advanced by Matza, who challenges the "blocked-out" subculture theory, stating that it explains too much delinquency. He believes that gangs exist because adolescents are in a state of suspension between childhood and adulthood; hence, they spend most of their time with peers and are anxious about both their identity as males and their acceptance by the peer group (gang). They conform to the norms of the gang because not to do so would threaten their status.[23] This theory is limited in explaining the continued involvement of adult and middle-aged *veterano* (veteran) gang members found in some Hispanic *barrios,* who are responsible family providers yet occasionally participate in some gang activities. All the above theories have merit and are applicable in many instances, as gangs are very complex and cannot be explained by any *one* theory.

The author proposes a fifth theoretical perspective. In a study of East Los Angeles Hispanic gang and non-gang probation juvenile camp graduates, I found that gang members, significantly more than non–gang members, came from families exhibiting more family breakdown, greater poverty, poorer housing, more alcoholism, drug addiction, and major chronic illness, and more family members involved with law enforcement and correctional agencies.[24] In the face of these overwhelming problems, the youngster turns to the gang as a *surrogate family.* Here, the gang member receives affection, understanding, recognition, loyalty, and emotional and physical protection. In this respect the gang is psychologically adaptive rather than maladaptive. It would not appear to be a coincidence that one of the largest Hispanic gangs in California is called *Nuestra Familia* (Our Family). Hispanic gang members call themselves *homeboys* or *homegirls,* labels consistent with a family and home orientation. Likewise, black gang members often refer to themselves as *brothers* or *sisters.* Close friends *can* be good medicine. But many gang members will often die or kill rival gang members for their gang or turf in the neighborhood. When this occurs, membership then becomes maladaptive. Adding to the powerful group cohesion of Hispanic gangs, which have existed in Chicago, El Paso, and East Los Angeles *barrios* for over seventy years—as have the socioeconomic conditions that produced them—is the reinforcement of the gang culture and tradition by older brothers, uncles, fathers, and even grandfathers.[25]

One also finds increasing evidence of Hispanic female gangs, estimated at 10 percent (about twenty to thirty gangs) in Los Angeles. This is significantly more than the five female gangs Thrasher found among his 1313 gangs. White middle-class family breakdown may also be one of the factors accounting for an increase in non-Hispanic white adolescent gangs.

TYPES OF GANGS

Youth gangs can be analyzed from the standpoint of their primary function, orientation or activity, organizational structure, age, ethnicity, race, and sex. Most social scientists investigating gangs today would agree that there are at least three types of gangs: the *criminal,* the *conflict,* and the *retreatist.* The author suggests that a fourth type of gang is emerging in recent years, which could be called the *cult/occult gang.*

The *criminal gang* has as its primary goal material gain through criminal activities. Success is obtained through the theft of property from premises or persons, extortion, fencing, and obtaining and selling illegal substances such as drugs. In the 1920s Thrasher discovered that some of the wealthiest youth gangs—which he called *beer gangs*—were involved in the liquor business during Prohibition.[26] Today gangs are making their money in drugs.

At an NAACP-sponsored conference on gang problems in Los Angeles in 1987, authorities reported that black street gangs controlled at least one hundred "rock houses" (rock cocaine), and that thousands of gang members were eager to cash in on a nationwide cocaine epidemic. According to police, gang members were now selling rock cocaine in Phoenix, Arizona, Portland, Oregon, Denver, Colorado, Las Vegas, Nevada, and Shreveport, Louisiana. Gwen Cordova, a community member commented:

> When a kid can make $3,000 a week selling drugs, why would he take a job at McDonald's for $3.50 an hour? In a capitalistic society they're taught to go after the best deal, and unfortunately, they do.[27]

The majority of criminal gangs in Los Angeles are black, and as Raymond Johnson of the NAACP warned:

> The Black gangs at this point in time are more organized and they are making the money. Eventually, the other gangs (Hispanic and Asian) are going to learn the technique and they will be doing the same thing.[28]

Asian gangs are similar to other racial/ethnic gangs, as they grew out of a need to protect their communities. However, according to authorities, contemporary Asian gangs are more likely the criminal type, as they are more concerned with generating profits from illegal activities (extortion, gambling, prostitution) within their communities rather than protecting their turf. The newest Asian gangs are composed of Korean and Vietnamese youth.[29]

The *conflict gang* is very turf-oriented and will engage in violent battle with individuals or rival groups that invade their neighborhood or commit acts they consider insulting or degrading. Respect is highly valued and defended. Hispanic gangs, in most cities, are highly represented among conflict gangs. Their mores, values, rituals, and codes are highly consistent in various neighborhoods and cities throughout the Nation and have existed in some areas for almost seventy years. As Sweeney learned in his work with conflict gangs:

> The Code of the *Barrio* means watching out for your neighborhood. This entails protecting your homeboys (and family) and the area designated as your "neighborhood." The Code demands absolute loyalty; every gang member must be willing to die for his *neighborhood* (homeboys and turf).[30]

Of the 600 gangs in Los Angeles, approximately two-thirds are Hispanic, and most of these are conflict-type gangs. Currently in Chicago, where Spergel identified fifty-five conflict gangs, thirty-three were Hispanic, fifteen were black, and seven were non-Hispanic white.[31]

The predominant feature of the *retreatist gang* is the pursuit of getting "loaded" or "high" on alcohol, marijuana, heroin, acid, cocaine, or other drugs. Retreatism is seen by Cloward and Ohlin as an isolated adaptation, characterized by a breakdown in relationships with other persons. The drug user has a need to become affiliated with other retreatist users to secure access to a steady supply of drugs.[32] What distinguishes the criminal gang involved in drugs from the retreatist gang is that the former is primarily involved for financial profit. The retreatist gangs' involvement with drugs is primarily for consumption.

The fourth type of adolescent delinquent group is the *cult/occult gang*.[33] The word *cult* pertains to a system of worshipping the devil or evil. *Occult* means keeping something hidden or secret, or a belief in mysterious or supernatural powers. Not all cult-occult devil or evil worship groups are involved in criminal activity or ritualistic crime. The Ku Klux Klan, for example, may be seen as a cult group, and some chapters, in spite of their hate rhetoric, are law abiding, whereas other chapters have committed criminal acts. The Charles Manson Family is perhaps one of the better known cult-occultic criminal groups. Some occultic groups place a great deal of emphasis on sexuality and violence, believing that by sexually violating a virgin or innocent child, they defile Christianity. One occultic group, called *OTO* (Ordo Templi Orientis), had eleven members convicted of felony child abuse in Riverside County, California.[34]

The majority of occultic groups, whether criminal or law abiding, are composed of adults. However, some juvenile groups are becoming interested in satanic and black magic practices and are using them for their own gratification of sadistic, sexual, and antisocial behavior. Their knowledge and application of rigid, ritualistic occultic practices, however, is often haphazard. Los Angeles has perhaps the largest number of these adolescent cult/occultic-type gangs, numbering about thirty-two.[35] These gangs are composed predominantly of white, non-Hispanic middle-class youths and a few middle-class Hispanics. They are not turf-oriented like conflict gangs, but are found in several middle-class locations. These gangs call themselves *Stoners,* such as the *Alhambra Stoners,* or the *Whittier Stoners.* Stoners from one location are allied with Stoners of other locations. They originally named themselves after the Rolling Stones, and valued getting "stoned."

Their philosophy is based on "Do what you will. The end is soon; live for today." Heavy Metal music is very popular with Stoners, and among their heroes are Aleister Crowley, leading occultist in the United States in the early 1900s, who advocated violation of every moral law from sexual perversion to homicide; Adolf Hitler; and Charles Manson. Some of the self-destructive activities in which Stoners participate, in addition to substance abuse, include sadism and masochism, and suicide. Their antisocial crimes are violence for violence's sake, ritual rape, ritual child abuse, and ritual homicide. Some examples of the graffiti of these groups are "666" (Biblical sign of the beast), "KKK," "FTW" (Fuck the World), and "SWP" (Supreme White People). Law enforcement officials are becoming more concerned about the growth of white middle-class Stoner-type gangs. The author suggests that these cult-occult gangs are a symptom of psychologically deteriorating middle-class Anglo white families. Economic pressures brought on by Reaganomics and now continued by President Bush often force both parents to spend many hours working, away from their children. In treating Stoners coming out of juvenile correctional institutions, the author has observed some of them to be quite emotionally disturbed, having been raised in families that physically abused them as children, or having had a parent or sibling with severe mental illness.

Another subtype of white cult-occult gang groups are the Skinheads, whose racist, anti-Semitic, homophobic "gay bashing," and other violent behavior has appeared in the South, Midwest, and West Coast. According to Spergel, their group structure and behavior comply with the gang pattern, including use of colors, tattoos, common dress and hairstyle, name, drug use, and criminal behavior (usually "hate" crimes). The majority of Skinheads come from middle-class and/or working-class white families.[36]

AGE LEVELS

The age levels of gang members are fairly consistent among the four types of gangs and seem to be related to maturational and natural developmental stages of growth. Thrasher in the 1920s described four general gang-age types as follows[37]:

Gang child:	6–12 years (child)
Gang boy:	11–17 (early adolescent)
Gang boy:	15–25 (later adolescent)
Gang man:	21–50 (adult)

In contemporary conflict and criminal gangs, a similar natural age-group phenomenon may be observed; however, with more specific age categories required by the gang. Small gangs may range in size from ten to twenty members, but in larger gangs with 200–300 members, age categories are more obvious as follows[38]:

Pee Wees:	8–12 years
Tinys:	12–14 years
Dukes:	14–16 years
Cutdowns:	16–18 years (or major name of the gang)
Veteranos:	18–20 years
Locos:	mixed ages (the "crazies")

Girls' gangs adopt similar age categories and gang names. For example, the Cloverettes will be from "Clover," where the Clover Street gang is found. Female adolescent gangs either assume a subordinate, supportive role to male gangs or are completely independent from the male gangs and, for defensive purposes, even engage in violent confrontations with male gang members from their own neighborhood. Female gang members have been known to murder both male gang members and rival female gang members.

The age levels of retreatist and cult/occult-type gangs are less formal, and female participation is minimal. The cult/occult gang age categories are more consistent with school grade levels, such as fifth and sixth grade, junior high, and high school. Older adolescent and young adult members, predominantly male, are often found in juvenile and adult correctional facilities.

HOMICIDE AS A HEALTH–MENTAL HEALTH CONCERN

In the following pages, an in-depth discussion of the etiology (causes) and epidemiology (frequency and distribution) of homicide will provide the reader with a contextual foundation of knowledge within which to better understand the meaning and significance of urban gang violence and homicide.

In 1984 the Secretary of Health and Human Services issued an annual report in which it was noted that the health and longevity of the U.S. population had continued to improve, but the prospect for living a healthy and full life was not shared equally by many minorities. For example, there is a gap of more than five years in life expectancy between blacks and whites. The Secretary called attention to the historical and persistent burden of disability, disease, and death experienced by minorities. One specific health area in which minorities had "excess deaths" was homicide.[39] Homicide is the eleventh leading cause of death for all ages and races combined. (Suicide is tenth.) According to a 1986 report of the Secretary's Task Force on Black and Minority Health, homicides in 1983 accounted for more than 19,000 deaths per year in the United States, a rate of eight homicides per 100,000 population. This is seven to eight times higher than any other industrialized European nation.[40]

The health profession is in the trenches when it comes to homicide and persons injured by the violent behavior of others. In addition to the unmeasurable emotional costs suffered by victims and survivors, the health costs of violence now amount to over 7 percent of national health care expenditures. Additionally, financial costs such as property damage, insurance payments, and foregone earnings amount to 2.3 percent of the Gross National Product.[41] At one hospital, one month's worth of violence-related injuries, that is, inpatient medical care for nine randomly selected victims (three gunshot victims, three stabbing victims, three assault victims) cost $655,595. The projected yearly cost would be $7.9 million, at one hospital.[42]

ETIOLOGY OF HOMICIDE

The United States has the highest rate of homicide of any developed country in the world, with blacks, Hispanics, and Native Americans generally having higher rates than the national average.[43] Excluding minorities from these homicide rates would not alter this nation's negative distinction. It is *not* that United States citizens are naturally born more violent than persons in other countries; rather, U.S. citizens are being raised in a social and cultural environment that encourages and conditions people to be more violent.[44] There is no *one* single factor causing violence and homicide; instead, this complex, biopsychosocial problem can be seen as having several independent and interrelated causes, ranging from micro- (individual) to macro- (societal) etiological factors. These factors can be arranged, from micro- to macro-level causes, into three major categories: (1) biological causes; (2) developmental-psychological causes; and (3) sociocultural-environmental causes.

Biological Causes

A significant amount of controversy exists in attempting to link biological factors to violence. At best it can be said that *some* biological factors, such as genetic conditions, hormonal imbalances, brain diseases, and brain chemistry dysfunctions, may predispose *some* individuals toward violence, under certain circumstances. One cannot predict who will be violent with any high degree of accuracy, only that given certain biological predisposition factors, the *potential* for violence exists.[45]

A growing body of brain chemistry research with animals and humans has demonstrated that pharmacologic modulation of neurotransmitter systems and electrical stimulation of certain regions of the brain can produce marked alterations in aggressive and violent behavior. Such treatment has been found to be successful in some institutionalized psychiatric patients and forensic prisoners.[46] However, even the most adamant proponents of the biological perspective maintain that social factors are by far the most significant determinants of violent behavior.[47]

Chemicals such as food additives, environmental pollutants, toxic metals, and vitamin deficiencies or imbalances have been known to trigger violent behavior or aggravate pre-existing tendencies toward violence in *some* people. Poor nutrition and/or substance abuse by a mother during pregnancy can negatively affect the fetus, causing low birth weight, premature birth, mental retardation, or abnormal brain development, conditions that are related to increased probability of violent behavior by the parent or child. Depressant drugs, such as barbiturates and alcohol, are highly conducive to violence. Alcohol use is associated with up to two-thirds of all violent situations. Drugs and violence often depend on the interaction of factors such as the type of drug substance and dosage, the personality of the user, user expectations of the drug experience, and the environmental situational context.[48]

The major physiological factors related to homicide concern age and gender. Almost 90 percent of homicide victims are males, mostly killed by other males. The majority of homicide victims and perpetrators are older juveniles, young adults, and adults up to thirty-five years of age.[49]

Psychological/Developmental Causes

In theory, a positive birth experience, characterized by a gentle, loving, and nontraumatic experience in every respect, increases the likelihood of healthy emotional, cognitive, and behavioral child development, and hence a nonviolent person. However, there is no *direct* link known to exist between the birth experience and violent behavior.[50] Quality of parenting, early childhood development, and experience may be more important in determining the nature of subsequent social relations. Many juvenile and adult violent criminal offenders had a history of childhood physical abuse (including corporal punishment) and neglect by their parents. These factors can lead to poor self-esteem, a negative or criminal self-image, and feelings of distrust, frustration, and powerlessness—feelings not uncommon among violent offenders.[51]

Unlike other health problems, homicide is the outcome of psychological thinking processes that result in conscious efforts to cause harm to another person. Although there are many psychological and psychiatric theories to explain violence and homicide, there is broad agreement, according to the Secretary's Task Force on Black and Minority Health, that persons who commit homicide and other violent crimes fall into a number of modal groups, as follows:

1. Normal, socialized persons exposed to extremely provocative or frustrating situations or circumstances, at times coupled with inhibition-lowering drugs or alcohol
2. Persons committed to a violent life style with supporting attitudes and values
3. Persons whose inhibitions against violence are impaired by functional (e.g., paranoia) or organic pathology (e.g., abnormal brain chemistry)
4. Overcontrolled persons, whose violence stems from excessive, inflexible inhibitions against the expression of normal aggressive behavior
5. Persons who are highly prone toward aggression or anger resulting from frustration, revenge, jealousy, and oppression
6. Persons who engage in violence as a means to achieve goals other than injuring the victim, such as robbers.[52]

Sociocultural-Environmental Causes

In analyzing the causes of citizen violence and homicide in the world's most violent nation, the social, cultural, and environmental context and values structure in which they occur must be examined. A nation founded on violence, preoccupied with power and oppression of Native Americans and other minorities, women, and the poor, occurring within the powerfully violent modeling context of wars, the advocacy and practice of capital punishment, and an obsession with the possession and use of firearms, all contribute to the creation of a violent citizenry.

There is evidence of an association between war and individual violence, as a society at war is teaching its members that such behavior is acceptable under certain circumstances. Warring nations are more likely to experience increases in homicide rates than nations not involved in war. The Nation's homicide rate more than doubled (4.5 per 100,000 in 1963, to 9.3 in 1973) during the Vietnam War years. Researchers found the fact of war as the most plausible explanation and the most influential variable in the causal equation.[53] Vietnam veterans, especially combat veterans, are more likely than nonveterans to be violence-prone; and evidence more social, psychological, and substance abuse problems than nonveterans.[54] Although the Persian Gulf War had about 200 casualties, scores more were wounded and/or witnessed violence. The traumatic psychological consequences of combat for U.S. male *and* female military personnel may visit violence upon their families, neighbors, and communities for many years to come.

Like war, capital punishment may have a negative effect on the public. One study concluded that publicized executions by the state, instead of deterring further violence, may incite imitative executionlike behavior in society.[55]

Of the homicides committed in the country, about three-fourths involve handguns. Whereas some industrialized nations permit their citizens to possess shotguns, rifles, and other hunting weapons, only the United States allows its citizens relatively unlimited access to and ownership of guns. The U.S. homicide rate by guns is, on average, fifty times higher than England, Germany, and Japan. It is estimated that the number of firearms in private hands nationwide is 120 million. And a firearm kept in the home is six times more likely to be used against a family member, accidentally or otherwise, than against an intruder.[56]

The U.S. media also play a significant role in modeling and influencing young minds. Children spend more time watching television than any other single activity, and by the age of 18 the average person has witnessed over 18,000 homicides on television. Sixty percent of prime-time TV programs contain violent solutions to conflict situations, with cartoons being among the most violent. Research findings do not support the notion that television violence has a cathartic effect on the viewer. In fact, children who watch TV violence are much less likely to stop other children from hurting one another than those who do not.[57]

The ultimate sexist act by a male is the homicide of a female during a rape. One of every ten female homicide victims in the United States is killed during a rape or other sexual attack. Rape victims claim that fear of being killed is a major reason for submitting to rape. As with other violent crimes, rape victims are more likely to be assaulted by a member of their own ethnic or racial group, and like their victims perpetrators are mainly from the younger age groups, with up to 70 percent being under twenty years of age. The high number of rapes in the United States results from sociocultural factors as well as individual psychological factors. Experts believe the existence of rape is associated with sexist culturally sanctioned and institutionalized values, attitudes, and sex-role norms.[58]

Contributing the most to the high rates of homicide and violence are the social factors pertaining to low socioeconomic status and institutional racism. *Institutional racism* may be defined as institutional behavior on a conscious, unconscious, or preconscious level that treats members of different ethnic and racial groups inequitably and differently from the majority.[59] High black homicide rates often have focused on greater poverty in the black population as the most important contributing factor. When socioeconomic status is taken into account, racial differences in homicide rates disappear. Poverty, therefore, unequivocally increases the risk of homicide.[60]

High minority-group homicides can also be attributed to the psychological scars caused by racism, particularly among the poor. The psychological harm expresses itself in feelings of low self-esteem, self-hatred, and rage that at times transform themselves to violence against others.[61]

To further analyze the relationship between institutional racism and economic factors, of the total work force, over twice as many blacks (13 percent) are unemployed as non-Hispanic white males (6 percent), with Hispanics at 8 percent. Blacks, as a group, in addition to being twice as likely to be unemployed, are more than three times as likely to be living below the poverty level. Rates of homicide and violent behavior are highest among young, black, poverty-stricken males who live in urban ghettos and are unemployed, untrained, subject to racism, thus hindered from achieving success.[62]

Federal data revealed that black and Hispanic males, in addition to experiencing more unemployment and underemployment than whites, were more likely to be overeducated for the jobs they held (37 percent for blacks, 19 percent for Hispanics, 23 percent for whites) and more likely to receive inequitable pay for comparable work (19 percent for blacks, 18.9 percent for Hispanics, and 13.8 percent for whites).[63] Noting the connection between institutional racism and economic factors, the California Commission on Crime Control and Violence Prevention stated in its public report to the people:

> High crime rates among some minority groups, particularly Black and Hispanic, may be due to the relegation of a substantial number of their members to a permanent underclass. Members of the underclass are denied participation in mainstream American life—economically and politically. This condition fosters alienation, deprivation and powerlessness, which in turn may lead to a negative form of adaptation whereby members of these groups react with violence.[64]

This observation appears to be applicable to minority community gangs that find themselves "blocked out" from mainstream society. In response, they develop their own contra-culture, and in a reaction-formation way to a state of powerlessness they become overly powerful, or violent.

HOMICIDE RATES

Contributing to the health status gap between whites and minorities is the remarkably high rates of homicide among certain minority populations, particularly blacks and Hispanics. These minority groups are six to nine times more likely than non-Hispanic whites to die from homicide. Including all ethnic and racial groups, the highest risk of homicide involves young males, most often killed by friends or acquaintances employing firearms (usually handguns) during the course of an argument.

During a fourteen-year period from 1970 to 1983, in every region of the United States, for both sexes and every age category, blacks were many times more likely than non-Hispanic white or persons from other ethnic/racial groups to die from homicide.[65] Whereas in 1983 homicide for non-Hispanic whites fifteen to twenty-four years of age was the third leading cause of death (with accidents #1, and suicide #2) and the fourth leading cause of death in the twenty-five to thirty-four years category (accidents #1, suicide #2, and cancer #3), among blacks homicide was *the* leading cause of death for both age categories.[66]

Approximately 60 percent of all Hispanics in the United States reside in the Southwestern states of Arizona, California, Colorado, New Mexico, and Texas. A Centers for Disease Control study in this geographical area, including the years 1976 through 1980, revealed that the Hispanic homicide rate was almost three times higher than non-Hispanic whites; specifically 21.6 per 100,000, compared to 7.7 per 100,000. The national rate in 1979 was 10.2 per 100,000. And Hispanic males had a higher homicide rate than non-Hispanic whites for every age group studied. The most dramatic difference occurred among males in the twenty to twenty-four years of age category, the category in which most homicides appeared for both groups. Here, non-Hispanic white males had a rate of 18.5 per 100,000, compared to Hispanic males with a rate of 83.3 per 100,000.[67]

The Indian Health Service (IHS), reporting on approximately 888,000 Native Americans (American Indians and Alaska Natives) residing in twenty-eight reservation states, revealed that overall, death rates from homicides, suicides, and unintentional injuries were higher among Native Americans than among the U.S. population as a whole. These deaths occur most often to male teenagers and young adults, and because Native Americans are a relatively youthful population, with 33 percent under fifteen years of age, the IHS believed that violent behavior by Native Americans was likely to remain high for the foreseeable future.[68] In 1974 the Native American homicide rate stood at 30.1 per 100,000, almost three times that of the general population. By 1980 the rate had declined, to 18.1, but it was still 70 percent higher than that of the general population (10.8).[69]

Homicide rates may be even higher for Native Americans in more urban areas than on reservations. For example, homicides in Bernalillo County, New Mexico, which includes Albuquerque, covering the five-year period from 1978 to 1982, revealed that in the 15 to 19, 20 to 24, and 25 to 29 age categories, Native Americans had rates of 50.4, 50.4, and 68.2 per 100,000 respectively. These were significantly higher than the rates for non-Hispanic whites in the same age categories, which were 5.8, 15.7, and 16.9 per 100,000 population.[70]

Homicide rates for Asian Americans in the United States are difficult to calculate because: (1) their population is very small; (2) they appear to commit very few homicides, far less than non-Hispanic whites; and (3) the few Asian American homicides that occur are often listed under the race/ethnic category of "other." For example, in a ten-year study of 4950 homicides in Los Angeles City from 1970 to 1979, 47.4 percent of victims were black, 27.1 percent were non-Hispanic white, 22.9 percent were Hispanic, and 2.6 percent were "other race/ethnic groups."[71] During the study period, Asian Americans numbered 100,000 to 700,000 persons. The little data that are available concerning Asian American homicides reveal that Asian Americans in Los Angeles are far more likely to be killed by a stranger with a handgun in a crime-related circumstance than are other ethnic-racial groups.[72] When a person is killed as the byproduct of a crime such as robbery or burglary, it is referred to as a *felony* homicide. A person killing another person where the primary intent is to cause harm, such as a spouse killing a spouse as the result of an argument, would be called a *criminal* homicide. Of 157,003 homicides occurring in the United States for the period 1976 to 1983, approximately two-thirds were *criminal* homicides.[73]

RELATIONSHIP OF VICTIM TO ASSAILANT

National homicide data for 1976 through 1983 reveal that black homicide victims knew their assailant in 59.8 percent of the cases, compared to 48.4 percent for "whites" and 48.8 percent for "other races." (It is not clear in which category Hispanics were included, "white" or "other races.") Among black male victims, the assailant was known in 58.3 percent of the cases, and in over three-fourths of these homicides, the perpetrator was an acquaintance, not a family member. Among black female victims, however, the assailant was known in 65.8 percent of the cases, and in 43.8 percent of these the assailant was a family member. Twenty-eight percent of black female victims were killed by family members, compared to 13.3 percent of black male victims. The pattern of a larger proportion of female than male victims being killed by family members also applied to whites and persons of other races, with 31.9 percent and 28.7 percent, respectively. Among white males and males of other races, the perpetrator was a family member in 12.1 percent and 11.4 percent of the cases.[74]

National data do not make the role of gangs in homicides clear; that is, the percentages of persons in each ethnic and racial group killed by gang perpetrators. These data are, however, beginning to be documented by some states and provide clear information about the seriousness of the problem in urban areas. The Illinois Criminal Justice Information Authority collected lethal violence data over a seventeen-year period (1965–1981) for Chicago. Females were found to have a lower risk of victimization than males, and females were far less prone to commit homicide whatever their race or ethnic background. More black wives killed their husbands than black husbands killed their wives. Homicide by wives or girlfriends constituted 13 percent of black male victims, compared to 5 percent of white males and 2 percent of Hispanic males being killed by women from their ethnic group. White males committed homicide less than blacks or Hispanics, but when white males killed, the victim was three times more likely to be a female as it was among blacks. Hispanic females are much less likely to be involved in homicide, either as victim or offender, than are members of any other group.[75]

The study revealed that violence against women, young children, and the elderly was very rare in the Hispanic population. Rape homicide, as an example, was virtually unknown among Hispanics as no rape homicide was attributed to Hispanic offenders during the entire seventeen-year period.[76]

Lower homicide rates among Hispanic families have also been found in California, perhaps indicating a traditional Hispanic cultural norm in which the family is valued and protected. This might represent the positive aspects of *machismo* (strong, responsible, family-oriented, protective husband and father), as opposed to the negative *macho* (irresponsible, drinking womanizer who physically abuses his wife and children). Table 15–1 represents 2947 homicides in California in 1988 by known relationship of victim to offender and by the race or ethnic group of the victim.[77]

In Table 15–1, it can be seen that black victims are more likely to be a friend or acquaintance (61.2 percent) of the offender than among non-Hispanic whites (53.2 percent) or Hispanic victims (56.7 percent). Non-Hispanic white victims, however, were significantly more likely to be the spouse, parent, or child of the perpetrator (21 percent) than either the black (8.4 percent) or Hispanic (7.4 percent) victims. Does the fact that non-Hispanic white family members are almost three times more likely than Hispanics and 2.5 times more likely than blacks to be killed by a family member reflect serious problems in Anglo-American culture, or is it a symptom of psychologically deteriorating middle-class Anglo-American families?

Wolgang and Ferracuti suggest that culturally learned patterns of behavior account for violence differences between racial groups; that blacks have learned to use violence in more situations, thus having higher homicide rates. According to this view, non-Hispanic whites have not internalized this learning, and hence have lower homicide rates.[78] Can it be said that non-Hispanic families have "learned" to use more violence *within* the family than Hispanic and black families? Comparing two predominantly Hispanic communities with two predominantly

TABLE 15–1   *Relationship of Victim to Offender Distributed by Race/Ethnic Group of Victim (Percentages)*

Victim*	Friend, Acquaintance	Spouse, Parent, Child	Other Relative	Stranger
White (not Hisp.)	53.2%	21.0%	3.9%	21.9%
Black	61.2	8.4	2.8	27.6
Hispanic	56.7	7.4	3.7	32.3

* The total number of homicides for the year was 2947.

Source: Homicides in California, 1988, Office of the Attorney General, Department of Justice/Division of Law Enforcement, Criminal Identification and Information Branch, Bureau of Criminal Statistics and Special Services.

non-Hispanic white middle-class communities in Los Angeles, the author found that the two Hispanic communities had significantly lower rates of homicide (4.2 and 6.1/100,000) than the two non-Hispanic white communities (9.4 and 22.8/ 100,000). What appeared to account for this dramatic difference was that the two Hispanic areas were *middle-class* communities. The two non-Hispanic white communities surpassed the two Hispanic communities in *five* of the "Seven Major Crimes" categories: homicide, forcible rape, burglary, larceny, and auto theft. The results were not definitive in the two remaining major crime categories, with the two Hispanic communities having aggravated assault rates of 535 and 381/ 100,000, compared to 563 and 263/100,000 for the non-Hispanic communities. Robbery was the final major crime category, with the Hispanic communities having a rate of 261 and 188/100,000, compared to 414 and 257/100,000 for the two white communities.[79] Socioeconomic factors, therefore, appear to play a significant role in Hispanic violence and major crime.

In Table 15–2, it can be seen that non-Hispanic whites were more likely than either blacks or Hispanics to have been victims of homicides in which the contributing circumstance was rape, robbery, or burglary (21 percent versus 12.5 and 14.2 percent respectively). Non-Hispanic whites and Hispanics, however, were more likely than blacks to have been killed as the result of an argument; 49.9 and 52.2 versus 40.6 percent. Blacks were much more likely than either Hispanics or non-Hispanic whites to have been victims of drug-related homicides (18.8 versus 8.3 and 6.2 percent respectively). The most dramatic difference between minorities and non-Hispanic whites concerning cause of homicide, however, was related to gangs. Blacks and Hispanics were sixteen to eighteen times more likely to have been victims of gang-related homicides than non-Hispanic whites (19.8 and 16.6 versus 1.1 percent, respectively). Gang membership appears to place minority youth at extremely high risk for death compared to nonminority youths. Gender also contributes to risk of victimization, as more males were killed by gangs (14.8 percent) than females (3.3 percent).[80]

TABLE 15–2   *Known Contributing Circumstance to Homicide, by Race/Ethnic Group of Victim (Percentages)*

Victim*	Rape, Robbery, Burglary	Argument	Gang-Related	Drug-Related	All Other
White (not Hisp.)	21%	49.9%	1.1%	6.2%	21.8%
Black	12.5	40.6	19.8	18.8	8.3
Hispanic	14.2	52.2	16.6	8.3	8.7

* The total number of homicides for the year was 2947.

Source: Homicides in California, 1988, Office of the Attorney General, Department of Justice/ Division of Law Enforcement, Criminal Identification and Information Branch, Bureau of Criminal Statistics and Special Services.

This pattern is also seen in other large urban areas such as Chicago, which reported in its seventeen-year study of 12,872 homicides that 25 percent of murderers of teen-agers *in general* involved "multiple offenders"; that is, a group attack. The risk of a gang-related homicide for Hispanics, however, was much higher than for non-Hispanic whites or blacks, whatever their age. More than half of murdered Hispanic youths were killed in gang-related altercations, and the trend was reportedly increasing,[81] as it is in Los Angeles. The Chicago Police Department defines a *gang-related homicide* as any homicide in which the motive for the killing was related to gang activity.[82]

(Note that the California homicide data do not define "gang-related homicide." There does not appear to be uniformity in criteria in reporting this information. Perhaps these decisions are made at the local law enforcement level. For more accurate reporting concerning "gang-related homicides," states will have to develop standard definitions and criteria within and among states.)

Large U.S. cities have comparable, high homicide rates per 100,000 population. For example, in 1981 Philadelphia had a rate of 22, New York City 26, Chicago 29, Los Angeles 29, Houston 39, and Detroit 42.[83] The more one focuses in depth in a specific area, the more one learns about what specific populations are at higher risk for homicide. Consider Table 15–3, which relates homicide rates from the national level to specific ethnic/racial communities with gangs.[84] In Table 15–3 it is seen that the *barrio* in East Los Angeles had a homicide rate three times higher than the nation but comparable to Los Angeles. The black community in the city's 77th Street police precinct had a rate almost six times higher than the Nation and almost twice the rate of the city as a whole. These figures become even more dramatic when gang homicides are analyzed, since the greatest number of gangs are found in poor, minority communities. Accepting

TABLE 15–3   *1983 Homicide Rates per 100,000 Population: U.S., California, and Los Angeles Gang Rates*

United States	8.0
California	10.5
Los Angeles	26.8
East L.A. Barrio (Hispanic area)	25.4
77th Street Precinct (black area)	46
Los Angeles Gangs[A] (300 gangs, 30,000 members, 200 homicides)	666
Los Angeles Gangs[B] (500 gangs, 50,000 members, 300 homicides)	600

A: Low estimate
B: High estimate

Sources: Department of Justice, "Homicide in California 1988," (Sacramento: State of California, Bureau of Criminal Statistics and Special Services, 1988); "Statistical Digest, 1983." Automated Information Division, Los Angeles Police Department; *State Task Force on Youth Gang Violence*, Final Report, California Council on Criminal Justice, January 1986.

law enforcement's estimate at that time that there were 300 to 500 gangs with 30,000 to 50,000 members who committed 200 to 300 homicides per year, one might be misled by thinking—in taking the lower figure—that 300 gangs committing 200 homicides averaged out to less than one homicide per gang per year.

However, since those who are more likely to be killed are *in* that 30,000 to 50,000 at-risk population, then the homicides rates per 100,000 population are astounding. For example, 200 homicides in a gang population of 30,000 = 666/100,000; or, 300 homicides in a gang population of 50,000 = 600/100,000. In the City of Los Angeles in 1986, 24 percent (187) of 777 homicides were committed by gangs.[85] The Los Angeles County figure was similar, with 60 gang homicides (23 percent) out of a total of 260 homicides for FY 1985–86. The vast majority of those killed by gangs were either gang members or involved in gang-related activities.[86] The Sheriff of Los Angeles County reported that in 1987 gang-related homicides increased to 387,[87] 452 in 1988, and over 500 gang-related homicides in 1989.[88] Gang homicide rates may now be at 700/100,000.

The magnitude of the urban gang homicide crisis perhaps can best be measured more accurately by the potential years of life lost annually. The number of years of potential life lost (YPLL) is measured by subtracting the age of death from age sixty-five.[89] Assuming that the 500 gang members averaged twenty years of age at the time of death and normally would have been expected to live up to the age of sixty-five, each victim therefore lost forty-five years of potential life, that is, 45 years × 500 victims = 22,500 years of potential life lost! Poor minority communities, therefore, are losing one of their most valuable resources, their youth. And inner-city gang homicides are killing the young at a far higher ratio of population than the dreaded AIDS.

GANG INTERVENTION APPROACHES

For over a century our society has developed different approaches in dealing with gangs, usually related more to the economic, emotional, racist, and political climate of the time rather than the comprehensive needs of the gang and its host community as symptoms of societal psychosocial and political neglect. A community case example demonstrating this involves one weekend evening in January, 1988, in the white, very affluent Westwood Village adjacent to the UCLA campus, when a spontaneous, very brief shooting conflict between rival gang members visiting the Village left one innocent female bystander dead. Local citizens were shocked to experience what is not an unusual experience in poor, minority communities. Overnight police patrols in Westwood were *tripled,* while screams of racism came from the poor communities charging that for years they had been asking for more police only to be told by law enforcement officials that their limited budgets prohibited this.[90] Prompted by the Westwood homicide, the L.A. City Council voted to expand its police force by 150 officers, at a cost of $9 million.[91]

Two weeks later in the inner city of Los Angeles, seven minority persons were shot (two died) in three separate drive-by shootings termed "probably" gang-related.[92] A "declaration of war" against gang mentality developed in the frustrated, five-member governing body of the County of Los Angeles known as the Board of Supervisors. Suggestions were made to use the National Guard against gangs and to urge the federal government to "declare war" on countries that support international narcotics trade feeding gangs. The Board voted to provide $1.5 million to expand the Sheriff's Department anti-gang program and place more deputies on patrol—a total increase of seventy-five officers.[93] Obviously, the approach to the problem was force in order to suppress the symptom, which *is* needed. However, how and *when* will the underlying causes be addressed, and who will do it?

It was twenty-five years earlier when angry, frustrated government officials literally sent in the National Guard and law enforcement to suppress the Watts Riots of August, 1965, in the black community in Los Angeles, which left thirty-four persons dead and over $40 million in property damage. Watts, which triggered hundreds of riots in 150 cities across the Nation, including six in the East Los Angeles Hispanic community in 1970–71,[94] indeed was a symptom of racism and societal neglect. The McCone Commission was appointed by the governor in 1965 to investigate the causes of Watts. The McCone report and recommendations were reviewed in 1985, producing the following findings:

> The overall conclusion of those testifying was that conditions are as bad, or worse, in South Central Los Angeles today as they were 19 years ago. As one speaker testified: 'a basic problem in South Central Los Angeles in 1984, as it was in 1965, is poverty—grinding, unending, and debilitating for all whom it touches.'[95]

In response to racism and societal neglect, anger in Watts was externalized and expressed through its youth and young adults against "whitey" with slogans of "Burn, baby, burn!" During the six 1970–71 Hispanic community riots, which covered a period of twenty months, there were no juvenile homicides. Instead, anger was projected onto police and white businesses in the *barrio.*[96]

With a few exceptions, in which innocent bystanders are killed, the epidemic gang violence of the 1990s by and large represents a fratricidal-like behavior, i.e., "homeboy" killing "homeboy," "brother" killing "brother." Homicidal anger and frustration are being internalized by gangs and directed at one's own people; more specifically at one's own image. Homicide is the flip side of suicide: many persons who kill others eventually kill themselves.

Different gang intervention approaches may have varied effects on the gangs, but most of the interventions are surface, short-term, symptom-oriented, remedial measures that at times may be of some benefit to society (increasing arrests of gang members) or the gang (the provision of social-recreational programs). The following represents some of society's responses in attempting to solve the gang problem.

Law Enforcement-Institutionalization Approach

The "send in the military," "get tough," "lock them up" approach, previously described as a governmental response to the gang problem, is not atypical. The public *does* have to be protected; violence suspects have to be arrested and have their day in court. If convicted, they should be incarcerated if the seriousness of the case warrants this disposition. The gang is seen as something evil and hence something to be destroyed. The gang will often be harassed and intimidated by the police, the intent being to discourage gang members from associating. The vast majority of gang youth are *not* violent, but they are *all* seen as violent, and frequently nongang minority youth are caught up in police dragnets. They are frequently arrested for even minor offences until there are sufficient arrests to warrant institutionalization. For example, a week after Los Angeles city and county officials decided to declare war on gangs and curtail gang violence, *200* additional officers were assigned to patrol gang areas. Between 6:30 P.M. on a Friday and 3:00 A.M. on Saturday (8½ hours), the special task force arrested 121 gang member suspects, on charges ranging from curfew violations to narcotics possession. Fifty-eight cars were impounded, 213 traffic citations were issued, and twenty grams of cocaine, twelve grams of marijuana, and eight handguns were seized. In spite of this impressive law enforcement suppression effort, two young men were killed and three others were wounded in gang-related shootings during this time period. No arrests were made related to the shootings.[97] Police officers are in a very difficult position and find themselves in a dilemma. Society expects them to solve the gang problem but does not provide resources to address the underlying social causes. If law enforcement admits that more police will *not* solve the problem, they may not receive additional resources. As was the case with the urban riots, police officers once again find themselves in a damned-if-you-do-or-don't position. They are assigned by the political power structure to sit on the lid of the TNT barrel.

A special effort is usually made by police, parole, and probation officers to rid the gang of its leader, the theory here being that if one takes away the leader of the gang, the gang will dissolve in confusion. These tactics are rarely if ever successful and could be even considered counterproductive, as a youngster's path toward criminalization is accelerated. (See Chapter 10).

Gang youth are frequently placed in juvenile detention facilities for their gang behavior. This delinquent behavior usually involves "joy-riding," curfew violations, alcohol and drug abuse, and misdemeanor and felony assault offenses. Gang youths respond very well to the requirements of the institution: a study revealed that they held the highest positions of authority in various probation camps. They were experts at group process and soon were running the institution. Following graduation from the institution, however, most gang members (75 percent) became recidivists within three months. There was rarely any carry-over of what they had learned in the institution and furthermore, they returned to the same oppressive conditions that were a major cause of their initial downfall.[98] The institutionalization "solution" becomes a revolving door, leading to more youths being incarcerated. As was seen in Chapter 10, California leads the Nation with this approach, and it is not working. Sixteen- and seventeen-year-old murderers are usually handled in adult court, and if convicted, are sent to state prison like adults.

Community Organization Approach

Community organization is a macro-level practice activity in which practitioners working within the network of human service agencies attempt to increase their effectiveness in meeting the needs of an identified population. In theory a community organization approach involves: (1) definition of the problem; (2) a needs assessment concerning the problem; (3) recommending resources addressing the needs of the problem to various private and public agencies, influential citizens, and politicians; and (4) obtaining and applying resources to the population in need, hence eliminating the problem.[99]

Following the 1965 Watts Riots, for example, the McCone Commission, in its investigation into problem areas related to the causes of the riots, developed recommendations concerning police–community relations, welfare and social services, employment, health, housing, transportation, and education. In its nineteen-year follow-up inquiry into the status of the McCone Commission recommendations, the city and county Human Relations Commissions found that the greatest improvements had been made in the public transportation system and the health area, where a major hospital and postgraduate medical school were built *in* the community seven years later. Police–community relations had improved, with an increase of black officers, but numbers of officers and their deployment became an issue of considerable discontent, especially as it concerned crimes against property and gang violence. Problems related to welfare, social services, and employment remained "critical," with housing continuing to be one of the "most critical" problems. Education problems were seen as "growing worse," as evidenced by greater racial isolation of blacks, overcrowding, overabundance of substitute teachers, chronic shortage of math and science teachers, and poor student academic achievement levels in comparison to other parts of the city.[100] Although the community was very satisfied with its new 480-bed hospital, the 1985 "McCone Revisited" testimony revealed that 83 percent of the patients using the hospital were there for the treatment of trauma wounds, primarily caused by handguns. Most of these violence and homicide victims were young, black males.[101] The report did not make it clear if they were gang-related homicides, but if one considers the numerous gangs in that community it is quite likely they were.

After studying the causes of hundreds of riots in 150 cities across the United States in the mid-1960s, the U.S. Riot Commission issued its findings, known as the Kerner Report, stating:

> White racism is essentially responsible for the explosive mixture which has been
> accumulating in our cities since the end of World War II.... The ghettos too
> often mean men and women without jobs, families without men, and schools
> where children are processed instead of educated, until they return to the
> street—to crime, narcotics, to dependency on welfare, and to bitterness and
> resentment against society in general and White society in particular.[102]

Similar findings were reached in a report commissioned by the Congress of Mexican American Unity and Chicano Moratorium Committee as the causes of the
Hispanic community riots in 1970–71 in East Los Angeles.[103]

Thrasher did not attribute the existence of 1313 gangs in Chicago in the
1920s to white racism—since the great majority of those gangs *were* "white"
(not Hispanic). However, he cited similar underlying causes as the McCone and
Kerner Commission reports, that is, failure of social institutions to function efficiently in a youngster's experience, as indicated by disintegration of the family,
"inefficiency of schools," political indifference, low wages, unemployment, and
lack of recreational opportunities. Thrasher added:

> The gang functions with reference to these conditions in two ways: It offers a
> substitute for what society fails to give; and it provides a relief from suppression
> and distasteful behavior. It fills a gap and affords an escape.... Thus the gang,
> itself a natural and spontaneous type of organization arising through conflict, is
> a symptom of disorganization in the larger framework. These conclusions, sug-
> gested by the present study, seem amply verified by data from other cities in the
> United States and in other countries.[104]

Thrasher, therefore, concluded that the gang was a function of specific conditions,
and "it does not tend to appear in the absence of these conditions."[105] Perhaps
the core problem is societal discrimination against the *poor,* which in turn is
compounded by ethnic and racial prejudice and *racism.* The "conditions" nevertheless continue to exist, as do gangs in these communities, that being the bottom
line. In *addition* to the chronic gang problem, spontaneous minority communal
riots make their appearance every ten or twenty years or so, when frustrations
peak, e.g., 1920s, 1940s, 1960s, and 1970s. What can be expected in the 1990s?

As was the case after past riots, broadly based "Blue Ribbon" committees
and commissions have to be appointed, to make comprehensive inquiries into
the gang problem, with society being prepared to make a commitment to allocate
resources to the problem. The government has on occasion appointed committees such as California's State Task Force on Youth Gang Violence to investigate
gang problems. These bodies, however, are usually organized by and are well
represented by criminal justice professionals, who understandably view the problem mainly from a law enforcement perspective. Hence they produce law enforcement–type recommendations, such as increasing incarceration penalties for
gang members, improving the effectiveness of prosecuting attorneys in handling
gang cases, adding training on gangs to criminal justice classes, and obtaining
increased federal funding for witness protection programs. The State Task Force

report, once again, did not address any of the underlying social and economic causes of the gang, despite its mandated goal to:

> ... recommend statewide policy, and legislative and budget priorities to the Governor and California State Legislature to combat youth gangs and youth gang violence.[106]

In 1972, a Los Angeles County Department of Community Services reported that community organization efforts be made to attack the basic social and economic problems seen as the underlying reasons for the existence of gangs. Nothing additional with regard to the community organization approach was offered— in short, nothing happened.[107]

Social–Recreational Approach

This traditional approach views the gang as being unhappy adolescents who lack social and recreational outlets. Attempts are made by social–recreational agencies to give the gang a positive identity as a result of their hard work in planning, having dances, and other social–recreational activities. Through various fundraising efforts, they eventually are able to purchase lettered jackets for themselves. This approach simply utilizes group processes to transform group values and behaviors. Thrasher cites examples of how in the 1920s they were able to transform violent, destructive youth gangs into Boy Scout Troops.[108] In other words, group cohesion is maintained, but its activities are redirected.

On the other hand, there is a theory that gang group cohesiveness and delinquency are related, that factors increasing gang cohesiveness (of which worker emphasis on group programming is one) will lead to increased gang recruitment and delinquency. This conclusion suggests that the gang group worker approach should be severely modified or abandoned.[109] The main problem with both of these approaches is that they are superficial; they do not deal with the *basic* causes of the gang.

Competitive sports is another social–recreational approach, as some believe that the underlying force in the gang is aggression.[110] It would seem logical, therefore, to channel this aggression into more positive outlets such as boxing. Some gang youth prefer boxing over what they consider to be less masculine team sports such as baseball, basketball, and football. The main drawback with this approach is the same as with the previous one, that is, that it only temporarily deals with the symptom. It also communicates to the youngster that this may be all he will ever be good for, to beat someone or be beaten. On the other hand, sports may be a way to at least initially gain the youngster's interest while other, more solid and promising career opportunities are worked out.

Other social–recreation gang intervention approaches involve a host of modest programs designed to impact on some aspects of the gang problem. There may be neighborhood meetings to educate parents about gangs; or antigang curriculum taught to elementary-aged children in the schools. Some programs focus on gang youth with regard to vocational/employment training and provide consultation to schools concerning gang problems occurring on school grounds. Teaching gang youths about art and music and developing these skills through mural painting and performing in musical groups is still another approach. Some gang members are organized into supervised groups and paid for removing graffiti from walls in their neighborhoods. All these programs have some value but are small in number, underfunded, and, like other programs, do not address the underlying causes of the problem.

Spiritual–Religious Approach

Religious groups representing various denominations have attempted to win over gang members in order to spiritually "rehabilitate" them. One such group having much success is called Victory Outreach, which has attracted some Hispanic gang members in Los Angeles. Victory Outreach was founded by Sonny Aguizoni, a former addict, who began the group in 1967 in East Los Angeles. The main function of Victory Outreach has been to bring the teachings of Jesus directly to drug addicts and gang members who are caught up in an "immoral" life. Many gang youth have joined this new Born-Again Christian movement and have become *barrio* missionaries for Christ.[111] Beginning with only one chapel and a handful of members, it has grown to at least twelve chapels and an estimated 5000 members throughout the Southwest. While no actual statistics exist to show its success rate in working with gangs and addicts, Victory Outreach has established a definite presence in some *barrios.* With many years of experience in working with gang members, I have found that when there is a major *structural* change in gang members' lives, such as entering into a marital relationship, having a child, obtaining a steady job, re-enrolling and attending school—or becoming a Born-Again Christian—they seem to abandon the gang. They, in effect, were empowered by a new group led by "the world's most powerful leader."

Street Worker–Counselor Approach

This intervention strategy, next to law enforcement gang suppression programs, is the most common traditional approach to reducing gang violence.[112] The street workers, or *street counselors,* as they sometimes are called, are often former gang members and serve as go-betweens for gangs and other community agencies and organizations. Following the Philadelphia Plan model, which was effective in reducing gang homicides in Philadelphia in the late 1970s, street counselors armed with beepers follow a crisis mode of intervention and immediately defuse potential violent confrontations between gangs by reducing rumors, anger, and, at times, calling the police. They often attempt to persuade warring gangs to sign "peace treaties." The primary goal of this approach is violence reduction; hence it is symptom-centered and not oriented toward addressing the basic causes of the gang.

Sociopolitical Approach[113]

Gangs are extremely cohesive units, and members have a dedication to one another that often surpasses their loyalty to their families. Such powerful cohesion, which gang members need for survival in a hostile, insensitive environment, can be enhanced, transformed, and directed toward efforts that will improve their community. The gang is politicized by the community's political activists, intellectuals, and respected, responsible former veteran gang members. They are helped to develop an even greater pride in themselves that extends beyond their cherished turf. Gang members gradually would become aware of the absence of community representatives on various boards of agencies that are supposed to serve them. Through political pressure they would eventually assume positions of authority in various agencies and have a direct hand in improving their community. This effort begins to change a youth's negative life style. By developing political consciousness, they do not have to feel powerless when faced with an insensitive welfare, health, law enforcement, and political system. Then gang members will engage in political activism, resulting in positive social change for their communities.

There is a precedent for this approach. In the Woodlawn area of Chicago in the late 1960s, the Blackstone Rangers, a black gang numbering 1800 members, were responsible for a 25 percent reduction in crime in their community. This gang was successful in signing treaties with other gangs and, in so doing, helped to prevent riots in their area. As a result of this accomplishment they were soon thereafter courted by political forces. Of equal if not greater importance is the fact that members of this gang developed an awareness of their power base which they could use to positive ends; in turn, they were able to organize businesses and obtain grants for projects that benefited the community. They were able to accomplish these objectives even in the face of an unremitting policy of harassment by a task force of the Chicago Police Department.[114]

A similar phenomenon occurred in numerous *barrios* throughout the Southwest in the late 1960s and early 1970s. Numerous Hispanic gang members joined an organization called the Brown Berets. They politicized their communities, protected them from what they perceived as police harassment and, in some *barrios,* established free clinics. As Dumont once said, "The line between destructive and constructive activism is much finer than the line between activism itself and passivity."[115] Few would disagree that a crucial element of mental health is a sense of environmental mastery, a feeling that some part of the environment, however small, is subject to the control and manipulation of the individual. This approach does not destroy the gang, but rather changes and redirects its activities and energies toward doing something about its environment. It begins to attack the basic cause of the gang. As a gang participates in political activities, it is no longer participating in activities that are harmful to the gang and/or others in the community. It therefore no longer can be defined as a gang. While in the 1920s gang group cohesion was maintained as the gang was transformed into a Boy Scout group, in the late 1980s and 1990s group cohesion may have to be used as an intervention approach on a selective basis to transform some gangs into positive political groups.

IMPLICATIONS FOR SOCIAL WORK

Of all the major helping professions, it appears that social work is best suited, from a values, knowledge, and skills perspective, to attempt to develop intervention strategies concerning one of the most serious psychosocial problems confronting many of the U.S.'s cities today—gangs. It was seen in Chapter 1 that social work is the professional activity of helping individuals, groups, or communities enhance or restore their capacity for social functioning and creating conditions favorable to that goal. Gangs, as a focus for practice, find the social worker helping individuals, groups, families, and the community, that is, are a micro- to macro-level intervention.

Micro Practice: The Individual and the Family

In addition to theories about gangs to explain crime and violence, there are also theories to explain individual crime and violence. Is the gang member, for example, participating in delinquent activities simply as a means of conforming to a subcultural group norm, and in this sense is he or she a "healthy" individual? Or is the gang member primarily acting out his or her individual psychopathology through the gang? In many cases these factors may be related. Based upon thirty-five years of work with gang members as a gang group worker, probation officer, and mental health therapist, I have found that the vast majority of gang members are not mentally disturbed. It is quite probable that the percentage of mentally disturbed gang members is comparable to that in the general population. If the social worker believes the gang member is relatively healthy, then a group intervention approach to modify the delinquent gang behavior will be indicated. If, however, the gang member is diagnostically psychotic, neurotic, or has a personality disorder or adjustment reaction to adolescence, then an individual intervention approach appropriate to the problem is indicated, along with involvement of the family as needed, or as much as *they* will permit. Although not identifying a specific diagnostic label, Johnson advocates an approach using both individual psychotherapy and a community treatment approach for gang members. Johnson states:

> The sociologist, in his enthusiasm for a therapeutic attack on a gang area, should not overlook those delinquents who have internal conflicts not susceptible to the techniques of therapy drawn from the community. It is necessary, therefore, diagnostically and therapeutically, that the sociologist and psychiatrist work together very closely.[116]

Berman sees the juvenile's antisocial behavior becoming more manifest as the youngster gets older, especially when he or she is confronted with the demands for social adaptation in school. Then the well-known symptoms of truancy, defiance of teachers, stealing, fire-setting, untruthfulness, irresponsibility, staying away from home, and fighting with other juveniles are observed. Berman suggests that treatment should involve the participation of the parents, especially the mother, for whom the juvenile holds intense hostility due to toilet-training difficulties. Psychotherapy requires active and direct collaboration on the part of the therapist. The juvenile is seen as reacting to the therapist with hostile, destructive behavior. Only gradually is it possible for the juvenile to trust the ego-syntonic support of the therapist. Berman adds that the correction of distorted object relations and the establishment of new identifications for the child can occur only when the therapist is neither seductive nor rejecting. It requires a benevolent, objective, incorruptible relationship in which the juvenile gradually feels he or she has the support and understanding of the therapist.[117]

The following case, seen by the author, is an example of an adolescent gang member experiencing family, sexual, and gang problems:

"Bluto," a large, 200-pound, fifteen-year-old male gang member, was referred to the mental health agency by the probation department for child molestation. He scored 67 on a WISC IQ test. Initial efforts to involve his parents in family therapy produced few results due to the father's chronic alcoholism. The father came to the only two family sessions red-faced and intoxicated and passively smiled during the mother's and worker's conversation. Bluto, also very quiet, was embarrassed by his father's behavior and was intimidated by his mother's articulate skills and aggressive manner. The father did not seem concerned about Bluto's behavior nor his own alcoholism and rejected the suggestion of a referral to an alcoholism treatment program. In several ways the parents were contributing to Bluto's feelings of inadequacy, expressed in his interest in little girls and over-compensated for in his participation in aggressive gang activities. He was involved in many fights. The intervention approaches with him were multiple and included some basic sex education sessions with a book, role playing, psychodrama, and socialization, the social worker being a positive role model and assisting him in developing verbal and physical coping skills. The treatment approach was supportive and mild to moderately insight-oriented. Bluto felt very proud when the social worker went to his church to witness his First Communion ceremony and was particularly happy when the social worker watched him play basketball in an organized league on a few occasions. Therapist after-hours efforts were sanctioned by the agency but were not financially reimbursable.

Bluto's participation in treatment sessions was excellent, as out of a total of thirty-five weekly sessions he had only one cancellation and two no-shows. He was dismissed from probation after his tenth session. He did not have any more arrests, and after nine months he left his gang. He played varsity football and graduated from high school.

Ideally, efforts should be made to involve the family in the treatment of the adolescent, especially in the case of latency-age or early-adolescent youngsters. In Bluto's case, however, because of the seriousness of the parents' problems, the social worker made a decision to focus more on Bluto, to help him develop his strengths, understanding of the stresses going on in his life, and the negative ways of coping that were threatening his life (gang fights) and bringing him to the attention of the authorities (sexual behavior). If the agency had had a social group work program, a worker would have been assigned to begin working with Bluto's gang if the gang did not already have one.

Micro Practice: The Group

In the case of Bluto, he himself was the primary social work practice unit of attention. In social group work, the unit of attention is primarily the group. The group worker requires a knowledge of group structure and processes, intervention approaches, individual members, group goals, nature of intragroup interaction, and needs, interests, and values of the members. The group worker also understands his or her role in the group, his or her minimal control over the group, and the group's right to self-determination. The group is seen as a microcosm in which positive gains made by the group through group process can produce growth and change in the individual, the group, and community through the group's social action, even in the larger environment.[118]

Fox points out that social work *can* adapt its social group work practice methodology to serve urban gang members and their community through the "detached worker" or gang group worker, engaged directly with the gang and supported through community-based agencies. Working with gangs requires that the social worker spend a significant amount of time in the client's (gang's) immediate environment rather than in the agency, hence the term *detached* or *street worker*. The author, having worked with gangs, agrees with Fox when he states that: (1) even though gangs have the same needs and rights to services as others, prejudice and distorted fear (countertransference) of inner-city minority group youth gangs prohibits many competent social workers from entering these communities; (2) most gang members are surprisingly receptive to a helping relationship and are usually quite willing to permit the worker to engage the gang as a group within the purposes of social work practice; and (3) the social worker can help urban youth gangs to change from being a destructive force to being a constructive contributor to the community while maintaining the gang's right to self-determination.[119]

One of the tasks of the worker is to assist the gang in obtaining resources in pursuit of its goals. In working toward this, the worker has an opportunity not only to help the gang obtain needed resources, but in the process also modify the negative image of the gang held by the community. This is illustrated in the following case:

> Gang members expressed boredom and frustration about the lack of athletic facilities in the neighborhood. Consequently, one of their favorite activities was harassing employees and destroying property at a nearby hospital.
>
> With the gang's consent, the worker approached the hospital's administration to suggest that part of the hospital's large paved parking lot be equipped with back-

boards and basketball court markings. The administration agreed to try this in
the hope that it would reduce harassment from the gang. The worker arranged
a meeting between several gang members and the hospital superintendent of
buildings and grounds for a semi-formal presentation of the court to the gang.
There was an immediate cessation of trouble from the gang, and the members
expressed great satisfaction with the new facility.[120]

In the above case, the group worker, while adopting an advocate and enabler
role, was able to create positive change in the gang *and* the institution, which
was helpful to both parties. The gang, through observing their group worker,
learned there were other ways of accomplishing goals in life than through the
use of intimidation and violence.

Macro Practice: The Community

The gang is, in the final analysis, a product and symptom of the community
indicating that some of the needs of youth are not being met by the family,
neighborhood, and traditional community institutions such as the police, school,
and religious and recreational institutions. To meet its needs the gang creates its
own institution—the gang. In pursuit of its needs the gang often functions in
delinquent ways, subjecting community members to antisocial acts, including
homicide. Their negative behavior contributes to social dysfunction and disorganization in the community.[121]

In developing a social work community intervention model concerning
gangs, Spergel recommends dealing with the problem at two levels, the larger
structural, and the local institutional. Attention has to be given to the major
underlying social, economic, cultural, political, and legal conditions that contribute to the gang problem—such conditions evolving at the national and international level. Spergel believes national-level problems that affect gang violence, such as housing segregation, unemployment, immigrant flow, and access
to handguns, can be modified through appropriate public policies.[122]

In addition to addressing the need for social policy changes at the national
level, attention also has to be focused on the local-community institutional and
program level. Institutional problems such as weak local community organization,
unsystematic police strategies, restrictive youth agency membership age policies,
and lack of young adult bridging mechanisms will require intervention. Weak
community organization is one of the contributing factors for the existence of
gangs and therefore has to be strengthened, according to Spergel. As part of the
structure of the community, the components of social controls (law enforcement)
and social opportunities (resources and services) have to be analyzed. There
needs to be a *balance* between law enforcement control and provision of resources, according to Spergel. Too much law enforcement emphasis, with resulting imprisonment, leads to increased criminal behavior of gang members; and
too much "do-goodism" can result in exploitation and manipulation of resources
by gangs, resulting in increased criminal behavior. Spergel believes if the community is more effectively organized, including the provision of adequate social

controls and social services, the violent gang as a transitional institution may no longer be necessary. Spergel offers a gang violence intervention operational model with five objectives, stated in brief form as follows:

1. Foremost is mediation of gang disputes and tensions that contribute to inter-gang violence. The objective is achieved through a process of crisis counseling and intergroup communication in the course of patrol and surveillance of the community during times when violent gang disputes are likely to erupt.
2. Mobilization of community groups and organizations to restrain gang violence, such as block clubs, local improvement organizations, mothers' groups, and church groups, who would intervene directly through patrols, marches, and closer communication with the police.
3. Assistance to various neighborhood groups and organizations to better target and utilize their resources concerning the needs of gang youth for education, training, jobs, family counseling, drug rehabilitation, and other services.
4. Prevention of gang violence and improved social adaptation of male gang members between thirteen and sixteen years referred to counseling by police for incipient violent gang activity.
5. Coordinated participation of key organizations, community groups, and justice system agencies in the development and evaluation of special programs focusing on gang violence reduction.[123]

Spergel sees these five objectives as interrelated. Appropriate staff time and resources have to be allocated in order for the model to be effective. An essential ingredient is the involvement of "grass roots" people, indigenous community workers, professional social workers, and graduate students. The creation of a community council, advisory board, or town hall group, comprised of members representing all concerned agencies, community people, gang members, and politicians, would then improve communication and strengthen the organization of the community.

CONCLUDING COMMENT

Violent, delinquent gangs have been part of the U.S. scene since at least 1842. It may very well be that gangs have never been more violent than they are today, with homicides at an unbelievable rate of 600 per 100,000 among that specific population in some urban areas. Gangs have always been primarily a law enforcement problem area. The 1920s to 1960s attracted some group work and community organization practice interest from the social work profession in gangs; however, beginning in the 1970s and now in the 1990s, the profession has been steadily moving away from criminal justice populations, gangs, and the urban social problems of poor minorities. Social work has increasingly taken a path toward private practice and industrial social work, becoming more "clinical" with a predominantly middle-class clientele.

The values, knowledge, and skills base of the social work profession places it in a unique position, compared to other helping professions, to seriously address the growing urban gang psychosocial crisis. For example, the profession has a historical knowledge base concerning group work with gangs and an impressive theory and practice foundation relating to community organization. Additionally, the profession's clinical skills have advanced significantly since the 1940s, and in specialized cases such as "Bluto" the social workers can be effective in treating gang members.

Fox's significant work with gangs reminds the profession that not only are gangs still present in the 1990s but also social group work skills. A community gang intervention model, developed by Spergel, provides the social work community organizer with a framework for practice that could reduce gang violence in any given community.

Urban gang violence is indeed a psychosocial crisis that will not go away. It *is* a challenge to the profession, an opportunity to demonstrate that social work is a unique micro- to macro-level practice discipline and *can* do some things that other helping professions cannot. Social work's values tell us that we have no choice but to help those most in need. And gang members have a right to social services.

SUGGESTED READINGS

EWING, CHARLES PATRICK. *Kids Who Kill* Lexington, Mass.: D.C. Heath, 1990.

FOX, JERRY R. "Mission Impossible? Social Work Practice with Black Urban Youth Gangs." *Social Work* 30 (January–February 1985): 25–31.

HOPPS, JUNE GARY. "Violence—A Personal and Societal Challenge." *Social Work* 32 (November–December 1987): 467–468.

MIDDLEMAN, RUTH R., and GOLDBERG, GALE. "Social Work Practice with Groups." *Encyclopedia of Social Work* 18th ed. vol. II Silver Spring, Md.: National Association of Social Workers, 1987, pp. 714–729.

MORALES, ARMANDO. "The Mexican American Gang Member: Evaluation and Treatment." In Rosina M. Becerra, Marvin Karno, and Javier Escobar, eds., *Mental Health and Hispanic Americans: Clinical Perspectives.* New York: Grune & Stratton, 1982.

Report of the Secretary's Task Force on Black and Minority Health vol. 5, U.S. Department of Health and Human Services, January 1986.

SPERGEL, IRVING A. "Violent Gangs in Chicago: In Search of Social Policy." *Social Service Review* 58 (June 1984): 199–226.

THRASHER, FREDERICK M. *The Gang: A Study of 1313 Gangs in Chicago.* Chicago: University of Chicago Press, 1963.

ENDNOTES

1. June Gary Hopps, "Violence—A Personal and Societal Challenge," *Social Work* 32 (November–December 1987): 467–468.

2. See E. Milling Kinard, "Child Abuse and Neglect," pp. 223–231; Barbara Star, "Domestic Violence," pp. 463–476, vol. I; and Andre M. Ivanoff, "Suicide," pp. 737–748, in *Encyclopedia of Social Work* 18th ed., vol. II (Silver Spring, Md.: National Association of Social Workers, 1987).

3. Ivanoff, p. 744.

4. Hopps, p. 468.

5. Gertrude Wilson, "From Practice to Theory: A Personalized History," in Robert Roberts and Helen Northen, eds., *Theories of Social Work with Groups* (New York: Columbia University Press, 1976), p. 11.

6. Ruth R. Middleman and Gale Goldberg, "Social Work Practice with Groups, *"Encyclopedia of Social Work* 18th ed., vol. II, p. 715.

7. Jerry R. Fox, "Mission Impossible? Social Work Practice with Black Urban Youth Gangs," *Social Work* 30 (January–February 1985): 25.

8. Another article was written by Irving A. Spergel, "Violent Gangs in Chicago: In Search of Social Policy," *Social Service Review* 58 (June 1984): 199–226.

9. Armando Morales, "The Need for Nontraditional Mental Health Programs in the Barrio," in J. Manuel Casas and Susan E. Keefe, eds., *Family and Mental Health in the Mexican-American Community,* Monograph No. 7 (Los Angeles: UCLA Spanish-Speaking Mental Health Research Center 1978), p. 133.

10. *State Task Force on Youth Gang Violence,* Final Report, California Council on Criminal Justice, January 1986, p. 4.

11. F. J. O'Hagan, "Gang Characteristics—An Empirical Survey," *Journal of Child Psychology and Psychiatry* 17 (1976): 305–314.

12. Saint Augustine, *Confessions* (New York: The Modern Library, 1949), p. 34.

13. A. Davis and M. Haller, eds., *The People of Philadelphia* (Philadelphia: Temple University Press, 1973), p. 78.

14. H. Asbury, *The Gangs of New York: An Informal History of the Underworld* (New York: Alfred A. Knopf, 1927), p. 29.

15. *State Task Force,* p. 30.

16. F. M. Thrasher, *The Gang: A Study of 1313 Gangs in Chicago* (Chicago: University of Chicago Press, 1963), p. 151.

17. *State Task Force,* p. viii.

18. Charles Patrick Ewing, *Kids Who Kill* (Lexington, Mass.: D.C. Heath, 1990), pp. 102–103.

19. Thrasher, pp. 31–35.

20. W. B. Miller, "Lower Class Culture as a Generating Milieu of Gang Delinquency," *Journal of Social Issues* 14 (1958): 5–19.

21. *Los Angeles Times,* Part I, April 12, 1983, p. 6.

22. See A. K. Cohen, *Delinquent Boys: The Culture of the Gang* (Glencoe, Ill.: Free Press, 1955); and R. A. Cloward and L. E. Ohlin, *Delinquency and Opportunity* (New York: Free Press, 1960).

23. D. Matza, *Delinquency and Drift* (New York: Wiley, 1964).

24. Armando Morales, "A Study of Recidivism of Mexican American Junior Forestry Camp Graduates, unpublished Master's thesis (School of Social Work, University of Southern California, 1963.)

25. A. Morales, "The Mexican American Gang Member: Evaluation and Treatment," in R. Becerra, M. Karno, and J. Escobar, eds., *Mental Health and Hispanic Americans: Clinical Perspectives* (New York: Grune & Stratton, 1982), p. 153.

26. Thrasher, p. 117.

27. *Los Angeles Times,* Part I, November 17, 1986, p. 18.

28. *Los Angeles Times,* Part I, January 11, 1987, p. 23.

29. *Report on Youth Gang Violence in California,* The Attorney General's Youth Gang Task Force, June 1981, pp. 16–20.

30. T. A. Sweeney, *Streets of Anger: Streets of Hope* (Glendale, Calif.: Great Western Publishing, 1980), p. 86.
31. I. A. Spergel, "Violent Gangs in Chicago: In Search of Social Policy," *Social Service Review* 58 (June 1984): 206.
32. Cloward and Ohlin, p. 178.
33. *State Task Force,* p. 8.
34. T. Kerfoot, "Crime and the Occult," *Peace Officers Association of Los Angeles County* (October 1985): 23.
35. M. Poirier, "Street Gangs of Los Angeles County," unpublished pamphlet, 1982.
36. Irving A. Spergel, "Youth Gangs: Continuity and Change," to be published in *Crime and Justice,* University of Chicago Press.
37. Thrasher, p. 60.
38. Morales (1982), p. 156.
39. Report of the Secretary's Task Force on Black and Minority Health vol. 5, U.S. Department of Health and Human Services (January 1986), p. v.
40. *Report of the Secretary,* p. 5.
41. E. Muñoz, "Economic Costs of Trauma, United States, 1982," *Journal of Trauma* 24 (1984).
42. Burnet B. Sumner, Elizabeth R. Mintz, and Patricia L. Brown, "Interviewing Persons Hospitalized with Interpersonal Violence-Related Injuries: A Pilot Study," in *Report of the Secretary,* pp. 305–306.
43. *Report of the Secretary,* p. 29.
44. "Ounces of Prevention: Toward an Understanding of the Causes of Violence," *1982 Final Report to the People of California,* Commission on Crime Control and Violence Prevention, State of California, p. 1.
45. *1982 Final Report,* pp. 81–82.
46. Burr Eichelman, "Toward a Rational Pharmacotherapy for Aggressive and Violent Behavior," *Hospital and Community Psychiatry* 39 (January 1988): 31.
47. *1982 Final Report,* p. 82.
48. *1982 Final Report,* p. 11.
49. *Report of the Secretary,* p. 32.
50. *1982 Final Report,* p. 13.
51. *1982 Final Report,* p. 6.
52. *Report of the Secretary,* pp. 29, 31.
53. Irwin L. Kutash, Samuel B. Kutash, and Louis B. Schlesinger, eds., *Violence: Perspective on Murder and Aggression* (San Francisco: Jossey-Bass, 1978), pp. 219–232.
54. *1982 Final Report,* p. 137.
55. *1982 Final Report,* p. 138.
56. *1982 Final Report,* pp. 139–140.
57. Ronald S. Prabman and Margaret H. Thomas, "Children's Imitation of Aggressive and Pro-Social Behavior when Viewing Alone and in Pairs," *Journal of Communication* 27 (1977): 199–205.
58. *1982 Final Report,* pp. 109–133.
59. Armando Morales, "Institutional Racism in Mental Health and Criminal Justice," *Social Casework* (July 1978): 387.
60. Centers for Disease Control, *Homicide Surveillance: High-Risk Racial and Ethnic Groups—Blacks and Hispanics, 1970–1983* (Atlanta: The Centers, November, 1986), p. 7.
61. Alvin Poussaint, "Black-on-Black Homicide: A Psychological-Political Perspective," *Victimology* 8 (1983): 161–169.
62. *1982 Final Report,* p. 51–52.
63. U.S. Commission on Civil Rights, *Unemployment and Underemployment among Blacks, Hispanics, and Women,* Clearinghouse Publication 74, November 1982.
64. *1982 Final Report,* p. 53.

65. Centers for Disease Control, p. 7.
66. Centers for Disease Control, pp. 14–15.
67. Centers for Disease Control, p. 16.
68. *Listening Post* 5 (February 1984, a periodical of the Mental Health Programs, Indian Health Service).
69. Indian Health Service, Chart Book Series, June 1984.
70. Cynthia Leyba, "Homicide in Bernalillo County: 1978–1982" (Paper commissioned by the Research Conference on Violence and Homicide in Hispanic Communities, University of California, Los Angeles, September 14 and 15, 1987) Table 6, p. 14.
71. University of California, Los Angeles, Centers for Disease Control, "The Epidemiology of Homicide in the City of Los Angeles, 1970–1979," Department of Health and Human Services, Public Health Service, Centers for Disease Control, August 1985, p. 18.
72. Fred Loya, Philip Garcia, John D. Sullivan, Luis A. Vargas, Nancy Allen, and James A. Mercy, "Conditional Risks of Types of Homicide among Anglo, Hispanic, Black, and Asian Victims in Los Angeles, 1970–1979," in *Report of the Secretary,* p. 123.
73. Centers for Disease Control, p. 5.
74. Centers for Disease Control, p. 5.
75. Carolyn Rebecca Block, "Lethal Violence in Chicago over Seventeen Years: Homicides Known to the Police, 1965–1981," Illinois Criminal Justice Information Authority, July 1985, p. 68.
76. Block, p. iv.
77. "Homicide in California, 1988," Department of Justice, Bureau of Criminal Statistics and Special Services, State of California, 1988, p. 8.
78. Marvin E. Wolfgang and Franco Ferracuti, *The Subculture of Violence: Toward an Integrated Theory in Criminology* (Beverly Hills, Calif. Sage Publications, 1982).
79. Armando Morales, "Hispanic Gang Violence and Homicide" (Paper commissioned by the Research Conference on Violence and Homicide in Hispanic Communities, Office of Minority Health, Department of Health and Human Services, the National Institute of Mental Health and the U.S. Centers for Disease Control, University of California, Los Angeles, September 14–15, 1987 (p. 30).
80. *Homicide in California, 1988,* p. 81.
81. Block, p. 69.
82. Carolyn Rebecca Block, "Specification of Patterns over Time in Chicago Homicide: Increases and Decreases, 1965–1981," Illinois Criminal Justice Information Authority, October 1985, p. 16.
83. Block, "Specification of Patterns Over Time," p. 87.
84. Sources: *Homicide in California, 1985;* "Statistical Digest, 1983," Automated Information Division, Los Angeles Police Department; *State Task Force on Youth Gang Violence,* Final Report, California Council on Criminal Justice, January 1986.
85. "Statistical Digest, 1986," Automated Information Division, Los Angeles Police Department.
86. "Fiscal Year 1985–86 Statistical Summary," Los Angeles County Sheriff's Department.
87. *Los Angeles Times,* Part II, February 24, 1988, p. 1.
88. Ewing, p. 101.
89. Centers for Disease Control, p. 3.
90. *Los Angeles Times,* Metro, Part II, February 6, 1988, p. 9.
91. *Los Angeles Times,* Metro, Part II, Wednesday, February 10, 1988, p. 1.
92. *Los Angeles Times,* Metro, Part II, February 14, 1988, p. 1.
93. *Los Angeles Times,* Metro, Part II, February 24, 1988, p. 1.
94. Armando Morales, *Ando Sangrando: I am Bleeding: A Study of Mexican American Police Conflict* (La Puente, Calif.: Perspectiva Publications, 1972), pp. 91–122.
95. "McCone Revisited: A Focus on Solutions to Continuing Problems in South Central Los Angeles," a Joint Report by the Los Angeles Country Commission on Human

Relations and the Los Angeles City Human Relations Commission, January 1985, p. 2.

96. Morales, *Ando Sangrando.*

97. *Los Angeles Times,* Metro, Part II, February 28, 1988, p. 2.

98. Morales, "A Study of Recidivism."

99. See Thomas M. Meenaghan, "Macro Practice: Current Trends and Issues," in *Encyclopedia of Social Work* 18th ed., vol. II, pp. 82–89; and Armando Morales and Bradford W. Sheafor, *Social Work: A Profession of Many Faces* 4th ed. (Needham Heights, Mass.: Allyn and Bacon, 1986), pp. 131–132.

100. "McCone Revisited," pp. 4–14.

101. "McCone Revisited," p. 7.

102. *Report of the National Advisory Commission on Civil Disorders* (New York: Bantam Books, 1968), p. 206.

103. Morales, *Ando Sangrando,* pp. 91–122.

104. Thrasher, *The Gang,* p. 33.

105. Thrasher, p. 35.

106. *State Task Force on Youth Gang Violence,* Final Report, California Council on Criminal Justice, January 1986, p. viii.

107. "A Program to Combat Gang Problems in Los Angeles County," Los Angeles County Department of Community Services, November 1972, p. 5.

108. Thrasher, p. 353.

109. Malcolm W. Klein, *Street Gangs and Street Workers* (Englewood Cliffs, N.J.: Prentice-Hall, 1971).

110. Jerome Singer, *The Control of Aggression and Violence* (New York: Academic Press, 1971).

111. "Victory Outreach Friendship Station," Newsletter, 1978.

112. "Early Gang Intervention," Transfer of Knowledge Workshop, Department of the Youth Authority, Office of Criminal Justice Planning, February 1985, p. 9.

113. Morales, "The Need for Non-Traditional Programs, pp. 133–141.

114. Matthew P. Dumont, *The Absurd Healer* (New York: Viking Press, 1968), p. 151.

115. Dumont, p. 151.

116. Adelaide M. Johnson, "Juvenile Delinquency," in Silvano Arieti, ed., *American Handbook of Psychiatry* (New York: Basic Books, 1959), p. 854.

117. S. Berman, "Antisocial Character Disorder," in Ruth S. Cavan, ed., *Readings in Juvenile Delinquency* 2nd ed. (New York: J. B. Lippincott, 1969), pp. 147–157.

118. Ruth R. Middleman and Gale Goldberg, "Social Work Practice with Groups," *Encyclopedia of Social Work,* pp. 718–719.

119. Fox, pp. 26–27.

120. Fox, p. 29.

121. Fox, p. 26.

122. Spergel, p. 220.

123. Spergel, pp. 221–222.

CHAPTER 16

The Impact of Macro Systems on Puerto Rican Families

Emelicia Mizio

PREFATORY COMMENT

This chapter by Emelicia Mizio highlights the importance of understanding the cultural heritage of Puerto Ricans and the extent of each family's identification with Puerto Rican or Anglo-American culture. A unique blending of these cultural factors is found in many of these families and individuals, which is also flavored by socioeconomic class factors. Since cultures rarely remain static, it is particularly important to be aware of evolving male/female roles and their functional and dysfunctional aspects as they concern subordination patterns. As is the case with most Hispanic cultures, Puerto Ricans value the extended family, and this should not be seen as a threat to a person's individuality. Mizio offers suggestions for the social worker in helping Puerto Ricans deal with oppressive external social systems through joint advocacy aimed at systems change.

Healthy families are the *sine qua non* of a healthy society. Well integrated families are critical to the preservation of our societal structure and its effective functioning. Families cannot exist in isolation and cannot maintain their health without societal supports. There is a reciprocity which must be recognized between society and its members (Zimmerman, 1976).

To understand a family and its operations, one must study its transactions with its environments. The family is an extremely vulnerable institution impacted

From Gloria Johnson Powell, Joe Yamamoto, Annelisa Romero, and Armando Morales, eds., *The Psychosocial Development of Minority Group Children* (New York: Brunner/Mazel, 1983).

by and responsive to societal conditions. The degree of a family's vulnerability relates closely to its socioeconomic status. The effects of poverty have been well documented in terms of physical and mental malaise and the overwhelming sense of helplessness, hopelessness and alienation. The generally poor, low-status Puerto Rican family is consequently in extreme jeopardy because its extended family system and differences in its values place it in conflict with a sociolegal system in this country which addresses itself basically to the nuclear family. Our society, in turn, jeopardizes itself when it does not meet the needs of its citizenry or provide necessary supports; hence, the problems of our inner cities. Major cities such as New York, Chicago, Philadelphia, Cleveland, Newark, and Boston have large Puerto Rican (and other minority) populations. The quality of life for Puerto Ricans (and other minorities) in key urban centers must be viewed as inextricably linked to the general quality of life in those cities (U.S. Commission on Civil Rights, 1976).

A coherent and just national family social policy must evolve and address itself to ethnic differences. Social policy deals with the kinds of benefits that are to be distributed, with the people to whom they are to be distributed, with the amount to be distributed, with the way in which they are to be financed, and with the cost of providing the specific benefit (Zimmerman, 1976). Ethnicity is defined as conscious and unconscious processes fulfilling a deep psychological need for security, identity, and sense of historical continuity. Within the family, it is transmitted in an emotional language, and it is reinforced by similar units in the community (Giordano, 1974). Ethnicity refers to a common culture. It operates on both conscious and unconscious levels and shapes basic values, norms, attitudes, and life styles of the group's members even as it is modified by such factors as class, race, religion, sex, region and generation (Giordano, 1976a). Social policy experts and planners and service-delivering professionals must make certain that they take these ethnic differences into account. Considerable research is now being conducted in this area (Giordano, 1976b).

THE EXTENDED FAMILY IN A NUCLEAR FAMILY SOCIETY

The family has been viewed as a goal-oriented, task-performing system. It has the following functions: (1) physical care and maintenance of its members; (2) addition of new members through reproduction and their relinquishment when they mature; (3) socialization of children for various roles as spouses, parents, workers, citizens, and members of social groups; (4) maintenance of order within the family and between the family and outside groups; (5) maintenance of family motivation and morale to facilitate performance of tasks in the family and other social groups; (6) production as well as distribution of services and goods necessary for maintaining the family (Zimmerman, 1976).

There are also different family types characterized by common residence. The one with which we are most familiar in the United States is the "model

American family," a nuclear family where special emphasis is placed on the conjugal bond. Typically, a nuclear family consists of wife and husband, and their offspring; kin are generally excluded (Murdock, 1968). In a nuclear family the family's decision making and reciprocal controls are weak since few mandatory exchanges are required (Goode, 1964). In the search for upward mobility, the nuclear family structure has freed its members to seek their fortunes without consideration of in-laws or other kin. It is often said that economic factors have shaped the "ideal" American family pattern.

A specific type of American humor centers around interfering in-laws who attempt to violate the sanctity of the nuclear family. Many mental health practitioners have not placed a high value on extended family ties. They have often correlated a successful analysis or course of treatment with the independence of individuals and their own procreated families from their families of origin. A study by the Jewish Family Service in New York showed that social workers often attempt to help the family change its kin relationships—usually in the direction of less involvement. Social workers were also found to be less kin-oriented than their clients. This fact leads to issues about the significance of value differences in therapeutic practice as well as, of course, in society (Leichter and Mitchell, 1967).

Policy makers, as well as mental health practitioners working with Puerto Rican families, must realize that the Puerto Rican family, in contrast to the American family, is an extended one, with strong ties that are in no way considered or experienced as pathological.

An extended family is a composite form of the nuclear family (Leichter and Mitchell, 1967). It is characterized by intense and frequent relationships. The Puerto Rican family is patriarchal, and roles are clearly defined and strictly monitored. There are important reciprocal obligations and strict fulfillment of each person's role responsibilities. Scheele (1969), for example, writes that a person in Puerto Rico, whether bootblack or bank president, by successfully fulfilling the expectancies of his or her various statuses, maintains *Dignidad*—one of the most important Puerto Rican values. The elderly are respected and have a place in this society. Children are deeply loved; they are not held accountable for the parents' "sins."

To visualize the Puerto Rican family, it is important to understand the interrelated Puerto Rican cultural values of *Dignidad, Respeto,* and *Personalismo.* For a fuller discussion of important Puerto Rican values, see Mintz (1973), Wagenheim (1970), Fitzpatrick (1971). A person automatically possesses *Dignidad* (dignity in a broadened sense). This is a belief in the innate worth and inner importance of each individual. The spirit and soul are more important than the body. The focus is on the person's qualities, uniqueness, goodness and integrity.

Persons are born into their socioeconomic roles and therefore, cannot be held accountable for their status. There is often a *fatalismo* (fatalism) about their position in life. Fatalism and Puerto Rican values should be examined in the context of Catholicism and colonialism. The notion of a "colonialized personality" is found throughout a good part of the literature. Some acquaintance with the history would be essential to an understanding of the Puerto Rican situations. (The beginning reader is referred to Wagenheim, 1970. For an interpretation from an independent point of view, see Maldonado-Denis, 1972. For an understanding of how fatalism comes into play in the helper/client relationship, see Vasquez de Rodriquez, 1973). They may see life's events as inevitable (*"Lo que Dios manda"*—What God wills). They feel themselves at the mercy of supernatural forces and are resigned to their fate. This life view is illustrated by a conversation between Piri Thomas, a Puerto Rican raised in the U.S., and his mother, who had spent her formative years in Puerto Rico. "Our parents were resigned to their life. But we, the youngsters, would say, 'Has this life gotta be for us forever?' I remember my own mother's answer one day when I asked her. 'Why can't we have a nice house like this?' showing her a picture in a magazine ... 'Of course, we can have it in heaven someday' " (Thomas, 1974).

It does not matter, therefore, what people have in this life or what their stations in life are. They possess status simply by existing. Rewards will come in heaven. A person is, however, entitled to be treated in this life with *respeto* (respect in a broadened sense) as long as they fulfill their role requirements and adhere to Puerto Rican values and norms. *Respeto* is the acknowledgment of an individual's personal attributes, uninfluenced by wealth or social position (Abad, Ramos and Boyce, 1974). *Respeto* also connotes hierarchal relationships. Elders and superiors of one form or another, are to be accorded respect. The superior, in turn, must always be cordial. There are prescribed cultural rituals to show respect. Puerto Ricans are very sensitive to affronts which would violate their *dignidad.* People who have been insulted must always handle themselves in an honest, dignified, and upright manner. An attempt is made to settle the situation *a la buena* (in a nice way). Generally, an attempt is made to avoid direct confrontation, with *"pelea monga"* ("passive resistance") often employed. Aggression is permitted when a man's machismo is challenged.

As previously stated, tied in with *dignidad* and *respeto* is the concept of *personalismo,* a strong preference for face-to-face contact and primary relationships. As an illustration of the importance and extent of this preference, while the supermarket may be a much cheaper place to shop, the *bodega* (neighborhood grocery store) is much more popular in many communities in the states, taking on the characteristics of a primary social institution (Vasquez, 1974). It is the individual in the organization or institution one trusts and deals with. The concept of a collective welfare generally has little meaning. One thinks instead of adverse or favorable effects on Pablo, José, and Juan. Even in terms of their ties to the church, Puerto Ricans experience special and individualistic relationships with the saints. Puerto Ricans do not want their unique personalities absorbed into committees and bureaucracies. Their participation in groups will depend on strong ties to individual group members rather than on ties to a cause per se (Roger, 1971). Puerto Ricans seem to seek charismatic leadership. A recent study comments on the high rate of participation in elections together with the tendency to idolize their leaders and to leave too much policy making and implementation to those they have elected. This relates as well to other leaders, labor and religious (Brameld, 1976). *Personalismo* requires that all social, economic, political relationships proceed on the basis of known face-to-face contact (Mintz, 1973).

Puerto Ricans feel most comfortable with a family style in their relationships. It is not surprising that the Puerto Rican extended family encompasses not only those related by blood and marriage, but also those tied to it by custom in reciprocal bonds of obligation and feeling. Important parts of the Puerto Rican family system are the *Compradazgo* and *hijos de crianza*.

The *Compradazgo* is the institution of *compadres* ("companion parents"), a network of ritual kinship whose members have a deep sense of obligation to each other. These responsibilities are taken quite seriously and include economic assistance, emotional support, and even personal correction. Sponsors of a child at baptism and confirmation take on the role of *Padrinos* ("godparents") to the child and *compadres* to the parents. Also assuming this role are witnesses at a marriage or close friends (Fitzpatrick, 1971). The relationship develops a significant religious and even mystical quality.

Hijos de crianza ("children of the upbringing") is the cultural practice of accepting responsibility for another's child, without the necessity of blood or even friendship ties. This child is raised as if it were one's own. Neither the natural parent nor the child is stigmatized for the relinquishment. There is also no stigma attached to an illegitimate child. Following the Roman legal tradition, there is no concept of illegitimacy; the child is viewed as a natural child (Fitzpatrick, 1971). This institutional practice serves as an economic and emotional safety valve for the family and often makes it possible for the child to enjoy a better life. The family, in all likelihood, will not be able to produce documents for the child. As Hidalgo (1972) points out, the helping professional must be prepared, if necessary, to battle the legal system. Previously stated and important to reiterate is that the Puerto Rican family is placed in immediate jeopardy as a result of described differences in family structure and values, bringing it into conflict with the sociolegal system of the U.S., which addresses itself basically to the nuclear family. Consider social security and income tax provisions as illustrations. Income tax regulations do not allow tax deductions for *Compadres* or consensual unions. In many parts of Puerto Rican society, consensual unions are a common and acceptable practice. Consensual unions must, however, be examined in the context of the economic situation. When one owns no property, there is little need for legal entanglements. It is interesting to note that with the rise of the middle class in Puerto Rico the percentage of consensual marriages has dropped and it is basically a phenomenon of the poor (Fitzpatrick, 1971).

Support of the *hijo de crianza* is credited by the Internal Revenue Service if the contribution has been more than half the year's total support. Social Security benefits are not paid to any of these groups. For those few fortunate Puerto Ricans who hold health insurance policies, coverage is defined without reference to the Puerto Rican concept of family.

There is a gross inequity in the amount of societal benefits and residual services provided to the Puerto Rican population. Young and old receive little from society. One need only look at the conditions in ghetto schools, hospitals, outpatient clinics and housing, at the lack of recreational facilities and activities, at the limited amount of police protection, at the types of jobs available and their salary range, along with the unemployment figures, to be struck by the harsh reality of the Puerto Rican condition. A society which provides so little to the Puerto Rican community also serves in many ways to render the minority impotent in its self-help efforts. Under existing societal conditions, mutual assistance, both financial and emotional, is essential. Puerto Ricans in the United States have been described as having lost their social assets; they are removed from the customary support of tradition, kin, and esteem of hometown neighbors. Housing patterns in New York show that Puerto Ricans scattered throughout the city at a faster rate than was true of other ethnic groups upon their arrival. Housing is not as easy to find as it was in the past. Puerto Ricans are thus exposed to the host culture more intensively and sooner. Isolation from their ethnic groups has been associated with increased rates of mental illness in minorities (Rabkin and Struening, 1976). It is imperative, therefore, that any remaining semblance of the extended family be preserved. Public policy and programs must lend support to the extended family. The extended family system should be viewed as important not only to the Puerto Rican, but to other ethnic groups as well. Moreover, the value placed on the extended family should not be assumed to be solely related to a poverty status. An examination of Anglo-American alternative life styles will frequently reveal attempts to create such an extended family group (Beck, 1976).

Society's restrictions on self-help affect the nearly two million Puerto Ricans and their descendants on the Mainland, most of whom live in New York City (*New York Times,* 1977). New York City Housing Authority regulations prohibit the public housing dweller from extending the traditional hospitality of an open door to their "kin" in need of a start in the new land; neither can they share the rent when it would be mutually beneficial in financial and child-caring terms. Among Puerto Rican families living in poverty, nearly 60 percent are headed by a woman (U.S. Commission on Civil Rights, 1976). The need for mutual aid arrangements within such families is especially critical. Lack of child care facilities for their children inhibits the participation of Puerto Rican women in the labor force (U.S. Commission on Civil Rights, 1976). Restrictions on apartment sharing occur at a time when it is virtually impossible to obtain an apartment in a project or to rent a decent apartment elsewhere. In attempting to qualify as foster parents, Puerto Rican families find that they face a serious problem in lack of housing space. Institutional care, rather than foster home care, is stressed by child welfare agencies (Valle Consultants Ltd., 1973). Can institutional care be considered better than the loving concern of a *Madrina* (Godmother) for an *hijo de crianza,* even if in substandard housing? To solve both the housing and child care problems, abandoned buildings in local neighborhoods might be refurnished and made available on a nonprofit basis to families who qualify as foster parents (Valle Consultants Ltd., 1973).

On the other hand, the author does not believe self-help efforts alone can suffice, nor is sharing a cramped apartment in New York. The Puerto Rican Family

Institute in New York has found that migrants may overstay their welcomes when they are unable to find a job or secure housing. Reliance for too long on a *Compadre* may lead to tension between the host and the newly arrived family (Gorbea, 1975). Certainly, day care or institutional programs are needed; however, their use should be dictated by need and cultural preference. Most importantly, the author should not be interpreted as denying society's responsibility to provide a humane standard of living for its poor. But if the poor are not to be helped, let them not be hindered in their communal efforts to solve the problems of their poverty.

SOCIETAL STRAINS ON THE PUERTO RICAN FAMILY

Points of tension in the Puerto Rican family have been classified as:

1. A traditional system of relationships based on social class and family background versus an industrial system based on competition, initiative, and conspicuous consumption as a basis for status.
2. High aspirations and low achievement.
3. The value of dignity, pride, and honor contrasted with the increasing emphasis on material wealth and consumption.
4. A value system that reveres the *jibaro* (an idolized folk hero of the Puerto Rican) (Wagenheim, 1970) as opposed to one that reveres the successful entrepreneur.
5. The present commitment to democracy compared to the traditional methods of power that prevailed in the colonial system (Vasquez de Rodriquez, 1971).

One cannot truthfully write about the Puerto Rican family living in the United States or in Puerto Rico as if a universal model existed. Families are affected by and deal with potential strains in different ways. The Puerto Rican family system must be viewed along a continuum from the extended family system to the American nuclear family system. There are many possible variations in between. It may be helpful to understand differences in Puerto Rican family structure and values as influenced by industrialization on one hand and by the penetration of the Anglo-American culture on the other (Mintz, 1973). Strains may be caused by either stream of influence. Traditional patterns are also often augmented by other friendships, such as work relationships (Wagenheim, 1970). Business firms may be quite paternalistic and highly centralized in authority, following a pre-industrial form (Scheele, 1969). A study dealing with acculturation among Puerto Rican women on the Mainland showed that even among those who score high on acculturation there is still respect for an adherence to traditional family-related values (Torres-Matrullo, 1976).

These points of tensions exist in Puerto Rico as well as in the United States. Under the impact of American colonialization, industrialization, and urbanization, the family in Puerto Rico has undergone considerable shock. Before emigrating, the poor family has often moved from a rural community to an urban area, where traditional values may have encountered "Americanization," and the effects of a clash of values may have already begun. The life style in a prosperous urban area in Puerto Rico is different from anything in their past experience. Families often find themselves living in urban shanties, sometimes in the shadow of sleek new office buildings. They exist by doing odd jobs and collecting meager welfare payments (Wagenheim, 1970).

The urban area stateside, especially in New York, is considerably more complex than in Puerto Rico. Lack of proficiency in English, limited education and occupational skills, and possible dark skin add to the problems of Puerto Ricans. Because they are automatically United States citizens, there is little preparation required for emigration to the States. They find themselves suddenly transplanted to an unfamiliar environment, and are expected to know how to negotiate business immediately in an American urban setting and to resolve the complexities of such a life style. The Puerto Rican Family Institute in New York has found that the newly arrived migrant needs assistance in dealing with the vital areas of housing, health, education, employment, and home management (Canabal and Goldstein, 1975). It is to be expected that many migrants would not know how to maneuver in this complicated environment that is so different in culture and institutional arrangements.

Families must be able to deal with an urban environment as well as to cope with major changes in values. These changes usually mean an increase in role failures. Family members will differ in their interpretations of role obligations, and strained relations may well ensue. Family members have not been prepared to fulfill the new expectations. Previously, roles in the Puerto Rican family had been clearly defined. In rural settings there was a sharp division of labor, with wage earning activities generally relegated to men. Women's freedom was severely limited and their relationships with men were limited to kin. The cults of virginity and machismo were combined, with men as innately superior to women, a view reinforced through the societal structure. Boys and girls in Puerto Rico had been basically segregated from each other and this pattern continued in adulthood. Parents had viewed their children as completely dependent, demanding obedience from them. Children should be quiet, submissive, and respectful; achievement is less important than conformity. These concepts were especially applicable to girls. In the middle and upper classes there is less emphasis on these subordination patterns, but they are still interwoven into the overall fabric of Puerto Rican society (Bucchioni, 1965; Stycos, 1952; Wagenheim, 1970). Wagenheim (1970) points to a phenomenon that was once taboo, that of a suburban wife in Puerto Rico driving and shopping alone; while she now shops alone, the same woman today will not venture out alone at night without her husband. While the double standard continues its hold among all classes in Puerto Rico, it is decreasing most rapidly in the urban class. The virginity cult, however, remains largely unmodified, even by the impact of more flexible continental standards (Brameld, 1976).

The traditional family structure and value system come into immediate conflict with the demands of the stateside environment. Women must act independently, work, and carry the same types of burdens as men. They are forced to deal with external systems such as school, police, hospitals, etc., and to be involved with non-kin men in lively interactions. Men cannot protect their women from external pressure. Children must also become assertive in order to survive and often continue this pattern by challenging parental views. While these exchanges and others like them need not become crises, they become critical when compounded by a society that denies access to resources which an individual needs to adequately play the newly defined role. American society denies such access to Puerto Ricans and then judges them by what they have been denied. This is indeed a crucial dilemma for Puerto Ricans. Rabkin and Struening's (1976) review of research on mental illness among New York City residents revealed that epidemiological studies consistently show higher rates of mental illness for Puerto Ricans than for other ethnic groups or for the total population.

It is important to note that the available statistics might not reflect accurately the degree of the problem. Puerto Ricans have great tolerance for the "peculiarities" of others and will lend support to keeping the person at home and in the community. Also, many Puerto Ricans have a belief system which differs from that of Anglos. Spiritualism flourishes hand in hand with Catholicism, the predominant religion of Puerto Ricans. Spirits are believed to be the cause of illness, and a person feeling his or her defenses tumbling may see a spiritualist and attend a seance. Such persons may find community support in dealing with their psychic problems, the origins of which are considered spiritual. However, for some not seeking psychiatric help may quickly precipitate a more severe breakdown. It is crucial for health practitioners working with the Puerto Rican population to have an understanding of this belief system, as well as of the way in which professionals can cooperate with spiritualism (Lubchansky, Egri and Stokes, 1970; Ruiz and Langrod, 1976).

Rabkin and Struening (1976) write that the development of mental illnesses in migrant populations relates to the amount of social change experienced in the transition from one setting to another. They view alterations in life style, family organization and role assessment, membership in social networks, and extent of community supports as each contributing to the individual's vulnerability to the experience of stress and illness. We have already noted the great number of social changes experienced by the Puerto Rican migrant. In general, all families handle stress differently. The fact that the great majority of families cannot be classified as mentally ill is a testimony to human resiliency. There are great differences in family structure and value systems. In the case of Puerto Ricans, differences relate in part to whether formative years were spent in the United States or in Puerto Rico, as well as to the level of education. When viewing Puerto Rican families along the continuum described earlier, one should not expect to find too many families at either the traditional or nuclear end. It is important to note, however, that certain Puerto Rican families in the United States may remain in a more traditional form than families in Puerto Rico because of their isolation from the wider society. This tendency may reflect needs to cling to the security of the familiar and to reject what appears to be so unaccepting of them.

To understand variations between families and family members, it is imperative that in our assessments we go beyond ego strength and pathology. It is critical to take into consideration the external systems with which the family and its members have been in transaction. How much stress can any family be expected to tolerate and still maintain a viable homeostatic balance? Families are open social systems and as "living systems are acutely dependent upon their external environment" (Katz and Kahn, 1966).

Sociologists have classified the family as having the following functions fundamental to social life: sexual, economic, reproductive, and educational (Murdock, 1968). The family, along with meeting instrumental needs, must be able to meet the expressive and affective needs of its members. One cannot evaluate the Puerto Rican family's ability to perform its functions or the way in which Puerto Rican culture structures these tasks without examining the environment of the Puerto Rican family in the United States. Goode (1964) pointed out that a family can continue to exist only as it is supported by the larger society. The society, as a larger social system, furnishes the family, as a smaller social system, with the conditions necessary for its survival.

THE PUERTO RICAN AS A MINORITY MEMBER

We have seen that the Puerto Rican family finds itself in a hostile environment which makes life a struggle for existence. Racist practices, along with a highly technological, stratified, closed society, inhibit the upward mobility of Puerto Ricans and relegate them and their family to the lower caste. The Puerto Rican family finds itself defined as a minority group, whereas in Puerto Rico it was part of a majority. Minority is synonymous with an out-group whose worth, culture, values, and life styles are deprecated and stereotyped. Minority is synonymous with blocked access to the fraternity of the in-group and the full benefits of the American way of life. Erickson (1959) notes that the shock of American adolescence is the standardization of individuals and the intolerance of difference. This destructive parochialism permeates the whole American scene. Society even attempts to force Puerto Ricans into defining themselves as white or black, the standardized categories for color in the United States, with no allowances for the Puerto Rican's mixed Indian, Spanish, and African heritage.

In fact, the Puerto Ricans' chances for success seem related to their ability, as individuals and families, to obscure their differences from the majority group. Puerto Ricans who, by placing themselves into the proverbial "melting pot," are able to metamorphose as white with an Anglicized name and life style can provide their families with an American standard of living. The price they must pay is denial of self and heritage, and sacrifice of personal integrity. Whether or not society permits them self-definitions, as white or black they are faced with an identity problem. There is no intention here to stigmatize or blame the victims, a procedure Ryan (1969) defines as an "intellectual process whereby a social problem is analyzed in such a way that the causation is found to be in the characteristics of the victim rather than in any deficiencies or structural defects in his environment."

As Longres (1974) points out, the racial experience in the United States goes beyond the individual and family and must be viewed as a collective one where all are forced to confront and question their racial identity. The color question persists as a psychological dilemma even among the seemingly assimilated. It is as if each day the Puerto Rican issue and color question come up even for those who can pass as Anglo. Again and again, one needs to decide whether to confront or let a remark about Puerto Ricans go by. Always at issue is how much racism one can accept in one's "friends." Also ubiquitous is the need to reassess the "fit" of the Puerto Rican stereotype and to place oneself and others in perspective.

This racism and its internalization also threaten Puerto Rican unity and can serve to divide Puerto Ricans along racial lines. For some a negative internalization of self may work against the interests of their own group in an attempt to deny their own heritage and to secure their new "chosen" identity.

The havoc society wreaks and the problems it creates for the individual and for the family by its measurement of worth in terms of color are vividly portrayed in *Down These Mean Streets.* Thomas's (1967) autobiography describes how his painful identity problem and destructive relationships with his siblings and father were related to the differences in color between him and his siblings and to feelings about self and others tied to these color differences:

> It wasn't right to be ashamed of what one was. It was like hating Momma for the color she was and Poppa for the color he wasn't ... Man do you know what it is to sit across a dinner table looking at your brothers that look exactly like paddy people? True, I ain't never been down South, but the same crap's happening here. So they don't hang you by your neck. But they slip an invisible rope around your balls and hang you with nice smiles, and "If we need you, we'll call you." I wanna feel like a "Mr." I can't feel like that just yet and there ain't no amount of cold wine and pot can make my mind accept me being a "Mr." part time ... You and James (his brothers) are like houses painted white outside and blacker'n mother inside. And I'm close to being like Poppa—trying to be white on both sides. (p. 8)

Thomas's identity crisis is unfortunately not atypical. How intense this crisis can be is indicated by the fact that admission rates to mental hospitals for non-white Puerto Ricans are the highest among the Puerto Rican group. Second generation Puerto Ricans have a higher total admission rate than their parents. This finding is surprising in its contrast to the usual pattern among immigrant groups (Rabkin and Struening, 1976). It may well be, however, that not being subject to minority status throughout one's formative years provides better insulation than growing up as a minority "non-person." First generation parents can probably maintain their *dignidad* and find comfort in their recollections of their past.

Identifying oneself as Anglo-white, black, or Puerto Rican serves as a focus of orientation to concepts of self and others, to values and to life styles. The kinds of identifications, confusions, and ambivalences experienced by Thomas unfortunately reflect malignancies in our society because individuals and their families comprise vulnerable and open social systems.

It is futile to enter into a debate about whether Puerto Ricans uncontaminated by American society are themselves racist. It is also futile to attempt to determine whether the prejudice observed in Puerto Rico relates to class, as is claimed, rather than to color. What is certain is that Puerto Ricans are totally unprepared to deal with the discrimination to which they are subjected upon arrival in the United States. Both in statistics and in literature, the devastating effects of color discrimination and ghetto existence on the Puerto Rican family in this country are clear. Thomas's excruciatingly painful identity struggle over what and who he was and his pathological relationships with his family over color differences would not have happened in Puerto Rico.

THE SEARCH FOR THE POT OF GOLD

The United States has traditionally attracted immigrants seeking their fortunes. Though the Puerto Rican has not found a fortune in the United States, Anglo-Americans have found a fortune in Puerto Rico. Puerto Ricans have filled labor shortages in many important stateside industries: in Illinois, electronic industries; in Wisconsin foundries; in the steel mills of Ohio, Indiana, and Pennsylvania; in East and Midwest farms; and in the textile and garment industries of New York (Migration Division, 1975). Puerto Ricans initially were recruited to serve as a source of cheap labor. Some employers now consider minorities an "excess population" because machines are increasingly being substituted for low-level positions. Current migration therefore differs from previous immigration in that the opportunities for work are no longer available.

White immigrants did not have to deal with the degree of racism that permeates our society with respect to "rainbow" people. There are other important differences which should be noted. For example, the Puerto Rican migration is an airborne one. It has a back and forth flow significant in that the feeling of need to adjust to the stateside environment tends to be less than if travel were more difficult. In fact, it is difficult to find a Puerto Rican adult who has not spent some time in the United States (U.S. Commission on Civil Rights, 1976).

Though Puerto Ricans come to the States for many reasons, migration has been seen to have an economic regulator (Migration Division, 1975) that serves as the primary motivation for migration. Puerto Rico's economic situation at present is devastating. It should be noted that the means of production, resources, and capital in Puerto Rico are mainly in the hands of North Americans. The dollar value of United States business holdings in Puerto Rico is exceeded only by its holdings in Britain, Germany, and Canada. Strategic considerations are also critical in Puerto Rico's proximity to Cuba and the Panama Canal. Also, Puerto Rico may prove in the future to be an oil resource, as preliminary seismic studies show potential deposits off the northwestern coast (*New York Times,* 1977).

In Puerto Rico present conditions are deplorable. The myriad economic problems necessitate a continuation of patterns that are cruel and divisive to the family. It is not uncommon to find wives separated from husbands and children, or vice versa, with children cared for an ocean away from their parents. With part of the family in Puerto Rico and part in the United States enough is earned to keep the family from starving. Yet, stateside, the Puerto Rican is by no means doing well. Puerto Ricans have had the dubious distinction of being poorer, having less education, and being more dependent upon welfare than the national average (U.S. Commission on Civil Rights, 1976). In the general population, about 64 percent of all persons 25 years old and over were high school graduates compared to 30 percent in the Puerto Rican population. By 1976, in the overall population, about 3.8 percent of all persons had completed less than 5 years of school; the figure was 18.7 percent for the Puerto Rican population (U.S. Bureau of Census, 1976).

We should, however, take note that official census figures often belie existing conditions. As an illustration, a 1966 report by the U.S. Department of Labor stated that the unemployment rate for Puerto Ricans in slum areas in New York was 33.1 percent, which contrasted with the 10 percent official unemployment rate (U.S. Commission on Civil Rights, 1976).

With reference to education, the dropout problem becomes acute in the 18–24 age group. In Chicago, a study showed that the dropout rate for Puerto Ricans in grammar and high school was 71.2 percent; 12.5 percent dropped out of grammar school while 58.7 percent dropped out of high school. It is important to understand that reasons for dropping out are not purely academic. Of the 30 percent of the Puerto Rican U.S. high school students who drop out each year, one-third have already completed most of their required courses and are in their senior year. Most dropouts are bored, feel the need to find a job, or find the school unresponsive to their cultural background.

Studies of schools in Chicago and New York revealed that schools with heavy Puerto Rican enrollments had students with reading averages lower than predominantly black or Anglo schools. Lags increased with each succeeding grade. Birthplace, language, and dropout rate were interwoven. Young Puerto Ricans born on the Island are more likely to be doomed to a life of poverty (U.S. Commission on Civil Rights, 1976). The Chicago report discussed its interviews of 140 dropouts (better termed "pushouts"). The pushout's personal reason for leaving school was a major crisis in self-identity that made staying in school more and more difficult. The pushout had learned that his or her position in society was clearly lower than that of an Anglo. This newly acquired consciousness of societal rejection was in violent opposition to the internalized sense of *respeto* and *dignidad.* "Social schizophrenia," a conflict of great intensity, resulted. The easiest way out was to dissociate oneself from school, a major establishment symbol. Aspirations for the future decreased and a sense of defiance developed. Some students joined gangs, which provided an environment where they could find recognition, new respect, and leadership roles. Such students concluded that academic achievement often does not bring the expected reward (Lucas, 1974).

While census figures and findings paint a grim picture of the Puerto Rican condition, what is perhaps of even greater concern is the fact that the situation has worsened greatly.

> The ... stresses and strains burdening the Puerto Rican family have resulted in an escalating increase in children without homes, delinquent children, addicted youth, and youth poorly prepared to compete for higher education or employment. It remains rather amazing that, despite these burdens, the majority of Puerto Rican families have been able to make an adjustment to their new environment, recreate some of their cultural ambience (for example, food, religion, and recreation), and create communal institutions and organizations that contribute to the community's well-being and progress. It is a strong, vibrant community, often resisting forces that attempt to assimilate it or eradicate it, linguistically or culturally. One commentator has suggested that the tenacity to exist as a distinctive group has been stubbornly embedded in Puerto Ricans as a result of 450 years of colonialism (Miranda, 1973).

To round out the picture, we should note that the situation is not uniformly bleak. One hundred and four thousand Puerto Ricans earned $10,000 or more in 1974. About 25,000 earned in excess of $15,000 and around 5,000 had earnings in excess of $25,000. Thousands of mainland Puerto Ricans are high school and university graduates. The figures for 1975 show 198,000 high school graduates, 12,000 college graduates, and more than 17,000 enrolled college students. Forty-two thousand Puerto Ricans held professional, technical, or managerial jobs in 1975. Three-fourths of the Puerto Rican families on the mainland are entirely self-sufficient and do not receive any government aid (U.S. Commission on Civil Rights, 1976).

Nevertheless, the overall statistical picture is a dismal one. The figures in human terms mean that it is often difficult for a Puerto Rican man or woman to find employment. When secured, jobs are frequently seasonal or temporary, and the norm is dead-end employment. Doors are often closed for reasons having nothing to do with willingness to work. Qualifications are unrelated to the task at hand. As an illustration written examinations for some sanitation workers require a college education; high school diplomas are required of airplane maintenance personnel; there is a height requirement for police personnel; Puerto Ricans in union construction jobs are token workers (U.S. Commission on Civil Rights, 1976); fluency in English is required for dishwasher jobs, etc. For a Puerto Rican seeking employment, discrimination exists at all levels, not only in the private sector but in public service as well as in employment and training programs. Discriminatory practices in government are well documented by the United States Commission on Civil Rights (1976). This is a matter of gravest concern, for how can Puerto Ricans expect to make gains in the private sector if they cannot rely on the governmental sector to set an example and enforce its own regulations?

A minority group woman can at times secure employment more easily than a man, perhaps as a sewing-machine operator or as a domestic, because our society still needs to have these functions performed. In those instances where a husband must stay at home to care for young children, family roles are reversed. Recall that in the Puerto Rican family system the male is expected to be the breadwinner and a dominant figure. Hence, role reversal is of tremendous importance in a family system where *machismo* is valued; the extent of valuation, of course, varies with the family. American psychiatrists have ethnocentrically defined *machismo* as "belligerent masculinity" and "sexual dominance" that such men are expected to display under any possible challenge or situation. They have viewed *machismo* in terms of sexual overcompensation, and as related to generic problems in masculine identification (Group for the Advancement of Psychiatry, 1970). *Machismo,* however, in its ramifications does not appear to be too different from the combination of male chauvinism, with its implications for female–male roles and rewards, and the double standard of sexuality (Sirjamaki, 1969).

The difference seems to be that Latin American *machismo* is not disguised or subtle so that its impact is more readily discernible. *Machismo* in its individualized expression can be viewed in the context of a society denying a male his manhood by societal castration. This situation has been found by social workers to create panic, confusion, marital discord, and the breakdown of family ties (Giordano, 1976a, 1976b).

A man needs to work. The significance of work to a man's self-concept is well understood. Peter Drucker states:

> Social effectiveness, citizenship, indeed even self-respect depend on access to a job. Without a job, a man in industrial society cannot possibly be socially effective. He is deprived of his citizenship, social standing, and of the respect of his fellow man, if not his family, and finally of self-respect (Mayfield, 1972, p. 108).

A man needs avenues for achievement. Being a *macho completo* (complete man) provides an avenue of gratification when there are few other opportunities for status or reward. This sense of being a *macho* must go hand in hand, however, with being able to provide for and protect one's family. It is not necessary that these functions be a man's exclusive domain. It is recognized that government has taken over more and more family functions. Consequently, the family's authority in relation to such concerns as parental discipline and legal systems has lessened. A Puerto Rican man with no employment, power, or status can be expected to be impotent in protecting his family in relation to these external systems. A principal strain on Puerto Rican family life is the disparity between the presumed dominance of the male and the actual facts of the situation (Group for the Advancement of Psychiatry, 1970).

Some women may experience contempt for their husbands because they can no longer view them as *machos.* A husband can be expected to strive to reassert his dominance, but due to all the external pressures, he will often in the end experience defeat and lose his sense of *dignidad.* Many women feel torn apart at seeing the men they love destroyed by forces over which they have no control.

Children, experiencing the friction in the home, seeing the family structure undermined, and probably having had no contact with successful Puerto Rican families, internalize contempt of parents, Puerto Ricans, and themselves. Funnye and Shiffman (1967) note that the ghetto imposes a pervasive sense of worthlessness on its children, with implications of undesirability and inferiority. There are situations in which the impact of these feelings is such that even after the parents' struggle to provide the child with a college education, the child is fearful of leaving the ghetto to achieve in the larger community.

In working with a group of Puerto Rican adolescents at Aspira, the author learned that for many youths the image of what a family should be was related to models derived from television. Media influences often mean that Puerto Rican parents and children, literally and figuratively, do not speak the same language in speech or in values. In the adolescent's eyes the Puerto Rican family can never be expected to compete with families in programs such as Life with Father. Studies conducted by Hickel among Afro-Americans revealed that young black television viewers regard whites as more competent than blacks, and model their conduct accordingly (*Newsweek,* 1977). Models on TV have been changing, with minorities, particularly Afro-Americans, being depicted in a more positive light. Yet the harsh realities of ghetto existence seem in many ways to be romanticized in the TV programming. Even with the limited changes, however, neither Afro- nor Anglo-American models are Puerto Rican models.

There are few Puerto Rican professionals in any area with whom the adolescents have contact and can identify. It is hoped that the further development of bilingual, bicultural school programs will help these adolescents establish goals for themselves and to recognize the worth of their family and their group. This author will never forget her first day on a job in a settlement as a Field Instructor of a student unit and as an Assistant Professor from a University. A youngster came running after her and said in disbelief, "Are you really Puerto Rican?"

Puerto Rican adolescents in contact with external systems in the larger society have been stripped of their cultural heritage.

> When Juan Ortiz began bringing his homework back from the second grade in Brooklyn, his mother noticed he had changed the spelling of his first name. "Well," the nine-year-old explained, "My teacher tells me my name isn't Juan, it's John." (*New York Times,* 1972)

The stripping process continues today. Many professionals are inadvertently guilty of taking part in this without any awareness of the racism involved. On one occasion the author served as speaker and discussion leader at a program designed to help social workers deliver relevant services to the Puerto Rican community. Under discussion were the difficulties students encountered in school in terms of both cultural and language issues. One day-care worker pointed out proudly how the children who were in her program would never face those difficulties, since from early infancy only English was spoken and Anglo values were stressed. The other professionals seemed convinced that the solution to Puerto Rican problems was socialization in the Anglo culture during infancy or at least in early childhood. They appeared taken aback when the author pointed out the racism in such an approach.

> Our definition of cultural pluralism must include the concept that our language and our culture will be given equal status to that of the majority population. It is not enough simply to say that we should be given the opportunity to share in the positive benefits of modern American life. Instead, we must insist that this sharing will not be accomplished at the sacrifice of all those traits which make us what we are as Puerto Ricans (U.S. Commission on Civil Rights, 1976).

In the futile search for the "pot of gold," children may often experience their parents' pain and feel tremendously responsible for the family's burdens and "failures." They often have had to learn to negotiate various systems for the family and may be crushed in the process. Some children exhibit acting-out behavior which may have primarily sociological determinants and great sociological and psychological ramifications (Cressey and Ward, 1969). Whatever the antecedents of Puerto Rican delinquency, for example, the authority of the parents, especially of the father, is destroyed. Clearly, not all families disintegrate. Great credit must be given to those families that maintain their strength and balance in a society where the "pot" discovered is not filled with gold but is a melting pot filled with stereotypes of the middle class Anglo-American family unit.

CASE ILLUSTRATIONS OF FAMILIES IN TRANSACTION WITH THEIR ENVIRONMENT

Several case vignettes from the files of family agencies demonstrate some of the transactions of the Puerto Rican family with the stateside environment.* No claim is made that these cases are a statistically representative sample of the Puerto Rican population stateside, but the situations are not atypical. Nor should these family agency clients be viewed as more or less pathological because of their relationship with the agency. Identifying data have been disguised so as to protect the client's right to confidentiality.

Case #1 (Gonzales)

Mr. and Mrs. Gonzales both came from Puerto Rico as adults. Both have some college education. Their financial situation is adequate in that their combined income makes it possible for them to live comfortably with their two children. They had just come back from a Florida vacation when they made contact with the family agency social worker. Mrs. Gonzales was working in a semiprofessional position in a day-care center, in an Eastern city, where a family agency worker

---

*The agencies are not being identified in the interest of protecting further the identity of the client. The author, however, would like to thank these agencies for their cooperation.

served as a consultant. When her 16-year-old daughter was arrested for shoplifting, she immediately turned for help to the family agency worker. An unsuccessful attempt was made to involve the father in the family sessions. Coming for help, especially to a female worker, seemed to be too great an affront to his machismo. His wife was quite accepting of the male–female role dichotomy in the home. Nevertheless, from the content of the sessions it was clear that Mr. Gonzales was very much involved in the counseling process and with his family. His affection and concern were very evident to the worker despite his difficulty in expressing his feelings directly.

The need for that clear communication by this family of feelings, ideas, and needs was also apparent to the worker. The daughter Dolores was feeling extremely lonely and misunderstood, and the parents in turn were feeling quite hurt. Dolores experienced herself as different from all her friends. She had stolen some clothing in order to dress like all the other teenagers and so that she could go to a school dance. The parents were very strict in keeping with the tradition of protecting the female. They did not approve of the typical teenage attire and the freedoms allowed to Anglos.

The parents came to see that they had to accept the reality of the stateside culture and that they would cripple their daughter were they to continue to deny her the right to participate in teenage activities. They gave up setting limits in an automatic way and tried to balance the traditional value system with the needs of their teenage daughter in an Eastern city environment. The 16-year-old daughter had internalized the traditional Puerto Rican value system with some modifications. Her rebellion against her heritage did not mean she was truly desirous of throwing it all off. She needed to feel she had options. She assessed her group of friends and recognized certain behaviors of which she did not approve. Nor did she herself truly wish to dress in any extreme fashion. The daughter was able to modify her dress in the way that was satisfactory to all. She pleased her parents and willingly went to family affairs. (All age groups socialize together in the Puerto Rican culture.) The parents recognized she needed to be allowed her own separate life.

Basically, what happened in this situation was a cultural clash that went beyond a clash of generations typical in families with teenagers. The family was able to handle a crisis by opening up channels of communication and build upon their foundation of love and caring. Fortunately, this was not a situation where poverty compounded the difficulties.

Case #2 (Garcia)

The Department of Public Assistance of an Eastern city referred Mr. Garcia to the family agency for a number of problems. The client was drinking heavily and showed no interest in the W.I.N. program to which he had been referred for employment. He needed assistance with his Medicaid eligibility and had great difficulty taking care of his 9-year-old daughter who was acting out. Also, they were living in a deplorable housing situation. Mr. Garcia, a man in his early fifties, had come to the States eight years ago, leaving a decent civil service job as a foreman in construction. His wife had moved herself and five children to the States against her husband's wishes.

Mrs. Garcia had insisted that in the States the family would have better economic and educational opportunities. Hoping to get his family to return to Puerto Rico, he took out a loan from a credit union and bought a home in Puerto Rico. Not succeeding in getting his wife to relent, he came to the States. His wife died from alcoholism shortly after his arrival. While in Puerto Rico he had had no idea of his wife's condition. The money that was left after selling the home in Puerto Rico and repaying the loan was used for her funeral expenses. The family had been receiving supplemental assistance while he was in Puerto Rico, as what he had been able to send was insufficient for their basic needs. He decided after his wife's death against returning to Puerto Rico and was able to secure a construction job to which he had to commute daily. Though his income was still inadequate, he withdrew the family from welfare on the basis that" ... if I can work to take care of my family, I don't want them acting like beggars." He had a series of layoffs and when he was no longer eligible for unemployment benefits he had to go on assistance. He tried hard looking for work. He picketed with the Puerto Rican construction workers for more jobs, having met up with job discrimination. When some jobs did finally open up, he was not able to obtain one because of his age. He was so defeated and depressed that he increasingly took to drink.

Mr. Garcia feels that basically he has been a happy man. He equates happiness with being in Puerto Rico where he feels he can function at his best. Puerto Rico is a memory which triggers a smile on his face. He does not speak, however, of returning to Puerto Rico. His children are very important to him and they intend to remain. His depression is clearly a reactive one.

It is not unusual for part of a family to come to the States and the other member(s) to feel forced to follow. A woman may very well take the lead in such a situation. Mrs. Garcia wanted what she thought would be the best for her family. She was especially concerned about educational opportunities. Puerto Ricans value education. Mr. Garcia valued his family and, despite the upheaval he knew it would cost him, came to reunite himself with his family. Little by little the force of circumstances and the environment tore this proud man down. All he had was in his past and like many Puerto Ricans he turned to his past for solace. He had not come to the States looking for handouts. He responded well to the combination of counseling, advocacy efforts and the concrete interventions of the family service worker. Importantly, through the worker's efforts he was again able to resume construction work, which gives him a sense of well-being. His daughter is doing well. It is a sad commentary on this society that a man should have to depend on a social worker to obtain employment.

Case #3 (Santos)

The Santos family was referred to the family service agency by the school their 11-year-old daughter attends. The mother was acting in a bizarre fashion and was interfering with the teacher's functioning and her daughter's schooling. The father is a factory worker. The mother was a former practical nurse in Puerto Rico and because of her inability initially to speak English worked on an assembly line for a while. Mrs. Santos has had a mastectomy, is terminally ill and undergoing chemotherapy. Due to her irrational behavior, there is fear that she may hurt herself as she wanders about or that she may hurt others as she is easily upset. When she takes her medication, she is under better control.

Mrs. Santos has always been a devoted mother and has become obsessed with her daughter. Until her illness the mother functioned well. She now no longer allows her daughter to visit girlfriends and limits all her activities.

The Santos are members of a Pentecostal congregation. The mother carries a Bible in her pocketbook and says, "God will help me," but will not discuss her condition. The minister and his congregation have been extremely supportive of the family. All the Santos find comfort and draw strength in the church experience. The minister takes the daughter to school and in an effort to contain and watch over Mrs. Santos the minister's wife has tried to stay with her during the day. Mr. Santos cannot continue to miss days from work without jeopardizing his job. If money is secured from Cancer Care, a member of the congregation will stay with Mrs. Santos. Plans are for the daughter to go and live with an aunt in Puerto Rico upon the death of her mother.

Mr. Santos is deeply concerned about his wife. He is at a loss about how to handle her. Under no circumstance, however, does he wish her institutionalized.

This family has ties to the Puerto Rican community in its affiliation with the Pentecostal Church, which is serving as a sustaining force in a difficult situation. The Pentecostal Church, a storefront variety, is a native organization and an important social institution both as a religious force and a community resource. This family, as many other Puerto Ricans have done, is able to draw emotional support from the religious experience. Mrs. Santos' belief that God will help her reflects the resignation to their fate that is not uncommon to many members of the Puerto Rican community.

Puerto Ricans, in general, have a wide tolerance for idiosyncratic behavior, which explains the acceptance of Mrs. Santos' irrationality. Families are willing to put up with a great deal and are not quick to institutionalize their own even when this seems absolutely necessary. A Puerto Rican social worker in New York recently reported to me how difficult it is to get families to accept placing the elderly in nursing homes when they, under their living conditions, cannot possibly care for them. There is tremendous guilt to work through. Nevertheless, it is my understanding from her that there is a long waiting list in Puerto Rico for nursing homes. Changes are clearly taking place. The hope is that the changes will reflect need and not the Anglo rejection of the elderly.

As to be expected, their daughter upon her mother's death will be cared for by family. Puerto Ricans are very protective of their female children. Mrs. Santos has become irrationally protective of her daughter. It is understandable that her anxiety over her impending death would manifest itself in this way.

Case #4 (Castro)

The family was referred to the family agency by the Visiting Nurses Association. The family is known to just about every social agency in the community, including protective services. Mrs. Castro's husband had deserted the family about a year ago, just prior to the birth of the youngest child. The oldest child is five years old. All children and Mrs. Castro appear retarded. The children have totally lacked stimulation. Mrs. Castro refuses to allow the children out of her sight. She is quite paranoid and has had a number of psychiatric hospitalizations. This is not to deny that some paranoia in a minority person is necessary for survival. Mrs. Castro carries a knife constantly in her skirt pocket and people are frightened of her. She has tremendous difficulty managing the care of her home which is in chaos. A student social worker had finally managed to gain Mrs. Castro's trust and, hopefully, there will be some changes in the home.

The family agency has tried to no avail to involve Mrs. Castro's blood kin and in-laws in an attempt to provide her with the emotional support of family, to avoid the possibility of placement, and in the hope of providing the children with the warmth of family contact and interaction. They say she is too crazy and refuse to involve themselves with her or to assume any responsibility at any level for the children. The relatives feel greatly burdened by their own difficult circumstances. They clearly state they do not want to take on anyone else's troubles or to involve themselves at all with this nuclear family. In fact, it is felt that Mrs. Castro's sister has actually stolen food stamps from her in the past. The extended family system has clearly broken down in this situation and traditional values seem to have no place. Neither is there stateside a community that can serve as a mechanism of social control which demands the meeting of one's obligation to one's family if one is to remain in good standing and in turn obtain community support. Environmental pressures can exert such force that the culture of poverty seems to have greater impact than ethnic roots and may destroy the humanity of people. This must not be allowed to continue to happen.

Many social agencies are now involved with this family and it is costing society huge sums of money for these residual-type services. Society will pay thousands to keep an individual in jail but not one cent for a guaranteed income. We can only speculate at this point about the kind of environmental and psychological stress that made Mr. Castro a runaway husband. One also needs to ask how much of the retardation of Mrs. Castro and the children relates to nutritional factors and how much to lack of intellectual development because of inadequate early stimuli. Projects such as the highly successful and replicated one originated by the Family Service Association of Hempstead, New York, need expansion. Trained personnel go into homes of two- and three-year-old children and attempt to foster verbal interaction by teaching mothers to play with their children. They demonstrate the use of toys and books. They work toward the development of a closer mother–child involvement and improvement of mother's self-image. The children's I.Q. scores have been shown to rise through such efforts. Preventive societal supports at all levels can enable families to make their proper contribution to society.

SUMMARY AND CONCLUSIONS

In attempting to understand the Puerto Rican family, it is important to gain knowledge of its cultural heritage and the degree of each family's identification with the Puerto Rican or Anglo cultures. A unique blending is found in each individual and family. Class factors enter into this blending. Gordon (1964) has formulated the term, "ethclass," a subsociety created when ethnicity and social class intersect. He speaks of two types of ethnic identification: historical, which primarily focuses on the ethnic group, and participational, which focuses on the ethclass. He points out that members of similar ethnic groups from different social classes share peoplehood (historical identification) but do not necessarily have similar behavioral styles (participational identification).

All classes in Puerto Rican society seem to maintain both the historical and participational identifications. The degree of the identifications varies with the individual and family. On the mainland, it is, of course, difficult to identify the numbers of those who have completely assimilated into an Anglo life style. No culture will remain static, especially if it is to remain viable. In addition, all cultures have functional and dysfunctional aspects. As in all societies, subordination patterns in male–female roles must continue to undergo changes without females developing into superwomen. Extended families remain critical to individual members in an alienated world. This should not, however, negate a person's individuality. The humanitarian value system of the Puerto Rican needs to influence Anglo culture. Nevertheless, Puerto Ricans should not accept that the fruits of their efforts will be rewarded only in heaven. A humane standard of living must be available to all.

Caution must be taken not to stereotype any individual, class or group. The author affirms Cafferty and Chestang's (1976) view that it is as dangerous to ignore an individual's ethnic identity as it is to assume certain behavioral characteristics based on that identity.

Therefore, the characteristics of the Puerto Rican culture that have been discussed in this chapter should be utilized as guidelines for comparisons and applied with a respect for the differences and similarities among Puerto Ricans and Anglo-Americans.

Most of what is written in the literature and experienced by the Anglo in relation to the Puerto Rican relates to the lower-class Puerto Rican. Because this is the case, it is critical to recognize that our knowledge of Puerto Rican culture, even with attention to ethclass, is insufficient without reference to the Puerto Rican's transaction with the environment. We know that external macro systems furnish the conditions for a family's existence. As members of a minority group, Puerto Ricans have suffered greatly from institutionalized racist practices.

Mayfield's (1972) definition of powerlessness distinguishes the type of powerlessness imposed from without. The ecological conception and redefinition of pathology are also relevant to the Puerto Rican family situation. Behavior is not seen as sick or well, but as transactional, the outcome of reciprocal interactions between specific situations and the individual (Kelly, 1969).

Admittedly, the helping professions by themselves cannot restructure society and achieve a more equitable distribution of opportunities and rewards. The helping professions can, however, help the Puerto Rican family deal with suffocating external systems and, through joint advocacy efforts, work toward systems change. Helping professionals are certainly in a position to examine with honesty their own delivery system to the Puerto Rican consumer, noting the ways in which their services are functional, dysfunctional, or nonexistent. Services must be culturally syntonic and not geared to an Anglo value system.

To avoid continued polarization between groups in our society (McGready, 1976), the helping professions must work toward an acceptance of the concept of social utilities as developed by Kahn (1969), building on the Wilensky and Lebeaux (1958) concept of institutional and residual services in social welfare. We need to accept that by the very nature and complexity of modern society, services and supports will be necessary. A social utility, then, is a social invention, a resource or facility designed to meet a generally experienced need in living. These services must be accessible and be non-stigmatized, in the manner of public utilities.

Social utilities must be delivered in culturally relevant ways. Flexibility must be allowed for in their neighborhood design and implementation. Minimally, the helping professions must advocate a public social policy and a delivery system which takes ethnic factors into account. This includes working toward helping the Puerto Rican community have a part in its definition of its problem. Solutions must not be superimposed.

The Puerto Rican family must be permitted and assisted to utilize its own strength, draw upon its humanitarian values, and support its kin and the Puerto Rican community at large. The helping professions must work as agents of change if they are to be instrumental in the Puerto Rican family's efforts to manage its tasks effectively, in harmony with its values and life style, as well as with the realities of the mainland environment and urban existence.

REFERENCES

ABAD, V., RAMOS, J., and BOYCE, E. "A model for delivery of mental health services to Spanish-speaking minorities." *American Journal of Orthopsychiatry,* 1974, 44, 584–595.

BECK, D. *Marriage and the Family Under Challenge: An Outline of Issues, Trends and Alternatives,* 2nd ed. New York: FSAA, 1976.

BETANCES, S. "Race and the mainland Puerto Rican." In A. P. Campos, ed., *Puerto Rican Curriculum Development Workshop: A Report.* New York: CSWE, 1974, pp. 55–66.

BRAMELD, T. "Explicit and implicit culture in Puerto Rico: A case study in educational anthropology." In J. I. Roberts and Akinsanya, eds., *Sociology in the Cultural Context.* New York: David McKay, 1976, pp. 44–57.

BUCCHIONI, E. "Home atmosphere and success in school: A sociological analysis of the functioning of elementary education for Puerto Rican children." (Unpublished doctoral dissertation, New School for Social Research, 1965, pp. 55–66.)

CAFFERTY, P. S. J., and CHESTANG, L., eds., *The Diverse Society: Implications for Social Policy.* Washington, D.C.: NASW, 1976.

CANABAL, J., and GOLDSTEIN, D. "The Puerto Rican family institute: A laboratory for therapeutic techniques to aid Spanish-speaking families." In D. J. Curren, ed., *Proceedings of Puerto Rican Conferences on Human Services.* Washington, D.C.: The National Coalition of Spanish-Speaking Mental Health Organizations, 1975, pp. 61–85.

CRESSEY, D. R., and WARD, D. A. *Delinquency, Crime, and Social Process.* New York: Harper & Row, 1969, especially pp. 244–253.

ERIKSON, E. *Identity and the Life Cycle.* New York: International Universities Press, 1959.

FITZPATRICK, J. J. *Puerto Rican Americans: The Meaning of Migration to the Mainland.* Englewood Cliffs, N.J.: Prentice-Hall, 1971.

FUNNYE, C., and SHIFFMAN, R. "The imperatives of deghettoization: An answer to Piven and Cloward." *Social Work,* 1967, 12, 5–11.

GIORDANO, J. "Ethnics and minorities: A review of the literature." *Clinical Social Work Journal,* 1974, 2, 207–220.

GIORDANO, J. "Introduction. Group identity and mental health." *International Journal of Mental Health,* 1976(a), 5, 3–4.

GIORDANO, J. "Ethnicity and community mental health." *Community Mental Health Review,* 1976(b), 1, 4–14.

GOODE, W. J. *The Family.* Englewood Cliffs, N.J.: Prentice-Hall, 1964.

GORBEA, C. "The institute's program for new arrivals." In D. J. Curren ed., *Proceedings of Puerto Rican Conferences on Human Services.* Washington, D.C.: The National Coalition of Spanish-Speaking Mental Health Organizations, 1975, pp. 73–79.

GORDON, M. *Assimilation in American Life.* New York: Oxford University Press, 1964.

Group for the Advancement of Psychiatry. *The Case History Method in the Study of Family Process.* New York: Group for the Advancement of Psychiatry, 1970.

HIDALGO, H. *Ethnic Differences, Series #4.* Washington, D.C.: National Rehabilitation Association, 1972.

KAHN, A. *Theory and Practice of Social Planning.* New York: Russell Sage Foundation, 1969.

KATZ, D., and KAHN, R. *The Social Psychology of Organizations.* New York: John Wiley and Sons, 1966.

KELLY, J. Ecological constraints on mental health services. In A. Bindman and A. Spiegel, eds., *Perspectives in Community Mental Health.* Chicago: Aldine, 1969, pp. 93–100.

LEICHTER, H. J., and MITCHELL, W. E. *Kinship and Casework.* New York: Russell Sage Foundation, 1967.

LONGRES, J. F., JR. "Racism and its effects on Puerto Rican continentals." *Social Problems,* 1974, 55, 67–75.

LUBCHANSKY, I., EGRI, G., and STOKES, J. "Puerto Rican spiritualists view mental health: The faith healer as a paraprofessional." *American Journal of Psychiatry,* 1970, 127, 88–97.

LUCAS, I. "A profile of the Puerto Rican dropout in Chicago." In A. P. Campos, ed., *Puerto Rican Curriculum Development Workshop: A Report.* New York: CSWE, 1974, pp. 20–30.

MALDONADO-DENIS, M. *Puerto Rican: A Socio-Historic Interpretation.* New York: Vintage Books, 1972 (Translation).

MAYFIELD, W. "Mental Health in the black community." *Social Work,* 1972, 17, 106–110.

McGREADY, W. "Social utilities in a pluralistic society." In P. S. J. Cafferty and L. Chestang, eds., *The Diverse Society: Implications for Social Policy.* Washington, D.C.: NASW, 1976, pp. 13–25.

MIGRATION DIVISION, DEPARTMENT OF LABOR, COMMONWEALTH OF PUERTO RICO. *Puerto Ricans in the United States,* 1975 (Xerox).

MINTZ, S. W. "Puerto Rico: An essay in the definition of national culture." In F. Cordasco and E. Bucchioni eds., *The Puerto Rican Experience: A Sociological Sourcebook.* Totowa, N.J.: Littlefield, Adams, 1973, pp. 26–90.

MIRANDA, M., ed., *Puerto Rican Task Force Report.* New York: CSWE, 1973.

MURDOCK, G. P. "The universality of the nuclear family." In N. Bell and E. Vogel, eds., *A Modern Introduction to the Family.* New York: The Free Press, 1968, pp. 37–44.

Newsweek, February 21, 1977.

New York Times, Jan. 9, 1977.

New York Times, July 30, 1972.

RABKIN, J. G., and STRUENING, E. L. *Ethnicity, Social Class and Mental Illness,* Working Paper
Series No. 17. New York: Institute on Pluralism and Group Identity, 1976.

ROGER, L. *Migrant In the City: The Life of a Puerto Rican Action Group.* New York: Basic
Books, 1972.

RUIZ, P., and LANGROD. "The role of folk healers in community mental health services."
Community Mental Health Journal, 1976, 12, 392–398.

RYAN, W. "Fretting about the poor." In W. Ryan, ed., *Distress in the City.* Cleveland: The
Press of Western Reserve University, 1969, pp. 262–267.

SCHEELE, R. "The prominent families of Puerto Rico." In J. Steward, ed., *People of Puerto
Rico.* Urbana: University of Illinois Press, 1969, pp. 418–462.

SIRJAMAKI, J. "Cultural configurations in the American family." In R. J. R. King, ed., *Family
Relations: Concepts and Theories.* Berkeley, Cal.: The Glendessary Press, 1969, 42–
54.

STYCOS, J. M. "Family and fertility in Puerto Rico." *American Sociological Review,* 1952,
17, 572–580. National Council on Family Relations, Reprint.

THOMAS, P. "Puerto Ricans in the promised land." *Civil Rights Digest,* January 1974, 6.

THOMAS, P. *Down These Mean Streets.* New York: New American Library, 1967.

TORRES-MATRULLO, C. "Accumulation and psychopathology among Puerto Rican women in
mainland United States." *American Journal of Orthopsychiatry* 1976, 46, 710–719.

U.S. BUREAU OF THE CENSUS. *Current Population Reports.* Persons of Spanish origin in the
United States, March 1975, Series P-20, No. 290. Washington, D.C.: U.S. Government
Printing Office, 1976.

U.S. BUREAU OF THE CENSUS. *Current Population Reports.* Persons of Spanish origin in the
United States, March 1976. Series P-20, No. 302. Washington, D.C.: U.S. Environment
Printing Office, 1976.

U.S. COMMISSION ON CIVIL RIGHTS. *Puerto Ricans in the Continental United States: An Uncertain Future.* October, 1976.

VALLE CONSULTANTS LTD. *What Holds Sami Back: A Study of Service Delivery in a Puerto
Rican Community.* New York: Valle Consultants Ltd., 1973.

VASQUEZ DE RODRIQUEZ, L. *Needs and Aspirations of the Puerto Rican People, Social Welfare
Forum,* 1971. New York: Columbia University Press, for the National Conference on
Social Welfare, 1971, 15–22.

VASQUEZ DE RODRIQUEZ, L. "Social work practice in Puerto Rico." *Social Work,* 1973, 18,
32–40.

VASQUEZ, J. D. "La Bodega—A social institution." In A. P. Campos, ed., *Puerto Rican Curriculum Workshop: A Report.* New York: CSWE, 1974, pp. 31–36.

WAGENHEIM, K. *Puerto Rico: A Profile.* New York: Praeger, 1970.

WILENSKY, H. L., and LEBEAUX. *Industrial Society and Social Welfare.* New York: Russell Sage
Foundation, 1958.

ZIMMERMAN, S. "The family and its relevance for social policy." *Social Casework,* 1976, 57,
547–554.

CHAPTER 17

Cultural Evolution of American Indian Families

John Red Horse

PREFATORY COMMENT

John Red Horse, a nationally respected expert concerning American Indians, reports that almost half (630,000) of American Indians reside in four states: California, Oklahoma, Arizona and New Mexico. There are nearly 500 different cultural tribes, and nationally almost one-quarter retain their native language. Indeed, American Indians are a very heterogeneous group.

Red Horse thoughtfully conceptualizes major types of family systems among American Indians, such as traditional, neotraditional, transitional, bicultural, acculturated, and panrenaissance families. These descriptive variations give the social worker greater understanding and appreciation of the differences within the American Indian special population.

American Indian family systems have drawn considerable attention during the past decade. Researchers during this period encouraged political activism in support of the Indian Child Welfare Act of 1978. They claimed that family systems were fractured by intrusions from child welfare professionals and proposed that due process of law could restore natural strengths of Indian families (Unger, 1977). After passage of the act, jurisdiction for selected child welfare matters was transferred to tribal courts. Red Horse (1982) noted that this transfer of jurisdiction was fraught with problems because of shortages of personnel with

From John Red Horse "Cultural Evolution of American Indian Families," in Carolyn Jacobs and Dorcas D. Bowles, eds., *Ethnicity and Race: Critical Concepts in Social Work* (Silver Spring, Md.: National Association of Social Workers, 1988), pp. 86–102.

appropriate clinical training, and he cited early indicators that suggested that removing American Indian children from their natural families would increase despite the act. Recent data have indicated that "the number of American Indian children in foster care has returned to—or has increased slightly above—the numbers which were cited prior to the passage of the Indian Child Welfare Act" (Sudia, 1986).

Social legislation alone cannot strengthen American Indian families. In addition, professionals armed with knowledge in American Indian family development must implement policies. To help social workers obtain such knowledge, this chapter addresses contemporary variations in American Indian family and individual behavior. The author uses traditional family systems as a benchmark for discussion but does not assume that persistence is preferable to change in traditional beliefs and customs. Adaptive behaviors are common among any cultural group exposed to new life situations; such behaviors among American Indians simply indicate a reframing, and in some cases a revitalization, of cultural beliefs through behaviors that vary from traditional life-styles.

This chapter includes discussion of several aspects of American Indian lifestyles. Demographic trends provide a macroscopic view of life circumstances among American Indians. Leading indicators suggest that families and individuals experience life situations that influence rapid change in behaviors and belief systems. Examples of the lives of several individuals capture discrete changes in behavior and aspirations that affect cultural maintenance across three generations and within the same generation. Two representative, existing resource manuals for training professional personnel then examine the art of diagnosis, assessment, and direct service to Indian families and individuals. A discussion of the spectrum of American Indian family systems examines permutations and combinations of behavior that emerge as revitalized cultural systems. A final, summary discussion examines implications for human service education and practice.

DEMOGRAPHIC TRENDS

Most American Indians became urban residents between the 1970 and 1980 census reporting periods (U.S. Department of Commerce, Bureau of the Census, 1983, 1984, and 1985). The 1970 census reported that 45 percent of the American Indian population resided in central cities or in urban areas proximate to central cities, and this group increased to 54 percent by 1980. The data also showed important variations among states. Forty-seven percent of the total American Indian population reside in four states: 201,369 (approximately 15 percent) in California; 169,459 (about 13 percent) in Oklahoma; 152,745 (about 11 percent) in Arizona; and 107,481 (about 8 percent) in New Mexico. Remarkable contrasts appear in residential patterns. California experienced rapid growth, and its American Indian population increased 118 percent between 1970 and 1980. The increase is attributed to migration patterns; 81 percent of California's Indian population resides in urban areas. This migration trend is less demonstrable in Oklahoma, but 59 percent of the American Indian population resides in or proximate to central cities. American Indians in Arizona and New Mexico, however, predominantly reside on reservations; in each state, only 30 percent of the American Indian population lives in urban areas. Eskimos and Aleuts in Alaska appear connected to traditional homelands—less than 30 percent of their in-state population (26 percent of their populations live outside the state) are urban residents.

Nationally, 24 percent of American Indians retain a native language. The 1980 census indicates that 333,000 American Indians ages five years and older speak a native language, and an estimated 15,000 native language speakers do not speak English at all. Native languages are spoken in 125,000 households. Again, state demographics vary dramatically for transmission of language. Forty-three percent of the total native language speakers reside in Arizona and New Mexico, and 33 percent of that group are from school-age populations, compared with only 15 percent from school-age populations in Oklahoma and 25 percent in Alaska. Language transmission across generations exceeded 75 percent in Arizona and New Mexico. In Oklahoma, the rate was 26 percent; in California, 27 percent; in Washington, 18 percent; and in Oregon, 15 percent.

Family structures are losing key members who previously were responsible for passing on traditional matters. Family systems in urban areas usually are nuclear household arrangements that are not influenced by extended kin on a daily basis. Mixed marriages increased 20 percent since 1970, and in 1980, more than 50 percent of all married American Indians had non-Indian spouses. Also, irrespective of urban or reservation residence, a disproportionate number of American Indian families are maintained by single parents (the rate exceeds 20 percent among the total American Indian population).

Demographic trends provide a macroscopic view of life situations. Residential status, language retention or loss, and marriage patterns are three critical variables associated with cultural maintenance. The immersion of families and individuals in urban environments that are distant from native homelands and traditional kin systems requires adaptations in personal life-style, aspirations, and behavior. These adaptive tendencies are not captured by census data, but the following examples of individuals' life choices show contrasting dynamics of cultural persistence and change.

EXAMPLES

Ogewabenais and Behmahseis: Across Three Generations

Ogewabenais was born 65 years ago in a remote, traditional village. He was introduced to ritual custom at a naming ceremony seven days after his birth. His American Indian name—Ogewabenais—means *Chief Eagle,* and he assumed a role as a bearer of ritual custom. He learned ritual songs for medicine drum ceremonies and became knowledgeable in medicinal herbs, roots, and tree barks. For most of his life, only the tribal language was spoken in his home.

Ogewabenais was not a cosmopolitan man by American standards. He did not travel much from his village. He did spend several years at a boarding school, which only strengthened his appreciation for traditional ways. Ogewabenais also was drafted into military service during World War II and spent three years in Europe. There, for the first time, he met white people who appreciated Indians, and he was tempted to make the military a career. Despite limited exposure to urban influences, Ogewabenais had an ability for cosmopolitan thinking. However, his skill in ritual healing puzzled medical doctors, and he could trace genealogy better than most professionals.

The path of life that Ogewabenais chose was tantamount to vows of poverty. By most standards in American society, Ogewabenais was a poor man—his lifetime earnings probably did not exceed $75,000, which he earned primarily during the heyday of the Office of Economic Opportunity. His livelihood derived mostly from traditional activities: gathering berries, working in wild rice paddies and cranberry marshes, and making maple syrup. During many summers, he supplemented this income by singing and dancing in a weekly show for tourists. By all standards in traditional American Indian society, however, Ogewabenais was a wealthy man. He knew ritual custom and passed it to namesakes for whom he served as role model and mentor. Ogewabenais died during the summer of 1986. More than 700 people attended his funeral. Most were extended kin and namesakes, who were testimony to his wealth; they were seeds of ritual tradition that he planted.

Behmahseis was born 17 years ago in a metropolitan hospital. He was introduced to ritual custom at a naming ceremony seven days after birth. His American Indian name—Behmahseis—means *child of harmony* and endows him with spirit powers to heal conflicts. Behmahseis spent seven years of childhood on the reservation and in a remote, traditional village. He served as keeper of the medicine drum, participated in ritual ceremonies, and spoke the language fluently. However, when he left the village, he developed other interests.

Behmahseis thrives in an urban life-style and has lived in four metropolitan areas. He comprehends formal science, understands profit margins, and commands Standard English. He aspires to a professional life and plans to become a lawyer or doctor. He was worked in wild rice paddies and cranberry marshes. However, he has decided that menial labor is not his future. Instead, he dreams of money, sports cars, and expensive homes and enjoys rock music and video games.

Behmahseis is preparing for success with meticulous care. He is an honor student in high school and is considering matriculating at Stanford or Harvard, but he has visited more than 30 university campuses in 28 states and Canada. His high school involvements show well-rounded achievement to improve his chances for university admission. He is a four-year letterman, is enrolled in college preparatory courses, is active in student government, and serves as an executive officer in the school's chapter of a national honor society.

By all standards in American society, Behmahseis exhibits attributes common to success; he is bright, motivated, and ambitious. However, he may die in poverty according to the standards of traditional American Indian society. His command of ritual knowledge and language is declining rapidly. He has not planted seeds of ritual tradition. Behmahseis has no namesakes and is too removed from kin to serve as a role model or mentor.

Ogewabenais respected Behmahseis's decision to pursue an individual path of life that departed from tradition. However, Ogewabenais planted tobacco every day while he lived and prayed that Behmahseis would return to traditional ways. This ritual was Ogewabenais' obligation because Behmahseis is his grandson.

This example paints a picture of contrasting persistence and change in behavior and aspirations as life experiences vary over generations. Both environment and personal choice influence patterns of cultural maintenance.

Helen and Marlene: Within a Generation

Helen is 32 years old. She is a traditional American Indian and she lives in a remote but well-developed area of her home reservation. Helen always was an exceptional student. She retained the native language, but acquired an admirable command of English. She graduated from college with a 3.54 undergraduate grade point average and earned a master's degree from a major research university. She experienced some difficulty in graduate school, particularly with theories and concepts in health care. Eventually she mastered health concepts that draw distinctions among primary and secondary institutions, but she no longer uses them, not because of a lack of intelligence but because of immersion in a traditional life-style that does not separate family, religion, and health care.

Helen struggled to retain ritual tradition while she completed her university work. She lived in metropolitan areas for seven years and did not visit a single health clinic, seek out a private doctor, or attend a counseling session to resolve personal stress. Instead, she made 63 trips home to receive health care at ritual ceremonies. Following graduation, she returned home and married a medicine man. They have three children who are becoming fluent in ritual custom and in their native language.

Helen's sister, Marlene, is 33 years old. She lived the first eight years of her childhood in the same traditional home setting. However, she went on educational placement at age nine and was away from family influence for 15 years. She is extremely intelligent and completed undergraduate studies with a grade point average of 3.62. Marlene did not attend graduate school.

Marlene adjusted to American society and lived in a white community. She joined the church that sponsored the educational placement and never went home for ritual ceremonies. She still has an ear for her native language and can understand conversations, but she has little need for the language in daily affairs. Consequently, she speaks it only haltingly and does not dream in it at all.

Marlene married a non-Indian who belongs to the same church, and the couple has four children. English is the language of preference in their home. The children neither speak their mother's native language nor attend ritual ceremonies. They visit grandparents occasionally, but they are not comfortable among extended kin. Also, they enjoy urban life and become bored on the reservation.

The contrasting behaviors of Helen and Marlene reverberate through their entire family of orientation. Their parents had nine children. Four stayed home and retained traditional ways. Five entered educational placement, disconnected from extended kin, and entered the American mainstream. The parents do not make judgments and supported educational placement. The children who stayed home to live according to tradition have mixed opinions about their siblings and find it difficult to reconcile departures from traditional ways.

TWO RESOURCE MANUALS

Several organizations have developed resource materials that blend discussions of Indian culture with professional concepts of family and individual services. This section examines two representative manuals prepared for distribution to American Indian and non-Indian audiences. One is intended primarily for child welfare professionals and serves a national audience (Anderson et al., 1983). The other is intended primarily for classroom teachers and serves a state audience (Arizona Department of Education, 1986).

Indian Child Welfare Resources and References (Anderson et al., 1983) provides an excellent overview of issues such as tribal sovereignty, intergovernmental relations, child welfare law, and program components in child welfare. However, it has limited value as a guide for clinical diagnosis, assessment, and treatment for Indian families and individuals. The manual explains American Indian behavior through a framework of five mutually exclusive life-styles that range from traditional to assimilated, but these five life-style types do not account for many life-style permutations and combinations that lead to behaviors not explained by the model. Such a limited model has serious implications for clinical service. Without some understanding of discrete behaviors that are possible among American Indians adapting to contemporary life stresses, child welfare professionals may reach dubious clinical decisions.

The Arizona Department of Education (1986) manual *A Varied People: Arizona's Indians* is one of the finest documents available. The manual details historical circumstances that shaped tribal diversity (such as custom, language, and life-styles), and it traces historical aspects of family development that link extended kin systems to traditional village organization. Lesson plans with teaching styles that can be adapted to individual children make it an excellent classroom guide for teachers. However, the manual disregards contemporary influences on family and individual development, as if cultural evolution has ceased. Culture systems are not static, however, and departures from traditional value orientations during the twentieth century have reshaped group attitudes among many American Indians. Attcity (1983), noted, for example, that three religious factions among Navajos on the reservation influence behaviors among families and individuals. Families in traditional factions retain a cultural view that one's relation to the physical world is sacred. Another faction modifies this to encourage a utilitarian view of the physical world. One faction retains a sacred view of language; another adopts an instrumental view. Thus, many elders raise concerns about the erosion in traditional understanding of the native language and attribute this erosion to the teaching of language in schools (Zah, 1984).

Both of these resource manuals are important contributions to the literature and serve as laudable efforts that can lead to further refinements. However, teachers and child welfare professionals need more discrete tools to guide their assessments of contemporary American Indian behaviors. Their professional observations in such areas of behavior as potential neglect and abuse, for example, have considerable impact on the lives of American Indian children.

SPECTRUM OF FAMILY SYSTEMS

American Indian family systems can be categorized on a continuum that organizes family typology and explicates modal behaviors for individuals and groups within family types (Table 17–1). The continuum of family typology includes traditional, neotraditional, transitional, bicultural, accultural, and panrenaissance family types. Modal behaviors common within family types include language of preference, religious beliefs, attitudes about land, kin system structure, and health behavior.

The traditional American Indian family is the benchmark for any discussion of American Indian family types. A demonstrable change in at least one modal behavior leads to the emergence of the neotraditional family type. More extreme changes in modal behaviors lead to the subsequent types. The spectrum provides for continuous reclassification during clinical service, so the service provider can update diagnosis and treatment on the basis of specific behavioral tendencies as families and individuals adapt to new life situations. The spectrum of types does not imply a linear phenomenon necessarily. In many instances, modal behaviors change for different situations, and families can move in either direction along the continuum.

Traditional Families

Traditional behavior derives from village structures that were common among tribal groups. Thomas (1982) noted three important attributes of these villages.

TABLE 17–1   *Spectrum of Indian Family Systems with Illustrative Modal Behaviors*

FAMILY TYPE	MODAL BEHAVIORS				
	LANGUAGE	KIN STRUCTURE	RELIGION	LAND	HEALTH BEHAVIOR
Traditional	Prefers use of native language in home, community relations, and ritual ceremonies. Exhibits homogeneity across generations.	Extended kin system organizes as basic unit of community structure. Kin are dominant in social relations, and community generally is closed to outsiders.	Practices native religion identified with historic custom. Bonds spiritual, human, and universal domains through ritual ceremonies. Retains clans and ritual names if applicable to custom.	Retains sacred view of land. Links to land through ritual ceremonies, including purification rites for residence.	Retains traditional beliefs regarding etiology of disease and seeks care through ritual ceremonies that recapture harmony among mind, body, spirit, and universe, includes use of prescriptive herbal medicines.
Neotraditional	Generally prefers use of native language in home, community, and ritual ceremonies. However, some have adopted second language, which is preferred and becomes dominant over the native language. Exhibits language homogeneity across generations.	Extended kin system may have been fractured through adoption of new religion, but modified kin system remains extended and community is closed. Kin dominate social relations.	Retains general beliefs associated with historic custom, but adopts new ritual procedures to act out beliefs.	Retains sacred view of land and links to land in a manner similar to traditional groups.	Retains traditional beliefs regarding etiology of disease. Adopts new ritual procedures and spiritual healers.
Transitional	Prefers native language in the home and intimate social relations, but not in community use and other external relations. Language homogeneity across generations declines.	Extended kin system is fractured, but modified system will be available if a colony is organized. Fractured, isolated groups form nuclear households. System opens to outsiders, particularly among children.	Retains beliefs associated with historic custom, but struggles to act them out on a daily basis because of absence of natural system. Travels frequently to homeland to reinforce religion through ritual ceremonies.	Retains sacred view of land and acts this out when visiting homeland. However, begins to acquire utilitarian view of residence and often other land in general.	Retains traditional sense of the etiology of disease and makes frequent trips to homeland for health care. Daily ritual behavior in health matters begins to deteriorate, and American institutional services begin to dominate.

TABLE 17–1 *(continued)*

Family Type	Modal Behaviors				
	Language	Kin Structure	Religion	Land	Health Behavior
Bicultural	English is preferred language in the home and community. Parents may know native language, but homogeneity across generations declines rapidly.	Nuclear household arrangements predominate, but a strong sense of American Indian identity leads to fictive extended kin structures. Prefers social relations with other American Indians and system is open to them.	Retains a symbolic sense of native religion, but does not practice it on a daily basis. Adopts new religion, but does not adapt it to traditional beliefs; hence, ritual customs are absent.	Aware of the symbolic meaning of the sacredness of land, but adopts utilitarian behaviors with respect to land in general.	Uses American institutional services, but prefers services that involve other American Indians. Has developed extensive parallel network of all-Indian services that mirror systems common to the general population. Prefers non-Indian view on etiology of disease.
Acculturated	English is preferred language in the home and community. Exhibits total loss of native language.	Nuclear households outside of general parameters of an identifiable American Indian community. Primary social relations are with non-Indians and no fictive system develops. System is open.	Converts to nonnative religion and loses ties to historic religious customs and practices.	Not generally concerned with sacredness of land. Except in narrow terms of secular views on conservation, land view is utilitarian.	Prefers American institutional care without need for all-Indian parallel systems. Adopts non-Indian view on the etiology of disease.
Panrenaissance	English generally is the primary language in the home and community. Language renewal is emphasized, but homogeneity across generations is low.	Nuclear household arrangements predominate, but a strong effort to reorganize natural extended kin systems prevails. Fictive kin arrangements are common and system is open.	Attempts to revitalize aspects of historic ritual custom. Generally organizes hybrid forms to replicate traditional religious beliefs.	Revitalizes the sacred view of land, but retains utilitarian views with respect to residence and other property in general.	Is extremely critical of American institutional system. Actively pursues expansion of all-Indian parallel networks of care. Attempts to revitalize historic beliefs around the etiology of disease.

First, they were extremely small, with a population range of 200 to 350 residents, and contact with outsiders was limited. Ritual events brought several villages together but did not alter social structures in the individual villages. Second, all village residents were members of an extended kin system, so social relations outside of family were limited. This attribute shaped behavior that generally was unobtrusive because maintenance of enduring family relationships was the basis of social control. Third, the villages were considered sacred societies, so life events and kin relationships were interpreted according to sacred law. Elders assumed respected roles because their accumulated wisdom was necessary to interpret lives and relationships according to a sacred context.

The attributes of village and kin structure explain many values that commonly are ascribed to American Indians. Family loyalty was strong, and important roles such as parenting were shared among grandparents, aunts, and uncles. Older children received considerable responsibility for child care. The nature of personal relationships facilitated behaviors that were nonjudgmental and noncompetitive among kin. However, nonjudgmental behavior was not necessarily the norm with people outside the kin systems—which, according to structural limitations common to villages, were organized as closed communities. Harsh opinion toward outsiders still is common today, and social workers familiar with American Indian behavior are aware of intergroup judgments made on the basis of blood quantum, reservation or urban residence, and religious beliefs. Also, value orientations that guided unobtrusive behavior did not allow deviant, irresponsible behaviors that could jeopardize kin. Social control could be exacting, and contemporary discussions on the role of noninterference in family relations often overlooked such control. Pipestem (1980) provides an example:

> Parenting was a sacred obligation in my tribe, and parents could be banished for child abuse and neglect. This was not used often, perhaps only once every generation, because it made a lasting impression. When this occurred, the entire village gathered in a double column as if to watch a parade. The neglectful parent was at the center of the village with a group of elders. They would march out from the heart of the village and move toward the land of strangers. A caller in the group would repeatedly announce the reasons for banishment and explain why the parenting behavior was not good for the village and why the parent must leave forever. This was like a public announcement of the findings of a court in current law. When the group reached the edge of the village, the parent was cast from family membership. No family member who remained in the village could ever again speak to the person that was banished.

Methods of social control among traditional families have changed with contemporary times, but modal behaviors influenced through early village structure remain reasonably constant. Most family households have close ties to extended kin systems, and traditional roles are intact. Grandparents, aunts, and uncles are parent figures who assume primary responsibilities in the lives of children. The families generally live in remote areas, whether on reservations or in rural areas, and the kin system organizes into a closed community. Closed communities are not penetrated easily by strangers; therefore, peer relationships outside of family are limited. Family membership expands through marriage, but spouses are expected to join the new family of orientation in a manner prescribed by custom.

Traditional families interpret life events in sacred terms. Individual behavior reinforces this daily, and traditional values structure sacred relationships among kin and with the universe. These relationships are expressed through ritual ceremonies, and depending upon tribal custom, these families are articulate with sacred bonds such as ritual names, clans, and namesakes. Ritual ceremonies, particularly in health care, generally are family affairs. Other American Indians may be invited as appropriate to custom, but non-Indians rarely are allowed to attend ritual events.

Most traditional American Indians are bilingual, but native language is preferred in the home, in community relations, and at ritual ceremonies. Language maintenance is intended to avoid intrusions from the outside world and is necessary to retain and transmit a precise understanding of a sacred past, present, and future. Ritual names, for example, are important bonds in traditional social structures. They link individuals with a sacred universe, pass spirit powers through the generations during healing ceremonies, and establish personal obligations among kin. As such, ritual names serve as sinews in a social structure that guides individual behavior, and their connotative meaning is lost when they are translated into English.

American Indian health services have introduced modern medicine to remote communities. However, traditional patterns of behavior change slowly, and customary health practices still are used widely among traditional families. Traditional American Indians mirror the general American population by seeking health care through the family system. However, their traditional beliefs concerning somatic and mental health are quite different from those held by the general population. Biological and psychological factors are not considered the only causes of disease, and the concept of health includes a sense of harmony among sociological structures and spiritual forces. Therefore, health care is holistic. Kin, ritual names, and clans play an important part in health care because medical practice includes both using prescriptive medicines and regaining harmonious balance of sociological structures and spiritual forces. Some government programs have acknowledged these important traditional beliefs and have integrated medicine men with doctors to deliver health services. Utilization rates improve among traditional families when such strategies are used (Kniep-Hardy and Burkhardt, 1977).

Neotraditional Families

Neotraditional families emerge most commonly through mass religious conversions. These families organize into closed kin and village structures and simply adopt new ritual procedures for sacred beliefs. Some conversions, such as the Native American Church, occurred with families in tribes from the Southwest to the upper Midwest. In some instances, entire tribes have been converted. The Yaquis, for example, blended native religion with Roman Catholicism. Neotraditional families retain most of the traditional modal behaviors, such as a sacred view of the universe and kinship roles. Yaquis, however, also changed language usage. They retain their native language in limited ways among younger generations, but Spanish is the dominant language in the home and the community.

Transitional Families

Transitional families emerge through geographic relocation away from extended kin systems. They attempt to retain modal behaviors similar to traditional groups, but actual retention varies according to the nature of change and the impact of that change on daily life. Some transitional families relocate as colonies with several members of an extended kin system moving together; they adapt to new living situations with minimal changes in modal behaviors. Other transitional families move as isolated household units, and they experience dilemmas across all modal behaviors. Parents generally retain native language use in the home, but language homogeneity decreases because children adopt English as a primary language. The family retains a sacred view of land, but the urban residence often is treated in a utilitarian manner. The extended kin system begins to fracture. Relationships are maintained through frequent travel to the reservation, but kin have considerably less influence with social roles and behaviors. Social relations in the urban community generally are with other American Indians, but families really do not retain the closed aspect of extended kin systems because urban peers are nonkin.

All transitional families retain traditional health behaviors and maintain frequent contact with their native homelands. A survey on health behavior in the San Francisco Bay area indicated that 28 percent of the sample population used medicine men at their home reservation when treatment was necessary (Kaufman, 1979). Transitional families are underserved by institutional care in urban areas, but certain health care strategies can modify their closed behavior. For example, a family and children's service in Oakland, California, noted that health care utilization rates among transitional families increased dramatically following employment of native language translators (Oakland Indian Child Resource Center, 1982).

Bicultural Families

Bicultural families make important shifts away from traditional modal behaviors. While transitional families reconcile disjunctions between life situations and preferred modal behavior, bicultural families face a dilemma between the symbolism of tradition and actual preferences in life-style. Typically, these families do not transmit specific traditional knowledge across generations. Parents often may understand their native language, but they do not maintain it as the language of preference in the home. Therefore native language use is declining rapidly among younger generations. Parents also are acquainted with ritual custom but have converted to non-Indian religions. Most children in bicultural families do not have ritual names, are not familiar with their clans, and do not have namesakes. This decline in attributes associated with specific ritual custom also leads bicultural families to favor institutional services common to American society. Finally, sacredness of land is acknowledged symbolically, but in actual practice, land is treated in a utilitarian manner.

Although bicultural families have acquired many characteristics of American society, they are not integrated socially. They prefer relationships with other American Indians and have introduced important adaptations that contribute to a construction of generalized American Indian values. Bicultural families often replicate traditional extended kin systems through fictive structures that incorporate nonkin into roles normally found in extended families. They manage geographic isolation by attending pow-wows in urban areas or on nearby reservations. Younger bicultural American Indians elevate pow-wows almost to ritual or ceremonial status, although pow-wows actually are social events that are open to the general public. The behavior, however, is an important form of cultural revitalization that reinforced and maintains a shared American Indian identity.

Acculturated Families

Acculturated families are assimilated and represent the most extreme departure from traditional life-styles. Families in this group differ from bicultural families by enacting social preferences that make them comfortable with non-Indians. They assume modal behavior similar to the American general population without any apparent personal dilemma. The English language is used by both parent and child generations. Acculturated families practice non-Indian religions and do not retain actual or symbolic sacred linkages to land, kin, or health behavior. Health behavior mirrors that of mainstream society. Nuclear households are the preferred family structures, and visits with kin are infrequent. Thus, peer relations generally are with non-Indians for both parents and children.

Panrenaissance Families

Panrenaissance families emerge as important cultural revival responses when external forces place families and individuals in jeopardy, and the emergence of such families and groups is not unique to contemporary American Indians. During the 1800s, for example, the ghost dance society emerged and spread rapidly as an attempt to revitalize American Indian religions that had been banned by the federal government. Contemporary panrenaissance families often exist in militant American Indian groups. Militant groups originally organized out of concern for civil rights, but they have expanded to include treaty rights, tribal sovereignty, and religious freedom, which indicates a shift in emphasis. Originally, the groups stressed cultural awareness, but they gradually included issues concerning language renewal and organized hybrid forms of traditional religion. Support for these activities is mixed. Language renewal generally is supported by traditional groups, but hybrid religions that change ritual custom are not popular.

Modal behaviors among panrenaissance families are similar to bicultural families in many respects. They prefer social relationships with other American Indians and reinforce kinship ties whenever possible, but they also maintain open structures as fictive kin systems. Symbolically, land is viewed with sacred meaning, but panrenaissance families seldom act out that view through daily rituals. The most notable behavior of such families is outspoken criticism of American Indian services designed by American institutions. Their tactics in areas such as child welfare are controversial, but the issues that they raise apply generally across a broad spectrum of American Indian families. Their efforts have led to the organization of several parallel institutional systems that provide American Indian–controlled services in education, social work, health care, and housing. Their efforts also have heightened awareness among American Indians and non-Indians alike, and they continue to publicize new, alarming matters, such as Indian genocide in Latin America.

SUMMARY AND RECOMMENDATIONS

The census data indicated important demographic shifts that affect the degree of cultural persistence and change among American Indian families and individuals. These shifts do not indicate uniform erosion of American Indian culture. However, variations among states and regions suggest that family proximity to native homelands fosters cultural maintenance through frequent contact with extended kin systems and language transmission across the generations. The census data, especially the large proportion of younger people among American Indians, suggest that traditional structures likely will experience rapid modification in years to come.

The spectrum of American Indian family systems describes variations in illustrative modal behaviors among American Indians. Although it is not an exhaustive model, it attributes variations in behavior within and across generations to personal choices that are made in response to external social forces. Thus, modal behavior suggests that personal variations can be situational, that bidirectional movement along with spectrum is common, and that families frequently replicate traditional social organization such as natural kin systems through fictive structures among urban groups. To show the range of the spectrum, accounting for permutations and combinations possible with the family typology and modal behaviors, families and individuals can exhibit 7,776 discrete behavior variations. This range raises implications for professional education, research, and practice that could be implemented through curriculum development, special programs of study, and partnerships between social service agencies and tribal governments.

Curriculum development should support the canons of scholarship. Current strategies in professional schools assume that minority content can be integrated with regular course offerings in human behavior and direct practice. This may be true for subpopulations that speak only one language within the group or have sacred beliefs that mirror organized religion in Western society. However, American Indians depart from the model. Estimates indicate that American Indians, excluding Alaskan natives, speak at least 149 different languages and are organized into several cultural groups with different customs and traditions (Red Horse, 1982). Although American Indians have beliefs about the etiology of health and disease, differences among American Indians affect health behaviors, ritual organization, and leadership in extended kin systems. Many behaviors are retained as American Indians move into the mainstream of American society (Miller, 1975). Integrated curricula simply reduce knowledge to a minimum level. A separate curriculum that provides opportunity for social service practitioners to examine Indian family development, track health behavior, and document effective practice methods is needed.

Special programs of study could be developed at selected professional schools in response to regional variations noted in the demographic trends. Such programs would allow appropriate investigation into American Indian life transitions and facilitate the integration of social service education with networks in health and social services that are common to American Indians. Study programs also would foster the development of research agenda specific to language and cultural groups within a region. The programs could organize independently or through consortia designed to share research and teaching resources among a number of schools. Such programs would provide scholarship opportunities in areas such as native American Indian languages and apply social work content in policy, administration, human behavior, and practice in a manner consistent with the Indian Child Welfare Act of 1978.

Partnerships between social service agencies and tribal governments could benefit both groups. Tribes would gain technical assistance to support the development of clinical programs, and professionals would gain knowledge of practice skills essential for service delivery to Indian families and individuals. Moreover, such structures could provide valuable insights to professional education and could be modeled to track effective practice and inform the profession about teaching models appropriate to American Indian family services.

WORKS CITED

ANDERSON, S. C., ET AL. *Indian Child Welfare Resources and References.* Norman, Okla.: University of Oklahoma, 1983.

ARIZONA DEPARTMENT OF EDUCATION. *A Varied People: Arizona's Indians.* Phoenix, Ariz.: Arizona Department of Education, 1986.

ATTCITY, S. "Navajo Religion and Culture." Symposium conducted during American Indian Week, University of Arizona, Tucson, April 1983.

KAUFMAN, J. *Patterns of Health Behavior Among Indians in the Bay Area.* Unpublished manuscript, 1979.

KNIEP-HARDY, M., and M. BURKHARDT. "Nursing the Navajo," *American Journal of Nursing,* 73 (1977).

MILLER, D. *Native American Families in the City.* San Francisco: Institute for Scientific Analysis, 1975.

OAKLAND INDIAN CHILD RESOURCE CENTER. "Toward a Theoretical Model in American Indian Mental Health." Symposium on Indian Child Welfare, Oakland, Calif., 1982.

PASSEL, J. S. "Provisional Evaluation of the 1970 Census Count of American Indians," *Demography,* 13 (1976).

PIPESTEM, B. Respondent panel. Colloquium on American Indian Families: Strengths and Stresses, Arizona State University, Tempe, 1980.

RED HORSE, J. G. "American Indian Community Mental Health: A Primary Prevention Strategy," in S. M. Manson, ed., *New Directions in Prevention among American Indian and Alaska Native Communities.* Portland, Oreg.: Oregon Health Sciences University, 1982.

——. "Clinical Strategies for American Indian Families in Crisis," *The Urban and Social Change Review,* 15 (1982), pp. 17–19.

SUDIA, C. "Analysis Compares Numbers of Indian Foster Children," in *Linkages for Indian Child Welfare Program* (pp. 1, 4), 1986.

THOMAS, R. "Mental Health: American Indian Tribal Societies," in W. L. Mitchell, ed., *American Indian Families: Developmental Strategies and Community Health.* Tempe, Ariz.: Arizona State University, 1982.

UNGER, S. *The Destruction of American Indian Families.* New York: Association of American Indian Affairs, 1977.

U.S. DEPARTMENT OF COMMERCE, BUREAU OF THE CENSUS. *1980 Census of Population: Characteristics of the Population, General Population Characteristics, U.S. Summary* (PC 80-1-B1). Washington, D.C.: U.S. Government Printing Office, 1983.

——. *1980 Census of Population, Volume I, Characteristics of the Population, Chapter D, Detailed Population Characteristics.* Parts 3, 4, 6, 7, 11, 14, 15, 17, 18, 24, 25, 26, 28, 29, 30, 32, 33, 34, 35, 36, 37, 38, 39, 43, 45, 46, 49, 51, 52, (PC 80-D3). Washington, D.C.: U.S. Government Printing Office, 1983.

——. *1980 Census of Population, Volume I, Characteristics of the Population, Chapter D, Detailed Population Characteristics, U.S. Summary* (PC 80-1-D1). Washington, D.C.: U.S. Government Printing Office, 1984.

——. *Census of Population, Volume 2, Subject Reports, American Indians, Eskimos, Aleuts on Identified Reservations and in the Historic Areas of Oklahoma (Excluding Urbanized Areas)* (PC 80-2-1D). Washington, D.C.: U.S. Government Printing Office, 1985.

——. *General Social and Economic Characteristics, U.S. Summary 1980* (PC 80-1-C1). Washington, D.C.: U.S. Government Printing Office, 1983.

——. *American Indian Areas and Alaskan Native Villages: 1980* (PC 80-51-13). Washington, D.C.: U.S. Government Printing Office, 1984.

——. *Marital Characteristics* (PC 80-2-4C). Washington, D.C.: U.S. Government Printing Office, 1985.

ZAH, P. "Mission of the Navajo Tribal Government." Symposium conducted during Navajo Divisional Direction Training Workshop, Arizona State University, Tempe, July 1984.

CHAPTER 18

Social Work Practice with Asian Americans

Man Keung Ho

PREFATORY COMMENT

This is a chapter developed for this volume by Man Keung Ho, who is a leading scholar on Asian Americans. He reminds readers that Asian Americans are not homogeneous but actually comprise several subgroups (Chinese, Filipino, Japanese, Korean, Vietnamese, Samoan, Guamanian), each having its own unique language and culture. Although there are some cultural characteristics common to Asian Americans, such as filial piety, respect for elders, and high value on the traditional family, there can be differences involving seeking physical health, mental health, and social services. Some Asian American groups feel shame in talking to strangers about personal problems.

Some Asian Americans have their own unique psychotherapy models, such as Morita therapy developed by the Japanese. This therapy emphasizes a "here and now" orientation with a focus on behavior rather than moods and feelings. Social workers need to become more aware of these cultural differences and therapeutic models if they are to become effective with Asian American clients.

Asian Americans are often perceived as sharing the same or similar characteristics, but they actually comprised many diverse groups: Chinese, Japanese, Korean, Filipino Americans, Samoans, Guamanians, Hawaiians, and other Pacific Islanders. Other groups include recent immigrants and refugees from Vietnam, Thailand, Cambodia, Laos, and Indonesia, persons from India, Pakistan, and Ceylon, and children of mixed marriages in which one parent is Asian.[1] There are obvious language, historical, social, and economic differences. Generational status (new immigrants versus third and fourth generation) among groups and individuals should not be overlooked. Before micro (direct) and macro (indirect) social work practice with Asian Americans is introduced, current demographics and ecosystems of Asian Americans are reviewed.

CURRENT DEMOGRAPHICS

Population

The Asian American population has doubled since 1970, now comprising about 2 percent of the total U.S. population (3.5 million) and continues to increase. The population distribution of Asian Americans in 1970 and 1980 is shown in Table 18–1.

In 1970 the most populous Asian American group was the Japanese (591,290), followed by the Chinese (435,062) and the Filipinos (343,060). In 1980, however, the Chinese were the most numerous (806,042), followed by the Filipinos (774,652) and the Japanese (700,974). The Koreans showed a five-fold increase, from an estimated 70,000 in 1970 to 354,593 in 1980. Other Asian groups identified by the U.S. Census, but who are not included in Table 18–1 are the Asian Indians (361,531) and the native Hawaiians (166,814). The Immigration Act of 1965 and the U.S. policy on refugees that resulted from the Vietnam War are primarily responsible for the rapid Asian American population increase in this country. Most Asian Americans live in West coast and East coast urban areas and in Hawaii. There was a concentrated effort by the U.S. government to scatter recent Southeast Asian immigrants throughout the country. The majority were resettled in California (135,308), Texas (36,198), and Washington State (16,286).

Socioeconomic Issues

Selected socioeconomic characteristics of Asian Americans are provided in Table 18–2.

TABLE 18–1   *Asian Americans in the United States, 1970 and 1980*

Year	Chinese	Filipino	Japanese	Korean	Vietnamese	Samoan	Guamanian
1970	435,062	343,060	591,290	70,000[a]	N.A.[b]	N.A.	N.A.
1980	806,042	774,652	700,974	354,593	261,729	41,948	32,158

[a] Estimated.

[b] N.A. = not available.

Source: U.S. Bureau of the Census, "U.S. Summary, Characteristics of the Population: 1980," vol. 1 (Washington, D.C.: U.S. Government Printing Office, May 1983), pp. 9–20.

TABLE 18–2   *Selected Socioeconomic Characteristics of Racial and Ethnic Groups in the United States, 1980 (percentages)*

	ETHNIC AND RACIAL GROUPS			
CHARACTERISTICS	WHITE	BLACK	ASIAN AND PACIFIC ISLANDERS	HISPANIC
Family Type				
Families with children under 18 years	49.4	61.0	61.5	67.8
Female-headed households; no husband present	11.1	37.3	10.9	19.8
Female-headed households with children under 18 years	56.1	68.8	56.5	72.6
Education				
Persons 25 years or older with less than a high school degree	31.3	49.4	25.8	56.7
Persons 25 years or older with at least a college degree	17.2	8.4	32.5	7.6
Employment				
Persons 16 years or older in labor force	62.2	59.2	66.3	63.4
Unemployed persons 16 years or older	5.8	11.7	4.8	9.1
Females 16 years or older in labor force	41.5	48.4	45.0	39.1
Income				
Median income	$20,840	$12,618	$22,075	$14,711
Persons living below poverty level in 1979	9.4	30.2	13.9	23.8
Persons who own homes	67.8	44.4	51.5	43.5

Source: U.S. Bureau of the Census, 1980 Census Population Supplementary Reports PHC 80-S1-1-Provisional Estimates of Social, Economic, and Housing Characteristics: States and Selected Standard Metropolitan Statistical Areas (Washington, D.C.: U.S. Government Printing Office, 1982), pp. 47, 100.

Asian American families are more likely than either black or white families to have children under age 18. One out of every ten Asian American households is headed by a female whose spouse is not present. Asian American households that are headed by women are less likely to include children than households headed by black and Hispanic women. Asian Americans make up the smallest proportion of people without a high school diploma and the largest proportion of those with at least one college degree.

Despite comparatively high national unemployment rates, a relatively large proportion of Asian Americans are part of the labor force. Asian American women are less likely to be employed outside the home than men. The median income of an Asian American household is $2,000 above the national average. Proportionally, Asian Americans own fewer homes than their white counterparts.

Health and Mental Health Risk Factors

Asian American patients have been found to be similar to white patients in mental health diagnoses, except they are more likely to receive psychotic diagnoses.[2] This difference may be explained by the fact that less severely disturbed Asian Americans avoid using mental health services.

Many investigators have suggested that Asian Americans as a group consume less alcohol and have fewer cases of alcoholism than whites and other ethnic groups.[3] This is attributed to the genetic-racial differences in alcohol sensitivity and aversion and Asian American attitudes and values toward the use of alcohol. Some observers have predicted that alcoholism among Asian Americans may increase in the future in response to urbanization, cultural conflict, and changes in family structure.

At the First National Asian American Conference on Drug Abuse Prevention, participants generally felt that drug abuse is as prevalent in Asian American communities as in other communities.[4] Lyman believes organized drug dealings in San Francisco's Chinatown provided revenues for the tongs (Chinese associations) and gained a foothold.[5] Among many of the early Chinese immigrants who were lonely and uncared for, Sung found that the suicide rate of Chinese Americans in San Francisco was four times greater than the rate for the city as a whole.[6] More Chinese American women than men resort to suicide as a means to resolve their personal and interpersonal problems. A high suicide rate may be attributable to the fact that Asian Americans tend to direct family discord and unhappiness inward toward the self.

Crime and juvenile delinquency is low in Asian American communities.[7] However, it is generally recognized that criminal acts in Chinatowns and other urban Asian American communities are underreported.[8] Youth gangs' violent activities have increased recently in various Chinatowns throughout the country. Lyman attributes the increased formation of gangs to: (1) an increase in the number of immigrant youths; (2) frustration over racism and powerlessness; (3) inability to succeed in school because of English-language problems and cultural conflicts; and (4) the financial gains obtained through gang activities.[9]

The process of immigration and cultural transition has created a severe health and mental health risk factor for Asian Americans. Immigration itself necessitates a large number of life changes over a short period of time that are associated with lowered well-being.[10] Five major factors have been identified as contributing directly or indirectly to the immigrational and cultural transitional difficulties that, in turn, increase physical and mental health risks of Asian Americans.[11] These factors include: (1) economic survival, (2) U.S. racism, (3) loss of extended family and support systems, (4) major cultural conflicts, and (5) cognitive reactive patterns to a new environment.

Two physiological systems, respiratory and digestive, have been found to be primary somatic targets for Asians experiencing immigrational stress.[12] Denial is the defense mechanism most frequently used by recent Vietnamese refugees. This denial defense is congruent with the Asian cultural values of self-sacrifice, submission for the common good, harmony, and consignment to fate. When the use of denial fails to protect a refugee from some of the harsh realities of immigration, and when previous support systems are unavailable, psychosocial destruction such as psychosis may occur.[13] A national Mental Health Needs Assessment found some alarming facts concerning stress among immigrants: (1) mental health problems among Southeast Asian immigrants who arrived in 1975 only began to surface several years later; (2) depression was the most frequently reported problem; (3) anxiety, marital conflict, and intergenerational conflict were prevalent; and (4) the stress of the uprooting and cultural adjustment led to many emotional problems.[14]

ECOSYSTEMS PERSPECTIVE

The practice of social work focuses on the interaction between the person and the environment. The goal of social work practice is to enhance and restore the psychosocial functioning of persons or to change oppressive or destructive social conditions that negatively affect the mutually beneficial interaction between persons and their environment. In assessing Asian Americans' needs for services, the social worker should seek to understand clients' feelings and attitudes about those oppressive and destructive factors and their negative impacts.

The ecosystem model of practice developed and advanced by Meyer, Germain, and Morales and Sheafor is adopted for analysis of psychological factors impacting on Asian Americans.[15,16,17] The ecosystem consists of five interconnected levels: (1) historical, (2) environmental-structural, (3) cultural, (4) family, and (5) individual. Analysis of each level as it affects the lives and social conditions of Asian Americans follows.

Historical Influences

The Chinese were the first immigrants from Asia to arrive in the United States during the 1840s. Their immigration from China was encouraged by the social and economic unrest in China at that time and by overpopulation in certain provinces.[18] During this period there was a demand in the United States for Chinese to help build the transcontinental railroad. However, a diminishing labor market and fear of the "yellow peril" made the Chinese immigrants no longer welcome. Chinese men were robbed, beaten, and murdered, especially if they tried to compete with whites in the mining districts of Western states. This anti-Chinese sentiment culminated in the passing of the Federal Chinese Exclusion Act of 1882, the first exclusion act against any ethnic group. This racist immigration law was not repealed until 1943, as a gesture of friendship toward China, who was an ally of the United States during the Second World War. The Immigration Act of 1965 finally abolished national-origin quotas. "Old-timer" immigrants were characterized primarily as uneducated peasants, unskilled laborers, and men. Post-1965 immigrants have been well-educated, urban families.[19]

Early Japanese immigrants came to the United States from 1890 to 1924, after the Chinese exclusion laws were passed. They left a rapidly industrializing country as "contract laborers" for the plantations in Hawaii. Legislation similar to the anti-Chinese acts was passed against the Japanese. Anti-Japanese prejudice culminated in the forced removal in 1942 of over 110,000 Japanese, 75 percent of them U.S. citizens, to guarded relocation centers. Unlike the Chinese, Japanese immigrants were allowed to start families, employing the "picture bride" (bride selected by photograph) method of marriage. Consequently, the acculturation process of their U.S.—born children occurred much earlier than for immigrant Chinese children. Hence, in general the Japanese are more acculturated than the Chinese, even though the Chinese have been in this country for a longer time.

The Filipino population in the United States grew most rapidly after the Immigration Act of 1965. As a result of the Spanish American War and the Treaty of Paris (1899), the Philippines at one time was actually a possession of the United States. The Tydings—McDuffie Independence Act conferred commonwealth status on the Philippines, and Filipinos then became aliens for the purpose of U.S. immigration. The earliest Filipino immigrants were unskilled laborers or students who were encouraged by the U.S. colonial government to attend U.S. colleges and universities.[20] Immigrants who came in the 1960s were mostly young professionals, both men and women. Many of them experienced difficulties in obtaining U.S. licenses to practice their profession. The majority of the surviving early Filipino immigrants are now retired, living in cheap one-room hotels and apartments. They experience health care problems, limited recreational opportunities, and physical and psychological isolation.

The number of Korean immigrants just prior to the Immigration Act of 1965 was slightly over 7000.[21] A high proportion of them were Christian, because U.S. missionaries in Korea played a major role in Korean immigration. Kim estimated that 90 percent of the Korean immigrants have been here less than fifteen years— since the Immigration Act of 1965 went into effect in 1968. The largest Korean community, with a population over 150,000, is in Los Angeles.[22] Generally, Korean post-1968 immigrants have had to endure less hostility and structural discrimination than early Chinese and Japanese immigrants.

The Pacific Islanders include groups such as Samoans, Tongans, Guamanians, and a small number from Tahiti and the Fiji Islands. Samoan immigration began to increase from 1951, when the U.S. Navy closed its island base. Guamanian immigration was facilitated by the 1950 Organic Act, which conferred U.S. citizenship on inhabitants of the territory of Guam. Because of their ties with the Church of Jesus Christ of Latter-Day Saints, many Tongans have settled near Salt Lake City, Utah. Pacific Islanders as a group are relatively few in number and have no visible, strong ethnic community in the United States today.

Southeast Asians from Cambodia, Laos, and Vietnam came to this country primarily as refugees. Statistics of 1980 indicate 415,238 Indochinese were in the United States, of which 78 percent were from Vietnam, 16 percent from Cambodia, and 6 percent from Laos. The majority of them have settled in California, Texas, and Washington.[23] Cambodia, Laos, and Vietnam were part of the old French colonial empire and were lumped together as French Indochina. Cambodian culture was influenced by India, whereas the people of Laos are mainly ethnic Thai. Vietnamese culture was heavily influenced by China. The exodus of Vietnamese refugees began in 1975 with the fall of Saigon and U.S. withdrawal from the country. The first wave of refugees were mostly professionals and well educated. A second wave was admitted to the United States after 1975 and consisted of less educated people. The latter group has experienced more difficulty than the first group in adjusting to the United States.

Environmental–Structural Factors

The designation of Asian Americans as a minority group that has experienced prejudice and discrimination is misunderstood by many, who fail to assess accurately the status of Asian Americans and to conceptualize racial discrimination. Asian Americans have had a history of exploitation and racism in the United States.[24] Federal legislation has often restricted Asian immigration, or as in the case of the 1924 Immigration Act, prohibited their immigration entirely. Asian immigrants were placed in the category of "aliens ineligible for American citizenship." Alien land laws completed the nightmare in that "aliens ineligible for citizenship" were denied the right to own property. Antimiscegenation laws, which prohibited interracial marriages, were passed. More than 110,000 Japanese Americans were relocated in detention camps during the Second World War.

Restrictions against Asian Americans covered many other areas of life as well. Employment and housing opportunities were limited, and the full use of public and private facilities was denied. Such structural, social, and psychological constraints relegated Asian Americans to second-class status.

Gains in civil rights and civil liberties occurred only after the Second World War. Today Asian Americans are often considered "model" minorities, but many still face discrimination and prejudice.[25,26]

Asian American Culture

Social workers should focus on understanding the cultural values, belief systems, and societal norms of U.S. culture as well as Asian traditional culture. In an attempt to understand Asian American clients and to work effectively with this unique ethnic group, Ho lists seven salient cultural values operating among Asian Americans.[27] These indigenous cultural values are:

1. *Filial piety.* The respectful love of parent is the cornerstone of morality and is expressed in a variety of forms. Oya-KoKo, a Japanese's version of filial

piety to parents, requires a child's sensitivity, obligation, and unquestionable loyalty to lineage and parents. An Asian child is expected to comply with familial and social authority even to the point of sacrificing his or her own desires and ambitions.

2. *Shame as a behavioral influence.* Shame (*tiu lien* in Chinese) and shaming are used traditionally to help reinforce familial expectations and proper behavior within and outside the family. If an individual behaves improperly, he or she will "lose face" and also may cause the family, community, or society to withdraw confidence and support. In Asian societal structures, where interdependence is very important, the actual or threatened withdrawal of support may shake a person's basic trust and cause him or her considerable anxiety at the thought of facing life alone.

3. *Self-control.* Self-discipline is another concept highly valued by Asian Americans. The value "enryo" requires a Japanese individual to maintain modesty in behavior, be humble in expectations, and show appropriate hesitation and unwillingness to intrude on another's time, energy, or resources. To "Yin-Nor" for a Chinese is to evince stoicism, patience, and an uncomplaining attitude in the face of adversity, and to display tolerance for life's painful moments.

4. *Middle-position virtue.* In training children Asian parents emphasize a social norm that cultivates the virtues of the middle position, in which an individual should feel neither haughty nor unworthy. Middle-position virtue is quite different from the perfectionism and individualism highly valued by the middle-class white U.S. population. Asian American emphasis on middle-position brings an individual in step with others, instead of ahead or behind others. Thus, it fosters the individual's sense of belonging and togetherness.

5. *Awareness of social milieu.* An Asian's concern for the welfare of the group also is related to his or her acute awareness of social milieu, characterized by social and economic limitations and immobility. The individual is highly sensitive to the opinions of peers and allows the social nexus to define his or her thoughts, feelings, and actions. In the interest of social solidarity, one subordinates himself or herself to the group, suppressing and restraining any disruptive emotions and opinions. Despite an individual's wealth and social status compliance with social norms, which provide him or her with social esteem and self-respect, is strictly observed.

6. *Fatalism.* Constantly buffeted by nature and by political upheaval over which they had little control, Asian Americans adopted a philosophical detachment. This resignation allowed people to accept their fate with equanimity. Other than trying to philosophize or ascertain underlying meaning in life events, the Asian met life pragmatically. It is unfortunate that this pragmatic adaptability, the very factor that contributed to success in the United States, later became a serious handicap. The Asian American's continuing silence only let him or her fall further behind in an alien U.S. culture that encouraged, and indeed demanded, aggressiveness and outspoken individualism. This fatalistic attitude of Asian Americans has partly contributed to their unwillingness to seek outside professional help.

Unfortunately, the Asian's pragmatic adaptability is often misconstrued as resistance by some mental health and social services providers.

7. *Inconspicuousness.* Fear of attracting attention was particularly acute among the thousands of Asian immigrants who came to the United States illegally. Experiences with racist segments of U.S. society further convinced the Asian immigrant of the need for and value of silence and inconspicuousness. Fear and distrust still linger today among the descendants of early immigrants. It is understandable why Asians are extremely reluctant to turn to government agencies for aid, even in cases of dire need. Asian Americans' silence and inconspicuousness tend to make them verbally passive members in politics, group work, and community activities.

Family Structure

The cohesive extended network of the traditional Asian American family is structured and prioritized, fed with male dominance, and having parental ties paramount. A male child has distinct obligations and duties to his parents that assume a higher value than obligations to his siblings, children, or wife. Sibling relationships are considered next in priority and are frequently acknowledged through cooperative adult activities. Concepts and teachings, such as working hard, responsibility, family obligations, and collaborations, pervade parent–child relationships. Members of the older generation are responsible for transmitting guidelines for socially acceptable behavior, educating younger people in how to deal with life events, and serving as a source of support in coping with life crises.[28] A traditional Asian American family becomes the primary caretaker of its members' physical, social, and emotional health.

The traditional Asian American family structure provided stability, interpersonal intimacy, social support, and a relatively stress-free environment for its members.[29] However, the process of immigration and cultural transition exerts a severe blow to these families. Relatives and close friends are often no longer available to provide material and emotional support to needy members. The traditional hierarchical structure and rigidity of family roles often make the expression and resolution of conflicts within the nuclear family very difficult. Little or no interpersonal interaction outside the nuclear family, in turn, forces greater demands and intense interaction *within* the nuclear family. This can leave members highly vulnerable and with many unresolved conflicts. Discrepancies in acculturation between husband and wife and between parents and children negatively affect the decision making and functioning of a family. An individual's acceptance of and compliance with Western values such as individualism, independence, and assertiveness, especially in attitudes related to authority, sexuality, and freedom of choice, make the hierarchical structure of a traditional Asian American family dysfunctional.

While an Asian American family undergoes several stages in its attempt to help its members, different families may have different service needs and help-seeking patterns. Generally, there are three types of Asian American families in the United States.[30]

Recently Arrived Immigrant Families.   Initial requests for services by this type of family tend to be predominantly requests for information and referral, advocacy, and other concrete services such as English-language instruction, legal aid, and child care. Due to cultural differences, unfamiliarity with mental health resources, and language barriers, these families seldom seek personal or psychological help.

Immigrant-American Families.   These families are characterized by foreign-born parents and U.S.–born children and the great degree of cultural conflict between them. They usually require help in resolving generational conflicts, communication problems, role clarification, and renegotiation.

Immigrant-Descendant Families.   These families usually consist of second (Japanese Nisei) or third (Japanese Sansei) generation U.S.–born parents and their children. They speak English at home and are acculturated to Western values. They can seek help from mainstream human service agencies, mental health centers, and private practitioners with some degree of comfort.

The Individual

Asian Americans face different problems with cultural conflict. Jones believes many forms of culture conflict are really manifestations of cultural racism.[31] Although there is nothing inherently wrong in acculturation and assimilation, he believes "when it is forced by a powerful group on a less powerful one, it constitutes a restriction of choice; hence, it is no longer subject to the values of the natural order." Sue and McKinney found young Chinese clients exhibited anxiety over the inability to reconcile the Western values of independence with their feelings of filial piety and family obligation.[32] Also reported were feelings of social isolation and feelings of passivity in social situations.

In an attempt to combat social isolation and gain a feeling of belonging and acceptance, an Asian American is forced to find reference groups in the United States. The Asian American may identify entirely with traditional Asian culture, or reject Asian culture as old fashioned and dysfunctional. He or she may adopt U.S. values exclusively, or become bicultural. Unfortunately, regardless of what value system an individual adopts, there are potential adjustment problems.

INTERVENTION STRATEGIES

Social workers who provide direct service, or micro-level social work intervention, and indirect service, or macro-level societal intervention, with Asian Americans need to have first-hand knowledge of how this unique ethnic minority group has traditionally responded to mental health and social services. It is also advisable for social workers to be familiar with traditional help-seeking behaviors of Asians. Many authors have warned that the client's orientation to the process of help-seeking and the "fit" between traditional paradigms and those utilized by providers may be critical to successful process and outcome.[33]

Mental Health and Social Service for Asian Americans

Studies indicate that Asian Americans seeking mental health treatment were more severely disturbed than Caucasians.[34] There is a tendency for Asian Americans to somatize, so that stress and tension are frequently turned into physical complaints.[35] On personality measures Asian Americans have indicated more feelings of isolation, loneliness, anxiety, and emotional distress than Caucasians.[36]

In spite of their many mental health and social service needs, Asian Americans do not generally turn to these institutions and services for assistance. Literature on minority counseling and social service indicates that Western modes of service delivery have not been effective.[37] Low utilization and early termination of services by Asian Americans support this premise.[38] Miranda and Kitano have identified several barriers to Asian American clients' utilization of mental health and social services.[39] They include: (1) fragmentation of services, so that clients are referred from one worker to another; (2) discontinuity between the life of the professional and that of the client; (3) inaccessibility of services, and (4) the primary focus of the professional on being accountable to fellow professionals rather than to the ethnic community.

Traditional Asian American Approach to Treatment of Psychological Problems

There are a number of therapeutic models traditionally used by Asians that should be of interest to social workers who provide mental health services to this group. Morita therapy is probably the best known Japanese therapeutic model for psychological problems. Morita therapy emphasizes a here-and-now orientation, behavior over moods and feelings, and the interdependence among individuals.[40] Further, Morita therapists place little emphasis on searching for the origins of neuroses, discourage verbal rumination of one's problems, and do not recommend elaborate treatment plans for recovery.

The Ajase complex, developed by the Japanese psychoanalyst Kosawa, is based on a figure described in Buddhist scriptures.[41] The most important concept of the Ajase complex is that of the ambivalent mother–child relationship, especially mother to son. During the process of separation and individualization, the child develops resentment based on his or her interpretation that the mother was unwilling to let go, and disappointment that he or she could not totally let go of the mother. The child's feeling of ambivalence is resolved upon the mother's unconditional forgiveness.

Naikan therapy focuses on enabling the individual to recapitulate significant others', especially the mother's, influence on him or her in the development of personhood.[42] Through the therapeutic process the sensei (teacher or therapist) guides the individual to a better understanding of his or her relationship with these significant others. Reciprocal role performance, obligation, indebtedness, forgiveness, and self-sacrifice also are focused on as integral parts of the therapeutic process. Through discussion and guidance the individual gains insight into his or her selfishness, which is considered the root of personal and interpersonal problems.

Ho'oponopono is a family-centered therapeutic approach practiced by Hawaiians to resolve family conflicts. Ho'oponopono is defined as "setting to right ... to restore and maintain good relationships among family, and family and supernatural powers."[43] The therapeutic process of ho'oponopono is as follows:

1. *Beginning phase,* characterized by prayer offering; general problems of identification, partialization of problems according to order of importance.
2. *Middle phase,* characterized by problem solving through open discussion, with minimal confrontation and negative emotional expression; sincere confession of wrongdoing; seeking forgiveness and restitution if necessary.
3. *Ending phase,* characterized by a summary of the therapeutic process by the leader, who is always a respected elder; reaffirmation of the family's strengths; commitment to the basic unit; closing prayer and family sharing food together.

Help-Seeking Patterns and Behaviors

To assist Asian Americans successfully, social workers need to understand their traditional cultural values toward dysfunctional behavior. The process of acculturation may have altered an individual's or a family's cultural values, but as Mass indicates, the influence exerted by the value patterns that were acquired throughout childhood is often considerable, even among those whose behavior is highly Westernized.[44] Asian Americans feel a stigma and shame in talking about personal problems. The terms *Hajj* for the Japanese, *Hijj* for the Filipinos, *Tiu lien* for the Chinese, and *Chaemyoun* for the Koreans indicate the shame and loss of face these Asian groups feel when talking about personal issues.[45] Most Asian Americans do not seek psychiatric dynamics and psychological theories to account for behavioral difficulty.[46] Instead, social, moral, and organic explanations are used. When an individual behaves dysfunctionally, he or she commonly identifies external events, such as physical illness, death of a loved one, or the loss of a job. The individual, therefore, is not to blame. Interpersonal duties and loyalties are held sacred by many Asian Americans. The dysfunction or suffering of an Asian American individual may be attributed to his or her violation of some duty, such as filial piety. Community elders or family members may be expected to exhort the individual to improve. In surveying a sample of Asian Americans in Los Angeles regarding their attitude toward mental health—seeking behavior, ministers, relatives, friends, and family doctors were mentioned as resources more frequently than professional workers.[47] Over one-half the sample indicated they would prefer to work out emotional problems on their own.

The following case examples are presented to illustrate how direct (micro) and indirect (macro) social work practice can be utilized to restore and enhance the psychological and social functioning of Asian American clients.

MICRO SOCIAL WORK PRACTICE

The Tran family was brought to the attention of the Transcultural Family Institute by a complaint from Mrs. Tran that their fourteen-year-old son Fen had been missing for more than three days. The intake interview with Mrs. Tran revealed that the family immigrated to the United States in 1975 after the fall of Saigon. The Tran family resides in a run-down neighborhood in Oklahoma City. There are about thirty Asian families in Tran's neighborhood. Most of them are refugees, some Cambodians, a few Laotians. Before the refugees moved in, the neighborhood was heavily populated with blacks and a few Hispanics.

Mr. Tran is fifty-one years old, a dentist trained in Saigon, and speaks fairly good English. Because he received his professional training in Vietnam, he has been unable to obtain a license to practice dentistry in Oklahoma City. Mr. Tran works as a store clerk in a neighborhood Asian food store.

Mrs. Tran was a housewife and never worked outside the home in Saigon. She is now employed in a day-care center serving mainly Vietnamese preschoolers. She has attended several English classes offered at her church.

The Trans have three children: A twenty-two-year-old daughter who is married and lives with her Vietnamese husband in Dallas, Texas; a nine-year-old daughter who Mrs. Tran describes as "very nice," and Fen. "Our son Fen is just the opposite of our nine-year-old. He gets into fights all the time at school and with neighborhood kids, especially the black kids," volunteered Mrs. Tran. Both Fen and his younger sister were born in Texas. The Trans moved to Oklahoma City two years ago, when Mr. Tran got his present job. Mrs. Tran also feared that Fen and his father "may hurt each other." "The men in our family are of a violent type," continued Mrs. Tran.

One day after the interview, Mrs. Tran called to inform the worker that Fen had returned home voluntarily and that her husband and Fen had gotten into a "big physical fight." Mrs. Tran asked if the worker would talk with her and her family before "something terrible" happened. I replied that I would assist the family and I indicated to Mrs. Tran that I would like to see Mr. Tran alone for the first meeting. I also suggested to Mrs. Tran that I would telephone Mr. Tran for the appointment.

When I telephoned Mr. Tran for an appointment next day, he expressed appreciation of my willingness to help. However, he said he doubted he could get off work and that he didn't know where my agency was located. I volunteered to meet with him at a Vietnamese restaurant two blocks from where he worked. He accepted my invitation.

Mr. Tran, a frail but gentle looking man, was early for the appointment, and he graciously ushered me to a corner table that was quieter. I expressed to him regret that I couldn't speak Vietnamese. Mr. Tran reciprocated by informing me that despite his Chinese/Vietnamese ancestry, he could speak only a few words of Chinese. (Perhaps his wife had informed him that I was Chinese.) As Mr. Tran was relating his background to me, he avoided eye contact by helping me with tea.

I asked Mr. Tran if his work at the store kept him busy. He immediately played down the importance of his present job. I empathized by letting him know that he must feel frustrated at not being able to practice his profession. Mr. Tran sighed that "my best years are over—they have been for quite some time." I remained silent but at the same time helped Mr. Tran with tea.

Mr. Tran continued to relate to me his immigration experiences, his love for his lost home and country, his extended family members who were left in Vietnam, and finally his beloved vocation as a dentist in Vietnam.

"I am happy for you that you still have your immediate family with you," I commented. "That's my greatest problem now," complained Mr. Tran. Mr. Tran then proceeded to tell the difficulty he was experiencing with his son, Fen, who was fluent in English but doing marginal work at school, not getting along with neighborhood kids, and refusing to defer to him as the father. Mr. Tran also complained that his wife had not been treating him with respect. He attributed this to his wife's "Americanization" and financial independence. Mr. Tran also disclosed that recently he had developed a colitis problem and that medication prescribed by the doctor did not help.

Before my interview with Mr. Tran ended, I summarized my understanding of his personal problems and family problem. Mr. Tran quickly told me his personal problems did not matter; it was his family problems he needed help with. I respected and supported his views and explained to him the manner in which I could assist the family, especially his son. Mr. Tran then related to me that his son had told him he would never see "no shrink" or social worker. I comforted Mr. Tran by letting him know that Fen's behavior could change without his actually seeing me. I emphasized that since Mr. Tran was the head of the family, I would need his help the most in order to help the family. Mr. Tran responded very positively and he assured me he would do whatever was needed in order to restore family harmony.

Over the following two weeks I saw Mr. Tran individually four times at my office. Our conversations centered around four major issues: (1) immigration and relocation experiences, (2) his father role and relationship with his son, (3) his role and relationship with his wife, and (4) his activities in the workplace, neighborhood, and home.

Having an opportunity to ventilate the loss associated with immigration and relocation, Mr. Tran realized he had a great deal of grief and unexpressed anger.

Mr. Tran admitted that "I have been a walking time bomb for some time." His pent-up feelings, coupled with his disappointment with his present job and his wife's lack of deference toward him, made him especially eager to assume the authoritarian, disciplinary father role toward his teen-age son.

Mr. Tran was helped to realize that he had been displacing all his disappointment and frustration onto his son. To support Mr. Tran and to help him understand adolescent characteristics, I reframed the situation by saying to him that he must have done a good job for his son to be adult enough to say "no" to him. Mr. Tran began to realize that Fen also was having a difficult time adjusting to family, school, friends, and the "American way of life." As I encouraged Mr. Tran to list the positive features about Fen, he relaxed more and commented, "Fen is not a bad boy, after all." I gave Mr. Tran positive strokes as a responsible and caring father, but he suddenly stopped and commented, "But I cannot allow Fen to say 'no' to me. If I had done that as a child, my father would have knocked my head off." I responded by agreeing that some Asian parents felt violence was the only way to control their children and get their children to mind them. I challenged that such disciplinary action may be antithetical to the love and care we originally intended to provide for our children. I later provided Mr. Tran with some other ideas and ways to discipline. I challenged him to exercise self-control in order for these new disciplinary ideas to work. Mr. Tran accepted my challenge.

At our last session, Mr. Tran invited his wife to come with him. Mrs. Tran was elated and volunteered that Fen was getting along well at home and at school. Fen and her husband had had no fights at all, and she and her husband also got along much better. The Trans invited me to their home for dinner as a way of expressing their appreciation. I accepted the invitation and had a wonderful dinner. As the evening ended, Mr. Tran told me he no longer had "stomach problems."

MACRO SOCIAL WORK PRACTICE

Three months after my last home visit with the Tran family, Mr. Tran called me at the office, requesting a private (individual) meeting. When we met, Mr. Tran was anxious to inform me that the "old" family problem was not why he called me. He insisted that everybody in the family was doing well and that he and his son Fen were getting along well. The reason for his wanting to talk with me was neighborhood disturbances, which had resulted in several violent incidents over the past months. In one of these incidents three Vietnamese and two black youths were badly hurt in a fight that required police intervention.

Additionally, there were more than three neighborhood vandalism cases involving both black and Vietnamese men. The Vietnamese, especially the women, were terrified by the violence and they did not feel safe walking alone on the streets.

Mr. Tran was very distressed over the unsafe environment in his neighborhood and that he lacked the means to relocate to another community. Mr. Tran insisted that nothing constructive in the prevention of crime had been accomplished, even though the police had been called each time. In fact, Vietnamese–black racial tension seemed to intensify after each time the police left the scene. Mr. Tran concluded that he was not sure if I could be of any assistance to him or to his neighborhood, but he needed to talk to somebody. I responded empathetically to him and his situation and explained that I would call him back in a couple of days with some suggestions.

After Mr. Tran left my office, I consulted with a black colleague who had good rapport with some of the black families in the Trans' neighborhood. My colleague was well aware of the racial tension there. He and I decided to work as a team to help reduce neighborhood racial tension and violence.

First, we each identified respected leaders among the blacks and the Asians in the refugee community. My colleague visited individually with the black leaders and I did the same with the Asian leaders. A meeting for all leaders (five blacks and five Asians) was set up, initially to identify and explore the problems as both sides perceived them. My colleague and I served as mediators for this first meeting. Each ethnic group felt others were as concerned as they were in establishing a harmonious and safe community.

It should be noted that care was taken in selecting the five Asian leaders. Mr. Tran, who served as a leader, helped me identify four other Asians. We sought community leaders who spoke English fluently and who were not afraid to express themselves, despite traditional Asian values like inconspicuousness.

The next joint meeting centered around plans and implementation strategies for improving black–Asian relationships. Prior to that meeting I met separately with the Asian representatives to prepare them. In addition to brainstorming for plans and implementation strategies, I prepared the Asian group for arriving at some consensus. We also rehearsed the actual presentation of ideas. Mr. Tran was elected spokesperson for the Asian group. My colleague held preparatory meetings with the black representatives.

The second black–Asian joint meeting proceeded smoothly, and the group had no difficulty in arriving at a consensus. Specifically, the group decided to employ education as a tool to break down racial stereotypes and prejudices. The Asian group initiated an invitation for the blacks to attend their Lunar New Year celebration. The blacks invited the Asians to their churches and concerts. Two Asian representatives, who were owners of a restaurant and a food store, agreed to employ black youths. A representative from the black group, who coached baseball, invited Asian youths to join the team. Each group's spokesperson served as a liaison and coordinator for these activities. My colleague and I agreed to serve as consultants when needed. The group decided to meet bimonthly until concrete improvements had been made.

The group met five more times in the next two and one-half months. Two youths, one from each racial group, were added to the group to ensure youth input. During the first two weeks the group met, there were two mild incidents between black and Vietnamese youths. Representatives from each group took part in mediating the event after it happened. There has been no violence reported since. Some blacks and some Asians actually began socializing, at churches, at baseball fields, and in stores and restaurants. Representatives from both groups made a conscious effort to socialize with each other, and this may have set the tune and direction for the rest of the community to follow. When both racial groups had shown signs of improvement in collaborative harmonious living, they decided to meet only when there was a need.

EMERGING ISSUES AND TRENDS

Using socioeconomic criteria to interpret Asian Americans' success image is inadequate for understanding the complex experiences of this group in the United States. Both native- and foreign-born Asian Americans have been shown to be segregated into certain occupations, industries, and specific firms.[48] Asian Americans generally experience a serious problem in transforming their high educational achievement into favorable occupations in the labor market, resulting in underutilization of their education. Asian Americans who are employed experience great difficulty in obtaining promotions and other benefits associated with career advancement.[49] Limited human capital resources are often blamed for minorities' labor market problems. Asian American experiences, however, indicate that high educational achievement and related human capital resources are insufficient to overcome minority status in the U.S. labor market.

Physical health, mental health, and welfare needs among Asian Americans have been underestimated. The appropriateness of the treated-case method of determining service needs is questionable. The untreated-case method would be more valid with Asian and Pacific Americans. Social work practice with Asian Americans has progressed past the general "descriptive-issues" stage. Drug abuse, alcoholism, bicultural identity, youth gangs, suicide, child abuse, and family violence are common problems social workers must help with.

With the large influx of Indochinese over the past decade, unique problems and issues are emerging. Due to a different political climate and economic conditions, these new immigrants are experiencing more difficulties than the immigrants of the 1800s. The newer Indochinese population is widely scattered around the United States and around both urban and rural areas. It is expected that immigrants who settled in the Midwest or Southwest, where fewer Asians have traditionally lived, may have more adjustment problems than immigrants in East and West coast urban centers.

As the Asian American population increases, its traditional "success image" becomes more visible and often more threatening to whites and other ethnic minorities. Interracial tensions and conflicts between Asian Americans and other minorities, especially blacks, have surfaced, particularly in the Southwest. The Indochinese's sudden, traumatic uprooting experience, lack of natural support systems, language difficulties, and hostile host environment, have made their settlement experience more difficult.

As the population and service needs of Asian Americans mount, resources available to them have dwindled because of cutbacks in federally funded programs. Because of language difficulties and cultural value conflicts, Asian Americans, especially newly arrived immigrants and refugees, need more bilingual and bicultural mental health and social service workers. But cutbacks in federal education funds have reduced the number of bilingual and bicultural workers. To combat the resources shortage and provide services consistent with the needs and desires of Asian Americans, social workers are challenged to strengthen or build "natural" resources within the community. Natural resources are those individual skills and strategies, interpersonal (family and friends) support systems, and institutional systems (churches, herbalists, family doctors, folk healers, etc.) available in everyday life and needed in times of stress. This concept of the natural resource is by no means strange to Asian Americans. Murase and Kim observed that existing indigenous organizations within the Asian community, such as churches, family associations, hometown clubs, and credit unions, and community caretakers, including ministers, physicians, teachers, merchants, and elders, have provided care for Asians in distress or in need of help.[50,51]

Asian Americans experience a multitude of social service needs. As with any other segment of the population, some of these needs are constant and familiar; others are unique and just emerging. Social work practitioners, educators, and students must be up-to-date on development trends and sensitive to Asian cultural values to ensure that all Asian American clients receive the help they deserve and have a right to.

ENDNOTES

1. J. Marishima, "The Asian American Experience: 1850–1975," *Journal of Ethnic and Special Studies* 2 (March 1978): 8–10.
2. S. Sue, "Community Mental Health Services to Minority Groups: Some Optimism, Some Pessimism," *American Psychologist* 32 (June 1977): 616–624.
3. E. Gomberg, "Special Populations," in *Alcohol, Science, and Society Revisited,* ed. E. Gomberg and J. Carpenter (Ann Arbor: University of Michigan Press, 1982), pp. 337–354.
4. Multicultural Drug Abuse Prevention Center, First National Asian American Conference on Drug Abuse Prevention (Los Angeles: Multicultural Resource Center, 1976).
5. S. Lyman, "Chinese Secret Societies in the Occident: Notes and Suggestions for Research in the Sociology of Secrecy," in S. Lyman, ed., *The Asian in North America* (Santa Barbara, Calif.: ABC-Clio, 1977).
6. B. Sung, *The Story of the Chinese in America* (New York: Macmillan, 1967).
7. H. Kitano, *Japanese Americans: The Evolution of a Subculture* (Englewood Cliffs, N.J.: Prentice-Hall, 1976).
8. W. Petersen, "Chinese Americans and Japanese Americans," in T. Sowell, ed., *Essays and Data on American Ethnic Groups* (Washington, D.C.: Urban Institute, 1978).

9. Lyman, p. 136.

10. T. Holmes and M. Masuda, "Life Change and Illness Susceptibility," in B. Dohrenwend, ed., *Stressful Life Events: Their Nature and Effects* (New York: John Wiley, 1974).

11. M. Ho, *Family Therapy with Ethnic Minorities* (Newbury Park, Calif.: Sage, 1987).

12. Holmes and Masuda, pp. 161–186.

13. M. Pfister-Ammeude, "Mental Hygiene in Refugee Camps," in C. Zwingmann, ed., *Uprooting and After* (New York: Singer, 1973).

14. Bureau of Research and Training, *National Mental Health Needs Assessment of Indochinese Refugee Populations* (Philadelphia: Pennsylvania Department of Public Welfare, Office of Mental Health, 1979).

15. C. Meyer, "What Directions for Direct Practice?," *Social Work* 24 (July 1979): 267–272.

16. C. Germain, "An Ecological Perspective in Casework Practice," *Social Casework* 54 (January 1973): 323–330.

17. A. Morales and B. Sheafor, *Social Work: A Profession of Many Faces* 4th ed. (Boston: Allyn and Bacon, 1986).

18. G. DeVos and K. Abbott, "The Chinese Family in San Francisco," MSW dissertation (Berkeley: University of California, 1966).

19. H. Lai, "Chinese," in S. Thernstrom et al., *Harvard Encyclopedia of American Ethnic Groups* (Cambridge, Mass.: Harvard University Press, 1980) pp. 217–334.

20. H. Melendy, "Filipinos," in Thernstrom et al., pp. 354–362.

21. H. Kim, "Koreans," in Thernstrom et al., pp. 601–606.

22. Ibid., p. 602.

23. D. Montero and I. Dieppa, "Resettling Vietnamese Refugees: The Service Agency's Role," *Social Work* 27 (February 1982): 74–82.

24. Lyman, p. 182.

25. Asian American Advisory Council, *Report to the Governor on Discrimination Against Asians* (Seattle: State of Washington, 1973).

26. B. Kim, *The Asian Americans: Changing Patterns, Changing Needs* (Montclair, N.J.: Association of Korean Christian Scholars in North America, 1978).

27. M. Ho, "Social Work with Asian Americans," *Social Casework* 57 (March 1976): 195–201.

28. G. Coelho and J. Stein, "Change, Vulnerability, and Coping: Stresses of Uprooting and Overcrowding," in G. Coelho, ed., *Uprooting and Development* (New York: Plenum Press, 1980) p. 21.

29. F. Hsu, *American Museum Science Book* (Garden City, N.Y.: Doubleday, 1972).

30. Ho, pp. 35–36.

31. J. Jones, *Prejudice and Racism* (Reading, Mass.: Addison-Wesley, 1922), p. 166.

32. S. Sue and H. McKinney, "Asian Americans in the Community Mental Health Care System," *American Journal of Orthopsychiatry* 45 (September 1975): 111–118.

33. See N. Mokuau, "Social Workers' Perceptions of Counseling Effectiveness for Asian American Clients," *Social Work* 32 (August 1987): 331–335; T. Owan, "Southeast Asian Mental Health: Transition from Treatment Service to Prevention—A New Direction," in T. Owen, ed., *Southeast Asian Mental Health: Treatment, Prevention, Services, Training, and Research* (National Institute of Mental Health), pp. 142–167.

34. D. Okimoto, *Asian Key Person: Survey on Drug Abuse,* Task Force Report of Seattle–King County Drug Commission (Seattle, Washington, 1975).

35. S. Sue and D. Sue, "Chinese American Personality and Mental Health," *Amerasia Journal* 1 (September 1971): 36–49.

36. D. Sue, S. Ino, and D. Sue, "Nonassertiveness of Asian-Americans: An Inaccurate Assumption," *Journal of Counseling Psychology* 30 (March 1983): 581–588.

37. M. Bromerly, "New Beginnings for Cambodian Refugees or Further Disruptions?," *Social Work* 32 (June 1987): 236–239; Mokuau, pp. 331–335.

38. D. Sue, *Counseling the Culturally Different: Theory and Practice* (New York: Wiley, 1981).

39. M. Miranda and H. Kitano, "Barriers to Mental Health: A Japanese and Mexican Dilemma," in N. Herandez, ed., *Chicanos: Social Psychological Perspectives* (St. Louis, Mo.: C. V. Mosby, 1976).

40. M. Miura and S. Usa, "A Psychotherapy of Neurosis: Morita Therapy," in T. Lebra and W. Lebra, eds., *Japanese Culture and Behavior* (Honolulu: University Press of Hawaii, 1974), pp. 407–430.

41. K. Okonogi, "The Ajase Complex of Japanese," *Japan Echo* 5 (March 1978): 88–105.

42. T. Murase, "Naikan Therapy," in T. Lebra and W. Lebra, eds., *Japanese Culture and Behavior* (Honolulu: University Press of Hawaii, 1974), pp. 431–442.

43. M. Pukui, E. Haertig, and C. Lee, *Nana I Ke Kumu* (Honolulu: Hui Hana, 1972), p. 85; L. Paglinawan, "Ho'Oponopono," in E. Shook, ed., *Ho'Oponopono* (Honolulu: University Press of Hawaii, 1983).

44. A. Mass, "Asians as Individuals: The Japanese Community," *Social Casework* 57 (March 1978): 160–164.

45. Kim, p. 198.

46. L. Lapuz, *A Study of Psychopathology* (Quezon City: University of the Philippines Press, 1973).

47. Y. Okano, *Japanese Americans and Mental Health* (Los Angeles: Coalition for Mental Health, 1977).

48. A. Cabezas, *Disadvantaged Employment Status of Asian and Pacific Americans* (U.S. Commission on Civil Rights, 1979), pp. 434–444.

49. W. Kuo, "On the Study of Asian Americans: Its Current State and Agenda," *Sociological Quarterly* 20 (June 1979): 279–290.

50. K. Murase, "State and Local Public Policy Issues in Delivering Mental Health and Related Services to Asian and Pacific Americans," in U.S. Commission on Civil Rights, *Civil Rights Issues of Asian and Pacific Americans: Myths and Realities* (Washington, D.C.: U.S. Government Printing Office, 1980).

51. T. Kim, "Statement on Census Issues—Impact and Reaction," in U.S. Commission on Civil Rights.

CHAPTER 19

Social Work Practice with Mexican Americans

Armando T. Morales and Ramon Salcido

PREFATORY COMMENT

This chapter was written specifically for this book. Mexican Americans are conspicuously absent from social work literature; only twenty-one articles concerning this distinct ethnic group appeared in the literature between 1964 and 1981. Eighty-one percent of these were written between 1971 and 1975. Most of the articles have been concerned with social justice for Mexican Americans rather than practice issues; that is, how to work with and help Mexican Americans.

The authors maintain that Mexican Americans do have mental health needs and do avail themselves of direct services when they are provided at minimum cost, in their primary language (Spanish), and near their homes. Given the regressive social and economic policies of recent government administrations in relation to the poor, Mexican Americans, specifically the "undocumented" Mexican immigrant, continue to be especially affected.

Armando T. Morales and Ramon Salcido offer practice suggestions that have implications for macro social work in the barrio, mobilizing various indigenous social support systems such as churches, neighbors, and the family. They also recommend the intervention strategy of advocacy to reduce institutional barriers to services for Mexican Americans.

Meeting the ever-increasing social service needs of disadvantaged groups, which are often isolated by class and cultural differences, is a continuing challenge to social work. If the social work profession hopes to be more viable among disadvantaged groups, especially among the Mexican American population, human service institutions must modify their service delivery systems. Moreover, social workers must understand the dynamics of both individual and institutional racism, which have discouraged or prevented Mexican Americans from availing themselves of existing services. At times those services have appeared impersonal, and even nonsupportive.

Despite the recent attention focused on the special needs of Mexican Americans, any explanation of their situation is complicated by the difficulty of defining this population as to size and demographic characteristics. More has to be learned about the variations within this group and its immigration pattern.

MEXICAN AMERICANS: A HETEROGENEOUS POPULATION

Mexican Americans are one of the most diverse ethnic groups in the United States in comparison to white ethnic groups and minority groups of color. On the one hand, like American Indians, Mexican Americans were an indigenous people who resided in the Southwest, were overpowered by Anglo settlers, and are therefore one of the *oldest* minorities. On the other hand, their continuing immigration from Mexico to the United States also makes them one of the *newest* and *largest* immigrant groups. Some are fully assimilated into Anglo society, and some reside almost exclusively in *barrios.*[1] Some retain strong ties to Mexico and return there frequently, while others prefer to remain in the United States. There are also those who partially integrate without assimilating but do not center their interactions exclusively within the *barrio.*[2]

With the Treaty of Guadalupe-Hidalgo in 1848, most of the Southwest, including California, became the possession of the United States. The actual number of Mexicans in the new Territory of the Southwest was relatively small. Harry Kitano reports that all laborers who were Mexicans, whether they were "pure" Spanish or not, were perceived as "half-breeds" and inferior by Anglos.[3] By 1900 these people were already a subordinated population; they lived in segregated enclaves and were controlled by the Anglos. From 1848 to 1910 very few Mexicans migrated to the United States. The relative ease of entry across a long, 3000-mile border; the difficulty in distinguishing between Spanish-speaking, U.S.-born people and Spanish-speaking immigrants from Mexico, both legal and illegal; and dubious official data make precise quantification impossible. However, the following official census figures on immigration of Mexicans to the United States are of some use:

to 1900	28,000
1901–1910	50,000
1911–1920	219,000
1921–1930	460,000
1931–1940	22,000
1941–1950	59,000
1951–1960	319,000
1961–1970	453,000

Significant migration of Mexicans to the United States did not take place until after 1910. It is estimated that fully 10 percent of the Mexican people immigrated to the United States early in the twentieth century, and the vast majority of them assumed agricultural work in the Southwest. This migration peaked in the 1920s but was curtailed during the years of the Great Depression, when large numbers of Mexicans, including those born in the United States, were repatriated (deported) by social service and immigration agencies. Many of those deported were U.S.-born children of the Mexican immigrants—U.S. citizens!

Moreover, as the Mexican American population of the United States grew, it remained highly localized, with almost 90 percent of the people located in the five Southwestern states. California's share of this population steadily increased, as Table 19–1 shows.

The next large influx of migrants arrived in the post–World War II period. The needs for agricultural laborers and unskilled workers to keep pace with economic expansion of the post-war years made Mexican immigration attractive to businesses and small industries. Business was the only contact between the two cultures; U.S. society was not concerned with housing conditions, lack of schooling, or availability of social services for Mexican Americans. This neglect, coupled with racism, caused Mexicans as well as Mexican Americans to maintain a distance from institutions and governmental agencies.

Certain social demographic characteristics have made the Mexican American experience unique in comparison to those of Europeans and Asians. This population is the second largest minority of color that is both indigenous and immigrant in character. Because of geographical proximity to Mexico, Mexican-born persons have followed a wide variety of migration patterns to the United States since the early part of the century. Generally, immigration to the United States has been greater from Mexico than from any other country in recent years. For example, Mexico has been the primary source of both legal and illegal immigration to the United States since the 1950s.

TABLE 19–1   *Mexican Population in the United States, 1910–1980*

YEAR	U.S. BUREAU OF THE CENSUS DEFINITION	TOTAL U.S.	TOTAL CALIFORNIA	PERCENT IN CALIFORNIA
1910	Mexicans of foreign-born and mixed parentage	382,002	51,037	13.4
1920	Mexicans of foreign-born and mixed parentage	731,559	86,610	17.4
1930	Mexicans	1,282,883	368,013	29.3
1940	Spanish mother tongue	1,570,740	416,140	32.9
1950	Spanish surname	2,281,710	591,540	35.8
1960	Spanish surname	3,464,999	1,141,207	40.1
1970	Spanish surname	9,600,000	2,222,185	23.1
1980	Spanish origin	14,605,883	4,543,770	31.1

The Mexican American population comprises at least three major subgroups: those who are born in the United States; those who are born in and emigrate legally from Mexico; and those who are born in and emigrate illegally from Mexico. The term *Mexican American* will be used to designate anyone having a Mexican heritage, regardless of time or place of arrival in the United States. During the highly political period of the 1960s and early 1970s, many persons of Mexican descent preferred the term *Chicano* rather than Mexican American. Some still prefer this designation today.

DEMOGRAPHIC PROFILE

The 1970 census showed that 9.6 million people of Spanish origin lived in the United States.[4] The 1975 population report showed an increase to 11.2 million Spanish people, and by March, 1988, census reports showed a jump to 19.4 million, or 8.1 percent of the U.S. population.[5,6] The 1988 population reports recorded that 12.1 million of the Hispanic populace were of Mexican origin; 2.5 million, Puerto Rican; 1.0 million, Cuban; 2.2 million of Central and South American origin, and 1.6 million of other Hispanic origin.[7] Added to these figures are an estimated 6 million undocumented aliens, predominantly from Mexico.[8] Although statistics vary widely on the basis of base lines and possible growth rates, demographers predicted (1) that Hispanics would be this country's largest minority by 1990; (2) that half the population in California and a third in Texas would be Spanish-speaking by the same date; and (3) that Hispanics could be the majority population group in three states by the year 2000.[9] However, the first two projected estimates did not occur by 1990.

Nevertheless, the Mexican American population is much larger than most figures indicate, primarily because of census undercount and continued immigration, both legal and illegal, to the United States from Mexico. Mexican Americans make up about 60 percent of the Hispanic population in the United States, and their numbers grew by 75 percent in the last decade. A recent government census found that Mexican Americans make up 19 percent of California's population and 28 percent of Los Angeles County, making Los Angeles the largest urban concentration of Mexicans outside Mexico City.[10]

The majority of Mexican Americans live in the states of California, Texas, and New Mexico. However, there are significant numbers in other states of the Southwest as well as in the Northwest and Midwest. Illinois, with its availability of manufacturing and agricultural jobs, has become home to many Mexican American migrants. Furthermore, contrary to stereotypes, the vast majority live in urban areas, with 46.3 percent residing in central cities, 34.7 percent residing in the suburbs, and the remaining 19 percent residing in rural areas.[11]

Compared to Anglos, Mexican Americans are a relatively young population. The median age of Mexican Americans is 19.8 years, compared to 28.6 years for the population overall.[12] Moreover, the 1975 census showed that the proportion of Mexican Americans over age 65 was only 4 percent, compared to 11 percent for the general population. The fact that there are few elderly Mexican Americans is a startling statistic.[13]

There is clear evidence that Mexican Americans have large families, a characteristic of lower socioeconomic status. National statistics show that the mean for Mexican Americans is 4.06 children and for non-Hispanics, 1.07. More specifically, statistics show that 41.9 percent of families of Mexican origin have three or more children, versus 22.3 percent of the total families in the United States.[14] Because of the large number of children, there are eighty persons in the dependent-age range (those under sixteen years old and over sixty-five years old) for every 100 Mexican American persons of working age; this compares to sixty-five persons in the dependent-age range for every 100 Anglos. The high rate of fertility among Mexican American women, especially combined with large family size, implies a high health risk for both mothers and children in this ethnic group.[15]

The reported income level for 1970 shows that 13.8 percent of Mexican Americans had incomes of less than $3000, while only 5.7 percent of Anglos reported such low incomes.[16] The median family income for families identifying themselves as "of Mexican origin" in the 1975 population survey was $9559, compared to $12,836 for all U.S. families.[17] The gap widened further: the 1980 median income for Hispanics was $12,952 compared to $19,116 for the entire population of the United States.[18] Furthermore, in 1978 about 2.5 million Hispanics (60 percent Mexican American), or 22 percent of the total Hispanic population, were below the poverty level in income, compared with 11 percent for the entire population of the United States.[19] By March, 1988, Hispanic median family income increased to $21,921, but the income gap between Hispanics and whites widened further, as whites now had a median family income of $35,953.[20] Whereas in 1978 about 2.5 million Hispanics (60 percent Mexican American), or 22 percent of the total Hispanic population were below the poverty level in income compared with 11 percent for the entire U.S. population, by 1987 the percent had increased to 32.1 versus 16.2.[21] The increased percentage of Hispanics below the poverty level was due to Reaganomics-type policies (favoring the rich) pursued by the previous and current Republican administrations. The poverty hits Hispanics harder, since they have larger families than Anglos.

Most Mexican Americans have occupations of low prestige. The 1975 population study conducted by the U.S. Bureau of the Census found that more than 60 percent of the occupations held by men of Mexican origin sixteen years of age and older were classified as blue-collar workers.[22] According to the 1978 U.S. Census, there were less than half as many white-collar workers among employed Mexican American males (18 percent) as among Anglo males (42.9 percent).[23]

The unemployment level of Mexican Americans generally is higher than that of the Anglo population. And during recessions, the unemployment rate difference becomes more exaggerated. In 1975, Hispanic unemployment (60 percent Mexican American) was 12.9 percent, compared to 8 percent for the white work force; and in 1976 Hispanic unemployment stood at 11.8 percent versus 8.9

percent for the white work force.[24] The disparities are even greater for youth. For instance, in 1974 30 percent of Hispanic youth sixteen to nineteen years of age were unemployed, compared to 18.4 percent of white youth.[25] In addition, according to the National Urban League, in the first quarter of 1978 teenage unemployment by race and ethnicity showed that 22.1 percent of Hispanic youth were unemployed, compared to 15.7 percent of Anglo youth.[26] Some reasons for the above-average unemployment among most groups of Hispanics, especially Mexican Americans, include educational disadvantages, language barriers, and discrimination. Furthermore, a significant number of Mexican American youth are employed as migratory farm workers, a sector of the economy that has high seasonal unemployment.

Despite the relative youth of the Mexican American population, school enrollment data indicate low educational attainment. Although 67 percent of non–Mexican American or non-Hispanic adults completed high school, only 34.3 percent of Mexican American adults completed high school.[27] Data concerning adults with less than five years of schooling again show this group trailing other minorities and Anglos. *U.S. News and World Report* stated that "a drop-out rate as high as 85 percent in some cities, to achievement scores that are two grade levels or more below national averages" are found in this population.[28]

Language is another important characteristic of the Mexican American population. According to information obtained from the 1976 *Survey of Income and Education Data*, 80 percent of Hispanic Americans lived in households where Spanish was spoken.[29] While there are few studies on Spanish-language usage, the small amount of data that do exist clearly illustrate the importance of language use by this group. The report of the National Center for Education Statistics, entitled *The Condition of Education for Hispanic Americans*, states, "The language one speaks is related to one's place of birth."[30] Among Mexican Americans born in Mexico, about two-thirds spoke Spanish as their primary language. Among those of corresponding heritage who were born in the United States, less than 20 percent usually spoke Spanish. The rest of the population of corresponding heritage was either monolingual or bilingual.

MEXICAN AMERICANS IN SOCIAL WORK LITERATURE

A survey of social work literature discussing mainly Mexican Americans written between January, 1964, and February, 1981, serves to exemplify the trends and volume available to the social work profession concerning this group. Much that has been written about Mexican Americans is of a descriptive nature, focusing on the value differences between Mexican American groups and the majority culture, and racism. The articles surveyed were obtained from the *Journal of Education for Social Work, Social Casework,* and *Social Work;* articles appearing in books or non–social work journals were not included.[31] The selection of articles was based on titles and abstracts specifically stating Mexican American or Chicano content. Using this criterion may have excluded other social work articles used in practice. Although this survey does not encompass all social work has to say about Mexican Americans, it does allow some inferences to be drawn about the state of Mexican American literature in social work practice.

Of the twenty-one articles about Mexican Americans published between 1964 and 1984, 81 percent were written between 1971 and 1975 (see Table 19–2). The remaining 29 percent were spread over eight of the fifteen years studied, with a greater number of articles written during the last years of the 1960s, and fewer articles written during the last half of the 1970s. No articles were published about Mexican Americans during the mid-1960s. Considering the Civil Rights Movement of the 1960s, it appears that the social work profession was slow to recognize the need to help Mexican Americans and to react in complying with that need. Recognition that this population did receive in the early 1970s rapidly diminished as the seventies came to a close.

The mid-1970s offered the most hope for achievement both within and outside the profession. The articles appearing between 1972 and 1976 were mostly concerned with social justice for Mexican Americans. The articles specifically emphasized the bilingualism and biculturalism of Mexican Americans, almost to the exclusion of other topics of interest to the profession. For example, one article focused on the elderly Mexican American. No articles were written about ex-offenders or gangs. Nor were any articles published about problems such as divorce, desertion, child abuse, wife abuse, and physical health/mental health needs. This pattern suggests that some subgroups and typical subjects of social work concern may have been overlooked because of the values and interests of the authors.

Table 19–3 clearly shows that cultural differences, experiences of racism, and family structure appeared more frequently than any other topics in the literature. These topics were for the most part not related to a discussion of how the social worker can use his or her knowledge of them in seeking to help Mexican Americans. Only one article discussed the application of knowledge in reporting a study of clients' perceptions of helping relationships formed with social workers of different ethnic backgrounds from their own. The study revealed that Anglo clients and Mexican American clients reacted positively to initial helping relationships with workers of different cultural backgrounds from their own. However, all the clients who spoke Spanish were excluded from the sample, as were documented and undocumented immigrants. Nor were the clients asked if they preferred social workers of the same ethnic background. No doubt all these factors would have influenced the results of the study had they been included.

TABLE 19–2   *Number of Articles on Mexican Americans/Chicanos, by Years*

Articles	1964–67	1968–71	1972–75	1976–80	Total
Mexican Americans/Chicanos	0	9 (43%)	8 (38%)	4 (19%)	21

TABLE 19–3 *Major Themes of Literature on Mexican Americans*

THEMES	NUMBER OF ARTICLES
Cultural Differences	6
Language	1
Warmth, Empathy, Genuineness	1
Experience of Racism	6
Social System Theory	1
Politics	0
Community Structure	1
Family Structure	3

Similar conspicuous absences appeared in articles about social work practice. Only three articles gave general suggestions for working with Spanish-speaking Mexican Americans but offered no general framework. Only one article presented a training model describing how knowledge of Mexican Americans could be applied to mental health training and incorporated in schools of social work. The period from 1981 to 1990 has resulted in less than a half-dozen articles, again indicating that the lack of articles prescribing methods is one of the major shortcomings of the available literature.

Although the literature is limited in usable practice frameworks, it is rich in identifying those areas of knowledge the authors deemed to be most significant for social work intervention. The authors were profoundly concerned with the effects of racism and cultural differences. These concerns provide the profession with practice knowledge regarding Mexican American issues that can be incorporated by social workers in their work with this population.

INTERVENTION STRATEGIES

The central task for a social worker is to help persons resolve existing or potential problems in psychosocial functioning. This process may involve helping the client resolve problems within themselves or with other people such as spouse, parent, children, friends, or coworkers. This focus is called *direct service* or *micro*-level social work intervention. Intervening in behalf of clients with larger social structure, such as the neighborhood, organizations, community, or even broader community—in effect all those social work activities that fall outside the domain of direct services—is referred to as *indirect service* or *macro*-level social work intervention. In work with the poor, who are often at the mercy of various social, economic, and political forces in society, both levels of intervention, micro and macro, are necessary for optimal helping effectiveness.

Direct Service Intervention

Direct service intervention has various modes, one of which is treatment, or *clinical* intervention. This is not to say that the poor are poor because of psychological problems; rather, their impoverished status may contribute to and exacerbate their stress. Indeed, it becomes a difficult task to help someone work through separation feelings regarding the loss of a loved one when they are starving, have no place to live, or are freezing to death. In this respect, certain basic human needs related to food, clothing, and shelter are universal, and a person's emotional response to stress also has universal qualities. The specific nature of that response and how it is handled, however, are related to the societal cultural context in which it occurs.

History of Treating Mental Illness. Societies throughout the world have developed various approaches for treating persons suffering from psychological problems. Three basic explanations and corresponding intervention strategies pertaining to psychological problems can be traced back to the earliest times: (1) the attempt to explain diseases of the mind in physical terms; that is, the organic approach ("It's in your blood/chemistry"); (2) the attempt to deal with inexplicable events through spiritual or magical approaches ("The devil/spirits made you do it"); and (3) the attempt to find a psychological explanation for psychological problems ("It's all in your mind"). Hippocrates (460–377 B.C.), the father of medicine, pioneered the organic approach, believing that black bile caused depression. Several centuries later, Cicero (106–43 B.C.), the Roman statesman and attorney, objected to the black bile theory, maintaining that depression was the result of psychological difficulties. He proclaimed that people were responsible for their emotional and psychological difficulties: in a psychological sense, *they* could do something about them. Cicero laid down the theoretical foundations for psychotherapy. The magical/spiritual approach found people treating the afflicted person through appeasement, confession, incantations, magical rituals, or exorcism.[32]

The effectiveness of any treatment approach often depends on the suggestibility of the person on whom the approach is worked, the suggestive power of the influencing practitioner, and the sympathetic connection (similarity) between the practitioner and the person seeking assistance. If a person strongly believes, for example, his or her headache, stomachache, or depression has as its basis a physical or chemical factor and that only a medical person can help, a physician or psychiatrist who prescribes medication may have the greatest likelihood of relieving that person's symptom. If, on the other hand, the person believes he or she is suffering certain symptoms because he or she has sinned and that only a minister or priest can help, the church's representatives may indeed have the greatest impact. And if the person believes his or her symptom has a psychogenic basis and can only be alleviated by talking to someone who can be "objective" in understanding the symptom or problem, the psychiatrist or perhaps social workers may offer the best help.

Mexico's Approach to Treating Mental Illness.   Mexican society, like other societies, also developed approaches to help people with psychological problems. The ancestors of Mexican Americans, the Aztecs, numbering 20 million persons in Central Mexico in the fifteenth century, created a wealthy, powerful, and progressive empire. Their culture was highly developed, and in that intellectual atmosphere flourished highly advanced forms of psychiatry and psychotherapy. Translations of Aztec literature reveal that Aztec therapy was provided by competent personnel and in institutions of high repute. They had an amazing grasp of psychology and developed concepts about ego formation similar to those advanced by Freud almost 500 years later. Those concepts appear in an Aztec document about dream interpretation. The Aztec psychiatrists knew how to recognize persons who were manic, schizoid, hysterical, depressive, and psychopathic—major mental disorder classifications not unlike the ones used today. Aztec patients were treated by a variety of methods, including an early form of brain surgery, hypnosis, "talking out" bad things in one's mind, and specific herbal potions for specific disorders.[33]

With the colonization of Mexico by Spain in the early sixteenth century came Spanish medicine based on European concepts. Spanish colonial physicians still held primitive ideas about the causes of disease, believing it was a punishment for sins caused by devils who had taken possession of the patient's body and spirit. Because military might was associated with racial superiority, Spanish medicine was also believed by Spaniards to be superior to that of the Aztecs. Had Spanish oppression not occurred, Aztec psychiatry might have made a very significant contribution to the mental health practices of the Western world. In spite of this overt conflict and clash over psychiatric approaches, however, the first hospital for the mentally ill founded in North America was in Mexico City, in 1567.[34] The first hospital for the mentally ill in the United States was founded 185 years later, in 1752 in Philadelphia, Pennsylvania.[35] The United States established two additional hospitals for the mentally ill during this period, one in Williamsburg, Virginia, in 1773, and the Bloomingdale Asylum in New York in 1821. In a comparable period, Mexico also established a hospital in Yucatán in 1625, the Manicomio de lä Canoa in Mexico City in 1687, the Hospital Civil in Guadalajara in 1739, Belém in 1794, and the Divino Salvado in Mexico City in 1796.

Other mental health milestones found Mexico establishing its first department of psychiatry in 1860 in Jalisco; the United States began its first program in 1906. Mexico began the systematic training of physicians in psychiatry in 1910; the United States initiated its training program in 1937. Mexico launched its community mental health movement in 1951, by establishing mental health programs in health centers. The United States initiated community programs in 1964, with the passage of the Federal Community Mental Health Act.[36] Today in Mexico the major mental health trends and various theoretical orientations are similar to those in other Western countries. No single therapy orientation prevails, and as in the United States psychiatrists are by and large in control of mental health programs, with psychologists, social workers, and psychiatric nurses having lesser roles. From the standpoint of mental health resources, the United States, being a much wealthier country, far overshadows Mexico in terms of mental health resources and manpower. The United States, for example, has 12.4 psychiatrists per 100,000, versus less than one psychiatrist per 100,000 in Mexico.[37]

Mental Health Treatment for Mexican Americans.   In the United States persons of Mexican descent have found it very difficult to obtain mental health services. One of the Nation's first community mental health programs specifically for persons of Mexican descent was established in East Los Angeles in 1967. The staffing pattern included four psychiatrists, four psychiatric social workers, three nurses, a clinical psychologist, a rehabilitation counselor, a community services coordinator, a community worker, and six secretaries. All but one of the staff were bilingual. In applying one measure of utilization (the percentage of Spanish surname population in the area, 76), the program was successful in that 90 percent of the clients seen had a Spanish surname. Clearly here there was an overutilization of services by Hispanics. The program offered traditional mental health services provided in the clients' primary language and at a fee ranging from 50 cents to $15.[38] There are a few other, rare examples of overutilization of mental health services by Hispanics,[39] but overall the utilization rate by this population rarely exceeds 50 percent. In other words, Hispanic receipt of services is one-half or less of their representation in the population.[40]

There are a number of reasons proposed to explain this underutilization. The literature is now making it increasingly clear that the major factors involved are structural in nature and pertain to the availability, accessibility, and acceptability of services to the very heterogeneous bilingual, bicultural characteristics of Hispanics.[41] When Hispanics finally do receive services, they are often of inferior quality, with diagnoses often based on assessment procedures developed for the middle-class Anglo population that have no validity or applicability to these people. Furthermore, Hispanics are more likely to receive somatic and medication treatment and less individual or group therapy. These experiences can and do result in premature treatment termination.[42] Another important factor, accounting for premature termination or resistance to treatment, is whether the Hispanic is a *voluntary* client seeking help for a problem *he* or *she* defines, or an *involuntary* client being referred for treatment regarding a problem of concern to the referring agency.[43] Racist and political policies and economic decisions (raising fees) by mental health agencies to deny services to "undocumented" or poor persons are other growing contributing factors related to the underutilization of services by Hispanics.

Indirect Service Intervention

A major problem in achieving practice goals for Mexican Americans is the conceptual constraints imposed by social work methods. In other words, social workers, as Nelsen points out, perceive phenomena exclusively and narrowly through the lenses of the methods in which they have been trained.[44] Often the focus is mainly a clinical or direct service one. Meyer believes the use of any methodological model as an anchoring or conceptual point of reference is like viewing something through the wrong end of the telescope—the view is too restricted and narrow to account for the breadth of the phenomena to be captured.[45]

Meyer adds that for years social work has been offering its well-honed methods only to those who could use them, instead of first finding out what was needed and then selecting the method from its intervention repertoire or inventing new methods. She believes the methods framework has been functional in maintaining social work's denial of what has to be done with regard to broader social problems. Meyer proposes the use of the ecosystems orientation to practice.[46]

Ecosystems Model.   Social work practice focuses on the interaction between the person and the environment. The term *person* may refer to an individual or may represent people in the context of a family, large or small group, organization, community, or even larger structure of society. Social work intervention might be directed at the person, the environment, or both. In each case, the social worker seeks to enhance and restore the social functioning of people, or to change social conditions that impede the mutually beneficial interaction between people and their environment.[47]

This orientation involves the application of ecology and general systems theory to professional tasks. In explaining the ecosystems perspective, Meyer points out that it allows social workers to look at psychological phenomena, account for complex variables, assess the dynamic interplay of these variables, draw conceptual boundaries around the unit of attention or the case, and then generate ideas for interventions.[48] At this point methodology enters in, because in any particular case—meaning a particular individual, family, group, institutional unit, or geographical area—any number of practice interventions might be needed.

This model of practice can promote social workers' understanding of: (1) the psychosocial problems experienced by Mexican American people, (2) the crippling effects of institutional racism, and (3) the oppressive environments in which these people struggle to survive. (The application of this model to a specific case was highlighted in Chapter 7, the Knowledge Base of Social Work.)

The Ethnosystem.   Assuming that social work abandons its constricted methods framework and adopts the ecosystems perspective, then this question must be asked: What other knowledge is needed in understanding the psychosocial problems of Mexican Americans that is specific about ethnic background? Solomon's framework provides one option for integrating Mexican American concerns into a practice framework.[49] She utilizes the ethnosystem and empowerment concepts as major integrative concepts. The *ethnosystem* is defined as a society comprising groups that vary in modes of communication, in degree of control over material resources, and in the structure of their internal relationships or social organization.[50] Moreover, these groups must be in a more or less stable pattern of relationships that have characteristics transcending any single group's field of integration; for example, the ethnosystem's political, educational, or economic subsystems. Solomon defines *empowerment* as a process whereby persons who belong to a stigmatized social category throughout their lives can be assisted to develop and increase skills in the exercise of interpersonal influence and the performance of valued social roles.[51]

The ethnosystems are the natural networks, the primary patterns of interaction, survival, and adjustment indigenous to societies. As used here, the concept of *natural networks* has its origins in several disciplines: social work, sociology, social psychology and anthropology, as well as in the mental health "community support—significant others" literature.[52] Social workers need to be aware that these natural networks and primary systems exist apart from the usual modes of secondary interactions that Mexican Americans have developed for survival within Anglo-urbanized systems, including the social establishment. There is a basic similarity between the ethnosystem with secondary interaction for coping with the Anglo society, and the concept of two environments, the immediate or nurturing environment and the wider environment. When, as Norton notes, the larger societal system rejects the minority group's immediate environment or ethnosystem, there is incongruence between the two (Solomon refers to this as negative valuation of a stigmatized collective), and power blocks are directed toward the minority individuals, groups, and communities.[53]

Barrio Service Systems.   Mexican Americans have been immigrating to *barrios* (Mexican neighborhoods) in U.S. urban areas in great and small waves. The *barrio* is a microcosm of the dominant society as well as an ethnosystem. Although the communities interrelate with external institutional structures such as the law enforcement system, the school system, and the public welfare system, *barrios* also have indigenous service systems that provide mutual aid and psychological support in time of need. Indigenous support systems include churches, neighbors, friends, the family, and alternate services.[54]

Many Mexican Americans, especially the elderly and immigrant groups, have strong religious ties and attend church on a regular basis. The church, whether Roman Catholic or Protestant, is an important spiritual support for many Mexican Americans and, in addition, a vehicle for disseminating information about *barrio* activities and services, reaching individuals who would be largely inaccessible to public agencies. There is trust in the church. For example, the parish priest or minister often knows of potential adoptive parents who would provide an excellent home for an unwed mother's child.

Concerned neighbors and friends also provide aid and act as a resource. Perceived as confidential sources of advice, these significant persons act as referral agents. Lee's study on the use of the services of a model neighborhood health center by Mexican Americans observed that some groups sought primary groups such as friends and neighbors as their major source of information about health care services.[55]

The family unit clearly plays an important role in providing economic, social, and psychological supports. Families also serve as adoptive parents for family members who are no longer able to care for their children. Especially in the case of older children, grandparents may care for and eventually adopt them. Other relatives, or the child's godparents or *compadres,* may also accept the responsibility of raising the child or children. Infants, of course, may also be adopted in the same manner. However, no matter how effective this network may be, it is the welfare agency, rather than the network itself, that has access at all times to the greatest amount of provision and greatest number of providers in the greatest geographical area; it is the agency that has legal responsibility for bringing services to the community.

As a result of the Chicano movement in the 1960s and 1970s, alternate service systems are being developed within the *barrio* to deal with the special needs of the Mexican American community. Although there are variations in the services offered in each *barrio,* common patterns in both structure and function are observable. Self-help groups, social action organizations, and specialized service agencies staffed exclusively by bicultural and bilingual personnel are considered the most essential aspects of the alternate service system.

Siporin writes that the ecological perspective is an "effort to improve the functioning and competence of the welfare service system of natural self-help mutual aid networks, and to improve the social functioning and coping competence of individuals and their collectivities."[56] This approach calls for the practitioner to broaden his or her view of the client. Intervention involves assessment of the total social, physical, psychological needs of the client and his or her network system. Intervention also calls for advocacy in the amelioration of identified problems related to barriers created by social welfare systems. Intervention strategies are initiated in anticipation of resolving psychosocial problems. Two examples of such macro-level strategies include networking and advocacy.

Support Networks.   Collins and Pancoast refer to *networks* as consisting of both people and relationships.[57] The social network is relatively invisible, though it is a real structure in which an individual, nuclear family, or group is embedded. The term *support systems,* as used here, parallels Caplan's conceptualization.[58] He states, "Support systems may be of a continuing nature, intermittent or short-term in the event of an acute need or crisis." Both enduring and short-term supports are likely to consist of three elements:

1. The significant others help the individual mobilize his psychological resources and master his emotional burdens;
2. They share his tasks; and
3. They provide him with extra supplies of money, materials, tools, skills, and cognitive guidance to improve the handling of his situation.[59]

Individuals usually belong to several networks at the same time. Networks can be based on kinship, friendship, employment, recreation, education, politics, ethnicity, religion, or whatever interests or elements individuals find in common.

The content of exchanges can also be varied.[60] Although the informal network is important, it cannot provide for all needs. Formal resources (social service agencies, medical services, and other service providers) are likely to be utilized. Social network intervention, therefore, is an approach to service delivery that involves significant individuals in the amelioration of identified psychosocial problems.

Social network intervention takes into consideration both formal and informal systems that are involved in the life of the family. Also of significance to Mexican Americans is that this approach incorporates the sociocultural components of the family. The utilization of support systems can be conceptualized into two main divisions: (1) to engage existing networks and enhance their functioning, and (2) to create new networks or "attach" a formerly isolated person or family to a network.[61]

The approach considers both psychological and environmental stresses and incorporates them into the total reality of a family. It focuses on rallying the life-sustaining forces of the individual and family. This viable system of self-help continues to function after the professional helper has been disengaged.

In social network intervention, the goal is to deal with the entire structure by rendering the network visible and viable and by attempting to restore its function. The social network for Mexican American families may include extended kin, *compadres* (coparents), friends, *curanderos* (folk healers), and other concerned individuals. These subsystems are identified because of their potential to provide emotional strength, support, and other types of assistance to the family. Social network intervention, therefore, emphasizes engagement of the family's network of support systems.

Advocacy. In cases where adequate services do not exist or are not accessible, the social worker can assume an advocacy function. As an advocate, he or she is concerned with making the social welfare system responsive to the unmet needs of the client. According to Briar, the social worker as advocate is the client's supporter, advisor, champion, and, if need be, representative in his or her dealings with the court, the police, the social agency, and other organizations that affect the client's well-being.[62]

Advocacy can be divided into five areas of practice: (1) family advocacy, (2) community advocacy, (3) legislative advocacy, (4) ombudsmanship, and (5) brokerage. In *family advocacy,* the social worker represents an individual or family and then fights the battle with the system; the ultimate goal is showing the client or family how to fight its own battles.[63] In *community advocacy,* on the other hand, a board or staff of an agency takes collective action to change a condition affecting the lives of the agency's clients. According to Patti and Dear, *legislative advocacy* refers to any individual agency or organization that attempts to influence the course of a bill or other legislative measure. *Ombudsmanship,* the least familiar of the practices, can also be used when practicing advocacy.[64] A recent report identifies ombudsmanship as an individual or office concerned with correcting administrative grievances and overcoming administrative problems and errors.[65] Finally, *brokerage,* based on knowledge of and experience with existing services, is a commitment to help each client reach the appropriate services.[66]

Social workers engaged in advocacy must be capable of using all forms of advocacy and able to select the one or combination of the five forms that best fits the client's specific situation. Social workers employed in hospitals and other social service institutions possess the knowledge and professional skills to function well in an advocacy service. In addition to utilizing existing resources, social workers must organize the services within the boundaries of the social service agency and use bilingual personnel to provide the services. The following example illustrates how advocacy intervention strategies can be applied when one confronts environmental and institutional barriers.

Political action and brokerage advocacy are the strategies a social worker employs to deal with environmental barriers. The social worker would be a partisan advocate for changes in present restrictive benefits. By lobbying directly with groups in the Mexican American community for these changes, the social worker can influence the legislative process at a governmental level useful to his or her clients.

Brokerage, on the other hand, entails acting as an intermediary between the client and existing services in the community. Brokerage, in this context, recognizes the dependence of the individual on his or her social environment and facilitates change by maximizing the resources available to the client. For example, a Mexican American seeking social services may be faced with inadequate housing, no medical or Social Security benefits, and no alien documentation. In such a case, the social worker should review the client's existing resources. If none exist, the worker would then seek out adequate resources and act as an advocate for the client. In this way, brokerage expands the role of the advocate beyond the boundaries of the health care institution to ensure that the client reaches the appropriate services.

Advocacy services that confront the barriers erected by the institution are both direct and indirect. Ombudsmanship and family advocacy deal directly with clients within the health care institution. Ombudsmanship is concerned with correcting administrative problems and errors within the health care institution. Unlike the broker, the ombudsman does not link up resources for his or her clients but pinpoints obstacles the institution presents to clients. Ombudsmanship provides a mediator to assist clients who feel their needs are not being met because of red tape or because the staff is insensitive to them.

Similarly, family advocacy is designed to improve life conditions for whole families or individual family members by linking direct and expert knowledge of family needs with a commitment to institutional change. According to Riley, family advocacy deals with institutional systems rather than with individuals.[67] Its purpose is to ensure that the institutional systems in closest contact with the clients work for them, rather than against them. Supportive networking, political action, brokerage, and family advocacy are all active practices in which social workers can engage and reasonably pursue within the social welfare system to ensure the maximum utilization of existing services.

The following case history demonstrates the efficacy of such a system. The services provided are supportive services and brokerage.

> Mr. A., age 60, is an undocumented alien from Guadalajara, Mexico. He speaks only Spanish. He has no schooling, so cannot read in Spanish or English. Mr. A. has no family in the area, only the friend who rents him a small room, and with whom he shares food.

> Mr. A. has resided in the U.S. for more than twenty years and has paid Social Security and taxes from his pay as a dishwasher, just as native-born Americans do. He presently draws $80 a month from the odd jobs he does in the neighborhood. Mr. A. is sick, yet he feels that he is not entitled to health and welfare benefits he supported with his taxes and Social Security contributions. He also fears deportation by the Immigration and Naturalization Service. Fortunately, he came to the attention of a social worker at the community health center. With assurances that he would not be turned over to the INS and that the services were free, Mr. A. received health screening at the center. Later, diagnosis revealed Mr. A. had severe diabetes.[68]

The social worker gained Mr. A.'s trust and recognized that his lack of financial resources was the major obstacle to his seeking the health care and other services he needed. The worker advised Mr. A. about current immigration laws that might make him eligible for resident alien status. As a resident alien, he would be eligible for welfare and health care provisions. After identifying Mr. A.'s reasons for not seeking health care and informing him of his rights under immigration law and as a consumer, the worker used brokerage to resolve his medical problems and to begin the paperwork for residency and welfare benefits.

> The worker's first concern was to obtain medication for Mr. A. The worker purchased the medication with petty cash funds allotted for that purpose. The worker then accompanied Mr. A. to a United Way funded agency for assistance in applying for resident status. The worker acted as a translator and as an advocate for Mr. A.'s immigration needs. A week later, the worker accompanied Mr. A. to the welfare office to provide support and to make sure he understood the necessary forms before signing them.[69]

Although the advocacy approach met some of Mr. A.'s needs, the fact that a social network was not available emphasized the importance of linking the client with a support system. The friend was encouraged to become more directly involved with the well-being of the client, by providing emotional support and seeking further assistance from trusted neighbors.

Mr. A. was helped by his support system in the following manner. First, he was successful in obtaining part-time employment as a gardener and maintenance man for two elderly people in the neighborhood. Second, Mr. A. was recruited by a *compadre* of the friend to provide cleanup service at a nominal fee at the family's restaurant. Finally, Mr. A. was linked by the social worker to a senior citizens' program in the *barrio,* where he had contact with persons who spoke Spanish and would socialize with him.

Mr. A.'s case shows how the social worker recognized the client's problem, overcame the language difficulty and lack of education, informed him of his legal and consumer rights, and showed him how to obtain the necessary services from the appropriate institutions. Advocacy provided Mr. A. with the medical treatment he needed and service to connect him with a supportive network.

CONCLUDING COMMENT

Mexican Americans are one of this country's most diverse ethnic groups. Because they were an indigenous population, in their own land, prior to the Anglo-American conquest of Mexico in 1848, they, like Native Americans, are one of the oldest minorities. On the other hand, continuing immigration from Mexico also makes them one of the newest and largest immigrant groups. They are a very heterogeneous Hispanic group, responding to all categories of any language and cultural scale. Mexican Americans primarily reside in urban areas in the Southwest, generally occupy a low socioeconomic status, and have large families, a high unemployment rate, and low educational attainments—all symptoms of working class exploitation, sexism, and racism. Mexican Americans have a small elderly population (4 percent), almost one-third the proportion of elderly whites, and a very large youthful population. Because their age profile is the opposite that of whites, their human services needs are different from whites', who are currently preoccupied with the needs of the elderly. As is the case with blacks, Hispanics are increasingly being caught up in the juvenile justice system, a field of practice in which social work has not expressed much of an interest.

The authors' survey of the social work literature pertaining to Mexican Americans revealed that much of it is of a descriptive nature, highlighting racism and value and cultural differences between Mexican Americans and whites. Only one article focused on the elderly Mexican American. With only an exception or two, there were no articles written specifically about juvenile and adult offenders, gangs, police–community conflict, stress caused by fear of deportation, divorce and separation, child abuse, family therapy, marital therapy, or mental health needs.

Mexican Americans *do* have mental health needs, and many do avail themselves of direct services when they are provided at modest cost, in their primary language, and near their homes. A rich psychiatric history, originating almost 700 years ago with the Aztecs, provides Mexican Americans with a foundation to build on, as both consumers and providers of mental health services. However, the current regressive trend in the United States, with its accompanying stresses, is creating new racism and poverty casualties among the poor and minorities. As needs for services increase, there is a corresponding increased effort to "economize" by "phasing out" or denying services to the poor. Mexican Americans are particularly affected by these trends, especially new Mexican immigrants and the "undocumented."

Practice suggestions were offered that may have implications for macro social work in the *barrio.* The *barrio* as an ethnosystem is comprised of indigenous social support systems such as churches, neighbors, friends, alternative services (self-help groups), and the family. Applying the concept of social network intervention to Mexican Americans signifies the inclusion of extended family members, *compadres* (coparents), friends, coworkers, and other concerned persons in their support systems. These subsystems have the potential to provide emotional strength, support, and other types of assistance to the family.

Complementing networking, the intervention strategy of advocacy and its five modes of practice (family advocacy, community advocacy, legislative advocacy, ombudsmanship, and brokerage) can assist Mexican Americans in reducing institutional barriers to human services.

SUGGESTED READINGS

CASAS, J. MANUEL, and KEEFE, SUSAN E. *Family and Mental Health in the Mexican American Community.* Los Angeles: Spanish-Speaking Mental Health Research Center, UCLA, 1978.

DE ANDA, DIANE. "Bicultural Socialization: Factors Affecting the Minority Experience." *Social Work* 29 (March–April 1984):101–107.

DE HOYOS, GENEVIEVE, DE HOYOS, ARTURO, and ANDERSON, CHRISTIAN B. "Sociocultural Dislocation: Beyond the Dual Perspective." *Social Work* 31 (January–February, 1986): 61–67.

GIBSON, GUADALUPE, ed. *Our Kingdom Stands on Brittle Glass.* Silver Spring, Md.: National Association of Social Workers, 1983.

GOMEZ, ERNESTO, ZURCHER, LOUIS A., FARRIS, BUFORD E., BECKER, AND ROY, E. "A Study of Psychosocial Casework with Chicanos." *Social Work* 30 (November–December 1985): 477–482.

HARDY-FANTA, CAROL. "Social Action in Hispanic Groups." *Social Work* 31 (March–April 1986); 119–123.

KUMABE, KAZUYE T., NISHIDA, CHIKAE, and HEPWORTH, DEAN H. *Bridging Ethnocultural Diversity in Social Work and Health.* Honolulu; University of Hawaii, School of Social Work, 1985.

"La Causa Chicana." *Social Casework* 52 (May 1971); 259–334; entire issue.

LEVINE, ELAINE S., and PADILLA, AMADO. *Crossing Cultures in Therapy: Pluralistic Counseling for the Hispanic.* Monterey, Calif.: Brooks/Cole, 1980.

MORALES, ARMANDO. "The Mexican American Gang Member: Evaluation and Treatment." In *Mental Health and Hispanic Americans: Clinical Perspectives,* ed. Rosina Becerra, Marvin Karno, and Javier Escobar. New York: Grune & Stratton, 1982.

ROTHMAN, JACK, GANT, LARRY M., and HNAT, STEPHEN A. "Mexican American Family Culture." *Social Service Review* 59 (June 1985): 197–215.

THE PRESIDENT'S COMMISSION ON MENTAL HEALTH. *Report of the Special Populations Subpanel on Mental Health of Hispanic Americans* vol. III. Washington, D.C.: U.S. Government Printing Office, 1978, Appendix.

ZUNIGA, MARIA E. "Chicano Self-Concept: A Proactive Stance." In Jacobs, Carolyn, and Bowles, Dorcas D., eds. *Ethnicity and Race: Critical Concepts in Social Work.* Silver Spring, Md.: National Association of Social Workers, 1988, pp. 71–85.

ENDNOTES

1. For the purposes of this chapter, a *barrio* is defined as a neighborhood or community area of a town or city occupied predominantly by persons of Mexican descent.
2. Harry H. L. Kitano, *Race Relations* (Englewood Cliffs, N.J.: Prentice-Hall, 1976), p. 242.
3. Ibid.
4. U.S. Bureau of the Census, "Persons of Spanish Origin in the United States: March 1976," *Current Population Reports,* Series P-20, No. 310 (Washington, D.C.: U.S. Department of Commerce, March 1977).
5. Ibid.
6. "The Hispanic Populations in the United States: March 1986 and 1987 (Advance Report)," U.S. Department of Commerce, Bureau of the Census, Series P-20, No. 416, August, 1987, p. 5.
7. U.S. Bureau of the Census, "The Hispanic Population in the United States: March 1988," *Current Population Reports,* Series P-20, No. 438 (Washington, D.C.: U.S. Department of Commerce, 1989), pp. 1–2.
8. Wayne A. Cornelius, *Illegal Mexican Migration to the United States* (Cambridge, Mass.: MIT Press, 1977).
9. *Business Week,* June 23, 1980, p. 86.
10. *Los Angeles Times,* August 4, 1981, pt. II, p. 1.
11. U.S. Bureau of the Census, *Current Population Reports,* 1980, p. 1.
12. Ibid., p. 1.
13. U.S. Bureau of the Census, *Current Population Reports,* 1977, p. 17.
14. U.S. Bureau of the Census, *Current Population Reports,* 1980.
15. Carmen A. Johnson, "Mexican American Women in the Labor Force and Lowered Fertility," *American Journal of Public Health* 66 (April 1976): 1186–1188.
16. U.S. Bureau of the Census, *Current Population Reports,* 1977.
17. Ibid.
18. U.S. Bureau of the Census, *Current Population Reports,* 1980.
19. U.S. Bureau of the Census, "Money, Income, and Poverty Status of Families and Persons in the United States: 1978," *Consumer Income,* Series P-60, No. 120 (Washington, D.C.: U.S. Department of Commerce, November 1979).
20. U.S. Bureau of the Census, "Marital Status and Living Arrangements: March 1988," *Current Population Reports,* Series P-20, No. 433 (Washington, D.C.: U.S. Department of Commerce, 1989), p. 42.
21. U.S. Bureau of the Census, *Marital Status and Living Arrangements,* p. 42.
22. U.S. Bureau of the Census, "Persons of Spanish Origin in the United States: March 1976," *Current Population Reports,* Series P-20, No. 310 (Washington, D.C.: U.S. Department of Commerce, July 1977).
23. U.S. Bureau of the Census, *Consumer Income,* 1979.
24. U.S. Bureau of Labor Statistics, Employment and Earnings (January 1978).
25. Ibid.
26. National Urban League, *Quarterly Economic Report of the Black Worker,* No. 11, First Quarter (June 1978).
27. U.S. Bureau of the Census, *Current Population Reports,* 1977.

28. *U.S. News and World Report.*

29. U.S. Department of Health, Education, and Welfare, National Center for Education Statistics, "Place of Birth and Language Characteristics of Persons of Hispanic Origin in the United States," *Survey of Income and Education Data,* No. 78-135 (Spring 1976).

30. National Center for Education Statistics, *The Condition of Education for Hispanic Americans* (Washington, D.C.: U.S. Department of Education, July 1980).

31. Lydia R. Aguirre, "The Meaning of the Chicano Movement"; Tomas C. Antencio, "The Survival of La Raza Despite Social Services"; John Florez, "Chicanos and Coalition as a Force for Social Change"; Alejandro Garcia, "The Chicano and Social Work"; Faustina Ramirez Knoll, "Casework Services for Mexican Americans"; Armando Morales, "The Collective Preconscious and Racism"; Phillip D. Ortego, "The Chicano Renaissance"; Faustina Solis, "Socioeconomic and Cultural Conditions of Migrant Workers"; and Marta Sotomayor, "Mexican American Interaction with Social Systems," all found in *Social Casework* 52, No. 5 (May 1971). See also Ignacio Aguilar, "Initial Contacts with Mexican American Families," *Social Casework* 17 (May 1972): 66–70; Miguel Montiel, "The Chicano Family: A Review of Research," *Social Work* 18 (March 1973): 21–23; R. J. Maduro and C. F. Martinez, "Latino Dream Analysis: Opportunity for Confrontation," *Social Casework* 55 (October 1974): 461–469; F. Souflee and G. Schmitt, "Education for Practice in the Chicano Community," *Journal of Education for Social Work* 10 (Fall 1974): 75–84; L. A. Santa Cruz and D. H. Hepworth, "News and Views: Effects of Cultural Orientation on Casework," *Social Casework* 56 (January 1975): 52–57; Teresa Ramirez Boulette, "Group Therapy with Low Income Mexican Americans," *Social Work* 20 (September 1975); David Maldonado, "The Chicano Aged," *Social Work* 20 (March 1975): 213–216; I. Aguilar and V. N. Wood, "Therapy through a Death Ritual," *Social Work* 21 (January 1976): 49; C. Medina and M. R. Neyes, "Dilemmas of Chicano Counselors," *Social Work* 21 (November 1976): 515–517; Armando Morales, "Institutional Racism in Mental Health and Criminal Justice," *Social Casework* 59 (July 1978): 387–396; Henry Ebihara, "A Training Program for Bilingual Paraprofessionals," *Social Casework* 60 (May 1970): 274–281; Ramon M. Salcido, "Undocumented Aliens: A Study of Mexican Families," *Social Work* 24 (July 1979); Ramon M. Salcido, "Problems of the Mexican American Elderly in an Urban Setting," *Social Casework* 10 (December 1979); 609–615.

32. Franz G. Alexander and Sheldon V. Selesnick, *The History of Psychiatry* (New York: Harper & Row, 1966), pp. 7–14.

33. Guido Belsasso, "The History of Psychiatry in Mexico," *Hospital and Community Psychiatry* 20 (November 1969): 342–344.

34. Ibid.

35. Alexander and Selesnick, p. 120.

36. Belsasso.

37. Ramon Parres, "Mexico," *World Studies in Psychiatry,* 2, No. 3 (Medical Communications, Inc., 1979).

38. Marvin Karno and Armando Morales, "A Community Mental Health Service for Mexican Americans in a Metropolis," *Comprehensive Psychiatry* 12 (March 1971): 116–121.

39. Morales, pp. 394, 395.

40. *Report to the President's Commission on Mental Health,* "Special Populations Sub-Task Panel on Mental Health of Hispanic Americans" (Washington, D.C.: U.S. Government Printing Office, 1978), p. 3.

41. Ibid.

42. Joe Yamamoto, Quinston James, and Norman Palley, "Cultural Problems in Psychiatric Therapy," *Archives of General Psychiatry* 19 (1968): 45–49.

43. Armando Morales, "Social Work with Third-World People," *Social Work* 26 (January 1981): 49.

44. Judith C. Nelsen, "Social Work's Fields of Practice, Methods, and Models: The Choice to Act," *Social Service Review* 49 (June 1975): 264–270.
45. Carol H. Meyer, "What Directions for Direct Practice?," *Social Work* 24 (July 1979): 267–272.
46. Ibid., p. 269.
47. Ibid., p. 271.
48. Ibid., p. 268.
49. Barbara Bryant Solomon, *Black Empowerment: Social Work in Oppressed Communities* (New York: Columbia University Press, 1976), p. 6.
50. Dolores G. Norton, *The Dual Perspective: Inclusion of Ethnic Minority Content on the Social Work Curriculum* (New York: Council of Social Work Education, 1978).
51. Solomon.
52. Ramon Valle, "Ethnic Minority Curriculum in Mental Health: Latino/Hispano Perspectives" (Paper presented at Mental Health Curriculum Development Conference sponsored by Howard University School of Social Work, November 16–18, 1979, Chicago.)
53. Norton.
54. Valle, p. 7.
55. E. P. Tsiaiah Lee, "The Pattern of Medical Care Use: Mexican American Patients at a Model Neighborhood Health Center in Los Angeles" (Doctoral thesis, University of California at Los Angeles, 1975).
56. Max Siporin, *Introduction to Social Work Practice* (New York: Macmillan, 1975).
57. Alice H. Collins and Diane L. Pancoast, *Natural Helping Networks: A Strategy for Intervention* (Washington, D.C.: National Association of Social Workers, 1976).
58. Gerald Caplan, *Support Systems and Community Mental Health* (New York: Behavioral Publications, 1974).
59. Ibid.
60. Collins and Pancoast.
61. Carol Swenson, "Social Networks, Mutual Aid, and the Life Model of Practice," in Carel B. Germain, ed., *Social Work Practice: People and Environment and Ecological Perspective* (New York: Columbia University Press, 1979), pp. 213–238.
62. Scott Briar, "The Current Crisis in Social Casework," *Social Work Practice* 1967 (New York: Columbia University Press, 1967), p. 28; also in Scott Briar, "The Casework Predicament," *Social Work* 13 (January 1968): 5–11.
63. Ronald V. Riley, "Family Advocacy: Case to Cause and Back to Case," *Child Welfare* 50 (January 1975): 374–383.
64. Rino J. Patti and R. B. Dear, "Legislative Advocacy: A Path to Social Change," *Social Work* 20 (March 1975): 108–109.
65. David Fritz, "The Advocacy Agency and Citizen Participation: The Case of the Administration on Aging and the Elderly" (Paper presented at the Annual Conference of the American Society for Public Administration, Arizona, 1978).
66. Ronald C. Federico, *The Social Welfare Institution: An Introduction* (Lexington, Mass.: D.C. Heath, 1976), p. 262.
67. Riley.
68. Ramon M. Salcido, "A Proposed Model of Advocacy Services for Mexican Aliens with Mental Health Needs," *Explorations in Ethnic Studies* 2 (July 1981): 210. (Published by the National Association for Interdisciplinary Ethnic Studies, California State Polytechnic University, 3801 W. Temple Ave., Pomona, California 91768).
69. Salcido, "A Proposed Model of Advocacy Services."

CHAPTER 20

Social Work Practice with Afro-Americans

Barbara Bryant Solomon

PREFATORY COMMENT

This chapter was written specifically for this book. The author states that people have a stereotypic view of the 25 million Afro-Americans residing in the United States; that is, that they are all criminally oriented. Like other minority group members, blacks are a very heterogeneous population, with more than half residing in central cities. The process of racism and discrimination, rather than urbanization, according to Solomon, contributed to the creation of a permanent underclass.

Solomon suggests social workers can increase their effectiveness in working with blacks by becoming actively involved in their educational, political, and cultural lives. In discussing black family structures and dynamics, Solomon points out that black families share mainstream cultural values and in many cases do not differ from those of other U.S. families. She adds, however, that blacks must deal with experiences that many other families do not confront, such as employment and educational discrimination and helping their children understand and learn to cope with racism and the negative self-images it generates. For those who suffer from powerlessness in their social environment, Solomon recommends the intervention strategy of empowerment, whereby the social worker engages in a set of activities with the client to reduce the powerlessness created by negative valuations based on membership in a group oppressed by discrimination.

Solomon is critical of social work's preoccupation with person variables, rather than system variables, and believes this factor has been an obstacle in developing effective intervention strategies with Afro-American clients. It would appear, therefore, that poor Third-World communities need a social worker who has the knowledge and skills to obtain needed direct services and is also able to intervene in larger social and community systems.

Social work is a profession that by definition must be responsive to changing social realities. It is not surprising that the often-dramatic events of the past two decades in regard to Afro-Americans in the United States affect the profession's priorities as well as its practice models. For example, all the following factors—the Civil Rights Movement; urban riots and political discontent; the War on Poverty; affirmative action; school busing to achieve integration; the Voting Rights Act; the new numerical dominance of blacks in major U.S. cities, and the proliferation of black mayors, city council members, school board members, and state legislators—symbolize the ferment of a minority group in transition. More important, these assaults on traditional social arrangements have required social workers to reappraise their emphasis on changing individuals versus changing collectives, on utilizing existing resources versus developing new ones, and on introspection versus systems analysis. In the process Afro-Americans have made it clear that social workers' old preoccupations with finding the source of problems in the individual psyche and in helping clients to "adjust" to inadequate social supplies are unacceptable.

WHO ARE THE AFRO-AMERICANS?

Police officers have often observed the predominantly black faces among the petty thieves, pimps, violence-prone families, and hardened felons with whom they are in constant contact, and made a quantum leap to the (erroneous) conclusion that these people are representative of Afro-Americans in general.[1] Social workers are guilty of a similar error. Since the probability is great that black clients are on welfare, on probation or parole, in poor housing, and in chaotic family situations, the generalization is made that all blacks share the same problems. The reality is that police officers, social workers, lawyers, or psychiatrists are most likely to encounter biased samples of the black population in their clientele. Knowledge of "other" blacks, that is, those for whom the client sample is not representative, is necessary if black persons are not to be perceived as acting out a predestined scenario.

Who, then, are these Afro-Americans, who constitute 12 percent of the population of the United States—some 31,025,000 individuals?[2] They are first of all descendants of slaves brought to the United States during the period before and after the Declaration of Independence. They are also descendants of blacks who immigrated later to the United States from the Caribbean, Central and South America, and to a lesser extent, Africa. Early in the Nation's history, black people were found in every state, though they were essentially a rural population located in the South. However, World War I marked the beginning of a great migration as large, segregated communities of Afro-Americans developed within many U.S. cities. The trend has continued into the 1990s: most Afro-Americans reside in metropolitan areas, and more than half reside in central cities. Gilder has even suggested that the large proportion of poor blacks who receive welfare, in comparison to poor whites, is the result of their concentration in urban areas where they are accessible to the pressures of social service bureaucracies that encourage their dependence.[3] Other authors have attributed this overrepresentation of blacks in welfare caseloads to the creation of a more or less permanent underclass through processes of discrimination and racism rather than urbanization.[4] Nevertheless, black urbanization has created a number of cultural, social, and political changes that have implications for social work practice.

Historically, the Urban League has been the social agency most clearly directed toward alleviating the negative conditions encountered by blacks in cities. The strong social work emphasis in the League and its local affiliates stimulated the development of a school of social work in predominantly black Atlanta University in 1921, as well as the provision of fellowships to black students for professional social work training in predominantly white universities.[5] Ironically, the League was strongly denounced during the 1960s and 1970s by more radical groups for its conservative approach to problems of racism and discrimination. For example, the League was more likely to use strategies of negotiation, advocacy, and coalition-building than confrontation and boycotts. Yet it can be argued that it was the League's support of social work education for Afro-Americans that provided the "critical mass" of social work professionals who moved into previously "lily white" social welfare settings, who finally answered the demands for more relevant services and more sensitive service providers among Afro-Americans.

Though migration patterns have been relatively easy to interpret, socioeconomic changes in the Afro-American population have been more difficult to characterize. For example, Wattenberg and Scammon contended in the early seventies that on the whole Afro-Americans had made considerable progress in the preceding decade and that, in fact, a majority could be considered "middle class."[6] This contention was based on 1970 census data and other statistics that attempted to demonstrate that during the preceding decade black family incomes had increased by nearly 100 percent, in contrast to 69 percent for white family incomes. Similarly, Gilder more recently has asserted that the income gap between blacks and whites has closed, so that differences are due to factors other than discrimination, despite the myths disseminated by "the politics of persecution."[7] On the other hand, Hill has called this same data base "the illusion of black progress."[8] His analysis of the data indicates that during the 1970s the number of poor blacks increased, whereas the number of poor whites declined. Utilizing standard budgets for urban families provided by the U.S. Bureau of Labor Statistics, the National Urban League Research Department in 1979 classified 10 percent of black families with incomes above the "higher" level ($30,317), 26 percent with incomes above the "intermediate" level ($12,517), and 46 percent with incomes above the "lower" level ($2,585). In contrast, 74 percent of white families had incomes above the "lower" level.[9] In 1988, the median family income for Afro-Americans was $18,500, versus $35,953 for white families.[10] The percentage of families with children living in poverty were greater for Afro-Americans than either Hispanics or whites, 37.3 versus 32.1 and 12.4 percent respectively.[11]

These data demonstrate the difficulties experienced by the social work practitioner who seeks to use social science information as the basis for developing intervention strategies. Social scientists disagree on the extent to which blacks experience discrimination as well as the extent to which dramatic changes have occurred in the relative incomes of black and white individuals and families. These disagreements necessarily create differences in intervention strategies aimed at increasing the effectiveness of social functioning among black families. A belief in the negative impact of discrimination results in more advocacy and social action; a belief in the lack of capacity to utilize opportunities provided leads to more intrapsychic, person-centered strategies.

Perhaps the most important characterization of Afro-Americans is their heterogeneity. The *majority* are employed and do not present major problems in social functioning. On the other hand, their overrepresentation among the poor implies that a disproportionate number are consumers of social services; that is, those programs made available by other than market criteria to ensure a basic level of health and welfare. Therefore, social workers who are the primary professionals in the social welfare field must be familiar with Afro-American culture, life styles, and help-seeking behavior if they are to be effective practitioners.

AFRO-AMERICAN CULTURE AND LIFE STYLE

The United States has been defined as an ethnosystem; that is, a composite of interdependent ethnic groups, each in turn defined by some unique historical and/or cultural ties and bound together by a single political system.[12] The largest ethnic group, Anglos, has successfully assimilated some groups who were ethnically distinct at the time of their extensive immigration to this country—the Dutch, German, Scandinavian, and Irish, for example. On the other hand, Afro-Americans for a variety of historical reasons have not been assimilated; the result has been the maintenance of a distinctive culture that possesses elements of the dominant culture, elements of other subcultural groups who have been oppressed, and elements that are a consequence of the unique Afro-American experience. This cultural distinctiveness may be observed in language and communication, in family structures, in religion, and in relationships with major social institutions. Knowledge of these distinctive cultural patterns should not encourage stereotyping but rather sensitize practitioners to a wide range of behavioral possibilities.

Language and Communication

There are different and sometimes conflicting ideas about how important it is to understand the vocabularies and communication styles of the various black subcultures from which Afro-American clients come. For example, since most blacks are at least bicultural, some assume that although the nonblack social worker may not understand the subtle nuances of language and communication styles current in black communities, the black client will understand the majority language of the social worker. Thus, the majority language must be the medium of communication in problem-solving activity. This attitude, however, ignores some dynamics of communication that transcend the simple issue of a common vocabulary. For example, a social worker is more likely to communicate feelings of warmth, understanding, and acceptance when clients view him or her as similar to themselves and as having problems, goals, and coping styles with which they can identify.[13] At the same time clients who view their counselors as similar to themselves tend to be more willing to freely disclose their thoughts, self-doubts, and concerns than they are with social workers whom they view as different from themselves.[14]

Block has found that blacks may have a tendency to communicate ideas and feelings by analogy rather than analysis.[15] Feelings of depression may be described as, "I feel like I do not have a real friend in the world," rather than, "I have feelings of intense loneliness." The client's tendency to give examples of his or her experience of a problem rather than to isolate and analyze specific factors is often considered reflective of a lack of insight or ability to abstract, rather than a style of communication. Furthermore, the kind of response the social worker makes to the client may cause additional problems. There is evidence that blacks who come for help expect the social worker to offer certain values and opinions on the issues they present. Though these opinions may differ from their own, clients expect that communication about differences will be a major aspect of the counseling process. The neutral counselor appears to be someone who has nothing to offer!

Lerner offers an example of the kind of consequences that can result when a helping person does not understand the language of the client served.[16] A white psychologist was required to make an evaluation of black school children. The evaluation procedures called for each child to be given one-half hour of unstructured play with blocks. Tinker Toys and beads were followed by a brief discussion between the child and psychologist about what the child had made. However, because the psychologist was unfamiliar with black dialect, he could not understand the child's answer to the question of what she had made. Thus, he repeated the question several times, thereby increasing the child's anxiety. When the child finally was able to make the psychologist understand the word "sticks," she was so relieved that she responded "sticks" whenever the question was asked, regardless of what she had actually made. After all, isn't it better not to frustrate the poor psychologist with words he cannot understand? Yet the child is likely to be assessed as having limited capacity to verbalize or limited ability to conceptualize on the basis of the psychologist's inability to communicate.

Banks has recommended that helping persons who work with black clients should recognize the heterogeneity of black culture and should become actively involved in the educational, political, and cultural life of different kinds of blacks.[17] Doing this would enhance the worker's ability to understand distinctive language patterns and communication styles, particularly if he or she spends some time in barbershops, churches, bars, and other places where people congregate within black communities. Social workers should familiarize themselves with these black communities and experience the texture of life so that they will be able to project a shared life space in verbal and nonverbal communication, regardless of how words may be accented.

Family Structures and Dynamics

Perhaps more has been written about black families than any other aspect of black life in the United States. Since the late nineteenth century influence of the psychoanalytic movement on social work and other helping professions, there has been an emphasis on the significance of the family in the etiology of problem behavior. For example, black families have been subject to sweeping generalizations about the effects of their behavior on problems experienced by family members. Much of the social science literature attempts to account for the overrepresentation of black families in certain problem categories—among the poor, the unskilled, the uneducated, and the poorly housed, for example. One view is that black and white families share the same cultural values and norms but differ because of socioeconomic class.[18] Another view is that lower socioeconomic class status is an outcome of culture, rather than its determinant.[19] Therefore, black families have different values and norms based on the harsh and oppressive experience of slavery, which developed behavior patterns that have persisted into the present and that have impaired the family's ability for social functioning. However, the most likely view is that black culture contains elements of "mainstream" white culture, elements from traditional African culture, and elements from slavery, reconstruction, and subsequent exposure to racism and discrimination.[20] Biculturalism serves to explain both similarities and differences in comparing black families with nonblack families.

Billingsley has pointed out that black families must teach their young members not only how to be human but also how to be black in a white society.[21] Pinderhughes has expanded on this idea by identifying what black families need in order to cope effectively with the "victim system" of racism, poverty, and oppression:

> What these families need are (1) flexible boundaries to deal with the outside systems, and (2) a family structure and process that reinforce a high degree of differentiation; effective leadership; and the ability to communicate and negotiate, tolerate differences in values and perceptions among members, function biculturally and build and use strong support systems such as the extended family.[22]

The concept of an ethnosystem also incorporates the idea of biculturalism as the primary force in the dynamics of black family behavior. Black families share mainstream cultural values to the extent that in many cases their family structures and process are no different from those of other U.S. families. At the same time, however, blacks are required to deal with experiences with which many other families do not have to deal, such as discrimination in access to educational and employment opportunities or helping their children understand how to deal with racism and the negative self-images it generates.

Certain aspects of family functioning are more characteristically encountered in black families and should be mentioned here. For example, the extended family is a common family pattern in which "base households" and "affiliate households" are interconnected in an extensive mutual-aid family network.[23] Although this structure and its various components vary from place to place and with the circumstances of individual families, it can serve to help identify possible sources of family support beyond the nuclear family, which is the essential functional family unit in middle-class, white culture. Studies of working-class and middle-class black families show that nurturing and provider roles in the family are frequently shared equally by husband and wife.[24] Black child-rearing patterns often emphasize individual uniqueness, assertiveness, early independence, and avoidance of early gender identity, all of which may create problems for the child in encounters with the white middle-class—dominated school.[25] Finally, in families that have become unstable because of excessive exposure to negative valuation from the oppressive social institutions, a variety of dysfunctional behaviors may be observed—extreme lack of motivation to achieve, apathy, negativism, irresponsibility, and violence.[26] Although most Afro-American middle-class families are able to cope with oppression better and have more resources to cope with oppressive social institutions than do poor Afro-American families, they do not escape entirely; thus, recognition of the vulnerability of their status has meant that middle-class black families do not function *exactly* as do white middle-class families.

Religion

No African religious cults were established in the United States during slavery. However, with the coming of Baptist and Methodist missionaries, the slaves found an avenue for the expression of emotion as well as bonds of kinship with their fellow slaves. After emancipation, the enlarged church organizations played an even more important role in the organization of the Afro-American communities. They promoted economic cooperation for the purpose of erecting and buying churches, establishing mutual assistance and insurance companies, and building educational institutions.[27] As the main form or focus of organized social life, the church has been both a secular and a religious institution, a fact that may well account for its playing a broader role in Afro-American communities than in white communities.

The role of the church in community life far beyond its strictly spiritual mission is exemplified by the campaign of 400 black ministers in Philadelphia in 1958 to end rigid patterns of job discrimination against blacks. This alliance of ministers brought an end to the more blatant forms of job discrimination by simply having members of their congregation boycott companies that practiced it. Since segregation had ensured that managers of the offending businesses were not members of the churches or their boards of trustees or even acquaintances, the ministers did not have to worry about pressure from these individuals. The strategy was effective, and the ministers, led by Reverend Leon Sullivan, went one step further and established the Opportunities Industrialization Centers to provide black people with the skills and training needed to fill the jobs selective patronage would open. Reverend Sullivan has attributed the success of this movement to prayer, moral initiative, black unity, and the appreciation of money as a prime determinant in human behavior.[28]

The spiritual side of the black church is far more personal than that of the traditional white church: God is never an abstraction apart from the here and now. He is personalized and included in daily life situations. It is not uncommon to hear Afro-Americans relate a conversation they have had with God or with His son, Jesus Christ. Prayer is a frequent response to everyday crisis, even by those who do not profess to any deep religious convictions. Comments like, "I prayed that my husband would find a job," or "I prayed that my child would get well," may be heard. The church provides significant services in black communities that can be utilized by creative social work practitioners seeking to enhance social functioning in those communities. For example, Leigh and Green point out that churches have served to develop leadership skills and mutual aid activities, as well as emotional catharsis for those in need of some release of emotional tensions.[29] If social workers routinely assess the significance of the church in the lives of black clients, they may find avenues for enhancing their service effectiveness through collaborative activity.

Relationships with Social Institutions

Although the family, neighborhood groups, and the church represent the primary institutions influencing the behavior of Afro-Americans, schools, social welfare agencies, health care institutions, and the justice system also influence the behavior of blacks. In contrast, however, these institutions are usually controlled by those committed to the dominant culture. Because Afro-Americans have had the historical experience of being subjected to negative valuations by these institutions, they are likely to view them defensively. For example, the schools have frequently perceived Afro-Americans as less capable of developing cognitive skills than whites; yet research has indicated that school failure is often a self-fulfilling prophecy reinforced by students' acceptance of the judgment. Students fail to expend the effort required to succeed, even in those instances in which that effort could certainly lead to success. The consequence is a high dropout rate among blacks and the accusation that "they lack interest in or appreciation for education." Yet failure in school is not a culture-based phenomenon.

Because health care institutions have long discriminated against Afro-Americans, blacks exhibit considerable distrust of health care practitioners. Jacquelyne Jackson has suggested that mainstream medical practitioners are most effective in treating urban blacks in emergency or critical situations and least effective in treating them in situations where much of the management of the illness is really the responsibility of the patient or his or her guardian.[30] The influence of the physician in those instances is somewhat small.

Particular targets of distrust are social welfare agencies, which have been given primary responsibility to help poor and disadvantaged persons. The policies of these agencies have contributed to their negative valuation by blacks; for example, welfare departments of Southern states have employed differential payment schedules for white and black clients in the belief that "blacks do not need as much as whites who have been accustomed to a higher standard of living." In addition to distrust, blacks exhibit feelings of anger, hostility, passiveness, and dependency in their dealings with welfare agencies. These constitute responses to the frustration and powerlessness that are experienced when opportunities are denied because of membership in a stigmatized collective. They do not reflect individual deficiency.

SOCIAL WORK INTERVENTION

Prior to the 1960s, *culture* in social work education and practice was primarily concerned with the esoteric groups and variables encountered in the works of Margaret Mead and Clyde Kluckhohn. Only token attention was given to the special problems or techniques of service delivery to blacks. When these concerns were discussed, the focus was more often on the effects of discrimination or the role of culture in general. Acts of discrimination were perceived as generating cultural attitudes and behaviors such as concern for immediate gratification, lack of interest in personal achievement, and lack of commitment to marriage and family. Moreover these supposed characteristics were viewed as deterrents to the involvement of blacks in problem-solving relationships with social work practitioners.

The Civil Rights Movement and subsequent Black Power Movement raised issues of self-determination and institutional racism that precipitated the development of more responsive social services and a more responsive social work profession. The literature of that era, which dealt with psychosocial services to blacks, focused primarily on consciousness-raising. However, the history of limited access to services and the ineffectiveness of traditional problem-solving processes received relatively little attention from the social work profession.

The rhetoric of the 1960s gave way during the 1970s to greater concern for the development of more appropriate theories of behavior and theories of practice for guiding social work intervention with black clients. Leigh and Green have identified three major criticisms of the existing theoretical frameworks:

1. Intervention based on psychodynamic theories is, at best, palliative and at worst counterproductive. Since the problems presented by black clients are

most often not ones of personal deficiency but of personal reactions to oppressive social institutions, an exclusive focus on the mental state of the black
client or on the worker's own intellectual and emotional problems in relating
to social issues diverts attention from system as source of the client's problem
and from the possible reasons that the client came to the attention of the
social worker in the first place.

2. The role of the black family as a source of strength rather than as a source of
   dysfunctional behavior patterns has been virtually ignored.

3. Indigenous social institutions, such as the black church, have also been overlooked as a natural support system for troubled black individuals and families.
   More effective strategies for social work intervention with black families would
   seek to remove the basis for these criticisms.[31]

Theoretical Frameworks

Recent social work literature has included several attempts to infuse a black
perspective into existing theoretical frameworks so that they serve to explain
behavior of blacks more accurately, especially in terms of how these people are
influenced by the larger social environment. For example, in addition to viewing
the social system in the United States as an ethnosystem, the literature now cites
power as the primary force governing the interrelationship between the dominant
Anglo group and negatively valued ethnic groups. Therefore, power is as significant a concept in understanding the individual or family's experience of problems
in psychosocial functioning as anxiety, guilt, or some other psychodynamic concept. The interrelationship of power, powerlessness, and human growth and development can be discerned most clearly through the basic process whereby
individuals develop skills in social functioning.

> The individual experiences a complex series of events monitored by the family
> or surrogate family which involves the self, significant others and the environ-
> ment. These experiences result in the acquisition of personal resources such as
> positive self-concept, cognitive skills, health, and physical competence. These
> personal resources lead to the development of certain interpersonal and technical
> skills such as sensitivity to the feelings and needs of others, organizational skills
> and leadership ability. The personal resources as well as the interpersonal and
> technical skills can then be used to perform effectively in valued social roles
> such as employee, parent or community leader.[32]

Racism, discrimination, and the general negative valuation of blacks may act directly or indirectly to decrease the individual's power to deal effectively with
psychosocial problems. For example, the negative valuations from more powerful
white persons in their environment are reflected in the family processes of many
rural and low-income urban blacks. Because these families accept society's label
of inferiority, they are prevented from developing such optimal personal resources as a positive self-concept or certain cognitive skills. In other instances,
powerlessness may be expressed as an inability to develop interpersonal or tech-

nical skills because of low self-esteem or underdeveloped cognitive skills, which in turn are a direct consequence of interaction in an oppressive society. The final step in this vicious circle would be a reduction of the black individual's effectiveness in performing valued social roles because of his or her lack of interpersonal and technical skills. Finally, the inability to perform valued social roles confirms and reinforces feelings of inferiority and of negative values, and the vicious circle begins again.

Some negative valuations do not result in powerlessness because strong family relationships or strong group relationships provide a cushion or protective barrier against them. Despite the experience of discrimination or disadvantages simply because they are black, some individuals are able to obtain and utilize a broad range of personal, interpersonal, and technical resources to achieve goals effectively. Not all blacks can be considered powerless or unable to function effectively in the wider social system. On the other hand, for those who do suffer that powerlessness, which has at least some of its source in the relationship between the individual and oppressive social institutions, empowerment is an important goal and process for social work with these clients.

> *Empowerment* is defined here as a process whereby the social worker engages in a set of activities with the client system that aim to reduce the powerlessness that has been created by negative valuations based on membership in a stigmatized group. It involves identification of the power blocks that contribute to the problem as well as the development and implementation of specific strategies aimed at either the reduction of the effects from indirect power blocks or the reduction of the operation of direct power blocks.[33]

This theoretical perspective on the relationship between blacks in the ethnosystem and its oppressive social institutions provides a basis for the generation of practice principles that are consistent with the definition of empowerment. These principles serve to specify the goals of social work intervention; that is, intervention should be directed toward:

1. Helping the client to perceive himself or herself as causal agent in achieving a solution to his or her problem or problems.
2. Helping the client to perceive the social worker as having knowledge and skills which he or she can use.
3. Helping the client to perceive the social worker as peer collaborator or partner in the problem-solving effort.
4. Helping the social worker to perceive the oppressive social institution (schools, welfare department, courts, and so forth) as open to influence to reduce negative impact.[34]

These objectives are not substitutes for other objectives that may be derived from other theoretical perspectives; for example, helping clients to gain insight into their emotional reactions to significant others in their social environment, or helping them to extinguish some problem behavior. However, the objectives related to empowerment take into account the fact that the problem may be created or exacerbated by the actions of external social institutions.

Presenting Problems

The criticism that traditional theoretical frameworks were not relevant to problem solving with black clients suggests that there is some inherent difference in the nature of the problems brought by black clients to social work agencies or settings. Social work has identified a broad range of problems in social functioning as amenable to change if subjected to application of social work skills. These problems are encountered not only in primary social work agencies (such as family agencies and adoption agencies) but also in host settings in health, education, law and justice, and income maintenance. Regardless of the setting, however, most black clients come to these agencies because they perceive them as a means for obtaining some needed material assistance or because they have been sent by agents of social control—judge, doctor, or educator—who have defined a problem for the client. Because most practice theories assume that the client will express a "felt difficulty," they are not very useful when the client expresses no felt difficulty or a very concrete one that, if accepted, requires only the connection of the client to the resource. In such cases, traditional practice theories indicate few options for intervention because they assume that the client is not motivated to help him- or herself. However, given the black experience in the ethnosystem, which generates little trust for social institutions, including those considered to be helping agencies, it should be expected that the majority of black clients will fall into the following two categories: (1) those people who have a mild to severe emotional and or social dysfunction but who perceive the social work practitioner as having no expertise for real assistance; or (2) those who perceive the "system" as a major contributor to the problem and believe it is not amenable to change or behavior modification. The incorporation of an empowerment goal in social work means that the social worker must intervene to change these attitudes of the client.

The distinctiveness of the presenting problems of black clients is not merely in their resistance to presenting the problems at all. In addition, even when the problems are clearly articulated by the client and not very different from problems presented by nonblack clients (parent–child conflict, adolescent school difficulties, inability to function effectively in the workplace, teen-age pregnancy, gang violence, marital conflict, schizophrenia, or depressive reactions), the chances are good that the experience of the client or family with oppressive social institutions will have created either direct or indirect power blocks to satisfactory functioning. Thus, the parent–child problem is exacerbated by the child's membership in a peer group that is spawned because of its negative valuation in the inner-city environment. Similarly, employment problems or adolescent school difficulties may be to some extent a consequence of low expectations and self-fulfilling prophecy. Depressive reactions may be a consequence to some extent of the cumulative frustration encountered in efforts to deal with school, employers, and social agencies. Eventually anger is turned inwards, and the depreciated self is created. The presenting problems of these black clients all involve stress from external systems. If the theoretical frameworks that serve to guide social workers all relate primarily to intrapsychic functioning as the determinant of ability to cope with one's environment, and not to institutional factors that might need to be changed instead or as well, the profession will have limited effectiveness in helping Afro-Americans.

Assessing the Problem

The social worker's initial problem-solving task is to assess (1) those factors that have contributed to the development and maintenance of the problem situation, and (2) the client's particular personal and social assets and liabilities that influence the problem-solving process. Black individuals and families are often perceived in biased ways that lead to erroneous conclusions about the source of the problem (for example, personal deficiency rather than environmental stress) and the degree to which they have the ego strengths (cognitive skills, language skills, and ability to relate to others) necessary to engage in effective problem-solving work. The social worker should operate from an empowerment perspective and attempt to discern and overcome the powerlessness felt by the client as a member of an oppressed minority group. However, the social worker must also assess the extent to which intrapsychic and or intrafamilial forces also contribute to feelings of powerlessness and impaired social functioning. This assessment must be a two-pronged one: that of the client's unique personal problems, and of the effect on him or her of negative valuation as a consequence of being black in a white-dominated society.

Certain elements of personality in black individuals have been directly connected with growing up black in a white-dominated ethnosystem. For example, Grier and Cobb have suggested several defensive postures that often characterize black–white relationships:

1. Cultural paranoia that assumes that anyone white or any social institution dominated by whites will potentially act against a black's best interests.
2. Cultural depression that is a consequence of life experiences and serves to define a black as less capable, less worthy than whites.
3. Cultural antisocialism that develops from a black's experience with laws, policies, and institutional procedures, which have no respect for him or her as an individual or blacks as a group; the black, in turn, has no respect for, or obligation to conform to, these laws, policies or procedures.[35]

Each of these defensive postures can be represented by a continuum: at one end there is just enough defensive posture to reduce the person's vulnerability to a potentially hostile social environment; at the other end there is so much defensive posture that the person is prohibited from functioning effectively.

The idea that personality development in blacks involves the task of achieving a balanced response to the experience of racism and discrimination is also found in Chestang's contention that blacks have dual personality components. One is a "depreciated" component that recognizes the low status society has ascribed to him or her and responds with feelings of worthlessness and hopelessness. The other is a "transcendent" component that seeks to overcome this low status and actualize the potential for successful psychosocial functioning. If either the depreciated or the transcendent component of the personality becomes too dominant, problems in social functioning are likely to arise. The overly depreciated personality projects the image of the deserving victim, whereas the overly transcendent personality projects a false power that has no basis in reality.[36]

The attitudes and behaviors exhibited by many blacks who come for help to social agencies are often labeled *resistance;* instead, these behaviors really reflect attempts at coping with discrimination and powerlessness. For example, because blacks often perceive delays in provision of service when requested from a counseling agency as indicative of indifference and/or low priority, they may not approach the agency again. Similarly, blacks may "drop out" because they view lengthy gathering of background information and nondirective, neutral counseling styles as signifying the social worker's disinterest in them or inability to deal with their problems. It is a mistake to label this dropping-out behavior as lack of motivation or resistance to dealing with the problem, since this behavior could just as easily signify resistance to the experience of negative valuation or being "put down" by those representing white-dominated social institutions or practice disciplines. Moreover, dropping out is not always the same as failure to cope with the problem. The client may have opted for a solution that may or may not be less functional; for example, attempting a self-help strategy or attempting to find help in the informal support network of family and friends.

In order to determine the *extent* to which the powerlessness expressed in a black individual or family's request for help stems from membership in the stigmatized collective, certain questions should be explored:

1. How has the client's family perceived the fact of being black in its life experiences (for example, quality of education, job opportunities, and marital relationships)?
2. What has been the interaction of social class and race in the formation of attitudes, beliefs, values, and behavior patterns?
3. How have formal and informal support systems within the black community been utilized by the individual and/or family?
4. To what extent does the individual consider it possible to change the outcome of his or her interactions with white-dominated social institutions?

In those instances where answers to these questions indicate that much of the powerlessness being experienced by the individual or family stems from negative encounters with social institutions, the social worker's role necessarily involves at least strengthening the client's ability to deal with these institutions and at most modifying the functioning of the institution.

Establishing a Working Relationship

Most black clients who come to social agencies for assistance have been sent by others who have defined their problem as requiring some type of social work intervention. For the most part, a social worker is viewed as synonymous with a welfare worker so that he or she is considered the one who is in a position to determine whether the client can receive or continue to receive concrete benefits such as financial assistance, food stamps, housing subsidies, and emergency shelter or referrals for employment, medical care, or educational programs. The social worker is not perceived as a therapist, nor is therapy often considered a solution to emotional problems. If the social worker insists on defining the problem only in psychological terms (the need for changes in the individual's emotional functioning), the client is likely to reject this definition. On the other hand, if the social worker focuses only on deficiencies in basic social supplies (such as food, clothing, and shelter), then any provision of help is unlikely to break the cycle of dependency created by dysfunctional attitudes, impaired intrafamilial and interpersonal relationships, and intrapsychic conflicts. A satisfactory working relationship can only be established for black clients when there is an expressed willingness on the part of the social worker to consider the multiple problems of clients as an interrelated whole.

Another aspect of establishing a satisfactory working relationship with black clients is to recognize the basis on which black individuals will permit the social worker to influence their life situation. Two major orientations to interpersonal relationships have been identified in sociological literature. One is the *gesellschaft* orientation, which is most characteristic of white, urban, middle-class individuals and identifies appropriate behavior according to the social status of the individuals involved. Therefore, these individuals would examine the social worker's educational attainment, credentials, and license in order to assess his or her competence to perform a helping role. Framed degrees or certificates, titles such as "doctor," and the location and decor of the offices would all have some bearing on the client's judgment of the practitioner. The other is the *gemeinschaft* orientation, which is more characteristic of rural, low-income, minority individuals for whom relationships are based on personal attributes of the individuals involved. For example, for these individuals, the social worker's answers to personal questions about marital status, number of children, religious beliefs, or time spent in the community may determine whether or not he or she is perceived as competent.

Establishing rapport between client and social worker is particularly difficult when ethnic boundaries are involved. Draper has suggested ways in which developing such rapport with low-income black clients may be more readily achieved:

> The white worker must try to enter the life space of the black client. He/she must listen to the expression of black language, its sounds and meaning. Read black literature and newspapers. Listen to black radio stations to get with the tempo and temper of blacks' feelings. Leave the office and walk around in black neighborhoods—look at the parts that are slums, but also acknowledge the blocks that are kept with pride.... Look at the addict and the pimp but also see those who carry themselves with dignity. Look at the hustler but also see the shopkeeper, the dentist, the doctor. Go with the black client to the hospital and the

> social service agency. Notice the very real differences in the way services are
> often given to black and white clients. . . . There is an infinite variety among blacks
> whether in the metropolis or the small town.[37]

A personalized approach to establishing relationships with black clients and a keen sensitivity to in-group diversity may overcome apparent obstacles. Attempts to encourage discussion of thought, feelings, and problems in an open manner by a white person may fail because of the black client's lifetime of conditioning in an opposite direction. The characteristic black–white relationship was based on white superiority and was not a peer relationship; that is, the black person was expected to defer to the white and to provide the white person with any information demanded, but at the same time was constrained from expecting similar deference or any information from the white person in return. This kind of relationship must be rejected totally; instead a peer–collaborator relationship, in which there is mutual respect and mutual sharing of information, must be established.

THE PROBLEM-SOLVING PROCESS

Social workers who are committed to an empowerment perspective in their practice constantly apply specific strategies aimed at helping clients to achieve a sense of control over their lives. They are particularly concerned with developing clients' abilities to influence the decisions of social institutions when such decisions will affect their lives.

The sense of control is often impaired by specific agency procedures. For example, clients of most social agencies are invariably required to answer myriad questions, often to satisfy the needs of the agency (for example, to identify client population). These questions have little relevance to the problem-solving process. Therefore, a client who comes to an agency to present a problem of parent–child conflict may in the initial session be required to indicate length of time in the community, place of employment, amount of family income, and religion—none of which at the time may be important to meeting the client's immediate need. Furthermore, revealing so much that may be negative (such as failed marriages, evictions, and last job) reinforces the client's sense of personal deficiency, which is often already a dysfunctional aspect of the personality of the Afro-American client. The helping process becomes part of the problem rather than part of the solution.

In order to counteract the problem, a guiding principle of social work practice from an empowerment perspective is to ask no questions that do not have direct bearing on the problem-solving work. This may mean that the social worker does not even ask the client for his or her telephone number. If arrangements have been made for a future appointment, the client may be asked, "In case anything happens and the appointment has to be changed, is there a way I can reach you?" Then the client has to option to give the telephone number, to indicate that he or she will call the agency to confirm the appointment, or take his or her chances. In such a case, clearly the client rather than the social worker will control the flow of information.

A client's sense of power over his or her life situation is also enhanced when the relationship with the social worker is a peer relationship. Each party brings a degree of expertise to the problem-solving process; that is, knowledge and/or skills that are necessary but not sufficient to reach a solution. For example, the client brings to the process first-hand knowledge of the problem he or she is experiencing, the strengths and weaknesses of the key actors (family members of the support network), and the consequences of past attempts at reaching a solution. The social worker brings to the process an understanding of human behavior and how people create problem situations, as well as how they can be influenced to change or modify them. It is the blending of separate areas of expertise that makes possible the eventual solution.

Because the problem-solving process is by definition a collaborative one, the client or client system must take responsibility for bringing about whatever change is sought. For example, if the problem is inability to maintain employment, the underlying reasons may include a variety of systemic forces (poor educational opportunities and discrimination in hiring, for example). If these forces are to be overcome, the client must take specific actions to counteract the negative impact of a hostile environment. These actions may be directed toward changes in the oppressive social institutions, such as the utilization of the legal and court systems to reduce discrimination or compensate for past discrimination. The social worker who is skilled in facilitating change at both the individual and larger system levels will have much more utility in black communities than the one who is skilled and comfortable in dealing only with individuals or small groups.

The social worker's role with Afro-American clients in the problem-solving process often is one of consciousness-raising so that the multiple forces that created problem situations can be acknowledged in order to relieve the demoralizing powerlessness stemming from an unconscious or conscious sense of personal deficiency. The question may be asked, "Why am I unable to make it when other people seem to be able to do so very well?" This question has become particularly problematic in more recent years, when the reduction in legalized discrimination has meant that some blacks have been able to take advantage of what Billingsley has referred to as "screens of opportunity." It is still necessary to educate many Afro-Americans about the systemic factors that mitigate against "winning" if one is poor and black in this society.

CONCLUDING COMMENT

There are unique issues involved in social work practice with Afro-American clients. Most blacks who come to social work agencies for help have been sent by schools, correctional authorities, or other agents of social control and do not have faith that the social worker has skills that can help in solving their social and emotional problems. It is not enough for the social worker to have an appreciation for cultural diversity; he or she must have basic knowledge regarding the life styles, communication patterns, and characteristic problems encountered by black individuals and families. This knowledge is required for accurate assessment of the client's strengths, resources, support network, and potential for collaborating in a problem-solving process. The preoccupation of social work practice with *person* variables rather than *system* variables is a particular obstacle in developing effective intervention strategies with Afro-American clients. Their problems are characteristically intertwined with the behavior of the oppressive institutions with which they come into contact. However, these institutions are not monolithic and invariant in the application of oppression; therefore, skills can be enhanced in order to deal with them. The goal of increasing a client's sense of control in the problem-solving process and in his or her life situation characterizes the approach to social work with Afro-American clients that has been identified as *empowerment.*

SUGGESTED READINGS

BILLINGSLEY, ANDREW. *Black Families in White America.* Englewood Cliffs, N.J.: Prentice-Hall, 1968.

BILLINGSLEY, ANDREW, and GIOVANNONI, JEANNE M. *Children of the Storm: Black Children and American Child Welfare.* New York: Harcourt Brace Jovanovich, 1972.

BOWLES, DORCAS D. "Development of an Ethnic Self-Concept among Blacks." In Carolyn Jacobs and Dorcas D. Bowles, eds., *Ethnicity and Race: Critical Concepts in Social Work.* Silver Spring, Md.: National Association of Social Workers, 1988, pp. 103–113.

GARY, LAWRENCE E., ED. *Black Men.* Beverly Hills, Calif.: Sage Publications, 1981.

GILBERT, GWENDOLYN C. "The Role of Social Work in Black Liberation." *The Black Scholar* (December 1974).

GLASGOW, DOUGLAS G. *The Black Underclass.* San Francisco: Jossey-Bass, 1980.

MILLER, HENRY. "Social Work in the Black Ghetto: The New Colonialism." *Social Work* 14 (July 1969).

MORALES, ARMANDO. "Social Work with Third-World People." *Social Work* 26 (January 1981): 45–51.

SOLOMON, BARBARA BRYANT. *Black Empowerment: Social Work in Oppressed Communities.* New York: Columbia University Press, 1976.

Special Issue, "Social Work and People of Color." *Social Work* 27 (January 1982).

ENDNOTES

1. Lawrence Rosen, "Policemen," in Peter I. Rose, Stanley Rothman, and William J. Wilson, eds., *Through Different Eyes: Black and White Perspectives on American Race Relations* (London: Oxford University Press, 1973), pp. 257–290.

2. Wetrogan, Signe I., "Projections of the Population of States by Age, Sex and Race," *Current Population Reports* Series P-25, No. 1053 (Washington, D.C.: U.S. Bureau of the Census, 1989): 15–22.

3. George Gilder, *Wealth and Poverty* (New York: Bantam Books, 1981), p. 160.

4. Douglas G. Glasgow, *The Black Underclass: Poverty, Unemployment and Entrapment of Ghetto Youth* (San Francisco: Jossey-Bass, 1980).

5. Guichard Paris and Lester Books, *Blacks in the City: A History of the National Urban League* (Boston: Little, Brown and Co., 1971), p. 78.

6. Ben J. Wattenberg and Richard M. Scammon, "Black Progress and Liberal Rhetoric." *Commentary* (April 1973): 35–44.

7. Gilder, *Wealth and Poverty*, pp. 155–156.

8. Robert Hill, "The Illusion of Black Progress," *Social Policy* (November–December 1978): 14–25.

9. Robert Hill, "The Economic Status of Black Americans," in James D. Williams, ed., *The State of Black America: 1981* (New York: National Urban League, January 14, 1981), pp. 58–59.

10. U.S. Bureau of the Census, "Marital Status and Living Arrangements: March 1988," *Current Population Reports* Series P-20, No. 433 (Washington, D.C.: The Bureau, 1989): 42.

11. U.S. Bureau of the Census, "Poverty in the United States: 1987," *Current Population Reports* Series P-60, No. 163 (Washington, D.C.: The Bureau, 1989): 1–4.

12. Barbara Solomon, *Black Empowerment: Social Work in Oppressed Communities* (New York: Columbia University Press, 1976), pp. 44–45.

13. A. A. K. Shapiro, E. Struening, E. Shapiro, and H. Barten, "Prognostic Correlates of Psychotherapy in Psychiatry," *American Journal of Psychiatry* (1976): 802–808.

14. R. R. Carkhuff and R. Pierce, "Differential Effects of Therapist Race and Social Class upon Patient Depth of Self-Exploration in the Initial Clinical Interview," *Journal of Consulting Psychology* 31 (December 1967): 632–634.

15. Carolyn B. Block, "Black Americans and the Cross-Cultural Counseling and Psychotherapy Experience," in Anthony J. Marsella and Paul B. Pedersen, eds., *Cross-Cultural Counseling and Psychotherapy* (New York: Pergamon Press, 1979), p. 183.

16. Barbara Lerner, *Therapy in the Ghetto: Political Importance and Personal Disintegration* (Baltimore: Johns Hopkins University Press, 1972), pp. 159–161.

17. W. M. Banks, "The Black Client and the Helping Professionals," in R. James, ed., *Black Psychology* (New York: Harper & Row, 1972), p. 210.

18. See particularly Jacquelyne Johnson Jackson, "Family Organization and Ideology," in Kent S. Miller and Ralph Mason Dreger, eds., *Comparative Studies of Blacks and Whites in the United States* (New York: Seminar Press, 1973); and Jerold Heiss, *The Case of the Black Family: A Sociological Inquiry* (New York: Columbia University Press, 1975).

19. See Robert Staples, "Toward a Sociology of the Black Family: A Theoretical and Methodological Assessment," *Journal of Marriage and the Family* (February 1971), pp. 119–138.

20. Barbara Bryant Solomon and Helen A. Mendes, "Black Families from a Social Welfare Perspective," in Virginia Tufte and Barbara Myerhoff, eds., *Changing Images of the Family* (New Haven, Conn.: Yale University Press, 1979), pp. 285–289.

21. Andrew Billingsley, *Black Families in White America* (Englewood Cliffs, N.J.: Prentice-Hall, 1968), p. 28.

22. Elaine Pinderhughes, "Family Functioning of Afro-Americans," *Social Work* (January 1982): 92.

23. Elmer P. Martin and Joanne Mitchell Martin, *The Black Extended Family* (Chicago: University of Chicago Press, 1978), pp. 5–16.

24. James W. Leigh and James W. Green, "The Structure of the Black Community: The Knowledge Base for Social Services," in James W. Green, ed., *Cultural Awareness in the Human Services,* (Englewood Cliffs, N.J.: Prentice-Hall, 1982), pp. 106–107.

25. Diane K. Lewis, "The Black Family: Specialization and Sex Roles," *Phylon* 36 (Fall 1975): 222.
26. Pinderhughes, pp. 92–94.
27. Leigh and Green, pp. 103–104.
28. C. Eric Lincoln, *The Black Church Since Frazier* (New York: Shocken Books, 1974), p. 121.
29. Leigh and Green, pp. 103–104.
30. Jacquelyne Johnson Jackson, "Urban Black Americans," in Alan Harwood, ed., *Ethnicity and Health Care* (Cambridge, Mass.: Harvard University Press, 1981), p. 117.
31. Leigh and Green, pp. 97–99.
32. Solomon, p. 17.
33. Ibid., p. 19.
34. Ibid., p. 26.
35. William H. Grier and Price M. Cobb, *Black Rage* (New York: Basic Books, 1968), pp. 200–213.
36. Leon Chestang, *Character Development in a Hostile Environment,* Occasional Paper No. 3 (Chicago: School of Social Service Administration, University of Chicago, 1972), pp. 7–8.
37. Barbara Jones Draper, "Black Language as an Adaptive Response to a Hostile Environment," in Carel B. Germain, ed., *Social Work Practices, People, and Environments* (New York: Columbia University Press, 1979), p. 279.

PART FIVE

The Future of
Social Work

*T*o examine the profession of social work thoroughly, one must not only study the past and current status of the field, but also seek a glimpse of the future. A few developing needs and trends offer some insight into the directions social work is likely to move in the next few years and suggest some challenges the profession will face as it continues to evolve in these areas.

Underlying discussion of the future of social work is the assumption that this profession will survive. Although several respected and knowledgeable social workers warn that social work may be eliminated as a significant helping profession,* there are strong arguments to refute this position.

First, although social work is still a relatively young profession, it has now achieved adequate maturity to allow social workers to become engaged in meaningful roles in a wide range of social agencies. This significant contribution is evident not only in agencies where social work is the primary or senior discipline, such as family service agencies and public welfare departments, but also in hospitals, schools, and other agencies where social work is a guest or secondary discipline. Despite some problems to be remedied if social work is to become an increasingly viable profession, social workers hold an important place in the delivery system of social services through the impact of their helping activities; they cannot be easily dislodged; their services are badly needed by the general public.

Second, the focus of social work on reconciling existing or potential problems between the person and the environment is not being accomplished successfully by any other professional group. The trend toward increased specialization and technology in most professions (with notable exception, the trend toward family practice in medicine) has

---

* Harry Specht, "The Deprofessionalization of Social Work," *Social Work* 17 (March 1972): 3–15; and Willard C. Richan and Allan R. Mendelsohn, *Social Work: The Unloved Profession* (New York: New Viewpoints, 1973), pp. 42–56.

moved them to focus on their unique practice areas and to become less concerned about the match between the person and the environment. Yet there is evidence that some emerging occupational groups are moving into this practice arena. The maintenance of social work as the primary profession with knowledge and skill for preventing or resolving problems in social functioning is critical to the successful provision of a comprehensive battery of social services to U.S. citizens. Unless extreme economic or physical disaster should force U.S. national priorities toward strict survival considerations to the neglect of consideration for the quality of life, this function will continue to be required.

Finally, its breadth allows social work to adjust its field at any one time toward greater emphasis on helping the person work more effectively with the environment or, conversely, toward making the environment more responsive to the person. A major factor in the survival of social work so far has been this ability to emphasize particular methodologies depending on the temper of the times. It is apparent that a strong social action emphasis would have damaged the development of the profession in the 1940s, when the psychoanalytic approach prevailed in the whole field of helping services. Yet in the 1960s social work was able to bring its social action skills out of mothballs to support the Civil Rights Move-

ment and antipoverty programs. In the 1970s the swing was back to a more balanced approach, ranging from clinical to social action roles for the social worker. This flexibility enables social work to avoid a narrow practice approach that could lead to the demise of the profession if conditions supporting the validity of any single practice approach change.

The six practice issues and developing trends presented in Chapter 21 serve to highlight concerns that will be confronting social work in the 1990s and directions in which the profession is likely to evolve. These issues and developments pertain to: (1) the concept of mental health primary prevention and how it can be applied in a cost-effective way to at-risk social welfare populations; (2) the role of social workers in ensuring a person's right to treatment, or nontreatment, and even preventing treatment abuse with involuntary clients; (3) the potential role of social work intervention in the prevention of violence and homicide in gangs; (4) the flow of social workers into industrial settings with a unique opportunity to implement primary prevention programs; (5) the application of advocacy and empowerment concepts in working with clients as a foundation to develop primary prevention strategies with nonclient populations; and (6) the continued development and testing in the courts of *class action social work* as a mental health primary prevention tool.

CHAPTER 21

Prevention as a New Direction: The Future of Social Work

PREVENTION: A CONCEPT FOR THE 1990s

As human services budgets were drastically reduced during the 1980s and into 1990, an increasing number of people continued to need services. Substance abuse, child abuse, crime and delinquency, homelessness, AIDS, and the breakdown of the family are social problems that are also increasing. Even in the most favorable economic periods for the human services, the mental health needs of the U.S. population have far surpassed the nation's financial and manpower resources to meet these needs. For example, it is estimated that there are anywhere from 1 to 2 million children in the United States each year who suffer physical or sexual abuse, or neglect. Considering that each case could cost society $7000 to treat, the total treatment expenditure might amount to $14 billion. The Department of Health and Human Services spends less than $30 million per year for child abuse and neglect. Federal and state agencies spend approximately $500 million per year for alcohol treatment services and treat less than 10 percent of all addicted alcohol abusers.[1] Accepting the fact that financial and professional manpower resources are limited, additional but less costly interventive approaches impacting large numbers of people have to be developed. Theories of *prevention,* therefore, have to be developed and applied.

In its most basic definition, *prevention* simply means to keep something from happening. As a helping concept in the field of social welfare, prevention is over 116 years old and dates back to 1874 and the case of Mary Ellen Wilson, a child who experienced abuse. Media coverage of the case caused intense public indignation and led to the founding of the New York Society for the Prevention of Cruelty to Children (NYSPCC) the same year. The NYSPCC annual report in 1894 claimed that in the twenty years following its creation, over 230,000 children had been placed in custody, thereby preventing them from becoming future "adult criminals."[2] In 1915 when Flexner's famous paper "Is Social Work a Profession?" was highlighted at the Proceedings of the National Conference of Charities and Corrections, six papers on prevention were also presented. The prevention papers dealt with topics such as sterilization of the insane, more institutions for the "feeble-minded," and reduced immigration. By today's standards, prevention concepts of 1915, which recommended the sterilization of schizophrenics to "prevent" schizophrenia, or restricting the flow of immigrants into the United States to solve the social problems of immigrants, appear crude.[3]

Richmond was actually discussing prevention in 1918, when she remarked that a good social worker not only helps people out of a ditch, but tries to find out what has to be done to get rid of the ditch.[4] By 1930 Richmond was defining prevention as one of the end results of a series of processes that included research, individual treatment, public education, legislation, and administrative adaptations.[5] Richmond was generalizing the potential of prevention from a single case basis to a broad societal level; that is, she was considering the range from micro to macro preventive intervention. Staulcup reports that Christian Carl Carstens, who served as the director of the Massachusetts Society for Prevention of Cruelty to Children from 1904 to 1920 and director of the Child Welfare League of America from 1920 to 1939, was a very persistent person, dedicated to preventing child abuse by seeking to strengthen the natural family. Staulcup believes the popularity of the Freudian psychoanalytic movement and the expansion and application of psychotherapy for the treatment of "social" psychosocial problems detracted from the development and refinement of prevention concepts until about the 1960s.[6]

Although there are various definitions of *prevention* that will be discussed later in greater detail, the concept has three basic stages: *primary prevention,* or the anticipation of future consequences and the purposeful manipulation to achieve desired ends or to prevent undesired ones; *secondary prevention,* which involves treatment; and *tertiary prevention,* which is rehabilitation. Within the framework of this definition Nance surveyed 762 articles in seven social work journals published between 1976 and 1980 and found that only eighteen articles pertained to primary prevention. Of the eighteen, two dealt with theory or research. The remaining sixteen described primary prevention as practiced through several social work methods. For example, five articles described the use of group work, three casework, three community organization, and five articles dealt with "multiple methods." Nance was of the opinion that the articles were conceptually weak in the area of primary prevention and that social work literature reflected the same overall lack of emphasis on primary prevention as did the mental health literature.[7]

Contemporary mental health conceptual formulations of prevention have as their foundation public health prevention theories and practice. In public health terms, prevention, as previously noted, has three stages. *Primary prevention* indicates actions taken prior to the onset of a problem to intercept its cause or to modify its course *before* a person is involved. It is the elimination of the noxious agent at its source. Through systematic spraying of affected ponds, for example, malaria-carrying mosquitoes, their eggs, and larva are destroyed before they have the opportunity to infect humans. *Secondary prevention* involves prompt efforts to curtail and stop the disease in the affected persons and the spreading of the disease to others. *Tertiary prevention* involves rehabilitative efforts to reduce the residual effects of the illness, that is, reducing the duration and disabling severity of the disease. In its most succinct form, therefore, prevention has three stages: prevention, treatment, and rehabilitation.

In 1977 the National Institute of Mental Health established an Office of Prevention to stimulate and sponsor large-scale programs of research on prevention. This Office has also assisted the Council on Social Work Education prepare curriculum materials about prevention.[8] The Director of the Office of Prevention developed the following definition of primary prevention within a mental health context:

> Primary prevention encompasses activities directed towards specifically identified vulnerable high risk groups within the community who have not been labeled psychiatrically ill and for whom measures can be undertaken to avoid the onset of emotional disturbance and/or to enhance their level of positive mental health.[9]

Primary preventive programs were for the promotion of mental health, as educational rather than clinical in conception and practice, with their ultimate goal being to help persons increase their ability for dealing with crises and for taking steps to improve their own lives.[10] Goldston identifies two goals in primary prevention: (1) to prevent needless psychopathology and symptoms, maladjustment, maladaptation, and "misery" regardless of whether the end point might be mental illness; and (2) the promotion of mental health by increasing levels of wellness among various defined populations.[11] This places an emphasis on strength and positive qualities, in contrast to the problem-centered focus found in the medical model.

In applying primary prevention to child abuse, for example, intervention program efforts can be developed at three different levels. On a macro, social-reform level, prevention interventions may include legislation to protect children's rights, abolishment of corporal punishment, advocacy for abortion, and a more equitable economic distribution of resources. A second level of primary prevention intervention, also macro in impact, may utilize educational approaches aimed at a variety of audiences. This may include, for example, educating and sensitizing society to basic issues in child abuse and its deterrents, the use of newsletters and "crash courses" to provide helpful information to young families, and teaching adolescents in public schools essential skills needed in their future parental roles. A more focused primary prevention practice strategy, which is directly concerned with the operation of intrafamilial variables, involves utilizing homemaker and home visitor services to provide support and crisis assistance to at-risk families with young children. The visitors could be hospital-based personnel, day care, child support workers, or community volunteers.[12] "Natural helpers" exist for most families. They are usually friends, neighbors, or relatives and have a relationship with the family not based on specific needs or problems of the family. With the family's sanction and the natural helper's cooperation, in at-risk families experiencing multiple problems requiring services, a preventive services worker may function as a case manager or consultant and attempt to coordinate the efforts of the various service providers. Child abuse may be prevented by assisting and meeting the needs of the at-risk family.[13]

The remainder of this chapter will examine several practice areas of concern to the future of social work, within a context of prevention theory and concepts. These areas relate to the prevention of treatment abuse, homicide prevention, the prevention implications of social work in industry, client advocacy and empowerment as prevention, and finally, class action social work as a macro-level strategy and tool.

PREVENTING TREATMENT ABUSE

In preparing this sixth edition of *Social Work: A Profession of Many Faces,* our survey of the literature and current trends in the helping professions suggested that the availability or lack of treatment is often linked to economic scarcity, political climate, and the devaluation of human services by the Reagan administration during the 1980–88 period, later followed by President Bush. It is interesting to note that concerned activists once advocated for a right to treatment and then later a right to nontreatment. Today the picture is mixed. There are some persons, such as the homeless (of whom 50 percent may be mentally ill), who need treatment and are not getting it, while some affluent white adolescents who do not want treatment are involuntarily committed by their parents to private psychiatric hospitals for behavioral problems. This paradox will be touched on later, following a discussion of the right to nontreatment.

The social worker must be concerned about the right of the client to refuse treatment. In order to understand the concept of the *right to nontreatment,* the concept of the *right to treatment* must first be considered. The latter concept was first publicly advocated for inmates of public mental institutions by Birnbaum in 1960. The constitutional basis for this concept is due process of law, that "a mentally ill person should not be deprived indefinitely of his liberty in what amounts to a mental prison if he is not receiving adequate care and treatment for his illness."[14]

One of the first landmark legal decisions inspired by the concept of right to treatment appeared in *Rouse* v. *Cameron* in 1966. Speaking for the majority, Chief Judge David Bazelon of the U.S. Court of Appeals for the District of Columbia affirmed the concept of a right to treatment for persons confined in public mental hospitals. He declared that the purpose of involuntary hospitalization was treatment, not punishment, since Congress had established a statutory right to treatment in the 1964 Hospitalization of the Mentally Ill Act.[15]

The first comprehensive attempt to establish and define a statutory right to treatment for mental patients in state institutions is best exemplified in a legislative bill entitled The Right to Treatment Law of 1968, introduced in the Pennsylvania General Assembly in December, 1967. By 1969 ten states and the District of Columbia had recognized a statutory right to treatment. Most statutes, however, tended to lack enforcement provisions and were little more than statements of policy—that the patient is entitled to medical care and treatment in accordance with the highest standards of the medical profession, although in fact limited by the facilities, personnel, and available equipment.[16]

Many subsequent court decisions upholding the right of institutionalized mental patients to adequate treatment have been made since 1960, but no guidelines have been promulgated. The right to treatment was not fully and conclusively applied until 1971–72, when the orders and decrees arising from *Wyatt* v. *Stickney* were given in the U.S. Middle District Court of Alabama. In this historic case the court clearly defined the purposes of commitment to public hospitals for the mentally ill and mentally retarded, affirmed the right of patients or residents to specific services and opportunities once a commitment had been effected, and established minimum standards of care and rehabilitation. It also established standards of staff qualification, appropriate staff–resident ratios, and appropriate approaches to transitional care and postinstitutional care. Commenting on the implications of *Wyatt* v. *Stickney* for social work, Prigmore and Davis stated:

> At one stroke, it seems that one of the cherished goals of social work—to provide a framework for individuals to attain their fullest potential—may have a good chance of early realization, at least for the institutionalized mentally ill and retarded.[17]

Prigmore and Davis pointed out that a footnote in the court decision raised the possibility that some day the court might be confronted with the question of whether the voluntarily committed resident, like the involuntarily committed resident, also has a right to treatment. Within the realm of that possibility, they believe it will probably follow that once government accepts responsibility for providing a social service, the recipient has a constitutional right to service that is adequate. They conclude that this responsibility may result in a restructuring and reorienting of U.S. social services.[18]

Szasz, however, saw several fallacies in the right-to-treatment concept. He states that publicly operated psychiatric institutions perform their services based on the premise that it is morally legitimate to treat "mentally sick" persons against their will.[19] The most fundamental and vexing problem, according to Szasz, is how a treatment that is compulsory can also be a right. He would prefer to ask the question, Which do involuntarily hospitalized mental patients need more— a right to receive treatments they do not wish, or a right to refuse such interventions (i.e., *the right to nontreatment*)? He felt the answer to such a question should come from the imprisoned patients rather than from the institutional psychiatrists.[20] Szasz noted:

It seems to me that improvement in the health care of poor people and those now said to be mentally ill depends less on declarations about their rights to treatment and more on certain reforms in the language and conduct of those professing a desire to help them. In particular, such reforms must entail refinements in the use of medical concepts, such as illness and treatment, and a recognition of the basic differences between medical intervention as a service, which the individual is free to seek or reject, and medical intervention as a method of social control, which is imposed on him by force or fraud.[21]

The concept of the right to treatment for the involuntarily committed patient is in many ways similar to the right to social services for the involuntary client. Both have as a goal a social control function. A social control process is present in the social services that a public welfare client receives—it's in the law! On the recommendations of the Ad Hoc Committee on Public Welfare, composed largely of social workers, Congress specified in the law in 1962 what was meant by *social services.* The services were defined by the purposes and qualifications of the personnel who provided them. The purposes were to strengthen family relations, to help families to become self-supporting, to rehabilitate dependent people, and to prevent dependency. The services were to be given by professionally trained social workers, and provision was made in the legislation to increase the supply of qualified workers. McEntire and Haworth maintain that the fundamental logic of combining social services with public assistance lies in the ideas that people who must depend on this "last resort" source of income are reduced to that extremity by personal or familial defects and that the application of professional knowledge and skill can remedy such defects so that these persons will become able to support themselves in some other manner.[22]

Social services *are* a form of social control to the extent that they encourage a welfare client to give up one set of behaviors for another set considered more appropriate in society. Cowger and Atherton assert that when social workers help clients find a job, apply for public aid, or manage the use of alcohol or other drugs, they are engaging in the process of social control. The objective is to enable clients to get along better within the social order.[23]

Miller perceives a "terrible dilemma" in the social work value of preserving the dignity and worth of the human being that at the same time demeans the person by imposing a social service on him or her:

> The wrong inheres in the assumption that we have a right to impose unsolicited advice upon another human being—*and he is not free to withdraw himself from the situation or even discount the advice.* If he is on welfare, his benefit is contingent on being counseled in the use of his money or more; if he is on probation or parole his physical freedom becomes a condition of his receptivity to counsel; if he hangs around on street corners, he is assaulted by the insinuations of the street workers; if he is insane and hospitalized, the duration of his confinement becomes a function of a willingness to be counseled.[24]

Miller believes through such actions the individual is deprived of the one primary freedom that endows people with the core of their dignity: the freedom to make a shambles of one's life. "This may sound like a strange doctrine," he states, "that people should be free to err, to make mistakes, to fail, to be 'ill.' "[25] He advocates that people be offered the possibility of choice—and that includes the choice of being maladaptive, deviant, or even ill. Thus, the individual has a right not to be treated. Prigmore reports that in the case of *Kainowitz* v. *Department of Mental Health of the State of Michigan,* the court found that involuntary psychotherapy was unconstitutional. The case is significant "because the right to treatment should logically be complemented by a corresponding right *not* to have treatment."[26] This movement for change is also affecting public welfare; in some states welfare is dispersed through an income maintenance section, while social services are offered in a casework section. The client is free to choose to be helped by social workers; or to ignore the help and continue to receive a check, as long as he or she is financially eligible. There are indications that welfare clients are not flocking to engage in therapy.[27]

Social workers are learning to live with the idea that their involuntary clients might not want their social services, and clients are not being penalized for refusing these services. In this respect, *the right to nontreatment,* as a phrase, might be newer to social workers than their familiarity with the ideology and application of the concept.

The development of the concept of the right to nontreatment has occurred over a very short period. This right will possibly have broader implications for social work and society as more people—particularly involuntary clients—become aware of the social control and political implications related to the definition of "deviant" behavior. For discussion purposes, one area of social work practice where this concept may have the greatest reform impact—social work practice with individuals, groups, and families—will be considered. To avoid confusion, the term *social casework,* rather than "social work practice with individuals, groups, and families," will be used in the following discussion.

Social casework, a tool in treatment that may be defined as a primarily psychotherapeutic method consisting of interviews dealing with the client's problems as defined by the client, in the context of the worker–client relationship,[28] is the largest segment of the social work profession.[29] It is also the primary mode of intervention used in the context of social service as previously defined. Social casework has been criticized consistently and most dramatically for its failure to demonstrate a clear effectiveness in helping clients.[30] In an analysis of eleven controlled studies of the effectiveness of social casework, Fischer found that nine of these clearly showed that professional caseworkers were unable to bring about any positive, significant, measurable changes in their clients beyond those that would have occurred without the specific intervention program or have been induced by nonprofessionals dealing with similar clients, often in less intensive service programs.[31] Fischer therefore concluded:

> Thus not only has professional casework failed to demonstrate that it is effective, but lack of effectiveness appears to be the rule rather than the exception across several categories of clients, problems, situations, and types of casework.[32]

Fischer pointed out that he was presenting research findings related to practice rather than an analysis of practice per se, and that most of the studies concentrated on work with children, juvenile delinquents, and low-income clients. He argued that the high rate of failure could have been an artifact of caseworkers' general inability to help clients when other, more powerful, environmental forces hold sway and that although the problem was important, the methods used may have been outdated.[33]

More recent research related to social casework has revealed positive results, indicating that effectiveness of casework may be related more to the problem and the client than to the method itself. In an analysis of thirty-two controlled studies on treatment outcomes of marital counseling, Beck found statistically significant, positive gains in all but one of the studies. The participants in many of the studies were young, white, and relatively well-educated middle-class couples.[34]

The clients in Beck's research represented a relatively homogeneous group dealing with one dominant social problem, in contrast to multiproblem families, and their principal problem did not require changes in the institutional structure or wider social context. With minor exceptions, the marital samples in the studies were restricted to couples who either were *actively seeking help* or were willing to volunteer.[35] In the Fischer studies, with one exception, all participants were involuntary clients. This evidence strongly suggests that when social workers do casework within a social control framework with involuntary clients, their interventive efforts are not as effective as when they serve voluntary clients who are actively seeking help with a specific problem.

In one instance, then, the state and its representatives—social workers—define the problem and goals for the involuntary client, while in the other, the voluntary client defines the problem and goals. Individuals who are not seeking to change their behavior usually do not change, whereas those who are seeking to change usually do. Imposing treatment on involuntary clients with questionable results, and perhaps even deterioration of the clients in slightly under 50 percent of the cases[36] (that is, iatrogenic effects of practice[37]), raises ethical questions for the social worker. Is the social worker performing a disservice to the involuntary client? Imposing treatment poses a dilemma for social workers because they are given legal sanction to carry out a social control function that does not have the sanction of the involuntary client and is inconsistent with the value social workers place on self-determination. Social workers, as representatives of the state, may feel more comfortable in intervening on behalf of the victim in a serious child abuse and maltreatment case than in interfering with a marijuana-smoking seventeen-year-old whose behavior is condoned by his parents. Imposed intervention as an act of social control should preferably be related to the seriousness of the specific case.

Social workers have a responsibility to people in need and should not permit themselves to be caught by and swing with the pendulum that is moved by political forces to extreme positions, ignoring the welfare of persons at risk. As Ladner cautioned social workers about the homeless,

> The civil libertarians leaned too far in ensuring the mentally ill's rights, so that now people are denied access to treatment even when they really need it and

ask for it. I think we need to recognize people's right to treatment as well as to short-term voluntary or involuntary hospitalization. And some will have to be put in asylums. But we have to stop going from one extreme to the other.[38]

The American Psychiatric Association's estimate that 25 to 50 percent of the country's estimated 3 million homeless are mentally ill may be a conservative figure. Lutheran Social Services in Washington, D.C., places the figure closer to 90 percent. Perhaps the most important issues are that the homeless have a need for various services and that social workers—according to the executive director of NASW—by far represent the largest number of professionals in one occupation who deliver these services.[39] Social workers have a key role to play on behalf of the homeless. On the one hand, they may still have to advocate for a right to nontreatment for those homeless who are still functioning, although marginally, and keep them from being institutionalized. Those who are gravely psychiatrically disabled and unable to care for themselves may need to be institutionalized against their will following due process in the courts.

In spite of the large estimates concerning the percentage of mentally ill among the homeless, the homeless by and large are *not* a homogeneous group. They vary from state to state and city to city, and are even different *within* a city. Their needs will vary too, requiring varied practice responses from the social worker. For example, a 1984 Los Angeles study by Ropers revealed that the homeless were not mostly "crazy, lazy, drunk or doped." Rather, Ropers saw them by and large as victims of deindustrialization, not deinstitutionalization, mental illness, substance abuse, or family problems. In comparing a Westside group to a downtown Skid Row group, he found more reported drug use in the Westside group (70.5 percent to 50.3 percent). The Westside homeless group was younger and better educated (56 percent "some college" versus 33 percent), with a median age of thirty-two, compared to thirty-nine for the Skid Row group. More than three-fourths were white, compared to less than half on Skid Row, and twice as many were likely to be women. There were no significant differences in the two groups concerning mental health, as about 20 percent reported previous psychiatric hospitalization; 28 percent had not seen a doctor or other professional for emotional or nervous problems, 14 percent reported they had been hospitalized for alcohol detoxification, 8 percent for drug detoxification, and 7 percent reported suicide attempts the previous year. Citing their reasons for being homeless, 52 percent said lack of money, 36 percent said lack of work, while a third major reason was domestic violence against women.[40] The homeless are indeed a heterogeneous group with various needs, who appear to be casualties of Reaganomics and the reduction in funding of human services programs.

From a mental health prevention standpoint, the moderately to severely psychiatrically impaired homeless will require tertiary prevention; that is, rehabilitation services to reduce the duration and disabling severity of their mental condition. For those with no prior or very little prior history of mental disorder who are now becoming symptomatic, secondary prevention (prompt treatment) will need to be initiated to curtail the emerging symptoms. Previously well-functioning homeless persons who temporarily find themselves out on the streets due to unforeseen circumstances beyond their control, who are not clinically symptomatic, would be provided primary prevention services. Primary prevention intervention for that high-risk group would involve, for example, helping the person obtain a job, re-enroll in school or return to their home town, in order to prevent needless psychopathology symptoms or maladjustment, and to increase their level of wellness.

Another at-risk population group with which social workers should be concerned are juveniles who in fact have *not* committed crimes, yet are involuntarily coming to the attention of private psychiatric hospitals and the public juvenile justice system. Congress enacted the Juvenile Justice and Delinquency Prevention Act of 1974 as a decriminalization and deinstitutionalization effort designed to prevent young people from entering a "failing juvenile justice system," and to assist communities in developing more sensible and economical alternatives for youths already in the juvenile justice system.[41] The Act was successful; arrests for status offenses or "crimes" which, had they been committed by adults, would not have been considered crimes (such as truancy, running away, or incorrigibility), declined 15.8 percent (569,481 arrests to 466,885 arrests) between 1974 and 1979.[42] The 1980s presented a mixed picture, as juvenile crime nationally was decreasing yet more juveniles were institutionalized. In Minnesota, for example, even though there was a decrease in institutionalization in public juvenile training institutions, there was a tremendous growth in the numbers of youths admitted "voluntarily" to in-patient psychiatric settings in private hospitals.[43]

In California there has also been a surge of these psychiatric facilities, related in part to California's 1977 Juvenile Reform Act, which, like the federal law, decriminalized status offenses. In Los Angeles alone there are twenty-eight such institutions, with a total of 820 beds—many having waiting lists. A study by Guttridge and Warren found that more than 70 percent of the admissions to these hospitals were for antisocial, depressive, runaway, drug abuse, or personality-disorder diagnoses. Less than one-fifth of the admissions were for psychosis.[44] The District Attorney's office questions the propriety of these hospitalizations, pointing out that experts do not agree on what exactly constitutes mental illness. A patients' rights advocate for the Los Angeles County Department of Mental Health believes hospitalization could create future and perhaps even more serious problems for the adolescents. They will suffer social stigma, especially from peers, and future employers may be reluctant to hire someone who has been in a "mental institution." Some view the adolescent's acting-out as symptomatic of the parents' relationship with the youth, considering that this relationship should be the focus of intervention. Many youths are admitted "voluntarily" to the hospital only because their parents volunteered them—perhaps as scapegoats. The admitting physician, who is also a hospital employee, is the person responsible for determining whether treatment is necessary.

The cost of hospitalization may range from $10,000–$20,000 per month, thereby making it the exclusive domain of the very affluent or well-insured. Insurance companies cover most of the cases, and since most prefer to cover in-patient rather than alternate forms of treatment, hospitalization becomes economically more attractive, according to Guttridge and Warren. There is a concern that adolescent wards have become profit-making ventures subsidized by the insurance companies; this has brought the mental health and insurance professions under criticism. Many allege that poor adolescents who are genuinely mentally ill but whose parents do not have the economic resources or insurance coverage are not receiving the specialized treatment that affluent youths with less severe problems receive, and are tracked instead into the public juvenile justice system.[45] Setting aside the potential economic conflict-of-interest issue for private hospitals and the double standard of treatment for the affluent and the poor, are the rights of hospitalized, affluent adolescents being abused?

Saul Brown, head of psychiatry at Cedars-Sinai Medical Center in Los Angeles, believes the issues of patients' rights is a misguided one and that giving adolescents the right to decide whether they need treatment abrogates a certain kind of parental reason. The United States Supreme Court ruled in 1979 that parents had the right to commit their children to a psychiatric facility if qualified medical professionals did the admitting. However, the ruling applied *only* to state hospitals. This situation has been referred to as a *legal twilight zone*. The California Supreme Court has asked the legislature to conduct an inquiry into psychiatric facilities being used by parents as "private prison hospitals for their incorrigible children."[46]

On the one hand, while some affluent white adolescents expressing behavioral disorder symptoms are being involuntarily committed by their parents to private psychiatric hospitals, risking the long-term psychosocio-political consequences of a psychiatric label, some poor adolescents—mostly minorities—who have not committed any crimes and are expressing behavioral disorder symptoms are being labeled criminal by law enforcement and tracked prematurely into the public juvenile justice system. They will have to suffer the long-term consequences of a criminal label. The U.S. Department of Justice has developed and funded the SHODI (Serious Habitual Offenders—Drug Involved) program in five cities: Oxnard and San José in California; Portsmouth, Virginia; Jacksonville, Florida; and Colorado Springs, Colorado. The purpose of the SHODI program, according to Oxnard Police Chief Robert Owens, is to (1) identify the most serious offenders, ages 13 to 17; (2) ensure they receive stiff sentences; and (3) keep the youths off the streets for the longest period of time. The criteria to be labeled a SHODI is three arrests in the last year and two previous arrests (three of the five arrests must be for felonies); or three arrests in the last year and seven previous arrests (eight of the ten arrests must be for petty theft, misdemeanor assault, narcotics, or weapons violations).[47]

The most controversial aspect of the program is that a juvenile who has never been convicted (on allegations found to be true and sustained in a juvenile court proceeding) of a crime could be classified by police as a habitual offender because criteria are based on arrests, *not convictions!* In Jacksonville, Florida, 22 percent of all youths classified as habitual offenders never appeared in court. With the SHODI label, probation officers are more likely to refer the case to court for prosecution. Judge McNally, former presiding judge of the Ventura County Juvenile Court (Oxnard area) disagrees with basing the SHODI criteria on arrests and believes some judges may overreact in a punitive manner when faced in court by a SHODI. The Public Defender's Office complained that Ventura County had a preoccupation with punishment and did not have adequate rehabilitation and treatment facilities. Approximately half the SHODI youths had drug problems—some chronic paint sniffers—but there were no drug treatment facilities for juveniles in the county. Eighty-three percent of the SHODI juveniles in Oxnard were either Hispanic or black. ACLU President Peggy Johnson believes basing the program on arrests rather than convictions results in more minorities being labeled SHODI, because minority youths are more likely to have contact with police.[48]

With reference to the affluent white and poor minority adolescents being prematurely labeled and tracked into the private psychiatric hospitals and public juvenile justice systems, the values social workers place on self-determination, right to nontreatment, opposing discrimination, and treatment abuse may require them to assume a position and take action. Those adolescents who are definitely a danger to themselves or others, who are severely psychiatrically disabled, or who chronically damage property or commit acts of violence, based on *convictions,* may indeed have to be institutionalized for their and/or society's protection. Social workers must support these detentions and make sure the youths receive proper treatment rather than punishment. This role would be consistent with *tertiary prevention.* However, for those youngsters whose acting-out is not harmful or who have numerous arrests that are related more to police deployment practices rather than predelinquent behavior of poor minority adolescents, social workers should assume a *secondary prevention* role as advocates encouraging intervention at the family and community level rather than harsher measures such as institutionalization. *Primary prevention* intervention involving educational and employment alternatives for at-risk families and youths might consist of evening workshops or seminars for affluent families concerning the stresses and pressures some affluent adolescents suffer; for example, the fear that they will not be able to achieve as well as their parents in a tight economy which places the cost of a home out of reach for many. For poor communities, primary prevention community education programs could focus on helping families learn to cope with the stresses of migration, urbanization, gangs, and drugs. Youths would be provided assistance in school or helped to obtain employment if they chose not to remain in school.

GANG VIOLENCE AND HOMICIDE PREVENTION

It was seen in Chapter 15 that the U.S. homicide rate was approximately 8 per 100,000, but that in a specific high-risk group—gangs in inner city communities—the rate can be in some areas as high as 600 per 100,000. A seventeen-year

Chicago study involving 12,872 homicides reported that more than half of Hispanic youth victims were killed in gang-related altercations.[49] In 1985, 10.5 percent of 2781 homicide victims in California were killed by gangs, and in Los Angeles 24 percent of 1037 homicides were gang-related.[50] Other large urban areas with gangs also have significant numbers of persons being assaulted and/ or killed by gangs. This violence exacts an extremely high toll in injuries, death, and emotional pain and adversely impacts the quality of life for thousands of poor residing in the inner cities.

The public health profession, with its focus on epidemiologic analysis and prevention, believes it can make a substantial contribution to solving problems of interpersonal violence. Former Surgeon General C. Everett Koop stated that "violence is every bit a public health issue for me and my successors in this century as smallpox, tuberculosis and syphilis were for my predecessors in the last two centuries."[51] The health professions are making their initial bold entry into this major problem area, following in the footsteps of criminology, sociology, and the criminal justice system. Psychiatry and psychology have been investigating the issue primarily from a biological (brain chemistry) and behavioral (modifying the behavior of *individuals*) perspective. Chapter 15 demonstrated how the social work profession, with its micro- to macro-level knowledge and skills base, was ideally suited to apply its techniques with individual gang members, gang groups, and the community to reduce urban gang violence and homicide. In addition to employing social work's traditional approaches in dealing with the problem, the present task is to devise ways in which prevention theory, with corresponding intervention models, can be applied.

It was stated earlier that *primary prevention* in a public health context involves averting the initial occurrence of a disease, defect, or injury. Primary prevention in homicide requires national efforts directed at social, cultural, educational, technological, and legal aspects of the macro environment, which facilitate the perpetuation of the country's extremely high homicide rate—indeed a tall order. A national strategy would involve public education on the seriousness and ramifications of violence, contributing factors, high-risk groups, and need for social policy as a physical health and mental health priority in the United States. The topic must become a higher priority in medical schools and schools of nursing, social work, and psychology. At the community level community self-help groups, social planning councils, and other civic groups need to work toward educating U.S. citizens about the causal relationship of alcohol, illegal drugs, firearms, and television violence to homicide and violence.[52] In theory these strategies, when directed at high-risk populations, are supposed to reduce those conditions that are seen as contributing to violence and homicide.

Secondary prevention in a public health context concerns the cessation or slowing down of the progression of a health problem. It involves the early detection and case-finding by which more serious morbidity may be decreased. Applying this concept to homicide, such case-finding requires the identification of persons showing early signs of behavioral and social problems that are related to increased risk for subsequent homicide victimization. Variables such as family violence, childhood and adolescent aggression, school violence, truancy or drop-ping out of school, and substance abuse are early indicators of many persons who later become perpetrators of violence and homicide. Secondary prevention in-tervention strategies with individuals already exhibiting these early symptoms interrupts a pattern that may later result in serious violence or homicide.[53]

Tertiary prevention pertains to those situations in which a health problem is already well established, but efforts can still be made to prevent further progress toward disability and death. In the case of homicide, the problems of greatest concern are those of interpersonal conflict and nonfatal violence, which appear to have a high risk for homicide. Aggravated assault is one early significant pre-dictor related to homicide.[54] In a study in Kansas, in 25 percent of the homicides either the victim or the perpetrator had previously been arrested for an assault or disturbance.[55] Victims of aggravated assault, such as spouses or gang members, are at especially high risk for becoming homicide cases.

Attempts have been made to develop program models aimed at preventing youth violence and homicide, although some of these programs are not specif-ically aimed at *gang* homicide prevention. These educational, court-, and com-munity-based programs seem to be functioning mainly at the primary (reducing conditions contributing to homicide) and secondary (identifying persons show-ing early signs of sociobehavioral problems) prevention levels. A few of these programs, as examples of prevention models, will be discussed.

Educational Prevention Models

The *Boston Youth Program* instituted in four Boston high schools had a curric-ulum on anger and violence. The ten-session curriculum provided: (1) infor-mation on adolescent violence and homicide; (2) the discussion of anger as a normal, potentially constructive emotion; (3) knowledge in developing alter-natives to fighting; (4) role-playing and videotapes; and (5) the fostering of non-violent values. Following the completion of the program an evaluation of a control group (no curriculum) and an experimental group (curriculum) revealed that there was a significant, positive change of attitude in the experimental group. The researchers cautioned, however, that further study had to delineate the actual impact the curriculum would have on actual *behavior,* and the longevity of the impact.[56] The Boston Youth Program was directed at minority students, but it was not indicated whether any of these students were gang members.

Peer Dynamics is another school-based program, sponsored by the Nebraska Commission on Drugs, which was designed to reduce the incidence of destructive risk-taking behaviors of juvenile delinquency and substance abuse among high school adolescents in fifty-six public schools. With the goal of developing im-proved self-esteem and better communication skills, the program trained and supervised students who participated in group interaction activities with other students. A follow-up evaluation found that in relationship to other students, program participants showed a noticeable drop in discipline referrals. The final evaluation noted that Peer Dynamics affected both sexes equally and that the greatest changes were noted in eighth, tenth, and eleventh grade students. No significant change in attitude toward themselves or others was reported in the control group.[57] Again, this was not a program designed specifically for gang youths, although some gang members may have been participants. The question remains, however, whether improved attitudes result in less violence and homicide.

A third school-based prevention program, functioning in the City of Paramount in Los Angeles County, is called the *Paramount Plan*. This was designed to be a "gang-prevention" model, and unlike the Boston Youth Program and Peer Dynamics, which target high school youths, it is an educational model directed at *all* fifth and sixth graders in the school district. The program consists of neighborhood parent meetings and an antigang curriculum taught to students in school for fifteen weeks. Prior to the program 50 percent of students were "undecided" about joining gangs. After the fifteen weeks, 90 percent said they would not join gangs.[58] No mention was made of the 10 percent of students who did not change their minds about joining gangs. In poor urban areas where there are gangs, it is only 3 to 5 percent of youths who become delinquents and/or join gangs. In other words, at least 95 percent of youths do not join gangs even without a gang-prevention program such as the Paramount Plan. Further research is needed to determine if those in the 10 percent who did *not* change their minds about joining gangs actually do, and second, whether they later become either perpetrators or victims of gang homicide. Perhaps one of the major research challenges is to be able to measure what was prevented.

Court- and Community-Based Programs

In Baltimore, Maryland, *Strike II* was developed as a court-based program linking juvenile justice with health care. Its "clients" were court adjudicated first-time offenders (secondary prevention) for violent crimes, assault, robbery, arson, and breaking and entering. Noninstitutionalized probationers were eligible for the program, which was a probation requirement. This multidisipline program employed paralegal staff, counselors, social workers, and psychiatrists. The juvenile probationers were involved in five programs: recreation, education, job readiness, and ongoing counseling and medical care as needed. These services were in *addition* to traditional probation supervision.

The recidivism rate for Strike II clients was only 7 percent, compared to 35 percent statewide and 65 percent for those leaving corrections institutions. The basic cost (excluding medical and job readiness services) was $100 per client.[59] The Strike II program dealt in large part with violent juveniles with a physical health/mental health, educational, employment, juvenile justice program, with impressive results. Although gang members were not mentioned specifically, it would appear that with a reduction in recidivism, these perpetrators would also have been at reduced risk for becoming violence/homicide victims.

Another community-based program, aimed specifically at gangs, was called *House of Umoja*. It was developed in Philadelphia in 1969 by two inner-city black parents whose son had joined a gang. His fellow gang members were invited to live with the family, following the model of an extended African family. In response to increased gang-related homicides in 1974 and 1975, the House of Umoja spearheaded a successful campaign to reduce gang violence by obtaining peace pledges from eighty youth gangs. From this experience evolved a community agency called Crisis Intervention Network that worked toward reducing gang violence through communication with concerned parties and organizational efforts.[60] This approach later was called the *Philadelphia Plan.*

In 1978 the state California Youth Authority reported its findings concerning its *Gang Violence Reduction Project* in East Los Angeles. The project's basic strategy was to: (1) promote peace among gangs through negotiation, and (2) provide positive activities for gang members. Directors maintain they reduced gang homicides in East Los Angeles 55 percent; from eleven homicides in seven months of one year, down to five homicides during a similar seven-month period the following year. The project researchers admitted that "any judgment that a relationship exists between the changes in a gang related homicide and violent-incident statistics and the activities of the Gang Violence Reduction Project must be based on inference."[61]

Another community-based peace-treaty program aimed at high-risk gang youth, patterned after the Philadelphia Plan, is the *Community Youth Gang Services Corporation* in Los Angeles. CYGS counselors in fourteen street teams were able to convince forty-four of 200 gangs they worked with to come to the table to develop a "peace treaty." During the period the peace agreement was in effect, from Thanksgiving of 1986 through the New Year's holidays of 1987, there was only *one* act of violence among the forty-four gangs. The peace-treaties model can "buy time" for all concerned, but if society does not respond with the needed resources (jobs, training, physical health–mental health services, education), peace treaties are very difficult to maintain. Obviously, *all* the above approaches are needed.

Gang Homicide Psychosocial Prevention Models

Continuing efforts have to be made in further refining homicide prevention models in order for them to correspond more closely with the specific type of homicide one wishes to prevent. There are different types of homicide that vary according to circumstances. Robbery, spousal, and gang homicide are all different and require different prevention strategies. If, for example, Asians are at extremely high risk for being robbed and murdered at 2 A.M. in Uptown, U.S.A., through a community education effort Asians would be informed about the high homicide risk in visiting Uptown at 2 A.M. Adhering to the warning could immediately reduce the number of Asian homicide victims.

In addition to attempting to get a "close fit" between the prevention model and the specific type of homicide, it is equally important that the high-risk person be clearly identified in order to maximize the impact of the prevention model. In the educational and community-based violence prevention models previously discussed, the focus of intervention appeared to be more on the perpetrator or the "pre-perpetrator" (the person showing early behavioral signs indicating he or she *might* become a perpetrator) who was at high risk for committing a violent act. In theory all potential victims in an *unspecified* population are spared victimization when the perpetrator ceases to be violent. Furthermore, there did not seem to be specific prevention programmatic strategies focusing on the violence *victim* or the person most likely to become a victim. What seems to be needed is a guideline or framework that assists in the identification of high-risk gang members.

With California as an example, Table 21–1 represents a "general to specific" profile framework for identifying and "zeroing in" on the high-risk gang members who will be the target population for homicide prevention.

For our purposes, we will attempt to develop a hospital-based and community-based youth gang psychosocial homicide prevention model in which social workers play a key intervention role. The focus of these prevention models will be on the gang member who actually becomes a violence or homicide victim of a gang and goes or is taken to the hospital. In Table 21–1 these victims would be gang members found in items 2b and 2c. In this respect the prevention models are largely tertiary in nature. However, they become primary prevention models when intervention strategies are aimed at younger children and latency-age siblings of the victim who are not yet gang members. By preventing children in high-risk families from becoming future gang members, they may significantly reduce the likelihood of the children being killed, since gang members are sixty times more likely to be killed than persons in the general population (600/100,000 versus 10/100,000).

Hospital-Based Model.   Health professionals in community clinics and hospitals are actually in the "trenches," dealing with thousands of violence and homicide casualties related to gang violence. These professionals are usually the first to touch these bodies, and in medical settings they function in a tertiary prevention role, literally trying to control bleeding and save lives. Wounded gang victims of gang violence are in reality a "captive audience," which creates an excellent intervention opportunity for secondary prevention.

Through the physician, social worker, nurse, or other health practitioners on the hospital emergency room team inquiring *how* the victim was injured (which may be confirmed by police, family members, or interested parties), professionals could ascertain if the incident was gang-related. Through in-service staff training concerning gangs and their culture, health staff would be able to determine whether the victim was a gang member. Specifically, dress codes, mannerisms, graffiti, language, tattoos, and other gang symbols could help establish or rule out the gang identity of the victim. Police, family members, peers, and/or witnesses could also be good sources for gang identity confirmation.

If the injuries were caused by gang members and the victim is a gang member, a designated health team member (the social worker) would be responsible for referring the matter to the hospital's SCAN Team. "SCAN Team" refers to Sus-

TABLE 21–1   *Area and Demographic Characteristics Related to Homicide Risk*

I. United States	One of the most violent countries in the world, ranked #5 out of 41 countries
II. California	Along with Southern states, ranks among the most violent states
III. Los Angeles	Among the more violent cities in the United States
IV. Inner City (L.A.)	The poorest areas, often the scene of most violent crime
A. Minority Groups	Overrepresented among the disadvantaged, poor, and those residing in the inner city
1. Profile of Perpetrators and Victims	
a. Males	4 to 5 times more likely than females to be killed
b. Age	15–25 age category at highest risk
c. Substance Abuse	Found in 50 to 66 percent of cases
d. Low Education	50 percent school drop-out rate not uncommon
e. Low Income	High unemployment, many living in poverty
2. Gangs	Quite prevalent in inner city and a product of social disorganization, classism, and racism
a. Minor Assaults	Gang members are at high risk for being assaulted
b. Aggravated Assaults	Gang members are at high risk for being victims of aggravated assault; occurs 20 to 35 times more often than homicide
c. Homicide	Gang members are at high risk for becoming homicide victims, rate being 600 per 100,000 in the 50,000 gang-member population

Sources: M. L. Rosenberg and J. A. Mercy, "Homicide: Epidemiologic Analysis at the National Level," *Bulletin of the New York Academy of Medicine* 62 (June 1986): 382; H. M. Rose, "Can We Substantially Lower Homicide Risk in the Nation's Larger Black Communities?," *Report of the Secretary's Task Force on Black and Minority Health* vol. 5 (Washington, D.C.: U.S. Department of Health and Human Services, January 1986); I. A. Spergel, "Violent Gangs in Chicago: In Search of Social Policy," *Social Service Review* 58 (June 1984): 201–202; A. Morales, "Hispanic Gang Violence and Homicide," Paper presented to the Research Conference on Violence and Homicide in Hispanic Communities, Los Angeles, September 14–15, 1987, p. 13.

pected Child Abuse and Neglect, or in some hospitals, Supporting Child Adult Network.[62] SCAN Teams, which are found in many hospitals, are composed of multidisciplinary health staff in which at least one member is a social worker. SCAN Teams were originally developed to investigate suspected child sexual or physical abuse or neglect cases coming to their attention in medical settings. In cases of suspected child abuse, for the protection of the child, SCAN Teams are required to take immediate action by involving law enforcement and the child-welfare department.

Our gang-homicide prevention model would require that gang violence victims also become a SCAN Team intervention priority. However, one additional social worker on the SCAN Team would be a gang "specialist" and have primary treatment-coordinating responsibility with the gang victim, his or her family, and the community.

Although not intended, the emergency room provides access to a high-risk population (victims and families) that is often too embarrassed, frightened, or reluctant to seek assistance from traditional social work agencies. The anonymity of a large, busy, impersonal hospital can be less threatening.[63] Additionally, medical crises may make some persons psychologically vulnerable, hence more amenable to change during the crisis period.

In working with gang members who have been seriously injured as the result of gang assault, the author has found that often this is when their psychological defenses are down, as they are suffering adjustment disorder or post-traumatic stress disorder symptoms (PTSD). In the acute stage of PTSD symptoms, victims may have recurrent, intrusive distressing recollections of the event, including nightmares, flashbacks, intense stress at exposure to events resembling the traumatic event, persistent avoidance of stimuli associated with the event, sleeping problems, hypervigilance, anxiety, and fear. They are sometimes reluctant to leave the home and even become fearful of their own friends in gang "uniform."

During this acute stage, which may last about six months, they are quite motivated to abandon "gang banging" (gang fighting). If the social worker is not the primary therapist, arrangements should be made for the youngster to receive prompt treatment for PTSD while hospitalized, as untreated PTSD may become chronic and last for years. It is at this point that the social worker can also obtain needed employment, educational, recreational, or training resources for the vulnerable gang member. The parents may also be emotionally vulnerable, having just gone through an experience in which they almost lost their son. They may be more willing to accept services for themselves if needed, and/or for younger siblings who might be showing some early behavioral signs of problems (deteriorating school performance, truancy, aggressiveness). Helping the family and young siblings is a primary prevention role, as these efforts may prevent future gang members (perpetrators or victims) from developing in this at-risk family.

There may also be situations in which the gang member arrives deceased at the hospital, or dies during or after surgery. These cases would still be referred to the SCAN Team social worker for service. The focus of help would be—with the family's permission—helping the parents and children deal with grief and other assistance they made need in burying their loved one. If there are adolescent gang members in the family, they may be quite angry and want to get even for their brother's or sister's death. If not already involved, the social worker would call on community gang group agencies to assist in reducing further conflict. If

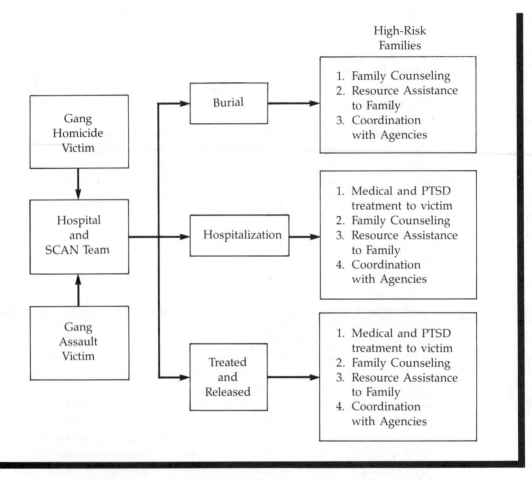

FIGURE 21–1   *Gang Homicide Psychosocial Prevention Model*

there are younger siblings in the family, an assessment would be made of their needs and efforts made to mobilize resources to meet these needs. These intervention strategies would have the objective of preventing future homicides in a high-risk family.

The preceding gang homicide prevention model operating from a medical-based agency is presented to illustrate how social work may be able to have intervention impact on a very serious problem shortening the life of many poor, inner-city youths. Figure 21–1 illustrates the various intervention strategies of the hospital-based gang homicide intervention model. Other models can be developed, such as a community agency–based model, described in the following paragraphs.

Community Agency–Based Model.   Other gang homicide prevention models can be developed, such as one that would be inner-city community agency–based, which the author is currently developing and implementing. The agency, Challengers Boys and Girls Club, founded in 1968, is located in a poor, predominantly Afro-American area in south-central Los Angeles. Within a three-mile radius of the agency are approximately 22,000 youths in a population of 379,000 persons, with 43 percent of the households headed by 15,000 single mothers over sixteen years of age with children up to eighteen years of age. This community has exceptionally high rates of school drop-outs (56% of seventeen-year-old Afro-American youths being functionally illiterate), AIDS, diseases of the heart, sexually communicated diseases, and homicide. Neighborhood homicide rates at 95 per 100,000 are almost twelve times the national rate, four times the Los Angeles rate, and at 600/100,000 *in* the neighborhood's gang population.

The agency, with 2100 enrolled families, has an average daily attendance of 400 boys and girls (ages 6 to 17) during the summer months, 200 during the rest of the year. Program services, in addition to athletic and recreational services, include tutoring, classes in basic math, reading comprehension and computers, photography, woodshop, job application training, a new basic dental and health examination program, and mental health crisis intervention.[64]

The mental health crisis intervention program, staffed by the author as a mental health consultant and full-time social worker, is available to those member families who experience a sudden, severe crisis such as the premature death of a family member brought on by an accident, suicide, or homicide. These tragic events are known to leave a spouse or parent emotionally immobilized for months, and at times even years. The death of a child results in a more severe grief reaction for a parent than that of any other family member.[65] The surviving siblings' loss may be double that of the surviving parent because they have lost not only an immediate family member but also the grieving parent(s) who is temporarily emotionally unavailable to them. During this time, depending on their prior adjustment, age, and emotional strength, these children are at high risk for emotional, educational, and behavioral problems. Prompt intervention (assessment, counseling, and possible referral in acute cases) may lessen and *prevent* a child from having more serious difficulties and problems of adjustment. In specific cases where the sibling was a gang member and the victim of a gang homicide, younger adolescent or pre-adolescent siblings are at especially high risk for becoming either future victims or perpetrators of gang violence and homicide.

Although this inner-city, agency-based gang-homicide psychosocial prevention model is only in the early months of development, two cases have already surfaced in the community that warrant comment. In one case, a fourteen-year-old Challengers member was the victim of a "drive-by" shooting outside his home by a gang group. The youth was not a gang member, yet met the general, stereotypic profile of a gang member held by many police and gang members; that is, he was a minority male adolescent residing in the poor, inner-city neighborhood. A bullet to his brain resulted in four months' hospitalization and permanent neurological impairments, including dependence on a wheelchair. Ongoing supportive visits were made with the youngster at the hospital, along with conversations with medical and social service staff, and his guardian aunt. (His mother had passed away three years previously due to illness, and his father was in a correctional facility.)

On release, efforts will be made to reintegrate the youngster into the Challengers program components, individual supportive counseling as needed, and assistance in applying for victim's assistance and Social Security benefits. The victim did not have younger or adolescent siblings, hence other family members were not at risk for gang homicide as future victims or perpetrators.

The second case concerned a ten-year-old suicidal boy, whose father had been killed by a robber twelve months previously, and his paternal uncle, three months before. The boy was experiencing school behavioral problems, sleep disturbance, and some somatic complaints, including vomiting. The mother had already taken the boy to a child guidance-counseling program and was now enrolling the youngster in the Challengers recreational program. The agency will make available to the mother an adult supportive counseling group led by the mental health consultant and social worker for family members who have lost a loved one due to a sudden, premature death. The mother herself will be seen individually until there are a sufficient number of affected families to begin a group. Such groups will also be established specifically for children and adolescents in the very near future. Once these programs are in place for the Challengers member families, an outreach effort will be made with law enforcement and other community agencies, hospitals, and churches, to identify high-risk families with children who had a child who was a gang member and was killed as the result of gang violence. These families, in their psychological state of vulnerability, will also be extended an invitation to become part of the Challengers program. As they begin to participate in the program and receive a host of social, recreational, educational, dental, health, and mental health services, it is anticipated that the cycle of gang violence and trauma, with its accompanying sequelae of psychosocial problems, will be lessened or stopped.

SOCIAL WORK IN INDUSTRY: PREVENTION IMPLICATIONS

It is ironic that as former president Reagan's fiscal policies drove unemployment to 9.4 percent in April, 1982, the highest since the 9.9 percent recorded in 1941, social workers began to find employment in business and industry.[66] The provision of social services in the business and industrial setting is a new practice arena for social work. This new practice turf is boundless, considering the fact that there are at least 100 million workers in the United States. When family members are included, workers constitute a massive target population. Business and industry organizations could hire *every* graduating social worker and hardly dent their employee rolls.[67]

A brief look at the history of social work's involvement with industry shows social worker Jane Addams, founder of Hull House, helping clothing workers in a strike in 1910 against Hart, Schaffner, and Marx in Chicago. During the 1930s some social workers, as union members, were active supporters of John L. Lewis's Congress of Industrial Organizations (CIO). Three social workers even managed to provide social services in the union halls of the National Maritime Union in New York. In the 1940s during the World War II, federal funds made it possible to expand the number of social workers in industry. Large numbers of women and minorities were being hired, and federal contracts provided services for these inexperienced workers. Following the war, however, there was a federal cutback in these services, since the primary interest was in the rehabilitation of the psychiatrically disabled veteran. Although there were a few surviving social work practitioners of industrial social work after the 1940s, it was not until the 1960s and 1970s that the profession and schools of social work began to take a more serious look at industry and business as an area of social work practice.[68]

The early 1960s saw the development of the Industrial Social Welfare Center at Columbia University's School of Social Work, which provided field placement opportunities for students in union settings. Industrial social work student placements were also offered at Boston College, Wayne State, and Hunter College School of Social Work in the late 1960s. In 1976 the Council on Social Work Education and the NASW introduced a nationwide project to examine business and industry as a potential area of social work practice intervention. Part of this effort resulted in the 1979 publication of *Labor and Industrial Settings: Sites for Social Work Practice,* by the Council on Social Work Education.[69] Between 1976 and 1979 social work schools having a business/industry social work practice concentration grew from four to fourteen.[70] These programs, both in schools and industry, are expanding rapidly and providing more careers for social workers in the world of business.

In general, employee benefit programs fall into three areas: (1) extra pay for time worked (overtime and work on holidays); (2) pay for time not worked (sick leave, vacations, and jury duty); and (3) payments for health, security, and welfare. Social work services provided to business and industry are within the framework of the third category.[71] There are five ways in which social services may be sponsored in industry:

1. Sponsorship by management in companies with or without a union.
2. Sponsorship by the union.
3. Sponsorship by both management and labor, with management employing social workers, and dual monitoring responsibility by management and labor.
4. Private consultantship by social worker under contract to union or management to provide services to workers and/or the organization.
5. Sponsorship by a community mental health center or family service agency having a specific contractual arrangement with the company.[72]

Social work intervention in the industrial setting may be on a micro and/or macro level. Micro-level practice finds the social worker providing treatment to the client, his or her family, employer, union representative, and coworkers. The focus is helping employees with problems related to work, self, and others. Work-related problems may include job performance, job dissatisfaction, absenteeism, and conflict with a supervisor or coworkers. Problems of self may relate to anxiety, depression, phobia, mental disturbance, and alcohol and drug abuse. Problems related to others may involve marital, parent–child, or family conflict.[73]

Macro-level social work practice in business and industry involves organizational intervention. Here the social worker provides individual and group consultation to supervisors and managers at all levels regarding human behavior. The focus is on the organization. For example, worker dissatisfaction may be the result of the way work activities are organized. Intervention, therefore, might take the form of proposing a new job design to replace boring, tedious, assembly-line work. One of the major goals of macro-level intervention is to help management and employees achieve a common understanding, make decisions together, share and enjoy the fruits of their labor, and feel they have a common destiny.[74] At present the majority of social workers in business and industry are involved in micro-level intervention activities. These practitioners report that casework is the most useful component in industrial social work.[75]

Balgopal would like to see an expanded role for clinical social workers in occupational settings. For example, Balgopal sees the social worker seeking to ameliorate hazardous environments through monitoring of Occupational Safety and Health Act compliance, lobbying for safety legislation, and persuading management to change work procedures that may threaten the physical and emotional well-being of employees.[76]

Considering the expansion of industrial social work courses in schools of social work and the increasing number of social work practitioners entering the business and industrial arena, one can definitely state that industrial social work will continue to be a trend for social work through the 1990s. Giving impetus to this trend is taxpayer revolt legislation, such as California's Proposition 13, in various states, Reagan's new federalism policies, and the related economic recession that is causing some social workers to lose their employment. Social workers, therefore, will be forced to seek new opportunities and territories of practice, such as the business and industry field.

This new opportunity and practice territory, however, presents several dilemmas for social work. Those favoring this new field argue that the working class is a population largely neglected by social services and that by providing services on the work site the profession begins to meet this need. Wherever there are people there is potential need.

Others argue that the values of social work and industry are in conflict. Bakalinsky states that what binds the social work profession

> ... is a humanistic philosophy that stresses the inherent dignity and worth of people. Concern for the well-being of people, individually and collectively, historically has been social work's trademark. Industry, on the other hand, places its primary value on production and profits. Its people are viewed as a commodity

having only instrumental value for the industry's central purpose. Detrimental conditions within industry are rarely considered in terms of the human cost involved. Or, more accurately, stressful and hazardous conditions may be considered, but their eradication is determined by financial rather than human cost.[77]

Social workers in business and industry inevitably face the risk of cooptation by rich and powerful representatives of the world of work. On the other hand, Kurzman and Akabas maintain the converse is equally likely. These authors believe social work in industry "holds promise of influencing not only the quality of work life, but the quality of life for workers and for *all* Americans."[78] In *theory* this may be true, and it parallels the "trickle-down" economic theory; that is, if government provides business with sufficient economic advantages, it will flourish, profit, expand, hire more people, and generally contribute to the economic well-being of the community and nation. So far the trickle-down economic theory apparently has not worked, considering the duration of poverty and the increasing and massive number of poor people in the Nation. In view of the current small number of social workers in industry, even if they could be increased a thousandfold, it would appear to be quite a task for them to influence the quality of life for *all* people in the United States.

Another issue for social work as it enters the field of business and industry is the question of whether it wishes to deploy its critical available work force to a more affluent target population. In other words, the new clients of industry social workers will have (according to new census data) a median annual income of approximately $35,953, compared to approximately $12,000 for the poor. Services therefore would be directed at the *middle class* rather than the lower class. Some social workers entering private practice have attempted to deal with this dilemma by working part-time in a public agency with low socioeconomic clients, and part-time with middle-class clients. Some, on the other hand, have chosen a full-time private practice and have accepted some low-fee clients. Social work practitioners in business and industry will not have this much flexibility available to them if they are employed full-time in an industrial setting. Perhaps a compromise is that social workers not enter the business and industry arena directly but provide services through existing resources such as family service agencies, community mental health centers, and private practice. These value dilemmas provide a challenge for the social work profession; given the new federalism policies that are resulting in a reduction of social work jobs, industry may offer social workers a temporary employment opportunity. Social work will survive; and when government once again makes a vigorous commitment to help the poor, social workers will be ready to redirect their energies to this population.

In the meantime, industry offers social work a unique opportunity for primary, secondary, and tertiary prevention. Early detection and prompt treatment of employee problems as a secondary intervention measure may prevent some workers from becoming more serious casualties, losing their jobs, and ending up on welfare rolls. Those who have developed serious problems such as chronic or acute substance addiction, for example, will require tertiary prevention intervention, that is, medical and psychosocial rehabilitation at a clinic or hospital facility. Primary prevention strategies in the workplace may take several forms. Educational programs and workshops for at-risk employees of the organization concerning topics such as learning about and coping with job-related stress, family and marital stress, substance abuse, and anxiety and depression, may be of benefit to many. If there are going to be large-scale layoffs, social workers could develop plans with management for new job training and placement at other companies as a means of softening the devastating emotional impact on employees and families often brought on by abrupt termination.

ADVOCACY, EMPOWERMENT, AND PREVENTION

Webster's Third New International Dictionary defines *advocate* (the noun) as "one that pleads the case of another" or "one that argues for, defends, maintains, or recommends a cause or a proposal." Briar defines the social worker advocate as one who is

> ... his clients' supporter, his advisor, his champion, and if need be, his representative in his dealings with the court, the police, the social agency, and other organizations that affect his well-being.[79]

On the other hand, Brager sees the social worker advocate as one who

> ... identifies with the plight of the disadvantaged. He sees as his primary responsibility the tough-minded and partisan representation of their interests, and this supersedes his fealty to others. This role inevitably requires that the practitioner function as a political tactician.[80]

Briar's concept represents advocacy on behalf of an *individual,* whereas Brager's concept represents advocacy on behalf of a group or *class* of people. The latter concept is similar to the role social workers would perform in *class action social work,* discussed later in this chapter.

Gilbert and Specht report that advocacy as a social work role (social change, versus psychological change) has presented a dilemma for generations of social workers. Each generation redefines this issue in its own terms. For example, in 1909 Richmond defined the issue in terms of the "wholesale" versus the "retail" method of social reform. Lee approached it in 1929 as "cause" versus "function," and in 1949 Pray perceived it as "workmanship" versus "statesmanship." In 1962 Chambers conceptualized the matter in terms of "prophets" versus "priests," and in 1963 Schwartz analyzed this conflict in terms of providing a service as opposed to participating in a movement.[81] In 1977, in a special issue of the journal *Social Work* on conceptual frameworks for practice, Morales perceived the issue differently. He saw social workers as persons armed with appropriate knowledge and skills that enabled them to do clinical work in poor communities as well as to intervene via social action and advocacy in larger community systems.[82]

The NASW has taken a clear position regarding the social worker as advocate. Its Ad Hoc Committee on Advocacy voiced the profession's commitment to advocacy as follows:

> The obligation of social workers to become advocates flows directly from the social worker's Code of Ethics. Therefore, why should it be difficult for a profession that is "based on humanitarian-democratic ideals" and "dedicated to service for the welfare of mankind" to act on behalf of those whose human rights are in jeopardy?[83]

The committee highlighted three dilemmas concerning the advocacy role in social work. First, in promoting a particular client's interests, the social worker may be injuring other aggrieved persons with an equally just claim. Gilbert and Specht suggest that a hard-and-fast rule should be followed, which is encompassed in the concept *primum non nocere,* a medical aphorism meaning "first of all, do no harm."[84] This dictum no doubt would apply to not harming other clients, but effective advocacy *is* going to cause harm to someone when any redistribution of power or resources is accomplished. Because of *Serrano* v. *Priest,* for example, poor children will ultimately benefit through increased educational resources resulting from a more equitable tax structure, and affluent children will be "hurt" as their privileges are eroded. This will be discussed further in *class action social work.*

The second dilemma mentioned by the committee involves conflict between two types of advocacy—on behalf of client or class. Because there are no hard-and-fast rules to govern these situations, social work advocates will have to be guided by ethical commitments and professional judgment.

The third dilemma presented by the committee concerns the choice between direct intercession by the worker and mobilization of clients on their own behalf.[85] Some would argue that it is a disservice to clients when social workers participate in advocacy on the clients' behalf, because it only makes them more dependent. There are cases for which this argument might be true, but advocacy on behalf of some powerless special populations, such as children or mentally ill jail inmates, might be appropriate. Where it is not appropriate, however, social workers can help clients help themselves through the application of concepts such as *empowerment.*

A new trend evolving in social work pertains to the concept of client empowerment. Solomon defines *empowerment* as

> ... a process whereby persons who belong to a stigmatized social category throughout their lives can be assisted to develop and increase skills in the exercise of interpersonal influence and the performance of valued social roles. Power is an interpersonal phenomenon; if it is not interpersonal it probably should be defined as "strength." However, the two concepts—power and strength—are so tightly interrelated that they are often used interchangeably.[86]

According to Solomon, empowerment, as a social work practice goal in working with black clients or other persons living in oppressed communities, implies the client's perception of his or her intrinsic and extrinsic value and the client's motivation to use every personal resource and skill, as well as those of any other person that can be commanded, in the effort to achieve self-determined goals. Solomon attempts to develop a conviction in the client that there are many pathways to goal attainment and that failure is always possible, but the more effort one makes the more probable success must be.[87]

Solomon suggests three practitioner roles that hold promise for reducing a client's sense of powerlessness and leading to empowerment: the resource consultant role, the sensitizer role, and the teacher/trainer role. The resource consultant role finds the practitioner linking clients with resources in a manner that enhances the clients' self-esteem and problem-solving capacities. Minahan and Pincus identify five specific practitioner tasks for accomplishing this.[88] In the sensitizer role the practitioner incorporates all the role behaviors that are designed to assist the client to gain the self-knowledge necessary for him or her to solve the presenting problem or problems. The teacher/trainer role, according to Solomon's conceptualization, finds the practitioner as manager of a learning process in which the principal aim is the completion of certain tasks or the resolution of problems related to social living.[89]

A *voluntary* relationship seems to be implied in Solomon's conceptualization when she speaks of the practitioner assisting the client gain self-knowledge to solve a problem or problems. The practitioner does not appear to be working from a social control perspective in which the presenting problem is defined by someone other than the client. Such "helping" transactions might make *involuntary* clients feel powerless.

According to O'Connell, advocacy and empowerment are related from the standpoint that through effective advocacy, power is secured and used. He adds that it is also natural that the most important aspect of effective advocacy is now being described as empowerment.[90] The movement toward empowerment—to use and transfer power so that the groups in need of services gain their own political and economic power enabling them to represent themselves effectively—in the final analysis is most important to society, since society benefits when *all* its members can contribute to the best of their ability.

In prevention theory a social worker helping *clients* through advocacy and empowerment concepts would seem to be using a secondary prevention strategy, since the target population is already identified as persons with problems. The social worker has a significant role and performs specific key tasks in advocacy and empowerment efforts with the client. In applying advocacy and empowerment concepts toward primary prevention goals, however, the social worker's role is not central, as it is in working with client populations. Rather, the role is multiple since the at-risk target population is comprised largely of nonclients or "normal" persons. The focus must be on strengths foremost in the target population, as opposed to problems, weaknesses, and inadequacies.[91]

One of the essential tasks of the social worker in working with an at-risk population toward primary prevention will be to network. *Network* may be defined as the process of developing multiple interconnections and chain reactions among support systems.[92] There are four levels of networking approaches: (1) personal networking, (2) networking for mutual aid and self-help, (3) human service organization networking, and (4) networking within communities for community empowerment.[93] The last approach will be highlighted, as it has primary prevention goals.

The community empowerment model and process has several goals. The first is to create community awareness of neighborhood strengths and needs, with emphasis on strengths as perceived by the target population. The second goal is to strengthen neighborhood helping networks by developing linkages among natural helpers in the community, among helpers and neighborhood leaders, and among neighborhood residents themselves. A third goal is to strengthen the professional helping networks by organizing a professional advisory committee in the target population area to advise this community empowerment-directed process. Fourth, linkages are formed between the lay and professional helping networks. The fifth goal is to form linkages between the lay and professional helping networks and the macro system. In a mental health primary prevention context, mental health professionals would help the target population put together a data base of information regarding federal, state, county, and local mental health and human services plans, or the macro system. The sixth and final goal would be to institutionalize the networking process, thereby creating a new mental health constituency, integrated into but not assimilated or taken over by the larger, bureaucratic human services system. Through such a networking process leading to community empowerment and an improvement in the quality of life, those problem areas that the professional system traditionally ends by treating (secondary and tertiary prevention) rather than preventing, the at-risk population may be spared unnecessary pain, stress, and anguish.[94]

CLASS ACTION SOCIAL WORK AND PREVENTION

The enormous mission of social work is to enhance the quality of life for all persons. Some of the injustices and obstacles that damage the quality of life are poverty, racism, sexism, and drug abuse; there are many more.[95] Social work's impact on these problems is sometimes limited by the clinical model, by inappropriate interventive strategies, and by the fact that it becomes too time-consuming and inefficient to try to help people on a case-by-base basis. On other occasions a referred client with a "problem" may not really have a problem. The problem may be in the referral system.

For example, a school may refer a problem student to a social worker to help him or her adjust to the requirements of the school system. The school system, however, may have serious defects that are the primary cause of the student's problem. The goal of the social worker should then be to help tailor the school system to meet the educational needs of the student. The student in this situation may represent a *class* of people, that is, a number of students in a similar predicament. Rather than the social worker working individually with each student to document the deficiencies in the school system, one student can represent all students in a *class action* suit to improve conditions in the school. Class action is a legal concept that has promising implications for social work. Closer working relationships will have to be cultivated with the legal profession to enable lawyers to conceptualize broad social work concerns and to translate these into legal class action suits. Such an approach can be called *class action social work.* Victories in the courts could provide relief for thousands of poor people.

There is precedent for an organized body of social workers and lawyers, with the potential for broader collaborative impact through class action suits on behalf of the poor. Recognition of matters of natural interconnection and mutual interest between lawyers and social workers led in 1962 to the creation of the National Conference of Lawyers and Social Workers, a joint committee composed of sixteen members, eight appointed from each parent organization. The Conference met twice a year.[96] In 1967 the Conference developed cooperative goals for the two professions to work toward in serving the needy. Some of these goals included:

1. Identification of needs requiring their individual or joint professional competencies.
2. Resolution of situations that involve both social and legal problems—including recognizing and reconciling respective professional orientations, especially with regard to the adversary role.
3. The development of machinery and procedures for effective referral relationships.[97]

The nine papers in *Law and Social Work,* one of the Conference's publications, envisioned a rather narrow role for social workers working with lawyers, following the traditional clinical, case-by-case model. For example, social workers defined their function as providing "expertise in psychosocial diagnosis including evaluation of the *individual's* potential for social functioning."[98] The collaborative potential of class action suits to help the poor on a broad scale is not mentioned in this 1973 document. Let it again be emphasized that the central theme of the Conference—"lawyers and social workers, as close collaborators in situations involving both social and legal problems, should seek to utilize to the full the resources of each profession to help the poor"—provides the foundation for social work to have a greater impact on social reform.

In some states social workers have already made pioneering efforts to enter the legal arena. In California, for example, the Greater California Chapter of the NASW presented an award to John Serrano, a social worker, for his actions as a concerned citizen in the widely publicized *Serrano* v. *Priest* case, which argued that the quality of a child's education should not be dependent on the wealth of a school district.[99] The California Supreme Court, in this class action suit filed by the Western Center on Law and Poverty, Inc., ruled 6 to 1 that the California public educational finance scheme, which relies heavily on local property taxes, violated the equal protection clause of the Fourteenth Amendment to the U.S.

Constitution. The court held that the financing system invidiously discriminated against the poor. The court also asserted that the right to a public education was a fundamental interest that could not be dependent on wealth, and it therefore applied the strict equal-protection standard. Finding no compelling state interest advanced by the discriminatory system, the court held it unconstitutional.[100]

The significance of the *Serrano* v. *Priest* decision transcends California boundaries because all states except Hawaii use similar educational finance systems. Wealthier districts are favored, to the detriment of poorer school districts. A direct relationship exists between the number of dollars spent per child and the quality of education available to that child. In *Serrano* v. *Priest* it was discovered that poor communities were paying two to three times as much school tax per $100 of assessed valuation as were wealthy communities, yet wealthy communities received two to three times as many educational dollars per child from the state as did the poorer communities.[101]

In *Serrano* v. *Priest* the court's policy considerations focused on the pervasive influence of education on individual development and capacity within modern society, and on education's essential role in the maintenance of free enterprise democracy. It was considered that the combination of these factors sufficiently distinguished education from other governmental services for it to merit recognition as a fundamental interest.[102] No court had previously placed education within the framework of interests meriting strict equal-protection scrutiny, and this decision represents the first time any type of governmental service has been held to involve fundamental interests.[103]

Considering the *Serrano* precedent, might not the areas of welfare, health, and mental health services also represent a set of circumstances as unique and compelling as education? A right to public education may not be maximally enjoyed if a child is poorly housed, impoverished, malnourished, and in need of physical and mental health care. *Serrano* v. *Priest,* as a social work class action concept, has the potential to be the cutting edge of social reform in a wide range of governmental services, including several in which social workers already have knowledge and experience. In view of the regressive social and economic policies of the last and current administrations, which even threaten legal services for the poor from time to time, the opportunity for class action collaboration between law and social work as a significant tool of intervention is somewhat constrained. However, the class action social work concept still holds promise, and its application is presently being tested by one of the authors in the courts as a mental health primary prevention activity.

Class action is a legal procedural device for resolving issues in court affecting many people. Those persons actually before the court represent the unnamed members of the class in a single proceeding in equity, thereby avoiding multiple case-by-case actions. *Class action social work* is a social work/legal profession collaborative litigation activity involving social work concerns, with the goal of obtaining a favorable court ruling that will benefit the social welfare of a group of socioeconomically disadvantaged persons. Class action social work in a mental health primary prevention context finds social workers and attorneys pursuing a court ruling that will have a positive psychosocial impact on a disadvantaged class of people who, prior to the ruling were at risk in developing psychological or psychiatric disorders or symptoms. Among the requirements needed to accomplish the primary prevention goals are—to borrow from public health terminology—a small sample of "infected" organisms, an identification of the suspected toxic agent, and a laboratory procedural test to show whether the toxic agent caused the infection in the organism. Translating this into class action mental health primary prevention terms in an actual case (*Nicacio* v. *United States INS*), the "infected organisms" were thirteen Hispanic plaintiffs (the injured, complaining parties) who were exhibiting psychiatric symptoms, allegedly caused by stressful interrogations conducted by patrol officers of the United States Immigration and Naturalization Service (INS). The courtroom becomes the laboratory in which the suspected toxic evidence (behavior of the INS officers) is analyzed as to potential harm. If found to be harmful, the court can issue an order terminating the toxic behavior of the INS, which then prevents psychosocial harm (psychiatric symptoms) in a specific at-risk population (millions of Hispanics residing in the Southwestern states or the State of Washington area, depending on court boundary definitions).

In *Nicacio* v. *United States INS,* the Hispanic plaintiffs brought suit contending that: (1) the border patrol agents of the INS were conducting roving motor vehicle stops in search of "illegal aliens" on the roadways of the State of Washington that were in violation of Fourth Amendment rights to be free from unreasonable searches and seizures, (2) that the actions of INS officials were unlawful, and (3) that the plaintiffs were entitled to money damages for humiliation, embarrassment, and mental anguish suffered as a result of a violation of their Fourth Amendment rights.[104] The facts of the case were that: (1) all plaintiffs were of Mexican descent and were either born in the United States, U.S. citizens, or permanent resident aliens who resided in the Yakima Valley area of the State of Washington; (2) the plaintiff class was defined by the court as "all persons of Mexican, Latin, or Hispanic appearance who have been, are, or will be traveling by motor vehicle on the highways of the State of Washington"; (3) at the time litigation was initiated, INS agents were regularly conducting roving patrol motor vehicle stops, detentions, and interrogations in the Yakima Valley area; (4) many of the stops were based solely on Hispanic appearance, or the agents' subjective feelings or intuition, or the suspected "illegal aliens'" innocuous behavior or appearance, traits; and (5) persons stopped were required in most cases to provide identification or documentation of legal presence in the United States.[105]

In attempting to document the amount of humiliation, embarrassment, and mental anguish suffered by the plaintiffs as a result of their contact with INS officers, plaintiffs' attorneys contacted one of the authors as an expert witness to conduct a mental health evaluation of all the plaintiffs. Having been sworn in by the court and qualified and accepted as an expert witness, the author rendered a DSM-III diagnosis of each plaintiff. The findings were that: (1) not one of the thirteen plaintiffs had ever been hospitalized or treated on an out-patient basis for a mental health problem, (2) eleven of the plaintiffs suffered adjustment disorder symptoms, either with depressed mood, anxious mood, or with mixed emotional features, (3) one plaintiff suffered acute post-traumatic stress disorder symptoms, and (4) one plaintiff was symptom-free.

The findings of the court were that: (1) the INS border patrol practices were unlawful, (2) plaintiffs and class action members were entitled to a declaratory judgment covering future conduct of INS officers in stopping vehicles on public highways, and (3) plaintiffs were *not* entitled to recover money damages for their suffering, since plaintiffs were unable to specifically identify the officers.[106] The favorable court ruling affected *all* persons of Mexican, Latin, or Hispanic appearance residing only in the State of Washington, rather than in the Southwestern states, as had originally been requested by plaintiffs' attorneys. Even so, the court order stopped the noxious activities of the INS directed at Hispanics in the State of Washington. *All* Hispanics in the State of Washington, therefore, will be spared INS-provoked psychiatric symptoms in the future. This case shows the growing potential of class action social work with a mental health primary prevention goal and outcome.

Class action social work, as a macro-level practice intervention prevention tool, can also be used to ensure that children receive the welfare benefits and services to which they are entitled. As more children are growing up poor and without stable families, Harris impresses on social workers and the social work profession that they must renew their commitment to child welfare and continue to play an important role in the development and formulation of public policy and child welfare services to strengthen the ability of vulnerable families to raise healthy children.[107]

In many instances, it is not necessary to develop and formulate *new* public policy concerning child welfare; simply creating new laws will not solve the problems. There may be many national and local situations in which child welfare laws and policies already exist to benefit children, but are not—for any number of reasons—being implemented. It is in these cases that class action social work intervention can be applied, to prevent children from experiencing harm when they are not receiving the services to which they have a right.

Stein suggests that child welfare agencies are vulnerable to class action suits alleging that clients are being deprived of constitutional guarantees or entitlements specified in federal or state policy. In this era of increased military spending at the continued expense of domestic programs, fiscal cuts, with related reductions in personnel and social services, increase welfare agency vulnerability to class action suits, since lack of funds *is not* a defense for failing to provide federal and state legally mandated services.[108]

Class action suits on behalf of children have charged that state agencies have failed to develop case plans; made inappropriate placements of children, ignoring racial/ethnic factors; failed to pursue adoptive placements; and failed to provide preventive services. Currently, two class action suits are pending that allege state failure to provide preventive services, and one suit alleging maltreatment of children in foster care and failure to develop and implement permanent plans.[109] The specific role of social workers in these class action suits is not clear, that is, whether they are defendants, expert witnesses, initiators and/or collaborators with the attorneys in the suits. It is when social workers are in the initiating, collaborating role with attorneys that it conforms to the earlier definition of class action social work.

Social workers need to pay careful attention to existing national and state benefits and welfare policies, and laws and regulations affecting vulnerable client groups, such as children, the homeless, welfare families, and institutionalized psychiatric and corrections populations, to ensure that they are receiving the services and benefits to which they are entitled. Continued denial of resources to clients by agencies, even after notification of mandated requirements, may have merits for attorney–social worker collaboration that eventually could result in a class action social work type of intervention. A favorable court remedy would prevent continued harm to the immediately affected client population (secondary prevention), and future client populations (primary prevention).

CONCLUDING COMMENT

In comparison to law and medicine, social work is a relatively young profession that, despite various growing pains, has survived and continues to be a viable profession in U.S. society. Six issues and trends affecting social work in the 1990s were discussed. These included: (1) the development and application of prevention concepts during a period of significant human need; (2) the prevention of treatment abuse while ensuring a person's right to treatment or nontreatment; (3) the expanding role of social workers in gang violence and homicide prevention; (4) the growth and expanding of social work roles in industry and social work's potential for mental health prevention work in industrial settings; (5) the further refinement and application of people-based helping concepts such as advocacy and client empowerment, and how these concepts can also result in primary prevention outcomes through networking; (6) the continued development of class action social work and its potential as a mental health primary prevention tool.

Although the forecast for social work has not been stable in view of Reagan's and Bush's economic policies continuing to reduce government commitment to social welfare programs, there are a few factors indicating a continuing need for social workers now and in the near future. First of all, there will continue to be a growing public recognition that formal education in social work prepares people to provide higher quality human services. This recognition should encourage the demand for professional education as a prerequisite for employment. Evidence does show that standards are increasing, given the fact that forty-seven states are licensing social workers. Furthermore, although there was a beginning of declassification of social workers in a few states, more specialized practice is being made available at the MSW level, such as gerontology and industrial social work, barring the encroachment of related disciplines into jobs emphasizing social work skills.

It is anticipated that social work will more fully incorporate the concept of a multiple-level profession over the next few years, whether or not social work's human resources increase. Appropriate knowledge, values, and skills will be brought to bear more effectively on the problems presented by clients. Along with greater acceptance in the field of a common base for social work practice has come the realization that a core of knowledge, values, and skills required for practice can be identified. The social worker with this core competence will be a generalist able to engage in practice ranging from individual services, to social reform on the community level. It is anticipated that all professional social workers will have a generalist foundation on which a methodological specialization can evolve, through advanced education and practice experience. In this manner social work will incorporate both the generalist and the specialist approaches to practice.

Escalating costs, coupled with increasing need for human services and the fact that there will never be sufficient mental health practitioners to meet these needs, requires the development and application of helping concepts such as primary prevention, designed to benefit large numbers of persons *before* they are symptomatic. Because social work is one of the helping professions most involved in interacting with and helping communities, it is anticipated that the profession will play an increasingly vital role in applying primary prevention concepts in the 1990s.

As social work emerges into multiple levels of practice, including both the generalist and the specialist approaches, issues such as the right to treatment, the right to nontreatment, and efforts to prevent treatment abuse pose interesting challenges to the profession. Social workers are more effective with voluntary clients; most of the time workers fail with involuntary clients, and even cause deterioration of the client's condition in slightly under 50 percent of cases. A social control framework restricts the therapeutic effectiveness of social work intervention. Involuntary clients, therefore, must have a right to nontreatment, and social workers must advocate this right. The only exceptions to this, however, involve persons such as infants, children, gravely psychiatrically disabled persons, and others who need help but are not capable of making treatment decisions for themselves.

Urban gang violence and homicide was highlighted in this chapter, to indicate to the social work profession that from a historical practice experience standpoint, it is best suited among the health and mental health professions to assume a leadership role in developing micro to macro intervention strategies to deal with a problem that is killing thousands of inner-city youths. Primary, secondary, and tertiary violence and homicide prevention programs were discussed and analyzed as to their impact on violence and gang homicide. A framework for identifying high-risk gang victims was developed, to correspond to a suggested hospital-based prevention program. Social workers are already employed in hospital emergency rooms and on SCAN teams, and in these settings there is potential for developing prevention models working with gang victims and their families. Special attention to meeting the needs of high-risk young siblings not yet gang members may prevent them from becoming future perpetrators or victims. An agency-based model was also highlighted, which holds promise in reducing and preventing gang violence and homicide.

As social workers enter the business and industry arena to practice, they will be challenged by an interesting dilemma. Involuntary clients do not exist only in the public sector. When social workers are sponsored by industry, how will they help an employee who is referred by a supervisor and feels he or she does not have a problem? The role of the social worker in these instances will be basically to communicate very clearly the rights and options available to the employee and the consequences of exercising the right to nontreatment. The final choice, therefore, is left with the employee. Treating employees away from the shop on a private-practice basis may give both the client and the practitioner greater autonomy and reduce the resistance level among those referred for help by an employer. Expanding the micro role of social workers to macro-level intervention, that is, improving the health, mental health, safety, and physical work environment, would be preventive (primary) in nature, as fewer related problems (no *new* cases) would be anticipated.

More and more social workers are leaving the public welfare arena, going into private practice, and shifting their target population to the middle class. Lacking public agency bureaucratic constraints, they are potentially free to help the poor through social action activities such as writing proposals, conducting needs surveys, or building coalitions to apply pressure on government. Related strategies of advocacy and client empowerment may result in a transfer of power so that client groups in need of services gain and exercise their own economic and political might. A community empowerment model built with networking methods can, in the final result, produce a mental health primary prevention outcome.

Class action social work, which was first introduced into the literature in this text in 1977, continues to show promise as a macro-level intervention strategy. *Serrano* v. *Priest,* a class action victory, established the precedent of the right to an equal education; it paved the road for the poor to fight for the right to health and welfare in order to maximize their new educational opportunity. Increasing an individual's opportunities through such assistance is in the best interests of the individual and society. The effectiveness of class action social work with a mental health primary prevention goal was demonstrated in *Nicacio* v. *United States INS,* in which a positive court ruling will have the effect of preventing literally thousands of at-risk Hispanics from developing psychiatric symptoms caused by discriminatory law enforcement practices. The recent exposure of police brutality as a national problem provides another unique opportunity for class action social work intervention and prevention. A rare opportunity for social work to help the poor on a broad scale seems very possible in light of *Serrano* and *Nicacio.* Examples were also provided to show how class action social work intervention can be applied on behalf of vulnerable client populations who are being denied legally mandated services. Collaboration with the legal profession should be vigorously pursued by social workers.

Social work has developed into a vital and important profession in the United States. The future of this profession and its success in helping people prevent or resolve problems in social functioning will depend on its ability to respond effectively to the challenges it faces today. The quality of that response can surely enhance the quality of life for many persons in the future.

SUGGESTED READINGS

ALBEE, GEORGE W., and JOFFE, JUSTIN M. *Primary Prevention of Psychopathology Volume I: The Issues.* Hanover, N.H. University Press of New England, 1977.

BALGOPAL, PALLASSONA R. "Occupational Social Work: An Expanded Clinical Perspective. *Social Work* 34 (September 1989): 437–442.

BARTON II, PRESTON N., and BYRNE, BRIDGET. "Social Work Services in a Legal Aid Setting." *Social Casework* 56 (April 1975): 226–234.

BURRIS, DONALD S., ED. *The Right to Treatment.* New York: Springer, 1969.

COWGER, CHARLES D., and ATHERTON, CHARLES R. "Social Control: A Rationale for Social Welfare." *Social Work* 19 (July 1974): 456–462.

COX, FRED M., ERLICH, JOHN L., ROTHMAN, JACK, and TROPMAN, JOHN E., EDS. *Tactics and Techniques of Community Practice* 2nd ed. Itasca, Ill.: F.E. Peacock, 1984.

HOPPS, JUNE GARY. "Violence—A Personal and Societal Challenge." *Social Work* 32 (November–December 1987): 467–468.

KRISBERG, BARRY, and SCHWARTZ, IRA. "Rethinking Juvenile Justice." *Crime and Delinquency* (July 1983): 333–364.

MIDDLEMAN, RUTH R., and GOLDBERG, GALE. "Social Work Practice with Groups." *Encyclopedia of Social Work* 18th ed., Vol. II. Silver Spring, Md.: National Association of Social Workers, 1987, pp. 714–729.

MORALES, ARMANDO. "The Mexican American Gang Member: Evaluation and Treatment." In Rosina M. Becerra, Marvin Karno, and Javier Escobar, eds., *Mental Health and Hispanic Americans: Clinical Perspectives.* New York: Grune & Stratton, 1982.

Report of the Secretary's Task Force on Black and Minority Health, Vol. 5, U.S. Department of Health and Human Services, January 1986.

SOLOMON, BARBARA BRYANT. *Black Empowerment: Social Work in Oppressed Communities.* New York: Columbia University Press, 1976.

SORICELLI, BARBARA A., and UTECH, CAROLYN LORENZ. "Mourning the Death of a Child: The Family and Group Process." *Social Work* 30 (September–October 1985): 429–434.

SPERGEL, IRVING A. "Violent Gangs in Chicago: In Search of Social Policy." *Social Service Review* 58 (June 1984): 199–226.

STEIN, THEODORE J. "The Vulnerability of Child Welfare Agencies to Class Action Suits." *Social Service Review* 61 (December 1987): 636–654.

ENDNOTES

1. H. John Staulcup, "Primary Prevention," in Aaron Rosenblatt and Diana Waldfogel, eds., *Handbook of Clinical Social Work* (San Francisco: Jossey-Bass, 1983), p. 1059.

2. Ibid., p. 1060.
3. Ronald A. Feldman, Arlene R. Stiffman, Deborah A. Evans, and John G. Orme, "Prevention Research, Social Work, and Mental Illness," *Social Work Research and Abstracts* 18 (Fall 1982): 2.
4. Edith Abbott, "The Social Caseworker and the Enforcement of Industrial Legislation," in *Proceedings of the National Conference on Social Work, 1918* (Chicago: Rogers and Hall, 1919), p. 313.
5. K. A. Kendall, "Discussion," *The Social Forum* (New York: Columbia University Press, 1969), p. 587.
6. Staulcup, pp. 1061–1062.
7. Kathy V. Nance, "Understanding and Overcoming Resistance to Primary Prevention," *Social Work Research and Abstracts* 18 (Fall 1982): 32–33.
8. Feldman et al., p. 6.
9. Stephen E. Goldston, "Defining Primary Prevention," in George W. Albee and Justice M. Joffe, eds. *Primary Prevention of Psychopathology* vol. I: The Issues (Hanover, N.H.: University Press of New England; 1977), p. 20.
10. Ibid.
11. Ibid., p. 21.
12. Steven L. McMurtry, "Secondary Prevention of Child Maltreatment: A Review," *Social Work* 30 (January–February 1985): 43.
13. Juliua R. Ballew, "Role of Natural Helpers in Preventing Child Abuse," *Social Work* 30 (January–February 1985): 40.
14. Morton Birnbaum, "A Rationale for the Right," in Donald S. Burris, ed., *The Right to Treatment* (New York: Springer, 1969), p. 77.
15. As cited by Thomas S. Szasz, "The Right to Health," in Burris, p. 64.
16. Nicholas N. Kittrie, "Can the Right to Treatment Remedy the Ills of the Juvenile Process?," in Burris, pp. 170–171.
17. Charles S. Prigmore and Paul R. Davis, "Wyatt v. Stickney," *Social Work* 18 (July 1973): 17.
18. Ibid., p. 18.
19. Szasz, p. 66.
20. Ibid., p. 67.
21. Ibid., p. 69.
22. Davis McEntire and Joanne Haworth, "The Two Functions of Public Welfare: Income Maintenance and Social Services," *Social Work* 12 (January 1967): 23–24.
23. Charles D. Cowger and Charles R. Atherton, "Social Control: A Rationale for Social Welfare," *Social Work* 19 (July 1974): 457.
24. Henry Miller, "Value Dilemmas in Social Casework," *Social Work* 13 (January 1968): 29–30.
25. Ibid., p. 30.
26. Charles S. Prigmore, "Points and Viewpoints," *Social Work* 18 (November 1973): 99.
27. Alexander B. Smith and Louis Berlin, "Self-Determination in Welfare and Corrections: Is There a Limit?," *Federal Probation* 38 (December 1974): 5.
28. Ann Hartman, "But What Is Social Casework?," *Social Casework* 52 (July 1971): 416.
29. Joel Fischer, "Is Casework Effective? A Review," *Social Work* 18 (January 1973): 5.
30. Scott Briar, "The Current Crisis in Social Casework," *Social Work Practice, 1967* (New York: Columbia University Press, 1967), pp. 19–33, as cited by Fischer.
31. Fischer, pp. 13–14.
32. Ibid., p. 14.
33. Ibid., p. 18.
34. Dorothy Fahs Beck, "Research Findings on the Outcome of Marital Counseling," *Social Casework* 56 (March 1975): 167.
35. Ibid., p. 168 (Emphasis ours.)

36. Fischer, pp. 14–16.
37. *Iatrogenic* is primarily a medical term denoting that a problem, condition, or disorder is induced, produced, or aggravated by the physician or healer—*iatro* (healer), *genic* (origin of).
38. *NASW News* 30, p. 8.
39. *NASW News* 30, p. 7.
40. *Los Angeles Times,* Westside, Part VIII, December 23, 1984, p. 6.
41. United States Senate Committee on the Judiciary, *Ford Administration Stifles Juvenile Justice Policy* (Washington, D.C.: U.S. Government Printing Office, 1975), p. 2.
42. Barry Krisberg and Ira Schwartz, "Rethinking Juvenile Justice," *Crime and Delinquency* (July 1983): 340.
43. Ibid., pp. 360–361.
44. Ron Schultz, "A New Prescription for Troubled Teens," *Los Angeles* 30 (January 1985): 159.
45. Ibid., p. 206.
46. Ibid., p. 205.
47. *Los Angeles Times* Part II, March 24, 1985, p. 2.
48. Ibid.
49. Carolyn Rebecca Block, "Lethal Violence in Chicago over Seventeen Years: Homicides Known to the Police, 1965–1981," Illinois Criminal Justice Information Authority, p. 69.
50. Department of Justice, "Homicide in California, 1985" (Bureau of Criminal Statistics and Special Services, State of California, 1985), p. 17; "Fiscal Year 1985–86 Statistical Summary," Los Angeles County Sheriff's Department; "Statistical Digest, 1986," Automated Information Division, Los Angeles Police Department.
51. N. Meredith, "The Murder Epidemic," *Science 84* (December 1984): 42.
52. Report of the Secretary's Task Force on Black and Minority Health vol. 5, U.S. Department of Health and Human Services, January 1986, pp. 43–44.
53. Report of the Secretary, pp. 46–50.
54. Report of the Secretary, p. 50.
55. Police Foundation, *Domestic Violence and the Police: Studies in Detroit and Kansas City* (Washington, D.C.: The Foundation).
56. The Boston Youth Program, Boston City Hospital, 818 Harrison Ave., Boston, Massachusetts, cited in *Report of the Secretary's Task Force,* pp. 235–236.
57. C. Cooper, "Peer Dynamics, Final Evaluation Report, 1979–1980, Nebraska State Commission on Drugs (Lincoln: Nebraska State Department of Health).
58. "Early Gang Intervention," Transfer of Knowledge Workshop, Department of the California Youth Authority, Office of Criminal Justice Planning, 1985, pp. 11–12; also see Tony Ostos, "Alternatives to Gang Membership," (Unpublished paper, Paramount School District, Los Angeles County, California, October, 1987.)
59. "Strike II," Hopkins Adolescent Program, Johns Hopkins Hospital, Park Building, Baltimore, Md.
60. Fattah Falaka, "Call and Catalytic Response: The House of Umoja," in R. A. Mathias, P. De Muro, and R. S. Allinson, eds., *Violent Juvenile Offenders: An Anthology* (San Francisco: National Council on Crime and Delinquency, 1984), pp. 231–237.
61. "Gang Violence Reduction Project, Second Evaluation Report: October 1977–May 1978," Department of the California Youth Authority, November 1978, pp. i, iii.
62. T. Tatara, H. Morgan, and H. Portner, "SCAN: Providing Preventive Services in an Urban Setting," *Children Today* (November–December 1986): 17–22.
63. Karil S. Klingbeil, "Interpersonal Violence: A Comprehensive Model in a Hospital Setting from Policy to Program," in *Report of the Secretary's Task Force,* p. 246.
64. Lou Dantzler, "Executive Summary, Challengers Boys and Girls Club," (Los Angeles, Calif., 1990), brochure.

65. Barbara A. Soricelli and Carolyn Lorenz Utech, "Mourning the Death of a Child: The Family and Group Process," *Social Work* 30 (September–October 1985): 429–434.

66. *Los Angeles Times,* May 8, 1982, Part I, p. 1.

67. Paul A. Kurzman and Sheila H. Akabas, "Industrial Social Work as an Arena for Practice," *Social Work* 26 (January 1981): 52.

68. Lou Ann B. Jorgenson, "Social Services in Business and Industry," in Neil Gilbert and Harry Specht, eds., *Handbook of the Social Services* (Englewood Cliffs, N.J.: Prentice-Hall, 1981), pp. 338–339.

69. Ibid., p. 340.

70. Ibid., p. 347.

71. Martha N. Ozawa, "Development of Social Services in Industry: Why and How?," *Social Work* 25 (November 1980): 464.

72. Copyright 1978, National Association of Social Workers, Inc. Reprinted with permission from "Industrial Social Work Movement Expanding; Practitioners Conference Planned for June," *NASW News* 23 (February 1978): 7.

73. Rosalie Bakalinsky, "People vs. Profits: Social Work in Industry," *Social Work* 25 (November 1980): 472.

74. Ozawa, pp. 468–469.

75. Jorgenson, p. 349.

76. Pallassona R. Balgopal, "Occupational Social Work: An Expanded Clinical Perspective, *Social Work* 34 (September 1989): 437–442.

77. Copyright 1980, National Association of Social Workers, Inc. Reprinted with permission from *Social Work* 25 (November 1980): 474.

78. Kurzman and Akabas, p. 58. (Emphasis ours.)

79. Briar, p. 28.

80. George A. Brager, "Advocacy and Political Behavior," *Social Work* 13 (April 1968): 6.

81. Neil Gilbert and Harry Specht, "Advocacy and Professional Ethics," *Social Work* 21 (July 1976): 288.

82. Armando Morales, "Beyond Traditional Conceptual Frameworks," *Social Work* 22 (September 1977): 393.

83. Ad Hoc Committee on Advocacy, "The Social Worker as Advocate: Champion of Social Victims," *Social Work* 14 (April 1969): 18.

84. Gilbert and Specht, p. 291.

85. Ad Hoc Committee, p. 19.

86. Barbara Bryant Solomon, *Black Empowerment: Social Work in Oppressed Communities* (New York: Columbia University Press, 1976), p. 6.

87. Ibid., p. 342.

88. Anne Minahan and Allen Pincus, "Conceptual Framework for Social Work Practice," *Social Work* 22 (September 1977): 348.

89. Solomon, p. 354.

90. Brian O'Connell, "From Service to Advocacy to Empowerment," *Social Casework* 59 (April 1978): 198.

91. Felix G. Rivera and John Erlich, "An Assessment Framework for Organizing in Emerging Minority Communities," F. M. Cox et al., eds., *Tactics and Techniques of Community Practice* 2nd ed. (Itasca, Ill.: Peacock, 1984).

92. Lambert Maguire, "Networking for Self-Help: An Empirically Based Guideline," in *Tactics and Techniques of Community Practice,* p. 198.

93. Maguire, p. 199.

94. Maguire, pp. 206–207.

95. Scott Briar, "The Future of Social Work: An Introduction," *Social Work* 19 (September 1974): 518.

96. National Association of Social Workers, *Law and Social Work* (Washington, D.C.: The Association, 1973), p. vii.

97. Ibid., p. 15.

98. National Association of Social Workers, *Law and Social Work,* p. 25. (Emphasis ours.)

99. NASW *Newsletter,* Greater California Chapter, April 1975, p. 1.

100. Robert B. Keiter, "California Educational Financing System Violates Equal Protection," *Clearinghouse Review* 5 (October 1971): 287.

101. Ibid., p. 297.

102. Ibid., p. 298.

103. Ibid., p. 299.

104. *Nicacio* v. *United States INS,* 595 F. Supp. 19 (1984), p. 19.

105. Ibid., p. 21.

106. Ibid., pp. 19, 25.

107. Dorothy V. Harris, "Renewing Our Commitment to Child Welfare," *Social Work* 33 (November–December 1988): 483–484.

108. Theodore J. Stein, "The Vulnerability of Child Welfare Agencies to Class Action Suits," *Social Service Review* 61 (December 1987): 636–654.

109. Ibid., p. 640.

Indexes

SUBJECTS